Uncle Sam's Guide to the Great Outdoors

Also by Inside Information

The Great American Web Book

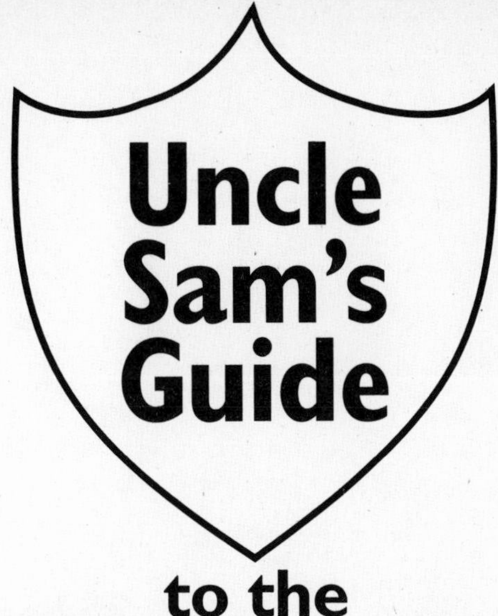

to the Great Outdoors

Raphael Sagalyn

and the Staff of Inside Information

RANDOM HOUSE NEW YORK

Staff

Uncle Sam's Guide to the Great Outdoors

Managing Editors

Raphael Sagalyn

Ethan Kline

Researchers

Nicolas Audy-Rowland

Chris Grams

Dan Kois

Sallie Locke

Amy Pastan

Howard Means

Jennifer Wells

Remy

Random House Editor

Jonathan Karp

 Published in the United States by Random House, Inc., New York, and simultaneously in Canada by Random House of Canada Limited, Toronto.

ISBN 0-679-77161-1

Random House website address: www.randomhouse.com

Printed in the United States of America on acid-free paper

9 8 7 6 5 4 3 2

This book is dedicated to everyone who cares for The Great Outdoors and strives to preserve it for generations to come.

A DISCLAIMER FROM THE STAFF OF INSIDE INFORMATION

We have researched this book with the primary mission to make public domain information about America's vast outdoors resources available to everyone. The descriptions and sidebars of the parks, forests and other sites, as well as "Sam's Tips," come from material provided by government agencies, rangers, naturalists, information officers and other staff of the individual sites themselves, and from the Websites maintained by the government agencies, especially the National Park Service, the U.S. Forest Service, the Bureau of Land Management and the Army Corps of Engineers.

Inside Information provides no warranty, expressed or implied, as to the accuracy, reliability or completeness of furnished data. The author and Inside Information cannot accept responsibility for any errors, omissions, misleading information, and/or potential travel disruption that may occur and we recommend that you verify information wherever appropriate.

We have done our best to confirm the accuracy of the addresses and phone numbers of all sites in this book. If there are any errors, please let us know by emailing us at UncleSam@cais.com. We'll be happy to include all changes in the next edition of the book.

CONTENTS

PROLOGUE XVII

THE NORTHEAST REGION I

THE ROCKY MOUNTAIN REGION 235

TERRITORIAL POSSESSIONS 503

TRAILS AND PARKWAYS 511

APPENDIXES 529

INDEX 584

PROLOGUE

If you've hiked down into the Grand Canyon, vacationed along the Cape Cod National Seashore or climbed the peaks of Rocky Mountain National Park, you've enjoyed a slice of America's Great Outdoors.

If you've driven along Shenandoah's Skyline Drive, photographed Yosemite's El Capitan, run the rapids of the Chattahoochee River in Georgia, or fished the lakes of Hiawatha National Forest in Michigan, you have participated in one of America's Great Outdoors' adventures.

From California and the Redwood forest to the Great Smoky Mountains in Tennessee, to paraphrase Woody Guthrie, this land truly is your land.

America's public lands—all 640 million acres of her mountains and forests, her rivers and seashores, her monuments and battlefields, and so much more—are the crown jewels of this nation's natural resources.

If you're planning a vacation or even a weekend trip, you'll find scores of books about national parks at your local bookstore or library to help you prepare for your adventure. What makes this book different?

First, most guidebooks to the Great Outdoors cover only the most well-known sites in America's backyard—national parks such as Glacier, Yosemite, Yellowstone, and the Grand Canyon—which are managed by the National Park Service (NPS), a division of the Department of the Interior. But the National Park Service is responsible for, at last count, 376 different elements, of which just 54 are national parks. Look at the accompanying sidebar and you'll see that the NPS also manages Uncle Sam's wild and scenic rivers, seashores, scenic trails and Civil War battlefields, among other sites. Interestingly, total acreage within the NPS exceeds 80 million acres but accounts for just 13 percent of all public lands in the United States.

When it comes to America's Great Outdoors, there's far more than just national parks. Over 500 wildlife refuges, 155 national forests, 28 national memorials, 19 national recreation areas, and thousands of cultural landmarks and treasure troves of history: these, too, are your public lands, rich with history, beauty, and recreational opportunities. And there's still more. If you live in the American West, you should know about another steward of American resources, the Bureau of Land Management, which is responsible for the greatest acreage of public land west of the Mississippi River (approximately 270 million acres) and includes an extraordinary number of fishing, hiking, off-road vehicle, hunting, swimming, and sailing opportunities. And finally, there are less

THE 376 ELEMENTS OF THE NATIONAL PARK SERVICE

The NPS is comprised of far more than the 54 famous National Parks such as Yosemite and the Grand Canyon. Here is a breakdown of the all the different elements of the NPS that are described in this book:

International Historic Sites—1
National Battlefields—11
National Battlefield Parks—3
National Battlefield Sites—1
National Historic Sites—74
National Historical Parks—38
National Lakeshores—4
National Memorials—28
National Military Parks—9
National Monuments—73
National Parks—54
National Parkways—4
National Preserves—16
National Recreation Areas—19
National Reserves—2
National Rivers—6
National Scenic Trails—3
National Seashores—10
National Wild and Scenic Rivers—9
Parks (other)—11

well-known agencies, such as the Bureau of Reclamation and the Army Corps of Engineers, which manage recreational resources at lakes, streams, and dams. Many of these sites are close to where you live, but may be entirely unfamiliar to you as you consider day trips for picnics, fishing, and other outings.

In preparing *Uncle Sam's Guide to the Great Outdoors,* we did extensive research to compile the most comprehensive guide to *all* federal lands. There's another distinguishing quality to this book. We'd like to introduce you to the recreational resource that can best help you plan and enjoy your next adventure in America's Great Outdoors. This expert produces many of the most authoritative and most comprehensive guides to the best-known and the lesser known parks and forests and monuments. We refer to the primary author of this book: Uncle Sam.

When we talk about Uncle Sam, we mean the tens of thousands of park rangers, naturalists, historians, biologists, superintendents, and information officers who are invaluable sources of information in planning your next outdoors experience. They work for the National Park Service, the U.S. Forest Service, the Fish and Wildlife Service, and other U.S. agencies, which means

ACREAGE OF UNCLE SAM'S GREAT OUTDOORS

Bureau of Land Management: 270 million
U.S. Forest Service: 191 million
Fish and Wildlife Service: 91 million
National Park Service: 80.7 million
Army Corps of Engineers: 11.6 million

they work for you and me, fulfilling a dual mission of protecting America's natural resources and educating her citizens.

In this book, we'll introduce you to your new travel agents and show you how to locate them by mail, phone, and on the World Wide Web.

Maps, Brochures, and So Much More!

When we started our research for this book, we wrote to over 150 national park, forest, and monument sites and asked for maps, brochures, helpful hints, and general guidebook information. We asked their staffs to send us materials that they thought would help visitors prepare for a trip to their site.

Within days, our mailbox was overflowing. From Glacier National Park in Montana came an oversize envelope stuffed with the National Park Service brochure of the site; more brochures on mule shoe outfitters, and cruises from Waterton Lake to Goat Haunt and other lakes; a tabloid-sized newspaper called *Nature with a Naturalist;* and flyers about Glacier's history, mammals, and geology.

From the Lewis and Clark National Forest, also in Montana, came a *Cabin and Lookout Directory,* which listed $20-per-day rustic cabin rentals, trail guides for hikers and bicyclists, and a *Pathways to the Past* brochure.

From Mammoth Cave National Park in Kentucky came all sorts of color brochures and flyers, our favorite being a guide for rigging a backyard home for nocturnal creatures, entitled *How to Build a Bat Box.*

From the Denali National Park and Preserve in Alaska came, among other printed matter, a list with phone numbers of local outfitters who will fly you from one remote region to another.

Many of these park rangers, naturalists, and information officers then called to see whether they could provide anything more. When we finished the manuscript, we wrote back to our expert friends asking them to verify the entry information for their respective sites. More than 90 percent of our requests were answered, usually with notes of thanks and encouragement. One of the hundreds to respond was an interpretive guide at the San Bernardino Forest in California, named Bob Loudon, who wanted to point out a little-known aspect of his site. San Bernardino, he wrote, is home to the Children's Forest Association where 3,400 acres are set aside and managed and interpreted for visitors by kids. Bob

DRIVING ACROSS AMERICA

Part of the pleasure of Uncle Sam's Great Outdoors can be found on the journey to get there. If you're traveling by car, minivan, or recreational vehicle, you'll want to drive along the most scenic roads possible. To help you plan your trip, you should know about a project called National Scenic Byways Online where you'll learn about scores of roads all across the country designated "National Scenic Byways" and "All American Roads." Included are navigation tips, driving times, and scenic highlights enroute. This Website, sponsored by the Federal Highway Administration (FHWA) and managed by the National Scenic Byways Online project at Utah State University, also features a clearinghouse of reference materials provided by the FHWA and the American Automobile Association. To access the Website, go to http://www.byways.org.

Loudon urged us to tell our readers to visit the forest and the Big Bear Discovery Center nearby.

Your new travel agents have mapped the parks, designed the campgrounds, studied butterflies, earthquakes, wildflowers, grizzly bears, and the migratory patterns of birds. And they have shared a remarkable amount of this knowledge in thousands of booklets, posters, maps, fact sheets, and books about the Great Outdoors. Much of this information is in the public domain, that is, it's freely available for any citizen's own use. Unfortunately, much of this knowledge is extremely hard to find.

Throughout this book, we have used this information in preparing site descriptions and recreational advice. And, we've relied on the expertise of specialists like Bob Loudon to give you authoritative, up-do-date, and sometimes just plain fun information to help prepare for your adventure.

Maps and camping and hiking information only touch the surface of the materials you can expect to receive from your parks and forests. You'll learn the fascinating histories of famous Americans such as Roger Williams, Mary McLeod Bethune, Frederick Douglass, and Frederick Law Olmsted and all our presidents; of the Lewis and Clark Expedition in the first decade of the nineteenth century; of Native Americans whose dwellings can still be found at the Aztec Ruins and Bandalier National Monuments in New Mexico. Natural history comes alive in scores of publications from Canyonlands National Park in Utah, the Chippewa National Forest in Minnesota, and the Florida Everglades.

Would you be interested in adopting a wild horse or a burro? Contact the Bureau of Land Management. How about observing an archeological dig? Contact scientists at the National Park Service. Do you want to volunteer or find a summer job at a National Forest or a National Park Service site? We'll tell you who to contact and how to accomplish all this.

We have been amazed by the quality and quantity of recreational information gathered from all these sources. Remarkably, much of this information is available either for free or at very low cost. These maps, brochures, and pamphlets have been paid for by your tax dollars and are available to anyone who asks—anyone who knows where to look for them.

Most satisfying of all has been the personal connections we've made. The rangers, historians, and other specialists could not have been nicer or more patient in tracking down our information requests, or making suggestions we could pass along to our readers. We urge you to meet them yourselves.

Names, Addresses, Phone Numbers, URLs!

In this book, we present more than 1,000 sites located on America's public lands. Some of them are well-known to you, but we predict that you'll be learning about the majority of them for the very first time. We offer the experts' brief overview of the site, but our emphasis is on giving you the tools for learning far more. You'll find the addresses and phone numbers of all sites, from Acadia National Park in Maine to Zion National Park in Utah. And in between you'll have access to regional offices and ranger districts within larger parks and forests. The people who staff them can be invaluable sources of still more information. We also introduce you to scores of nonprofit organizations—in particular, the cooperating associations, interpretive associations, and historical societies that are affiliated with America's public lands and work closely with their managers to produce excellent guidebooks that are not often found in your local bookstore.

Finally, we take advantage of the awesome capabilities of the World Wide Web. The National Park Service (http://www.nps.gov) has a superior website that describes the features and recreational opportunities of all elements of the NPS. All other government agencies that manage public land, such as the Forest Service (http://www.fs.fed.us), Bureau of Land Management (http://www.blm.gov), and Fish and Wildlife Service (http://www.fws.gov) have developing websites that will guide you through fascinating points of interest.

Our book is packed with hundreds of phone numbers of sites, visitor centers, cooperating and interpretive associations, licensed concessionaires, regional offices of public land agencies, 800 numbers, park site, and website addresses—all now available in one volume to help you get the most up-to-date and topical information. We have done the hard part—assembling all this information. All that is left is for you to take advantage of it and participate in an adventure in Uncle Sam's Great Outdoors.

PARKS IN PERIL

For all their beauty and recreational pleasure, America's natural treasures are in increasing peril. From the traffic jams of Yosemite to the polluted forests of the Smokies, from the vanishing monuments at Gettysburg to the budget shortfalls at scores of historic sites, the National Park Service faces an enormous challenge to maintain our nation's greatest natural resources.

In 1995, the General Accounting Office (GAO) prepared a report to Congress entitled, "National Parks: Difficult Choices Need to Be Made about the Future of the Parks." In it, the GAO found there was legitimate cause for concern about the condition of the national parks for both visitor services and resource management, that services were being cut back and the condition of many trails, campgrounds, and other facilities were declining.

Eleven of the 12 parks reviewed by GAO had cut visitor services. For example, at Shenandoah National Park in Virginia, programs to help visitors understand the park's natural and scenic aspects were cut by more than 80 percent from 1987 to 1993. At Ellis Island in New York, 32 of 36 historic buildings had seriously deteriorated. At Hopewell Furnace National Historic Site, an 850-acre park in Pennsylvania that depicts part of the nation's early industrial development, the Park Service had never performed a complete archaeological survey to identify and inventory the park's cultural resources.

One of the most startling facts about our national parks is their rise in popularity. In 1980, for example, there were a little less than 200 million visitors to the parks. In 1996, that number grew to 270 million, an increase of 35 percent. At the same time, funding as measured in constant dollars dropped from $989 million to $630 million.

These statistics come from the Natural Resources Defense Council, a leading environmental advocacy group based in Washington, D.C., which, together with the National Trust for Historic Preservation, has produced a startling report on America's Great Outdoors, titled "Reclaiming Our Heritage: What We Need to Do to Preserve America's National Parks." It's both an alarming and comprehensive look at the deteriorating conditions of our national parks and a call to action for lawmakers and citizens alike to protect them. We recommend this study which can be viewed online at: http://www.nrdc.org/nrdcpro/roh/rohinx.html. A key part of the report consists of case studies of more than 20 national parks. To access these in-depth reports, go to: http://www.nrdc.org/find/laroh.html.*

Among the specific problems cited by the study:

- Air pollution at Acadia National Park. Smog and acid rain have become so severe that visitors are advised to avoid strenuous exercise such as hiking and bicycling.
- Disintegrating monuments at Gettysburg National Military Park. The 1,300 monuments, markers, and memorials at Gettysburg are gradually disappearing due to environmental factors. (Moreover, according to an article in *U.S. News & World Report,* the park's archives of precious letters, maps, guns, and other artifacts are stored in leaky maintenance buildings, unprotected from fire and humidity.)

* For printed copies of this report, send $10.50 plus $3.50 shipping and handling to: NRDC, Publications Department, 40 West 20th Street, New York, NY 10011. California residents must add 7.25 percent sales tax. For further information, contact NRDC Headquarters in New York City, 212-727-2700.

TOP TWENTY MOST VISITED NATIONAL PARKS (1996)

1. Great Smoky Mountains (TN)	9,265,667 visits
2. Grand Canyon (AZ)	4,537,703
3. Yosemite (CA)	4,046,207
4. Olympic (WA)	3,348,723
5. Yellowstone (WY)	3,012,171
6. Rocky Mountain (CO)	2,923,755
7. Grand Teton (WY)	2,733,439
8. Acadia (ME)	2,704,831
9. Zion (UT)	2,498,001
10. Mammoth Cave (KY)	1,896,829
11. Glacier (MT)	1,720,518
12. Shenandoah (VA)	1,571,019
13. Haleakala (HI)	1,553,344
14. Hot Springs (AR)	1,538,105
15. Mount Rainier (WA)	1,338,961
16. Bryce Canyon (UT)	1,269,600
17. Hawaii Volcanoes (HI)	1,231,557
18. Death Valley (CA)	1,189,215
19. Joshua Tree (CA)	1,095,046
20. Badlands (SD)	1,024,705

- Crumbling ancient dwellings at Mesa Verde National Park. Weather, age, and a lack of routine maintenance threaten many prehistoric cliff dwellings at Mesa Verde, built in the thirteenth century. At the famous Cliff Palace, ground water has damaged the original walls and plaster.
- Pest invasion at Shenandoah National Park. Non-native insects such as gypsy moth caterpillars have defoliated many of the park's hardwood trees and are causing the rapid decline of the eastern hemlock stands in the park. Unfortunately, there is no known solution to these problems.
- Vandalism. Examples include the theft of Civil War relics and tons of petrified wood, and the defacing of monuments.

Overcrowding, underfunding, overdevelopment, pollution, and vandalism—these are some of the woes that will not be easy for the park service to solve. What can be done? The NPS is experimenting with higher park entrance fees, which will help reinstate visitor services and rebuild some deteriorating structures. In addition, the NPS has issued a proposal that would require Yosemite visitors to leave their vehicles outside the park boundaries and take a bus into the valley. The park service's most controversial plan, announced in November 1997, concerns Gettysburg National Military Park where the

NPS would allow a developer to build a new visitor center and museum in exchange for the right to operate a giant-screen movie theatre and private shops in the new complex.

As the NPS, Forest Service, and other public agencies devise ways to overcome these problems, some of the burden must shift to us, the resource users who, it has been said, are "loving their parks to death." After all our research, we have three simple bits of advice we'd like to impart to our readers:

- *Plan ahead.* If you spend a little more time preparing for your trip, by calling or writing well in advance of your travel, by getting campground reservations or hiking permits or finding out prime fishing spots, you'll ease the strain on individual sites and have an even better outdoors experience.
- *Discover lesser known areas.* As magnificent as our 54 national parks are, there are hundreds of forests, lakeshores, scenic rivers, historic sites, and wildlife refuges that will satisfy all types of recreational activities for people of all ages. If your destination is Yosemite National Park, for example, be sure to consider a day or more at either Sierra National Forest or Stanislaus National Forest, just a few miles away. You may be relieving traffic congestion at the same time you easily find an available campground while all those at Yosemite are sold out.
- *Respect the Great Outdoors and preserve its splendor for generations to come.* Throughout this book, we've included tips about many worthy programs that aim to conserve the flora and fauna of the Great Outdoors. For those readers unfamiliar with programs such as "Leave No Trace" and "Tread Lightly!" or groups such as the Student Conservation Association and the National Forest Foundation, we urge you to heed the counsel of those who do such a fantastic job of caring for the land and maintaining our natural treasures.

By following these three tips you can do your part to protect our greatest natural resource, our public lands.

GREAT OUTDOORS RECREATIONAL PAGES (GORP)

Throughout this book, we've focused exclusively on government publications and Websites to better inform and prepare readers for their outdoors adventure. But we would be remiss in not directing our readers to one especially valuable non-governmental resource in particular. That is the well-named GORP, which stands for Great Outdoor Recreational Pages. GORP is a perfect supplement to this book in that it, too, encompasses all the many dimensions of public lands and has scores of other web features. Of all the superb private sector Websites that guide you through American's recreational adventures, GORP stands above the rest. The address is http://www.gorp.com.

GETTING TO KNOW YOUR NEW TRAVEL EXPERTS

Responsibility for managing all of America's public lands is shared among a number of different government agencies, primarily divisions of the Departments of Agriculture and the Interior. In this book, we'll introduce you to all of them and show you how to access information at a number of levels, from national headquarters in Washington, D.C., to regional offices and the recreational sites themselves. Let's take a minute to introduce the players and to better understand their missions, their range of publications, and their visitor centers on the World Wide Web.

The National Park Service

On March 1, 1872, the U.S. Congress established Yellowstone National Park in the Territories of Montana and Wyoming "as a public park or pleasuring ground for the benefit and enjoyment of the people" and placed it under the control of the Secretary of the Interior. In subsequent years, other national parks and monuments were authorized, mostly carved from the federal lands of the American West. At the same time, other natural and historic areas were administered by other government agencies such as the War Department and the Forest Service, which is part of the Department of Agriculture.

Forty-four years later, on August 25, 1916, President Woodrow Wilson signed an act creating the National Park Service within the Department of the Interior giving the NPS the mandate to protect the 40 national parks and monuments then in existence and those yet to be established. This "Organic Act" of 1916 states that the NPS would promote and regulate these federal lands "by such means and measures as conform to the fundamental purpose of the said parks, monuments and reservations, which purpose is to conserve the scenery and the natural and historic objects and the wild life therein and to provide for the enjoyment of the same in such manner and by such means as will leave them unimpaired for the enjoyment of future generations."

In 1933, an Executive Order transferred 63 monuments and military sites from the Forest Service and the War Department to the NPS, setting in motion the management of "superlative natural, historic, and recreation areas" under one government umbrella. Today, when we think of the National Park Service, we think of national parks like Yosemite, the Grand Canyon, and the Great Smokies. But did you know that most Civil War battlefields are the responsibility of the NPS as well? So are Harper's Ferry National Historic Park in West Virginia, Assateague Island National Seashore in Maryland; Golden Gate National Recreation Area in California;, Big Thicket National Preserve in Texas; and the most famous sites in Washington, D.C., including the White House, the Vietnam Veterans Memorial, and the Jefferson and Lincoln Memorials.

There is an incredible diversity of outdoor sites managed by the NPS. Some of the designations ascribed to these sites—reserves or preserves, historical parks or historical sites—can be confusing, so we've included a sidebar to show how the National Park Service distinguishes between them.

NPS Publications

The National Park Service has produced an extraordinary array of books, maps, brochures, checklists, posters, and recreational information for campers, hikers, picnickers, mountain climbers, boaters—just about everybody who enjoys the outdoors.

Where should you begin your publication search? Each NPS site has prepared an NPS *Map and Guide,* which is an essential resource for any park visitor. You're probably familiar with these brochures; they are usually handed out for free at entrance stations to all NPS sites. Each *Map and Guide* has a full-color map of the park showing the location of visitor centers and landmarks and features an overview of the purpose, history, and unique characteristics of the site. The brochures can be ordered for $1.25 from a number of places, including the Consumer Information Center in Pueblo, CO, any field office of the NPS, or specific NPS sites. But, we've found that a personal letter requesting a particular *Map and Guide,* addressed to the Publications Officer of the particular site might well get a free copy into your mailbox within a week.

Other fine general publications include the *National Parks Index* ($6.50, stock #024-005-01182-0), a 125-page book with state-by-state descriptions of each NPS site and with lists of affiliated areas, wild and scenic rivers, and national trails; *Lesser Known Areas* ($1.75, stock #024-005-01152-8), a 48-page guide to the NPS sites that are not yet famous and overcrowded, with information on locations, accommodations, and attractions; and the *National Trails System Map and Guide* ($1.50, stock #024-005-01111-1), a map with brief descriptions of each of the National Scenic and Historic Trails in the United States. These publications are often available from NPS regional offices, or you can send your order with payment to the Superintendent of Documents, PO Box 371954, Pittsburgh, PA 15250.

National Park Service Handbooks

We strongly recommend the series of *National Park Service Handbooks* that are available for over 60 NPS sites. These *Handbooks* are printed on thick, high-quality paper, with full-color illustrations, maps, and photos. They are the most in-depth publications produced by Uncle Sam and they are hard to find in any traditional bookstore. Prices range from $1.50 to $8.00. For a complete list of available titles, contact the Superintendent of Documents, U.S. Government Printing Office, Washington, DC 20402; 202-512-1800, and ask for the National Park Service Handbook Subject Bibliography. Or visit the NPS World Wide Web publications catalog (http://www.nps.gov/hfc/index.html).

National Park Service on the World Wide Web

At ParkNet (http://www.nps.gov) you'll find answers to the most frequently asked questions about the NPS (largest/smallest/most visited, and so on), a wealth of information on Civil War battlefields, a register of national historic places, online collections of national park museums, and other material about the science, culture, and history of NPS sites.

All elements in the NPS have a homepage that offers background and practical information ranging from campground facilities to hours of operation. You can search for information by state or region, or even by theme. A number of sites have developed "virtual visitor centers" that feature maps, detailed campground information, natural history, and ecological features of the parks, and more.

Forest Service

National Forests were first established primarily for watershed protection and wood production by the Organic Administration Act of 1897. The Multiple Use-Sustained Yield Act of 1960 expanded these original uses to include outdoor recreation and wildlife habitat. Over the years, other emphasis areas, such as wilderness, fisheries, and heritage resources have been added to the Forest Service's mission. All of these benefits are managed by the U.S. Department of Agriculture (USDA) so they, too, can be enjoyed by generations to come.

The largest part of the USDA, the U.S. Forest Service oversees 155 national forests encompassing 191 million acres—the size of California, Oregon, and Washington combined. Recreational opportunities range from wilderness to urban adventures, from individual boating to hunting and fishing, from guided auto tours along forest roads to white water rafting, from backpacking to volunteering on archaeological projects. In fact, a 1992 USDA report found that the national forests are the leading provider of total outdoor recreation use in the United States, offering 43 percent of all visitor days on public lands. The National Park Service provides 17 percent of recreational opportunities for visitors.

The Forest Service also administers 17 national grasslands as well as 96 of the 153 rivers that are part of the National Wild and Scenic River System.

Publications

A terrific starting point is *A Guide to Your National Forests.* Like the NPS's *Official Map and Guide,* this foldout features a map of all locations as well as addresses for obtaining information on all of the forests. To obtain a copy, write to any Forest Service regional office, or contact the Forest Service headquarters in Washington: USDA Forest Service, Auditor's Building, 201 14th Street SW, PO Box 96090, Washington, DC 20090-6090; 202-205-1760.

Another good primer is *Discover Special Places in Your National Forests,* which lists all of the recreation areas, scenic areas, and monuments within the forests. Locations in this guide are the most spectacular in the forest system, and include Mount St. Helens in the Gifford Pinchot National Forest, Hells Canyon in the Ashley National Forest, and Flaming Gorge in the Wallowa Whitman National Forest. Somewhat more specialized is a brochure titled *Fishing in Your National Forests,* which lists not only the addresses for each

NATIONAL PARK COOPERATING ASSOCIATIONS

Cooperating associations began four years after the National Park Service itself was established. The need for educational and orientation material, in addition to what the park could afford to provide, was first recognized by Ranger Ansel T. Hall at Yosemite National Park. By 1920, Hall's plan for a museum and "visitor contact center" providing inexpensive guides and maps was realized. In 1925, the Yosemite Natural History Association took responsibility for the daily running of the center and so became the first cooperating association. By the early 1930s, a dozen other national parks had formed similar cooperating associations of their own. In 1948, the Eastern National Park and Monument Association was established and was the first organization to support a number of small parks and historic sites. Currently, there are associations at more than 350 areas managed by the National Park Service and other agencies.

Cooperating associations are nonprofit, tax-exempt organizations recognized by the U.S. Congress to aid the National Park Service and other agencies in their mission of education and service. Cooperating associations service millions of visitors to national parks, monuments, historic sites, forests, wildlife refuges, and recreation areas. The revenue generated by cooperating associations from the sales of merchandise (both printed matter and theme-related goods) and memberships is returned to the parks and used to enhance programs and publications. Cooperating associations also underwrite costs incurred by special events, field seminars, and educational exhibits; sometimes, they underwrite research in biology, archaeology, and history. In 1995 alone, cooperating associations returned $16 million to the NPS and other land management agencies; since 1920, their contributions have exceeded $130 million.

Every cooperating association will send you a brochure or catalog of products for sale. Generally, these magnificent books, movies, and posters will supplement the information you receive from the site itself.

For a complete list of cooperating associations and the sites they serve, write to: Conference of National Park Cooperating Associations (CNPCA), 8375 Jumpers Hole Road, Suite 104, Millersville, MD 21108 (phone: 410-647-9001; fax: 410-647-9003).

Or, at the NPS Website, go to http://www.nps.gov/coop/coophome.htm for a history of cooperating associations and a directory of the sites they serve, sorted alphabetically and by state.

forest, but also different types of fish that the forest is known for, and the best way to catch them. These are just two of our favorite brochures related to our forests and you'll likely get them for free by writing to headquarters in Washington or any regional office.

National Forests on the World Wide Web

The Forest Service has a useful though rudimentary website. From the homepage, click on the section called "Enjoy the Outdoors" to find your gateway to the national forest nearest your home or your recreation destination. You'll find a great deal of practical information ranging from waterfall locations to fish and camping spots. Not all of the forests are online yet. You'll also find information about caring for forests, global conservation, and fire management and even a Fall Color Hotline giving weekly seasonal updates during foliage season in each part of the country. The web address is: http://www.fs.fed.us.

National Wildlife Refuge System

The National Wildlife Refuge System is the world's largest and most diverse collection of lands set aside specifically for wildlife. The refuge system began in 1903 when President Theodore Roosevelt designated 3-acre Pelican Island, a pelican and heron rookery in Florida, as a bird sanctuary.

Today, national wildlife refuges have been established from the Arctic Ocean to the South Pacific, from Maine to the Caribbean. Varying in size from half-acre parcels to thousands of square miles, they encompass more than 92 million acres of the nation's best wildlife habitats. The vast majority of these lands are in Alaska, with the rest spread across the rest of the United States and several U.S. territories.

Managed by the U.S. Fish and Wildlife Service (FWS), Uncle Sam's national wildlife refuges also play a vital role in preserving endangered and threatened species. Among the refuges that are well-known for providing endangered species habitat are Aransas in Texas, the winter home of the whooping crane; the Florida Panther refuge, which protects one of the nation's most endangered mammals; and the Hawaiian Islands refuge, home of the Laysan duck, Hawaiian monk seal, and many other unique species.

National wildlife refuges offer the public a wide variety of recreational and educational opportunities. Many refuges have fishing and hunting programs, visitor centers, wildlife trails, and environmental education programs. Nationwide, some 25 million visitors annually hunt, fish, observe, and photograph wildlife or participate in interpretive activities on refuges.

On the 511 refuges throughout the country, fishing is perhaps the most popular activity, and unlike the National Park Service, the FWS allows hunting under very stringent regulations. At this time, 268 refuges are open to public hunting (142 allow waterfowl hunting, 149 allow big game hunting) and 253 refuges are open for fishing. Over 1 million people hunt on wildlife refuges each year, and over 5 million people fish. Write or call the wildlife refuge you are interested in visiting to get specific information on local hunting and fishing policies, as well as permit, regulation, and facility information.

Publications

The FWS has a free publications catalog that is available from its Office of Public Affairs, U.S. Fish and Wildlife Service, Mail Stop 130 Webb Building, 4401 North Fairfax Drive, Arlington, VA 22203; 703-358-1711. The best overview is *National Wildlife Refuges: A Visitor's Guide,* which is the *Map and Guide* for the wildlife refuges, listing addresses and locations of all refuges with visitor opportunities. More detailed information on national wildlife refuges can be obtained by writing any of the offices listed at the back of this brochure.

Two excellent introductory publications are: *The National Wildlife Refuge System,* a short historical and educational brochure; and *National Wildlife Refuges: Conserving Habitat and History,* an overview of historic and archeological sites. Ask for these brochures at the Public Affairs Office listed above.

Fish and Wildlife Service on the World Wide Web

Use the regional map of the FWS just off the homepage (http://www.fws.gov) to access refuges closest to you. The highlight of the FWS website is the National Wildlife Refuge System, at http://bluegoose.arw.r9.fws.gov, which features beautiful online brochures about plants and wildlife.

Bureau of Land Management

Less well-known than the National Park Service and the National Forest Service, the Bureau of Land Management (BLM) oversees the largest land mass in the United States primarily in the 11 Western states and Alaska. BLM manages the land and its resources on the principles of multiple use and sustained yield, meaning that lands can be used for grazing, mining, timber, wildlife, and/or recreation. Visitors will discover that BLM lands are some of the most wild and untouched places in the United States and have excellent opportunities for primitive outdoor adventures.

An agency within the U.S. Department of the Interior, BLM manages a vast expanse of land held in ownership by the U.S. government for the American people. The original 1.8 billion-acre public domain stretched from the Appalachian Mountains to the Pacific Ocean—so much land that Western historian Frederick Jackson Turner called it "the richest free gift that was ever spread out before civilized man."

Of these 1.8 billion acres, two-thirds was transferred from federal ownership to individuals, corporations, and states. Other land was set aside for national forests, national parks, and other public purposes, leaving the BLM to manage 270 million acres that were once called "the land nobody wanted" because nineteenth-century Western settlers—the homesteaders—had passed it by.

Land under BLM management comprises one-eighth of America's land surface and amount to 41 percent of the land under federal ownership.

The BLM, formed during a government reorganization in 1946, is a successor to two former federal agencies—the General Land Office and the U.S. Grazing Service. Besides protecting and managing the public lands for a variety of uses, the BLM also maintains custody of nearly 9 million pages of historic land documents. These documents include copies of homestead and sales patents, survey plats, and survey field notes.

Headquartered in Washington, D.C., the BLM has about 9,000 employees, most of whom work in field offices throughout the 12 western states.

The regional offices and the Washington Office of Public Affairs (Bureau of Land Management, Office of Public Affairs, 1849 C Street NW Room 5600, Washington, DC 20240; 202-452-5125) are the best places to get general information about recreation opportunities on BLM lands. Ask for the *Recreation Guide to BLM Lands* which, like the NPS *Map and Guide;* gives you the addresses for all district offices, as well as the locations of all public lands, campgrounds, visitor centers, National Wild and Scenic Rivers, National Wilderness Areas, National Historic Trails, and National Scenic Trails administered by BLM. Other fine titles include: *Camping on the Public Lands, the Bureau of Land Management's Recreational Rivers, America's Treasures: Rivers and Streams on the Public Lands, National Backcountry Byways,* and *Fish and Wildlife Resources on the Public Lands.*

For more publications about the Bureau of Land Management, contact the Superintendent of Documents, U.S. Government Printing Office, Washington, DC 20402; 202-512-1800, and ask for the Bureau of Land Management Subject Bibliography.

The BLM on the World Wide Web

The most useful material about recreation opportunities on BLM lands is located one step off the homepage under the heading "National Map: BLM Points of Interest." Point your browser to http://www.blm.gov.

Bureau of Reclamation

An agency of the Department of the Interior, the Bureau was created in 1902 to help develop and sustain the economy of the Western United States by providing reliable water and energy supplies through the development of dams and hydroelectric powerplants. What's key for outdoors enthusiasts is that the USBR oversees more than 300 recreation areas in 17 Western states, containing 5 million acres of water and land surface. Nearly 200 of these recreation areas are managed by nonfederal entities such as state and county parks. Included under USBR's domain are 8 National Recreation Areas such as Lake Mead and Grand Coulee. USBR also offers guided tours at some of its major sites, such as Hoover Dam near Las Vegas, and Grand Coulee Dam near Spokane.

USBR Publications

The Bureau of Reclamation has over 100 useful full-color brochures and guides available to outdoors enthusiasts. For a complete catalogue, contact the Office of Public Affairs (Bureau of Reclamation, Office of Public Affairs, 1849 C Street NW, Room 7642, Washington, DC 20240, Phone: 202-208-4662). We particularly recommend a guide called *Bureau of Reclamation Recreation Areas,* which features a map, regional addresses, and the types of facilities available at each individual recreation area. Another useful brochure is *Your Guide to Fishing at Reclamation Reservoirs* which includes information on where and when to fish, as well as directions to prime angling spots. To order these and other specific brochures, contact NTIS (Department of Commerce, Springfield, VA 22161, Phone: 703-605-6000, http://www.ntis.gov).

The Bureau of Reclamation on the World Wide Web

The USBR website is not as well-developed as its siblings at the Interior Department. It still may be useful to visit, so mark the address: http://www.usbr.gov.

Army Corps of Engineers

The U.S. Army Corps of Engineers records the second largest visitation figure among all federal agencies. Corps projects provide over 30 percent of the recreational opportunities on Federal lands, with only 9 percent of the federal funds expended for recreational resources, and on less than 2 percent of the federal land base. The Corps is the largest provider of water-based recreation with over 25 million individuals visiting a Corps project at least once each year.

Development of Corps of Engineers projects during the decades of the 1940s and the 1950s occurred typically in rural settings. Suburban sprawl was in its infancy. The development of Corps lakes nationwide soon attracted so many visitors that the Congress began to include recreation and fish and wildlife management as a project purpose. The Flood Control Act of 1944 gave the Corps specific authority to provide public outdoor recreation facilities at its projects.

Continued national growth, with its attendant increase in disposable income and leisure time, resulted in increased public use of Corps projects. Improved roads and automobiles came quickly, and the cities grew out to meet and surround the once rural projects. Currently about 80 percent of the Corps 459 lakes which contain 4,290 recreation areas (53 percent managed directly by the Corps), are within 50 miles of major metropolitan areas; 94 percent are within a two-hour drive. The Corps currently administers approximately 11.7 million acres of land and water.

The U.S. Army Corps of Engineers operates more than 450 water resource development projects in 43 states. Recreational opportunities such as boating, fishing, and camping are balanced with wildlife management at the reservoirs and artificial lakes that are typical of Corps sites.

Army Corps of Engineers Publications

Outdoor recreation opportunities are available at 4,300 public use areas on Corps-managed lands. There's no single publication that addresses the recreational opportunities of each project, so you may need some prior knowledge of the recreational area to request specific information. ACE does have brochures for each of their ten regions so we urge you to contact a regional office to make your request.

Army Corps of Engineers on the World Wide Web

Recreational information for ACE sites is found primarily at the regional offices. You'll find them off the homepage of the Army Corps's homepage located at http://www.usace.army.mil. An alternative is to use the Search function at the homepage, type in "Recreation," and then choose from a long list of regional options.

Tennessee Valley Authority

The Tennessee Valley Authority's system of dams and reservoirs, initially designed for flood control and navigation, includes 30 lakes with 11,000 miles of shoreline. The TVA is an increasingly popular source of recreation with some facilities managed privately, and others by local, state, or federal governments.

For specific information about TVA sites, write: Land Between the Lakes (100 Van Morgan Drive, Golden Pond, KY 42211-9001; 502-924-2000, the largest TVA recreation area. Ask for TVA brochures about Recreation on TVA Lakes.

Fishing and Hunting on TVA Lands

Fishing is permitted year round on TVA lakes, but the best catches are in the spring and late fall. The principal game fish are largemouth, smallmouth, spotted, white, and striped bass; crappie; walleye; sauger; and sunfish. Rainbow trout can be found in several of the deepest lakes and below some dams. All hunting on TVA lands must be conducted in accordance with applicable federal and state laws and regulations.

Trails, Camping, and Recreation Maps

Many TVA reservoirs have trails for backpacking, hiking, jogging, and bicycling. The brochure *TVA Trails: A Trail Guide to the Great Lakes of the South* lists the best of these trails. For this brochure or for complete maps of individual TVA lakes (including camping information and boat navigation maps) write to TVA Map Sales, Haney Building 1A, 1101 Market St., Chattanooga TN 37402 for a free catalog.

U.S. Geological Service

Since 1879, the U.S. Geological Service (USGS) has served the public by collecting, analyzing and publishing information about the nation's land, mineral and water resources. Think of USGS as Uncle Sam's mapmaker, for it produces maps of all kinds, from satellite images to elevation maps to city maps. Hundreds of catalogs filled with relatively low-priced maps covering every part of the country are available from either the central office or a regional office of USGS.

You should get acquainted with one of USGS's most valuable resources, the Earth Science Information Center (Box 25046, Federal Center, Mail Stop 504, Denver, CO 80225-0046; 800-USA-MAPS), which is the Service's primary map store. A publication called *USGS Maps* will describe in more detail all of the different types of maps and help you decide which ones you would like. ESIC will also send you a map catalog for any particular state that includes a list of every available map and an order form. ESIC's useful website is at http://www-nmd.usgs.gov/esic/esic.html.

Geological Survey on the World Wide Web

USGS has an extensive site on the World Wide Web. Teachers can download lesson plans (with maps and text) for class activities focusing on maps and geology. The Cartographic Technology Laboratory has virtual exhibits (including animation and sound) that discuss the research being done on map applications. Other interesting things to see are recently declassified satellite images from the 1960s, the latest earthquake information at the National Earthquake Information Center, photos and activities at three volcano labs (including one at Mount St. Helens), and 3-D pictures of undersea canyons at the Marine and Coastal Geology Center. Point your web browser to http://www.usgs.gov.

HOW TO USE THIS BOOK

For easy reference, the following icons are used to designate key information throughout the book:

 Cooperating Associations Shield

 Sam's Tips

 Site-Specific Sidebars

 General Interest Sidebars

Different government agencies manage the thousand or more different sites that are described in this book. We organized the book to reflect six different regions of the country—the Northeast, Southeast, Midwest, Rocky Mountain, Southwest, and Pacific—and then listed alphabetically the states within each region and the sites within each state—all the parks, forests, monuments, battlefields, and the like. Each entry is broken down into the following elements:

Location

Rather than give driving directions, we have located the site geographically within the state or have given the approximate mileage from recognizable cities or highways.

DEFINITIONS

National Park

A national park has generally been assigned to the greatest natural attractions of the National Park System. The term is meant to imply a large, spectacular natural place having a wide variety of attributes, at times including significant historic assets. Hunting and mining are not authorized.

National Monument

President Theodore Roosevelt proclaimed and reserved the first national monument, Devils Tower (WY) in 1906. National monuments are smaller than national parks and lack the diversity or range of attractions that national parks have.

National Memorial

A national memorial is purely commemorative of a particular historic person or episode. The first NPS property classified as a national memorial was the Washington Monument, begun in 1848.

National Battlefield

The parks under this general title include national battlefields, national battlefield parks, national battlefield sites, and national military parks.

National Historic Site

This designation, derived from the Historic Sites Act of 1935, applies to the second largest number of units in the National Park System. The title has been applied to an array of historic sites from forts to the homes of notable Americans. In general, a national historic site contains a single historical feature that was directly associated with its subject.

National Historical Park

The National Historical Park designation has generally been applied to parks that extend beyond single properties or buildings, such as Independence National Historical Park in Philadelphia with its several structures; Boston National Historical Park with nine separate components; and Colonial National Historical Park in Virginia (originally a national monument) with its separate Jamestown and Yorktown units.

National Preserve

In 1974, Big Cypress (FL) and Big Thicket (TX) became the first of the national preserves. Ten national preserves are in Alaska, all established by the Alaska National Interest Lands Conservation Act of 1980. Seven of these preserves border national parks of the same name; all allow sport hunting which is prohibited in the national parks. Many of the existing national preserves would, without sport hunting, otherwise qualify for designation as national parks.

National Recreation Area

The first unit with this designation was Lake Mead National Recreation Area, called Boulder Dam National Recreation Area when the National Park Service assumed responsibility for it in 1936. Twelve national recreation areas in the NPS are centered on large reservoirs. The first urban national recreation areas were Gateway and Golden Gate, authorized by Congress in 1972. These urban parks combine scarce open spaces with the preservation of significant historic resources and important natural areas in locations that can provide outdoor recreation for large numbers of visitors.

National Seashore

Cape Hatteras National Seashore (NC) was the first such area to be authorized, in 1937. Nine more have been established on the Atlantic, Gulf, and Pacific coasts, the last being Canaveral National Seashore (FL) in 1975. Some national seashores have roads, parking and other facilities to accommodate heavy beach visitation. Some are in a relatively primitive state and include wilderness areas.

National Lakeshore

Congress authorized Pictured Rocks National Lakeshore (MI) in October 1966, and Indiana Dunes (IN) in November in the same year. The last two national lakeshores, Apostle Islands (WI) and Sleeping Bear Dunes (MI), were authorized in 1970. The lakeshores, all on the Great Lakes, closely parallel the seashores in character and use.

National Scenic River

The first area with this title was authorized in 1964—Ozark National Scenic Riverways—extending 140 miles along two rivers in Missouri. Other river units bear variations of this title reflecting their differences—national river and recreation area, national scenic river, national recreational river, and wild river, as well.

Wild and Scenic River Designation

To be eligible for WSR designation, a river must be free flowing and contain at least one "outstandingly remarkable value." These resources may include scenery, recreation, geological, fish, wildlife, historic, or cultural resources, and other similar values. Although most rivers are designated by an Act of Congress, the Secretary of the Interior can also designate a river upon a State Governor's request.

National Parkway

Four units of the NPS fall into this classification, although none is designated as national parkway. The first, George Washington Memorial Parkway in Virginia, dates from 1930. The Blue Ridge Parkway and the Natchez-Trace Parkway, each more than 400 miles long, were begun in the mid-1930s. John D. Rockefeller, Jr., Memorial Parkway, linking Yellowstone and Grand Teton national parks, was designated in 1972. The title parkway refers to the parkland paralleling the road as well as the roadway itself.

National Scenic Trail

The Appalachian National Scenic Trail, the first such park in the National Park System, was so designated by the National Trails System Act of 1968. The trail extends some 2,100 miles from Katahdin, ME, to Springer Mountain, GA. The title aptly describes these linear parklands and their use.

Wilderness Area

Congress passed the Wilderness Act that created the National Wilderness Preservation System in 1964. The legislation stated that wilderness is "an area where the earth and its community of life are untrammeled by man, where man himself is a visitor who does not remain." It provided for use and enjoyment of wilderness, but in a manner that leaves such areas unimpaired for future use and enjoyment as wilderness.

Address

Be aware that the mailing address is not always the same as the visitor center or the highlight of the site. In most cases, we've included the site's homepage on the World Wide Web. Scores of these sites still have only a minor web presence, if any. As we went to press, for example, the Forest Service was planning to significantly upgrade its website with the Department of Agriculture, and every month during our research, a new forest had added extremely useful new information and features, such as electronic visitor centers and maps and reservation information. In this first edition of Uncle Sam's Guide to the Great Outdoors, we've included the primary Forest Service Website—http://www.fs.fed.us—for most forests, except in those cases where a forest had developed a significant online presence.

Cooperating Association

Most sites are affiliated with a cooperating, interpretive or a historical association, each of which offers extremely worthwhile publications, videos and other information and products. We've done our best to link each association with the appropriate site, listing name, address, and phone number.

Site Description

Most site descriptions are drawn directly from the government publications gathered from a variety of sources (e.g., National Park or Forest Service headquarters, a regional office, or the sites themselves) and generally present the unique physical, cultural, or historic characteristics of the site.

Sam's Tips

This section gives you the inside skinny on the best and most interesting things to see and do at the site. We spoke or corresponded with hundreds of rangers and naturalists and asked them for any suggestions and highlights that we could pass along to visitors. These tips range from the best hiking trails to unique landmarks. We're grateful to all those with whom we corresponded and we trust that the information they supplied will be helpful to you.

Sidebars

Hundreds of sidebars are sprinkled throughout the book. Some are site-specific, meaning that they pertain to the history or geology or etymology of a particular monument, battlefield, forest, or wildlife refuge. Other sidebars pertain more generally to endangered species, volcanoes, historical episodes or people, volunteer programs, and safety. Sidebars are our favorite feature because they give us a chance to highlight things that simply interested, amused, or enlightened us. We hope they enlighten you as well.

Points of Interest

You'll note another feature called "Points of Interest" at the end of each state listing. These are drawn primarily from one of four public land managers—the

Army Corps of Engineers, the Bureau of Land Management, the Fish and Wildlife Service, and the Bureau of Reclamation—which are responsible for hundreds of smaller, recreational sites such as dams, lakes, marinas, grasslands, and rivers. They offer ideal opportunities for a daylong or weekend adventure or perhaps an afternoon picnic. We encourage readers to write to the agency's regional field office for further information.

The Northeast Region

NATIONAL PARK SERVICE HANDBOOKS—THE NORTHEAST REGION

National Park Service handbooks highlight popular visitor sites across the country. Use them to learn about the historic significance and natural beauty of your next vacation destination. All are generously illustrated with photos, maps, and diagrams. Sites in the Northeast for which these authoritative handbooks are available include:

Site	*Stock No.*	*Price*
Antietam National Battlefield (MD)	024-005-00892-6	$2.50
Appomattox Court House (VA)	024-005-00778-4	6.00
Assateague Island National Seashore (MD)	024-005-00776-8	7.50
Cape Cod (MA)	024-005-01126-9	5.00
Gettysburg National Military Park (PA)	024-005-00196-4	2.75
Independence National Historic Park (PA)	024-005-00913-2	3.25

You can place an order by phone (202-512-1800) or fax (202-512-2250), or by writing to: Superientendent of Documents, PO Box 371954, Pittsburgh, PA 15250-7954. (Use stock number when ordering. Prices may change.) There are 24 government bookstores located around the country which carry titles of regional interest. Check the Appendix section of this book for the one nearest to you.

NATIONAL PUBLIC LANDS DAY

National Public Lands Day is an annual volunteer program designed to bring thousands of citizens to national parks, national forests, Army Corps of Engineers recreation areas and Bureau of Land Management sites for hands-on restoration work and conservation education. These lands are part of the 640 million acres of public lands owned equally by every American.

National Public Lands Day offers citizens an opportunity to make a difference by giving something back to the lands where they retreat for recreation and relaxation. Since 1994, thousands of individuals have helped with trail restoration, wildlife habitat improvement, stream bank restoration, and other high-priority projects on public land sites. The value of this volunteer work to the agencies that manage the public lands increases each year as federal budgets get tighter.

Public Lands Day takes place on the last Saturday in September. To learn more about how to become a National Public Lands Day volunteer, contact: The Bureau of Land Management, Office of Environmental Education and Volunteers, 849 C Street, NW, MS-1275, Washington, DC 20240.

CONNECTICUT

WEIR FARM NATIONAL HISTORIC SITE

40 miles west of New Haven, CT; 60 miles northeast of New York City.

735 Nod Hill Road
Wilton, CT 06897
203-834-1896
http://www.nps.gov/wefa

The Weir Farm Heritage Trust. (write to the address above or call 203-761-9945)

Weir Farm has been inspiring artists and art lovers for more than 100 years. The American Impressionist painter Julian Alden Weir (1852–1919) purchased this 153-acre farm in 1882 for ten dollars and a painting. This was his primary summer studio for 40 years. The Farm suggested subject matter for much of Weir's work and for his wide circle of friends, including such leading figures in American art as Albert Pinkham Ryder, John Twachtman, and Childe Hassam.

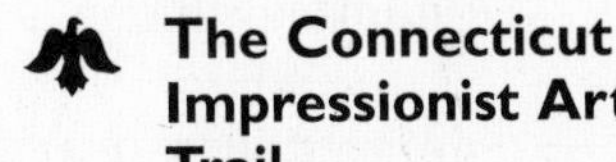

The Connecticut Impressionist Art Trail

Not for hiking! This "driving" trail covers eleven museums and other sites important to the American Impressionist movement. The sites include the Weir Farm, the New Britain Museum of American Art, the Yale University Art Gallery, and the Wadsworth Atheneum in Hartford. For more information and a brochure, call the numbers listed above.

Sam's Tips

- Artists are encouraged to bring their easels and sketchbooks. Beginners can borrow large pads of paper and crayons at the visitor center.
- Take the Historic Painting Sites Trail, where you are invited to compare landscape sites with those inspired by Weir, Hassam, and Ryder.
- The Weir Farm Heritage Trust sponsors art classes, lectures, exhibitions, and a Visiting Artist Program. Call the park for more information.

IN THE EVENT OF A NATURAL DISASTER . . .

Natural disasters—from hurricanes, to earthquakes, to flooding—can strike anytime, anywhere. One of the first places to turn is the Interactive Weather Information Network (http://iwin.nws.noaa.gov/iwin/main.html), part of the National Weather Service, where you will find up-to-date National Warnings for floods, hurricanes, and tropical and winter storms. Sites on specific disasters include the National Earthquake Information Center (http://wwwneic.cr.usgs.gov/), the National Landslide Information Center (http://gldage.cr.usgs.gov/html_files/nlicsun.html), and the Cascades Volcano Observatory (http://vulcan.wr.usgs.gov/).

Points of Interest

U.S. ARMY CORPS OF ENGINEERS

BLACK ROCK LAKE
Located next to Black Rock State Park, the 21-acre Black Rock Lake is crossed by a portion of the Mattatuck Trail. From Thomaston, go 2 miles west on CT 109.

COLEBROOK RIVER LAKE
This 750-acre lake is used as a standby water supply and is available seasonally for fishing and boating. A large boat ramp is available. From Winsted, go 6 miles north on CT 8.

HANCOCK BROOK LAKE
The project includes a shallow 40-acre lake and streamside environment good for canoeing, fishing, and hunting. From Plymouth, take CT 262 south to South Main Street to the lake.

HOP BROOK LAKE
A popular day-use area with swimming and picnicking facilities, an athletic field, and a picnic shelter. The 21-acre lake is stocked with trout by the State. From Naugatuck, go 3 miles north on CT 63.

MANSFIELD HOLLOW LAKE
A popular day-use park; managed by the State around a 450-acre lake. A large picnic area and playing fields serve as a nucleus to miles of hiking and cross-country skiing trails. Hunting and fishing opportunities are available. From Hartford, take I-84 and then US 6 to CT 195.

NORTHFIELD BROOK LAKE
A popular day-use park; offers swimming in the 7-acre lake, and picnicking and hiking in the environs. The reservoir area is open for fishing. From Thomaston, go 2 miles north on CT 254.

THOMASTON DAM
Vista picnic area offers visitors an excellent view of the dam and portions of the Naugatuck River Valley. The streamside environment is popular for fishing, hunting, trail bike riding, and snowmobiling. From Thomaston, go north on CT 222 to the dam.

WEST THOMPSON LAKE
Excellent camping in a rustic campground with wooded sites near the 200-acre lake. There are modern bathrooms with hot showers, a trailer dump station, and resident campground attendants. A picnic area, hiking, hunting, and fishing opportunities are available.

MAINE

ACADIA NATIONAL PARK

275 miles northeast of Boston, 100 miles east of Augusta, Mount Desert Island is on Maine Route 3.

PO Box 177
Bar Harbor, ME 04609
207-288-3338
http://www.nps.gov/acad

 **Eastern National.** (same address)

Thanks to summer residents of Mount Desert Island who, in the early 1900s began purchasing the land that now forms the park, Acadia National Park is one of New England's last undeveloped coastal stretches. This was the first area east of the Mississippi to be incorporated into the national park system, and it is the only national park in the northeast. The park has a rocky coastline (occasionally home to over 300 species of bird), lakes, ponds, meadows (over 500 types of wildflowers), and mountains (more than 15 rocky peaks including the 1,530-foot-high Cadillac Mountain). The forest, which survived a large fire in 1947, consists of spruce, fir, and pine. An extensive system of carriage roads (57 miles) and hiking trails (120 miles) makes Acadia's diverse and species-rich wilderness easy to explore.

 **Sam's Tips**

- Take one of the most beautiful carriage tours in America on the scenic Rockefeller carriage roads. Six daily routings depart from Park Loop Road, one-half mile south of the Jordan Pond House. Contact the Wildwood Stables from mid-June to mid-October, PO Box 241, Seal Harbor, ME 04675.
- A variety of boat tours, ranging from fishing trips to wildlife watching to scenic dining cruises, are available from private concessionaires in and around the park. Ask for a list of cruise operators from the park.
- Visit the Islesford Historical Museum and The Blue Duck, located on Little Cranberry Island. Besides commemorating those who lived on the Cranberry Islands, they preserve a part of the history of maritime New England.
- If you enjoy camping in remote areas, consider Isle au Haut. This island is accessible only by the daily mailboat ferry from Stonington. For schedules, contact the Isle au Haut Ferry Company, Stonington, ME 04681; 207-367-5193.

Rockefeller's Roads

The carriage roads that weave throughout Acadia National Park were the gift of John D. Rockefeller, Jr., who wanted car-free lanes to run into the heart of Mount Desert Island. Rockefeller developed his love of road building from his father, who had constructed and landscaped carriage roads on his Ohio and New York estates. The roads in the park are broken stone roads, a type commonly used at the turn of the century. Three layers of rock, stone culverts, wide ditches, and a substantial six- to eight-inch crown ensure good drainage. Acadia's carriage roads are the best example of broken stone roads left in America today.

- Thunder Hole (a chasm in the rocks where the water rushes in and makes a loud noise like thunder), Otter Cliffs (sheer 100-foot granite cliffs that dive straight down to the ocean), Cadillac Mountain, and the Puffin Cruises (taking visitors out into the Atlantic to view puffins) are some of the major attractions.
- Scuba diving in the park is a great way to see its abundant marine life. But be sure to bring a full wet suit; the sea water temperature does not climb above 55 degrees Fahrenheit. The inland lakes, however, are significantly warmer. There are lifeguards on duty in the summer at two locations: Echo Lake (freshwater) and Stone Beach (saltwater).
- Visit the shore at low tide, and see why park interpreters call Acadia "the living shores." Explore the fascinating world of tidepools, teeming with life and found all over the park's rugged coastline. Access is limited and slippery, so watch your step, and remember to clear out before the tide comes in.

SAINT CROIX ISLAND INTERNATIONAL HISTORIC SITE

80 miles northeast of Bangor, 206 miles northeast of Portland.

c/o Acadia National Park
PO Box 177
Bar Harbor, ME 04609
207-288-3338

The island, location of an unsuccessful French settlement in 1604, is in the Saint Croix River, which forms part of the U.S.–Canadian border. The site, which commemorates the settlement and the founding of New France, is managed by the National Park Service in cooperation with the Canadian government.

Sam's Tips

- There are wayside exhibits on both the American and Canadian sides of the St. Croix River, but the island itself is inaccessible to the public.

NATIONAL FOREST FOUNDATION

The National Forest Foundation (NFF) is a nonprofit organization that supports the U.S. Forest Service in managing 191 million acres of public land. It plants trees, runs youth camps and urban tree houses, and raises funds to benefit forests. For membership and project information, contact: National Forest Foundation, 1099 14th Street, NW, Suite 5600-W, Washington, DC 20005 (phone: 202-501-2473; fax: 202-219-6585; Website: http://www.nffweb.org).

MARYLAND

ANTIETAM NATIONAL BATTLEFIELD

17 miles south of Hagerstown, 70 miles east of Baltimore; on Maryland Route 65.

PO Box 158
Sharpsburg, MD 21782-0158
301-432-5124
http://www.nps.gov/anti

Parks and History Association. (126 Raleigh Street SE, Washington, DC 20032; 800-990-7275)

The battle of Antietam (or Sharpsburg), on September 17, 1862, was the result of Confederate General Robert E. Lee's first attempt to carry the war into the North. About 40,000 Southerners were pitted against the 87,000-man Federal Army of the Potomac under General George B. McClellan. In the ensuing battle—known as "the bloodiest single-day battle of the Civil War"—Federal losses numbered 12,410, and Confederate losses were 10,700. Neither side gained a decisive victory, but Lee's failure to advance into the North caused Great Britain to postpone recognition of the Confederate government. The battle also gave President Abraham Lincoln the opportunity to issue the Emancipation Proclamation which, on January 1, 1863, declared free all slaves in the states still in rebellion against the United States. Now the war had a dual purpose: to

CIVIL WAR SOLDIERS AND SAILORS SYSTEM

The Civil War Soldiers and Sailors System will be a computerized database—accessible through a National Park Service Website—containing: very basic facts about servicemen, on both sides, during the Civil War; a list of regiments in both the Union and the Confederate armies; identifications and descriptions of 384 significant battles of the war; references that identify the sources of the information in the database; and suggestions for where to find additional information. The first phase of the Civil War Soldiers System is complete, and more than 235,000 names of soldiers who served in African American units in the Civil War are now available. The CWSS System is made possible by partnerships with the Federation of Genealogical Societies, the Genealogical Society of Utah, the United Daughters of the Confederacy, and other partners. Additional information about soldiers, sailors, regiments, and battles, as well as prisoner-of-war records and cemetery records, will be added over time. The Website is located at http://www.itd.nps.gov/cwss/.

preserve the Union and to end slavery. Amid the fields and farmlands of the battlefield, visitors can easily envision the bloody events that took place there. The Antietam Creek runs along the edge of the camping area, and Burnside Bridge, the park's best known landmark, is nearby.

SAM'S TIPS

- There are interpretive markers at Turner's, Fox's, and Crampton's Gaps on South Mountain (scenes of preliminary fighting) and at the Shepherdstown Ford, where Lee's army recrossed the Potomac.
- Before starting your tour of the battlefield, stop at the visitor center's exhibits and audiovisual programs, which provide an introduction to the battle and the Maryland Campaign.

ASSATEAGUE ISLAND NATIONAL SEASHORE

7 miles south of Ocean City, 160 miles east of Washington, DC.

7206 National Seashore Lane
Berlin, MD 21811
410-641-1441
http://www.nps.gov/asis

Eastern National. (446 North Lane, Conshohocken, PA 19428; 800-355-5566)

Assateague Island is a mix of white sandy beaches along the Atlantic Ocean side and dunes, pine forests, salt marshes, and sheltered coves on Chincoteague Bay. The 37-mile-long barrier island, located off the Maryland and Virginia mainland, is a favorite haunt of nesting shorebirds and migrating waterfowl. Several bands of wild ponies roam the island.

SAM'S TIPS

- Ask at a visitor center for fishing information. Naturalists present surf-fishing demonstrations in summer for anglers new to the sport. Clamming is best at the island's Maryland end. The favored method here is raking while wading in the generally shallow water.
- Approximately half of the Refuge trails are paved for bicyclists, including the Wildlife Loop and Woodland Trail.
- If you are coming from the Maryland end, make the Barrier Island Visitor Center your first stop. It features exhibits, publications, and an aquarium.
- In Maryland, the park offers two campgrounds, Oceanside and Bayside, with some sites available year-round.

Wild Horses

Two herds of wild horses known as "ponies" make their homes on Assateague Island. The herds are separated by a fence at the boundary between Maryland and Virginia. In Maryland, horses are often seen around roads and campgrounds. In Virginia, look for them in Black Duck Marsh from observation platforms along Beach Road and Woodland Trail.

Primitive outdoor facilities include chemical toilets, drinking water, and cold-water showers. A campsite reservation system is available from May 15 to October 15.

- For information about the the Chincoteague Refuge, visit the Refuge Visitor Center at the Virginia end, or contact the Refuge Manager, Chincoteague National Wildlife Refuge, PO Box 62, Chincoteague, VA 23336; 757-336-6122. The refuge offers wildlife-oriented interpretive walks, as well as narrated land and boat tours. On summer weekends, holidays, and during Pony Penning Week, local wildlife artists exhibit their work in the historic Lighthouse Oil Shed, a short walk up the Lighthouse Trail.
- Be sure to bring mosquito repellent. Assateague's little stingers are almost as famous as its ponies.

CATOCTIN MOUNTAIN PARK

The park is 25 miles northwest of Frederick, 70 miles northwest of Washington, DC.

6602 Foxville Road
Thurmont, MD 21788-1598
301-663-9388
http://www.nps.gov/cato

Parks and History Association. (126 Raleigh Street SE, Washington, DC 20032; 800-990-7275)

Men once logged, farmed, and made moonshine deep in the hills of this low-slung portion of the Appalachian Mountains range. Today, campers and day-trippers come for a quiet woodland visit. Creeks flow through the hills, and white-tailed deer are commonplace.

Sam's Tips

- About 25 miles of trails, many leading to outstanding vistas, are set aside for hiking, cross-country skiing, and snowshoeing. Four trails—Hog Rock, Browns Farm Environmental Study Area, Cunningham Falls, and Renaissance—are self-guiding and nature-oriented.
- The Blue Blazes Whiskey Still has interpretive talks on selected weekends. Dates are published in the park's events calendar.
- Rustic cabins are available for rent from mid-April through the last weekend in October. For reservations and information, call 301-271-3140.
- For a driving tour, stop by the visitor center on Route 77 for suggestions on routes and times. A scenic overlook on the east side of Hunting Creek Lake (in Cunningham Falls State Park) offers a panoramic view of the water and woods.

CHESAPEAKE AND OHIO CANAL NATIONAL HISTORICAL PARK

Parallel to the Potomac River, on the Maryland side; from Georgetown in Washington, DC, to Cumberland, MD, 184.5 miles to the northwest.

Box 4
Sharpsburg, MD 21782
301-739-4200
http://www.nps.gov/choh/co_visit.htm

Parks and History Association. (126 Raleigh Street SE, Washington, DC 20032; 800-990-7275)

The park preserves remnants of America's transportation history. A towpath paralleling the entire canal provides a nearly level byway for hikers and bicyclists. The canal's watered sections provide quiet refuge to canoeists, boaters, and anglers. For many years, the Chesapeake and Ohio Canal was the lifeline for communities and business along its route as it floated coal, lumber, grain, and other products to market.

SAM'S TIPS

- The National Park Service operates information centers at Georgetown (1057 Thomas Jefferson Street, NW, Washington, DC 20007; 202-653-5190), Great Falls Tavern (11710 MacArthur Boulevard, Potomac, MD 20854; 301-299-3613), Hancock (326 E. Main Street, Hancock, MD 21750; 301-678-5463), Williamsport (205 W. Potomac Street, Williamsport, MD 21795; 301-582-0813), and Cumberland (Canal Street, Cumberland, MD 21502; 301-722-8226). For general information, write or call the Superintendent at the Sharpsburg, MD, address.
- A museum in the historic Great Falls Tavern includes an exhibit about the canal's operation.
- You can relive the canal's heyday, afloat on mule-powered barges, in the Georgetown and Great Falls areas. Boats run from mid-April to mid-October. Tickets go on sale two hours before each trip.
- Canal canoeing and boating are popular in watered levels, or sections, between Georgetown and Violettes Lock. You must portage around each lock. Canoes, as well as boats and bicycles, can be rented at Swains Lock (301-299-9006), Thompson's Boat Center (202-333-4861), and Fletcher's Boathouse (202-244-0461).
- The U.S. Weather Bureau provides a taped message on river conditions in the lower Potomac Valley. Call 703-260-0305.

CLARA BARTON NATIONAL HISTORIC SITE

10 miles northwest of Washington, DC, adjacent to Glen Echo Park.

5801 Oxford Road
Glen Echo, MD 20812
301-492-6245
http://www.nps.gov/clba

Parks and History Association. (126 Raleigh Street SE, Washington, DC 20032; 800-990-7275)

The Clara Barton National Historic Site was the headquarters of the American Red Cross from 1897 to 1904 and the home of its founder from 1897 until her death in 1912. This unusual 41-room building is furnished with original and period artifacts commemorating Barton and the American Red Cross. The house is open from 10 A.M. until 5 P.M. every day, and the 30-minute guided tours, which are the only way to see the house, are available every hour until 4 P.M. The site is a small one, but the neighboring Glen Echo Park has more extensive facilities.

Clara Barton and the Red Cross

In 1869, recovering from a breakdown in her health, Clara Barton traveled to Europe for rest. It was there that she first heard of the International Red Cross. During the Franco-Prussian War, she worked with the group to provide relief for the war-stricken civilians of France and Germany. Ten years of further poor health, uncooperative government officials, and public apathy could not dampen her determination to carry the organization's ideal to this country. In 1882, the U.S. Senate ratified the Treaty of Geneva, which officially established the Red Cross in the United States.

FORT MCHENRY NATIONAL MONUMENT AND HISTORIC SHRINE

Baltimore, MD.

End of East Fort Avenue
Baltimore, MD 21230
410-962-4299
http://www.nps.gov/fomc

 **Evelyn Hill Corporation.** (same address; 410-625-2330)

Starting in the early morning of September 13, 1814, some 1,500 to 1,800 shells and rockets were fired at Fort McHenry during a ferocious British naval attack. In the morning of September 14, it became clear that the defense of the fort had been successful. As the British sailed away, the American soldiers at the fort fired the morning gun and hoisted a large U.S. flag. An influential young Washington lawyer named Francis Scott Key witnessed the entire battle scene from the deck of a U.S. truce ship and jotted down some notes. He finished the poem on his return to Baltimore. The "Defense of Fort McHenry" was published the

Flag Facts

Key's star-spangled banner measured 42 feet wide and 30 feet long. The original is now in the Smithsonian, but Fort McHenry has a replica. Because of its size, it can be flown only in certain conditions. In winds less than 5 miles per hour, the flag cannot unfurl, and in winds of more than 12 miles per hour, the flagstaff is at risk of being broken.

next day and was soon being sung to the tune of "To Anacreon in Heaven." Key's lyrics and their imported melody became the official National Anthem of the United States. Fort McHenry never again came under enemy fire, although it continued as an active military post for the next 100 years. During the Civil War, it was used as a temporary prison for captured Confederate soldiers, Southern sympathizers, and political prisoners. From 1917 to 1923, U.S. Army General Hospital No. 2 was located here to serve WWI veterans. In 1925, it was made a National Park; 14 years later, it was redesignated a national monument and historic shrine. It is the only park in the country to have this double distinction.

SAM'S TIPS

- Exhibits of historical and military memorabilia are displayed in the restored barracks and Visitor Center.
  It takes roughly 30–40 minutes to visit all five historical structures.
- Don't miss the inspiring film, *The Defense of Fort McHenry,* in the Visitor Center. This 16-minute captioned film highlights the events that inspired Francis Scott Key to write "The Star-Spangled Banner" and ends with a rendition by the U. S. Naval Academy Choir.
- The daily flag change at the fort preserves the truly "living quality" of the old fort. Following a 20-minute talk, visitors actively participate with the park staff in hoisting or taking down the fort's flag. This "hands-on" activity gives visitors a true appreciation of sacrifice and patriotism at Fort McHenry. The flag changes are held daily, weather permitting.
- The park also offers special talks for children, who may walk the ramparts, explore a soldier's equipment, practice loading a cannon, or learn why artifacts are important. It is recommended that groups schedule an appointment at least one month prior to their arrival.
- Annual celebrations are held on Flag Day, June 14, and Defenders Day, held on the second Sunday in September. These free performances involve live music and fireworks.

TAKE THE PATUXENT BIRD QUIZ

A terrific Website at the Patuxent Wildlife Research Center (part of the Biological Services Division of the U.S. Geological Survey) is a must for any birder. See beautiful pictures of common U.S., Canadian, and Central American birds, and hear their songs and calls on audio. You can also take an interactive Bird Quiz to test your knowledge. Go to: http://www.mbr.nbs.gov/bbs/trend/birdquiz.html.

BOX SCORE OF ENDANGERED SPECIES

Scientists, researchers, and others will find a very informative "boxscore" of all endangered and threatened species in the United States at the Fish and Wildlife Website: http://www.fws.gov/~r9endspp /boxscore.html. Total U.S. threatened species: 222 (111 animals, 111 plants). Total U.S. endangered species: 858 (335 animals, 523 plants).

FORT WASHINGTON PARK

The Maryland side of the Potomac River, south of Washington, DC.

13551 Fort Washington Road
Fort Washington, MD 20744
301-763-4600
http://www.nps.gov/fowa

Parks and History Association. (126 Raleigh Street SE, Washington, DC 20032; 800-990-7275)

The Treaty of Paris, which ended the American Revolution, did not settle all the problems between the former colony and Great Britain. In 1808, to protect the national capital, the United States began work on Fort Warburton, on the Maryland side of the Potomac River, across from Mount Vernon. This first incarnation of Fort Washington fell after British forces landed at Benedict, Maryland, on August 19, 1814, and marched overland to Washington, DC. Less than a month after its demolition, Fort Warburton began to rise from its own ashes. Pierre Charles L'Enfant was commissioned to design the new structure, which was renamed Fort Washington. During the Civil War, the development of armored ships and rifled cannon altered the nature of warfare. The answer was concrete batteries that housed larger rifled cannon with a greater range. Even though the batteries were located away from the river, they were as effective as the earlier brick structure had been against wooden ships. Fort Washington is not just one structure but several that were built to meet the changing demands of strategy and technology.

Sam's Tips

- On weekends, park interpreters, dressed in authentic U.S. Army uniforms, recreate the life of a 19th-century military garrison. They demonstrate how to load and fire muzzle-loading weapons, talk about the everyday life of an enlisted man, and conduct military ceremonies. These programs take place only at specified times, so call 301-763-4600 for a schedule of events.
- Fort Foote is often overlooked by park visitors. This dirt fort was part of the circle of forts around the nation's capital, and it houses two of the biggest smooth-bore cannons ever used by the U.S. Army. The fort is connected to the rest of the park by a hiking trail which leads to a really nice sandy beach right on the Potomac.

GLEN ECHO PARK

10 miles west of Washington, DC.

7300 MacArthur Boulevard
Glen Echo, MD 20812
301-492-6229
http://www.nps.gov/glee

Parks and History Association. (126 Raleigh Street SE, Washington, DC 20032; 800-990-7275)

For over 100 years, the land now designated as Glen Echo Park has been dedicated to public use—first, in 1891, as a National Chautauqua Assembly, a center where people could participate in the sciences, arts, languages, and literature; then, until 1968, as a famous amusement park. Now, the park has come full circle as a place that emphasizes the arts and cultural education for the community.

SAM'S TIPS

- Classes are taught year-round by artists and educators, some of whom are members of the artist residency program. Visits to artists' studios are encouraged. Call the park for a catalog and more information about this and the May–June and September–October cultural events series.
- The antique, hand-carved, and hand-painted Dentzel Carousel operates on every Wednesday, Thursday, and weekend during the summer.

GREENBELT PARK

10 miles north of Washington, DC.

6565 Greenbelt Road
Greenbelt, MD 20770-3207
301-344-3948; 301-344-3944 (weekends)
http://www.nps.gov/gree

This woodland retreat in the greater Washington, DC, metropolitan area allows urban dwellers to go camping and get away from the pressures of city life without going far from home. Situated on the rolling hills of the Piedmont coastal plain, the park's hardwood forests are a natural sanctuary for raccoons, squirrels, red fox, bobwhite quail, and many other birds.

SAM'S TIPS

- Visit the Airport Museum at the College Park Airport, the world's oldest, continually running airport. It was established in 1909 when the Wright brothers brought their aeroplane to the field in order to teach Army officers how to fly.

- Another off-beat stop is the Beltsville Agricultural Research Center. Tour the 7,000-acre facility by calling in advance 301-504-9403.
- In Greenbelt Park, three marked nature trails introduce visitors to the park's flora, ecology, and human history: The 1.3-mile Azalea Trail connects the three picnic areas and passes through plant communities that grow along streams and hillsides. The Perimeter Trail is primarily for horseback riding. This 6-mile loop circles the park's western section and leads to some of the most picturesque areas of the park. The 1.4-mile Dogwood Trail begins at the parking area on Park Central Road.

HAMPTON NATIONAL HISTORIC SITE

10 miles north of Baltimore.

535 Hampton Lane
Towson, MD 21286
410-823-1309
http://www.nps.gov/hamp

This 18th-century, 33-room mansion, built between 1783 and 1790, remains one of the largest and most ornate Georgian houses in America. Hampton Hall's design follows the traditional balanced five-part plan: a main house, two flanking wings, and "hyphens" or enclosed passages that connect the wings to the central structure. The interior of the mansion is decorated with original furniture, paintings, and other material culture representing the major periods of Ridgely family occupancy. Surrounding Hampton Hall are beautiful formal gardens and numerous exotic trees. A tearoom (serving luncheon) and a gift shop are located in the mansion.

MONOCACY NATIONAL BATTLEFIELD

Frederick, MD.

4801 Urbana Pike
Frederick, MD 21701-7307
301-662-3515
http://www.nps.gov/mono

Parks and History Association. (126 Raleigh Street SE, Washington, DC 20032; 800-990-7275)

If judged by its consequences rather than its size, the Battle of Monocacy ranks among the most important battles of the American Civil War. On July 9, 1864, on a checkerboard of gold wheat fields and green cornfields just outside Frederick, MD, Confederate forces under General Jubal Early defeated Union forces under General Lew Wallace. The battle cost Early a day's march and his chance to capture Washington, DC. Thwarted in the attempt to take the capital, the Confederates turned back to Virginia, ending their last campaign to carry the war into the north. The preserved battlefield includes a small visitor center and five monuments that are accessible by the public roads.

PISCATAWAY PARK

Maryland side of the Potomac River, across from Mount Vernon, downstream from Woodrow Wilson Bridge.

Fort Washington Park
13551 Fort Washington Road
Fort Washington, MD 20744
301-763-4600
http://www.nps.gov/pisc

Alice Ferguson Foundation and Hard Bargain Farm Environmental Center. (2001 Bryan Point Road, Accokeek, MD 20607; 301-292-5665)

Accokeek Foundation and National Colonial Farm. (3400 Bryan Point Road, Accokeek, MD 20607; 301-283-2113)

Piscataway Park stretches for 6 miles from Piscataway Creek to Marshall Hall on the Potomac. Waterfowl come to feed in the wetlands and along the shore, white-tailed deer browse in upland areas, and an occasional bald eagle or other raptor soars overhead. The National Colonial Farm and Hard Bargain Farm, working with the National Park Service, offer interpretive programs about the park's historic and natural resources.

Hard Bargain Farm

Adjacent to the northern end of the park, the Alice Ferguson Foundation operates the 330-acre Hard Bargain Farm Environmental Center. Here, a cooperative program developed by the Foundation and the National Park Service teaches thousands of children to protect and preserve the natural environment. By arrangement, youngsters come to explore a working farm and study the wildlife found along the river. Except for special events held several times a year for all comers, Hard Bargain Farm is open only to group participants or by special arrangement through the Foundation.

THOMAS STONE NATIONAL HISTORIC SITE

40 miles southeast of Washington, DC.

6655 Rose Hill Road
Port Tobacco, MD 20677
301-934-6027
http://www.nps.gov/thst

Haberdeventure, a Georgian mansion built in 1771 near Port Tobacco, MD, was the home of Thomas Stone (1743–1787), a signer of the Declaration of Independence and a delegate to the Continental Congress.

Points of Interest

U.S. ARMY CORPS OF ENGINEERS

CHESAPEAKE AND DELAWARE CANAL
The Old Lock Pumphouse in Chesapeake City was built in 1837 at the site of the original canal. A major fossil area is found near the Summit RR Bridge. From Wilmington, DE, go south on US 13, west on US 40, south on MD 213 to Chesapeake City, MD, and follow the signs to the Canal Museum and Project Office.

MEET YOUR PARK RANGERS

The National Park Service has a varied and experienced staff of national stature—rangers, natural resource managers, archaeologists, historians, interpreters, landscape architects, engineers, and planners—who protect our land and legacy, conduct research, and educate the public. Throughout this book, we'd like to introduce you to some of them.

Deb and Jay Liggett, a dual career couple, are, respectively, Superintendent at Devils Tower, Wyoming, and Chief Ranger at Theodore Roosevelt National Park, North Dakota. Deb and Jay have worked in many parks, though not always together. As newlyweds, they both worked as seasonals at the Grand Canyon. However, they were assigned different housing—Deb on the rim and Jay at the bottom of the canyon. "We stayed in good shape hiking in and out on our days off," Jay said. Fifteen years and seven parks later, they now live 255 miles apart. "Why do we do it? It's a job worth doing. The NPS is our life. Do we like living apart? No. If there was a better or easier way to do it, we would choose that route. But in order for us to work in jobs that are challenging, for a mission that's 'worth doing,' we have to take risks. Each time one of us moves, we take a risk. So far we have been fairly lucky. The risks have paid off. Who knows what the next move entails. . . . "

MASSACHUSETTS

ADAMS NATIONAL HISTORIC SITE

10 miles south of Boston.

135 Adams Street
PO Box 531
Quincy, MA 02269-0531
617-770-1175
http://www.nps.gov/adam

This site includes the birthplaces of John and John Quincy Adams and the "Old House," home to four generations of the Adams family. The nearby United First Parish Church, still an active parish, contains both presidents' and their first ladies' tombs. The 18th-century formal garden, the historic orchard, and 30,000 artifacts provide a setting for visitors to explore and reflect upon this remarkable family of presidents, public servants, writers, and historians.

Sam's Tips

- All trips begin at the Visitor Center (1250 Hancock Street, in Quincy). The 13-acre park—including the birthplaces, the Old House, and its library, gardens, and stables—is open to the public from April to November. Transportation to the historic homes is via a trolley bus. Tour space is limited and is filled on a first-come, first-served basis.
- The Old House's gardens and gravel paths feature horticultural wonders, such as the white York rose, which Abigail Adams brought back from a 1788 trip to England and which still thrives today.

The Adams Family

The political and intellectual contributions of the Adams family to our nation are unmatched by those of any other family. President John F. Kennedy said, in 1961, that the successive Adamses' "vitality" and "devotion to the public interest" run like a "scarlet thread through the entire tapestry" of American history. We owe our knowledge of this remarkable record to the care and foresight of the Adamses themselves, who were well aware of the hand of history on their shoulders. "Whatever you write, preserve," John Adams instructed two grandsons who were sailing in 1815 to join their father, John Quincy Adams, the new American minister to London. Toward the end of the 19th century, a visitor reported that, after surveying the crowded shelves of Adams archives running around three sides of the family library, he had seen "the manuscript history of America in the diaries and correspondence of two Presidents and of that Minister to England [Charles Francis Adams] who spoke the decisive word which saved England and America from a third war."

- There are several local picnic/park areas. Faxon Park is one of the closest. (Directions: At the intersection of Franklin Street and Independence Avenue, bear left on Franklin Street to the first set of lights at Kendrick Road and then go left. Kendrick Road becomes Faxon Park at the top of the hill. The entrance will be on your right.)

BOSTON AFRICAN AMERICAN NATIONAL HISTORIC SITE

Downtown Boston.

46 Joy Street
Boston, MA 02114
617-742-5415
http://www.nps.gov/boaf

The Boston African American National Historic Site explores the history of Beacon Hill's 19th-century black community. The 1.6-mile Black Heritage Trail, winding through what is now one of Boston's most fashionable neighborhoods, highlights 15 pre-Civil War sites with close ties to the history of the city's African American community.

Sam's Tips

- The Black Heritage Trail begins at the Shaw Memorial across from the State House. Black and brown signs identify sites. The Shaw Memorial, sculpted by Augustus Saint-Gaudens, is a tribute to Robert Gould Shaw and the 54th Regiment Massachusetts Volunteer Infantry, which was featured in the film *Glory*.
- The site sponsors historical reenactments, living history encampments, speeches, and parades. Reenactments include the 54th Regiment's 1863 departure from Boston, with speeches by Frederick Douglass, and a Civil War Encampment on the Boston Common. Call or write for dates.
- When you walk the trail, be sure to visit the African Meeting House at 8 Smith Court, Beacon Hill, the oldest standing African American church building in the country. It was there that William Lloyd Garrison founded the New England Antislavery Society in 1832.

PLANTS NATIONAL DATABASE

Courtesy of the U.S. Department of Agriculture, the PLANTS Database provides a single source of standardized information about the plant kingdom. A magnificent resource, featuring scores of images, PLANTS is one of the most attractive Websites in Uncle Sam's domain. A necessary tool for natural resource managers, scientists, forest biologists, and other professionals, PLANTS is also invaluable for backyard gardeners. To access the Database on the World Wide Web, go to: http://plants.usda.gov.

BOSTON NATIONAL HISTORICAL PARK

Downtown Boston and Charlestown (1.5 miles from downtown), and South Boston (3 miles from downtown).

Charlestown Navy Yard
Boston, MA 02129
617-242-5644
http://www.nps.gov/bost

 **Eastern National.** (446 North Lane, Conshohocken, PA 19428; 800-355-5566)

This large, urban park contains 16 sites connected by Boston's 2.5-mile-long Freedom Trail: numerous historic homes, churches, public buildings, the Charlestown Navy Yard, and the Bunker Hill Monument. Together, these sites reflect the ideas that influenced the events surrounding the Revolutionary War and the founding of our nation.

 **Sam's Tips**

- Allow a day to walk the Freedom Trail from its beginning at the Boston Common to its end across the harbor at the Charlestown Navy Yard. The trail is marked by a red line on the sidewalk or by red brick or granite paving stones.
- The National Park Service offers guided tours of the best known sites along the Freedom Trail. Ranger tours start at the Boston National Park Visitors Center across from the Old State House (15 State Street) and take you to Faneuil Hall, the Old State House, the Old South Meeting House, the Paul Revere House, and the Old North Church.

CAPE COD NATIONAL SEASHORE

100 miles southeast of Boston.

South Wellfleet, MA 02663
508-349-3785
http://www.nps.gov/caco

 **Eastern National.** (446 North Lane, Conshohocken, PA 19428; 800-355-5566)

One of America's most popular vacation destinations, this hook-shaped peninsula, a quintessential seashore environment, contains woodlands, marshes, wildlife, dramatic dunes, and 40 miles of sandy beaches. Swimming, fishing, hiking, biking, and whale watching are popular activities, but there's also a lot to learn about maritime history, architecture, and even communications at the Marconi Wireless Station at Wellfleet.

SAM'S TIPS

- Several historic buildings are open for tours in the summer. The Old Harbor Lifesaving Station was moved from Chatham to Race Point in 1977; Captain Edward Penninman's 1868 house in Eastham is atypically ornate and reminiscent of the once-profitable whaling era; Nauset Light is one of five lighthouses within the seashore; and the Atwood-Higgins House, built around 1730, represents the typical Cape Cod dwelling.
- The Cape is a glacial deposit that is constantly undergoing natural changes as winds and water move sand along the shorelines. You can get a good sense of how quickly the land is diminishing at the Marconi Wireless Station at Wellfleet, where the peninsula is only a mile wide.
- Great Island, once a secluded area where whalers would congregate, is now connected to the peninsula and accessible by the Great Island Trail. Be aware, however, that the land south of Great Island becomes submerged during all but the lowest tides.
- Whale-watch cruises operate from April to October. Cape Cod Cruises, located at the Fisherman's Wharf in Provincetown, can be reached at 508-747-2400. Or try Hyannis Whale Watcher Cruises at 800-287-0374 or 508-362-6088.
- There are two main visitor centers: Salt Pond Visitor Center on US 6 in Eastham and Province Lands Visitor Center on Race Point Road in Provincetown. Ranger-guided walks, talks, and evening programs are offered daily in the summer. Free printed schedules are available upon request.

THE 10 ESSENTIALS FOR HIKING

Proper equipment can mean the difference between fun and tragedy. The White Mountain National Forest (NH) recommends taking these 10 essential items on every hike:

1. Map.
2. Compass.
3. Warm clothing.
4. Extra food and water.
5. Flashlight or headlamp.
6. Matches.
7. First aid kit.
8. Whistle.
9. Rain gear.
10. Pocket knife.

The King of Suburbia

Olmsted was a prophet of suburbia, believing that "no great city can long exist without great suburbs." During the course of his career, he designed more than a dozen suburban communities outside cities like Baltimore and Chicago. They were intended to be places where people could express their individuality and practice the art of gardening while retaining convenient access to the commerce and amenities of the city. As in his public parks, Olmsted's ideals were reflected in his vision of the private landscape, which "fosters delicacy of perception and of sentiment, strengthens family ties and feeds the roots of patriotism."

FREDERICK LAW OLMSTED NATIONAL HISTORIC SITE

Brookline is a suburb west of Boston.

99 Warren Street
Brookline, MA 02146
617-566-1689
http://www.nps.gov/frla

Eastern National. (446 North Lane, Conshohocken, PA 19428; 800-355-5566)

Perhaps more than any other person, Frederick Law Olmsted affected the way America looks. Olmsted, designer of New York's Central Park and many other of the nation's best known green spaces, is considered the father of American landscape architecture. From 1883 to 1979, his firm was based at "Fairsted" where Olmsted, his sons, and their associates worked on thousands of projects from coast to coast. Today, visitors can tour the historic design office and see samples of the over 140,000 drawings and work spaces used in the early 20th century. The recently restored grounds offer an excellent example of Olmsted's design theory, which characterized his great urban parks.

JOHN FITZGERALD KENNEDY NATIONAL HISTORIC SITE

Brookline is a suburb west of Boston.

83 Beals Street
Brookline, MA 02146
617-566-7937
http://www.nps.gov/jofi

Eastern National. (446 North Lane, Conshohocken, PA 19428; 800-355-5566)

Joseph and Rose Kennedy began their family life in this modest home on a quiet tree-lined street. John F. Kennedy, 35th President of the United States, was born in the upstairs front bedroom in 1917 and lived there until age four. Many of the furnishings are original. An audiotape of Rose Kennedy relating tales of family history is used during guided tours through the home. A neighborhood walking tour takes you to nearby points of significance in the early years of the Kennedy family.

LONGFELLOW NATIONAL HISTORIC SITE

Cambridge is 5 miles from downtown Boston.

105 Brattle Street
Cambridge, MA 02138
617-876-4492
http://www.nps.gov/long

 **Eastern National.** (446 North Lane, Conshohocken, PA 19428; 800-355-5566)

 **Friends of the Longfellow House.** (same address as historic site)

The Vassal family of British sympathizers fled this house when General George Washington came to Cambridge to take command of the colonial forces. Used by Washington as his headquarters in 1775–1776, the house later became the home of Henry Wadsworth Longfellow (1837–1882). Literary friends Nathaniel Hawthorne and Ralph Waldo Emerson were among his notable guests. The "Chestnut Tree" chair, a gift to Longfellow from local school children, remains in his study.

LOWELL NATIONAL HISTORICAL PARK

Lowell is 26 miles north of Boston.

67 Kirk Street
Lowell, MA 01852
978-970-5000
http://www.nps.gov/lowe

 **Eastern National.** (446 North Lane, Conshohocken, PA 19428; 800-355-5566)

Lowell—once called "Spindle City"—ushered America into the Industrial Age. Starting in the 1820s, water from the Merrimack River was harnessed to power cotton textile mills. At the Boott Cotton Mills Museum you can experience the clatter and heat early workers endured, and enjoy the many interactive exhibits on labor and immigrant history. Explore the story of the Yankee "Mill Girls" at the restored boarding house, and see a working turbine at the Suffolk Mill Exhibit. Replicas of 1901 streetcars connect the park sites, from April through November.

Francis Lowell

America's Industrial Revolution began in New England, in the early 19th century, with the development of the textile industry. Francis Cabot Lowell (1775–1817) was a pioneer textile manufacturer who designed and built the first power loom in America. After his death, his financial backers transformed East Chelmsford (renamed Lowell) into the nation's first planned factory town. By 1840, Lowell had become a major textile center, with nine mill complexes and 4,000 looms.

SAM'S TIPS

- For information about interactive workshops for children grades 4–12, professional development workshops for teachers, and programs in topics related to industrial history, contact the Tsongas Industrial History Center (Boott Cotton Mills Museum, 400 Foot of John Street, Lowell, MA 01852; 978-970-5080).
- On the last full weekend of July, the park suspends its regular tour schedule to offer the Lowell Folk Festival, a celebration of traditional music and dance, with street parades, dance parties, and ethnic foods. The festival takes place on six outdoor stages, in the streets, and along the canals of historic Lowell.
- The Lowell Summer Music Festival features concerts throughout the summer.

MINUTE MAN NATIONAL HISTORICAL PARK

Concord is 20 miles west of Boston.

174 Liberty Street
Concord, MA 01742
978-369-6944 or 6993
http://www.nps.gov/mima

 **Eastern National.** (446 North Lane, Conshohocken, PA 19428; 800-355-5566)

On April 19, 1775, the American Revolution began in earnest when citizen-soldiers fired "the shot heard 'round the world" at Concord's Old North Bridge. You can follow the British retreat to Boston along Battle Road with stops at the restored Hartwell Tavern, Daniel Chester French's famed Minute Man statue, the North Bridge, and the historic garden at the Buttrick Mansion Visitor Center.

SAM'S TIPS

- The pre-Revolutionary Old Manse (Box 572, Monument Street; 978-369-3909) was the home of Emerson, Ripley, and Hawthorne. Canoe or just walk around Walden Pond State Reservation (Walden Street, Route 126; 978-369-3254). Recreational activities include a hiking trail that leads to the site of Thoreau's cabin.
- At the Orchard House (399 Lexington Road; 978-369-4118), home of the Alcotts, Louisa May Alcott wrote *Little Women*.
- The interior of the Emerson House (28 Cambridge Turnpike; 978-369-2236), home of Ralph Waldo Emerson, has been maintained with original furnishings.

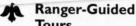

Ranger-Guided Tours

Harnessing the Merrimack: Journey through the Pawtucket Canal, through Guard Locks, and onto the Merrimack River to discover how the river was diverted and controlled to provide water for Lowell's textile industry.

Run of the Mill Tour: Travel to the Suffolk Mill to see a working 19th-century turbine and an operating power loom. Learn how new technology and labor sources made Lowell's factory system work.

Pawtucket Canal Tour: Travel by foot, trolley, and boat to the Francis Gate and Guard Locks on the Pawtucket Canal to see how Lowell's planners integrated transportation with flood control, and harnessed water for industrial purposes.

- In the Sleepy Hollow Cemetery (Route 62), you will find the graves of Thoreau, Emerson, Hawthorne, and the Alcotts.
- The Wayside (455 Lexington Road; 978-369-6975) was home to literary giants Louisa May Alcott and Nathaniel Hawthorne.

SALEM MARITIME NATIONAL HISTORIC SITE

Salem is 20 miles northeast of Boston.

174 Derby Street
Salem, MA 01970
978-740-1650
http://www.nps.gov/sama

 **Eastern National.** (2 New Liberty Street, Salem, MA, 01970; 978-745-6668)

Salem is well known as the site of the 17th-century witch trials. Less well known is the fact that Salem was once the sixth largest city in the United States; its name was famous among merchants and traders throughout the world. Today, the city's maritime history can be relived through a collection of restored harbor structures that include three wharves. The Salem story is a saga of enterprising and daring Yankee sea captains, privateers, and merchants who transformed a tiny, uncertain settlement into a rich and powerful world port.

SAM'S TIPS

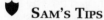

- The restored buildings include the Custom House (1819), the Scale House (1829), which sheltered the large scales used by Customs Service to weigh and tax the innumerable shiploads of goods, and the West India Goods store (1800).

Captain's Responsibilities

A trusted captain was allowed much discretion by Salem shipowners. On a typical voyage, he sailed with a full cargo of American and West Indian goods. After selling or trading part of the cargo at Capetown, South Africa, he continued on to Île de France, where, if the prices were right, he traded the rest for coffee, pepper, and tea, or sold the whole ship and took the cash home. If prices were low, he sailed on to Bombay, where indigo and cotton were much desired.

- A trip to Salem is not complete unless you visit the nearby House of Seven Gables, made famous by Nathaniel Hawthorne, a native of Salem.
- A Maritime Festival is held annually in July.

SAUGUS IRON WORKS NATIONAL HISTORIC SITE

10 miles north of Boston.

244 Central Street
Saugus, MA 01906
781-233-0050
http://www.nps.gov/sair

Eastern National. (446 North Lane, Conshohocken, PA 19428; 800-355-5566)

The first successfully integrated iron works in North America was established here to supply iron for the American colonies. Originally called "Hammersmith," this iron-making community was in operation from 1646 to 1668. Seven operational waterwheels powered the furnace bellows, forge bellows, 500-pound trip hammer, and rolling and slitting mill. The Iron Works House is a 17th-century building on a site that may have been the residence of the Iron Master. It consists of three furnished rooms and two exhibit rooms and was restored by Wallace Nutting in 1915. Tours are offered daily, May 1–October 31.

Arms for the Nation

Springfield Armory is responsible for the development and manufacture of such rifles as the Model 1903 Rifle used by American troops in World War I, and still considered one of the most accurate rifles ever made. Another original Springfield development is the M-1 Rifle, which was issued to millions of servicemen in two wars. At its peak during the Civil War, Springfield Armory employed 3,400 persons who were producing 1,000 muskets a day. The armory ceased to be active in 1968.

SPRINGFIELD ARMORY NATIONAL HISTORIC SITE

Springfield is 95 miles west of Boston, 30 miles north of Hartford, CT.

One Armory Square
Springfield, MA 01105
413-734-8551
http://www.nps.gov/spar

President George Washington created the Springfield Armory in 1794 as the first national armory. The site includes one of the world's largest collections of military small arms with many one-of-a-kind weapons. The Armory museum interprets the story of women ordinance workers, and the development of the American system of manufacture, featuring antique and modern machinery.

The "Organ of Muskets," made famous by Longfellow's poem "The Arsenal at Springfield," can be seen here.

POINTS OF INTEREST

U.S. ARMY CORPS OF ENGINEERS

BARRE FALLS DAM

Trout and pheasant are stocked by the state at this streamside environment. From Gardner or MA 2, take MA 68 south to MA 62, then two miles west to the dam.

BIRCH HILL DAM

The Lake Dennison recreation Area, on an 82-acre natural lake, contains campgrounds, a beach, and a picnic area. From MA 2, take US 202 six miles north to find Lake Dennison. The dam is on MA 68, four miles west of US 202.

CAPE COD CANAL

The gateway to Cape Cod, popular for bicycling, fishing, and camping. Take I-195 from Providence, RI, or MA 3 from Boston.

CHARLES RIVER NATURAL VALLEY STORAGE

Over 3000 acres, available for hiking, canoeing, skiing, and fishing. Accessible from I-90, I-95 and I-495.

KNIGHTVILLE DAM

Excellent trout streams and rich game habitat stocked by the state, a seasonal visitor center, and picnic areas. From Westfield, take US 20 west to MA 112. Take a right on MA 112 and follow it north to the dam.

WEST HILL DAM

This park allows picnicking, hiking, hunting and fishing. It also offers an offshore swimming hole. From Worcester, follow MA 122 to North Uxbridge, then take Hartford Avenue east to the dam.

"CHANGING LIVES THROUGH SERVICE TO NATURE"

That is the motto for the Student Conservation Association (SCA). Since 1957, SCA volunteers have worked on Uncle Sam's private lands, restoring fire damaged areas at Yellowstone, or removing debris from the Everglades after Hurricane Andrew, or leading anti-graffiti campaigns in urban areas. A nonprofit organization, SCA sponsors programs that include teaching wilderness work skills and the requirements for careers in conservation. For more information, contact SCA Headquarters, PO Box 550, 689 River Road, Charlestown, NH 03603 (phone: 603-543-1700; fax: 603-543-1828; Website: http://www.sca-inc.org).

NEW HAMPSHIRE

SAINT-GAUDENS NATIONAL HISTORIC SITE

60 miles northwest of Concord, 105 miles south of Burlington, VT.

RR 3, Box 73
Cornish, NH 03745-9704
603-675-2175
http://www.nps.gov/saga

 **Eastern National.** (446 North Lane, Conshohocken, PA 19428; 800-355-5566)

Augustus Saint-Gaudens, America's foremost sculptor during the late 19th and early 20th centuries, lived and worked here at Aspet, often in the company of writers, musicians, and other artists. The park preserves his home, studios, gardens, and some original sculptures. In addition to a sculptor-in-residence program, there are concerts and art exhibitions.

WHITE MOUNTAIN NATIONAL FOREST

120 miles east of Burlington, VT, 100 miles west of Portland, ME.

Federal Building
719 Main Street
Laconia, NH 03246
603-528-8721
http://www.fs.fed.us

 **White Mountain Interpretive Association.** (33 Kancamagus Highway, Conway, NH 03818; 603-447-5448)

The White Mountains, featuring some of the highest peaks in the East, rise in dramatic relief just north of New Hampshire's central plateau. The Presidential Range culminates in the bare granite summit of 6,300-foot Mount Washington. Mounts Adams, Jefferson, Monroe, and Madison also exceed 5,000 feet in elevation.

FOREST SERVICE SCENIC BYWAY

Kancamagus Highway:

Kancamagus Highway covers 28 miles on State Highway 112 through the White Mountain National Forest from Conway to Lincoln. One of the best highways in America for viewing fall foliage, it also offers a wide array of recreational opportunities. *Contact White Mountain National Forest.*

POINTS OF INTEREST

U.S. ARMY CORPS OF ENGINEERS

BLACKWATER DAM

The streamside environment includes a meandering 8-mile stretch of the Blackwater River, an excellent canoe stream stocked with trout. Hunting and snowmobiling opportunities. From Concord, go 8 miles north on I-93 and take Exit 17 onto US 4 North.

EDWARD MACDOWELL LAKE

A 165-acre shallow lake with adjacent lands for fishing and hunting. A picnic area is located next to the dam. From Nashua, take US 3 to Exit 7, west on NH 101A and 101 to Peterborough; follow signs to the dam 4 miles west.

EVERETT LAKE

Clough State Park offers swimming and boating (motors prohibited) on the 130-acre lake. Fishing, hunting, picnicking, and snowmobiling are popular, too. From Manchester, take Everett Turnpike to Exit 10, then NH 101 west to NH 114, then to NH 13 north; follow the signs to Clough State Park and Everett Dam.

FRANKLIN FALLS DAM

A 15-mile stretch of the Pemigewasset River flows through a reservoir area managed by the state for fish and wildlife. From Concord, go 20 miles north on I-93 to Exit 22, then south on NH 127 for 3 miles to the dam.

HOPKINGTON LAKE

Elm Brook Park, with a 220-acre shallow lake, offers swimming, picnicking, and boating. Areas for group outings are available by special use permit on a first-come, first-served basis by calling 603-746-4775. The reservoir area and Stumpfield Marsh provide canoeing, wildlife observation, fishing, and hunting. From Concord and I-93, go north on I-89 to Exit 6, then south on NH 127.

OTTER BROOK LAKE

The park offers swimming, picnicking, and boating (no motors) at the 70-acre lake. From Keene, go east 2 miles on NH 9 to the recreation area.

The Cog Railroad

Boarding the Cog Railway to the summit of Mount Washington, the tallest peak in the Northeast, will take you back to America's pre-electric, pre-automotive steam train culture. This was the world's first mountain-climbing cog railway, and today it's the only one still powered entirely by steam. The three-mile route to the summit of Mount Washington is the second steepest railway track in the world. One trestle, called "Jacob's Ladder," climbs an incredible 37 percent grade. On this journey to the summit, each locomotive consumes a ton of coal and a thousand gallons of water while pushing passenger cars (with tilted seats to compensate for the steep grade) to the top of the mountain.

Adopt-A-Trail

With more than 1,200 miles of hiking trails in the White Mountain National Forest, trail maintenance is a big job. Many volunteers help get the job done by "adopting" a trail or section of a trail. Adopters take care of basic maintenance, such as cleaning drainages and cutting brush along the trail. Volunteers work at their own pace; training sessions and tools can be provided. Help keep White Mountain trails open. Call 603-528-8721.

SURRY MOUNTAIN LAKE

The park has a large beach and picnic area on the shore of the 260-acre lake; 10-hp limit for boats. From Keene, go 6 miles north on NH 12A.

Short Hikes in the White Mountain Forest's Pemigewasset Ranger District

1. Basin Cascade Trail. This trail starts at the Basin in Franconia Notch State Park and terminates at the intersection of Cascade Brook Trail. It's a short (1mile; 50 minutes), moderate uphill hike that parallels Cascade Brook and features many scenic cascades, including Kinsman Falls and Rocky Glen Falls.
2. Lincoln Woods Trail. The main access into the Pemigewasset Wilderness Area is this abandoned railroad grade for hauling logs to a mill in Lincoln. It follows the East Branch of the Pemigewasset River for 2.8 miles and terminates at the wilderness boundary, where it becomes the Wilderness Trail. An easy goal for a short day hike is Franconia Falls, a massive granite ledge with a water chute, or Black Pond.
3. Greely Ponds Trail. This trail runs from the Kancamagus Highway to Waterville Valley. Greeley Ponds Scenic Area is located about 1 mile (1 hour) from the highway. Both ponds offer trout fishing and picnicking. The trailhead on the Kancamagus Highway is located 9 miles east of Exit 32 on I-93.
4. East Pond/Little East Pond. These are small mountain ponds located in a sylvan setting. East Pond's crystal-clear water hosts trout. Diatomaceous earth (also known as tripoli) was once mined from this pond. This hike starts on Tripoli Road, 5 miles east of Exit 31 on I-93. The complete loop to both ponds is 5 miles (about 3 hours).
5. Mount Osceola Trail. This moderately difficult 3.5-mile hike starts at Thornton Gap on the Tripoli Road, 7 miles east of Exit 31 on I-93. The climb to the summit of Mount Osceola takes about 3 hours.
6. Welch/Dickey Mountain Trail. A loop trail that provides a very scenic hike to the summits of Welch Mountain (2,605 feet) and Dickey Mountain (2,734 feet). The complete loop is 4.5 miles (about 3½ hours). Location: Follow NH 49 east 6 miles from Exit 28 on I-93. Turn left, cross bridge, and follow Upper Mad River Road 0.7 mile. Turn right on Orris Road and go 0.6 mile to parking area.

NEW JERSEY

EDISON NATIONAL HISTORIC SITE

90 miles northeast of Philadelphia, 20 miles west of New York City, off I-280.

Main Street and Lakeside Avenue
West Orange, NJ 07052
201-736-0550
http://www.nps.gov/edis

 **Eastern National.** (446 North Lane, Conshohocken, PA 19428; 800-355-5566)

After he invented the electric light system, Thomas Alva Edison bought Glenmont, a 13.5-acre estate with a 29-room house, and built his new laboratory complex in West Orange, New Jersey. Visitors to the lab can see a full-scale replica of the Black Maria, an early motion picture studio, and listen to Edison's favorite invention, the phonograph. A remarkable number of furnishings remain at both the home and the laboratory, which are seen by guided tour only.

SAM'S TIPS

- A busy urban area has grown up around the West Orange labs, and all but one of the poured-concrete factory buildings that surrounded them are gone. But the old complex remains a quiet enclave where you can sense the spirit of new ideas and the excitement of new technology that drove Edison and his staff.

GREAT EGG HARBOR SCENIC AND RECREATIONAL RIVER

30 miles east of Philadelphia, the designated portion of the Great Egg Harbor River crosses 12 municipalities from Winslow Township to Upper Township.

National Park Service
Conservation Assistance Group
U.S. Custom House
200 Chestnut Street, Third Floor
Philadelphia, PA 19106
215-597-7018
http://www.nps.gov/greg

 **Eastern National.** (446 North Lane, Conshohocken, PA 19428; 800-355-5566)

The Great Egg Harbor River begins in suburban towns and meanders 59 miles in the heart of New Jersey's Pinelands Reserve. Dissolved iron and tannin, a product of fallen leaves and cedar roots, produce the river's tea-colored "cedar water." The watershed has been occupied since prehistoric times; traditionally, the Lenape Indians lived there before occupation by Europeans in the early

A PARK IN YOUR OWN BACKYARD?

Is there an abandoned railroad bed behind your house that would make a good walking path? A scenic stretch of river nearby that is disappearing? Are the fish dying out at your favorite fishing spot?

The Rivers, Trails, and Conservation Assistance (RTCA) Program, part of the National Park Service, helps local communities protect rivers and trails on lands outside the federal domain. By lending the skills and credibility of the NPS to local projects, the RTCA might be able to help your community turn that railroad bed into a trail, preserve the scenic river, or figure out how to bring back the fish.

For more information, contact your local National Park Service office or the program itself:

National Park Service
Rivers, Trails, and Conservation Assistance Program
1849 C Street, NW, Room 3606
Washington DC, 20240
202-565-1200

1700s. The river flows through land that is primarily privately owned, therefore river access is limited. This river is the largest canoeing river in the Barrens, and lies relatively near the urban centers of Philadelphia (PA), Trenton and Camden (NJ), and Wilmington (DE).

MAURICE SCENIC AND RECREATIONAL RIVER

From Buena Vista Township through Vineland, Millville, Maurice River, and Commercial Townships.

National Park Service
Conservation Assistance Group
U.S. Custom House
200 Chestnut Street, Third Floor
Philadelphia, PA 19106
215-597-7018
http://www.nps.gov/ccso/maurice.htm

The Maurice Scenic and Recreational River includes the Maurice and Manumuskin Rivers, and the Menantico and Muskee Creeks. As part of the Atlantic flyway, its clean waters and related habitats are vitally important to the migration of shorebirds, songbirds, waterfowl, raptors, rails, and fish. Historically, the Maurice is home to a rich fishing, boating, and oystering heritage. Serving as the western boundary of the Pinelands, the Maurice River is a critical link between the Pinelands National Reserve and the Delaware Estuary.

MORRISTOWN NATIONAL HISTORICAL PARK

80 miles northeast of Philadelphia, 35 miles west of New York City.

Washington Place
Morristown, NJ 07960
973-539-2085
http://www.nps.gov/morr

 **Eastern National.** (446 North Lane, Conshohocken, PA 19428; 800-355-5566)

During two winters, Morristown sheltered the main encampment of the Continental Army. In 1777, George Washington overcame desertion and disease to build an army capable of taking the field against William Howe's veteran Redcoats. During 1779–1780, the hardest winter in anyone's memory, the enemies Washington faced at Morristown were starvation, lack of clothing, and outright mutiny on the bleak hills of Jockey Hollow. Never was Washington's leadership more evident as he held together the small, ragged army that represented the country's main hope for independence. You can visit the Jockey Hollow Encampment area, the Ford Mansion (Washington's headquarters), the newly landscaped Fort Nonsense, the Wick House Farm, and the restored Pennsylvania Line soldier huts.

SAM'S TIPS

- Jockey Hollow Encampment Area is the site of the 1,200 simple huts built to house soldiers from New York, Maryland, New Jersey, Rhode Island, Pennsylvania, Connecticut, Massachusetts, and even Canada. Reconstructed huts give a sense of the soldiers' daily life.
- The park's museum is an important orientation point for the events that happened at Morristown. Exhibits of numerous military and other artifacts afford glimpses of the Continental Army in winter quarters.

NATIONAL PARK SERVICE SITES HONORING AMERICAN ARTISTS AND WRITERS

- Eugene O'Neill National Historic Site Danville, CA.
- Weir Farm National Historic Site Ridgefield, CT.
- John Muir National Historic Site Martinez, CA.
- Frederick Law Olmsted National Historic Site Brookline, MA.
- Longfellow National Historic Site Cambridge, MA.
- Saint-Gaudens National Historic Site Cornish, NH.
- Carl Sandburg Home National Historic Site Flat Rock, NC.
- Edgar Allan Poe National Historic Site Philadelphia, PA.

NEW YORK

CASTLE CLINTON NATIONAL MONUMENT

In Battery Park, at the southern tip of Manhattan.

26 Wall Street
New York, NY 10005
212-344-7220
http://www.nps.gov/cacl

Completed in 1811, Clinton Castle was built to defend New York after the British attack on the frigate *Chesapeake* in 1807. At the end of the War of 1812, the fort became the headquarters for the Third Military District and was named Castle Clinton in honor of a former Mayor of New York. In June of 1824, the Castle was leased by the city as a place of public entertainment, and it soon became Castle Garden, one of the favored "places of resort"—the setting for band concerts, fireworks, an occasional balloon ascension, and demonstrations of the latest scientific achievements. In August 1855, the Castle was transformed into an immigrant landing depot, providing information about travel routes, medical care, and honest currency exchange. Between 1855 and 1889, more than 8 million immigrants—two out of every three persons immigrating to the United States in this period—passed through the Castle. With the opening of Ellis Island on January 1, 1892, the Castle was altered yet again to become the New York City Aquarium. Today, with the aquarium relocated to Coney Island, Castle Clinton hosts visitors to the harbor areas's historic sites.

TREAD LIGHTLY!

Tread Lightly! is an educational program dedicated to increasing awareness of how to enjoy public and private lands while minimizing impacts. It emphasizes responsible use of off-highway vehicles, other forms of back-country travel, and low-impact principles applicable to outdoor recreation activities. Tread Lightly! unites federal and state land management agencies with the private sector, user groups, and individuals who share a basic commitment to care for our valuable resources. Through Tread Lightly!, recreationists can learn to recreate with care, so the land will always be available to enjoy.

The Tread Lightly! pledge:

Travel only where permitted.
Respect the rights of others.
Educate yourself.
Avoid streams, meadows, and wildlife.
Drive and travel responsibly.

ELEANOR ROOSEVELT NATIONAL HISTORIC SITE

5 miles north of Poughkeepsie, 90 miles north of New York City.

519 Albany Post Road
Hyde Park, NY 12538
914-229-9115
http://www.nps.gov/elro

Roosevelt–Vanderbilt Historical Association. (PO Box 235, Hyde Park, NY 12538; 914-229-9300)

Mrs. Roosevelt used this rural estate, "Val-Kill," as a retreat from her public life and, with her husband, Franklin, to entertain dignitaries in a casual atmosphere. Originally a furniture factory, it was converted for her use in 1937. An earlier retreat on the grounds, Stone Cottage (1925), was built for her by FDR. Val-Kill's grounds include woods, ponds, meadows, and swamps; a filmed biography is shown regularly.

The First Lady of the World

A few days after FDR died in April 1945, a reporter hailed his widow outside her home and asked for a statement. "The story is over," she replied. True, Eleanor Roosevelt's many years as the most influential First Lady in history ended suddenly, but her own story continued for nearly two more decades. Vigorously promoting the humanitarian causes so close to her heart, this unassuming woman earned the title—in the words of President Harry S Truman—"First Lady of the World."

FEDERAL HALL NATIONAL MEMORIAL

Wall Street is located at the southern tip of Manhattan Island in New York City.

26 Wall Street
New York, NY 10031
212-283-5154
http://www.nps.gov/feha

 **Eastern National.** (446 North Lane, Conshohocken, PA 19428; 800-355-5566)

Built in 1703 as the first City Hall for New York, Federal Hall was witness to John Peter Zenger's "freedom of the press" trial (1735), the Stamp Act Congress (1765), the Second Continental Congress (1785), and George Washington's first presidential oath (1789). The original building no longer stands. On the site now is a Greek revival structure, completed in 1842, that first served as a U.S. Custom House, then a treasury repository. On occasion, its front steps still host political and social rallies. Various exhibits in the building depict the role this site played in the history of our nation.

ACREAGE OF PUBLIC LAND ASSIGNED TO FEDERAL AGENCIES

Bureau of Land Management: 270 million
U.S. Forest Service: 191 million
Fish and Wildlife Service: 91 million
National Park Service: 80.7 million
Army Corps of Engineers: 11.6 million

FINGER LAKES NATIONAL FOREST

70 miles southeast of Rochester, 80 miles southwest of Syracuse.

5218 State Route 414
Hector, NY 14841
607-546-4470
http://www.fs.fed.us

Like the fingers on a pair of outstretched hands, the Finger Lakes extend north and south across central New York. This area, which was once divided into 600-acre military lots and distributed to Revolutionary War veterans as payment for their services, contains the smallest of the 155 national forests in the National Forest system—the 16,000-acre Finger Lakes National Forest, which stands on a ridge between Lake Seneca and Lake Cayuga. The Finger Lakes region contains dozens of gorges that conceal deep pools; cliffs covered in moss; and waterfalls, including Taughannock Falls, the highest perpendicular waterfall in the northeastern United States. Driving through the forest takes you over ridge-top topography and through open pastures with rich and varied vistas.

It's No Three-Star Hotel, But . . .

There are three developed campgrounds in the forest:

1. Blueberry Patch Campground has a picnic area, nine sites for tents or self-contained recreational vehicles, cooking grills, a hand-pump well, and vault toilets.
2. Potomac Group Campground is intended for groups of 10 to 40 people. Cooking grills, a hand-pump well, and vault toilets are available near the open picnic shelter. Reservations must be made in advance.
3. Backbone Trailhead is designed for picnicking or overnight camping by horseback riders. Facilities include parking areas with hitching posts, vault toilets, and cooking grills.

FIRE ISLAND NATIONAL SEASHORE

Southern part of Long Island, 60 miles east of New York City.

120 Laurel Street
Patchogue, NY 11772
516-289-4810
http://www.nps.gov/fiis

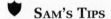

Eastern National. (446 North Lane, Conshohocken, PA 19428; 800-355-5566)

Fire Island is a 32-mile-long barrier island that protects Long Island from the Atlantic Ocean. The park offers beachcombing, fishing, swimming, and limited camping. The Sunken Forest, the restored Fire Island Lighthouse and keeper's quarters, and the national wilderness area (1,300 acres) make the seashore much more than "just a beach." Also, the estate of Declaration of Independence signer William Floyd, at Mastic Beach, is open seasonally.

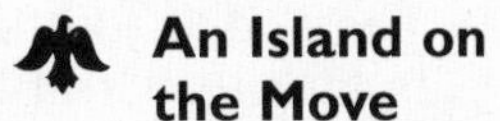

An Island on the Move

Every day, more than 10,000 waves pound the beaches of Fire Island, shoveling sand into currents that carry 500,000 cubic yards westward each year. The bulk is transported in the winter and during storms. Witness to this migration is the Fire Island Lighthouse; built in 1858 at the island's western end, it is now nearly 5 miles east of Democrat Point.

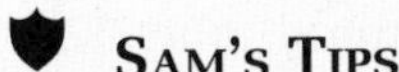

- The Watch Hill area has a 188-slip marina, coin pumpout, 50-amp electricity, elevated boardwalk nature trail across the salt marsh, tidal estuary programs, and limited canoe trips. For ferry services, call 516-475-1665; for marina information, call 516-597-6644; for camping, call 516-597-6633.
- The Sailor's Haven area has a 42-slip marina, electricity, coin pumpout, maritime forest exhibits, elevated boardwalk nature trail, and visitor center. For additional information about ferry services, call 516-589-8980; for the marina, call 516-597-6171 from May 1 to October 15.

TRAVELING LIGHT

The U.S. Forest Service reports that experienced backpackers pride themselves on being able to travel light and will cut towels in half and saw the handles off toothbrushes to save ounces. They measure out just the necessary amount of food and store it in plastic bags. They carry scouring pads with built-in soap to eliminate dish soap and a dishcloth. How much should you carry? It all depends on your physical condition and experience, the terrain to be covered, the length of the trip, and the time of year. The maximum recommended weight for women is 30 pounds, and for men, 50 pounds. When figuring out weight, count all items: the cup on your belt, the camera around your neck, and the keys in your pockets.

FORT STANWIX NATIONAL MONUMENT

50 miles east of Syracuse, 20 miles northeast of Utica.

112 East Park Street
Rome, NY 13440-5816
315-336-2090
http://www.nps.gov/fost

 **Eastern National.** (446 North Lane, Conshohocken, PA; 800-355-5566)

The Fort is located in Rome, NY, which lies next to an ancient water route linking the Great Lakes with the Atlantic Ocean. Except for the short portage across nearly level ground between the Mohawk River and Wood Creek, a traveler in colonial times could journey by water all the way from New York City to Canada and back again. Because of its strategic location, the Fort and city soon became a passageway for commerce, settlement, and military activity. In August 1777, American soldiers at the Fort stood fast against a combined force of Redcoats, American loyalists (who outnumbered the British regulars), and the allied Iroquois tribe, and helped to repulse a British invasion from Canada. The Fort has been almost completely restored to its 1777 appearance.

GATEWAY NATIONAL RECREATION AREA

Entrance to the New York–New Jersey estuary in New York Harbor: Brooklyn, Queens, and Staten Island in New York, and Sandy Hook, New Jersey.

Floyd Bennett Field, Bldg. 69
Brooklyn, NY 11234
718-338-3338
http://www.nps.gov/gate

 **Eastern National.** (446 North Lane, Conshohocken, PA 19428; 800-355-5566)

Gateway National Recreation Area, America's first urban national park, contains 26,000 acres stretching across two states. These resources include wildlife sanctuaries, marshes, recreational and athletic facilities, and indoor and outdoor classrooms. In addition, the park contains old military installations, airfields, and a lighthouse. All of these give visitors the chance to learn more about the natural environment and the cultural history of the New York/New Jersey metropolitan area.

Sam's Tips

- The *Breezy Point/Jamaica Bay Unit* is made up of the Breezy Point and Jamaica Bay Districts. The Breezy Point District, located on the Rockaway Peninsula near the mouth of New York Harbor, includes Jacob Riis Park (ocean beaches, bathhouse, boardwalk, and concessions), Fort Tilden (a historic military fort, ballfields, and other recreational opportunities such as birdwatching, bicycling, and fishing), and the Jamaica Bay Wildlife Refuge (one of America's finest bird sanctuaries). The Jamaica Bay District in Brooklyn includes historic Floyd Bennett Field (first NYC municipal airport; site of many aviation records, historic hangars), now the site of many special events, birdwatching, organized environmental education programs, picnicking, and community gardens. Concessions operated within the Jamaica Bay District include miniature golf, tennis courts, a marina, horseback riding, and a restaurant at Canarsie Pier.

- The *Staten Island Unit* extends along the south shore of Staten Island and includes: Miller Field (a World War I Army Air Corps airbase, athletic fields, picnic areas), Great Kills Park (swimming, marina, boat ramp, model airplane field, athletic activities, bicycling and hiking, outdoor concerts, and more), and Fort Wadsworth, (a historic fort overlooking New York Harbor and the Verrazano Narrows Bridge; limited Ranger-led tours available).
- The *Sandy Hook Unit* (New Jersey) is a long barrier peninsula. It includes miles of ocean beaches, hiking trails, and salt marshes. The unit includes historic Fort Hancock (oldest lighthouse in the country, site of the first U.S. Army Proving Ground, and Fort Hancock), the Sandy Hook Museum (former post guardhouse, bookstore), and History House (1898 Lieutenant's residence, exhibits).

GENERAL GRANT NATIONAL MEMORIAL

In New York City's Riverside Park at 122nd Street and Riverside Drive.

122nd Street and Riverside Drive
New York, NY 10024-3703
212-666-1640
http://www.nps.gov/gegr

 **Eastern National.** (446 North Lane, Conshohocken, PA 19428; 800-355-5566)

Popularly known as Grant's Tomb, the memorial to General Grant is one of the largest mausoleums in the world, rising 150 feet on a bluff overlooking the Hudson River. Its construction was a mammoth undertaking at the time: Hundreds of men worked on the structure between 1892 and 1897, using over 8,000 tons of granite. The great size of the tomb was meant to express the admiration Americans felt for the Civil War commander who later became President. The design of Grant's Tomb incorporates elements from the tomb of King Mausolus at Halicarnassus, the tomb of the Roman Emperor Hadrian, Napoleon's Tomb in Dome des Invalides, and the Garfield Memorial in Cleveland, OH.

HAMILTON GRANGE NATIONAL MEMORIAL

In New York City, at Convent Avenue and West 141st Street.

c/o General Grant National Memorial
122nd St. and Riverside Drive
New York, NY 10024-3703
212-666-1640
http://www.nps.gov/hagr

 **Eastern National.** (446 North Lane, Conshohocken, PA 19428; 800-355-5566)

When Alexander Hamilton, the first Secretary of the Treasury, moved his family to The Grange, it was far from the heat, noise, and disease of the city. Eventually, the house was purchased by St. Luke's Episcopal Church and was moved two blocks southeast to its present location. When it was moved, the architecture was substantially altered; perhaps the biggest changes were the removal of the front and side porches and the rotation of the house on its site. In 1924, the American Scenic and Historic Preservation Society acquired the Grange and opened it to the public. Since 1962, the National Park Service has managed the site as a National Memorial and intends to restore it to its appearance during the Hamiltons' residence there.

At present, Hamilton Grange National Memorial is closed for renovations. It is being administered by General Grant National Memorial. Please contact them for general information and to see when Hamilton Grange will re-open.

HOME OF FRANKLIN DELANO ROOSEVELT NATIONAL HISTORIC SITE

6 miles north of Poughkeepsie, 90 miles north of New York City.

519 Albany Post Road
Hyde Park, NY 12538-1997
914-229-9115
http://www.nps.gov/hofr

Roosevelt–Vanderbilt Historical Association. (PO Box 235, Hyde Park, NY 12538; 914-229-9300)

Overlooking the Hudson River, "Springwood" was Franklin D. Roosevelt's birthplace (1882) and "Summer White House" during his four presidential terms. Built in the early 1800s, the house was purchased by Roosevelt's father in 1867. The home is decorated with original furnishings and memorabilia recalling such famous visitors as Winston Churchill. The former president and his wife Eleanor are buried in the garden adjacent to the home. His presidential library is nearby.

FDR planted a variety of trees on the grounds, eventually turning large sections of the estate into experimental forests. Some of his work is still in evidence. The house, too, retains his stamp. Four times, he stood on the terrace on election nights to greet well-wishers. Many presidential duties were conducted from his home-office. In the main hall are his boyhood collection of stuffed birds, and a bronze sculpture of him at age 29, when he was serving his first term in the New York State Senate.

 **SAM'S TIPS**

- Reserve some time for the FDR Library, administered by the National Archives and Records Administration. Designed by FDR himself, the stone Dutch-Colonial building holds a museum of FDR memorabilia, such as FDR's cradle and presidential desk and chair. The library holds 40,000 books, manuscript collections, photographs, recordings, and films. A separate gallery is dedicated to Eleanor Roosevelt.

MARTIN VAN BUREN NATIONAL HISTORIC SITE

25 miles south of Albany.

PO Box 545
Kinderhook, NY 12106-0545
518-758-9689
http://www.nps.gov/mava

 **Eastern National.** (446 North Lane, Conshohocken, PA 19428; 800-355-5566)

 **Friends for Lindenwald.** (Kinderhook, NY 12106; 518-758-7600)

The Martin Van Buren National Historic Site contains the home and surrounding lands of the eighth President of the United Sites. Early 19th-century politics was a whirlwind of boisterous characters and opposing interest groups. Van Buren artfully positioned himself in the eye of the storm, persistently advocating the principles of the Jeffersonian Republicans: states' rights, strict constitutional construction, and civil liberties. During the administration of Andrew Jackson, Van Buren was a top adviser. As the eighth President—the first born under the U.S. flag—Van Buren continued the era of Jacksonian Democracy. Van Buren was defeated for reelection in 1840 and returned to his native Kinderhook. He ran twice more for the presidency, but not until his defeat for the presidency in 1848 did Van Buren give up public life. In 1862, Van Buren succumbed to bronchial asthma and was buried at Kinderhook.

SAGAMORE HILL NATIONAL HISTORIC SITE

Oyster Bay is on the north shore of Long Island, 40 miles east of New York City.

20 Sagamore Hill
Oyster Bay, NY 11771-1899
516-922-4788
http://www.nps.gov/sahi

 **Eastern National.** (446 North Lane, Conshohocken, PA 19428; 800-355-5566)

 **Friends of Sagamore Hill.** (Oyster Bay address above)

Sagamore Hill was built by Theodore Roosevelt during 1884 and 1885 and remained his permanent home for the rest of his life. The house is a rambling 23-room Victorian structure of frame and brick. Today, it is little changed from the time when it was known as the "Summer White House." Furnishings throughout the house are original Roosevelt pieces.

On the south and west sides of the house is the spacious piazza from which Roosevelt looked out over Oyster Bay Harbor and Long Island Sound. On the grounds are landscaped gardens. In 1950, two years after the death of Roosevelt's second wife Edith, Sagamore Hill, its contents, and 83 acres of land were purchased by the Theodore Roosevelt Association, the group that eventually declared the estate as a gift to the American people.

Sam's Tips

- The Old Orchard Museum, a Georgian revival home built for Gen. Theodore Roosevelt, Jr., is open to the public and includes exhibits relating to Roosevelt's political career, family life at Sagamore Hill, and the lives of his six children. Film programs are presented on a regular schedule all year.
- The Theodore Roosevelt Memorial Park and Theodore Roosevelt Gravesite and Sanctuary are both located nearby.
- The Independence Day Celebration includes Patriotic Music, a Cavalry Demonstration, a Teddy Bear Exhibition, a Patriotic Film Festival, and reenactments of TR's greatest speeches.

SAINT PAUL'S CHURCH NATIONAL HISTORIC SITE

20 miles north of New York City.

897 South Columbus Avenue
Mount Vernon, NY 10550
914-667-4116
http://www.nps.gov/sapa

Society of the National Shrine of the Bill of Rights at St. Paul's Church, Eastchester, Inc. (same address)

In 1665, Thomas Pell brought ten families to settle a small community soon to be known as Eastchester, which had agreed to hire a Congregational minister to preach to them every other week. In 1763, construction on the extant church began. The churchbell is the Freedom Bell, the less famous "twin" of the Liberty Bell, which was cast in the same London foundry. Completion was delayed by the beginning of the Revolutionary War, at which time the adjacent village green was the setting for events linked with John Peter Zenger's fight for freedom of the press. Following the battle of Pell's Point, in October 1776, the unfinished church was used as a hospital for wounded British and German soldiers. A mass burial ground at the back of the church contains more than 100 Hessian (German) mercenaries who died while being treated at the hospital. After the Revolution, the church was used as a courthouse; Aaron Burr practiced law there in 1787. In 1805, the church was finally completed.

Sam's Tips

- The burying ground, containing an estimated 9,000 interments dating from 1665 to the present, encompasses approximately 5 acres and a fascinating variety of gravestone markings and imagery, from stones bearing only initials to phonetically spelled full names in the 1800s. Special tours are given on the last Sunday of each month at 2:00 P.M.

MEET YOUR PARK SUPERINTENDENTS

The National Park Service has a varied and experienced staff of national stature—rangers, natural resource managers, archaeologists, historians, interpreters, landscape architects, engineers, and planners—who protect our land and legacy, conduct research, and educate the public. We'd like to introduce you to one of them.

Diane H. Dayson, Superintendent, Roosevelt–Vanderbilt National Historic Site, New York, says: "I am second generation in the Park Service. My father was an interpreter and then a maintenance worker for 35 years, all over the New York area. He ate, slept, breathed the parks, and we got sick of hearing about it. He said NPS was home for him. I took a summer seasonal job but then said, 'This is it; I'm outta here.' I wanted something different. But I found that the Park Service was in my blood. They say it's just like family, and it is." (Her brother works in law enforcement at Gateway National Recreational Area, New York.) " I wasn't sure what a government agency with all its traditionalism had to offer a woman and a minority. It has been a lot of sacrifices and balancing. But what better place than the Park Service? A lot of my friends make four or five times what I do. But their pressures are different and they're not happy. I go out and enjoy the resource; I'm not trapped in an office."

SARATOGA NATIONAL HISTORICAL PARK

30 miles northeast of Albany.

648 Route 32
Stillwater, NY 12170-1604
518-664-9821
http://www.nps.gov/sara

 **Eastern National.** (446 North Lane, Conshohocken, PA 19428; 800-355-5566)

British General John Burgoyne's surrender to American General Horatio Gates here in 1777 was the turning point of the Revolutionary War and one of the decisive campaigns in world history. Burgoyne's army had arrived from St. Johns, Canada, and was pushing forward to Albany. On September 13, England's Crown Forces, over 9,000 strong, crossed to the west bank of the Hudson at Saratoga and began marching southward. Four miles north of the village of Stillwater, the British came upon an equal force of Americans. Following battles on September 19 and October 7, the British were forced to withdraw northward to Saratoga. There, surrounded by more than 10,000 American soldiers and militia, Burgoyne surrendered on October 17th.

Sam's Tips

- A nine-mile auto tour of the battlefield includes ten stops. Interpretive markers on the battlefield and maps help you understand the battles of Saratoga.
- General Philip Schuyler's country home and the 155-foot Saratoga monument are a short drive away, in Schuylerville.

STATUE OF LIBERTY NATIONAL MONUMENT AND ELLIS ISLAND

Liberty Island is off the southern tip of Manhattan, located approximately halfway between New York and New Jersey.

Liberty Island
New York, NY 10004
212-363-3200 (recorded information)
http://www.nps.gov/stli

Roosevelt–Vanderbilt Historical Association. (PO Box 235, Hyde Park, NY 12538; 914-229-9300)

"Liberty Enlightening the World," the original name of the 151'1" copper statue bearing the torch of freedom was given by the French people in 1886 to commemorate the alliance of the two nations in the American Revolution. Designed by Frederick Bartholdi, the statue came to symbolize freedom for immigrants and resident Americans alike.

Ellis Island was opened on January 1, 1892, and served until 1954 as the main entry site for immigrants coming to the United States. In 1990, after extensive restoration, the site was reopened to the public as the nation's only museum devoted entirely to immigration. The three-story main building on the northern portion of the island contains exhibits, audio/visual displays, and a film telling the story of the nearly 15 million immigrants who passed through its portals.

Sam's Tips

- For a schedule of ferry service in New York from Battery Park in lower Manhattan, call 212-269-5755; for service from Liberty State Park in New Jersey, call 201-435-9499. The first ferries leave at 9:30 A.M. and continue at half-hour intervals in the summer. To avoid crowds in summer, take the Circle Line ferry from Liberty State Park in Jersey City, NJ.
- The crown of the statue can be reached by climbing the 354 steps (the equivalent of 22 stories). Visitors taking the elevator will have access only to the pedestal, not the crown. Avoid the climb if you are asthmatic, claustrophobic, or afraid of heights.
- Half-hour-long ranger-guided tours of the statue are available throughout the day on a first-come, first-served basis. Tours are outdoors except in winter and inclement weather. Check the information board at the statue for details.
- At the Ellis Island Immigration Museum, visitors can view the Great Hall registry room, a restored Board of Special Inquiry, and a dormitory room, as well as artifacts such as clothing, tickets, passports, and ships' manifests. Allow about three hours to tour the museum and take advantage of the special activities, which include tours, a film, and a play.

An Expensive Endeavor

Only one condition was placed on France's gift to America: The younger nation was to provide the statue's foundation and pedestal. Public appeal for donations began in 1877, and in 1883, work began on the foundation, the largest concrete mass of its time. The statue was finished by 1883, but donations were not as generous as expected, and the completion of the pedestal was in jeopardy. Many of those who could have afforded large contributions objected to the statue on aesthetic grounds, and ordinary citizens regarded the statue as New York's problem or a frivolity that the rich should underwrite. Joseph Pulitzer, a Hungarian immigrant and the publisher of the *New York World,* took on the job of raising the necessary money. In his paper, he blasted the rich for not donating and stressed the symbolic importance of the statue, soliciting donations from the masses. The completed pedestal and statue were dedicated on October 28, 1886.

- There are 45-minute, ranger-guided tours of the museum's highlights, offered free throughout the day on a first-come, first-served basis. The documentary film *Island of Hope, Island of Tears,* by Oscar-winning film director Charles Guggenheim, is shown in Theaters 1 and 2 (accompanied by a 15-minute ranger talk). Theater 3 hosts the play *Ellis Island Stories,* performed by the Hypothetical Theater Company from May to October, and based on actual interviews between inspectors and immigrants in the museum's Oral History Project. Get performance times and free tickets at the Information Desk.
- The *Ellis Island Oral History Project* has conducted over 1,500 interviews of immigrants and immigration officials since 1973. The collection is open to the public and can be searched by name, date of immigration, passenger ship, and country of origin. For a small fee, copies of the transcripts and tapes are available.
- The NYNEX Learning Center, a 30-minute interactive multimedia program on the immigration process, is open for school groups Monday though Friday, by reservation only. Frequent 40-minute ranger-guided overview tours are available daily. Times are subject to change due to staffing levels.

BUREAU OF LAND MANAGEMENT—BY THE NUMBERS

Acres of reservoirs: 198,000
Acres of lakes: 4.1 million
Sites listed on the National Register of Historic Places: 228
Number of recorded caves and cave systems: 897
Miles of fishable streams: 174 thousand
Number of designated wild and scenic rivers: 33
Miles of designated rivers: 2,020
Number of designated wilderness areas: 136
Acres of designated wilderness areas: 5.2 million
Acres of waterfowl habitat: 23 million
Acres of small game habitat: 215.6 million
Acres of big game habitat: 198.9 million
Big game animals—approximate populations:

- Deer (whitetail, blacktail, and mule deer): 1.54 million
- Antelope: 365 thousand
- Elk: 248 thousand
- Bighorn sheep (Rocky Mountain, Dall, California, and Desert bighorn sheep): 25 thousand
- Bear (black, grizzly, and brown bears): 21 thousand
- Moose: 40 thousand

THEODORE ROOSEVELT BIRTHPLACE NATIONAL HISTORIC SITE

28 East 20th Street, in Manhattan.

26 Wall Street
New York, NY 10005
212-260-1616
http://www.nps.gov/thrb

Eastern National. (446 North Lane, Conshohocken, PA 19428; 800-355-5566)

Theodore Roosevelt Association. (PO Box 719, Oyster Bay, NY 11771; 516-921-6319)

Theodore Roosevelt was born here in 1858. In 1916, the family home was demolished to make room for a larger commercial structure. After Roosevelt's death at Sagamore Hill in 1919, the birthplace was reconstructed on its original site. Opened as a museum in 1925, the site now contains an extensive collection of original and family-owned furnishings.

Teddy's Bears . . .

In November of 1902, President Theodore Roosevelt and some friends went on a hunting trip to Mississippi. After hours of searching, the group finally tracked down and surrounded a helpless bear. One of the guides offered the President a chance to shoot the bear but the President refused, and news of his kind act spread throughout the country. When Morris Micthom, a store owner in Brooklyn, saw a Clifford Berryman cartoon depicting Roosevelt's rescue of the bear, he decided to make toy bears to sell in his shop. He asked President Roosevelt for permission to use the name "Teddy's Bear" for his toys.

THEODORE ROOSEVELT INAUGURAL NATIONAL HISTORIC SITE

Buffalo, NY.

641 Delaware Avenue
Buffalo, NY 14202-1079
716-884-0095
http://www.nps.gov/thri

On September 14, 1901, in the library of the Wilcox home, Theodore Roosevelt was sworn in as the 26th President of the United States 8 days after the shooting of President William McKinley and hours after his death. The site, which includes a museum, contains many original furnishings and exhibits. It also contains a room commemorating the events that took place between September 5, when President McKinley arrived in Buffalo to attend the Pan-American Exposition, and President Roosevelt's inauguration.

Dressing on the Run

As President McKinley lay dying in Buffalo from two bullet wounds, the Vice President was vacationing in the Adirondacks. In his rush to Buffalo, Roosevelt had no time to gather up formal attire. Instead, he pieced together an outfit of gray trousers, a waistcoat, and a black four-in-hand tie from those invited to attend the swearing-in ceremony. A long frock coat, borrowed from his friend Ansley Wilcox, is on display at the site.

UPPER DELAWARE SCENIC AND RECREATIONAL RIVER

60 miles northeast of Scranton, PA; 110 miles northwest of New York City.

RR 2, Box 2428
Beach Lake, PA 18405-9737
717-685-4871
http://www.nps.gov/upde

Eastern National. (446 North Lane, Conshohocken, PA 19428; 800-355-5566)

The Upper Delaware Scenic and Recreational River is 73 miles of clear, free-flowing water winding through a valley of swiftly changing scenery. Old buildings, remains of a once busy canal, bald eagles, and the oldest existing wire suspension bridge in the United States are just some of the sights to be enjoyed in the river valley. Numerous privately owned liveries rent canoes, rafts, tubes, and other watercraft along the river. This National Park Service unit is a working partnership of private individuals and local, state, and federal governments.

The Zane Grey House and Museum

Considered by many to be the father of the western novel, Zane Grey once made his home here. Grey was also a world-renowned fisherman and outdoorsman who held ten saltwater fishing records. The house and museum contain displays commemorating the author's work, including the chair on which he sat while writing his novels. For information about the museum, call 717-685-4871.

VANDERBILT MANSION NATIONAL HISTORIC SITE

10 miles north of Poughkeepsie, 90 miles north of New York City.

519 Albany Post Road
Hyde Park, NY 12538
914-229-9115
http://www.nps.gov/vama

Roosevelt–Vanderbilt Historical Association. (PO Box 235, Hyde Park, NY 12538; 914-229-9300)

From a high bluff, the Indiana limestone country home of Frederick and Louise Vanderbilt overlooks the Hudson River. Under construction between 1896–1898, the mansion is an opulent example of the great estates developed by the financial and industrial tycoons during the Gilded Age. Although the house was only used as a spring and fall cottage, 54 rooms were ornately furnished by the leading decorators of the time. The mansion and its contents remain unchanged from the time that the Vanderbilts resided here.

WOMEN'S RIGHTS NATIONAL HISTORICAL PARK

40 miles west of Syracuse, 50 miles east of Rochester.

136 Fall Street
Seneca Falls, NY 13148-1517
315-568-2991
http://www.nps.gov/wori

 **Eastern National.** (446 North Lane, Conshohocken, PA 19428; 315-568-2991, ext. 13)

In 1847, Elizabeth Cady Stanton moved to Seneca Falls from Boston with her family and began her quest to establish equal rights for women. In addition to petitioning for the 1848 Married Women's Property Act, Stanton, along with fellow reformers, drafted at the M'Clintock House the "Declaration of Sentiments" for the first Women's Rights Convention. The Declaration listed 18 grievances, including the denial of the right to vote. The park consists of Stanton's home and the Wesleyan Chapel in Seneca Falls, and the M'Clintock House in nearby Waterloo, NY.

 **SAM'S TIPS**

- The park has developed Classroom Kits, an interdisciplinary teaching unit with one to two weeks of activities describing women's struggle for equal rights. The kit includes a video, books, lesson plans, and a corset. Call the park to reserve the dates you'd like to use the kit. For $25 and shipping fees, kits can be loaned for one-month periods.
- Junior Girl Scouts can earn Women's Stories Badges through a program of previsit, onsite, and postvisit activities. The program focuses on the lives of women in 1848 and today, pointing out similarities and differences. Call the park for more information.

 **Celebrate '98**

July, 1998 marks the 150th anniversary of a significant event in American history—the first Women's Rights Convention held in Seneca Falls in 1848. At that time, women didn't vote, hold elective office or attend college. If married, they could not make legal contracts, divorce an abusive husband or gain custody of their children. Elizabeth Cady Stanton, a Seneca Falls housewife and mother of three, joined with a group of Quaker and abolitionist women and called for a Convention to help right these wrongs.

A not-for-profit organization called Celebrate '98 honors these women and the first Women's Rights Convention over a four day period, July 16–19, 1998. The event will feature many speakers, exhibits, films and performances. Go to the Women's Rights National Historical Park Website to see the calendar of events.

Points of Interest

U.S. ARMY CORPS OF ENGINEERS

EAST SIDNEY LAKE
Located in New York's rolling dairy country. The annual canoe slalom is held downstream of the dam during October. From Binghamton, go east on I-88 to Unadilla and 5 miles east on NY 357 to the park.

MOUNT MORRIS DAM
Located on the Genesee River, this flood control project features a dry lake. The adjacent Letchworth State Park, famous for its scenic deep gorge and waterfalls, offers camping. From Rochester, go south on US 15, west on NY 20A, south on NY 36, and south on NY 408.

WHITNEY POINT LAKE
In the hills of south central New York, the lake provides a productive sport fishery and excellent hunting for small game. From Binghamton, go 19 miles north on I-81 and 3 miles north on NY 26 to the park.

TOP TWENTY MOST VISITED NATIONAL PARK SERVICE SITES (1996)

1. Blue Ridge Parkway (VA)	17,169,062 visits
2. Golden Gate National Recreation Area (CA)	14,043,984
3. Lake Mead National Recreation Area (NV)	9,350,847
4. Great Smoky Mountains National Park (TN)	9,265,667
5. Gateway National Recreation Area (NY)	6,381,502
6. George Washington Memorial Parkway (VA)	6,126,490
7. National Capital Parks (DC)	6,094,875
8. Natchez Trace Parkway (MS)	6,088,610
9. Cape Cod National Seashore (MA)	4,901,782
10. Delaware Water Gap National Recreation Area (PA, NJ)	4,657,735
11. Grand Canyon National Park (AZ)	4,537,703
12. Statue of Liberty National Monument (NY)	4,494,076
13. Yosemite National Park (CA)	4,046,207
14. Castle Clinton National Monument (NY)	3,753,944
15. San Francisco Maritime National Historic Park (CA)	3,670,972
16. Jefferson National Expansion Memorial (MO)	3,649,308
17. Chattahoochee River National Recreation Area (GA)	3,540,375
18. Cuyahoga River National Recreation Area (OH)	3,455,878
19. Olympic National Park (WA)	3,348,723
20. Colonial National Historic Park (VA)	3,145,039

PENNSYLVANIA

ALLEGHENY NATIONAL FOREST

115 miles south of Buffalo, NY, 150 miles north of Pittsburgh.

PO Box 847
Warren, PA 16365
814-723-5150
http//www.penn.com/~anf

 **Eastern National Forests Interpretive Association.** (PO Box 70, East Tawas, MI 48730; 517-362-7511)

Located in the northwestern Pennsylvania counties of Elk, McKean, Forest, and Warren, the Allegheny National Forest comprises some 513,161 acres of forest, streams, and trails. The hardwood forest includes stands of black cherry, yellow poplar, white ash, red maple, and sugar maple. For recreation, there are trails for hiking, cross-country skiing, all-terrain vehicles (ATVs), and snowmobiles, as well as hunting grounds and over 500 miles of streams for fishing.

SAM'S TIPS

- The Allegheny reservoir is a 12,000-acre lake with 91 miles of shoreline. The forest surrounds the lake on the Pennsylvania side, where camping and boat-launching facilities are available. On the New York side, the Allegheny State Park (716-354-2182) offers similar facilities.
- The forest is divided into three Ranger Districts. These districts administer camping, hunting, and fishing sites, and have trails open to mountain bikes and snowmobiles. For brochures about specific activities and areas, contact the main address.
  1. The Marienville Ranger District (814-927-6628) is in the southern part of the forest. The popular Marienville All Terrain Vehicle Trail connects with a system of ATV trails that weave throughout this forest. The trail is open Memorial Day to September 24, and December 20 to April 1.
  2. The Bradford Ranger District (814-362-4613), in the northeastern part of the forest, includes the Morrison Trail, which offers fascinating geological sights.

Orienteering

Orienteering involves using a map and compass to find your way in unfamiliar terrain. The object is to select and follow the best route to a series of designated points where markers (controls) will be located. The Orienteering Course is located at the Hearts Content Recreation Area 15 miles southwest of Warren, PA, just outside the Hickory Creek Wilderness.

Allegheny National Recreation Area

USDA Forest Service
222 Liberty Street, Box 847
Warren, PA 16365

The recreation area consists of two separate units. The first is along the Allegheny River southwest of Warren and adjacent to the Allegheny Islands Wilderness area. The second unit, along the New York–Pennsylvania border, includes part of the Allegheny Reservoir, with campgrounds (accessible by boat) and other recreational sites. Both areas are generally unroaded and covered with cherry, maple, and oak forests.

3. The Ridgway District office (814-776-6172), in the southeastern part of the forest, includes the Laurel Mill Cross-Country/Hiking area. The only trail that is groomed in the winter, it offers skiing for all ages and levels of ability.

ALLEGHENY PORTAGE RAILROAD NATIONAL HISTORIC SITE

90 miles east of Pittsburgh. Off US 22, 12 miles west of Altoona.

PO Box 189
Cresson, PA 16630-0189
814-886-6150
http://www.nps.gov/alpo

 **Eastern National.** (446 North Lane, Conshohocken, PA 19428; 800-355-5566)

Though only a short section of the Pennsylvania Main Line of Public Works, this 1834–1857 railroad portage over the Allegheny Mountains was a crucial link between the canals of eastern and western Pennsylvania. Canal boat passengers and goods were placed on rails and towed by teams of horses, locomotives, and stationary steam engines up a huge staircase of five inclined planes and five level sections. On the descent, they were let down five more planes and six levels, then transferred again to the Main Line canal. This engineering marvel was rendered obsolete by the advance of railroads.

How the Inclined Plane Works

Much like the cable car system of San Francisco, the engines stayed in one place and towed the railcars via hemp ropes. Sheds at the top of inclines housed twin 35-hp steam engines, used one at a time, with the other as a backup. Each pulled the continuous rope that ran between the rails. The cable was kept taut by pulleys. A water brake on the crankshaft kept descending cars from picking up too much speed. A safety buck, or brake car, prevented cars from rolling downhill if a rope broke.

Sam's Tips

- The Engine House 6 Exhibit Building preserves the remains of the original engine house foundation and features a life-size model of the stationary steam engine, as well as exhibits on the railroad operation.
- Several of the ten original inclines, as well as the Staple Bend Tunnel, the country's first railroad tunnel, are open to the public.
- The 47-mile drive between Altoona and Johnstown, part of a longer auto tour dubbed the "Path of Progress," includes the Horseshoe Curve, Railroaders Memorial Museum, Johnstown Flood National Memorial, and the Johnstown Flood Museum.

DELAWARE WATER GAP NATIONAL RECREATION AREA

100 miles north of Philadelphia, 65 miles west of New York City.

Bushkill, PA 18324
717-588-2435
http://www.nps.gov/dewa

Eastern National. (446 North Lane, Conshohocken, PA 19428; 800-355-5566)

Camping areas are scattered throughout the long valley of the Delaware River, which carved the Delaware Water Gap through this hardwood region of the Appalachian Mountains. Nearby tributary streams cascade down to the river through deeply eroded gorges. Stone houses and other historic structures built by early Dutch settlers are preserved and open to the public. The park encompasses more than 20 lakes and ponds, scenic gorges, and beautiful waterfalls, 25 miles of the Appalachian Trail, and 40 miles of the Delaware National Scenic River.

Winter Eagles

A small group of 10 to 15 bald eagles are a regular part of the winter community at the Gap, but bring your bincoculars if you want to see one. Some of the best viewing areas in Pennsylvania are: Smithfield Beach access, Bushkill boat access, Dingmans Ferry access, and Milford Beach. From the New Jersey side, try the Kittatinny Point Visitor Center and the Poxono boat access.

EDGAR ALLAN POE NATIONAL HISTORIC SITE

Downtown Philadelphia at the corner of 7th and Spring Garden, 6 blocks north of Market Street.

532 North Seventh Street
Philadelphia, PA 19123-3502
215-597-8780
http://www.nps.gov/edal

Eastern National. (446 North Lane, Conshohocken, PA 19428; 800-355-5566)

Poe's life and work are commemorated at the house where he and his family resided in 1843–1844. His short stories, "The Black Cat," "Tell-Tale Heart," and "Gold Bug" were published while he lived here. Of his several Philadelphia homes, this is the only one that survives. Exhibits include ranger-guided tours, a reading room, and an eight-minute slide program that interprets the author's literary career. Special events and programs are offered throughout the year.

For Kids

The Area's Junior Naturalist Discovery Pack includes a magnifying lens, a 2-in-1 telescope-microscope, a ruler, leaf and track identification cards, a dip net, a bug box, and a compass/thermometer. You can borrow a pack at the Visitor Center, and use its contents to complete the Junior Naturalist Booklet. After you've become a Junior Naturalist, you can become a Junior Ranger by filling out another booklet, also available at the Visitor Center. If you complete it all, you'll have earned a Junior Ranger Badge that looks just like the ones real Rangers wear!

Other Sites that Honor Edgar Allan Poe

The Edgar Allan Poe House and Museum: Poe's Baltimore home from 1832–1835 is operated by Baltimore City under the Commission for Historic and Architectural Preservation. For additional information, contact: Curator, Poe House Room 601, Baltimore City Hall, Baltimore, MD 21202; 301-396-4866.

Edgar Allan Poe Cottage: The final home of the author is administered by the Bronx County Historical Society (3266 Bainbridge Avenue, The Bronx, NY 10467; 212-881-8900).

Poe Museum: Not a Poe home, but dedicated to telling Poe's story. Operated by the Poe Foundation at 1914–16 East Main Street, Richmond, VA 23223; 804-648-5523.

EISENHOWER NATIONAL HISTORIC SITE

130 miles west of Philadelphia, 60 miles northwest of Baltimore, MD.

97 Taneytown Road
Gettysburg, PA 17325
717-338-9114
http://www.nps.gov/eise

 **Eastern National.** (95 Taneytown Road, Gettysburg, PA 17325; 717-334-4474)

The only home ever owned by Gen. Dwight D. Eisenhower and his wife, Mamie, this served as a refuge when Ike was President and as a retirement home after he left office. The site includes a barn (where the President bred prize-winning Angus cattle), the 2-room guest house, the main house with 8 bedrooms/bathrooms, and the guardhouse, formerly occupied by Secret Service agents. The reception center celebrates Ike's life on the farm and uses publications, exhibits, and an orientation program to tell his story. Visitors must obtain tickets and board the shuttle bus at the visitor center in Gettysburg.

FORT NECESSITY NATIONAL BATTLEFIELD

60 miles south of Pittsburgh, 35 miles north of Morgantown, WV, 11 miles east of Uniontown, PA, on US 40.

1 Washington Parkway
Farmington, PA 15437-9514
412-329-5512
http://www.nps.gov/fone

 **Eastern National Bookstore.** (same address)

On July 3, 1754, Virginia troops commanded by 22-year-old Colonel George Washington were defeated here in the opening battle of the French and Indian War. In addition to the reconstructed fort, the early 19th-century Mount Washington Tavern stands nearby. General Braddock's grave and Jumonville Glen are a short drive west.

FRIENDSHIP HILL NATIONAL HISTORIC SITE

3 miles north of Point Marion, PA on Route 166.

RD 1, Box 149A
Point Marion, PA 15474
412-725-9190
http://www.nps.gov/frhi

Gallatin House, the two-story brick house located on Friendship Hill, was once the home of Albert Gallatin. An entrepreneur, politician (he was the longest-serving treasury secretary), diplomat, and scholar—and nearly forgotten today—Gallatin stood alongside Thomas Jefferson, James Madison, and James Monroe as they hammered out a political philosophy that defined our government in its first decades. The house contains exhibits on Albert Gallatin's private and public life.

GETTYSBURG NATIONAL MILITARY PARK

50 miles northwest of Baltimore, MD, 80 miles north of Washington, DC.

PO Box 1080
Gettysburg, PA 17325
717-334-1124
http://www.nps.gov/gett

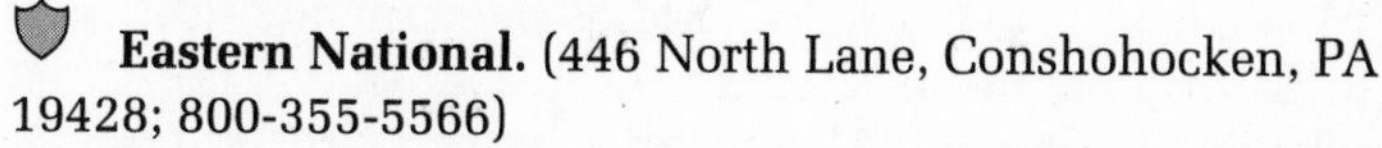
Eastern National. (446 North Lane, Conshohocken, PA 19428; 800-355-5566)

The great Civil War Battle of Gettysburg, fought here July 1–3, 1863, repulsed the second Confederate invasion of the North and claimed more lives than any other battle fought in North America before or since. Many of the Union soldiers who died here are buried in Gettysburg National Cemetery, which adjoins the park. It was at the dedication of the cemetery, on November 19, 1863, that President Abraham Lincoln delivered his timeless Gettysburg Address.

Philadelphia's Yellow Fever Epidemics

"It is too distressing and affecting a scene, for a person young in life to bear" wrote 23-year-old Isaac Heston, a law clerk in the office of John Todd, at Fourth and Walnut Streets. The letter Heston wrote to his brother survives as a testament to the events of that fateful summer and conveys the horror of the yellow fever epidemic that broke out in late July 1793 in the alleys and dim, crowded houses along Water Street, near the Philadelphia docks. Panic ensued, and those who could afford to leave the city sought refuge in outlying communities. Heston himself died ten days after writing his letter.

Sam's Tips

- A self-guided auto tour takes two to three hours to complete. Most of the numbered stops have markers that describe significant actions during the three days of battle.
- The Library of Congress home page (http://www.loc.gov) has an electronic exhibit on the Gettysburg Address that includes digitized versions of early drafts of Lincoln's address, as well as rare related documents.
- The Cyclorama depicts the South's 12,000-man assault, commonly known as Pickett's Charge, through Paul Phillippoteaux's painting. As you stand in the middle of the large circular painting—356 feet by 26 feet—a sound and light program recreates the scene of the fighting and highlights points of interest on the canvas.
- The 750-square-foot Electric Map, located in the Visitor Center, uses a taped narration and 600 colored lights to explain movements of both sides. This is an ideal way to begin your tour.

HOPEWELL FURNACE NATIONAL HISTORIC SITE

Eastern Pennsylvania, off route 345.

2 Mark Bird Lane
Elverson, PA 19520
610-582-8773
http://www.nps.gov/hofu

 **Eastern National.** (446 North Lane, Conshohocken, PA 19428; 800-355-5566)

Hopewell Furnace was built by Mark Bird in 1771 to take advantage of eastern Pennsylvania's abundant raw materials, water power, and religious tolerance. The furnace immediately began casting stove plates, despite a British ban. When the Revolution began, Bird was a supplier of cannon and shot to the Continental Army and Navy. Debt, acquired by his adamant support of the

Gloria Dei Church National Historic Site

Gloria Dei (Old Swedes') Episcopal Church in South Philadelphia is the oldest church building in Pennsylvania and among the oldest in the country. Constructed of Flemish bond, and black header brick, the church was built between 1698 and 1700 for Swedish settlers. After serving as the Swedish Lutheran Church for almost 150 years, Gloria Dei became a part of the Episcopal Church in 1845. Gloria Dei Church was designated as a National Historic Site in 1942, six months before Independence Hall. The Gloria Dei congregation owns and maintains the church and the related buildings, its ministry, and the grounds. The National Park Service has provided the church with additional land to help preserve the site.

For more information contact: Independence National Historical Park, Public Affairs, Office, 313 Walnut Street, Philadelphia, PA 19106; 215-597-0060.

revolutionary cause, forced Bird to sell the furnace. Because the furnace's original appearance was too poorly documented to reconstruct, the site has been restored to the period 1820–1840.

INDEPENDENCE NATIONAL HISTORICAL PARK

In Philadelphia, the Visitor Center is on 3rd and Chestnut Streets.

313 Walnut Street
Philadelphia, PA 19106
215-597-8974
http://www.nps.gov/inde

Eastern National. (446 North Lane, Conshohocken, PA 19428; 800-355-5566)

Independence National Park is perhaps the most significant historical property in the United States. The park, located in central Philadelphia, includes over three dozen buildings and sites associated with the American Revolution and the founding of the United States. Among them: Independence Hall, Congress Hall, Old City Hall, the Liberty Bell Pavilion, the First and Second Banks of the United States, and Franklin Court. Most sites are a short walk from the Visitor Center.

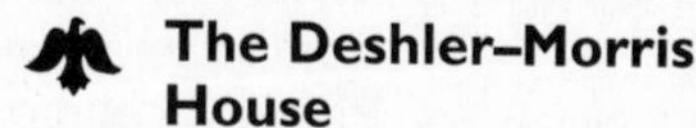

The Deshler–Morris House

The Deshler–Morris House, named for its first and last owners, is the oldest presidential residence still in existence and was the home of George Washington for two periods during his second term. The President sought a house in Germantown, a few miles outside of the capital, to escape the yellow fever epidemic of 1793 that killed close to 10 percent of the population in a three-month period.

Sam's Tips

- At the Visitor Center, a 28-minute film called *Independence* will familiarize you with the historic events that took place here.
- The City Tavern, once called the "most genteel" tavern in America by John Adams, was one of the social, political, and economic centers of late-18th-century Philadelphia. Today, the reconstructed tavern serves lunch and dinner daily in an 18th-century ambience.
- The Park Service offers a handsome 62-page guide to Independence National Historical Park. Contact the cooperating association.

JOHNSTOWN FLOOD NATIONAL MEMORIAL

80 miles east of Pittsburgh.

PO Box 355
St. Michael, PA 15951-0355
814-495-4643
http://www.nps.gov/jofl

Eastern National. (446 North Lane, Conshohocken, PA 19428; 800-355-5566)

"The dam is becoming dangerous and may possibly go," was the last telegraph warning sent to Johnstown on May 31, 1889. Minutes later, the earthen South

"Our Misery Is the Work of Man"

Why weren't the people of Johnstown warned? They *were*, three times, in the hours before the dam broke. But years of similar warning had inured them to the danger. The South Fork Dam, one of the largest earthen dams in the world, had always held during high water. After all, the dam was being maintained by some of the richest and most powerful men in America.

The exclusive South Fork Fishing and Hunting Club was comprised of wealthy Pittsburgh industrialists and businessmen—legendary capitalists like Andrew Carnegie and Andrew Mellon. The club had purchased the abandoned reservoir, repaired the old dam, then raised the level of the lake and built a clubhouse and cottages. Members enjoyed hunting, sailing, and even two excursion steamers plying the lake. But their careless maintenance of the dam weakened it dangerously.

Angel of the Battlefield

Clara Barton, "Angel of the Battlefield," and her staff of 50 doctors and nurses arrived in Johnstown 5 days after the flood. It was the first test of her newly formed American Red Cross. After surveying the injured, she set up hospital tents, built six "Red Cross hotels" for the homeless, and distributed food, clothing, and medicine. Though she was 67, she worked tirelessly, remaining in Johnstown until October. Visit the Clara Barton National Historic Site in Glen Echo, MD.

Fork Dam gave way, sending 20 million tons of water racing at 40 miles an hour into Johnstown. Most residents never saw anything until the 36-foot wall of water, boiling with huge chunks of debris, rolled over them. The worst inland flood in the nation's history claimed over 2,200 lives and virtually wiped out Johnstown. Property damage was $17 million. Bodies were still being found months—and in a few cases, years—after the flood.

Sam's Tips

- The visitor center features the award-winning film *Black Friday* and exhibits that relate the story of the 1889 flood.
- Hike the North Abutment Trail, which begins behind the Unger house (located behind the visitor center) and leads to the remains of the South Fork Dam. The upper portion of the trail is steep and strenuous.
- The South Abutment Trail leads down through the gap of the broken dam. This half-mile trail descends into the old lake bed via an easy trail and climbs back to the parking lot via a series of stairs.

STEAMTOWN NATIONAL HISTORIC SITE

In Scranton, 140 miles north of Philadelphia.

150 South Washington Avenue
Scranton, PA 18503-2018
717-340-5200
http://www.nps.gov/stea

Museum Store, Steamtown Volunteer Association. (150 South Washington Avenue, Scranton, PA 18503-2018; 717-346-7275 or 888-856-2345)

Steamtown National Historic Site occupies 52 acres of the Scranton railroad yard of the Delaware, Lackawanna and Western Railroad, one of the earliest railroads in northeastern Pennsylvania. At the heart of the park is a large collection of standard-gauge steam locomotives and freight and passenger cars. The locomotives range in size from a tiny industrial switcher engine built in 1937 to a huge Union Pacific Big Boy built in 1941. The park has a large museum complex: History Museum, the remaining portion of the 1902–1937 roundhouse, a 90-foot-diameter turntable of the type used here after 1900, and a Technology Museum. Park rangers offer daily tours of the yard, roundhouse, and locomotive repair shops. On certain days, steam train rides are offered, including a main line two-and-a-half-hour excursion, or a short trip to the nearby Scranton Iron Furnaces.

THADDEUS KOSCIUSZKO NATIONAL MEMORIAL

In downtown Philadelphia, at 301 Pine Street, on the corner of 3rd and Pine Streets.

c/o Independence NHP
313 Walnut Street
Philadelphia, PA 19106-2278
215-597-9618
http:/www.nps.gov/thko

 **Eastern National.** (446 North Lane, Conshohocken, PA 19428; 800-355-5566)

One of the first foreign volunteers to come to the aid of the American revolutionary army, Kosciuszko (KOS-CHOOS-KO) arrived in Philadelphia just a few weeks after the Declaration of Independence was adopted and was soon serving

Trainer Extraordinaire, Friedrich von Steuben

When Washington's army marched into camp at Valley Forge, it was tired, cold, and ill-equipped. Yet, after enduring a ravaging winter, that claimed over 2,000 lives, it was able to pursue and successfully engage the British army at the Battle of Monmouth in New Jersey six months later. Credit for this remarkable transformation goes to Friedrich von Steuben, once a member of the elite General Staff of Frederick the Great of Prussia, who had offered his military skills to the patriot cause. Impressed with the Prussian, Washington immediately assigned him the task of developing and carrying out an effective training program.

Von Steuben, who spoke little English, drafted training manuals in French. They were then translated by his aides, copied, and passed to the individual regiments, which carried out the prescribed drill the following day. Von Steuben shocked many American officers by breaking tradition and working directly with the men, often acting as a drill sergeant.

as an engineer with the rank of colonel. Kosciuszko's selection and fortification of Bemis Heights, overlooking the Hudson River near the village of Saratoga, contributed greatly to the pivotal surrender of 6,000 British troops under General John Burgoyne. Kosciuszko's next assignment, and perhaps his greatest achievement, began in March 1778, when he was entrusted with the defense of the Hudson River at West Point. For 28 months, Kosciuszko planned and built fortifications at West Point which were so solid and ingenious that the British never dared to attack. When the United States Military Academy was established at West Point in 1802, the first monument erected was a tribute to Thaddeus Kosciuszko. Today, he is memorialized by this house, which served as his residence during the winter of 1797–1798.

VALLEY FORGE NATIONAL HISTORICAL PARK

20 miles northwest of Philadelphia, 45 miles west of Trenton, NJ.

PO Box 953
Valley Forge, PA 19481
610-783-1000
http://www.nps.gov/vafo

 **Valley Forge Park Interpretive Association.** (PO Box 953, Valley Forge, PA 19482; 610-783-1076)

REVOLUTIONARY WAR-RELATED SITES

1. Boston National Historical Park (MA)
2. Bunker Hill Monument (MA)
3. Colonial National Historical Park (VA)
4. Cowpens National Battlefield (SC)
5. Dorchester Heights Monument (MA)
6. Fort Stanwix National Monument (NY)
7. Fort Sumter National Monument (SC)
8. George Rogers Clark National Historical Park (IN)
9. Guilford Courthouse National Military Park (NC)
10. Independence National Historical Park (PA)
11. Kings Mountain National Military Park (SC)
12. Longfellow National Historic Site (MA)
13. Minute Man National Historical Park (MA)
14. Moore's Creek National Battlefield (NC)
15. Morristown National Historic Park (NJ)
16. Ninety-Six National Historic Site (SC)
17. Overmountain Victory National Historic Trail (TN, NC, SC)
18. Saratoga National Historic Park (NY)
19. Valley Forge National Historical Park (PA)

Of all famous sites associated with the War for Independence, none is a more forceful reminder of the suffering, sacrifice, and ultimate triumph of the Continental Army than Valley Forge. No battles were fought here, but hundreds of American soldiers died here during the winter of 1777–1778 as they struggled against hunger, disease, and the unrelenting force of nature. Nonetheless, Washington was able to transform the army into an effective and well-trained force; some consider the American army to have been born here. The park contains General Washington's headquarters, original earthworks, a variety of monuments and markers, and recreations of log huts and cannons.

Sam's Tips

- The Visitor's Center provides an 18-minute film, which gives an overview of life during the encampment. The extensive George C. Newmann Collection of firearms, swords, and accessories is the focal point of the exhibit area.
- A self-guided tour route, keyed to numbered stops on the map, will take you past extensive remains and reconstructions of major forts and lines of earthworks, the Artillery Park, Washington's Headquarters, and the Grand Parade where General von Steuben rebuilt the army.

Points of Interest

U.S. ARMY CORPS OF ENGINEERS

AYLESWORTH LAKE

A 4-acre lake featuring a beach, a picnic area, and hiking trails near East Jermyn, in Lackawanna County. From Scranton, go about 10 miles upstream on US 6.

ALVIN R. BUSH DAM

Surrounded by high mountains in a wild, scenic area, Kettle Creek State Park provides the recreational facilities at this project. From Renovo, go west 5 miles on PA 120 to Westport and north 8 miles on the unmarked state road.

BELTZVILLE LAKE

Fossils of early marine life are found in outcroppings in this project area. From Allentown, go north on PA Turnpike NE Extension to Exit 34, cross PA 209, and take Township Route 444 to the project.

FOSTER JOSEPH SAYERS DAM

Bald Eagle State Park provides a marina, campground, picnic areas, and beach at this 1,730-acre lake. A historical village is under restoration. From I-80, Exit 23, go north 10 miles on PA 150.

MAHONING CREEK LAKE

Another lake set in the rugged hills of western Pennsylvania. Hiking, hunting, and fishing are among its attractions. Follow project signs south from New Bethlehem.

MAXWELL LOCK AND DAM

This dam provides a 24-mile pool, ideal for recreational boating, and receives more recreational use than any other on the Monongahela. From Brownsville, go south 8 miles.

YOUGHIOGHENY RIVER LAKE

Releases from the dam allow some of the best whitewater canoeing in the East. Visit spectacular Ohiopyle Falls. From Confluence, go south 1.5 miles on PA 281.

PROMPTON LAKE

The passage of glaciers in the vicinity has left numerous depressions in which small lakes and swamps have developed. From Scranton, go east on US 6 through Honesdale and then north on PA 170 to the project.

RAYSTOWN LAKE

On this vast and twisting lake, the largest entirely within Pennsylvania, you will find boating, fishing, camping, hiking, swimming, and scenic beauty. Park headquarters is at Hesston, 2 miles east of PA 26.

MEET YOUR PARK CONSERVATIONISTS

The National Park Service has a varied and experienced staff of national stature—rangers, natural resource managers, archaeologists, historians, interpreters, landscape architects, engineers, and planners—who protect our land and legacy, conduct research, and educate the public. We'd like to introduce you to one of them.

Steve Golden, Chief, Conservation Assistance Division, Rivers, Trails, and Conservation Program, Massachusetts, was described by his local newspaper recently as having "the best job in the conservation movement," and Steve wholeheartedly agrees. Steve has worked for the NPS 19 years, most recently for the Rivers, Trails, and Conservation Program. Steve has this to say about his job: "Every day I am in contact with people working to save their rivers, their trails, their open space lands, and eager for NPS help. From the South Bronx to the wilds of Maine, I have had the chance to hear the dreams of people struggling to make their communities better places in which to live and work. We are lucky that the NPS has the courage to work outside of confined boundaries and tight regulations. Every day, we win new friends by participating in the broad conservation agenda of the region. Although my family thinks of me as a bit of an outdoor nut, a grown-up Boy Scout, I can't imagine a closer fit between one's vocation and one's avocation."

RHODE ISLAND

ROGER WILLIAMS NATIONAL MEMORIAL

Downtown Providence, RI.

282 North Main Street
Providence, RI 02903
401-521-7266
http://www.nps.gov/rowi

 **Eastern National.** (446 North Lane, Conshohocken, PA 19428; 800-355-5566)

This green oasis marks the original settlement of Providence in 1636. Most important, it honors Roger Williams, the colony's founder and statesman, who believed in religious freedom for all. The beautiful landscape features a well commemorating the spot of the spring where Williams and his followers obtained fresh water for their colony. The visitor's center is in the historic Antram–Gray house.

 **SAM'S TIPS**

- Less than 20 minutes away from the park is the Haffenreffer Museum of Anthropology. Built near the site of Massasoit's winter encampment, the museum houses artifacts from Native American tribes throughout North America. For more information, contact the museum (300 Tower Street, Bristol, RI 02809; 401-253-8388).

The Apple Tree That Ate Roger Williams—A Folktale

Roger Williams died around 1683, but over the next 175 years people gradually forgot where he was buried. In 1860, a group of citizens decided to build a monument to Williams and his wife, Mary, and to relocate his remains to the site. While the approximate location of Williams' grave was known, the exact spot turned out to be in the middle of an apple orchard. As his grave was being dug out—so the story goes—it was discovered that a nearby apple tree had pushed one of its main roots into the coffin. The root had worked its way around the place where his skull had been, and then had grown in a straight line where his backbone had been. At Williams' hips, the root divided into two branches, each one following a leg bone all the way to the heels. From here, each of the roots turned upward toward the toes. One of the branches had a slight crook in it, just where Williams' knee would have been. The apple tree, it seems, had eaten Roger Williams. Today, the tree root is owned by the Rhode Island Historical Society.

Blackstone River Valley National Heritage Corridor

The Blackstone River Valley is one of the best preserved examples of America's "Age of Industry." Once called the "hardest working river in the world," the Blackstone begins in Worcester, MA, and flows through two dozen Massachusetts and Rhode Island towns. Along its 46 miles, the river drops 438 feet, making it an excellent source of power. Samuel Slater's cotton spinning mill (1793) in Pawtucket, RI, the first factory in America, ushered in the American Industrial Revolution and resulted in this sprawling river valley's becoming the first industrialized area in the nation.

For more information contact: 1 Depot Square, Woonsocket, RI 02895; 401-762-0250; http://www.nps.gov/blac

Touro Synagogue National Historic Site

85 Touro Street
Newport, RI 02840
401-847-4794

This synagogue, designed by Peter Harrison, is one of the finest examples of colonial religious architecture. It is still an active place of worship. Benefiting from the religious tolerance of Roger Williams, founder of the colony that became Rhode Island, the first Jewish community in Rhode Island, and the second in the United States (the first was New York City's Congregation Shearith Israel), was founded here in 1658. Construction of the present synagogue was completed in 1763. The classical and ornate interior contrasts sharply with the outward simplicity of the building. The National Park Service provides technical assistance for the preservation of the building under a cooperative agreement with the congregation. From the synagogue, it's a short walk up Touro Street to the old burial ground, the inspiration for Longfellow's poem "The Jewish Cemetery at Newport."

VERMONT

GREEN MOUNTAIN NATIONAL FOREST

90 miles north of Albany, NY, 170 miles west of Boston, MA.

231 North Main Street
Rutland, VT 05701
802-747-6700
http://www.fs.fed.us

Eastern National Forests Interpretive Association. (PO Box 70, East Tawas, MI 48730; 517-362-7511)

The 355,000-acre Green Mountain National Forest, located in central Vermont, is comprised mostly of 60- to 100-year-old hardwoods, such as beech, birch, and maples. In addition to camping, canoeing, and fishing opportunities, there are numerous wildlife observation sites (marked with binocular signs) where visitors can study the various habitats and ecosystems present in the forest and in its ponds and rivers.

Sam's Tips

The Green Mountain National Forest includes several Wilderness and Recreation areas. Among them are:

- The Hapgood Pond Recreation Area (8 miles northeast of Manchester, VT) has 28 campsites, a sandy beach, a bathhouse, and an .8-mile nature trail that winds around the north edge of the pond. Canoes and small boats are allowed, and a boat launch provides easy access. Fishing requires a valid state license. The Hapgood Pond Recreation Area is operated by the Vermont Youth Conservation Corps under a special use permit by the U.S. Forest Service. Contact the Corps (103 South Main Street, Waterbury, VT 05671; 802-241-3699) for additional information. The Vermont Institute of Natural Science (VINS) also presents weekly nature programs. For schedules and more information about the VINS, call or write: RR 2, Box 532, Woodstock, VT 05091; 802-457-2779.
- The Chittenden Brook Recreation Area (8 miles southwest of Rochester, VT) includes a campground with 17 secluded, wooded sites. Tent pads, tables, fire grates, garbage and recycling bins, and outhouses are available. Hiking and cross-country skiing trails and a wetlands area are also open to the public. For more information, contact: Green Mountain National Forest, Rochester Ranger District, Route 100, Rochester, VT 05767; 802-767-4261.

Developing Fish

Fishery biologists are developing a native strain of the Atlantic Salmon in the White River drainage. This is an important step in establishing a viable and permanent salmon population. The White River National Fish Hatchery produces about 400,000 newly hatched salmon fry every year in order to stock the river system. The Hatchery is located on Route 107, in Bethel, VT, and is open to the public. Call 802-234-5400 for more information.

White Rocks National Recreation Area

USDA Forest Service
RR 1, Box 1940
Manchester Center, VT 05255
802-362-2307

White-rock cliffs and ice beds are major attractions of the White Rocks National Recreation Area. The Appalachian Trail and the Catamont Nordic Ski Trail traverse the area. Cultural resources include prehistoric hunting camps, a quarry site for arrowhead quartz, and historic farms. Recreation opportunities can be found at three local lakes.

- The Grout Pond Recreational Area, situated in Stratton township (10 miles east of Arlington, VT), is made up of 1,600 acres of semiprimitive land and a 79-acre pond, which is ideal for canoeing and wind surfing. The pond has bass, pickerel, perch, sunfish, and bullhead. Other nearby fishing opportunities are at Branch and Beebe ponds, Somerset Reservoir, Black Brook, and the East Branch of the Deerfield River. Five camping sites are situated immediately around the pond, but they are accessible only by trail or canoe. For more information, contact the Manchester Ranger District, Routes 11 & 30, RR 1, Box 1940, Manchester Center, VT 05255; 802-362-2307.
- For hikers, the Long Trail winds its way along the ridge line of the main range of the Green Mountains for 264 miles from Massachusetts to the Canadian border. The trail system contains a network of shelters spaced approximately one-day's hike apart. The Appalachian National Scenic Trail and the Long Trail share the same route for some 97 miles.

MARSH–BILLINGS NATIONAL HISTORICAL PARK

Woodstock, VT.

c/o National Park Service
Office of Communications
15 State Street
Boston, MA 02109
617-223-5200
http://www.nps.gov/mabi

This was home to pioneer conservationist George Perkins Marsh in the early 1800s. In 1869, attorney and railroad tycoon Frederick Billings bought the property, reforested it, and started scientific farming methods based on Marsh's environment-saving principles. Billings's granddaughter, Mary, and her husband, conservationist Laurence S. Rockefeller, donated the mansion and woodlands for the park. The Marsh–Billings National Historical Park is located on land currently owned by the Rockefeller family. The Rockefellers will give the land to the National Park Service when they no longer use it. Call the Office of Communications for more information on the mid-1998 opening date.

Points of Interest

U.S. ARMY CORPS OF ENGINEERS

BALL MOUNTAIN LAKE

Winhall Brook Campground offers streamside campsites, modern restrooms with hot showers; a trailer dump station, and resident campground attendants. The river and 75-acre lake offer fishing, and reservoir lands are open for hunting. From Brattleboro, go north on VT 30 to Jamaica and to the dam. The campground is 5 miles north of the dam, off VT 100.

NORTH HARTLAND LAKE

At the upper end of the reservoir, the Ottaquechee River flows through sheer-faced, 165-foot-deep Quechee Gorge, one of the outstanding natural spectacles in the state. An overlook area and state-managed campground are nearby. A park with a small beach offers swimming, picnicking, and boating at the 215-acre lake. From White River Junction, go south 5 miles on US 5.

NORTH SPRINGFIELD LAKE

The 100-acre lake and 65-acre Stoughton Pond offer excellent warm-water fishing (small boats only). A small park on Stoughton Pond has a beach and picnic area. Reservoir lands are open for hunting and snowmobiling. From Springfield, go north on VT 106 and follow signs to the dam.

TOWNSHEND LAKE

This 95-acre lake provides an attractive setting for the day-use area with swimming, picnicking, hiking, and boating. A historic covered bridge is located downstream. From Brattleboro, go north 18 miles on VT 30.

UNION VILLAGE DAM

A streamside environment with excellent fishing and hunting. Small day-use areas with picnicking facilities. Two scenic covered bridges nearby. From White River Junction, go north on US 5 and turn left on VT 132.

WEST VIRGINIA

BLUESTONE NATIONAL SCENIC RIVER

100 miles southeast of Charleston, WV.

PO Box 246
Glen Jean, WV 25846
394-465-0508
http://www.nps.gov/blue

 **Eastern National.** (446 North Lane, Conshohocken, PA 19428; 800-355-5566)

To be included under the Wild and Scenic Rivers Act of 1968, a river must possess "outstandingly remarkable" values. For this 10-mile section of the Bluestone River, eligibility was never in question. The Bluestone begins on East River Mountain in Virginia and flows 77 miles to its confluence with the New River at Bluestone Lake near Hinton, West Virginia. Along the way, it passes through the Bluestone Gorge between Pipestem and Bluestone State Parks, and it's this part that has been set aside as a National Scenic River.

Sam's Tips

- The 8-mile Bluestone Trail is ideal for hikers to observe birds and wildlife. A new bridge eliminates the need to ford the Little Bluestone River on the trail that connects Pipestem and Bluestone State Parks.
- Much of the Bluestone is managed as hunting and fishing grounds by the West Virginia Department of Natural Resources. Hunting is permitted during the fall, winter, and spring, in accordance with state laws. Be sure to wear bright orange in these seasons.

GAULEY RIVER NATIONAL RECREATION AREA

70 miles east of Charleston, WV, 225 miles south of Pittsburgh, PA.

PO Box 246
Glen Jean, WV 25846
394-465-0508
http://www.nps.gov/gari

Eastern National. (446 North Lane, Conshohocken, PA 19428; 800-355-5566)

> **The Good Old Days**
>
> Modern whitewater rafters like to boast of their encounters with the challenging rapids of the Gauley and Meadow rivers, but turn-of-the-century residents of the area most likely would consider today's rafters tame; during floods, they rode the Gauley's rapids on railroad ties.

The 25 miles of the Gauley River and 6 miles of the Meadow River pass through some of West Virginia's most scenic gorges and valleys. Dropping 26 feet per mile through a gorge that averages 500 feet in depth, the Gauley is noted for its outstanding whitewater rafting and, for kayakers, is one of the most technically challenging rivers in the nation. The Meadow River gradient averages 71 feet per mile. Although much of the land within the park boundaries is privately owned, several high cliff walls offer outstanding rock-climbing opportunities for the public.

Favorite Names of Local Rapids

Pure Screaming Hell Rapids
Heaven Help You Rapids
Insignificant Rapids
Pillow Rock Rapids

HARPERS FERRY NATIONAL HISTORICAL PARK

65 miles northwest of Washington, DC, and 20 miles southwest of Frederick, MD.

PO Box 65
Harpers Ferry, WV 25425
304-535-6298
http://www.nps.gov/hafe/

Harpers Ferry Historical Association, Inc. (PO Box 197, Harpers Ferry, WV 25425; 800-821-5206)

Harpers Ferry lies at the confluence of the Shenandoah and Potomac rivers, which have carved a natural water gap from steep ridges of quartzite and shale. It was the site of abolitionist John Brown's famous 1859 raid in an attempt to seize 100,000 rifles to wipe slavery from the nation. During the Civil War, Harpers Ferry changed hands eight times. After the war, Storer College, one of the earliest integrated schools, was founded here to educate former slaves.

Sam's Tips

- The park's bookshop contains over 2,000 titles, with special emphasis on the Civil War; African American history; transportation and industry; and official National Park Service handbooks and videos. (For more information, call 800-821-5206.)
- The park's exhibits and museums include the Wetland Exhibit, the John Brown Museum and Fort, the Storer College Museum, Black Voices Museum, Civil War Museum, an Industry Museum, the Harper House, and Jefferson Rock, named for Thomas Jefferson, who once proclaimed the view from the rock, above the merging rivers, "worth a voyage across the Atlantic."
- Virginius Island features the ruins of a once thriving 19th-century industrial community. Allow 1–2 hours for exploring the ruins.
- The Appalachian Trail Club's Headquarters is located adjacent to the park, in the town of Harpers Ferry.

MONONGAHELA NATIONAL FOREST

The borders of West Virginia, Virginia, and Maryland.

200 Sycamore Street
Elkins, WV 26241-3962
304-636-1800
http://www.fs.fed.us

 **West Virginia Highlands Conservancy.** (PO Box 306, Charleston, WV 25321)

Begun in 1915 with the purchase of 7,200 acres, the Monongahela National Forest has expanded in size to over 909,000 acres of public land. The moist western side of the Allegheny Front of the Appalachian Mountains forms the character of the forest and contains northern hardwoods such as cherry and maple mixed with oak on the drier ridges and yellow poplar in the coves. The drier eastern side contains cedars and even cactus. The Monongahela features hundreds of miles of small streams, including the headwaters of five major river systems, full of both native and stocked trout. In the spring, during high water, some of the rivers may be run by whitewater enthusiasts. Although located within a day's drive of much of the East Coast, the forest remains secluded and quiet.

 **FOREST SERVICE: SCENIC BYWAY**

Highland Scenic Highway

The Highland Scenic Highway, in the Monongahela National Forest, extends 45 miles through the rugged landscape of the Allegheny Highlands and offers spectacular views of ridgetops, broad valleys, and mountain streams. *Contact Monongahela National Forest.*

NEW RIVER GORGE NATIONAL RIVER

60 miles southeast of Charleston, WV.

PO Box 246
Glen Jean, WV 25846
304-465-0508
http://www.nps.gov/neri

 **Eastern National.** (446 North Lane, Conshohocken, PA 19428; 860-355-5566)

Each year, more than one million visitors come to admire the rugged New River, which flows through deep canyons and—despite its name—is among the oldest rivers on the continent. The 52-mile section from Hinton to Fayetteville is abundant in natural, scenic, historic, and recreational features. Visitors also come to use the park's many recreational opportunities, including whitewater rafting and boating, fishing, hiking, mountain biking, and rock climbing.

Sam's Tips

The following visitor centers provide information services, exhibits, and interpretive activities:

- The main falls of the popular Sandstone Falls scenic area is 1,500 feet wide and drops 10 to 25 feet. This is also one of the best fishing areas on the New River for catfish and smallmouth bass. Short trails lead off the boardwalk to wildlife habitats and fishing beaches. A boat access below the falls is available.
- Rock climbing is a popular activity at the park. The Bridge area (located near the Canyon Rim Visitor Center) is the best place for first-time visitors. Most routes in the gorge are rated 5.9 and harder, so be sure to obtain a guidebook. Some favorite names of climbing routes are Throw Down Those Childish Toys, The Spamling, Blood Donors, and Mean, Mean Girl.
- The New River Bridge boasts the world's longest single-arch steel span (3,030 feet). It is also the second highest in the country (876 feet above the river bed). On the third Saturday of October, the Fayette County Plateau Chamber of Commerce hosts "Bridge Day," during which the bridge is open to pedestrians and draws up to 250,000 people.

Points of Interest

U.S. ARMY CORPS OF ENGINEERS

BEECH FORK LAKE

Small lake nestled in the hills of West Virginia with boating and camping opportunities, and solar energy information center. Located 7 miles south of Huntington, just off WV 152.

BLUESTONE LAKE

Many artifacts remain from a large Indian town once located on project land. Located at Hinton on WV 3 and 20.

BURNSVILLE LAKE

Numerous recreation opportunities include excellent hunting. A historical complex with a Civil War battle site is part of this project, which is easily accessible from I-79 at the Burnsville exit.

SUTTON LAKE

With 45 miles of shoreline, this lake attracts fishing and boating enthusiasts. Located in the wooded hills of central West Virginia, a mile east of Sutton.

TYGART LAKE

The Tygart State Park supplements Corps facilities at this lake in the West Virginia mountains 3 miles south of Grafton, on County Road 9.

R.D. BAILEY LAKE

Beautiful lake in rugged terrain with visitor center overlooking the lake and many recreational opportunities. Located near Justice, just off US 52.

EASTERN NATIONAL (COOPERATING ASSOCIATION)

Cooperating associations are on the front lines as providers of vital information to millions of visitors to America's national parks, forests, and other public lands. These nonprofit associations work closely with the management of the parks and forests toward the production of quality publications, maps, videos, and theme-related merchandise. One of the largest associations is:

Eastern National
446 North Lane
Conshohocken, PA 19428
800-355-5566
http://www.easternnational.org

This Association provides information on these public lands:

Abraham Lincoln Birthplace National Historic Site (KY)
Acadia National Park (ME)
Adams National Historic Site (MA)
Andersonville National Historic Site (GA)
Andrew Johnson National Historic Site (TN)
Apostle Islands National Lakeshore (WI)
Appomattox Court House National Historic Park (VA)
Assateague Island National Seashore (MD)
Big South Fork National River and Recreation Area (TN)
Blue Ridge Parkway (VA)
Booker T. Washington National Monument (VA)
Boston National Historical Park (MA)
Canaveral National Seashore (FL)
Cape Cod National Seashore (MA)
Cape Hatteras National Seashore (NC)
Cape Lookout National Seashore (NC)
Caribbean National Forest (Puerto Rico)
Carl Sandburg Home National Historic Site (NC)
Chattahoochee River National Recreation Area (GA)
Christiansted National Historic Site (Virgin Islands)
Colonial National Historic Park (VA)
Cumberland Island National Seashore (GA)
Cuyahoga Valley National Recreation Area (OH)
Delaware Water Gap National Recreation Area (PA)
Edgar Allen Poe National Historic Site (PA)
Edison National Historic Site (NJ)
Effigy Mounds National Monument (IA)
Eisenhower National Historic Site (PA)
Fire Island National Seashore (NY)
Fort Caroline National Memorial (FL)
Fort Mantanzas National Monument (FL)
Fort Necessity National Battlefield (PA)

Fort Pulaski National Monument (GA)
Fort Smith National Historic Site (AR)
Fort Stanwix National Monument (NY)
Fort Sumter National Monument (SC)
Frederick Law Olmsted National Historic Site (MA)
Fredericksburg/Spotsylvania County National Military Park (VA)
George Rogers Clark National Historical Park (IN)
Gettysburg National Military Park (PA)
Gulf Islands National Seashore (MS)
Harry S Truman National Historic Site (MO)
Herbert Hoover National Historic Site (IA)
Hopewell Culture National Historic Park (OH)
Hopewell Furnace National Historic Site (PA)
Horseshoe Bend National Military Park (AL)
Hot Springs National Park (AR)
Independence National Historic Park (PA)
Indiana Dunes National Lakeshore (IN)
Jimmy Carter National Historic Site (GA)
John F. Kennedy National Historic Site (MA)
Johnstown Flood National Memorial (PA)
Kings Mountain National Military Park (SC)
Lincoln Boyhood National Memorial (IN)
Longfellow National Historic Site (MA)
Lowell National Historic Park (MA)
Mammoth Cave National Park (KY)
Manassas National Battlefield Park (VA)
Martin Luther King, Jr. National Historic Site (GA)
Minute Man National Historic Park (MA)
Natchez National Historical Park (MI)
Petersburg National Battlefield (VA)
Pictured Rocks National Lakeshore (MI)
Richmond National Battlefield Park (VA)
Russell Cave National Monument (AL)
San Juan National Historic Site (Puerto Rico)
Saratoga National Historic Park (NY)
Shiloh National Military Site (TN)
Sleeping Bear Dunes National Lakeshore (MI)
Springfield Armory National Historic Site (MA)
Theodore Roosevelt Birthplace National Historic Site (NY)
Tuskegee Institute National Historic Site (AL)
Upper Delaware Scenic and Recreation Area (NY)
Vicksburg National Military Park (MI)
Virgin Islands National Park (Virgin Islands)
William Howard Taft National Historic Site (OH)
Women's Rights National Historic Park (NY)
Wright Brothers National Memorial (NC)

The Southeast Region

NATIONAL PARK SERVICE HANDBOOKS—THE SOUTHEAST REGION

National Park Service handbooks highlight popular visitor sites across the country. Use them to learn about the historic significance and natural beauty of your next vacation destination. All are generously illustrated with photos, maps, and diagrams. Sites in the Southeast for which these authoritative handbooks are available include:

Site	*Stock No.*	*Price*
Fort Sumter (SC)	024-005-00919-1	$3.25
Great Smoky Mountains National Park (TN)	024-005-00815-2	6.50
Richmond National Battlefield (VA)	024-005-00182-4	2.75
Vicksburg and the Opening of the Mississippi River (MS)	024-005-00976-1	4.50

You can place an order by phone (202–512-1800) or fax (202–512-2250), or by writing to: Superintendent of Documents, PO Box 371954, Pittsburgh, PA 15250–7954. (Use the stock number when ordering. Prices may change.) There are 24 local government bookstores located around the country which carry titles of regional interest. Check the Appendix section of this book for the one nearest to you.

TRASH TALK: HOW LONG DOES IT LAST?

Park Rangers urge you to do the right thing and put litter in its proper place (and be sure to recycle what you can). Simple acts of carelessness can leave a lasting impression on the land. Just how long does litter last?

Orange and banana peels	Up to 2 years
Cigarette butts	1–5 years
Plastic-coated paper	5 years
Plastic bags	10–20 years
Plastic film container	20–30 years
Leather	Up to 50 years
Aluminum cans and tabs	80–100 years
Plastic six-pack holders	100 years
Glass bottles	1,000,000 years
Plastic bottles	Indefinitely
Styrofoam	Indefinitely

Litter removal along park roads and trails costs taxpayers millions of dollars every year. That money could be better spent on other park programs.

ALABAMA

HORSESHOE BEND NATIONAL MILITARY PARK

12 miles north of Dadeville and 18 miles northeast of Alexander City.

Route 1, Box 103
Daviston, AL 36256
205-234-7111
http://www.nps.gov/hobe

 **Eastern National.** (446 North Lane, Conshohocken, PA 19428; 800-355-5566)

On March 27, 1814, at the "horseshoe bend" of the Tallapoosa River, General Andrew Jackson and the 3,000 Tennessee frontier troops and U.S. regulars under his command defeated about 1,000 Upper Creek Indians led by Chief Menawa. Soon thereafter, Creek lands comprising three-fifths of the present State of Alabama and one-fifth of Georgia were added to the United States and opened for white settlement. One year after his election to the Presidency, partly as a result of his fame from the battles at Horseshoe Bend and New Orleans, Andrew Jackson signed the Indian Removal Bill, forcing all tribes east of the Mississippi River to move to Oklahoma, a journey the Cherokees named the "Trail of Tears."

LITTLE RIVER CANYON NATIONAL PRESERVE

110 miles northeast of Birmingham, AL, 50 miles south of Chattanooga, TN.

2141 Gault Avenue North
Fort Payne, AL 35967
205-845-9605
http://www.nps.gov/liri

In Cherokee and Dekalb Counties, near Lake Weiss (known as the "Crappie Capital of the World"), lies one of the deepest canyons east of the Mississippi. Flowing through the canyon is Little River, the only body of water in the United States that flows its entire length on a mountain before crashing down Little River Falls to Little River Canyon. The area is in the very early stages of development, and there are no visitor facilities yet, but the park is open for hiking, kayaking, and other activities.

 **Sam's Tips**

- Contact the Little River Canyon Field School (700 Pelham Road, N., Ayers Hall, Suite 216, Jackson State University, Jacksonville, AL 36265; 205-782-5697) to find out about workshops on the local environment and culture. Most of the workshops are free.

- Call or write the nearby Desoto State Park Resort (Route 1, Box 210, Fort Payne, AL 35967; 205-845-5380) to learn about the facilities, including campgrounds, furnished cabins, resort lodges, picnic trails, and so on.

NATIONAL FORESTS IN ALABAMA: CONECUH, TALLADEGA, TUSKEGEE, WILLIAM B. BANKHEAD

Conecuh National Forest is 140 miles northeast of Mobile and 100 miles south of Montgomery.

Talladega National Forest is comprised of three separate ranger districts, about 45 miles northwest of Montgomery.

Tuskegee National Forest is 45 miles east of Montgomery.

William B. Bankhead National Forest is 40 miles northwest of Birmingham.

2946 Chestnut Street
Montgomery, AL 36107
334-832-4470
http://www.fs.fed.us

Cradle of Forestry in America Interpretive Association. (100 South Broad, Brevard, NC 28712; 704-884-5713)

The four separate national forests in Alabama collectively feature ecosystems and landscapes that range from the rugged Talladega mountain range to rolling coastal plains. These national forests provide both developed and dispersed recreational activities, including hunting, fishing, boating, canoeing, hiking, and off-road vehicle riding.

Sam's Tips

- Each forest has nearby points of interest:
  1. Conecuh National Forest: Thomas E. McMillan Museum, Brewton.
  2. Talladega National Forest: Cheaha State Park, Talladega Motor Speedway, Butler's Mill, U.S. Army Chemical Corps Museum, Fort McClellan, DeSoto Caverns, near Childersburg.
  3. Tuskegee National Forest: Tuskegee Institute National Historic Site.
  4. William B. Bankhead National Forest: Alabama Space and Rocket Center Museum, Huntsville; Clarkston (Legg) Covered Bridge, Culman County; General Joe Wheeler Home; Hillsboro/Natural Bridge of Alabama, Winston County Dismals Wonder Garden.

RUSSELL CAVE NATIONAL MONUMENT

In northeastern Alabama, 7 miles northwest of Bridgeport and 45 miles west from Chattanooga, TN.

3729 County Road 98
Bridgeport, AL 35740
205-495-2672
http://www.nps.gov/ruca

 **Eastern National.** (446 North Lane, Conshohocken, PA 19428; 800-355-5566)

Thousands of years ago, nomadic Indians stumbled on Russell Cave in the hill country of northern Alabama. The cave was a great boon to these Indians because it provided ready protection from the elements. Successive bands of hunters, gatherers, and their children took shelter in this cave until 1000 A.D. When the last occupants departed, Russell Cave held beneath its surface the record of at least 9,000 years of human life on this continent, but the first of these relics were not discovered until 1953, when four members of the Tennessee Archaeological Society began digging in the cave. They realized the significance of their discovery and turned to the Smithsonian Institution for assistance. The land was passed to the National Geographic Society, which donated it to the National Park Service in 1961.

TUSKEGEE INSTITUTE NATIONAL HISTORIC SITE

40 miles east of Montgomery, and 50 miles west of Columbus, GA.

PO Drawer 10
Tuskegee Institute, AL 36087
205-727-3200
http://www.nps.gov/tuin

 **Eastern National.** (446 North Lane, Conshohocken, PA 19428; 800-355-5566)

Tuskegee Institute was founded for African Americans in 1881 by Booker T. Washington. Born into slavery, Washington entered Hampton Institute, worked his way through as a janitor, and graduated in 1875 with honors. Six years later, he moved to Tuskegee, Alabama, to create the Tuskegee Normal and Industrial Institute. It continues today as Tuskegee University. Preserved here are many historic buildings constructed of bricks made and laid by the institute's students. The National Historic Site, located on the campus, includes: a museum devoted to scientist George Washington Carver, who joined the Tuskegee faculty in 1896; The Oaks, home of Booker T. Washington; and Tuskegee's Historic Campus District, which contains more than 27 historically significant landmarks. Here, too, is The Daniel "Chappie" James Center for Aerospace Science and Health Education. James was a Tuskegee student who went on to become the nation's first African American four-star general.

Points of Interest

U.S. ARMY CORPS OF ENGINEERS

ALABAMA RIVER LAKES

This project consists of three lakes with campgrounds, primitive sites, day-use areas, and swimming beaches. Directions:

- R. E. Woodruff Lake: From Montgomery, take US 80 for 30 miles to Benton.
- William Dannelly Lake: From Camden, take Highway 28 west for 9 miles to the dam.
- Claiborne Lake: From Grove Hill, take Highways 84 east and 41 north, then County Road 17 to the dam.

BLACK WARRIOR—TOMBIGBEE RIVER LAKES

These six lakes have been important commercial waterways since the earliest settlers moved inland. Today, historic sites and picturesque terrain welcome visitors year-round to the 47 recreation areas on this 453-mile project. Directions:

- Bankhead, Holt, and Oliver Lakes: From Tuscaloosa, go 10 miles east on AL 216 to Peterson.
- Warrior, Demopolis, and Coffeeville Lakes: From Demopolis, take US 80 west 2 miles to Lock & Dam Road.

NATIONAL PARK SERVICE SITES ASSOCIATED WITH EARLY AMERICAN SETTLERS

- DeSoto National Monument (FL), named for the Spanish explorer DeSoto.
- Fort Raleigh National Historic Site (NC), for the first English colony in North America.
- Tumacacori National Monument (AZ), for a Spanish Catholic Mission.
- Arkansas Post National Memorial (AR), for the French settlers of 1686.
- Cabrillo National Monument (CA), for Portuguese explorers.
- Fort Caroline National Monument (FL), for the French Huguenots.
- Homestead National Monument of America (NE), for the pioneers who settled the West.
- Pipe Spring National Monument (AZ), for Mormon pioneers.

ARKANSAS

ARKANSAS POST NATIONAL MEMORIAL

95 miles southeast of Little Rock.

1741 Old Post Road
Gillett, AR 72055
870-548-2207
http://www.nps.gov/arpo

 **Eastern National.** (446 North Lane, Conshohocken, PA 19428; 800-355-5566)

Founded in 1686, this site, which has come to be known as the birthplace of Arkansas, marked the first permanent French settlement in the Lower Mississippi Valley. Because of its important strategic location on the Arkansas River, the Post saw battles during the Spanish Regime, the American Revolution, and the Civil War. In its long history, the exact location of Arkansas Post changed many times; historians have identified at least seven different forts and three settlements associated with the Post. Although many of these are not within the present park, the 389-acre National Memorial does encompass the sites of several early forts and the territorial capital.

 **SAM'S TIPS**

- The Memorial is also a wildlife sanctuary. Walking tours might lead to sightings of alligators, white-tailed deer, turkeys, eagles, and other animals native to the area.

BUFFALO NATIONAL RIVER

Harrison is 135 miles north of Little Rock.

PO Box 1173
Harrison, AR 72602-1173
870-741-5443
http://www.nps.gov/buff

 **Eastern National.** (446 North Lane, Conshohocken, PA 19428; 800-355-5566)

Originating high in the Boston Mountains, the swift-moving Buffalo River meanders past many nearby camping areas on its 150-mile journey through the Ozark Mountains. The watercourse is lined with bluffs as high as 440 feet. Riverside stands of willow, sycamore, river birch, and cottonwood blend into upland forests of oak and hickory. The river, one of the few free-flowing unpolluted rivers in the lower 48 states, is popular for float trips and sport fishing.

 **SAM'S TIPS**

- River guides, maps, and regional books are available at the park headquarters in Harrison and at the visitor center and ranger stations.
- Short hiking trails are located at Lost Valley, Pruitt, Tyler Bend, and Buffalo Point. For more challenging trails, hikers should try the Ponca and Lower Buffalo Wilderness Areas.
- The river offers some outstanding fishing opportunities for smallmouth, largemouth, and spotted bass; catfish; and a variety of other panfish. Float fishing is most common on the lower (eastern) half of the river. A license is required.

FORT SMITH NATIONAL HISTORIC SITE

Fort Smith is 125 miles northwest of Little Rock, in the mid-northwestern part of the state, against the Oklahoma border.

PO Box 1406
Fort Smith, AR 72902
501-783-3961
http://www.nps.gov/fosm

 **Eastern National.** (446 North Lane, Conshohocken, PA 19428; 800-355-5566)

One of the first U.S. military posts in the Louisiana Territory, Fort Smith served as a base of operations for enforcing federal Indian policy from 1817 to 1896. The park contains the remains of two frontier military forts and a federal court. Judge Isaac C. Parker served here for 21 years, protecting the rights of Native Americans and helping to bring law and order to Indian Territory.

 **SAM'S TIPS**

- The main building housing the Visitors' Center will be closed for renovations until 1999. However, visitor facilities can be found in a temporary building across the street; only the Fort's jail will remain closed during the renovations.

ASK-A-GEOLOGIST

Have you ever wondered why California has so many earthquakes, and New York does not? Why is there so much oil in Texas but not in Wisconsin? What are the deepest canyons in the United States? What would you like to know about volcanoes, earthquakes, glaciers, or rivers? Why not ask a geologist for an answer?

The U.S. Geological Survey (USGS) offers an Internet e-mail service—Ask-A-Geologist. General questions on earth sciences may be sent by electronic mail to the Internet address: Ask-A-Geologist@usgs.gov. Be sure to include an Internet-accessible return address in the body of your message.

HOT SPRINGS NATIONAL PARK

55 miles southwest of Little Rock.

PO Box 1860
Hot Springs National Park, AR 71902-1860
501-624-3383, ext. 640
http://www.nps.gov/hosp

 **Eastern National.** (446 North Lane, Conshohocken, PA 19428; 800-355-5566)

Hot Springs is the oldest area in the national park system. The naturally pure 143-degree water that gushes out from the earth at a rate of 850,000 gallons a day is rain that fell more than 4,000 years ago. When it opened in 1915, the Fordyce Bathhouse offered a wide range of medical therapies and leisure. Today, this elegant structure, built in the architectural style of Spanish Renaissance Revival, is a visitor center with attractively furnished rooms. The park has a full range of traditional and nontraditional bathhouse amentities, such as tub and pool baths, showers, steam cabinets, hot and cold packs, whirlpool, and massage.

 **SAM'S TIPS**

- Exhibits and films at Fordyce Bathhouse (in the 300 block of Central Avenue) help orient visitors to Hot Springs and tell the story of thermal water bathing.
- The park's campground is in Gulpha Gorge, 2 miles northeast of downtown. Tables and fireplaces are provided, but there are no electrical, shower, or water connections.
- Four of the traditional bathhouses are in nearby hotels, all within walking distance of the visitor center. Nontraditional bathhouses are also available.

 **FOREST SERVICE SCENIC BYWAY**

Arkansas Highway 7

Turnouts such as the Rotary Ann Overlook offer vistas of high mountain meadows and hardwood forests along this 61-mile byway on two national forests. Visitors will find easy access to geological features such as the Alum Cove Natural Bridge, Sam's Throne, and Pedestal Rocks. *Contact Ouachita National Forest.*

OUACHITA NATIONAL FOREST

The forest stretches from near the center of Arkansas (about 40 miles west of Little Rock) to southeastern Oklahoma.

Federal Building
PO Box 1270
100 Reserve Street
Hot Springs, AR 71902
501-321-5202
http://www.fs.fed.us/oonf/ouachita.html

Ozark Interpretive Association. (PO Box 1279, Mountain View, AR 82560; 870-757-2211)

Talimena Scenic Drive Interpretive Association. (PO Box 548, Talimena Chamber of Commerce, Talimena, OK 74571; 918-567-3434)

This 1.7-million-acre forest comprises almost 6,000 miles of roads and 700 miles of trails. Although primarily a pine forest, the Ouachita is also home to a variety of native plant species and serves as a natural habitat for wildlife. Its recreational opportunities include scenic byways, shooting ranges, float camps, the Robert S. Kerr Memorial Arboretum and Nature Center, and trails dedicated to hiking, biking, horseback riding, and all-terrain vehicles. Almost 65,000 acres are divided into six wilderness areas for visitors to enjoy peace and solitude in a primitive environment.

SAM'S TIPS

- A great way to enjoy the forest is through one of its self-guided auto tours. The Buffalo Gap, Crystal Vista, Poteau Mountain, and Winona auto tours are 15 to 25 miles in length and take 45 minutes to 3 hours to complete.
- The campground of the Cedar Lake Equestrian Camp is a popular starting point for its more than 70 miles of equestrian trails. For more information, contact the Choctaw Ranger District, HC-64, Box 3467, Heavener, OK 74937; 918-653-2991.
- The Dry Creek Wilderness preserves natural conditions by keeping human influence to a minimum. There are no trails or roads. Use of motorized or mechanized equipment is prohibited. Contact the Cold Springs Ranger District, 2190 E. Main Street, PO Box 417, Booneville, AR 72927; 501-675-3233.
- The Crystal Vista crystal collection area is on top of Gardner Mountain. The steep trail that leads to the area

Good Hunting Grounds

The Ouachita Mountains were inhabited by Indian tribes when Spaniard Hernando De Soto's exploration party first came through in 1541. French explorers followed, flavoring the region with names like Fourche La Fave River. "Ouachita" (Wash-a-taw) is the Francophone spelling of the Indian word "Washita," which translates into "good hunting grounds."

starts at the base of the mountain and takes about 30 to 40 minutes to negotiate. Contact the Womble Ranger District, PO Box 255, Highway 270 E, Mount Ida, AR 71957; 870-867-2101.

- Hunting is permitted anywhere in the Ouachita National Forest except within developed recreation sites or otherwise posted areas. All state hunting and fishing regulations apply. For more information on these regulations, contact the Arkansas Game and Fish Commission, #2 Natural Resources Drive, Little Rock, AR 72205; 501-223-6351.

OZARK–ST. FRANCIS NATIONAL FORESTS

Ozark National Forest is 65 miles northwest of Little Rock; St. Francis National Forest is 60 miles southwest of Memphis, TN.

Ozark–St. Francis National Forests
605 W. Main Street
Russellville, AR 72801-3614
501-968-2354
http://www.fs.fed.us/oonf/ozark.html

Ozark Interpretive Association. (PO Box 1279, Mountain View, AR 72560; 870-757-2211)

The Ozark–St. Francis National Forests are two separate and quite distinct forests. Located mostly in northwestern Arkansas, the "Ozarks" are really part of the Boston Mountains and the southern end of the Springfield Plateau. They are characterized by narrow V-shaped valleys bordered by steep-sided slopes and vertical bluffs of sandstone and limestone beside clear streams. The St. Francis Forest, located on the east central edge of the state, lets visitors experience the grandeur of the Mississippi River from the shoreline.

Sam's Tips

- The 165-mile Ozark Highlands Trail traverses the Ozark Forest from the western end at Lake Fort Smith State Park near the Oklahoma border to the Buffalo National River on the eastern end.
- Each year, in June, the Forest cosponsors "Take a Kid Fishing" derbies at all ranger districts, in observance of National Fishing Week. Contact the Forest for more information.
- The Blanchard Springs Caverns, located in the Sylamore Ranger District 14 miles northwest of Mountain View, AR, offer visitors a view of a subterranean world. Several guided tours are available.
- Storm Creek and Bear Creek Lakes, along with the St. Francis and Mississippi rivers, contain striped bass, largemouth bass, crappie, catfish, and bream.

 FOREST SERVICE SCENIC BYWAYS

Mount Magazine Scenic Byway

Truly a winding mountain drive through a variety of landscapes and wildlife, the 20-mile Mount Magazine Scenic Byway on the Ozark National Forest takes visitors away from the surrounding river valleys' hot summer weather to the top of Mount Magazine, the highest point in Arkansas. *Contact Ozark–St. Francis National Forest.*

Ozark Highlands Scenic Byway

The 35-mile Ozark Highlands Scenic Byway offers panoramic views, colorful flora, and rugged terrain. Wildlife is abundant; it is not uncommon to see deer, turkey, and black bear. Old and new homesteads, as well as Civilian Conservation Corps facilities built in the 1930s and 1940s, offer a glimpse of history. *Contact Ozark–St. Francis National Forest.*

Pig Trail Scenic Byway

The Ozark National Forest's Pig Trail Scenic Byway crosses 19 miles of Arkansas, showing sketches of rural America along with spectacular panoramas, timber-covered mountains, rugged landscapes, clear mountain streams, and colorful spring flowers or autumn foliage. Pig Trail is the popular route of students and sports fans who wander, as the wild pigs once did, to and from Fayetteville, home of the University of Arkansas Razorbacks. *Contact Ozark-St. Francis National Forest.*

St. Francis Byway

Located atop Crowley's Ridge, the 20-mile St. Francis Scenic Byway offers spectacular views of the surrounding forest and river delta lands. Travelers can follow the route of the DeSoto Expedition, visit the scene of Civil War action, and learn about the early pioneers. *Contact Ozark–St. Francis National Forest.*

Sylamore Scenic Byway

The S.S.B. traverses 26.5 miles on Ozark National Forest and provides views of white oak–hickory forests, rocky limestone cliffs, mountain vistas, and stands of shortleaf pine. Special features along the route include Blanchard Springs Caverns, one of the most beautifully decorated caves in the world, and Blanchard Amphitheater, where summer night programs highlight the folklore, culture, and forest resource management. *Contact Ozark–St. Francis National Forest.*

PEA RIDGE NATIONAL MILITARY PARK

Northwestern Arkansas, 35 miles north of Fayetteville and 10 miles north of Rogers on Highway 62.

PO Box 700
Pea Ridge, AR 72751-0700
501-451-8122
http://www.nps.gov/peri

 **Eastern National.** (446 North Lane, Conshohocken, PA 19428; 800-355-5566)

Control of Missouri, a prime objective of both Union and Confederate forces during the first year of the Civil War, led to the clash at Pea Ridge on March 7–8, 1862. The Union Army won the battle and prevented the Confederate Army from invading Missouri. Two regiments of Cherokee Indians fought under the Confederate flag, making the Battle of Pea Ridge the first Civil War battle in which organized regiments of American Indians participated.

POINTS OF INTEREST

U.S. ARMY CORPS OF ENGINEERS

BEAVER LAKE

Located in the picturesque Ozark Mountains, Beaver Lake is noted for excellent fishing and hunting. There are caves and museums nearby. From Fayetteville, go 22 miles north on US 71, then east on US 62.

BLUE MOUNTAIN LAKE

In the Ouachita Mountains of western Arkansas. Excellent crappie fishing in the shadow of Mount Magazine, the tallest mountain between the Rockies and the Allegheny Mountains. From Fort Smith, go 50 miles east on AR 10.

BULL SHOALS LAKE

A popular area with anglers for its lunker bass. Float trips and trout fishing are available on the White River nearby. A state park borders the lake. From Little Rock, go 135 miles north on US 65, 50 miles east on US 62 to Flippin, and 4 miles north to the lake. From Springfield, MO, go south on US 65, then east on AR 14.

DEGRAY LAKE

A relatively new lake with excellent public use facilities. The state park on the lake has a lodge, marina, golf course, and campground. From Little Rock, go 55 miles south on I-30 to Caddo Valley, and 2 miles north on US 67.

DEQUEEN LAKE

Located on Rolling Fork River about 4 miles northwest of DeQueen, 4,000 acres are open to hunters. White-tailed deer is the principal game. Other wildlife includes squirrel, cottontail and swamp rabbit, raccoon, bobwhite quail, and duck. From DeQueen, go 8 miles north on US 71, then 5 miles west to the lake.

GILLHAM LAKE

On the Cossatot River about 6 miles NE of Gillham, there is good hunting on 5,400 acres. Game includes whitetail deer, squirrel, cottontail and swamp rabbit, and bobwhite quail. Most waterfowl are found in the downstream flood plain. From DeQueen, go 15 miles north on US 71, then 5 miles east to the lake.

GREERS FERRY LAKE

A highly developed and popular recreation area. Sugar Loaf Nature Trail, on an island in the lake, has received many awards for scenic beauty. From Little Rock, go 15 miles north on US 67-167, then 50 miles north on AR 5.

LAKE GREESON

Chimney Rock, an outstanding geological formation, and a cinnabar mine nature trail are located at the project. From Little Rock, go 60 miles south on I-30 to AR 26, then go 37 miles west to Murfeesboro, and 6 miles north on AR 27.

NIMROD LAKE

A hunting and fishing paradise, Nimrod offers largemouth bass, channel cat, crappie, and bream. The project includes a duck hunting area, a wildlife refuge, and a goose sanctuary. Food and cover plots have been developed for quail. From Hot Springs, go 40 miles north on AR 7.

LAKE OUACHITA

High in the Ouachita Mountains, near the resort spa of Hot Springs, the exceptionally clear water of Lake Ouachita is popular with skin divers. From Hot Springs, go 13 miles west on AR 227.

DISTRICT OF COLUMBIA

CONSTITUTION GARDENS

Behind the Jefferson Memorial, in downtown Washington, DC.

c/o National Capital Parks, Central
900 Ohio Drive, SW
Washington, DC 20242
202-426-6841
http://www.nps.gov/coga

Parks and History Association. (126 Raleigh Street SE, Washington, DC 20032; 800-990-7275)

This 40-acre park was constructed during the American Revolution Bicentennial. On an island in a lake is a memorial to the 56 signers of the Declaration of Independence.

FORD'S THEATER NATIONAL HISTORIC SITE

Downtown Washington, DC.

511 10th St. NW
Washington, DC 20004
202-426-6924
http://www.nps.gov/foth

Parks and History Association. (126 Raleigh Street SE, Washington, DC 20032; 800-990-7275)

On the night of April 14, 1865, President Abraham Lincoln was shot in Ford's Theater by John Wilkes Booth. The President died in the early hours of April 15 in the small back bedroom of the Petersen House across the street from the theater, where the pillow and the bloodstained pillow cases Lincoln died on can still be seen. The museum beneath the theater contains portions of the Olroyd Collection of Lincolniana, and the Peterson House contains authentic and period furniture.

SAM'S TIPS

- Besides being a memorial to Abraham Lincoln, Ford's is also an active theater, putting on a full schedule of plays during the year. For box office information, call 202-347-4833.

OUR GROWING FAMILY

With the dedication of the Franklin Delano Roosevelt Monument on May 2, 1997 the National Park Service family grew to 375 units on over 83 million acres! Here are 5 new parks added under the 1996 Omnibus Parks and Public Lands Management Act, and where to call or go for more information on each:

1. New Bedford Whaling National Historical Park (MA)
   508-996-4165, http://www.nps.gov/nebe
2. Boston Harbor Islands National Recreation Area (MA)
   617-727-7676, http://www.nps.gov/boha
3. Tall Grass Prairie National Preserve (KS)
   316-273-8494, http://www.nps.gov/tapr
4. Nicodemus National Historic Site (KS)
   316-285-6911, http://www.nps.gov/nina
5. Washita Battlefield National Historic Site (OK)
   405-497-3929, http://www.nps.gov/waba

In late 1997, the NPS family grew to 376 units with the Oklahoma City National Memorial which commemorates those who died in the 1995 bombing.

FRANKLIN DELANO ROOSEVELT MEMORIAL

Along the cherry tree walk that rims the Tidal Basin in West Potomac Park.

c/o National Capital Parks, Central
900 Ohio Drive, SW
Washington, DC 20242
202-426-6841
http://www.nps.gov/fdrm/index2.htm

Parks and History Association. (126 Raleigh Street SE, Washington, DC 20032; 800-990-7275)

Dedicated in the spring of 1997, the Memorial is an artistic narrative history of FDR's presidency (1933–1945). Located in a parklike setting of four outdoor rooms representing each term of office, the Memorial depicts the great social, economic, and cultural upheavals that marked the Roosevelt presidency. The FDR Memorial is unique among presidential memorials in two respects: (1) it is the first to honor a First Lady (a bronze statue of Eleanor Roosevelt is in the fourth room) and (2) it is the only one that resulted from a collaborative effort of architect and artists. Conceived as an interactive monument, with granite walls, statuary, inscriptions, waterfalls, and thousands of plants, shrubs, and trees, the Memorial takes its place of honor as the fourth monument to an American President on the National Mall.

Sam's Tips

- Try to plan a visit for late March, when you can enjoy the cherry trees in bloom.
- The memorial is about 10 minutes' walk from the Lincoln Memorial and the Vietnam Veterans Memorial.
- Other FDR-related sites in the national park system include: a plaque, the size of his desk, outside the National Archives in Washington, DC—the only memorial he ever sanctioned; the Roosevelt–Campobello International Park in New Brunswick, Canada; the Home of Franklin Delano Roosevelt National Historic Site, Hyde Park, NY; and the Eleanor Roosevelt National Historic Site, Hyde Park, NY.

FREDERICK DOUGLASS NATIONAL HISTORIC SITE

14th and W Streets, SE.

1411 W Street, SE
Washington, DC 20020-4813
202-426-5960/1
http://www.nps.gov/frdo

Parks and History Association. (126 Raleigh Street SE, Washington, DC 20032; 800-990-7275)

Born in slavery, Frederick Douglass became an outstanding author, orator, and champion of civil rights. From 1877 to the end of his life in 1895, Cedar Hill was his home. Original furnishings in the house represent Douglass's late years, when he was U.S. Minister to Haiti, as well as the upper-middle-class standards of the neighborhood in the 1880s. The visitors center has exhibits and regularly shows a film.

KOREAN WAR VETERANS MEMORIAL

Adjacent to the Lincoln Memorial.

900 Ohio Drive, SW
Washington, DC 20242
202-426-6841
http://www.nps.gov/kwvm

Parks and History Association. (126 Raleigh Street SE, Washington, DC 20032; 800-990-7275)

The Korean War Veterans Memorial was authorized on October 28, 1986, to honor members of the United States Armed Forces who served in the Korean War. The Memorial is located adjacent to the Lincoln Memorial, directly across the Reflecting Pool from the Vietnam Veterans Memorial. The Memorial has two components, a triangular Field of Service and a Pool of Remembrance. In the Field of Service, 19 battle-clad foot soldiers are portrayed advancing toward the flag. A polished granite wall reflects the scene, intermingling the soldiers' reflections with etched faces of supporting forces. The names of the 22 nations that supported the United Nations' military action in Korea are etched on a low curb. Beyond the flagpole, a grove of linden trees surrounds the circular Pool of Remembrance, which provides a setting for quiet reflection.

LINCOLN MEMORIAL

At the foot of 23rd Street, NW.

c/o National Capital Parks, Central
900 Ohio Drive, SW
Washington, DC 20242
202-426-6841
http://www.nps.gov/linc

Parks and History Association. (126 Raleigh Street SE, Washington, DC 20032; 800-990-7275)

Although Congress incorporated the Lincoln Monument Association in March 1867 to build a memorial to the slain President, no progress was made until 1901, when the McMillan Commission chose West Potomac Park as the site for the memorial. This decision expanded on the ideas of Pierre L'Enfant, who laid out the Federal City and envisioned an open mall area from the Capitol to the Potomac River. Congress agreed on a design for the memorial submitted by New York architect Henry Bacon, and construction began on February 12, 1914. Daniel Chester French designed the epic statue of the seated Lincoln, and the Piccirilli brothers of New York carved it from 28 separate blocks of white Georgia marble. Murals painted by Jules Guerin, depicting principles evident in Lincoln's life, adorn the north and south walls of the memorial, above inscriptions of Lincoln's Gettysburg Address and his Second Inaugural Address.

NATIONAL PARK SERVICE SITES HONORING AFRICAN AMERICANS

National Park Service sites devoted to the lives and accomplishments of black Americans are:

- Maggie L. Walker National Historic Site, in Richmond, VA.
- Frederick Douglass National Historic Site, in Washington, DC.
- Martin Luther King, Jr. National Historic Site, in Atlanta, GA.
- Boston African American National Historic Site, in Boston, MA.
- Booker T. Washington National Monument, in Hardy, VA.

MARY MCLEOD BETHUNE COUNCIL HOUSE NATIONAL HISTORIC SITE

Downtown Washington, DC.

1318 Vermont Avenue, NW
Washington, DC 20005
202-673-2402
http://www.nps.gov/mamc

Parks and History Association. (126 Raleigh Street SE, Washington, DC 20032; 800-990-7275)

This site—headquarters of the National Council of Negro Women, established by Mary McLeod Bethune in 1935—commemorates Bethune's leadership in the African American women's rights movement. Bethune was also a founder of Bethune–Cookman College in Florida.

NATIONAL MALL

In Washington, DC.

c/o National Capital Region
900 Ohio Drive, SW
Washington, DC 20242
202-426-6841
http://www.nps.gov/nama

Parks and History Association. (126 Raleigh Street SE, Washington, DC 20032; 800-990-7275)

This landscaped park, extending from the Capitol to the Washington Monument, was envisioned as a formal park in Pierre Charles L'Enfant's 1791 plan for the capital city. Rows of elms mark the sweep of the greensward, which is bounded by the Lincoln Memorial on the west side and the U.S. Capitol to the east. Footpaths, bikeways, information and map kiosks, and refreshment stands line the Mall. Bordering the Mall are the Department of Agriculture, the Castle—the central Smithsonian Institution building—and nine Smithsonian museums: The National Gallery of Art, The Freer Gallery, The Sackler Gallery, The Museum of African Art, The Arts and Industries Building, The Hirshhorn Museum and Sculpture Garden, The Air and Space Museum, The Museum of American History, and The Natural History Museum.

SAM'S TIPS

- Parking is extremely limited on the Mall. It is best to use public transport. Should you take the Metro, the stop is Smithsonian Station.

- For detailed Smithsonian information, call 202-357-2700 or visit its extraordinary Website at http://www.si.edu, to learn about current exhibits, hours of operation, and much more.

OLD POST OFFICE TOWER

Downtown Washington, DC.

Pennsylvania Avenue and 12th Street, NW
Washington, DC 20566
202-606-8691
http://www.nps.gov/opot

Parks and History Association. (126 Raleigh Street SE, Washington, DC 20032; 800-990-7275)

This 315-foot tower keeps watch over downtown Washington. The granite fortress opened its doors in 1899 as the headquarters for the Postmaster General and a mail depot for the city. Its rugged architecture soon fell from favor, however, and the "Old Tooth," as it was dubbed by critics, was to be replaced with offices styled to match the rest of the Federal Triangle. Preservationists waged a successful campaign to save the landmark, and the tower was completely renovated. Where postal clerks once sorted mail in the skylit courtyard, performers now offer daily entertainment, and a variety of shops create an urban-mall atmosphere. A glass elevator located at the Northwest Corner of the Old Post Office Pavillion glides visitors up the nine-story atrium to a spectacular view of the city's skyline and to the tower's bell chamber.

PENNSYLVANIA AVENUE NATIONAL HISTORIC SITE

Pennsylvania Avenue, in Washington, DC.

c/o Pennsylvania Avenue Development Corporation
1331 Pennsylvania Avenue, NW
Suite 1220N
Washington, DC 20004-1703
202-724-9091
http://www.nps.gov/paav

Parks and History Association. (126 Raleigh Street SE, Washington, DC 20032; 800-990-7275)

This site includes a redeveloped portion of historic Pennsylvania Avenue near The White House and encompasses Ford's Theater National Historic Site, several blocks of the Washington commercial district, the Old Post Office Tower, and a number of federal structures. See site-specific entries for details.

ROCK CREEK PARK

Winding north through the District from The Kennedy Center.

3545 Williamsburg Lane NW
Washington, DC 20008
202-282-1063
http://www.nps.gov/rocr

Parks and History Association. (126 Raleigh Street SE, Washington, DC 20032; 800-990-7275)

One of the largest urban parks in the United States, this wooded preserve contains a wide range of natural, historical, and recreational features in the center of Washington. The Old Stone House, Montrose Park, Dumbarton Oaks Park, Glover Archbold Park, the Fort Circle Parks, Meridian Hill Park, Rock Creek, Potomac Parkway, and other green spaces in the city, are all administered by the park.

Sam's Tips

- The Rock Creek Nature Center gives guided nature walks daily and has nature exhibits and planetarium shows. Demonstrations at Pierce Mill illustrate the working of a 19th-century gristmill. In Georgetown, tours are given of the Old Stone House, which is the oldest dwelling in Washington.

Pierce Mill

When the main shaft of the Pierce Mill broke in 1897, it ended many years of milling along Rock Creek. From the 1780s, Pierce Mill and eight others ground as many as twelve wagon loads of wheat a day. Using waterwheels powered by Rock Creek, millstones measuring about 4½ feet across and weighing about 2,400 pounds turned wheat to flour. The mill was renovated and opened to the public in 1970. Today, visitors can see a largely completed flour mill that operates throughout the year. Pierce Mill is on Tilden Street near Beach Drive, 1 mile north of the National Zoo.

SMOKEY BEAR

In 1944, the U.S. Forest Service and the War Advertising Council introduced a bear as a campaign symbol to promote the prevention of accidental forest fires. A year later, Albert Staehle, a noted animal illustrator, first painted "Smokey Bear." The first poster carried the caption, "Smokey says: Care will prevent 9 out of 10 forest fires."

For a complete history of Smokey's 50-plus years as a vital part of forest preservation, go to his Website at the Oregon Department of Forestry, where you can order your very own 3 × 5 Smokey Bear collector cards for free, courtesy of an online order form:
http://www.odf.state.or.us/smokey/smokey.htm.

Smokey even has his own page on the World Wide Web:
http://www.smokeybear.com.

THEODORE ROOSEVELT ISLAND

Washington, DC, off the northbound lanes of George Washington Memorial Parkway, just north of Theodore Roosevelt Bridge.

c/o George Washington Memorial Parkway
Turkey Run Park
McLean, VA 22101
703-285-2598
http://www.nps.gov/this

Parks and History Association. (126 Raleigh Street SE, Washington, DC 20032; 800-990-7275)

On this wooded island sanctuary in the Potomac River, trails lead to an imposing 17-foot bronze statue of Roosevelt, the conservation-minded 26th President who often sought isolation here. Roosevelt's tenets on nature, manhood, youth, and the state are inscribed on four 21-foot granite tablets. Three major biological communities—marsh, swamp, and upland forest—provide a refuge for a variety of native plants and animals.

SAM'S TIPS

- The parking area is reached from the northbound lanes of George Washington Memorial Parkway, on the Virginia side of the Potomac River. A footbridge connects the island to the Virginia shore.

THOMAS JEFFERSON MEMORIAL

Downtown Washington, DC, on the south bank of the Tidal Basin.

c/o National Capital Parks, Central
900 Ohio Drive, SW
Washington, DC 20242
202-426-6841
http://www.nps.gov/thje

Parks and History Association. (126 Raleigh Street SE, Washington, DC 20032; 800-990-7275)

Jefferson's importance in the nation's history demanded a memorial site of equal prominence with the Washington Monument and the Lincoln Memorial. Placing the Jefferson Memorial on the Tidal Basin, directly south of the White House, achieved this by creating a north–south axis to complement the east–west axis of the National Mall. The classical circular colonnaded structure was dedicated in 1943 on the 200th anniversary of Jefferson's birth. Breathtaking views of the memorial come in early spring, when the Japanese cherry trees, a gift from the Japanese government, shroud the area in pink and white blossoms.

Roosevelt on . . .

The park has these words from FDR chiseled in granite:

Nature: "There are no words that can tell the hidden spirit of the wilderness, that can reveal its mystery, its melancholy, and its charm. The Nation behaves well if it treats the natural resources as assets which it must turn over to the next generation increased and not impaired in value. Conservation means development as much as it does protection."

Manhood: "A man's usefulness depends upon his living up to his ideas in so far as he can. It is hard to fail, but it is even worse never to have tried to succeed. All daring and courage, all iron endurance of misfortune make for a finer and nobler type of manhood. Only those are fit to live who do not fear to die; and none are fit to die who have shrunk from the joy of life and the duty of life."

Youth: "I want to see you game, boys, I want to see you brave and manly, and I also want to see you gentle and tender. Be practical as well as generous in your ideals. Keep your eyes on the stars, but remember to keep your feet on the ground. Courage, hard work, self-mastery, and intelligent effort are all essential to successful life. Alike for the Nation and the individual, the one indispensable requisite is character."

The State: "Ours is a government of liberty by, through, and under the law. A great democracy has got to be progressive or it will soon cease to be great or a democracy. Order without liberty and liberty without order are equally destructive. In popular government results worth having can be achieved only by men who combine worthy ideals with practical sense. If I must choose between righteousness and peace I choose righteousness."

UNITED STATES HOLOCAUST MEMORIAL MUSEUM

On 14th Street, South of the Washington Monument.

100 Raoul Wallenberg Place, SW
Washington, DC 20024-2150
202-488-0400
http://www.ushmm.org

The United States Holocaust Memorial Museum is dedicated to the victims of Nazi tyranny from 1933 to 1945. The Museum's primary mission is to remember those who suffered and died and to inspire visitors to contemplate the moral implications of their choices and responsibilities as citizens in an interdependent world. The Museum, chartered by a unanimous act of Congress in 1980 and opened in April 1993, contains a permanent exhibition that presents a comprehensive history of the Holocaust through artifacts, photographs, films, and eyewitness testimonies. The hexagonal Hall of Remembrance is America's national memorial to the victims of the Holocaust. There are also special exhibitions and a research institute that sponsors academic programs and fellowships and includes a library and archival collections of historic documents, photographs, oral histories, films, and videos.

SAM'S TIPS

- Most Museum programs are suitable for visitors 11 years and older. Images and artifacts in the exhibitions have been chosen carefully, and the most difficult images in the Permanent Exhibition are behind privacy walls.
- The museum is often very crowded, so tickets are sometimes required. For same-day tickets, arrive at the box office early; it opens at 10 A.M. For advance tickets, call 202-488-0400 for information on how they may be obtained.
- For information about group visits of more than ten people, write to the Museum's schedule coordinator. Because of heavy demand, it is best to make reservations for group visits at least six months in advance.

THE PARKS AND HISTORY ASSOCIATION

Parks and History Association
126 Raleigh Street, SE
Washington, DC 20032
800-990-7275
http://www.parksandhistory.org

This Association produces material about these public lands:

Antietam National Battlefield (MD)
Arlington House, The Robert E. Lee Memorial (VA)
Arlington National Cemetery (VA)
Catoctin Mountain Park (MD)
Chesapeake and Ohio Canal National Historic Park (MD)
Clara Barton National Historic Site (MD)
Frederick Douglass National Historic Site (DC)
Ford's Theatre National Historic Site (DC)
Fort Washington Park (MD)
George Washington Memorial Parkway
Glen Echo Park (MD)
Great Falls Park (VA)
Lincoln Memorial (DC)
Monocacy National Battlefield (MD)
National Capital Parks (DC)
Old Post Office Tower (DC)
Rock Creek Park (DC)
Thomas Jefferson Memorial (DC)
Washington Monument (DC)
Wolf Trap Farm Park for the Performing Arts (MD)

VIETNAM VETERANS MEMORIAL

21st Street and Constitution Avenue, NW.

c/o National Capital Parks, Central
900 Ohio Drive, SW
Washington, DC 20242
202-426-6841
http://www.nps.gov/vive

Parks and History Association. (126 Raleigh Street SE, Washington, DC 20032; 800-990-7275)

The memorial's polished black granite walls are inscribed with the names of more than 58,000 persons who gave their lives or remain missing in the Vietnam War. The names of the service men and women are inscribed "in the order they were taken from us," although alphabetical directories are available to help visitors find specific names by panel and number. The memorial was designed by Maya Ying Lin, who, at the time, was a 21-year-old student at Yale University. A flagstaff and bronze statues of three American servicemen in Vietnam, sculpted by Fredrick Hart, and a tribute to the women who served sculpted by Glenna Goodacre, are included in an entrance plaza.

WASHINGTON MONUMENT

Downtown Washington, DC; Constitution Avenue at 15th Street, NW.

c/o National Capital Parks, Central
900 Ohio Drive, SW
Washington, DC 20242
202-426-6841
http://www.nps.gov/wamo

Parks and History Association. (126 Raleigh Street SE, Washington, DC 20032; 800-990-7275)

At more than 555 feet, the Washington Monument towers over everything in the nation's capital and underscores George Washington's contribution to the republic. The cornerstone was laid July 4, 1848, and the monument rose steadily to 152 feet until funds raised by the Washington Monument Society ran out in 1853. It stood unfinished for nearly 25 years until President Ulysses S. Grant approved an act authorizing the federal government to complete the project. In December 1884, a 3,300-pound marble capstone was placed on the obelisk and topped with a 9-inch pyramid of cast aluminum, a rare metal in 1884.

Sam's Tips

- An elevator takes visitors to the 500-foot level. You may also wish to walk down the 898 steps, from which the 190 memorial stones donated by local, state, and foreign governments can be seen, but arrangements to use the stairs must be made prior to your visit.
- Free tickets can be obtained at the ticket kiosk in front of the monument. Tickets are required and can be obtained daily from 8:30–4:30.

THE WHITE HOUSE

At 1600 Pennsylvania Avenue, NW, in Washington, DC.

National Capital Region Public Affairs Office
1100 Ohio Drive, SW
Washington, DC 20242
202-208-1631
http://www.nps.gov/whho

The White House Historical Association. (740 Jackson Place, NW, Washington, DC 20560)

The White House is the oldest public building in the District of Columbia, and 1600 Pennsylvania Avenue is the nation's most famous address. Here, every President except George Washington has conducted the government of the nation. The White House itself has been altered, adapted, or enlarged to suit the needs of the residents and the demands of a growing nation. After the British burnt it down in 1814, the building was reconstructed between 1815 and 1817 on the same foundation. The Jacqueline Kennedy Garden and the Rose Garden are often used for formal ceremonies and bill signings.

Sam's Tips

- Tours of The White House are offered year-round, Tuesday through Saturday, although this access can change with minimal notice to accommodate official functions. It is important to call beforehand: 202-208-1631. For the self-guided walk-through tours, tickets are required. Tickets are free and must be used on the day they are issued. One person may claim no more than four tickets. Ticket distribution starts at 7:30 A.M., at The White House Visitors' Center at 1450 Pennsylvania Avenue South, NW, a block east and south of The White House itself. (Look for the three American flags and blue awnings.) Once visitors have obtained their tickets, they are free to do other things until the time of the tour stated on the ticket. For the guided tour, reserved tickets may be obtained by writing to the local office or the Washington, DC, office of your Congressional representative or Senator eight to ten weeks in advance. These tickets are free. Tours start between 8:15 A.M. and 8:45 A.M. and last approximately one half hour.

- For information on the seasonal events at The White House, such as garden tours in the spring and fall, candlelight tours during the Christmas season, and the Easter Egg Roll, call the 24-hour White House Visitor Information Line at 202-456-7041. This number also provides information on all tours (updates and all ticket information) and accessibility.
- Tours of the Old Executive Office Building—part of the White House complex—are available on Saturday mornings only. Reservations are required and can be made by phone at 202-395-5895 between 9 A.M. and 12 P.M. Tuesday through Friday or by fax at 202-395-1051. It is necessary to give your name, date of birth, and social security number when you make a reservation.

PARKS AS CLASSROOMS

Imagine reading "The Raven" in Edgar Allan Poe's house or learning about the Executive Branch of the government at the White House. Picture yourself learning or teaching natural science in the Everglades or Yellowstone, or in urban natural areas in San Francisco or New York City. See history come alive at Gettysburg or Valley Forge. No matter what the subject—art, science, history, social studies, or even math or physical education—it is probably easier to teach and learn when you are dealing with "the real thing." National parks are places where people of all ages can learn about the natural world and the people and events that shaped this nation.

Understanding that not everyone can visit all of the national parks, the National Park Service's Parks as Classrooms program takes this concept one step further. Park service personnel work directly with educators to provide learning materials and experiences that accentuate existing curriculum requirements.

Parks as Classrooms programs and materials include: curriculum materials, videos, accredited teacher training, traveling trunks and kits, teacher and student resource packets. These materials have resulted from a partnership between a particular national park site(s) and neighboring school district(s), but the final products often have wide applications and utility to schools across the nation.

To find out more about specific programs and materials, you can contact the NPS Center for Teaching and Learning at the University of Massachusetts Lowell, or by accessing "The Guidebook to Excellence" produced by the Eisenhower National Clearing House for Math and Science at Ohio State University (http://www.enc.org), or by contacting your local national park site.

For more information, please contact the National Park Service's Parks as Classrooms coordinator on the Internet at: bob_huggins@nps.gov.

FLORIDA

APALACHICOLA NATIONAL FOREST

Situated in the panhandle of Florida bordering Tallahassee; the forest extends westward to the Apalachicola River.

Woodcrest Office Park
325 John Knox Road, Suite F-100
Tallahassee, FL 32303
904-942-9300
http://www.fs.fed.us/

Cradle of Forestry in America Interpretive Association. (100 South Broad, Brevard, NC 28712; 704-884-5713)

Much of the 564,000 acres of the Apalachicola National Forest is wet lowland dressed with cypress, oaks, and magnolias. On the upland, flatwoods, slash, longleaf pine, and turkey oak dominate the vegetation. White-tailed deer, turkey, black bear, and squirrel are favored game here. Fishermen can expect to catch bass, bream, and catfish in the numerous rivers, streams, and lakes. The Apalachicola National Forest is also the habitat for many endangered species, such as the Florida alligator, the red cockaded woodpecker, the indigo snake, and the southern bald eagle. The Leon Sinks, Fort Gadsden, and the Florida National Scenic Trail are other features on the forest.

BIG CYPRESS NATIONAL PRESERVE

60 miles west of Miami, roughly the same distance southeast of Naples.

HCR 61, Box 110
Ochopee, FL 33943
941-695-2000
http://www.nps.gov/bicy

The Big Cypress Swamp, on which the Preserve is located, is something of a misnomer. The land consists of sandy islands of slash pine, mixed hardwood hammocks, wet and dry prairies, marshes, and mangrove forests. Adjoining the northwest section of the Everglades National Park, this ancestral home of the Seminole and Miccosukee Indians teems with subtropical plant and animal life. The Preserve contains 31 miles of the Florida Trail, a national scenic trail that travels the length of Florida. National Preserve status allows special activities such as offroad vehicle (swamp buggies, airboats) use in the back-country, as well as hunting for deer and turkey.

FOREST SERVICE SCENIC BYWAY

Apalachee Savannahs Scenic Byway

Travelers along this 31-mile stretch can view landscapes of savannahs, swamps, riverine systems, and the longleaf pine lands surrounding them. Rare and unusual plant communities with spectacular seasonal wildflower displays provide an example of ecological diversity and attract a growing number of visitors each year. *Contact Apalachicola National Forest.*

SAM'S TIPS

- In Big Cypress Swamp, winter is known as "the dry season," and those looking to escape snow and ice will find that water here is evaporating into the ground rather than falling from the sky. To obtain additional information on hunting, or permits for off-road vehicle use, contact the Oasis Visitor Center at 941-695-4111.
- Limited services are found around the Preserve's access areas. Nine campgrounds are available (but with no water or facilities); all allow tent camping and most accommodate mobile homes. A dump station with potable water is located at the Dona Drive campground. Big Cypress is the only south Florida national park area where ORVs, including airboats, are allowed.
- The wood stork, snail kite, southern bald eagle, red-cockaded woodpecker, Arctic peregrine falcon, Cape Sable sparrow, West Indian manatee, and Florida panther all are endangered species that live in the Preserve. The Loop Road and Turner River Road provide the best opportunities to view swamp wildlife. Trails suitable for mountain biking can be found in the northern portion of the Preserve.
- Take the 26-mile, single-lane Loop Road Scenic Drive, which affords passage through different habitats. From your car windows, you can view birds and alligators in roadside canals during seasonal low water.

The Florida Trail

The concept of a Florida Trail began in 1966, when a group of outdoor enthusiasts proposed a hiking trail running the length of Florida. These volunteers designed the Trail's path using public lands where possible and forming partnerships with private landowners. It begins at Gulf Islands National Seashore, located in the panhandle, and extends eastward to the Osceola National Forest, then south to Big Cypress National Preserve. For information about the Florida Trail, contact the Florida Trail Association, PO Box 13708, Gainsville, FL 32604; 800-343-1882.

BISCAYNE NATIONAL PARK

37 miles south of Miami; 9 miles east of Homestead.

PO Box 1369
Homestead, FL 33090
305-230-7275
http://www.nps.gov/bisc

Florida National Parks and Monuments Association (10 Parachute Key, #51, Homestead, FL 33034-6735; 305-247-1216)

Florida's Geology

Many of Florida's lakes, swales, caverns, natural depressions, and sinkholes, including Leon Sinks, are examples of "karst," terrain changed by water's dissolving underlying limestone bedrock. Florida's limestone base was formed millions of years ago when the land that is now Florida lay beneath the ocean. Over time, vast deposits of skeletal material accumulated and compacted to form limestone that is close to a mile thick in some places. After being thrust above sea level, the limestone began to be eroded by water. As the limestone dissolved, the earth above it caved in. The Floridian aquifer—the source of drinking water for most of the state—was created in just this way.

At the northern end of the Florida Keys lies Biscayne National Park, a living rock garden of coral reefs. Biscayne's waters include the northernmost living coral reefs in the continental United States, including both the chain of outer or "rubble" reefs and the small patch reefs that lie behind them, and the nearly 50 islands separating the bay from the Atlantic Ocean. The bay is relatively shallow, so its floor is flooded with light, allowing the reefs, and the over 200 species of fish and other creatures they sustain (e.g., dolphins, manatees, sea turtles, and crocodiles) to thrive.

Sam's Tips

- A park concessionaire offers glass-bottom boat tours of the bay and reefs, snorkeling and scuba diving trips to the reefs, and occasional island excursions for picnicking and hiking. All tours leave from Convoy Point. Contact Biscayne National Underwater Park, Inc., PO Box 1270, Homestead, FL 33090-1270; 305-230-1100. Call ahead for boat reservations because seats fill up quickly.
- Subtropical islands of the Florida Keys provide remote camping areas not far from the city of Miami. The islands are 7 miles off the Florida mainland. Island access is by boat only. Contact the park for more information.

CANAVERAL NATIONAL SEASHORE

Situated on the east coast of central Florida between New Smyrna Beach and Kennedy Space Center.

308 Julia Street
Titusville, FL 32796
407-267-1110
http://www.nps.gov/cana

Eastern National. (446 North Lane, Conshohocken, PA 19428; 800-355-5566)

Canaveral is located on a 150-mile-long barrier island, occupied in part by the Kennedy Space Center. Because the National Aeronautics and Space Administration (NASA) owns a part of the property in Canaveral National Seashore and all of Merritt Island Wildlife Refuge, the southern portion of the seashore is closed three days prior to space launches.

Canaveral's undeveloped beach, dunes, lagoon, marshes, and coastal hammocks are a sanctuary to many species of endangered or threatened plants and animals. Wildlife species include sea turtles, West Indian manatees, southern bald eagles, peregrine falcons, gopher tortoise, scrub jay, and eastern indigo snake. Popular activities at the national seashore include swimming, beachcombing, boating, hiking, and fishing. Horseback riding and back-country camping require special permits, obtainable at the North District Ranger office (904-428-3384).

Sam's Tips

- The park does not have facilities for recreational vehicle (RV) camping. Numerous motels, campgrounds, and RV parks are located in and around Titusville and New Smyrna Beach. For more information, contact: Titusville Chamber of Commerce (2000 S. Washington Avenue, Titusville, FL 32780; 407-267-3036) or New Smyrna Beach Chamber of Commerce (115 Canal Street, New Smyrna Beach, FL 32168; 904-428-2449).
- Seashore areas may be closed when parking lots are filled or during shuttle launch activities at Kennedy Space Center. For recorded information on launch closures at Playalinda Beach call 407-867-4077.
- For refuge information or hunting permits, contact the Refuge Manager of the Merritt Island National Wildlife Refuge, PO Box 6504, Titusville, FL 36504; 407-861-0667.

CASTILLO DE SAN MARCOS NATIONAL MONUMENT

St. Augustine, FL.

1 South Castillo Drive
St. Augustine, FL 32084-3699
904-829-6506
http://www.nps.gov/casa

 **Eastern National.** (446 North Lane, Conshohocken, PA 19428; 800-355-5566)

The Castillo de San Marcos was for many years the northernmost outpost of Spain's vast empire in the New World. Over three centuries old, it is the oldest masonry fort and the best preserved example of a Spanish colonial fortification in the continental United States. Begun in 1672 and completed by 1695, the Castillo replaced nine successive wooden fortifications that had protected St. Augustine since its founding. The fort's commanding location on the west bank of Matanzas Bay allowed its guns to protect not only the harbor entrance but the ground to the north against a land attack. Except for the period 1763–83, when the area now known as Florida was under English rule, Spain held the fort until 1821, when it was ceded to the United States. The Americans renamed the Castillo Fort Marion and used it to house Indian prisoners during the Seminole War of 1835–1842. Confederate troops occupied it briefly during the Civil War, and Indians captured it in military campaigns held there later on. It was last used during the Spanish American War as a military prison.

DE SOTO NATIONAL MEMORIAL

65 miles south of Tampa, 150 miles southwest of Orlando.

PO Box 15390
Bradenton, FL 34280-5390
941-792-0458
http://www.nps.gov/deso

 **Eastern National.** (446 North Lane, Conshohocken, PA 19428; 800-355-5566)

This memorial marks the approximate place where, in 1539, over 600 Spanish conquistadors and crew under the command of Don Hernando de Soto landed with dreams of wealth and conquest in "La Florida." A small contingent of soldiers remained on the coast while De Soto led the main body of his army inland, searching for gold. This search lasted four years and covered over 4,000 miles throughout what is presently the southeast of the United States. His group wandered as far as present-day Tennessee and Texas. By the end of the expedition, De Soto and most of his men were dead. The remaining few managed to escape by floating down the Mississippi. De Soto's expedition left a trail of torture, death, famine, disease, and social disorder in the various Indian villages that they encountered.

DRY TORTUGAS NATIONAL PARK

In the Gulf of Mexico, 68 nautical miles west of Key West. The islands can be reached by boat or seaplane from the Key West area.

PO Box 6208
Key West, FL 33041-6208
305-242-7700
http://www.nps.gov/drto

 **Florida National Parks and Monuments Association** (10 Parachute Key, #51, Homestead, FL 33034-6735; 305-247-1216)

Ninety-nine percent of the park's 64,657 acres are submerged. The cluster of seven coral reefs called the Dry Tortugas, along with the surrounding shoals and waters, is noted for marine life, several species of nesting birds, and hundreds of species of migratory birds. Fort Jefferson, America's largest 19th-century coastal fort, was established in 1846 to help control the Florida Straits and served as the Civil War military prison that once held four of the Lincoln assassination conspirators. The Fort, the visitor center, and the park headquarters are located on Garden Key. Nearby Loggerhead Key is home to the Loggerhead Lighthouse, as well as the ruins of the Carnegie Laboratory.

 **The Dry Turtles**

First named "The Turtles" (Las Tortugas) by Spaniard Ponce de Leon in 1513 because of the great number of sea turtles he found there, these reefs soon read "Dry Tortugas" on mariners' nautical charts to warn they had no fresh water.

Sam's Tips

- The park offers outstanding scuba diving, snorkeling, and fishing, although spear fishing and fishing for lobster are prohibited.
- If you plan to visit by private boat, be sure to have at least two anchors and beware of the possibility of extremely rough seas. The National Park Service authorizes charter boats and air taxis to the park from Miami and Key West. Ask the park for a list of authorized carriers.
- Anything you plan to consume must be brought with you, including water. There are no bathing facilities at the park, although a 10-site primitive campground is available on a first-come, first-served basis.

EVERGLADES NATIONAL PARK

Less than 35 miles west of Miami, the park comprises most of the tip of southern Florida. Take the Florida Turnpike (Route 821) to the Florida City exit, turn right at the first traffic light and follow the signs to the main park entrance.

40001 State Road 9336, SW
Homestead, FL 33034-6733
305-242-7700
http://www.nps.gov/ever

Florida National Parks and Monuments Association (10 Parachute Key, #51, Homestead, FL 33034-6735; 305-247-1216)

Originally called Pa-Hay-Okee, or "River of Grass," by native Indians, this watery lowland provides a sanctuary for alligators, the Florida panther, myriad birds, and many tropical plants. The park's inland waterways divide open Everglades prairies and mangrove forests and lead to remote Everglades spots. The park has been designated a Biosphere Reserve, a World Heritage Site, a Wetland of International Importance, and an Outstanding Florida Water.

The sprawling Everglades National Park was created in 1947 for preservation of this unique landscape, but it is considered one of the most endangered protected areas in the United States. The threats are many and complex but stem from the disturbance of the natural systems of water quality and distribution in the Everglades' ecosystem. Long Pine Key, Flamingo, and Chekika campgrounds offer drinking water, picnic tables, restrooms, grilles, and tent and trailer sites.

For Teaching the Everglades

A complete multimedia curriculum teaches students about the Everglades ecosystem as well as the National Park Service. The kit includes a 60-minute video, a 175-page activity and resource guide, and three prepackaged activities. Designed for fourth-grade teachers, it is easily adaptable for the fifth and/or sixth grade. To order the kit, contact the cooperating association.

Sam's Tips

- The best way to visit the park is to walk the boardwalks and trails along the main park road and to join in ranger-led events. Naturalists give talks and lead hikes, canoe trips, tram tours, and campfire programs.

- To enjoy a tram tour of the park, call the Shark Valley Tram Tours at 305-221-8455 for information or to make reservations. The tour winds through a sawgrass prairie and stops at a 65-foot tower for spectacular views. Birding tram tours are also offered.
- Set aside time for a boat tour at Flamingo, which features the marine feeding and nursery grounds of Florida Bay as well as the mangrove back-country wilderness. During the winter, sailing cruises to Cape Sable and Whitewater Bay are available. The Mangrove Wilderness Trip, another guided boat trip through a portion of Florida's Ten Thousand Islands, which might be thought of as a "water wilderness," lasts about two hours. Trip highlights include twisting and turning creeks, a view of ancient Native American shell mounds, and plentiful birdlife.

FORT CAROLINE NATIONAL MEMORIAL

13 miles northeast of downtown Jacksonville.

12713 Fort Caroline Road
Jacksonville, FL 32225
904-641-7155
http://www.nps.gov/foca

 **Eastern National.** (446 North Lane, Conshohocken, PA 19428; 800-355-5566)

The 140-acre park memorializes the historic French Huguenot colony of La Caroline (1564–1565). Here, the French and Spanish began two centuries of colonial rivalry in North America. This was the second attempted French settlement within the United States. Popular thought has the original site of La Caroline located on a river plain (today the St. Johns River) which was washed away after the river channel was deepened and widened in the 1880s. The construction of the Memorial's fort was based on a 16th-century sketch by Jacques le Moyne, the colony's artist and mapmaker. The Memorial is part of the Timucuan Ecological and Historic Preserve.

FORT MATANZAS NATIONAL MONUMENT

Fort Matanzas is 14 miles south of St. Augustine.

c/o Castillo de San Marcos National Monument
1 Castillo Drive East
St. Augustine, FL 32084
904-471-0116
http://www.nps.gov/foma

 **Eastern National.** (446 North Lane, Conshohocken, PA 19428; 800-355-5566)

"Slaughters" is the English translation for Matanzas. Here, on September 29 and October 12, 1565, 200 to 300 Frenchmen, all Huguenots, were put to the sword by the Spaniards. These Frenchmen were less than half the force that had set out from Fort Caroline to attack St. Augustine. Their ships had been scattered and wrecked by a hurricane. The Spanish fort was built in 1740–1742 to prevent enemy vessels from reaching St. Augustine from the Matanzas River. The fort is on Rattlesnake Island and is accessible only by boat.

GULF ISLANDS NATIONAL SEASHORE

Pensacola, FL and Ocean Springs, MS area.

1801 Gulf Breeze Parkway
Gulf Breeze, FL 32561
904-934-2600 (FL); 601-875-0821 (MS)
http://www.nps.gov/guis

 **Eastern National.** (446 North Lane, Conshohocken, PA 19428; 800-355-5566)

Stretching 150 miles along the northeastern Gulf of Mexico from West Ship Island, Mississippi, to the east end of Santa Rosa Island in Florida, this chain of barrier islands features sparkling white-sand beaches, historic forts, and nature trails. The Seashore is divided into a variety of units.

Sam's Tips

- A number of the park's facilities, as well as Highway 399 east of Pensacola Beach, have been closed since Hurricane Opal struck in 1995. Restoration efforts continue. Call the park for up-to-date information.
- In Mississippi, the Seashore includes the offshore barrier islands of Horn, Petit Bois, and East and West Ship Islands. The mainland headquarters and visitor center are in Ocean Springs on Davis Bayou. There, kids can see a video about Fort Massachusetts or go on a short trail hike and see the alligator pond. The islands are 9 to 12 miles off the coast and can be reached only by boat. If you have time to visit only one island, take a concession boat from Gulfport and visit Fort Massachusetts on West Ship Island.
- In Florida, there are historical forts and beaches. The Visitor Center is at Naval Live Oaks Area, east of Gulf Breeze on US 98. Other Seashore locations in Florida are Perdido Key Area, the Okaloosa area, and Fort Barrancas, located on the Pensacola Air Station.
- The Fort Pickens 200-site campground area and the fort itself are on the west end of Santa Rosa Island. It's a short walk from the campground to the Gulf of Mexico and Pensacola Bay.
- The Santa Rosa area, 7 miles east of Pensacola Beach on Highway 399, offers swimming and other recreational activities. Facilities, severely damaged by Hurricane Opal, are being rebuilt.

OCALA NATIONAL FOREST

30 miles west of Daytona Beach, 55 miles north of Orlando.

Ocala National Forest
10863 East Highway 40
Silver Springs, FL 34488
352-625-7470
http://www.fs.fed.us/

 **Eastern National.** (446 North Lane, Conshohocken, PA 19428; 800-355-5566)

The Ocala is the oldest national forest east of the Mississippi River, and the southernmost in the nation. Three rivers flow through the forest, offering excellent canoeing and boating opportunities. Major camping, picnicking, and swimming facilities are located at the three springs that feed the rivers. The forest's proximity to destinations such as Daytona Beach, Walt Disney World, the Kennedy Space Center, and Silver Springs contributes to its popularity.

OSCEOLA NATIONAL FOREST

Northeastern Florida, 50 miles west of Jacksonville.

Osceola National Forest
PO Box 70
Olustee, FL 32055
904-752-2577
http://www.fs.fed.us/

Cradle of Forestry in America Interpretive Association. (100 South Broad, Brevard, NC 28712; 704-884-5713)

Pine flatwoods and cypress hardwood swamps are the forest's predominant vegetation. The 200,000-acre forest contains Ocean Pond, a nearly 2,000-acre lake that lures campers, anglers, and boaters. Olustee Beach Day-Use Area and Ocean Pond Campground are the two principal developed recreation sites in the forest. Olustee Beach shares its name with the largest Civil War battle fought in Florida, the Battle of Olustee, which is reenacted every February. A 22-mile segment of the Florida National Scenic Trail passes through Osceola. In several areas, the trail is blazed on old railroad trams that once hauled timber. There are also boardwalks for crossing the swamps and wetland areas common to the flatwoods.

TIMUCUAN ECOLOGICAL AND HISTORIC PRESERVE

15 miles east of Jacksonville.

13165 Mount Pleasant Road
Jacksonville, FL 32225-1227
904-641-7155
http://www.nps.gov/timu

 **Eastern National.** (446 North Lane, Conshohocken, PA 19428; 800-355-5566)

Created in 1988 to protect wetlands and historic and prehistoric sites, and named for the Native Americans who lived here for more than 3,000 years, the 46,000-acre Timucuan Ecological and Historic Preserve encompasses Atlantic coastal marshes, islands, tidal creeks, and the estuaries of the St. Johns and Nassau rivers. Besides traces of Indian life, the site preserves the remains of European colonial ventures as well as 18th- and 19th-century American settlements.

 **Sam's Tips**

- The Kingsley Plantation features the oldest plantation buildings still existing in Florida, including the Planter's residence (which contains the visitor center), garden, barn, and slave quarters. These buildings date back to 1798.
- The Theodore Roosevelt Area is a 600-acre natural preserve with over 4 miles of hiking trails through one of northern Florida's most pristine settings.

Points of Interest

U.S. ARMY CORPS OF ENGINEERS

LAKE OKEECHOBEE AND OKEECHOBEE WATERWAY

Located in Florida's heartland, Lake Okeechobee is Florida's largest lake. The 152-mile waterway offers excellent boating, bass fishing, and waterfowl hunting. This convenient commercial link with the Florida coast also offers recreational boaters protected waters, peaceful anchorages, and pleasant shore stops. Corps-managed boat-in camping areas are available at St. Lucie Lock and the W. P. Franklin Lock. Other camping and day-use areas are available at the following locations:

- St. Lucie Lock: From Stuart, go 6 miles south on US 1, off FL 76.
- Port Mayaca Lock: From Stuart, go 20 miles west on FL 76.
- Moore Haven Lock: From Miami, go 130 miles north on US 27 to Moore Haven.
- Ortona Lock: From Fort Myers, go 33 miles east on FL 80, paved road to lock, 778.
- W. P. Franklin Lock: From Fort Myers, go 12 miles east off US 80.

BUREAU OF LAND MANAGEMENT

TAMPA BAY AREA

The Anclote Key Lighthouse, just north of Tampa Bay, sits on an island within Florida's Anclote Key Preserve and played an important role in the settlement and development of the Tampa Bay area. This wrought-iron lighthouse is in the process of being restored according to national preservation standards.

Phone: 601-977-5400

PALM BEACH COUNTY

The Jupiter Inlet Area of Critical Environmental Concern consists of about 86 acres of land associated with the Jupiter lighthouse. The tract contains one of the five largest stands of coastal scrub remaining in the county, and it supports many sensitive plant and animal species and numerous cultural resources, including a historic military barracks building.

Phone: 601-977-5400

For more information contact:

BLM Eastern States Office
7450 Boston Boulevard
Springfield, VA 22153
703-440-1600
http://www.blm.gov/eso

THE GREAT OUTDOORS ON THE WORLD WIDE WEB

Here are your essential Web sources for information about Uncle Sam's Great Outdoors:

Bureau of Land Management	http://www.blm.gov
Department of Agriculture	http://www.usda.gov
Department of the Interior	http://www.doi.gov
National Biological Survey	http://www.nbs.gov
National Park Service	http://www.nps.gov
National Wildlife Refuge System	http://bluegoose.arw.r9.fws.gov
Tennessee Valley Authority	http://www.tva.gov
U.S. Army Corps of Engineers	http://www.usace.army.mil
U.S. Bureau of Reclamation	http://www.usbr.gov
U.S. Fish and Wildlife Service	http://www.fws.gov
U.S. Forest Service	http://www.fs.fed.uv
U.S. Geological Survey	http://www.usgs.gov

GEORGIA

ANDERSONVILLE NATIONAL HISTORIC SITE

120 miles south of Atlanta, and 50 miles southeast of Columbus, GA.

Route 1, Box 800
Andersonville, GA 31711-9707
912-924-0343
http://www.nps.gov/ande

 **Eastern National.** (446 North Lane, Conshohocken, PA 19428; 800-355-5566)

This Civil War prisoner-of-war camp commemorates the sacrifices borne by American POWs not only in the 1861–1865 conflict but in all wars. Of the 45,000 Union soldiers who were confined here, almost 13,000 died from disease, poor sanitation, malnutrition, and overcrowding. The park includes the Andersonville National Cemetery, which has 18,000 interments.

Sam's Tips

- The Visitor Center contains exhibits on Andersonville prison, the National Cemetery, and the systems of exchange and parole used during the Civil War. A National Prisoner of War Museum is scheduled to open in April 1998.

CHATTAHOOCHEE–OCONEE NATIONAL FORESTS

Mostly in the middle and northernmost part of the state.

Chattahoochee–Oconee National Forests
1755 Cleveland Highway
Gainsville, GA 30501
770-536-0541
http://www.fs.fed.us/conf

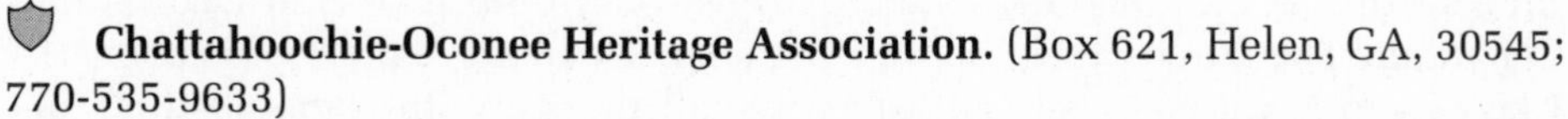

Chattahoochie-Oconee Heritage Association. (Box 621, Helen, GA, 30545; 770-535-9633)

Cherokee Indians made this area their home from the 1500s to the 1800s, after they were pushed out of their earlier sites by gold-seeking white settlers. The Chattahoochee National Forest is made up of 749,000 acres stretching from the wild and scenic waters of the Chattooga River on its northeastern border through the Blue Ridge Mountains into the Cohutta Wilderness and across the ridges and valleys of northwest Georgia. The 114,000-acre Oconee National Forest is located in the rolling Piedmont of middle Georgia. These two forests offer more than 500 developed campsites, 200 picnicking sites, 10 wildernesses, 6 swimming beaches, thousands of acres of lakes and streams, and more than 500 miles of trails. Hunting and fishing are allowed under state regulations.

FOREST SERVICE SCENIC BYWAY

Russell–Brasstown Scenic Byway

This 38-mile byway takes travelers from the picturesque hamlet of Helen through the Chattahoochee National Forest to Brasstown Bald, Georgia's highest mountain. Along the way, sportspersons will find sparkling streams with native wild trout, and photography buffs can spend countless hours at scenic overlooks and tumbling waterfalls, or watching for wildlife in quiet woodland coves. *Contact Chattahoochee National Forest.*

Sam's Tips

- Recreational gold panning is allowed in both forests. In most cases, streambed gold does not exist in sufficient quantity to constitute economically recoverable deposits. Usually, no more than a few cents' worth of gold can be panned out in an hour, although there's always the chance of finding a stray nugget. Contact the District Ranger office to be sure the stream you wish to pan is on National Forest land.

CHATTAHOOCHEE RIVER NATIONAL RECREATION AREA

Headquarters are in Dunwoody, 10 miles northeast of Atlanta.

1978 Island Ford Parkway
Atlanta, GA 30350
770-399-8070
http://www.nps.gov/chat

Eastern National. (446 North Lane, Conshohocken, PA 19428; 800-355-5566)

This national recreation area is comprised of 14 separate land sites along a 48-mile section of the Chattahoochee River between Buford Dam at Lake Sidney Lanier and Peachtree Creek, near the Atlanta city limits. The river is primarily Class I and II water—a few riffles and small rapids, with some obstructions, such as rocks and downed trees.

Sam's Tips

- To find out about latest river conditions, contact: Buford Dam, 770-945-1466, or Morgan Falls Dam, 770-329-1455.
- The Chattahoochee Outdoor Center (770-395-6851) rents several types of boats and provides a shuttle service between river takeout points and parking lots.
- Upland ridge trails in the Palisades Unit lead to panoramas of the river gorge and down through wooded forests to flood plain trails, sandy beaches, and expanses of shoal water.

CHICKAMAUGA AND CHATTANOOGA NATIONAL MILITARY PARK

8 miles south of Chattanooga, TN.

PO Box 2128
Fort Oglethorpe, GA 30742
706-866-9241
http://www.nps.gov/chch

 **Eastern National.** (446 North Lane, Conshohocken, PA 19428; 800-355-5566)

This military park, the oldest and largest in the country, was created by the Civil War veterans who fought here. The park commemorates the battles between Union and Confederate armies during the fall of 1863 in some of the hardest fighting of the entire war. The prize was Chattanooga, a key rail center and the gateway to the heart of the Confederacy. A major Confederate victory at Chickamauga in September was countered by Union victories at Orchard Knob, Lookout Mountain, and Missionary Ridge in November.

Sam's Tips

- Lookout Mountain contains monuments, historical tablets, hiking trails, scenic vistas, and the historic Cravens House, the scene of fierce fighting during the battle of Lookout Mountain. Be sure to see James Walker's huge (13′ x 33″) painting, "Battle Above the Clouds."
- Kids between 6 and 13 have the opportunity to become a Chickamauga Battlefield Junior Ranger; all it takes is about 90 minutes spent on the battlefield.
- Visit with Johnny Reb and/or Billy Yank as they show you Civil War equipment and talk about army life as a common soldier. The talks conclude with a rifle-firing demonstration. These talks are scheduled seasonally, primarily during the summer (June through mid-August) and during weekends in the spring and fall.

CUMBERLAND ISLAND NATIONAL SEASHORE

St. Marys is 50 miles north of Jacksonville, FL, and 110 miles south of Savannah. The island is accessible only by boat or ferry.

PO Box 806
St. Marys, GA 21558-0806
912-882-4335
http://www.nps.gov/cuis

 **Eastern National.** (446 North Lane, Conshohocken, PA 19428; 800-355-5566)

St. Marys, the largest of Georgia's Atlantic barrier islands and a favorite spot of former U.S. President Jimmy Carter, is characterized by unspoiled beaches and dunes, maritime forests, salt marshes, and freshwater lakes. In the central and northern sections of the island, pine trees tower over mixed hardwood forest. On the western side, saltwater marshes follow the tidal flow. Deer, bobcat, turkey, alligators, and numerous shorebirds and songbirds can be found on the island. Sea turtles nest on the beaches in the summer. Cumberland's horse herds graze openly in the marsh and forest areas of the island.

Sam's Tips

- A ferry transports passengers between St. Marys and Cumberland Island. To make reservations or to find out about ferry schedules, contact the park.

FORT FREDERICA NATIONAL MONUMENT

12 miles east of Brunswick, 75 miles south of Savannah.

Route 9, Box 286-C
St. Simons Island, GA 31522-9710
912-638-3639
http://www.nps.gov/fofr

Fort Frederica Association. (same address and number)

Located on the island of St. Simons, Fort Frederica was established by General James E. Oglethorpe as a fortified English settlement in 1736, during the struggle between England and Spain for what is now the southeastern United States. Settlement was one of Oglethorpe's purposes; another was defense against the Spanish. Spain saw the Georgia settlements as a threat to her interests in Florida. Spanish Commander Manuel de Montiano led a force north but was ambushed at the Battle of Bloody Marsh outside of Frederica, which ended the Spanish threat to Georgia.

THE OFFICIAL NPS EMBLEM

On July 20, 1951, the Secretary of the Interior authorized the arrowhead insignia as the official emblem of the National Park Service (NPS). In 1965, the U.S. Patent Office registered it as the official emblem of the entire national park system.

The *arrowhead* represents the historical and archaeological sites the NPS preserves.

The *Sequoia tree* represents the vegetation the NPS conserves.

The *bison* represents the wildlife the NPS protects.

The *mountain range and water* represent the scenic and recreational aspects of the NPS.

Sam's Tips

- Because of its extensive path system, St. Simons Island is ideal for running or biking. The Golden Isles Track Club (PO Box 20651, St. Simons Island, GA 31522) puts out a free brochure with maps for loops that range from 1 to 15-plus miles with water stops and other tips.
- Bloody Marsh Battle Site, a detached unit of the park, is 6 miles south of Frederica. Nearby are the remains of Fort St. Simons, built on the south end of the island, and the old military road that connected the fort with Frederica.

FORT PULASKI NATIONAL MONUMENT

13 miles east of Savannah.

PO Box 30757
Savannah, GA 31410-0757
912-786-5787
http://www.nps.gov/fopu

 **Eastern National.** (446 North Lane, Conshohocken, PA 19428; 800-355-5566)

This fort, built between 1829 and 1847, was named for Count Casimir Pulaski, the Polish hero who lost his life in the unsuccessful siege of Savannah in 1779. The structure took 18 years and 25 million bricks to build. Its masonry walls, measuring 7½ feet thick, were thought to be impregnable; the fort itself was considered to be the ultimate defense. In 1862, Union troops established a base for operations against Fort Pulaski at Tybee Island at the mouth of the Savannah. The Confederates were not particularly alarmed; the Union guns were a mile away, more than twice the effective range for heavy ordnance of that day. But roughly 30 hours of new experimental rifle-cannon fire tore great gaping holes in the fort's walls, forcing the Confederate garrison to surrender.

Sam's Tips

- The fort has prepared brochures for students on the technical details of the Civil War soldier. Themes include Organization and Training, Uniforms and Accouterments, Army Rations and Food Preparations, and a suggested reading list on related topics. Write to the park for copies.

JIMMY CARTER NATIONAL HISTORIC SITE

10 miles west of Americus, GA.

100 Main Street
Plains, GA 31780
912-824-3413
http://www.nps.gov/jica

Jimmy Carter's Firsts and Favorites

According to a park brochure, here are some interesting facts and firsts about the former president:

- *Favorite Musicians: Bob Dylan, Allman Brothers, Paul Simon, and Marshall Tucker Band.*
- *Favorite Hymns: "Amazing Grace," "Blest Be the Tie That Binds," "My Son," and "The Navy Hymn." At Annapolis, Midshipman Carter was paddled and hazed for refusing to sing General Sherman's battle hymn, "Marching through Georgia."*
- *First Car: 1948 blue Studebaker "Commander." Drove it cross-country in 1948.*
- *Favorite Room in the White House: The Treaty Room, on the second floor.*
- *Firsts for a President: First President to be born in a hospital; first (and only) President to live in low-income federal housing.*
- *Favorite Philosophers: Tillich, Niebuhr, Kierkegaard.*

 **Eastern National.** (446 North Lane, Conshohocken, PA 19428; 800-355-5566)

This site provides access to President Carter's boyhood home and high school. The town railroad depot served as campaign headquarters during the 1976 election. The Visitor Center and museum are in the Plains High School. The Jimmy Carter National Preservation District, separate from the park, includes part of the town of Plains and its environs. Together, they demonstrate the rural southern culture of Plains, Georgia, which revolves around farming, church, and school, and had a large influence on molding the character of the 39th President of the United States.

KENNESAW MOUNTAIN NATIONAL BATTLEFIELD PARK

30 miles northwest of Atlanta.

900 Kennesaw Mountain Drive
Kennesaw, GA 30152-4855
770-427-4686
http://www.nps.gov/kemo

Kennesaw Mountain Historical Association, Inc. (same address; 770-422-3696)

In June 1864, General William Tecumseh Sherman's advance toward Atlanta was delayed for two weeks at Kennesaw Mountain by a Confederate force led by General Joseph E. Johnston. Fifty years later, surviving veterans dedicated a monument to their fallen comrades. The park has 16 miles of trails, historical markers, two designated picnic areas, and three designated activity fields for ballplaying and kite flying.

Sam's Tips

- The mountaintop features a panoramic view of the surrounding area, including downtown Atlanta and Stone Mountain.
- Be sure to visit Cheatam Hill, site of the fiercest fighting. Along a short trail to the imposing Illinois Monument are Confederate earthworks and markers where prominent Union soldiers fell. Near the base of the monument is the entrance to a tunnel begun by Union soldiers intending to blow up the Confederate position with a mine.

Named After the Mountain

The eccentric and irascible Kennesaw Mountain Landis was named by his father after the bloody Civil War site where Kennesaw's grandfather had lost his leg. Judge Kennesaw Mountain Landis is best known as one of Teddy Roosevelt's most zealous trust-busters and as the first Commissioner of Baseball.

MARTIN LUTHER KING, JR. NATIONAL HISTORIC SITE

Atlanta, GA.

450 Auburn Avenue, NE
Atlanta, GA 30312
404-331-5190
http://www.nps.gov/malu

Eastern National. (446 North Lane, Conshohocken, PA 19428; 800-355-5566)

The birthplace, church, and grave of civil rights leader Dr. Martin Luther King, Jr., all are situated within the park. The neighborhood also includes the Martin Luther King, Jr., Center for Nonviolent Social Change, Inc. The surrounding 68-acre preservation district includes Sweet Auburn, the economic and cultural center of Atlanta's black community during most of the 20th century.

OCMULGEE NATIONAL MONUMENT

85 miles southeast of Atlanta.

1207 Emery Highway
Macon, GA 31201
912-752-8257
http://www.nps.gov/ocmu

Ocmulgee National Monument Association. (same address and phone)

Between 900 and 1100 A.D., a skilled farming people lived on the site of the Ocmulgee National Monument.

The Ancient Creeks and Ocmulgee

When the early English explorers and traders first encountered the people who are now called Creek Indians, they were living in the valley of the Ocmulgee River. In those times, the river was known to the English as Ochese Creek and the Indians living in the area were called Ochese Creek Indians. Over time, the name became shortened to be simply Creek Indians. Among themselves, the Creeks used the name Muscogee. Ocmulgee (OAK-MUL-GHEE) is derived from the Hitchiti tongue and means "boiling water."

Known to us as early Mississippians, they were a sedentary people who lived mainly by farming bottomlands for corn, beans, squash, pumpkins, and tobacco. The park interprets and preserves traces of 12,000 years of southeastern culture, from the Ice Age Indians to the historic Creek Confederacy, and includes the massive temple mounds of a Mississippian Indian ceremonial complex. A later Mississippian period town, the Lamar Mounds and Village, is the site of the only spiral mound still known to exist in this country.

Sam's Tips

- The Visitor Center houses a major archaeological museum with many artifacts that were found nearby. The museum, earthlodge—a restored ceremonial building with an original floor approximately 1,000 years old—and other exhibits are designed for self-guiding tours.
- The Dr. Charles Fairbanks Memorial Discovery Lab provides teachers and other group leaders a hands-on resource to enhance the experience of students during field trips to the park. A written guide and video are available. The Lab is divided into stations devoted to archaeology, history, nature, and crafts.

Points of Interest

U.S. ARMY CORPS OF ENGINEERS

ALLATOONA LAKE

Located in the foothills of the Blue Ridge Mountains, this is the oldest Corps lake in the southeastern United States. Camping, hiking, marinas, and cabins are available, and historic Civil War battlefields are nearby. From Atlanta, go 45 miles north on I-75 to Exit 125, east on GA 20, then south on GA 294 to the dam.

GEORGE W. ANDREWS LAKE

Located in an area of historical archaeological significance; Indian trails and battlegrounds are well marked. The lake features a scenic waterfall. From Albany, go 60 miles west on GA 62 to Hilton, then follow signs to dam.

LAKE SEMINOLE

In a rural setting, this lake features rugged ravines, cypress ponds, limesinks, and hardwood and pine forests, and is nationally known for its largemouth bass and wide variety of plant and animal life. From Tallahassee, go 42 miles west on US 90 to Chattahoochee, FL, then 1 mile north to dam.

LAKE SIDNEY LANIER

The combination of recreation facilities, panoramic views, climate, and proximity to Atlanta has attracted more visitors to this large lake than to any other Corps project. From Atlanta, take I-85 north to I-985 and Exits 1 through 7 west.

WALTER F. GEORGE LAKE

The area features Indian trails and mounds, battlegrounds, antebellum homes, and a restored village of the 1850s. From Albany, go 24 miles west on GA 62 to Leary, 36 miles west on GA 37 to Fort Gaines, and 2 miles north on GA 39 to the dam.

FISH AND WILDLIFE SERVICE

BLACKBEARD ISLAND NATIONAL WILDLIFE REFUGE

Situated about 18 miles off the coast of McIntosh County, GA, this is one of seven refuges within Savannah Coastal Refuges. It is one of the oldest refuges in the country, having been in continuous federal ownership since 1800, when the island was acquired by the Navy Department at public auction for $15,000. The refuge comprises an area of 5,618 acres of interconnecting linear dunes thickly covered by oak/palmetto vegetation interspersed with numerous ponds and savannas. In the years 1880–1910, the island was the South Atlantic Quarantine Station for victims of yellow fever. The southern refuge is reserved as a wilderness area. There are approximately 1,163 acres of open freshwater or freshwater marsh, 2,000 acres of regularly flooded salt marsh, 2,115 acres of noncommercial forest, and 340 acres of sand beach.

WEST POINT LAKE

Designed as a recreation demonstration project, this lake has fishing piers for the handicapped and other special features. There is excellent camping and good fishing. From Atlanta, take I-85 south to US 29.

BURIED TREASURY

Blackbeard Island was named for Edward Teach, alias Blackbeard the Pirate. Legend tells of his murderous and plundering activities along the coast and his periodic retreats to the island for "banking" purposes. Rumors of Blackbeard's buried treasure still flourish, but no evidence of his fortune has ever been discovered.

For information on this site, contact:

Refuge Manager, Savannah Coastal Refuges
1000 Business Center Drive, Suite 10
Savannah, GA 31405
912-652-4415
http://www.fws.gov

For information on Georgia's ten other wildlife refuges, contact:

US Fish and Wildlife Service Public Affairs Office
1875 Century Boulevard
Atlanta, GA 30345
404-679-7287

LOUISIANA

CANE RIVER CREOLE NATIONAL HISTORICAL PARK AND HERITAGE AREA

A 30-mile area approximately 1 mile on either side of Cane River Lake.

PO Box 536
Natchitoches, LA 71458
318-352-0383
http://www.nps.gov/cari

The Cane River Creole National Historical Park, a cultural "island" illustrating the French and Spanish Creole cultures in Louisiana, contains 34 historic structures that are currently undergoing restoration. The park is expected to re-open in 1998. The Heritage area further includes three state commemorative areas: Fort Jesup at Many, LA; Los Adaes near Robeline, LA; and Fort Saint Jean Baptiste in Natchitoches. The park contains numerous plantations (some are open to the public) as well as museums.

JEAN LAFITTE NATIONAL HISTORICAL PARK AND PRESERVE

Throughout southeastern Louisiana. Individual sites listed below.

365 Canal Street, Suite 2400
New Orleans, LA 70130-1136
504-589-3882
http://www.nps.gov/jela

 **Eastern National.** (446 North Lane, Conshohocken, PA 19428; 800-355-5566)

Rather than focus on a single theme, Jean Lafitte Park and Preserve encompasses the lower Mississippi Delta. Six sites within the park interpret the many diverse cultures of the region: (1) Barataria Preserve, south of New Orleans, with trails and canoe waterways through bottomland hardwood forests, swamps, and marshes; (2) Chalmette Battlefield, east of New Orleans, the scene of the 1815 Battle of New Orleans; (3) the French Quarter Visitor's Center which interprets the diverse heritage of the Delta; (4) the Prairie Acadian Cultural Center at Eunice; (5) the Wetlands Acadian Cultural Center at Thibodaux; and (6) the Acadian Cultural Center at Lafayette. The latter three interpret Cajun culture and history. Several other cultural centers operate within the park through cooperative agreements.

Sam's Tips

- The French Quarter Visitor's Center, at 916 North Peters Street (504-589-2636) in New Orleans, offers free interpretive tours of the French Quarter and the Garden District.
- The three Acadian sites explain the role and life of the Acadian people who were relocated from Nova Scotia to the Mississippi Delta region during 1765–1785. Contact the Acadian Cultural Center (318-232-0789), which serves as headquarters for the Acadian sites; the Prairie Acadian Cultural Center (318-262-6862); or the Wetlands Acadian Cultural Center (504-448-1375). Check with the park for locations and driving directions to these cultural centers.
- The Barataria Preserve (504-589-2330) encompasses about 20,000 acres of hardwood forest, cypress swamp, and freshwater marsh. Eight miles of boardwalk and hard-surfaced trails and over 20 miles of waterways allow exploration.
- The Chalmette Battlefield (504-589-4430) preserves the site of the January 8, 1815, Battle of New Orleans, a decisive American victory over the British, ending the War of 1812.

Jean Lafitte, Pirate or Patriot?

Jean Lafitte's life is veiled in mystery and legend. It is believed he was born around 1780 in southwestern France. Jean and his older brother Pierre migrated to the West Indies and then to the Louisiana Territory, probably as French privateers (individuals granted special licenses by governments). Known as letters-of-marque, these licenses bestowed the right to legally prey on enemy ships. After being privateers for some time, the Lafitte brothers moved to New Orleans as early as 1802 and soon became agents for the pirates that frequented the Gulf Coast, operating smuggling operations from Grand Terre Island through a swampy region south of New Orleans called Barataria. In 1814, the British offered Jean a bribe and a commission in the Royal Navy if he would help them capture the city of New Orleans. Lafitte forwarded the information to the American Governor, who in turn informed Major General Andrew Jackson of the imminent invasion. Jackson responded by refusing Lafitte's help, and subsequently the U.S. Army and Navy raided Grand Terre Island and arrested 80 Baratarian pirates. Lafitte again offered his help, and this time Jackson accepted. The Baratarians were released to fight for the United States. President Madison gave a full pardon in 1815 to all men who participated in the American victory, and Jean and Pierre Lafitte were celebrated as patriots.

KISATCHIE NATIONAL FOREST

Central and northern Louisiana.

PO Box 5500
Pineville, LA 71361
318-473-7160
http://www.fs.fed.us

Ozark Interpretive Association. (PO Box 1279, Mountain View, AR 72560; 870-757-2211)

Located in the piney hills and hardwood bottoms of seven central and northern Louisiana parishes, the Kisatchie National Forest is composed of dense stands of mixed hardwood and pine, meadows, occasional clearings, and rock out-croppings mixed with many streams, bayous, and lakes. The 600,000-acre Kisatchie has six ranger districts geographically separate from one another. The Vernon, Catahoula, Winn, and Evangeline Districts are relatively flat, but the Caney and Kisatchie Districts are located in rolling hills, some of which are quite steep and rocky. The forest offers more than 40 developed recreation sites and over 100 miles for hiking, biking, and horseback riding. Other activities include camping, swimming, fishing, boating, and hunting.

SAM'S TIPS

- Saline Bayou was designated a national scenic river in the fall of 1986. A 13-mile water trail has been developed on the Bayou for forest visitors.
- The Wild Azalea National Recreation Trail in the Evangeline District is popular for its spectacular native flowers.

NEW ORLEANS JAZZ NATIONAL HISTORICAL PARK

365 Canal Street, Suite 2400
New Orleans, LA 70130-1136
504-589-3882
http://www.nps.gov/neor

The New Orleans Jazz National Historical Park was initiated to preserve the history and increase the public understanding and appreciation of America's indigenous art form—jazz. To find out more about an opening date and what this park will contain, use the contact information above.

FOREST SERVICE SCENIC BYWAY

The Longleaf Trail Scenic Byway

The Longleaf Trail wanders for 17 miles through the rugged Kisatchie Hills and offers outstanding views of mesas, buttes, and sandstone outcrops against a background of longleaf pine. *Contact Kisatchie National Forest.*

POVERTY POINT NATIONAL MONUMENT

North of Natchez on LA 577.

c/o Poverty Point State Commemorative Area
PO Box 276
Epps, LA 71237
318-926-5492
http://www.nps.gov/popo

Department of Culture, Recreation and Tourism, Office of State Parks. (PO Box 44426, Baton Rouge, LA 70804; 504-342-8111)

Poverty Point National Monument contains more than 400 acres of the Poverty Point site, a prehistoric Indian center dating from about 1800 B.C. to 700 B.C. Over 7.5 miles of artificial ridges remain in the complex, ridges forming a gigantic semi-circle that surrounds a 37½ acre plaza. Artifacts and village debris are found along the ridge crests, which originally rose six to ten feet. Poverty Point was a major ceremonial and trade center and is the largest known site of the Poverty Point culture, which is represented in over 150 sites found mainly in Louisiana, Arkansas, and Mississippi. One of three World Heritage Archaeological sites north of Mexico, Poverty Point is recognized worldwide for its archaeological significance. The Monument is managed by the State of Louisiana and state park facilities are open to the public. There are no Federal facilities.

POINTS OF INTEREST

U.S. ARMY CORPS OF ENGINEERS

OUACHITA-BLACK RIVERS NAVIGATION PROJECT

Two navigation pools provide seventeen recreation areas along the 322-mile system. Recreational areas stretch from the Louisiana-Arkansas state line to the Jonesville Lock and Dam, located on LA 24, 12 miles south of Jonesville.

PEARL RIVER LOCK NO. 1

This recreational area is used primarily for fishing, hunting, and boating. However, it's also a great spot for bird watching and nature study. From Hattiesburg, MS, take I-59 south for 76 miles, then trun north on LA 41 and follow it to the access road, 12 miles away.

MISSISSIPPI

The Six National Forests in Mississippi

Bienville, Delta, DeSoto, Holly Springs, Homochitto, and Tombigbee are the six national forests of Mississippi. In each of them, visitors may wander through lush cypress swamps filled with insect-eating pitcher plants, centuries-old virgin pines and towering oaks, or blooming dogwood and giant magnolia trees. Secluded areas for hunting and camping; meandering streams for canoeing; lakes for swimming, boating, and fishing; and tree-lined trails for hiking or horseback riding are found in all six forests.

BIENVILLE NATIONAL FOREST

45 miles east of Jackson, 45 miles west of Meridian.

3473 Highway 35 South
Forest, MS 39074
601-469-3811
http://www.fs.fed.us

Ozark Interpretive Association. (PO Box 1279, Mountain View, AR 72560; 870-757-2211)

Established in 1934, the forest was named after the French-Canadian colonist and soldier Jean Baptiste Bienville, who founded Mobile in 1702, Natchez in 1716, and New Orleans in 1718. Forest visitors can enjoy a variety of outdoor recreational activities—camping, picnicking, swimming, hiking, fishing, hunting, and visits to many historically significant sites.

BRICES CROSS ROADS NATIONAL BATTLEFIELD SITE

115 miles southwest of Memphis, 170 miles northeast of Jackson.

2680 Natchez Trace Parkway
Tupelo, MS 38801
800-305-7417
http://www.nps.gov/brcr

Eastern National. (446 North Lane, Conshohocken, PA 19428; 800-355-5566)

On June 10, 1864, a small Confederate force led by General Nathan Bedford Forrest engaged Union troops at Brices Cross Roads in an attempt to sever Union General William T. Sherman's railroad supply line from Nashville to Chattanooga. The Confederate cavalry was employed with extraordinary skill, the battle ended in a rout—the Union lost five men to every Southern casualty—and General Forrest's troops captured needed supplies. The battle was considered a major tactical victory for the Confederacy, but Forrest had not severed the Union's supply lines, and Sherman continued the Atlanta campaign.

 **SAM'S TIPS**

- There are no facilities or personnel at Brices Cross Roads, but park interpreters at the nearby Tupelo Visitors Center of the Natchez Trace Parkway can answer your questions.

DELTA NATIONAL FOREST

25 miles north of Vicksburg.

The Sharkey Ag Building
402 Highway 61 North
Rolling Fork, MS 39156
601-873-6256
http://www.fs.fed.us

Ozark Interpretive Association. (PO Box 1279, Mountain View, AR 72560; 870-757-2211)

Located in the delta floodplain of the Mississippi River, the Delta National Forest is one of the few hardwood stands remaining in the Mississippi Delta and the only bottomland hardwood National Forest in the nation. During America's early settlement, the rich natural resources of the area permitted such an extensive prehistoric Indian population that the Delta is sometimes called the cradle of cultural development in North America. The forest lies within the Mississippi Waterfowl Flyway and is an excellent place to watch the habits of migratory species of waterfowl. The 60,000-acre bottomland hardwoods, which are flooded in the winter, provide excellent duck habitat. The forest also contains three virgin research natural areas and several large waterfowl reservoirs.

DESOTO NATIONAL FOREST

Southeastern Mississippi, 5 miles north of Biloxi and 10 miles south of Laurel.

DeSoto Ranger District
654 W. Frontage Road
PO Box 248
Wiggins, MS 39577
601-928-5291
http://www.fs.fed.us

Chickasawhay Ranger District
418 S. Magnolia Street
PO Box 426
Laurel, MS 39411
601-428-0594

 **Ozark Interpretive Association.** (PO Box 1279, Mountain View, AR 72560; 870-757-2211)

The DeSoto National Forest, an area of more than 500,000 acres, contains both of Mississippi's wilderness areas and a Scenic River. It is managed by the two Ranger Districts noted above. The forest covers a gently rolling terrain with stands of longleaf, slash, and loblolly pine, and it harbors abundant game, including deer, turkey, and quail. Streams are often tea-colored because tannic acid leaches from tree leaves and bark in the wooded swamps. One of the most popular activities here is floating on the winding streams in a canoe or a raft. Fishing, and camping are available.

GULF ISLAND NATIONAL SEASHORE

See description in Florida section.

HOLLY SPRINGS NATIONAL FOREST

60 miles northwest of Tupelo, and 60 miles southeast of Memphis.

1000 Front Street
Oxford, MS 38655
601-236-6550
http://www.fs.fed.us

Ozark Interpretive Association. (PO Box 1279, Mountain View, AR 72560; 870-757-2211)

About 155,000 acres of Forest Service lands are intermingled with private lands from Ashland to Holly Springs and from Oxford to Coffeeville. Within the forest are over 40 lakes constructed by the Soil Conservation Service. Even though their purposes are flood prevention and erosion control, the lakes provide abundant recreational opportunities, especially warmwater fishing from the banks or from small boats.

HOMOCHITTO NATIONAL FOREST

60 miles south of Jackson, 60 miles north of Baton Rouge, LA.

Route 1, Box 1
Meadville, MS 39653
601-965-4391
http://www.fs.fed.us

Ozark Interpretive Association. (PO Box 1279, Mountain View, AR 72560; 870-757-2211)

The first National Forest in Mississippi, the Homochitto, or "the Heartland," as it is called, was named for the Homochitto River, an Indian name meaning "big red river." France, England, Spain, and the United States strongly influenced the area of land around what is now the Homochitto National Forest. The forest is a leading timber-producing area in the South. For nearly 50 years, exploration for oil and gas has taken place on the forest land. About 86 percent of the producing wells on National Forest land in Mississippi are located within the Homochitto. Immense wildlife is found in this forest, so hunting is a particularly popular sport.

NATCHEZ NATIONAL HISTORICAL PARK

Downtown Natchez, in southwestern Mississippi.

PO Box 1208
Natchez, MS 39121
601-446-5790
http://www.nps.gov/natc

 **Eastern National.** (446 North Lane, Conshohocken, PA 19428; 800-355-5566)

European settlement of Natchez began with a French trading post in 1714. In the decades before the Civil War, Natchez became a commercial, cultural, and social center of the South's "cotton belt." Its power and wealth were unmatched by any other southern town of comparable size. The city of Natchez today represents one of the best preserved concentrations of significant antebellum properties in the United States. Among them is the home of William Johnson, a prominent free Black who lived in Natchez during the antebellum era.

Sam's Tips

- Each May the Natchez Literary Celebration—sponsored by the Copiah–Lincoln Community College, the Mississippi Department of Archives and History, and the National Park Service—features internationally acclaimed speakers and literary figures. For dates and other information, call the Natchez Convention and Visitors Bureau at 800-647-6724 or 601-446-6345.

TOMBIGBEE NATIONAL FOREST

Northeast Mississippi.

Highway 15 South
Route 1, Box 98A
Ackerman, MS 39735
601-285-3264
http://www.fs.fed.us

Ozark Interpretive Association. (PO Box 1279, Mountain View, AR 72560; 870-757-2211)

The Tombigbee National Forest, in northeast Mississippi, contains about 66,000 acres in two units, most of which house watershed lakes designed for flood control. Both 200-acre Davis Lake and 100-acre Choctaw Lake were built for recreation in 1937. Several archaeological sites of Indian origin are located in the area.

TUPELO NATIONAL BATTLEFIELD

In the town of Tupelo, on Main Street (which is also Highway 6).

c/o Natchez Trace Parkway
2680 Natchez Trace Parkway
Tupelo, MS 38801
601-680-4025 and
800-305-7417
http://www.nps.gov/tupe

 **Eastern National.** (446 North Lane, Conshohocken, PA 19428; 800-355-5566)

This one-acre site commemorates the last major Civil War battle in Mississippi. The engagement at Tupelo, July 14–15, 1864, was part of the effort on the part of Union forces to keep General Nathan Bedford Forrest in northeast Mississippi and away from General William T. Sherman's supply line, which ran from Nashville to Chattanooga. Federal forces under General A. J. Smith occupied the town of Tupelo. Forrest and his commander, General Steven D. Lee, realizing that Smith could take control of the Mobile and Ohio Railroad, moved troops to Tupelo for a two-day battle that ended ultimately in a draw. But the Union objective had been achieved: Sherman's supply line in eastern Tennessee remained open, allowing Sherman to continue his march to the sea. The site contains two cannons, a monument to the battle, and an interpretive wayside.

VICKSBURG NATIONAL MILITARY PARK

42 miles west of Jackson, 70 miles north of Natchez.

3201 Clay Street
Vicksburg, MS 39180
601-636-0583
http://www.nps.gov/vick

 **Eastern National.** (446 North Lane, Conshohocken, PA 19428; 800-355-5566)

Reconstructed forts and trenches evoke the 47-day siege of Vicksburg that ended in the city's surrender on July 4, 1863, and helped secure Union control of the Mississippi River. The Civil War ironclad gunboat *U.S.S. Cairo,* which has the dubious honor of being the first ship ever to be sunk by an electrically detonated mine, is on display. The nearby Vicksburg National Cemetery is the final resting place for 17,000 Union soldiers, more than any other burial ground in the country.

The Civil War's Best-Kept Secret . . .

. . . or one of them, anyway, is the result of a highly successful deception accomplished by an obscure soldier who fought at Vicksburg and throughout the Civil War. Private Albert D. J. Cashier was on the roll of Company G of the 95th Illinois Infantry Regiment. The 95th compiled an impressive record as a hard-hitting and often bloodied unit. During the assault of May 19, 1863, the 95th Illinois was part of the only brigade of General McPherson's Corps to directly attack the Confederate defense line. The unit weathered blistering fire to reach a point less than 100 yards from the enemy position. The 95th remained there until ordered to withdraw the following morning. In this action, the unit suffered 62 casualties. During the major Federal assault, three days later, the 95th advanced under a murderous fire that cost them 109 casualties. Private Cashier was fortunate enough to escape the ravages of combat and disease. Barely 5 feet tall, thin, laconic, Cashier made no effort to mingle with peers and preferred to sit apart from the others while smoking a pipe in silence. Members of the unit characterized Cashier as one always ready for duty, never sick, and capable of enduring long marches. In return for assistance in tasks involving heavy lifting, Cashier would sew on buttons and mend torn clothing. At the end of the war, Cashier retired to Saunemin, a small village near Chicago. In 1911, Cashier was struck by an automobile. A physician, summoned to the scene, examined the old soldier, noted a broken leg, then looked for further injuries. To his astonishment, he discovered that Cashier was a woman. Her grave site in Sunny Slope Cemetery reads:

Albert D. J. Cashier
Co.G, 95 Ill Inf Civil War
Born
Jennie Hodgers
In Clogher Head, Ireland
1843–1915

Sam's Tips

- Orientation to the park begins with an 18-minute film presented at the Visitor Center. Visitors can then drive the historic 16-mile tour road along Union and Confederate lines.
- After being sunk during the Civil War, the *Cairo* lay in the river for over 100 years before it was raised and restored. The nearby U.S.S. Cairo Museum houses military and personal artifacts from the boat.

Points of Interest

U.S. ARMY CORPS OF ENGINEERS

ARKABUTLA LAKE

Known for its large crappie, this lake offers camping, swimming, and excellent sailing. Special events include the Fall Arts and Crafts Fair. From Memphis,

TN, go 12 miles south on I-55 to Hernando, MS, then 13 miles west on Scenic Loop 304.

ENDID LAKE

Just off I-55, below the dam, this lake has a fishing pier for the handicapped, an equestrian trail, and numerous campsites and day-use facilities. From Memphis, TN, go 56 miles south on I-55.

GRENADA LAKE

Features include a Civil War redoubt, tennis courts, a fitness trail, and a visitor center. From Memphis, TN, go 82 miles south on I-55 to Grenada, then 3 miles east on MS 8.

OKATIBBEE LAKE

An irregular, wooded shoreline offers attractive recreation. A 5,000-acre managed hunting area is open to the public. From Meridian, go 7 miles north on MS 19.

SARDIS LAKE

Has a large swimming beach and beach house and a state park with a swimming pool, recreation hall, and cabins. From Memphis, TN, go 38 miles south on I-55 to Sardis, then 7 miles east on MS 315.

TENNESSEE–TOMBIGBEE WATERWAY

This 234-mile system of locks and dams forms a chain of ten lakes reaching from the Tennessee River in the north to Demopolis, AL, in the south. It is just a scenic shortcut to the Gulf of Mexico. The "Tenn Tom" offers excellent fishing, hunting, and lakeside recreation.

- Bay Springs Lake and Divide Section/Upper Canal Section: From Dennis, take MS 4 west for 5 miles to Bay Springs Visitor Center.
- Lower Canal Section, Aberdeen and Columbus Lakes: From Columbus, take Highway 82 west to Waterway Management Center.
- Aliceville and Gainesville Lakes. From Pickensville, AL, take Route 14 south 1 mile to Tom Bevill Visitor Center.

NORTH CAROLINA

CAPE HATTERAS NATIONAL SEASHORE

100 miles south of Norfolk, VA; 200 miles east of Raleigh, NC.

Route 1, Box 675
Manteo, NC 27954
919-473-2111
http://www.nps.gov/caha

 **Eastern National.** (PO Box 427, Kill Devil Hills, NC 27948; 919-441-6181)

"Graveyard of the Atlantic" and "Torpedo Junction" are two names given by sailors for the waters off the Outer Banks of North Carolina. Throughout history, more than 600 ships have been victims of shallow shoals and storms—and German U-boats during WWII. Today, the Cape Hatteras National Seashore (the first in the country) includes three barrier islands—Bodie, Hatteras, and Ocracoke—with long stretches of beach, sand dunes, marshes, and woodlands.

MEET YOUR PARK MAINTENANCE CHIEFS

The National Park Service has a varied and experienced staff of national stature—rangers, natural resource managers, archaeologists, historians, interpreters, landscape architects, engineers, and planners—who protect our land and legacy, conduct research, and educate the public. We'd like to introduce you to one of them.

Mike Shields, Chief of Maintenance, Denali National Park and Preserve, Alaska, recalls: "I joined the NPS in 1960 as a seasonal laborer, and in the ensuing years have been a Trails Leader, Ranger, Interpreter, General Foreman, Facility Manager, and Chief of Maintenance. My career has taken me from Olympic to Grand Canyon, Big Bend (twice), canyonlands, natural bridges, North Cascades, Sequoia–Kings Canyon, Rocky Mountain, and now Denali. . . . Like most of my peers, I'm here to help preserve the premier examples of America's natural and cultural heritage for today's and tomorrow's public, and to help educate that public to the enduring but often intangible values of this heritage. It is a calling, not just a job—a form of public service that invites willing subservience of personal interests to a longer and more lasting goal. It's no easy task to attempt balancing the long-term protection needs of a finite resource against the virtually infinite shorter-term desires of the public owners of that resource, but I wouldn't trade a bit of the last 35 years for any other task."

Lighthouses You Can Visit

These lighthouses are open to the public:

Bald Head "Old Baldy" Light
Location: Bald Head Island/Cape Fear River
Nearest city: Southport
Current use: Museum
Museum open daily
Access: Ferry from Southport
910-457-5000

Bodie Island Light
Location: 4 miles north of Oregon Inlet/ Outer Banks
Nearest city: Nags Head
Current use: Active aid to navigation/ National Park
Museum open daily in summer
Access: Cape Hatteras National Seashore/Route 12
919-473-2111

Cape Hatteras Light
Location: North of Cape Hatteras Point/Outer Banks
Nearest city: Buxton
Current use: Active aid to navigation/ National Park
Visitor Center open daily
Access: Cape Hatteras National Seashore/ Route 12
919-996-4474

Cape Lookout Light
Location: Core Banks
Nearest city: Beaufort
Current use: Active aid to navigation/National Park
Visitor Center open daily
Access: Ferry from Harkers Island
919-728-2250

Currituck Beach Light
Location: Outer Banks/Whale Head Bay
Nearest city: Corolla
Current use: Active aid to navigation/Museum
Easter through Thanksgiving
Access: US 158 to NC 12
919-453-8152

Ocracoke Island Light
Location: Ocracoke Inlet/Outer Banks
Nearest city: Ocracoke
Current use: Active aid to navigation/ National Park
Grounds only
Access: Rural Road 1326
919-473-2111

Sam's Tips

- Ask at the Seashore for a copy of *In the Park,* a publication that covers attractions and summertime activities, plus articles written by park rangers and ranger historians.
- The grounds of Cape Hatteras, Bodie, and Ocracoke lighthouses welcome visitors and are popular destinations. Only the Cape Hatteras light, however, is open for climbing, from Easter to Columbus Day.
- Popular surfing sites are at the Cape Hatteras Lighthouse and Pea Island. For windsurfing, the best site is one mile north of the village of Buxton. Rental

equipment is available locally. Certain areas also allow off-road vehicle use. To obtain more information and a permit, call one of the visitor centers.

- On Coquina beach lie the ruins of the shipwrecked *Laura A. Barnes,* not far from where she went aground in 1921.
- For information about the ferry linking Ocracoke Island and Hatteras Island, call 800-BY-FERRY.

CAPE LOOKOUT NATIONAL SEASHORE

The park can be reached only by ferry or boat from Harkers Island, located 160 miles southeast of Raleigh.

131 Charles Street
Harkers Island, NC 28531
919-728-2250
http://www.nps.gov/calo

 **Eastern National.** (446 North Lane, Conshohocken, PA 19428; 800-355-5566)

Cape Lookout National Seashore is a low, narrow ribbon of sand running from Ocracoke Inlet on the northeast to Beaufort Inlet on the southwest. These barrier islands consist mostly of wide, bare beaches with low dunes covered by scattered grasses; flat grasslands bordered by dense vegetation; and large expanses of salt marsh alongside the sound. Wind, waves, and currents are continually at work reshaping these low-lying islands. One strong storm can create extensive changes.

CARL SANDBURG HOME NATIONAL HISTORIC SITE

26 miles south of Asheville and 3 miles south of Hendersonville.

1928 Little River Road
Flat Rock, NC 28731-9766
704-693-4178
http://www.nps.gov/carl

 **Eastern National.** (446 North Lane, Conshohocken, PA 19428; 800-355-5566)

Poet and author Carl Sandburg spent the last 22 years of his life at his home, Connemara, where, in addition to writing, he ran a goat farm. Sandburg's works include his Pulitzer Prize-winning biography of Abraham Lincoln, plus poetry, biography, autobiography, history, children's literature, books on American folk music, and a novel. The house and grounds have been maintained, and the property still functions as a goat farm.

CROATAN NATIONAL FOREST

60 miles north of Wilmington.

141 East Fisher Avenue
New Bern, NC 28560
919-638-5628
http://www.fs.fed.us

Cradle of Forestry in America Interpretive Association. (100 South Broad, Brevard, NC 28712; 704-884-5713)

Located on the coastal part of the state, the 157,000 acres of the Croatan National Forest cover an area between Morehead City and New Bern.

SAM'S TIPS

- The Cedar Point Tideland Trail offers a good view of an estuary. This National Recreation Trail meanders through hardwood and pine forests, crossing a salt marsh on boardwalks.
- Brices Creek is a blackwater stream lined with cypress tress. This is a great place for fishing, canoeing, wildlife watching, and photography. A fishing pier and boat ramp provide easy access to the creek.

FORT RALEIGH NATIONAL HISTORIC SITE

140 miles south of Norfolk, VA; 180 miles east of Raleigh, NC (at the headquarters for the Cape Hatteras National Seashore on Roanoke Island).

c/o Cape Hatteras National Seashore
Route 1, Box 675
Manteo, NC 27954-2708
919-473-5772
http://www.nps.gov/fora

Eastern National. (PO Box 427, Kill Devil Hills, NC 27948; 919-441-6181)

Sir Walter Raleigh led the first attempted English settlement here in 1585. Based in what had been named by the English the "Land of Virginia," after the Virgin Queen, the first settlement had failed due to hunger and poor relations with local Indians. The surviving colonists then returned to England. By 1586, Raleigh was already planning another colony in Virginia. The three ships that sailed in May 1587 carried 117 colonists and included 17 women and 9 children. This was to be a long-term, self-perpetuating settlement. In July, the ships arrived at Roanoke Island to pick up 15 men whom Sir Richard Grenville had left there in 1586 to guard the fort. The ships' pilot insisted that the summer was too far advanced to go any farther, so the coloniests were left at Roanoke instead of their original destination. Three months later, the colony's leader, artist

John White, was forced to return to England for badly needed supplies. Upon his arrival, his ship was immediately put into service against the threat of the Spanish Armada. When White finally returned to the colony, three years later, he found no sign of the colonists except for the letters CRO carved on a tree. As his party approached the settlement, there was only silence. The houses had been taken down and a palisade had been constructed, on one post of which was carved "Croatan," the name of a nearby island. This message had been agreed on in the event the colonists had to leave, but there was no Maltese cross to signal that trouble had forced their departure. No other trace of the colonists was found, and their fate will probably never be known.

Sam's Tips

- At the visitor center, exhibits on Elizabethan life include a reconstructed 16th-century manor house room, artifacts from the site, and copies of watercolors by John White. Be sure to ask for the *In the Park* brochure, listing all the interpretive activities of the Cape Hatteras Group.
- *The Lost Colony,* which has been running since 1937, combines drama, music, and dance to tell the story of the ill-fated 1587 Roanoke colony. The play was written by Pulitzer Prize-winning dramatist Paul Green, who built this mostly fictional narrative from first-hand accounts. The play is produced each summer, in the outdoor Waterside Theater, by the Roanoke Island Historical Association. For tickets and reservations, call the box office at 919-473-2414 or 800-488-5012.

GUILFORD COURTHOUSE NATIONAL MILITARY PARK

6 miles north of downtown Greensboro, NC (off US 220 North).

2332 New Garden Road
Greensboro, NC 27410-2355
910-288-1776
http://www.nps.gov/guco

Eastern National. (446 North Lane, Conshohocken, PA 19428; 800-355-5566)

On March 15, 1781, the American army of General Nathanael Greene was defeated in a fierce two-hour battle at Guilford Courthouse, NC, by the British army of Lord Charles Cornwallis. The costly British victory was a crucial link in the chain of events that led to Cornwallis's defeat at Yorktown, VA, and to the end of the American Revolution.

Begun in 1887, the 220-acre park was established, in 1917, as the first battleground of the American Revolution to be preserved as a national military park. Monuments and graves of Revolutionary soldiers and statesmen, including two signers of the Declaration of Independence, are located within the park.

The large statue of Nathanael Greene on horseback, which stands near the Visitor Center, is a fitting monument to the general who was the strategist of the

Southern Campaign. "We fight, get beat, rise, and fight again," said Greene of that war within a war. As early as 1848, local citizens were thinking of raising a monument to Greene's memory. After some efforts over the decades, Congress appropriated the funding for the monument in 1911. The monument's sculptor was Francis H. Packer, a follower of the realist movement in American art. The monument was unveiled in 1915.

MOORES CREEK NATIONAL BATTLEFIELD

20 miles north of Wilmington via US 421, and 90 miles north of Myrtle Beach, SC, via US 17.

200 Moores Creek Drive
Currie, NC 28451
910-283-5591
http://www.nps.gov/mocr

 **Eastern National.** (446 North Lane, Conshohocken, PA 19428; 800-355-5566)

This 90-acre park preserves the site of the first Patriot victory of the American War for Independence. The battle was fought on February 27, 1776, between Patriots and Loyalist militia. The Patriots' victory resulted in North Carolina's becoming virtually free of British control for over four years, and the first colonial government to call for total independence (on April 12, 1776). Original remains include the bridge site, a stretch of the old Negro Head Point Road and remnants of earthworks built by Col. Alexander Lillington's troops. The earthworks were rehabilitated in the late 1930s.

Sam's Tips

- Points of interest at the Visitors' Center include artifacts, displays, a diorama depicting the bridge site, a video program, One Mile History Trail, and the quarter-mile Tarheel Trail (interpreting the naval stores industry). There are special weekend events, and an annual Anniversary Celebration, held on the last weekend of February, features reenactors, a colonial militia encampment, weapons demonstrations, period music, and a memorial program.

NANTAHALA NATIONAL FOREST

Southwestern North Carolina.

PO Box 2750
160A Zillicoa Street
Asheville, NC 28802
704-257-4200
http://www.fs.fed.us

Cradle of Forestry in America Interpretive Association. (100 South Broad, Brevard, NC 28712; 704-884-5713)

The Nantahala National Forest covers 515,000 acres south of Great Smoky Mountains National Park and features many waterfalls, including the 441-foot Whitewater Falls, the highest in the East.

SAM'S TIPS

- The Mountain Waters National Scenic Byway covers more than 60 miles through Appalachian hardwood forest and rural countryside from Highlands nearly to Bryson City. It passes through the Cullasaja Gorge, with its four waterfalls, and Nantahala Gorge, famous for its whitewater rafting.
- The Joyce Kilmer Memorial Forest is a magnificent 3,800-acre remnant of old-growth cove hardwood forest. Enormous yellow poplar, hemlock, basswood, beech, and other trees tower over the two loop trails. The forest is named for Joyce Kilmer, the teacher, journalist, soldier, and poet best known for his poem "Trees."
- A chain of mountain lakes offers boating, skiing, fishing, and recreation areas.

PISGAH NATIONAL FOREST

In the mountains of western North Carolina, 70 miles northwest of Charlotte.

PO Box 2750
160 A Zillicoa Street
Asheville, NC 28802
704-257-4200
http://www.fs.fed.us

Cradle of Forestry in America Interpretive Association. (100 South Broad, Brevard, NC 28712; 704-884-5713)

The Pisgah National Forest, in western North Carolina, is a land of mile-high peaks, cascading waterfalls, and heavily forested slopes. The Pisgah is primarily a hardwood forest and produces some of the best timber in the United States. Both the Appalachian Trail and the Blue Ridge Parkway run through the forest.

Sam's Tips

- This "Cradle of Forestry in America" was formerly a part of George Washington Vanderbilt's estate. It is located on the site where Dr. Carl Schenk, hired by Vanderbilt to oversee his vast private forest lands, established the Biltmore Forestry School in 1898. Open May 1 to November 1, exhibits in the Center show the importance of forests in America.
- The Roan Mountain forms the boundary between Tennessee and North Carolina. The Roan's hundreds of acres of natural rhododendrons create a blooming spectacle in June.
- The 79-mile Forest Heritage Scenic Byway is a specially designed loop linking many popular attractions such as the Looking Glass Falls, the Cradle of Forestry, and Sliding Rock.
- To obtain a newsletter called Carolina Connections, call 704-257-4200 (in Asheville).

FOREST SERVICE SCENIC BYWAY

Forest Heritage Scenic Byway

This 79-mile loop through the Pisgah National Forest, where American forestry was born, encompasses mountain valleys and rural countryside. The byway, rich in the history of the Southern Appalachians' exploration and settlement, features attractions such as the Cradle of Forestry, Looking Glass Falls, and Sliding Rock. *Contact Pisgah National Forest.*

UWHARRIE NATIONAL FOREST

40 miles northeast of Charlotte, 50 miles northwest of Fayetteville.

Route 3, Box 470
Troy, NC 27371
910-576-6391
http://www.fs.fed.us

Cradle of Forestry in America Interpretive Association. (100 South Broad, Brevard, NC 28712; 704-884-5713)

Named after its mountain range, the 46,000-acre Uwharrie National Forest ranges over low hills and rolling uplands and includes several meandering rivers—the Uwharrie, Yadkin, and Pee Dee. The forest is an important regional producer of pulp and other wood products. The first gold found in America was discovered in 1799 just south of the Uwharrie National Forest. Along the forest's streams, you can still enjoy noncommercial gold-panning.

WRIGHT BROTHERS NATIONAL MEMORIAL

Kill Devil Hills, between Kitty Hawk and Nags Head.

Route 1, Box 675
Manteo, NC 27954
919-473-2111
http://www.nps.gov/wrbr

 **Eastern National.** (PO Box 427, Kill Devil Hills, NC 27948; 919-441-6181)

The first sustained flight in a heavier-than-air machine was made here by Wilbur and Orville Wright on December 17, 1903. The park's Visitor Center tells the story of the Wright brothers through exhibits and full-scale reproductions of their 1902 glider and 1903 flying machine. One of the 1903 camp buildings duplicates the one used by the brothers as a hangar for the 1903 flyer. The other is similar to the one used as a workshop and living quarters in 1903.

 **SAM'S TIPS**

- Appropriately enough, you can reach this site by plane. The park's 3,000-foot paved airstrip was added in 1963 to accommodate small aircraft. Parking at the airstrip's limited tie-down area is restricted to 24 consecutive hours or a total of 48 hours during any 30-day period. Pilots who wish to stay longer may tie down at the Dare County Regional Airport, where gas and rental cars are available. Call the park for more information.
- On December 17th of each year, the public is invited to commemorative ceremonies.

 **The Lost Colony and the Wright Brothers**

The Fort Raleigh National Historic Site, 3 miles north of Manteo, NC, on US 64/264 (8 miles west of Whalebone Junction), commemorates the "Lost Colony," the first English attempt to settle the New World in the 1580s. The Wright Brothers National Memorial at Kill Devil Hills, milepost 8½ (9 miles north of Whalebone Junction), commemorates the Wright Brothers' famous 1903 flight.

POINTS OF INTEREST

U.S. ARMY CORPS OF ENGINEERS

B. EVERETT JORDAN DAM AND RESERVOIR

This 13,900-acre lake is located within a 45-minute drive from Raleigh and Durham. Boat launching, picnic, swim beach, and public marina facilities are available for public use. From Raleigh, go 30 miles south on US 1.

CAPE FEAR RIVER LOCKS AND DAMS

Located in the tobacco country of eastern North Carolina, on the improved channel between Wilmington and Fayetteville, the facilities are equipped for day use, boating, and picnicking. Shad fishing is popular; swimming and camping are not permitted. Directions:

- Pool No. 1: From Wilmington, go 2 miles west on US 74–17, 16 miles west on US 74–76, then 15 miles northwest on NC 87, and 1 mile northeast on State Road to the lock.
- Pool No. 2: From Elizabethtown, go about 1 mile southeast on NC 87 and 1 mile northeast on State Road to the lock.
- William O. Huske Pool: From Fayetteville, go about 17 miles south on NC 87.

FALLS LAKE

This 12,500-acre lake is located within a 30-minute drive from Raleigh and Durham. Boat launching, public marina, swim beach, and picnic facilities are available. From Durham, go 25 miles east on NC 98.

JOHN H. KERR RESERVOIR

This 50,000-acre lake on the Virginia border, one of the largest manmade lakes in the southeast, is noted for its record striped bass catches and camping facilities. Camp areas are operated by the Corps, the states of North Carolina and Virginia, and private concessionaires. From Raleigh, go north on US 1 to I-85, then north to VA 4.

W. KERR SCOTT DAM AND RESERVOIR

Located in the heart of scenic country, with Moravian and Cascade Falls in the immediate vicinity and the Blue Ridge Parkway 28 miles away, this area has many historical and cultural attractions. Day-use facilities and modern camp sites are available for public use. From Winston-Salem, go west on US 421 to Wilkesboro, then 5 miles west on NC 268.

FISH AND WILDLIFE SERVICE

GREAT DISMAL SWAMP NATIONAL WILDLIFE REFUGE

Located in southeastern Virginia and northeastern North Carolina, the refuge consists of almost 107,000 acres of forested wetlands greatly altered by drainage and repeated logging operations. Lake Drummond, a 3,100-acre natural lake, is located in the heart of the swamp. Visitors' activities include hiking, biking, photography, wildlife observation, fishing, and boating.

Biking/Hiking A variety of unpaved roads provide opportunities for hiking and biking. Washington Ditch Road is the best suited for bicycle traffic. The Boardwalk Trail, located on Washington Ditch Road, meanders almost a mile through a portion of the swamp.

Fishing/Boating These activities are permitted year-round on Lake Drummond. A Virginia fishing license is required. Access is via the Feeder Ditch, which connects Lake Drummond with the Dismal Swamp Canal. A public boat ramp is located north of the Feeder Ditch.

ANNUAL RECREATIONAL VISITS TO THE NATIONAL PARK SYSTEM

Year	Visits
1916	358,006
1920	1,058,455
1930	3,246,656
1940	16,755,251
1950	33,252,589
1960	79,229,000
1970	172,004,600
1980	198,014,710
1990	263,234,120
1996	265,796,163

Hunting A white-tailed deer hunt is held during the fall. Permits are required. Portions of the refuge are closed during the fall deer hunt.

Educational Opportunities A refuge orientation, film presentations, slide programs, and outdoor classroom activities are available to organized school, civic, and professional groups. Advance reservations are required for all programs.

Directions: South of Suffolk, VA, on Route 13 to Route 32, south for 4.5 miles, then follow signs. A boat access is adjacent to Route 17 at Dismal Swamp Canal.

For further information, contact:

Refuge Manager, Great Dismal Swamp
National Wildlife Refuge
PO Box 349
Suffolk, VA 23434-0349
804-986-3705
http://www.fws.gov

FREE BOOKLETS AND POSTERS FROM THE USGS

Uncle Sam's mapmaker, the U.S. Geological Survey, distributes over 100 free booklets and posters about the USGS's major activities, products, and services. Sample titles include:

- *Helping Your Child Learn Geography*
- *How Maps Can Help You Trace Your Family Tree*
- *Finding Your Way with a Map and Compass*
- *Naming (and Misnaming) of America*
- *Collecting Rocks*
- *Earthquakes*
- *Marine Geology: Research Beneath the Sea*
- *Elevations and Distances in the United States*
- *Geology of Caves*
- *Geysers*
- *Monitoring Active Volcanoes*
- *The Interior of the Earth*
- *The San Andreas Fault*
- *Why Is the Ocean Salty?*
- *Mapping Research in Antarctica*
- *Geologic History of Cape Cod*
- *Landforms of the United States*
- *Gold*

Ordering information for these and other USGS products can be found on the World Wide Web at http:/www.dwatcm.wr.usgs.gov/gen.interest .cat.html and http://www.usgs.gov/education/edulist.html

SOUTH CAROLINA

CHARLES PINCKNEY NATIONAL HISTORIC SITE

1254 Long Point Road in the town of Mount Pleasant, east of Charleston, SC.

c/o Fort Sumter National Monument
1214 Middle Street
Sullivans Island, SC 29482
803-883-3123
http://www.nps.gov/chpi

 **Eastern National.** (446 North Lane, Conshohocken, PA 19428; 800-355-5566)

The Charles Pinckney National Historic Site is one of the newest units of the National Park Service to open to the public. Charles Pinckney (1757–1824) fought in the Revolutionary War and became one of the chief framers of the Constitution. He served four terms as Governor of South Carolina, was a member of both the U.S. Senate and House of Representatives, and was President Thomas Jefferson's minister to Spain. The site is a 28-acre remnant of what was once a 715-acre plantation. An 1828 low-country cottage houses museum exhibits detailing Pinckney's accomplishments and daily life on an 18th-century plantation.

CONGAREE SWAMP NATIONAL MONUMENT

25 miles southeast of Columbia, SC.

200 Caroline Sims Road
Hopkins, SC 29061
803-776-4396
http://www.nps.gov/cosw

 **Eastern National.** (446 North Lane, Conshohocken, PA 19428; 800-355-5566)

Congaree Swamp contains the last significant tract of southern bottomland hardwood forest in the United States. The rich diversity of plant and animal species supported by this alluvial floodplain includes about 90 tree species, roughly half the number found in all of Europe. Activities and facilities at the park include a ranger station, interpretive programs, nature and hiking trails, canoe trails, backcountry camping, boating, fishing, primitive camping, and a picnic area.

Morris Island and the Massachusetts 54th

As the "Cradle of Secession," Charleston was a primary target of the Northern high command. After a failed attempt to conquer the city, Union commanders realized that there were five possible lines of approach. Two of them were through Sullivans Island, which was heavily guarded, or Morris Island, which was more accessible. The key to Morris Island's defense was Battery Wagner; armed with more than a dozen cannon, it presented a formidable obstacle. At dusk on July 18, 1863, the Union infantry advanced up the beach toward Wagner. Spearheading the attack was the 54th Massachusetts, a regiment of free Blacks from the North, led by Colonel Robert G. Shaw, who was White. The Massachusetts 54th's role in the attack on Morris Island was the subject of the film *Glory.* To learn more about the Massachusetts 54th, visit the Boston National Historical Park.

COWPENS NATIONAL BATTLEFIELD

17 miles north of Spartanburg, 70 miles west of Charlotte, NC.

PO Box 308
Chesnee, SC 29323-0308
864-461-2828
http://www.nps.gov/cowp

 **Eastern National.** (446 North Lane, Conshohocken, PA 19428; 800-355-5566)

Here, on January 17, 1781, General Daniel Morgan led his army of Continentals and backwoods militia against British General Banastre Tarleton's larger force of British regulars. It was all over in an hour. The British losses were staggering—110 dead and 500 captured—while Morgan lost only 12 killed and 60 wounded in a victory as complete as any in the war. Cowpens was one of the links in the chain of British disasters in the South that ultimately led to the final defeat at Yorktown.

FORT SUMTER NATIONAL MONUMENT

On a manmade island in Charleston Harbor, accessible only by boat.

1214 Middle Street
Sullivans Island, SC 29482
803-883-3123
http://www.nps.gov/fosu

 **Eastern National.** (446 North Lane, Conshohocken, PA 19428; 800-355-5566)

Fort Sumter, one of a series of coastal fortifications built by the United States after the War of 1812, was the site of the first engagement of the Civil War, on

April 12, 1861. The park also embraces Fort Moultrie, scene of a Patriot victory on June 28, 1776—one of Britain's earliest defeats in the Revolutionary War. Together, the forts reflect 171 years of coastal defense.

 **Sam's Tips**

- Private boaters may dock at the fort during park operating hours. Public transportation to the fort is available by concessionaire-operated tour boats. For schedules and information, contact Fort Sumter Tours, Inc., at 17 Lockwood Boulevard, Charleston City Marina, Charleston, SC 29401; 803-722-1691.

FRANCIS MARION NATIONAL FOREST

20 miles northeast of Charleston, SC.

4931 Broad River Road
Columbia, SC 29210-4021
803-561-4000
http://www.fs.fed.us/r8/fms

Cradle of Forestry in America Interpretive Association. (100 South Broad, Brevard, NC 28712; 704-884-5713)

The nearly flat Francis Marion National Forest, which rises from sea level to only 50 feet, provides an ideal setting to enjoy open long-leaf pine stands and large bottomland hardwood swamps. The forest is home to the largest population of the endangered red-cockaded woodpecker in the world as well as to swallow-tailed kites and many seasonal songbirds.

KINGS MOUNTAIN NATIONAL MILITARY PARK

60 miles northeast of Greenville, SC; 30 miles west of Charlotte, NC.

PO Box 40
Kings Mountain, NC 28086
864-936-7921
http://www.nps.gov/kimo

 **Eastern National.** (446 North Lane, Conshohocken, PA 19428; 800-355-5566)

Kings Mountain is a rocky, wooded outlying spur of the Blue Ridge, rising some 60 feet above the plain around it. On October 7, 1780, the plateau at its summit, about 600 yards long, was the site of a vicious battle between British loyalists, led by Major Patrick Ferguson, and North and South Carolina militia, who surprised the British by encircling the mountain. The Patriot victory delayed by three months General Cornwallis's plan to take the fighting north into Virginia.

 **SAM'S TIPS**

- Camping is permitted in the nearby Kings Mountain State Park. Contact the State Park at 1277 Park Road, Blacksburg, SC 29702; 803-222-3209.

NINETY SIX NATIONAL HISTORIC SITE

60 miles southeast of Greenville, 75 miles west of Columbia.

PO Box 496
Ninety Six, SC 29666-0496
864-543-4068
http://www.nps.gov/nisi

 **Eastern National.** (446 North Lane, Conshohocken, PA 19428; 800-355-5566)

The siege of Ninety Six, a colonial back-country trading post, grew out of one of the great dramas of the Revolution: the second British attempt to conquer the South. The post was essential to British influence in the region. The ruins of the star-shaped fort survived in remarkably good condition well into the 20th century and provided one of the best examples of 18th-century fortification. The Patriots' siege lines were reconstructed in the 1970s.

The first settler here was Robert Gouedy, whose thriving market rivaled some Charleston merchants'. He grew grain and tobacco, raised cattle, served as a frontier banker, and sold cloth, shoes, beads, gunpowder, tools, and rum.

 **Etymology of Ninety Six**

No one is certain how the village got its name. One explanation is that traders out of Charleston thought this stopping place was 96 miles from the Cherokee town of Keowee, in the foothills of the Blue Ridge Mountains.

 **SAM'S TIPS**

- To see the main attractions of the park, take the mile-long Gouedy Trail. Features along this natural trail include Robert Gouedy's Trading Post, Gouedy family grave sites, and The Charleston Road, one of the oldest roads in upper South Carolina.

 **FOREST SERVICE SCENIC BYWAY**

SC State Highway 107

A 12-mile segment of SC State Highway 107, near Walhalla, crosses the mountains of the Sumter National Forest, which offer scenic vistas, beautiful fall colors, and access to major recreation areas such as the Chattooga National Wild and Scenic River, Oconee State Park, and the Ellicot Rock Wilderness. *Contact Sumter National Forest.*

SUMTER NATIONAL FOREST

Spread throughout northwestern SC.

4931 Broad River Road
Columbia, SC 29210-4021
803-561-4000
http://www.fs.fed.us

Cradle of Forestry in America Interpretive Association. (100 South Broad, Brevard, NC 28712; 704-884-5713)

The Sumter's piedmont portion has trails and gravel roads traversing rolling terrain covered with upland hardwoods and loblolly pine. Several recreation areas adjacent to lakes provide camping facilities as well as swimming, fishing, and interpretive trails. Reaching elevations up to 3,200 feet, the mountainous portion of the Sumter National Forest provides cooler temperatures during the summer. The Chattooga Wild and Scenic River provides an ideal setting for scenic hiking.

POINTS OF INTEREST

U.S. ARMY CORPS OF ENGINEERS

J. STROM THURMOND LAKE

This is the largest Corps lake east of the Mississippi River. J. Strom Thurmond provides excellent striper and black bass fishing, and its large wildlife management areas offer some of the South's best hunting and wildlife observation opportunities. The visitor center and public overlook are located at the Natural Resource Management Center. From Augusta, GA, go north 20 miles on GA 28 or 104 to GA 150.

HARTWELL LAKE

This lake in the upstate region of Georgia and South Carolina is rich in historical lore. Clemson University adjoins the lake. The Natural Resource Management Center is located 5 miles north of Hartwell, GA, on US 29, and 100 miles east of Atlanta, on I-85. Several lake access areas are easily reached from the Hartwell, Anderson, or Clemson exits on I-85.

RICHARD B. RUSSELL LAKE

The Corps' newest lake project on the Savannah River, lying between J. Strom Thurmond Lake to the south and Hartwell Lake to the north, Russell, is one of the finest fishing lakes in the Southeast. From Calhoun, go west 8 miles on US 72.

FISH AND WILDLIFE SERVICE

CAPE ROMAIN NATIONAL WILDLIFE REFUGE

Several small rivers feed into the refuge's 22-mile coastline. Spring is the best time of the year to visit the refuge. You can see painted buntings and other songbirds and warblers, as their migration peaks in March and April. Shorebirds also return at this time. Summer is a hot and humid period; temperatures sometimes reach above 100° F. Fall temperatures begin to cool, and fall colors then appear in the maritime forest. Endangered peregrine falcons move through, and, in September, ducks begin to arrive in preparation for their winter stay. Winter is the season for hunting and fishing. Channel bass runs peak in November, and deer hunts occur in November and December. January and February are prime times to gather clams and oysters.

Sewee Visitor Center. On the night of September 21, 1989, Hurricane Hugo swept through the area and destroyed nearly all old-growth timber and most recreational facilities on the refuge and in the adjoining Francis Marion National Forest. Completed in 1996, the Sewee Visitor Center promotes public appreciation of the natural and visual riches of the Cape Romain Refuge and the Francis Marion Forest. It is located at the forest on US 17, approximately 18 miles north of Charleston, SC.

For information contact:

Refuge Manager
Cape Romain NWR
5821 Highway 17N
Awendaw, SC 29429
803-928-3368
http://www.fws.gov

ANGLERS' CODE OF ETHICS

We all have a responsibility to respect and protect the resources that enrich our lives. The Bureau of Land Management offers this voluntary Angler's Code. While enjoying the sport of fishing, the ethical angler:

Supports conservation efforts.
Practices catch and release where needed.
Doesn't pollute, and properly recycles and disposes of trash.
Practices safe angling and boating.
Obeys fishing and boating regulations.
Respects other anglers' rights.
Respects property owners' rights.
Shares fishing knowledge and skills.
Doesn't release bait into waters.
Promotes ethical sport fishing.

TENNESSEE

ANDREW JOHNSON NATIONAL HISTORIC SITE

Downtown Greenville, at College and Depot Streets.

PO Box 1088
Greenville, TN 37744-1088
423-638-3551
http://www.nps.gov/anjo

 **Eastern National.** (446 North Lane, Conshohocken, PA 19428; 800-355-5566)

Andrew Johnson's two Greenville houses, tailor shop, and gravesite illuminate the life and political career of the 17th President, the only one acquitted of misconduct in an impeachment trial. The Early Andrew Johnson Home is located on Depot Street. A block and a half away, on Main Street, is the Homestead, where the Johnsons lived beginning in 1851. Ten rooms, furnished with many original family possessions, are open to visitors. Less than half a mile away is the National Cemetery where Andrew and Eliza Johnson are buried with other family members.

BIG SOUTH FORK NATIONAL RIVER AND RECREATION AREA

65 miles northwest of Knoxville, TN, in Tennessee and Kentucky.

4564 Leatherwood Road
Oneida, TN 37841
423-569-9778
http://www.nps.gov/biso

 **Eastern National.** (446 North Lane, Conshohocken, PA 19428; 800-355-5566)

The free-flowing Big South Fork of the Cumberland River and its tributaries passes through 86 miles of scenic gorges and valleys containing a wide range of natural and historical features and offering a broad range of recreational activities. It was the first combined National River and Recreation Area.

SAM'S TIPS

- The gorge of the Big South Fork of the Cumberland River is renowned for its Class III (and above) rapids. Bring your own equipment or rent from a commercial licensed outfitter who can provide you with the proper equipment. Contact the park for a list of commercial outfitters.
- Because the park is in two states, you must obtain the correct licenses for the state in which you plan to hunt or fish.

A Ghost Town with Voices

Big South Fork's popular Blue Heron relives the existence of the hundreds of people who worked in the isolated mining community of Blue Heron, or Mine 18, from 1937 to 1962. Key stops along the tour include the train depot, bathhouse, residencies, the tipple and bridge, a company store, community school house, and church.

When the Stearns Coal and Lumber Company closed out the community in 1962, the buildings were either removed or allowed to decay. As a result, no original architecture was intact when the town was recreated in the 1980s. Ghost structures—metal beams outlining the size, shape, and location of the original buildings—were built, and they accent the "ghost town" feel one might have during the tour. Audio tapes of scripted recollections of Blue Heron citizens add to the town's ghostly aura.

- The park abounds with dramatic cliffs, arches, and rock shelters. One of the most popular sites is the Twin Arches, whose trailhead is approximately 20 miles (35 minutes' drive) from the Bandy Creek Visitor Center.
- Special yearly events at Big South Fork, including nature photography workshops, a mountain bike race, mountain dulcimer concerts and workshops, and astronomy workshops, are held from late spring through early fall. Contact the park to receive a copy of a guide that is published yearly.

CHEROKEE NATIONAL FOREST

The forest stretches along Tennessee's eastern border from Georgia to Virginia and is divided by the Great Smoky Mountains National Park.

2800 N. Ocoee Street
PO Box 2010
Cleveland, TN 37320
423-476-9700
http://www.fs.fed.us

Cradle of Forestry in America Interpretive Association. (100 South Broad, Brevard, NC 28712; 704-884-5713)

The Cherokee National Forest, the largest tract of public land in Tennessee, hosts 9 million visitors annually. The forest's 650 miles of hiking trails include a 170-mile section of the Appalachian Trail, which enters the forest from Virginia and leaves it at the Great Smoky Mountains National Park. The trail contains a network of shelters spaced about one day's hike apart. The forest also has 11 wilderness areas for hiking, camping, hunting, and fishing in solitude. Major rivers within the forest's boundaries include the well-known Oconee River, which has been the site of national whitewater championships as well as the 1996 Olympics canoe and kayak events.

FOREST SERVICE SCENIC BYWAY

Oconee–US 64

This, the very first National Forest Scenic Byway, is located in the Cherokee National Forest and consists of 26 miles of US Highway 64 in Polk County. Passing through scenic areas dominated by rock bluffs, mountain peaks, and Lake Oconee, the highway offers ready access to whitewater rafting, boating, swimming, and historical sites related to the Civil War and the Cherokee Indian culture. *Contact Cherokee National Forest.*

NATIONAL PARK SERVICE CIVIL WAR-RELATED SITES

1. Andersonville National Historic Site (GA)
2. Antietam National Battlefield (MD)
3. Appomattox Court House National Historic Park (VA)
4. Arlington House, The Robert E. Lee Memorial (VA)
5. Brices Cross Roads National Battlefield Site (MS)
6. Chickamauga and Chattanooga National Military Park (GA, TN)
7. Fort Donelson National Battlefield (TN)
8. Fort Pulaski National Monument (GA)
9. Fort Sumter National Monument (SC)
10. Fredricksburg and Spotsylvania County Battlefields Memorial National Military Park (VA)
11. General Grant National Memorial (NY)
12. Gettysburg National Military Park (PA)
13. Harper's Ferry National Historical Park (WV, MD)
14. Kennesaw Mountain National Battlefield Park (GA)
15. Manassas National Battlefield Park (VA)
16. Monocacy National Battlefield (MD)
17. Pea Ridge National Military Park (AR)
18. Pecos National Historical Park (NM)
19. Petersburg National Battlefield (VA)
20. Richmond National Battlefield Park (VA)
21. Shiloh National Military Park (TN)
22. Stones River National Battlefield (TN)
23. Tupelo National Battlefield (MS)
24. Ulysses S. Grant National Historic Site (MO)
25. Vicksburg National Military Park (MS)
26. Wilson's Creek National Battlefield (MO)

FORT DONELSON NATIONAL BATTLEFIELD

80 miles northwest of Nashville, TN.

PO Box 434
Dover, TN 37058
931-232-5706
http://www.nps.gov/fodo

 **Eastern National.** (446 North Lane, Conshohocken, PA 19428; 800-355-5566)

The first major victory for the Union Army in the Civil War occurred here, in February 1862, under the leadership of Ulysses S. Grant. This victory opened the way into the heart of the Confederacy and brought national attention to Grant. Fort Donelson (Dover) National Cemetery, which has 1,842 interments, adjoins the park.

SAM'S TIPS

- On the weekend closest to February 16, the park hosts a living encampment to commemorate the battle.
- The Dover Hotel, built between 1851 and 1853, served during the battle as Confederate General Simon Buckner's headquarters. Here, on the morning of February 16, 1862, Confederate Buckner surrendered his army to Grant.

GREAT SMOKY MOUNTAINS NATIONAL PARK

60 miles southeast of Knoxville, TN; 230 miles northeast of Atlanta, GA.

107 Park Headquarters Road
Gatlinburg, TN 37738
423-436-1200
http://www.nps.gov/grsm

The Great Smoky Mountains Natural History Association. (115 Park Headquarters Road, Gatlinburg, TN 37738; 423-436-0120)

The Great Smoky Mountains, the majestic climax of the Appalachian Highlands, are a wildlands sanctuary preserving the world's finest examples of temperate deciduous forest. The name *Smoky* comes from the smokelike haze enveloping the mountains, which stretch in sweeping troughs and mighty billows to the horizon. The Smokies offer a wide range of activities in beautiful, unspoiled forests similar to those encountered by early pioneers, although the woods are more crowded now than then. East year, as many as 9 million people come to this most visited park in the country. The diversity of its flora is world-renowned. You'd have to hike the entirety of the Appalachian Trail—from Georgia to Maine—to encounter the variety of trees you will find by walking from mountain base to peak in the Smokies. The park also preserves structures representing southern Appalachian mountain culture.

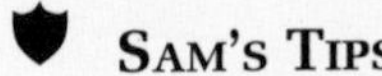

Sam's Tips

- From the Tennessee side, make your first stop the Sugarlands Visitor Center. Publications, information, exhibits, and a film are offered here at the intersection of the Newfound Gap and Little River Roads.
- From the North Carolina side, visit the Oconaluftee Visitor Center, open year-round. Adjacent to the Visitor Center, the Mountain Farm Museum lets you see how the early mountain people lived.
- The park publishes a newspaper, *Smokies Guide,* which is an excellent introduction to activities, trails, and resources available within the park.
- Just over half of the 800 miles of hiking trails also permit horseback riding. Five stables are located around the park.
- If you plan to only drive through the area, take Newfound Gap Road (Highway 441) and enjoy the majestic vistas.
- The most popular camping sites are Elkmont and Cades Cove in Tennessee and Smokemont in North Carolina. For quieter accommodations, check out the often overlooked northeastern part of the park, near Cosby, TN. Hike the Old Settlers Trail and see remnants of 19th- and 20th-century mountain life and other historical monuments.
- Though not the highest peak, Mount LeConte, near Gatlinburg, is a great place to see fall colors, which are usually most vivid in the last two weeks of October.
- October can be a very busy time on park roads, with many visitors out to see the fall colors. To avoid the crowds, try some of these lesser known roads and destinations:

  Foothills Parkway.
  Balsam Mountain Road.
  Cataloochee Valley.
  Rich Mountain Road.
  Gatlinburg Bypass.
  Greenbrier Cove.

Only in the Smokies . . .

The elevation and orientation of the Great Smoky Mountains foster a wide variety of plant and animal communities. In a small distance, changes in altitude, temperature, and moisture create ecosystems that are entirely different from those of the surrounding areas. The result is over 1,500 types of wild flowers, 200 species of birds, more species of trees than in all of Europe, and 27 kinds of salamanders. In fact, the Smokies have the distinction of hosting the most diverse salamander population anywhere in the world.

Smokies Weather

Spring: March has the most changeable weather; it may be sunny and in the 70s one day, and snowing the next. Backpackers are often caught off guard by bitter cold. By mid to late April, the weather is milder and more predictable.

Summer: By mid-June, heat, haze, and humidity are the norm. Most precipitation occurs as afternoon thundershowers.

Autumn: In mid-September, a pattern of warm sunny days and crisp, clear nights often begins. However, cool rainy days also occur. Dustings of snow may fall at the higher altitudes in November.

Winter: Days during this fickle season can be sunny and 70°F. or snowy with highs in the 20s. In the low elevations, snows of 1 inch or more occur up to five times a year. At Newfound Gap, annual snowfall averages 69 inches. Lows of -20°F. are possible in the high country.

OBED WILD AND SCENIC RIVER

Wartburg is 40 miles west of Knoxville, TN.

PO Box 429
Wartburg, TN 37887
423-346-6295
http://www.nps.gov/obed

Eastern National. (446 North Lane, Conshohocken, PA 19428; 800-355-5566)

"Wild" and "scenic" accurately describe the Obed river system, which includes sections of four streams: Daddy's Creek, Clear Creek, Emory River, and the Obed River. For centuries, these rivers have been cutting into the sandstone of the Cumberland Plateau, creating a rugged panorama of wild land and turbulent water seldom found east of the Mississippi. The Obed and its tributaries have carved spectacular gorges with cliffs rising as much as 500 feet above the water. Huge sandstone boulders, once part of the cliff face, now dot the streams and create obstacles to the water rushing by. Activities at the park include swimming, fishing, hunting, and primitive camping.

Rock climbers can take advantage of the area's sandstone cliffs; the three primary climbing areas are the Obed, North Clear Creek, and South Clear Creek. Although there are opportunities for casual floating on quiet stretches of water, this is one of the best and most difficult whitewater regions in the eastern United States, with rapids ranging from Class I to Class IV.

SHILOH NATIONAL MILITARY PARK

150 miles southwest of Nashville.

Route 1, Box 9
Shiloh, TN 38376
901-689-5275
http://www.nps.gov/shil

 **Eastern National.** (446 North Lane, Conshohocken, PA 19428; 800-355-5566)

On April 6, 1862, Confederate forces attacked unsuspecting Union troops encamped at Pittsburgh Landing. One day later, a bolstered Federal army retook lost ground near Shiloh Church, compelling the Southerners to retreat to their base at Corinth, Mississippi. Within the park, both the Shiloh National Cemetery (3,584 interments) and the Shiloh Indian Mounds National Historical Landmark overlook the Tennessee River.

STONES RIVER NATIONAL BATTLEFIELD

25 miles southeast of Nashville.

3501 Old Nashville Highway
Murfreesboro, TN 37129-3094
615-893-9501
http://www.nps.gov/stri

 **Eastern National.** (446 North Lane, Conshohocken, PA 19428; 800-355-5566)

The battle that took place here, from December 31, 1862, to January 2, 1863, marked the beginning of an offensive that split the Confederacy and paved the way for General Sherman's "March to the Sea." After the battle, the Union army constructed Fortress Rosecrans, the largest earthen fort constructed during the war.

POINTS OF INTEREST

U.S. ARMY CORPS OF ENGINEERS

CENTER HILL LAKE

Located in the Cumberland Mountains of middle Tennessee, this lake offers excellent smallmouth bass, walleye, and white bass fishing. Deep, clear water provides recreationists a beautiful setting for nearly any activity. Fancher and Burgess Falls provide beautiful scenic views. Bluffs and steep, forested hillsides enrich the natural beauty of the lake. From Nashville, go east 50 miles on I-40 to the Center Hill exit, then south 6 miles on TN 141.

CHEATHAM LAKE

This project passes through middle Tennessee and features a 2,700-acre waterfowl refuge and game management areas. The lake meanders through Nashville and past Opryland. Fort Nashboro and Riverfront Park overlook the lake in downtown Nashville. From Nashville, go west 32 miles on TN 12.

CORDELL HULL LAKE

Located at the base of the Highland Rim of middle Tennessee, the lake boasts modern campgrounds and day-use areas, opportunities for hunting and fishing, and trails for hikers, backpackers, and horseback riders. Canoeing is excellent on the Roaring River section of the lake. From Nashville, go east on I-40, then north on TN 43 to Carthage.

J. PERCY PRIEST LAKE

At this lake, located near metropolitan Nashville, good fishing is enhanced by the rockfish stocked by the Tennessee Wildlife Resources Agency. Multipurpose recreation areas dot the shoreline, offering good access and recreational enjoyment. From Nashville, go east 5 miles on I-40 to the Stewarts Ferry Pike exit. Turn right on Stewarts Ferry Pike and left on Bell Road.

OLD HICKORY LAKE

This extensively developed lake is located northeast of Nashville. Sailing and yachting are popular, and numerous regattas are held on the lake. The Old Hickory Nature Trail, a part of the National Trails System, provides interesting features for all age groups. From Nashville, go north on I-65 to the Madison exit, then east on TN 45 to the lake.

THE CORPS WANTS YOU

The Army Corps of Engineers has a volunteer program for people of all ages and talents. Here are some things a volunteer might do:

- Recover archaeological artifacts.
- Stabilize shorelines and streams.
- Build and install artificial fish habitats.
- Develop and build interpretive displays.
- Install and survey animal nesting structures.

The Army Corps of Engineers Volunteer Clearinghouse can help you find an opportunity near you. Call 800-VOLTEER, or write to this address:

U.S. Army Corps of Engineers Volunteer Clearinghouse
PO Box 1070
Nashville, TN 37202-1070

VIRGINIA

APPOMATTOX COURT HOUSE NATIONAL HISTORICAL PARK

92 miles west of Richmond, 18 miles east of Lynchburg.

PO Box 218
Appomattox, VA 24522-0218
804-352-8987
http://www.nps.gov/apco

 **Eastern National.** (446 North Lane, Conshohocken, PA 19428; 800-355-5566)

Here, on April 9, 1865, Robert E. Lee, commanding general of the Army of Northern Virginia, surrendered his army to Ulysses S. Grant, general-in-chief of United States forces, effectively ending the Civil War. Today, uniformed park rangers and interpreters in period dress tell the story of this community and how it was affected by the war. The park includes historical buildings such as the Jailhouse and the Clover Hill Tavern, and the Richmond–Lynchburg Stage Road where, on the fourth anniversary of the firing on Fort Sumter (National Monument, SC), Confederate troops laid down their weapons and furled their battle flags.

SAM'S TIPS

- Outside the village lie several spots associated with the events of the surrender. The site of Lee's headquarters is northeast of the village, a 5-minute walk from a small parking lot on VA 24. In the opposite direction from the village is the site of Grant's headquarters. Park programs show how the people of the village lived, catching drinking water in rain buckets and sharpening sickles, scythes, and axes on grindstones.

ARLINGTON HOUSE, THE ROBERT E. LEE MEMORIAL

About a 15-minute walk from the Arlington National Cemetery Visitor Center, in Arlington, VA.

c/o George Washington Memorial Parkway
Turkey Run Park
McLean, VA 22101
703-557-0613
http://www.nps.gov/arho

Arlington House, the nation's memorial to Robert E. Lee, is linked to the Lincoln Memorial by Memorial Bridge, symbolizing the reunion of North and South. From boyhood, Robert E. Lee was a frequent visitor to Arlington House. Its owner, George Washington Parke Custis, was the step-grandson of the first U.S. President. In 1831, Lee married Mary Custis, Custis's only surviving child.

For 30 years, Arlington House was their home while Lee pursued a career in the United States Army. That phase of his military career ended in 1861, when he resigned his Army commission to help defend his native state, Virginia. During the Civil War, Federal troops occupied Arlington House. In 1864, Arlington National Cemetery was established on a portion of the Arlington estate. Today, the 26-room house is being restored to its 1860–1861 condition with original and period furnishings.

BOOKER T. WASHINGTON NATIONAL MONUMENT

35 miles southwest of Lynchburg, 22 miles southeast of Roanoke.

12130 Booker T. Washington Highway
Hardy, VA 24101-9688
540-721-2094
http://www.nps.gov/bowa

 **Eastern National.** (446 North Lane, Conshohocken, PA 19428; 800-355-5566)

Booker T. Washington's birthplace and the farm on which he lived in slavery for his first nine years serve as a tribute to this 19th-century African American educator and statesman. Booker T. Washington left the Burroughs farm in 1865 at age 9—poor, uneducated, and newly freed. When he returned for a visit in 1908, he was a college president and influential statesman. In 1957, 101 years after Booker T. Washington was born, the national monument was established.

WHAT'S IN A NAME?

The names that we give to our parks, forests, rivers, and other regions are a central part of Uncle Sam's living heritage. According to the U.S. Geological Survey, the origins and meanings of geographic names derived from many languages show national, personal, and social ingredients of life both past and present. Some of the oldest names found on U.S. maps are from Native American languages: Adirondack, Chippewa, Chesapeake, Shenandoah, Choctaw, Yukon, and the names of 28 States. Other names reflect the European naming traditions of the early settlers. New London, Yorktown, Putney, Grover Hill, and Lancaster reflect English heritage; Fond du Lac, Baton Rouge, Marietta, La Salle, and St. Louis, French; El Mirage, Guadalupe, Rio Grande, San Francisco, and De Soto, Spanish. Names are often rich in description, local color, and national history. For example, names like Stone Mountain, Ragged Ridge, Big Muddy River, Carmel-by-the-Sea, Grandview, and Long Island are descriptive word pictures of the places, features, and areas they represent. Last Chance, Hell's Canyon, Liberty, Thief Lake, Enterprise, Rattlesnake Creek, Dread and Terror Ridge, and Paradise Flats evoke the dreams, fear, and color of the frontier.

 **SAM'S TIPS**

- The Plantation Trail is a .25-mile loop through the historic area. It passes by reconstructions of the 19th-century slave cabins and farm buildings similar to those that stood on the Burroughs Plantation when Booker T. Washington lived here as a boy.
- The Jack-O-Lantern Branch Heritage Trail is a 1.5-mile loop through the rolling hills characteristic of the Virginia Piedmont. These fields and forests were once part of the land worked by Booker and other slaves.

COLONIAL NATIONAL HISTORICAL PARK

50 miles southeast of Richmond, 50 miles northwest of Norfolk.

PO Box 210
Yorktown, VA 23690
804-898-3400
http://www.nps.gov/colo

 **Eastern National.** (446 North Lane, Conshohocken, PA 19428; 800-355-5566)

Within a distance of a few miles, visitors to Colonial National Historical Park can set foot on sites that were of great importance in the history of the Republic. The park encompasses most of Jamestown Island, site of the first permanent English settlement; Yorktown, scene of the culminating battle of the American Revolution in 1781; and Cape Henry Memorial, the approximate site of the first landing of Jamestown's colonists in 1607. The 23-mile Colonial Parkway connects Jamestown and Yorktown and includes restored Colonial Williamsburg and other historic spots along its route.

 **Virginia, Tobacco, and Kings . . .**

In the year 1604, His Majesty James I of England wrote a pamphlet against "this base and vile use of taking tobacco in our kingdom." He found it "loathsome to the eye, hatefull to the nose, harmefull to the braine, and dangerous to the lungs." Historians have not recorded what His Majesty said when he discovered, a few years later, that a settlement of his subjects in the New World had embarked upon an economy based on the raising and sale of that most noxious weed.

 **SAM'S TIPS**

- The events of the Revolutionary War siege at Yorktown and the story of the Town of York are presented in a theater program and exhibits at the Yorktown Visitor Center. Military tents used by George Washington during the Yorktown campaign, part of a reconstructed British frigate, and objects recovered from the river are on display.
- The first glass manufactured by Englishmen in the New World was produced at the small glass factory at Jamestown in 1608. Today, craftsmen show visitors how it was done.

FREDERICKSBURG AND SPOTSYLVANIA COUNTY BATTLEFIELDS MEMORIAL NATIONAL MILITARY PARK

50 miles south of Washington, DC; 55 miles north of Richmond, VA.

120 Chatham Lane
Fredericksburg, VA 22405
540-371-0802
http://www.nps.gov/frsp

 **Eastern National.** (446 North Lane, Conshohocken, PA 19428; 800-355-5566)

Fredericksburg and Spotsylvania National Military Park commemorates four major actions of the Civil War: the battle of Fredericksburg (December 11–13, 1862), the Chancellorsville Campaign (encompassing the battles of Chancellorsville, Second Fredericksburg, and Salem Church, April 27–May 6, 1863), the Battle of the Wilderness (May 5–6, 1864), and the Battle of Spotsylvania Court House (May 8–21, 1864). Fredericksburg National Cemetery, site of 15,333 interments, lies within the park's boundaries.

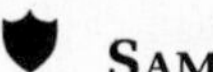

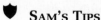

SAM'S TIPS

- The park is divided into seven major units and contains two visitor centers. One is located at the Fredericksburg Battlefield, the other at Chancellorsville. The self-guided tour of all four battlefields and three historic buildings begins at the Fredericksburg Battlefield Visitor Center, located on Lafayette Boulevard.

GEORGE WASHINGTON BIRTHPLACE NATIONAL MONUMENT

38 miles east of Fredericksburg.

Route 1, Box 717
Washington's Birthplace, VA 22442-9688
804-224-1732
http://www.nps.gov/gewa

George Washington Birthplace National Memorial Association. (Route 1, Box 718, Washington's Birthplace, VA 22443; 804-224-7895)

When George Washington was born, on February 22, 1732, in a middle-size plantation manor house along the banks of Popes Creek, Virginia was the largest and among the most powerful colonies. Washington's father, grandfather, and great-grandfather were solidly entrenched in the affairs of the colony and in Tidewater culture, and young George rapidly absorbed the principal values of both his family and the region—a sense of public duty and a love of farming. This monument contains the birthplace site and Popes Creek Plantation.

 **SAM'S TIPS**

- Living history interpreters demonstrate the endless task of tobacco growing on the plantation. Eighteenth-century farming techniques and domestic crafts are demonstrated year-round.

GEORGE WASHINGTON AND JEFFERSON NATIONAL FORESTS

See individual entries.

Forest Headquarters
5162 Valleypointe Parkway
Roanoke, VA 24019-3050
540-265-6054
http://www.fs.fed.us/gwjnf

Cradle of Forestry in America Interpretive Association. (100 South Broad, Brevard, NC 28712; 704-884-5713)

The George Washington and Jefferson National Forests occupy most of the mountainous western part of Virginia. The Jefferson National Forest extends for 218 miles, from the James River on its northern side to the Kentucky state line on its southern border. In addition to the easy walking/mountain biking Virginia Creeper trail, the forest contains 300 miles of the Appalachian National Scenic Hiking Trail, 11 wilderness areas, 8 fishing lakes, and over 400 miles of trout streams. "The Jeff," as it is commonly called, is interspersed with thousands of small clearings. Maintained for wildlife, these are excellent observation points for those who prefer to hunt with a camera. Other activities at the forest include hunting, boating, canoeing, and camping.

The George Washington National Forest, an area of more than 1 million acres, stretches westward across the Blue Ridge, Massanutten, Shenandoah, and Allegheny mountain ranges. In addition to activities similar to those offered at the Jeff, "the GW" contains four rifle ranges and four ATV trail systems. Situated along the 38th parallel, the forests are a meeting ground for hundreds of plants and animals usually seen only in the north or only in the south.

SAM'S TIPS

- There are 950 miles of hiking and riding trails in the Jeff. Four are especially noteworthy:
  1. The Appalachian National Scenic Trail: 300 miles of this 2,000-mile hiking trail pass through the Jefferson National Forest.
  2. The Cascades National Recreation Trail: A particularly scenic 4-mile round-trip hike passes by a 70-foot waterfall.
  3. The Mount Rogers National Recreation Trail: A scenic 4-mile hike stretches from the Fairwood Valley to the Appalachian Trail near Mount Rogers, the highest point in Virginia.

FOREST SERVICE SCENIC BYWAYS

Big Walker Mountain Scenic Byway

Winding 16 miles through the countryside surrounding the mountain from which it takes its name, the Big Walker Mountain Scenic Byway showcases year-round scenic beauty—frozen winter wonderlands, the wildflowers of springtime, and spectacular fall color. Summer is an excellent time to enjoy camping, hiking, picnicking, and fishing (especially for trout) along the byway. *Contact George Washington and Jefferson National Forests.*

The Highlands Scenic Tour

In addition to panoramic views and a variety of wildlife—white-tailed deer, songbirds, wild turkey, squirrel, and black bear—visitors to the 20-mile Tour can travel back in time to the site of an early iron-mining operation. Though idle since the early 1900s, parts of the mines, iron furnaces, and narrow-gauge railroad operations are still in evidence. *Contact George Washington and Jefferson National Forest.*

Mount Rogers Scenic Byway

These 55.5 miles of the George Washington and Jefferson National Forest offer views of the Mount Rogers National Recreation Area as well as open rural countryside. *Contact George Washington and Jefferson National Forest.*

4. The Virginia Highlands Horse Trail: A 68-mile trail designed for horseback riding and wagon trains. A corral and primitive camping area are available for those who trailer horses.

- A special area for hikers and horseback riders is the Pine Mountain high country adjacent to Mount Rogers. Closed to motor vehicles, the 5,000-acres of open grassy meadows, huge rock outcrops, fields of flowering rhododendron, and drainages lined with blueberries are a favorite place for visitors to southwest Virginia.

LYNDON BAINES JOHNSON MEMORIAL GROVE

In Ladybird Johnson Park, on the Potomac River.

Turkey Run Park, c/o George Washington Birthplace Memorial Parkway
McLean, VA 22101
703-285-2601
http://www.nps.gov/lyba

Parks and History Association. (126 Raleigh Street SE, Washington, DC 20016; 800-990-7275)

This living memorial to the 36th president lets visitors walk among white pines, in solitude, only minutes from downtown Washington, DC.

MAGGIE L. WALKER NATIONAL HISTORIC SITE

At 110½ East Leigh Street, in Richmond.

c/o Visitor's Center
600 N. Second Street
Richmond, VA 23223-1981
804-771-2017
http://www.nps.gov/malw

 **Eastern National.** (446 North Lane, Conshohocken, PA 19428; 800-355-5566)

Maggie Lena Walker rose from humble beginnings to achieve national prominence as a businesswoman and community leader. The first woman in the United States to found a bank, and a lifelong supporter of beneficial burial societies, Walker brought tangible improvements for African Americans and women. Visitors may tour the 25-room, 2-story brick row house that was the residence of Maggie L. Walker and her family from 1904 to 1934. The house has been restored to its 1930s appearance and is furnished with Walker family pieces.

 **Sam's Tips**

- Educational materials for young children about Maggie L. Walker and her life are available from the park. A visitors' center opened in April 1997.

MANASSAS NATIONAL BATTLEFIELD PARK

26 miles southwest of Washington, DC.

12521 Lee Highway
Manassas, VA 20109
703-754-1861
http://www.nps.gov/mana

 **Eastern National.** (446 North Lane, Conshohocken, PA 19428; 800-355-5566)

The Battles of First and Second Manassas, also known as the Battles of Bull Run, were fought here July 21, 1861, and August 28–30, 1862. The 1861 battle was the first test of Northern and Southern military prowess. Both armies were confident that this would be the only battle of the war and that the other side would run at the first shot. Ten hours of heavy fighting swept away any notion that the war's outcome would be decided quickly. The three-day Battle of Second Manassas produced far greater carnage—3,300 killed—and brought the Confederacy to the height of its power.

 **SAM'S TIPS**

- The First Manassas Battlefield is best seen on foot. The one-mile self-guided walking tour, with taped messages and interpretive signs, tells the story of the battle. The tour begins on the rear terrace of the visitor's center.
- The Second Manassas Battlefield—four times larger than the first—is best seen via a 12-mile driving tour designed to cover 12 sites that figured prominently in the second battle.

MOUNT ROGERS NATIONAL RECREATION AREA

Stretches from a point 60 miles southwest of Roanoke to the Tennessee border.

Route 1, Box 303
Marion, VA 24354
540-783-5196

 **Mount Rogers Interpretive Association.** (same as above)

The Mount Rogers National Recreation area—which features Mount Rogers, the highest point in Virginia—is a 114,000-acre part of the Jefferson National Forest that has been dedicated to outdoor recreation.

 **The Virginia Creeper Trail**

The 33.4-mile Virginia Creeper National Recreation Trail is a multiple-use trail connecting Abingdon, VA, with the Virginia–North Carolina line 1.1 miles east of Whitetop Station, VA. The trail began as an Indian footpath. Later, it was used by pioneers, including Daniel Boone. By 1907, W. B. Mingea had constructed the Virginia–Carolina Railroad from Abingdon to Damascus. In its day, the line hauled lumber, iron ore, supplies, and passengers. It got its nickname, Virginia Creeper, from the early steam locomotives' slow struggle up steep grades.

PETERSBURG NATIONAL BATTLEFIELD

23 miles south of Richmond, VA.

1539 Hickory Hill Road
Petersburg, VA 23803
804-732-3531
http://www.nps.gov/pete

 **Eastern National.** (446 North Lane, Conshohocken, PA 19428; 800-355-5566)

In 1864–1865, the Union Army waged a 34-week campaign to seize Petersburg. The park contains 2,460 acres and is made up of ten units, including Appomattox Manor, in Hopewell, VA; Poplar Grove (Petersburg) National Cemetery (6,315 interments); Flank Road; Five Forks Unit; and Confederate Fort Gregg.

 **SAM'S TIPS**

- Start your visit at the Visitor Center of the main unit, which contains Confederate Battery 5, the site of the opening battle. You'll also see the site of the charge of the First Maine heavy artillery, which suffered the largest number of casualties in one unit in one action of the war.

- The 4-mile auto tour of the park's main unit has wayside exhibits, audio stations, and short, interpretive walking trails.

PRINCE WILLIAM FOREST PARK

32 miles south of Washington, DC; 22 miles north of Fredericksburg, VA.

18100 Park Headquarters Road
Triangle, VA 22172-0209
703-221-7181
http://www.nps.gov/prwi

Parks and History Association. 126 Raleigh Street, SE, Washington, DC, 20032; 800-990-7275)

During World War II, this park was a top-secret training ground for the Office of Strategic Services (OSS), and was patrolled by armed guards with the order to "shoot to kill" any trespassers. After the war, the OSS became the CIA, which relocated closer toWashington, and the park was opened to the public. The Piedmont forest of the Quantico Creek watershed serves as a sanctuary for plants and animals and offers visitors hiking trails, campgrounds, playing fields, and five Civilian Conservation Corps-era camp districts. The park intersects two major physiographic provinces: the Piedmont Region, and, in the park's eastern section, a small portion of the coastal plain.

Civilian Conservation Corps Cabins

During the 1930s, the Civilian Conservation Corps built five cabin camps that are on the National Register of Historic Places. The cabins rent for $20/night and the camps rent for $200/night.

Cabin Branch Pyrite Mine

In 1890, the Cabin Branch Mining Company opened a Pyrite mine on the north branch of the Quantico. Pyrite, known as "fools' gold" because of its gold nuggetlike appearance, was valued for its high sulfur content. The mine was closed in 1920 because sulfur from the mine had ruined the soil, but a successful reclamation program (still in progress) has reversed much of the damage, and the park staff hopes to reopen it sometime soon.

Sam's Tips

- Ask the park for the monthly *Turkey Caller,* a newsletter that announces schedules and activities such as ranger-led interpretive nature walks.
- The Streamside Walk, at Parking Lot A, is an easy path to the South Branch of the Quantico Creek. Upstream, discover the different creatures that live in and along the creek. Downstream, you'll see the Scenic Drive's wooden bridge, which originally came in a kit. Look closely and you will find some of the assembly letters engraved on the timbers.
- Fun activities for kids include visits to beaver ponds and weekend evening campfire programs during the summer and sometimes in the spring/fall. Special ranger-led activities also can be arranged; contact the visitor center 2 to 4 weeks in advance.

RICHMOND NATIONAL BATTLEFIELD PARK

In Richmond and surrounding area; Visitor Center is at 3215 East Broad Street.

3215 East Broad Street
Richmond, VA 23223
804-226-1981
http://www.nps.gov/rich

 **Eastern National.** (446 North Lane, Conshohocken, PA 19428; 800-355-5566)

From the beginning of the Civil War, "On to Richmond" was the rallying cry of Union troops. Richmond was the Confederacy's capital, its principal manufacturing and medical center, and its primary supply depot for the Eastern theater. Seven military drives were hurled at the beleaguered city, and two of the assaults brought Union troops within sight of the Capitol. The park's ten units commemorate battles for Richmond. At Cold Harbor, well-preserved trenches and fortifications cost the Federal forces several thousand casualties in 30 minutes of fighting. Together, these sites give visitors an understanding of the 1861–1865 defense of the Confederacy's capital.

SAM'S TIPS

- A complete tour of the park, which consists of ten units and the Visitor Center, involves an 81-mile drive. Uniformed park interpreters stationed at the Visitor Center will answer your questions and provide you with historical information.

SHENANDOAH NATIONAL PARK

75 miles southwest of Washington, DC; headquarters offices are on Route 211, 3 miles west of Thornton Gap, 4 miles east of Luray, VA.

3655 US Highway 211 E
Luray, VA 22835-9036
540-999-3500
http://www.nps.gov/shen

Shenandoah Natural History Association, Inc. (same address as above; 540-999-3581)

Shenandoah National Park lies within a beautiful section of the Blue Ridge, part of the eastern rampart of the Appalachian Mountains. In the valley to the west is the Shenandoah River, from which the park gets its name, and between the north and south forks of the river is Massanutten, a 40-mile-long mountain. To the east lies the rolling Piedmont country. Skyline Drive, a winding road that runs along the Blue Ridge through the length of the park, provides vistas of spectacular landscapes. The park has campgrounds, mountain cottages, lodges, restaurants, fishing, horse rentals, picnic spots, 101 miles of the Appalachian Trail, and 500 miles of park trails. The park's nine waterfalls are among the most popular hiking destinations.

Sam's Tips

- The park's publication, *Shenandoah Overlook,* contains articles and information about seasonal activities. Rangers at the two visitor centers and at one Information Center give programs and are happy to provide information and directions.
- By far the greatest number of people enjoy Shenandoah's scenic beauty from the 105-mile Skyline Drive along the Blue Ridge. Numerous parking overlooks present panoramas of the Piedmont to the east and the Shenandoah Valley to the west.
- An "Explorer Backpack" of field equipment, such as hand lenses, binoculars, field guides, and drawing supplies, can be rented at the visitor centers.
- Guided tours on horseback are available through a concessionaire; visitors may bring their own horses and ride the designated trails. Pets are allowed on most trails, but only if kept on a leash at all times.
- Most facilities, including the visitor centers, are closed during the winter months.

UNITED STATES MARINE CORPS WAR MEMORIAL

Off Fort Meyer Drive and Meade Street near the Rosslyn Metro station in Arlington, VA.

Superintendent
George Washington Memorial Parkway
c/o Turkey Run Park
McLean, VA 22101
703-285-2600
http://www.nps.gov/gwmp

Parks and History Association. (126 Raleigh Street, SE, Washington, DC 20032; 800-990-7275)

The Marine Corps Memorial stands as a symbol of this nation's esteem for the sacrifices of the United States Marine Corps. The sculpture depicts one of the most famous incidents of World War II—Marines raising the American flag on Iwo Jima—and is dedicated not just to World War II casualties but to all Marines who have given their lives in defense of the United States since 1775.

WOLF TRAP FARM PARK FOR THE PERFORMING ARTS

25 miles west of Washington DC; outside the Capital Beltway (I-495) between Route 7 and Route 267/Dulles Toll Road.

1551 Trap Road
Vienna, VA 22182
703-255-1800
http://www.nps.gov/wotr

Parks and History Association. (126 Raleigh Street SE, Washington, DC 20032; 800-990-7275)

The Filene Center, an open-air performing arts pavilion, can accommodate an audience of 7,000 including 3,200 on the sloping lawn, in a setting of rolling hills and woods. The stagehouse is 10 stories high, and the stage is 125 feet wide and 70 feet deep. Performances range from dance, opera, and symphony to jazz, pop, musicals, country-western, and bluegrass.

Sam's Tips

- Contact the park to receive information on preperformance talks and off-season backstage tours. For information about tickets, directions, performances, group sales, and gift certificates, call 703-255-1860.
- Performances for children are sponsored by the National Park Service during July and August in the Theater-in-the-Woods amphitheater. This program uses music, songs, dance, mime, puppets, and plays to introduce children to the world of live performing arts. For information, call 703-255-1827.

Points of Interest

U.S. ARMY CORPS OF ENGINEERS

ATLANTIC INTRACOASTAL WATERWAY

Two canal routes link the Chesapeake Bay at Norfolk with Albemarle Sound in North Carolina and form part of the inland waterway from Miami to New England. Great Bridge Lock, in Chesapeake, on the historic Albemarle and Chesapeake Canal, features picnic areas for day use. It is located 4.5 miles east of I-64 on VA 168. Deep Creek Lock, located in Chesapeake, on the Dismal Swamp Canal 3 miles west of I-64 on US 17, also has day-use picnic areas.

GATHRIGHT DAM (LAKE MOOMAW)

Situated within the George Washington National Forest, the dam's recreational facilities are managed by the US Forest Service. From Covington, go north on US 220 to VA 687, then follow the signs to the dam site.

JOHN H. KERR RESERVOIR

This 50,000-acre lake, one of the largest manmade lakes in the East, is noted for its record striped bass and camping facilities. Camp areas are operated by the Corps, the states of Virginia and North Carolina, and private concessionaires. From Petersburg, go 70 miles southwest via I-85 or US 1, then west on US 58 or VA 4.

JOHN W. FLANNAGAN RESERVOIR

Project lands adjoin Jefferson National Forest. Nearby Breaks Interstate Park contains massive geological features. Seven miles from Haysi, take VA 63, VA 614, and then VA 739.

NORTH FORK OF POUND LAKE

This hikers' paradise lies adjacent to the wooded hills of Jefferson National Forest. From Pound, go southwest for one mile on VA 630.

PHILPOTT LAKE

Nestled in the rugged foothills of the Blue Ridge, the lake adjoins Fairy Stone State Park. Canoe to campsites on Deer Island. From Roanoke, go south on US 220, west on VA 57, and north on VA 904.

HUGGING YOUR FAMILY TREE

The Bureau of Land Management (BLM) operates the Automated Land Records System of historic land documents, including copies of homestead and sales patents, survey plats, and survey field notes. This system facilitates genealogical research through last name and title searches. Perform searches of your homesteading ancestors who bought their land in the Northwest Territory or the Deep South from the federal government. Or search the Historic Land Patents (1787–1908) file, where homestead entries, cash sales, military warrants, and other documents have been filed. The Secretary of the Interior's copies include more than five million patents and warrants, and more than four million land survey records for Alabama, Arkansas, Florida, Illinois, Indiana, Iowa, Louisiana, Michigan, Minnesota, Missouri, Mississippi, Ohio, and Wisconsin.

For more information, contact:

David Henry, Public Access Team Leader
BLM Eastern States' Office
7450 Boston Boulevard
Springfield, VA 22153
703-440-1600
http://www.blm.gov/nhp/map/es/esglo.html

The Midwest Region

NATIONAL PARK SERVICE HANDBOOKS— THE MIDWEST REGION

National Park Service handbooks highlight popular visitor sites across the country. Use them to learn about the historic significance and natural beauty of your next vacation destination. All are generously illustrated with photos, maps, and diagrams. Sites in the Midwest for which these authoritative handbooks are available include:

Site	*Stock No.*	*Price*
Apostle Islands (WI)	024-005-01023-8	$3.75
Scotts Bluff National Monument (NE)	024-005-00891-8	3.50

You can order these documents by phone (202-512-1800) or fax (202-512-2250), or by writing to: Superintendent of Documents, PO Box 371954, Pittsburgh, PA 15250-7954. (Use the stock number when ordering. Prices may change.) The 24 local government bookstores located around the country carry titles of regional interest. Check the Appendix for the one nearest to you.

Illinois and Michigan National Heritage Corridor

In 1673, the first Europeans to venture into the area, Louis Jolliet and Father Jacques Marquette, noticed that an area now called the Chicago Portage could connect the Chicago and Des Plaines Rivers and provide an uninterrupted water route from the Great Lakes to the Gulf of Mexico. The canal was started in 1836 and opened in 1848; in the decade after its opening, the population of Chicago soared over 600 percent. Use of the canal dwindled with the rise of the railroad, and in 1933, with the opening of the canal's modern successor, the Illinois Waterway, the canal was closed. The remains of the canal have been preserved along with historic sections of over 40 cities and towns along the 120-mile corridor, plus nearly 20 Chicago neighborhoods. It includes rare natural areas, state and local parks and forest preserves, and acreage set aside for picnicking, hiking, cross-country skiing, fishing, canoeing, and camping. For more information contact: 15701 South Independence Boulevard, Lockport, IL 60441; 815-740-2047; http://www.nps.gov/ilmi

ILLINOIS

LINCOLN HOME NATIONAL HISTORIC SITE

Springfield, IL.

413 S. Eighth Street
Springfield, IL 62701
217-492-4241, ext. 221
http://www.nps.gov/liho

 **Eastern National.** (446 North Lane, Conshohocken, PA 19428; 800-355-5566)

In April 1837, Abraham Lincoln moved to Springfield, Illinois, and remained there until he left for Washington to become President of the United States in 1861. The house that he occupied for 17 of those years—framed in pine, hickory, walnut, and oak—is open to visitors. An exhibit, "What a Pleasant Home Abe Lincoln Has," is located in the Dean House, across Eighth Street from the Lincoln Home.

SHAWNEE NATIONAL FOREST

120 miles southeast of St. Louis, MO; 15 miles south of Harrisburg.

50 Highway 145 South
Harrisburg, IL 62946
800-699-6637
http://www.sitc.org/shwnfor1.html

 **Eastern National Forest Interpretive Association.** (PO Box 70, East Tawas, MI 48730; 517-362-7511)

Chicago Portage National Historic Site

The Great Lakes, called the "five keys" to the Continent, and the Mississipi River Drainage System were separated by a continental divide that had to be crossed by a land "portage" during the dry seasons. This portage route, discovered by Father Jacques Marquette and Louis Jolliet in 1673, became known as the Chicago Portage. It encouraged additional settlers and underlined the need to connect these waterways. Recognizing this need, the federal government authorized the Illinois and Michigan Canal, which was completed in 1848 and has been credited for the growth of the city of Chicago. For more information contact The Chicago Portage National Historic Site
Forest Preserve District of Cook County, 536 N. Harlem Ave., River Forest, IL 60305; 708-771-1335.

At the southernmost tip of Illinois, the Shawnee National Forest encompasses 273,800 acres from the state's eastern border, the Ohio River, to the state's western border, the Mississippi River. This relatively small national forest features a variety of landscapes: forested hills, lakes, and spectacular outcroppings of sandstone and limestone. Popular sightseeing locations in the forest include: the Garden of the Gods Recreation Area, Little Grand Canyon, High Knob, Shawnee Hills on the Ohio Scenic Byway, and LaRue Pine Hills Scenic Area. There are many lakes and ponds in the forest ideal for swimming, boating, and other recreational activities.

POINTS OF INTEREST

U.S. ARMY CORPS OF ENGINEERS

CARLYLE LAKE

Water-oriented outdoor recreation abounds on Illinois's largest lake. A favorite spot for sailboating. On US 50, about 50 miles east of St. Louis, MO.

KASKASKIA LOCK AND DAM

Provides a riverside picnic area and visitor overlook at the confluence of the Kaskaskia and Mississippi rivers. Located 3 miles south of IL 3, near Modoc, IL.

LAKE SHELBYVILLE

Sandy beaches, hiking trails, marinas, and popular lakeside campsites make this an ideal vacation spot. A resort offers rooms, convention facilities, and a championship golf course. Located 60 miles southeast of Springfield, just off IL 16 and IL 128.

REND LAKE

Water-oriented recreation opportunities include picnicking, swimming, camping, boating, fishing, and hunting. Well known for waterfowl hunting and wildlife viewing. Located near Mount Vernon, IL, 15 miles south of the junction of I-64 and I-57

INDIANA

GEORGE ROGERS CLARK NATIONAL HISTORICAL PARK

50 miles north of Evansville, off US Highway 41 at the Willow Street exit.

401 South Second Street
Vincennes, IN 47591
812-882-1776
http://www.nps.gov/gero

 **Eastern National.** (446 North Lane, Conshohocken, PA 19428; 800-355-5566)

George Rogers Clark, an organizer of the Kentucky militia, a hero of the Revolutionary War, and a close friend of Thomas Jefferson, was also one of the infant nation's greatest explorers. He was the older brother of William Clark, who partnered with Merriweather Lewis on the famed Lewis and Clark Expedition. A circular granite memorial supported by 16 columns was dedicated in 1936 to pay tribute to this soldier and trailblazer. A larger-than-life statue of Clark is surrounded by murals of his military accomplishments.

HOOSIER NATIONAL FOREST

65 miles southwest of Indianapolis; 55 miles northwest of Louisville, KY.

811 Constitution Avenue
Bedford, IN 47421
812-275-5987
http://www.fs.fed.us

Eastern National Forests Interpretive Association. (PO Box 70, East Tawas, MI 48730; 517-362-7511)

A major attraction to visitors from nearby Chicago, Indianapolis, Louisville, Evansville, and Cincinnati, the Hoosier National Forest covers 194,000 acres of oak and hickory woods standing alongside wetlands. The forest came into being in the late 1930s, when the Great Depression stirred the farmers in the area to migrate, generally abandoning their eroded farms. As the amount of tax-delinquent land grew, the State Legislature asked the federal government to purchase the land for National Forest purposes. Unique attractions include: Hemlock Cliffs, the Pioneer Mothers Memorial Forest, and the Lick Creek Settlement, the home of the first African American settlers in the area. The Little Blue River, which runs through the southern part of the forest, is especially popular for canoeing.

INDIANA DUNES NATIONAL LAKESHORE

45 miles west of South Bend; 50 miles southeast of Chicago.

1100 North Mineral Springs Road
Porter, IN 46304-1299
219-926-7561
http://www.nps.gov/indu

 **Eastern National.** (446 North Lane, Conshohocken, PA 19428; 800-355-5566)

Formed by centuries of erosion and other natural forces, the Indiana Dunes National Lakeshore includes sand dunes that rise 126 feet above Lake Michigan's southern shore. Walking through the dunes, visitors will find a variety of ecosystems: sandy beaches, bogs, marshes, swamps, and prairie remnants. The sands of the dunes are known as "singing sands" because the uniformity of the dunes' size and roundness results in an even distribution of grains. The grains move over one another "in harmony" and create a ringing sound along the beach. Historic sites include a French fur trader's homestead and the Chellberg Family farm (c. 1900), where visitors can participate in historic farming techniques and quotidian domestic tasks. Also located here is the Paul H. Douglas Center for Environmental Education.

 **SAM'S TIPS**

- The Pinhook Bog Trail, a short boardwalk trail, passes through one of the last remaining bogs in Indiana. This wetland is an example of a quaking kettle-hole bog, more typical of the northeastern United States. Because it is such a fragile environment, the bog is open for weekly programs by reservation only. The park also includes many self-guided trails, including the Lycukiwe Trail, the West Beach Succession Trail, and the historic Bailly Chellberg Trail.

LINCOLN BOYHOOD NATIONAL MEMORIAL

30 miles northeast of Evansville; 60 miles southwest of Louisville, KY.

Lincoln City, IN 47552
812-937-4541
http://www.nps.gov/libo

 **Eastern National.** (446 North Lane, Conshohocken, PA 19428; 800-355-5566)

In 1816, 7-year-old Abraham Lincoln and his family moved to Indiana from Kentucky. He stayed in this area until 1830, when he left for Illinois and began a career that would carry him to the White House. The Lincoln Living Historical Farm depicts pioneer life in the 1820s and features a cabin and other log buildings, livestock, gardens, and crops. From May through September, park rangers dressed in period clothing perform day-to-day chores of the 1820s.

Sam's Tips

- Abraham Lincoln's mother, Nancy Hanks Lincoln, who died in 1818, is buried in a cemetery just north of the Visitor Center. The Trail of Twelve Stones connects Lincoln's boyhood home site with his mother's grave. The twelve stones, donated by various groups, represent major events in Lincoln's life and career. The seventh stone, for example, is from the White House in Washington, DC.

Points of Interest

U.S. ARMY CORPS OF ENGINEERS

CAGLES MILL LAKE

The lake features the largest waterfall in the state, a rock cut showing a number of geologic ages, native hardwood trees, a state park, and a nearby covered bridge. From Terre Haute, 30 miles east on I-70, 5 miles south on IN 243.

CECIL M. HARDEN LAKE

Fall forest colors are vivid in October, when Parke County holds its nine-day Covered Bridge Festival. Turkey Run State Park is 20 miles away. From Indianapolis, 55 miles west on US 36.

FALLS OF THE OHIO WILDLIFE CONSERVATION AREA

This is the only congressionally designated Wildlife Conservation Area managed by the Corps. The site is world-renowned for extensive Devonian period fossil beds. Birdwatching is popular in both the spring and fall; more than 245 species of birds have been observed here. From Louisville, KY, north across the Ohio River on I-65 to Clarksville, IN, then take Exit 0 west on Riverside Drive.

SALAMONIE LAKE

Attractions include Hanging Rock, located 2 miles downstream from the dam, and Old Canal Locks at Lagro. From Wabash, south on IN 15, east on IN 124, and then north on IN 105 to Lost Bridge recreation sites.

IOWA

EFFIGY MOUNDS NATIONAL MONUMENT

60 miles northwest of Dubuque; 3 miles north of Marquette, IA.

151 Highway 76
Harpers Ferry, IA 52146
319-873-3491
http://www.nps.gov/efmo

 **Eastern National.** (446 North Lane, Conshohocken, PA 19428; 800-355-5566)

The 1,475-acre Effigy Mounds National Monument is a tribute to more than 2,000 years of prehistoric Indian burial and ceremonial mound building. Within the monument's borders are 191 known prehistoric mounds; 29 are in the form of bear and bird effigies, and the remainder are conical or linear. Some mounds are monumental; the Great Bear Mound is 70 feet across the shoulders and forelegs, 137 feet long, and 3½ feet high.

SAM'S TIPS

- Hiking trails go past the mounds to a series of scenic overlooks on the high bluffs, 300 feet above the Mississippi River. Because the mounds are still considered sacred by many people, camping and picnicking are prohibited within the monument.

Effigy Mounds

Although prehistoric Indian burial mounds are fairly common in North America, "effigy" mounds, or mounds resembling animals, were built only in southern Wisconsin and in nearby areas in Minnesota, Illinois, and Iowa. Archaeologists believe that the mounds were built between 500 B.C. and A.D. 1300 by Woodland Indians, who used the mounds for social and religious purposes, and also perhaps to delineate hunting and gathering territories. The Indians were hunter-gatherers and survived by collecting wild rice, nuts, fruits, berries, fresh water mussels, and fish. These prehistoric people did not have any tribal affiliations. No one knows whether the Effigy Mounds people departed the region or stayed in place and underwent cultural change. We do know that the people who lived here during the 1400s gained much of their sustenance from agriculture, a way of life quite different from any of the other mound-building groups.

HERBERT HOOVER NATIONAL HISTORIC SITE

30 miles southeast of Cedar Rapids on I-80, exit 254.

Box 607
West Branch, IA 52358
319-643-2541
http://www.nps.gov/heho

 **Eastern National.** (446 North Lane, Conshohocken, PA 19428; 800-355-5566)

The Herbert Hoover National Historic Site celebrates the life of the 31st President of the United States. Highlights of the park include Hoover's Birthplace Cottage, a blacksmith shop, a Friends meetinghouse, a schoolhouse, the Presidential Library and Museum, and the gravesites of President Hoover and his wife, Lou.

Remodeled in 1992, the Herbert Hoover Presidential Library and Museum features a Humanitarian Gallery, which highlights President Hoover's international efforts. Visitors can play the Hoover Quote Game, an electronic history game, and peek into the President's fishing cabin.

POINTS OF INTEREST

U.S. ARMY CORPS OF ENGINEERS

COALVILLE LAKE

Recreation opportunities are available at five federal recreation developments and the adjacent Lake MacBride State Park. From I-80, take Dubuque Street (Exit 244) north to the Coralville Lake turnoff.

LAKE RED ROCK

Six major park developments offer camping and day-use activities. A state wildlife management area provides refuge and public hunting. It is located 4 miles southwest of Pella, on County Road T15.

RATHBURN LAKE

Over 1,000 campsites are available at this 11,000-acre lake in the rolling hills of southern Iowa. The excellent fishing, hunting, sailing, state fish hatchery, and floating restaurant are major attractions. From Des Moines, 85 miles southeast on IA 5.

SAYLORVILLE LAKE

In the heart of Iowa, 11 miles north of Des Moines. The 14 recreational areas offer camping and a variety of other outdoor activities. From Des Moines, I-235 west, then I-35 north to IA 141.

FISH AND WILDLIFE SERVICE

WALNUT CREEK NATIONAL WILDLIFE REFUGE

Located in Jasper County, the refuge recreates 8,000 acres of tallgrass prairie and oak savanna, plus the native plant and animal communities that existed in central Iowa prior to Eurasian settlement in the 1840s. The Refuge Prairie Learning Center facilities include a visitor center with a bookstore, a theater, classrooms, and an exhibit area. Outside, miles of trails radiate from the Center as does an 800-acre drive-through bison enclosure. Teachers' workshops, birding, hiking, biking, mushrooming, and wildlife watching are featured activities. The address is:

Walnut Creek National Wildlife Refuge–Prairie Learning Center
PO Box 399
Prairie City, IA 50228
515-994-2415

For more information on Iowa's other National Wildlife Refuges, contact:

Public Affairs Office
1 Federal Drive, Federal Building
Fort Snelling, MN 55111-4056
612-725-3519
http://www.fws.gov/~r3pao

BAT BARRACKS

Maintaining abandoned mines for bats is both simple and cost-effective. To protect these crucial bat habitats, the U.S. Forest Service is installing iron grates over abandoned mine entrances. These "bat-gates" serve two primary purposes: they protect the public from stumbling into a mine, and they provide habitat for bats. With approximately 25,000 abandoned mines on Forest Service lands and an estimated 200,000 across the United States, there is great potential to make a significant positive impact on bat populations through this method of protection.

Abandoned mines have become key year-round resources for bats for rearing young in summer, hibernating in winter, and resting during migration. Without the mines, many species' migratory mortality could greatly increase.

During hibernation, bats, due to their colonial nature, are especially vulnerable to vandals and to rapid mine closures. The Canoe Creek State Park limestone mine in Pennsylvania was reopened in the nick of time to save its bats and now shelters the largest bat hibernating population in the state. The difference that protecting and stabilizing even one mine shaft can make is tremendous.

KANSAS

BROWN V. BOARD OF EDUCATION NATIONAL HISTORIC SITE

Topeka.

424 South Kansas Avenue, Suite 220
Topeka, KS 66603-3441
913-354-4273
http://www.nps.gov/brvb

The landmark 1954 Supreme Court decision, stating that "separate educational facilities are inherently unequal," effectively ended racial segregation in the public schools of this country. That decision is commemorated at Monroe School, the segregated school attended by Linda Brown, in whose name the suit was brought. Brown was represented before the Supreme Court by Thurgood Marshall, who later became its first African American Justice. Presently, The Monroe Elementary School is not open to the public. Tours are scheduled by special requests only to the above phone number.

FORT LARNED NATIONAL HISTORIC SITE

140 miles northwest of Wichita; 6 miles west of Larned, on State Highway 156.

Route 3
Larned, KS 67550
316-285-6911
http://www.nps.gov/fols

Southwest Parks and Monuments Association. (221 N. Court Avenue, Tucson, AZ 85701; 520-622-1999)

Between 1822 and 1880, the Santa Fe Trail—connecting Independence, Missouri, and Santa Fe, New Mexico—was a key route for settlers and commercial traffic. To help protect the trail from Indian raids, the US Army established Fort Larned (named for the Army Paymaster-General, Benjamin Larned) on the bank of the Pawnee River, in October 1859. The fort also served as an agency of the Bureau of Indian Affairs. Today, visitors can tour the fort's main buildings, including the barracks (now a visitor center), the officers' quarters, and the commissaries, or walk along the portion of the Santa Fe Trail that passes by the site.

FORT SCOTT NATIONAL HISTORIC SITE

90 miles south of Kansas City, KS, at the intersection of U.S. Highways 69 and 54.

Old Fort Boulevard
Fort Scott, KS 66701-1471
316-223-0310
http://www.nps.gov/fosc

Southwest Parks and Monuments Association. (221 N. Court Avenue, Tucson, AZ 85701; 520-622-1999)

Fort Scott served many different purposes over its history—a peacekeeper on the Indian frontier, a Union supply center during the Civil War, and a security division for the protection of railroad workers. Today, visitors can explore 20 reconstructed and restored fort buildings and learn more about how the fort operated during each of these periods. Fort Scott offers educational programs to visiting school groups, including guided tours, living history programs, and "Life on the Frontier," a special program introducing aspects of life at the fort to children in grades K–5.

POINTS OF INTEREST

U.S. ARMY CORPS OF ENGINEERS

COUNCIL GROVE LAKE

Named for the nearby town of Council Grove, where the Osage Indians signed a treaty to establish the Old Santa Fe Trail. From Topeka, 30 miles south on KS Turnpike, then west on US 56.

EL DORADO LAKE

An overlook provides an unobstructed view of this 8,000-acre lake. From Wichita, about 20 miles northeast via I-35, then 6 miles east on KS 54, and 1 mile north on KS 177.

ELK CITY LAKE

A rock bluff marks the north margin of the river for several miles above the dam site. The State of Kansas uses 11,680 acres of project lands for wildlife management and public hunting. From Independence, 7 miles north on US 75, 4 miles west and 2 miles south on Country Road.

HILLSDALE LAKE

This newly developed lake is located in the transition zone between the western prairie lands and the eastern hardwood forests, which makes it attractive to all types of wildlife. From Kansas City, 26 miles south on I-35, 12 miles south on US 169, and 2 miles west to Hillsdale Lake.

KANOPOLIS LAKE
The nearby Fort Harker Museum at Kanopolis and the Rogers Art Gallery and Museum at Ellsworth portray the settlement of the American West. From Salina, 26 miles southeast on KS 140, then 10 miles south on KS 141.

MELVERN LAKE
Located on the east edge of the Flint Hills region, Melvern features a 12-mile equestrian trail. From Topeka, 39 miles south on US 75. From Kansas City, 72 miles southwest on I-35.

PERRY LAKE
Hikers will enjoy the scenic beauty of the 30-mile National Recreation Trail, which follows the eastern shoreline. From Topeka, 17 miles northeast on US 24 to Perry.

POMONA LAKE
Located near the Santa Fe Trail, this 4,000-acre lake features scenic beauty as well as an abundance of wildlife. From Topeka, 24 miles south on US 75, 7 miles east on KS 268.

WILD RESOURCES, EDIBLE PLANTS?

The National Park Service reports that, of the estimated 250,000 to 750,000 plant species, only a handful have been studied for their medicinal value. Almost one quarter of all prescription drugs sold in the United States (an $8 billion-a-year market) contain natural substances. Alkaloids, plant substances especially common in tropical plants, are used in cancer-fighting drugs, painkillers, blood-pressure boosters, antimalarials, and musclerelaxants. Aspirin and penicillin, two of the best known drugs, also have natural origins.

There are almost 80,000 species of edible plants, but fewer than 20 produce 90 percent of the world's food. When diseases or climate changes decimate commercial crops, farmers rely on genetic infusions from the natural world to create new, hardier, disease-resistant strains. Likewise, commercial fishing, a $75 billion-a-year industry, relies on estuaries and protected coastal areas for continued fish spawning. National parks and other preserves are necessary to ensure that vital wild resources and their genetic information will continue to exist.

U.S. BUREAU OF RECLAMATION

CEDAR BLUFF RESERVOIR

Box 76A, Ellis, KS 67637; 913-726-3212. Located 15 miles south of WaKeeney. Nearest highway: Kansas 283. Reservoir open 24 hours. Good access roads. Fishing season year-round.

CHENEY RESERVOIR

Cheney State Park, RR 1, Pretty Prairie, KS 67570; 316-542-3664. Nearest main highway: US 54. Nearest major city: Wichita. The lake is about 9,500 acres of open water, accessible from numerous roads. Several boat ramps, camping facilities. Open to fishing year-round.

KIRWIN RESERVOIR NATIONAL WILDLIFE REFUGE

Route 1, Box 103, Kirwin, KS 67644; 913-543-6673. Located 5 miles southeast of Philipsburg. Nearest highway: Kansas 183. Reservoir open 24 hours. Good access roads. Fishing season year-round.

KEITH SEBELIUS RESERVOIR

Norton Wildlife Area, Box 431, Norton, KS 67654; 913-877-2953. Located 4 miles southwest of Norton. Nearest highway: US 36. Reservoir open 24 hours. Good access roads. Fishing season year-round.

LOVEWELL RESERVOIR

RR 1, Box 66A, Weber, KS 66970; 913-753-4971. Located 10 miles south of Superior, NE. Nearest highway: Kansas 14. Reservoir open 24 hours. Fair access roads. Fishing season year-round.

WACONDA RESERVOIR

Box 298, Glen Elder, KS 67446; State Park 913-545-3345 or Wildlife 913-781-4884. Located 2 miles east of Downs. Nearest highway: US 24. Reservoir open 24 hours. Good access roads. Fishing season year-round.

KENTUCKY

ABRAHAM LINCOLN BIRTHPLACE NATIONAL HISTORIC SITE

3 miles south of Hodgenville, KY.

2995 Lincoln Farm Road
Hodgenville, KY 42748
502-358-3137
http://www.nps.gov/abli

 **Eastern National.** (446 North Lane, Conshohocken, PA 19428; 800-355-5566)

Abraham Lincoln was born in a cabin at Sinking Spring Farm, Kentucky, in 1809. Today, visitors to the area can take a walking tour that includes the Sinking Spring (now a large depression), trails that pass many of the plants and animals on which the family depended, and the Memorial Building. The cabin on display in the Memorial Building was once thought to be the actual cabin in which the 16th U.S. President was born. Outside experts have expressed doubts, but the National Park Service research indicates otherwise. The cabin is now referred to as the "symbolic" birthplace cabin. The Lincoln Museum and the Lincoln Boyhood Home, Knob Creek Farm, are nearby.

CUMBERLAND GAP NATIONAL HISTORICAL PARK

In parts of Kentucky, Virginia, and Tennessee. The Visitor Center is located in Middlesboro, KY.

Box 1848
Middlesboro, KY 40965
606-248-2817
http://www.nps.gov/cuga

 **Eastern National.** (PO Box 156, Middlesboro, KY 40965; 606-248-2817)

This tri-state park covers more than 20,000 acres. For northern and mid-Atlantic colonists, the Appalachian Mountains presented a formidable barrier to westward travel. In the South, however, Cumberland Gap had long been used to cross the Appalachians. Indians learned of it by following the buffalo, and it became a major route to the hunting grounds of Kentucky. Raiding parties were so common in the Gap that its path was said to be marked by the bleached bones of slain enemies. Daniel Boone marked the trail through the Gap that became known as the Wilderness Road. By the 1820s, other routes across the Appalachians had opened, and the Gap began to decline in importance. But it had already overseen the opening of the American West.

DANIEL BOONE NATIONAL FOREST

40 miles east of Lexington; 30 miles east of Winchester.

1700 Bypass Road
Winchester, KY 40391
606-745-3100
http://www.fs.fed.us

Cradle of Forestry in America Interpretive Association. (100 S. Broad Street, Brevard, NC 28712; 704-884-5713)

The Daniel Boone National Forest, formerly known as the Cumberland National Forest, was renamed in 1966 for the famed woodsman who explored the Kentucky wilderness and returned with other pioneers to establish a settlement at Fort Boonesboro. Located in the eastern Kentucky mountains, the forest covers portions of 21 counties and contains more than 690,000 acres. The land is generally rugged, with steep slopes, narrow valleys, and cliffs. In the south end of the forest, slopes are not as steep and ridgetops are generally more flat. The Red River Gorge Geological Area, which surrounds the river's middle section, contains more than 80 major natural arches formed by wind and water erosion over the past 70 million years.

Sam's Tips

- The most spectacular natural bridge at the Red River Gorge Geological Area is Sky Bridge, a solid rock span stretching along the top of a thin ridge. This geological area also contains the Clifty Wilderness.
- Near-record catches have established Cave Run Lake as one of the top muskie fishing holes in the country.
- The Sheltowee Trace National Recreation Trail starts at the northern end of the forest and runs for approximately 269 miles through deep canyons, along narrow ridgetops, and through areas of strikingly beautiful rimrock cliffs. "Sheltowee," an Indian word meaning Big Turtle, was the name given to Daniel Boone by Chief Blackfish when he adopted him as his son into the Shawnee Tribe.
- The Beaver Creek Wilderness contains numerous "rock houses" or cliff overhangs once used as shelter by Native Americans.

FOREST SERVICE SCENIC BYWAY

Zilpo Road

Zilpo Road travels for 9 miles through the Daniel Boone National Forest, alongside Cave Run Lake and Zilpo Recreation Area. The road is popular for viewing seasonal color and wildlife. *Contact Daniel Boone National Forest.*

LAND BETWEEN THE LAKES NATIONAL RECREATION AREA

Golden Pond, in the middle of the area, is 35 miles southwest of Hopkinsville, KY.

100 Van Morgan Drive
Golden Pond, KY 42211-9001
502-924-2000
http://www.lbl.org

 **Land Between the Lakes Association.** (same address as above; 502-924-5897)

Created by President John F. Kennedy, in 1963, as the country's only "national demonstration area" to blend environmental education, outdoor recreation, and natural resource management, Land Between the Lakes, located in western Kentucky and Tennessee, has more than 170,000 acres of rolling hills and 300 miles of undeveloped shoreline bordering about a quarter million acres of water. Boat, swim, and fish in secluded bays; camp at developed or primitive sites; and hike, bike, or ride horses along forested trails. The largest continuous block of public land east of the Mississippi, Land Between the Lakes is operated by the Tennessee Valley Authority.

Sam's Tips

- The Nature Station has a large "backyard" where you can find live specimens of native wildlife, including red wolves, golden and bald eagles, and more common species. It also includes an indoor learning center with interactive exhibits and video presentations. Programs are provided for prescheduled groups. One of the most popular programs is "Habitat Gardening," which demonstrates how to attract hummingbirds, butterflies, wildlife, and insects to a garden—even if the garden is a window box.
- The Golden Pond Planetarium, located inside the Visitor Center, offers a variety of astronomy programs and seasonal specials for audiences of all ages.
- The Buffalo Herd, begun in 1969 with 19 animals from the Theodore Roosevelt National Memorial Park in North Dakota, is now the largest publicly owned herd in the eastern United States. The herd has been so popular for wildlife viewing (the most popular activity here), that the Land Between the Lakes established a 750-acre enclosed Elk and Bison Prairie Habitat, a 3.5-mile loop drive, featuring approximately 29 elk and 40 buffalo. Tokens for the drive are available at all facilities and at the Prairie Habitat itself. Other opportunities for wildlife viewing are provided by bicycle, canoe, and van tours. If you didn't bring your own, rentals are available: mountain bikes at Hillman Ferry Campground, road bicycles at the Nature Station, and canoes at the Nature Station and the Energy Lake campground. Guided horseback tours and guided trail rides (for the horseless) are conducted from J Bar J Stable at Wranglers Campground, the premier horse camp in the mid-South region. Primitive log cabins also are available here and at Piney Campground.

- For a strong taste of the region's 19th-century culture, visit The Homeplace—1850: A Living History Farm. This working recreation of a local homestead farm features period log buildings, minor breeds of farm animals, and guides in period clothing performing the daily chores. This is not a look-but-don't-touch museum; there is lots here to do. Visitors can help with the chores, from quilt making to butter churning to tending the garden of heirloom plants. The Family Living History Weekend permits families to join in and even to dress in period clothes. Place reservations at the address above.
- The Turkey Bay Off-Highway Vehicle Area, the first federally designated area for off-highway vehicle riding, offers terrain for various skill levels.

MAMMOTH CAVE NATIONAL PARK

The visitor center is 85 miles southwest of Louisville, KY.

Mammoth Cave, KY 42259-0007
502-758-2328
http://www.nps.gov/maca

 **Eastern National.** (446 North Lane, Conshohocken, PA 19428; 800-355-5566)

Beneath the sandstone-capped ridges of Mammoth Cave National Park lies the most extensive cave system on Earth, much of it still unexplored. Geologists estimate that there could be as many as 600 miles of undiscovered passageways. The cave itself, with approximately 130 forms of life, is the world's most diverse cave ecosystem. Mammoth Cave was one of the nation's first tourist attractions. Tours began in the early 1800s; it became a National Park in 1926. The Green River, which flows through the park, is one of North America's most biologically diverse rivers.

Mammoth Cave's History

Native Americans discovered Mammoth Cave about 4,000 years ago. Archaeological evidence indicates that these early cavers explored about 10 miles of the passageways and collected crystals and other salts found in the cave. Exploration and use of the cave ceased some 2,000 years ago and did not begin again until its rediscovery by settlers in the early 1800s. During the War of 1812, slaves mined sediments for salt to be used in the manufacture of gunpowder. Tours began in 1816.

By 1941, just 40 miles of passageways had been mapped. As surveying techniques improved, great strides were made in describing and understanding the overwhelming extent of the cave system. To date, 350 miles of passages have been surveyed in the Mammoth Cave system. Several caves in the park have been found to be connected, and the cave system is known to extend well beyond the park's boundary.

The Caves, the Water, and the Ecosystems

Like most major caves, Mammoth Cave was formed by the slow dissolution of limestone by groundwater. As rainwater falls and infiltrates soil, it picks up small amounts of carbon dioxide gas. The carbon dioxide reacts with the water to form a weak solution of carbonic acid, making the groundwater itself a mildly acidic solution.

Over time, as the groundwater dissolved the limestone, it formed underground streams. These streams converged and created the large underground rivers of Mammoth Cave. The cave streams follow lower routes up to 360 feet below the surface, creating the network of cave passages. Rain that falls outside the park travels underground and sculpts Mammoth Cave daily. Plants and animals that live in the cave depend on the quantity and quality of this water, and if human activities outside the park pollute the water supply, the cave and its life are threatened. Today, the National Park Service and its neighbors are working together to help protect the cave and the life inside.

Sam's Tips

- The park offers a number of extremely popular guided tours, both on the surface and underground.
- On the "Trog Tour," designed specifically for children 8 to 12 years old, parents must accompany the children for the first 15 minutes. It includes a nature walk above ground and a journey into cave passageways. Children must be prepared to do some crawling. Helmets and lights are provided. To find out more about this and other cave tours, go to the Mammoth Cave's Expanded World Wide Web page: http://www.nps.gov/maca/tours.htm.
- More than 60 miles of above-ground trails are open for horseback riding. Horses may be rented from a concessionaire outside the park.
- One-hour boat cruises are available from April through October, weather permitting, aboard the *Miss Green River II.* Buy tickets in advance at the Visitor Center.

Points of Interest

U.S. ARMY CORPS OF ENGINEERS

BARREN RIVER LAKE

A 10,000-acre lake in the slightly rolling, timbered countryside. From Louisville, 95 miles south on I-65 to Cave City, 10 miles south on KY 90 to Glasgow, 5 miles south on US 31 to KY 252, and 9 miles south to the dam.

DALE HOLLOW LAKE

Located in the Highland Rim section of northern Tennessee and southern Kentucky, Dale Hollow's crystalline waters are ideal for virtually all water sports, including scuba diving. A federal fish hatchery and Standing Stone State Park are nearby. From Nashville, 69 miles east on I-40, 17 miles north to TN 56, 23 miles north on TN 53 to Celina, and then follow the signs.

GRAYSON LAKE

Vertical rock cliffs rim the lake's 40 miles of shoreline. See the well-preserved log cabin at the project and visit the caves at nearby Carter Caves State Park, 7 miles south of Grayson on KY 7.

GREEN RIVER LAKE

In the hills of central Kentucky. An interpretive center at the dam site acquaints visitors with the geology, culture, and history of the area. Tebbs Bend, a Civil War battlefield area, is nearby. Located 90 miles southeast of Louisville via I-65 and KY 61, KY 210, and KY 55.

LAKE CUMBERLAND

Cumberland Falls, located on the upstream end of this lake in southern Kentucky, is famous for a "moonbow" that can be seen on clear, moonlit nights. Restored Mill Springs Mill adds a touch of living history to an area rich in local legend. Canoeing opportunities are numerous and include the famous Big South Fork and Rockcastle River. From Somerset, KY, 5 miles south off US 27 on Boat Dock Road.

LAUREL RIVER LAKE

Located in the heart of Daniel Boone National Forest, this lake has clear water and excellent largemouth bass fishing. Recreational facilities include campgrounds, boat ramps, picnic areas, hiking trails, and more. From London, KY, 20 miles west on KY 1193.

MARTINS FORK LAKE

Fed by the clear waters of Martins Fork Creek, this small but attractive 340-acre lake offers excellent recreational opportunities in the scenic mountainous terrain of Harlan County, 16 miles southeast of Harlan on KY 987.

MICHIGAN

HIAWATHA NATIONAL FOREST

Michigan's Upper Peninsula, 95 miles northeast of Green Bay, WI.

2727 N. Lincoln Road
Escanaba, MI 49829
906-786-4062
http://www.fs.fed.us

 **Eastern National Forests.** (PO Box 70, East Tawas, MI 48730)

Tucked among three of the Great Lakes and within the central and eastern portions of Michigan's upper peninsula, the Hiawatha National Forest is divided into an eastern portion stretching north from St. Ignace (along Lakes Michigan and Huron) to the shore of Lake Superior, and a western portion extending from Rapid River (along Lake Michigan) to the town of Munising on the shore of Lake Superior. The forest is comprised of hills thick with northern hardwoods, white pine, and hemlock; flatland covered by red pine, jack pine, and aspen; and large open and tree-covered wetlands.

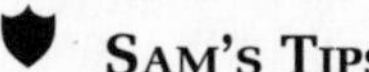

Sam's Tips

- Three lighthouses lie within the boundaries of the forest; two of them, Point Iroquois and Peninsula Point, are open to visitors.
- The 100-foot-long Naomikong Suspension Bridge spans the Naomikong River, which delivers water to Lake Superior. Naomikong Point was once an important fishing ground and was the location of a mission outpost during the 1800s. "Naomikong" is an Ojibwa Indian word meaning "where the breakers strike the shore."

Grand Island National Recreation Area

Located in Lake Superior, a half mile offshore from Munising, MI, Grand Island has probably been inhabited for the past 2,300 years. Recent investigations indicate that it was an important center for the Ojibwa people in the 16th century. Fur trading posts were established in the late 1700s and early 1800s, and the first permanent European settlers came to the island in 1840. The Forest Service's newest Recreation Area, Grand Island, can be reached by scheduled ferry during the summer and by snowmobile when the lake is frozen. The island's North Light is said to be the highest lighthouse above sea level in the world. For more information contact: Grand Island National Recreation Area, 400 East Munising Avenue, Munising, MI 49862; 906-387-3700.

FOREST SERVICE SCENIC BYWAY

Whitefish Bay Scenic Byway

Within a day's drive from Detroit, Milwaukee, or Grand Rapids, the Whitefish Bay Scenic Byway in the Hiawatha National Forest follows the south shore of Lake Superior's Whitefish Bay, where sandy beaches, hardwood-covered sand dunes, and glacial moraines abound. Points of interest include Point Iroquois Lighthouse and a wide range of recreational facilities. *Contact Hiawatha National Forest.*

- When completed, the North Country National Scenic Trail will be the longest continuous footpath in the United States, traveling for 90 miles through the Hiawatha National Forest among northern hardwoods and coniferous forests.
- The straits of the Great Lakes act as a funnel for bird migrations in the spring and fall. Rare wildlife includes the Cerulean warbler, northern goshawk, sandhill crane, loggerhead shrike, bald eagle, and timber wolf. Waters surrounding and within the forest create microclimates in habitats that support threatened and endangered plants. Some special plants found in the forest include heart's tongue fern, pitchers thistle, dwarf lake iris, Houghton's goldenrod, and monkey-flower.

HURON–MANISTEE NATIONAL FORESTS

100 miles north of Grand Rapids, on US Highway 131.

1755 South Mitchell Street
Cadillac, MI 49601
616-775-2421
800-821-6263
http://www.fs.fed.us

Eastern National Forests Interpretive Association. (PO Box 70, East Tawas, MI 48730; 517-362-7511)

Located in the northern lower peninsula of Michigan, the Huron–Manistee National Forests—two national forests, combined in 1945—cover approximately 964,413 acres of wetlands, rivers, and wilderness. The Huron–Manistee area is home to five wild and scenic rivers: portions of the PereMarquette, Au Sable, Pine, Manistee, and Bear Creek rivers. The forest is home to rare regional fauna, such as the Kirtland's warbler, which has had a record number of recent sightings. The Loda Lake Wildflower Sanctuary is home to rare regional flora.

FOREST SERVICE SCENIC BYWAY

River Road

These 22 miles along the south bank of the Au Sable River offer panoramic views of reservoirs surrounded by forests as high as 150–200 feet, and opportunities to view bald eagles and spawning salmon. *Contact Huron–Manistee National Forest.*

ISLE ROYALE NATIONAL PARK

In Lake Superior, 22 miles from Grand Portage; 50 miles north of the Keweenaw Peninsula; 13 miles from Ontario.

800 East Lakeshore Drive
Houghton, MI 49931
906-482-0984
http://www.nps.gov/isro

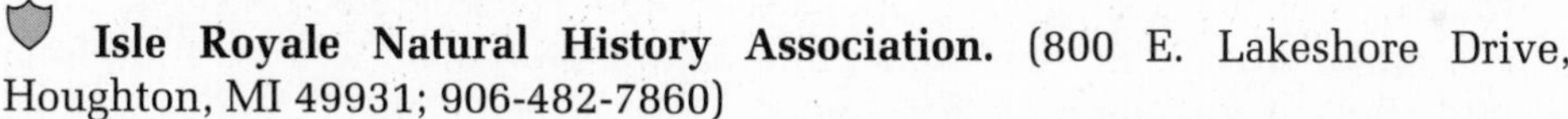

Isle Royale Natural History Association. (800 E. Lakeshore Drive, Houghton, MI 49931; 906-482-7860)

Isle Royale, accessible only by boat or floatplane, is the largest island (40 miles long) in Lake Superior, the largest freshwater lake in the world. One of the few national parks that is almost 100 percent wilderness, the island is a roadless land of almost unspoiled forests, inland lakes, and rugged, scenic shores. Part of an archipelago made of lava and sandstone, this area is rich in flora and fauna. So rich and pristine (99 percent of the island is legally designated wilderness) and so varied are its habitats (bogs, swamps, and marshes, in addition to thickets and forests), that it has been declared an International Biosphere Reserve for its capacity to maintain the native life and natural processes of the north woods. Long before Europeans saw Isle Royale, Indians mined here for copper. Archaeologists have excavated their shallow mining pits, some dating back 4,500 years. Today, the island is home to one of the largest herds of moose in the United States, as many as 200 species of birds and several packs of Eastern timber wolves that crossed an ice bridge formed between Canada and the island during the bitter-cold winter of 1948–1949.

SAM'S TIPS

- Transportation to the island is available aboard the National Park's boat, *Ranger III,* from Houghton, MI (906-482-0984); the *Isle Royale Queen III,* from Copper Harbor, MI (906-289-4437); and the *Voyageur II* and *Wenonah,* from Grand Portage, MN (715-392-2100). Seaplane service is also provided from Houghton, MI. Call 906-482-8850 (late May through September) for advance reservations.

- Three types of camping are available at Isle Royale: three-sided shelters (maximum, 6 people), tent sites (6 people) for 1 to 3 tents, and group sites (parties of 7 to 10 people). Groups may not exceed 10 at any time while hiking or camping. An organized group may bring 20 people at any one time to the island. Each group must submit a separate itinerary that will not overlap any of their overnight stays on the island. Advance reservations are required for all camping parties of 7 to 10 people and for all organizations visiting the park with 7 or more people.
- The island is known for its excellent cold-water scuba diving and historic shipwrecks. At least 10 major shipwrecks, most dating back to the late 1800s and early 1900s, are within a few miles of the island.
- Three park highlights are: (1) Ojibwa Tower, with a scenic view of the island's topography; (2) the Edisen Fishery, a restored commercial fishery near the Rock Harbor Lighthouse, which was built in 1855 to guide ships safely to ports on the island; and (3) the Windigo Self-Guiding Trail, which is one of the most preferred "Watchable Wildlife" sites in the country.
- From June through September, guests can stay in the Rock Harbor Lodge, which is located along the shore of Rock Harbor. The resort features lodge rooms, as well as cottages, equipped with a refrigerator, electric stove, utensils, and dishware. For additional information or to make a reservation from mid-May to September, contact: National Park Concessions, Inc., PO Box 405, Houghton, MI 49931-0405; 906-337-4993. For information or reservations during the rest of the year, contact: National Park Concessions, Inc., Mammoth Cave, KY 42259-0027; 502-773-2191.

KEWEENAW NATIONAL HISTORICAL PARK

175 miles north of Green Bay, WI.

PO Box 471
Calumet, MI 49913
906-337-3168
http://www.nps.gov/kewe

Keweenaw Tourism Council. (1197 Calumet Avenue, Calumet, MI 49913; 906-337-4579)

The Keweenaw National Historical Park was established in 1992 to commemorate the heritage of copper mining on the Keweenaw Peninsula—site of America's first mineral rush, several years before the famed California Gold Rush. Keweenaw has been mined for 7,000 years, longer than anywhere else in the Western Hemisphere. In the Calumet unit of the park, visitors can follow wayside exhibits through the grounds and town of what was America's most productive copper mine. The Quincy unit features the world's largest steam hoist, a panoramic tram ride, and tours of the underground workings of the Quincy Mine. The walking tour of Laurium's historic residential district takes visitors to homes of prominent leaders of the mining industry as well as local hero George Gipp ("the Gipper"), who played football for the University of Notre Dame.

OTTAWA NATIONAL FOREST

Michigan's Upper Peninsula, 210 miles northeast of Green Bay, WI.

2100 East Cloverland Drive
Ironwood, MI 49938
906-932-1330
http://www.fs.fed.us/r9/ottawa

Ottawa Interpretive Association. (PO Box 276, Watersmeet, MI 49969; 906-358-4724)

The one million acres of the Ottawa National Forest feature magnificent views of rolling hills studded with lakes, rivers, and spectacular waterfalls. Elevations range from 600 feet at the Lake Superior shoreline to more than 1,800 feet in the Sylvania Wilderness. The most dramatic changes come near Lake Superior, where the upward shift of the land exposes bedrock, and the resulting bluffs provide homes for cliff-nesting peregrine falcons. Approximately 118 miles of the North Country National Scenic Trail cross the forest.

Sam's Tips

- Winter sports thrive on the area's 200-plus inches of annual snow. Popular activities during the season include Alpine and Nordic skiing, snowmobiling, dog sledding, and ice fishing.
- The Black River Scenic Byway features waterfalls, old-growth Eastern white pine and hemlock, and the historic Black River Harbor Village.
- Anglers will enjoy more than 500 lakes and nearly 2,000 miles of rivers and streams. The forest hosts several festivals during the year, including fishing derbies in June, the Upper Peninsula Championship Rodeo in July, and the Log Jamboree in September.

PICTURED ROCKS NATIONAL LAKESHORE

140 miles northeast of Green Bay, WI.

PO Box 40
Munising, MI 49862
906-387-3700
http://www.nps.gov/piro

 **Eastern National.** (446 North Lane, Conshohocken, PA 19428; 800-355-5566)

Pictured Rocks, the first national lakeshore in the United States, hugs the upper peninsular coast of Lake Superior for more than 40 miles. The 73,000-acre park, only 3 miles across at its widest point, offers multicolored sandstone cliffs, beaches, sand dunes, waterfalls, inland lakes, wildlife, and the forest. The Pictured Rocks themselves rise up from Lake Superior at heights of 50 to 200 feet. Years of erosion have sculpted the rocks into caves, arches, and formations that seem to change as the sun's rays move over them throughout the day.

Sam's Tips

- At Pictured Rocks, the most popular attractions are: Munising Falls, a 50-foot waterfall nestled in a cool, shaded valley; Sand Point Beach, popular for watching the sunset over Munising Bay; Miners Castle Trail, which leads to breathtaking overlooks of Lake Superior and Grand Island; the Grand Sable dunes, 4 square miles of dunes deposited between Grand Sable Lake and Lake Superior; and Au Sable Light Station, built in 1874 and currently being renovated by the National Park Service.
- The Alger Underwater Preserve, containing large, colorful rocks, a dozen shipwrecks, and lots of fish, extends from just west of Munising to Au Sable Point.

Beachcombing for Shipwrecks

More than 50 ships have been lost in the rough waters within Sleeping Bear Dunes. Most of these were driven into shallow water and torn to pieces by the waves and ice. Divers explore these shipwreck sites in the Manitou Passage State Underwater Preserve, but you don't have to be a diver to share the excitement of discovering and exploring shipwrecks. You will not find a complete ship washed ashore, but sections of timber frames and planking often survive intact along the beach. Look for large timbers of white oak (recognizable as black when wet and white when dry); large metal fasteners such as spikes, rods, pegs, and bolts; and hardware such as iron rings, chains, cleats, and hawsers. Some wrecks may remain visible for only a few days and then are covered up again by shifting sand. But with a little luck and perseverance, you may uncover a piece of history.

SLEEPING BEAR DUNES NATIONAL LAKESHORE

125 miles northwest of Grand Rapids.

9922 Front Street
Highway M-72
Empire, MI 49630-0277
616-326-5134
http://www.nps.gov/slbe

Eastern National. (446 North Lane, Conshohocken, PA 19428; 800-355-5566)

Chippewa Indian Legend

Long ago, in the land that today is Wisconsin, a mother bear and her two cubs were driven into Lake Michigan by a raging forest fire. They swam and swam, but soon the cubs tired and lagged far behind. The mother bear finally reached the opposite shore and climbed to the top of a bluff to watch for and await her offspring. But the cubs drowned. Today, "Sleeping Bear," a solitary dune in Michigan, overlooking Lake Michigan, marks the spot where the mother bear waited. Her hapless cubs are the Manitou Islands.

The humid, temperate summer climate of Michigan, along with high winds, make the state's lakeshores ideal places for sand dunes to form. At Sleeping Bear Dunes National Lakeshore, named after a solitary dune overlooking Lake Michigan, visitors can scramble up the towering Dune Climb, hike through the back-country, and enjoy the beaches. The Lakeshore area includes: a 35-mile stretch of Lake Michigan's eastern coastline, as well as North and South Manitou Islands; an 1871 lighthouse; three former Life-Saving Service/Coast Guard Stations; a Maritime Museum; and Cannery Historic Boat Museum. Charter operators from Traverse City offer scuba diving trips to shipwrecks in nearby Manitou Passage State Underwater Preserve.

POINTS OF INTEREST

U.S. ARMY CORPS OF ENGINEERS

LOWER KEWELENAW ENTRY WATERWAY
This entrance for Great Lakes shipping is used as a shortcut and refuge from storms on Lake Superior. Day-use facilities. From Chassell, 4 miles east on US 41.

ST. MARY'S FALLS LOCKS AND VISITOR CENTER
The world-famous "Soo Locks" were a private enterprise until transferred to the U.S. government in 1881. Visitors can see Great Lakes freighters over 1,000 feet long and "salties" (oceangoing ships) from around the world as they lock through between Lakes Superior and Huron. The waterway forms the international border between the United States and Canada in the cities of Sault Ste. Marie, MI, and Sault Ste. Marie, Ontario.

FISH AND WILDLIFE SERVICE

SHIAWASSEE NATIONAL WILDLIFE REFUGE

The Refuge comprises over 9,000 acres in central lower Michigan, approximately 25 miles southwest of Saginaw Bay. Four rivers converge in the Refuge: the Tittabawassee, Flint, Cass, and Shiawassee. The Saginaw River and its tributaries flow along the northeastern edge of the Refuge. Nature trails are restricted to hiking, biking, and cross-country skiing. The Woodland Trail at the east end of Stroebel Road is just over 3.5 miles long and has a shorter 1-mile loop. The Ferguson Bayou Trail (a National Recreation Trail) at the west end of Curtis Road is just over 4.5 miles in length and has a shorter 1.5-mile loop. The Ferguson Bayou Trail provides views of Refuge agricultural lands, moist soil units, pools, sloughs, and forested wetland areas. Two wildlife observation decks with permanently mounted spotting scopes provide added wildlife-watching opportunities.

For more information on this site, contact:

6975 Mower Road
Saginaw, MI 48601
517-777-5930

For more information on the other refuges in Michigan, contact:

Public Affairs Office
1 Federal Drive, Federal Building
Fort Snelling, MN 55111-4056
612-725-3519
http://www.fws.gov/~r3pao

BIRD AND BUTTERFLY CHECKLISTS OF THE UNITED STATES

Get to know the Northern Prairie Wildlife Research Center, a part of the U.S. Department of the Interior, accessible on the World Wide Web at http://www.npsc.nbs.gov.

Two of the Center's features to capture every aviary interest are:

The Bird Checklists of the United States. A comprehensive, state-by-state, up-to-date guide to information on bird distribution. Invaluable for both the amateur and the expert birdwatcher. Print out these lists and take them into the field with you. For further information, go to: http://www.npsc.nbs.gov/resource/othrdata/chekbird/chekbird.htm.

Butterflies of the United States. Again, courtesy of the Northern Prairie Wildlife Research Center, a similarly comprehensive guide to individual butterfly species in the United States. State maps even identify species by specific counties. Best of all are the stunning photos of butterflies at adult and caterpillar stages. For further information, go to: http://www.npsc.nbs.gov/resource/distr/lepid/bflyusa/bflyusa.htm.

MINNESOTA

CHIPPEWA NATIONAL FOREST

170 miles northwest of Minneapolis.

Route 3, Box 244
Cass Lake, MN 56633
218-335-8600
http://www.fs.fed.us/r9/chippewa

 **Lake States Interpretive Association.** (3131 Highway 53, International Falls, MN 56649-8904; 218-283-2103)

The Chippewa National Forest, more than half of it water, was the first national forest established east of the Mississippi River. Over 700 lakes, 920 miles of streams, and 150,000 acres of wetlands are remnants of the ancient glaciers that once covered the land. The forest boasts the largest breeding population of bald eagles in the lower 48 states; they often can be seen soaring over the larger lakes in the forest. There are 23 developed campgrounds and extensive opportunities for recreational fishing, hiking, canoeing, mountain biking, and more.

GRAND PORTAGE NATIONAL MONUMENT

145 miles northeast of Duluth.

PO Box 668
Grand Marais, MN 55604
218-387-2788
http://www.nps.gov/grpo

 **Eastern National.** (PO Box 668, Grand Marais, MN 55604; 218-387-2788)

Between 1784 and 1803, the North West Company ran the most profitable fur trading operation on the Great Lakes. The company's headquarters at Grand

FOREST SERVICE SCENIC BYWAY

Avenue of Pines

The 39-mile byway earned its name from a section lined with large red and Norway pines planted in the 1930s by the Civilian Conservation Corps. Many lakes add to the scenic beauty and to water activities such as fishing, canoeing, and water skiing. The area is home to nearly 300 nesting bald eagles, as well as osprey, black bear, gray wolf, deer, and raccoon. *Contact Chippewa National Forest.*

Portage was the largest fur trading post within hundreds of miles. Today, the buildings have been reconstructed and furnished to reflect those early, profitable times. Visitors can tour the Great Hall, the kitchen, a fur press, the lookout tower, and the canoe warehouse to learn more about trappers and life on the frontier in the late 1700s. Passenger boats depart from here to Isle Royale National Park.

MISSISSIPPI NATIONAL RIVER AND RECREATION AREA

Centered in St. Paul, MN.

175 E. 5th Street
Suite 418, Box 41
St. Paul, MN 55101-2901
612-290-4160
http://www.nps.gov/miss

The Mississippi National River and Recreation Area is in the first stages of becoming an operational National Park Service site. The area consists of more than 350 parks representing important examples of America's natural and cultural heritage. The river's long history has inspired Mark Twain, jazz musicians, guitar and banjo players, and the music of Native Americans. To showcase the talent that has flowed along with the river, the park sponsors an annual program series. Past programs have included: "New Songs of the Mississippi River" and "Exploring the Mississippi River Through Song." For more information, contact the park at the main address. An advocacy group, Friends of the Mississippi River, a source of useful information, may be contacted at: 26 East Exchange Street, Suite 215, St. Paul, MN 55101-2264; 612-222-2193.

PIPESTONE NATIONAL MONUMENT

165 miles southwest of Minneapolis.

36 Reservation Avenue
Pipestone, MN 56164
507-825-5464
http://www.nps.gov/pipe

Pipestone Indian Shrine Association. (PO Box 727, Pipestone, MN 56164; 507-825-5463)

Ceremonial pipe smoking was a central spiritual activity of the people who lived and worshipped along the Plains. As America grew westward, pipes found their way into White society through trade. Pipestone National Monument is a tribute to the land that produced the precious carving stones needed to make ceremonial pipes. The Upper Midwest Indian Cultural Center sponsors demonstrations of pipemaking by native craft workers, using the stones from the quarry.

SUPERIOR NATIONAL FOREST

Headquarters are in Duluth. The forest lies 60 miles to the north.

PO Box 338
Duluth, MN 55801
218-720-5324
http://www.gis.umn.edu/snf

Lake States Interpretive Association. (3131 Highway 53, International Falls, MN 56649-8904; 218-283-2103)

Spanning 150 miles of the United States–Canada border, the Superior National Forest is rich with northern pine and sizable populations of moose, deer, and bear. The forest is also one of the last strongholds of the gray wolf—a predator that has long symbolized the wildness of the north woods. About 300–400 timber wolves still roam the expanses of this wild, remote country.

One of the distinctive features of the forest is the Boundary Waters Canoe Area Wilderness, a series of interconnected lakes unparalleled in the contiguous United States. This area's recreational value has been recognized since the last part of the 19th century and was a prime reason for the establishment of the forest in 1909.

SAM'S TIPS

- The park contains more than 2,000 lakes, including those in the Boundary Waters Canoe Area Wilderness. Many have boat launches. Permits are required for summer travel in the Wilderness. They may be obtained up to 24 hours before a trip by calling 800-745-3399.

The Voyageurs

As the fur trade expanded westward, it relied heavily on voyageurs, the French-Canadian canoemen who moved pelts and trade goods between Montreal and the Canadian Northwest. Their route was so well established that the 1783 treaty ending the American Revolutionary War stipulated that the international boundary should follow their customary waterway between Lake Superior and Lake of the Woods.

The voyageurs' character has been described as daring if not brave, knowledgeable though uneducated. Above all, they were colorful. Daniel Harmon, a partner in the North West Company, wrote of them in 1819: "[The] Canadian Voyageurs possess lively and fickle dispositions; and they are rarely subject to depression of spirits of long continuance, even when the circumstances are most adverse. Although what they consider good eating and drinking constitutes their chief good, when necessity compels them to it, they submit to great privation and hardship, not only without complaining, but even with cheerfulness and gaiety. . . . Trifling provocations will often throw them into a rage, but they are easily appeased when in anger, and they never harbor a revengeful purpose against those by whom they conceive that they have been injured."

VOYAGEURS NATIONAL PARK

135 miles northwest of Duluth.

3131 Highway 53
International Falls, MN 56649-8904
218-283-9821
http://www.nps.gov/voya

Lake States Interpretive Association. (3131 Highway 53, International Falls, MN 56649-8904; 218-283-2103)

Voyageurs National Park, more than 40 percent of it water, is named for the French-Canadian trappers and traders (voyageurs) who moved furs and other trade goods between Montreal and the Canadian Northwest in their handmade birch-bark canoes. Visitors leave their cars behind and travel through the park by water, just as the voyageurs did during the fur trade heyday in the late 18th and early 19th centuries. These interconnected northern lakes, 30 of them, are dotted with islands and surrounded by forests. Between the lakes and adjacent rocky knobs and ridges extend bogs, marshes, and beaver ponds. Visitors can see kingfishers, loons, bald eagles, osprey, and great blue heron. In winter, snowmobilers and cross-country skiers travel across the frozen lakes.

Sam's Tips

- Most visitors travel park waters by motorboat, although many also travel by canoe, kayak, sailboat, or houseboat. If you'd prefer to have a guide or need to see an outfitter during your trip, ask the park for a copy of its newspaper, *Rendezvous,* which can give you specific information on outfitters, guides, charters, lodging, and other services.
- The park is the heart of the only region in the continental United States where the Eastern timber wolf survives. The park is also a prime location for birders to observe ospreys, eagles, and great blue herons, and for fishermen to catch walleye, northern pike, and smallmouth bass.
- Deep in the heart of the forest is the Kettle Falls Hotel, a former brothel for local lumberjacks, built between 1910 and 1913. A 13-mile boatride from the nearest road, it's one of the few places in the United States where you can look *south* into Canada. For information and reservations, call 800-KF-Hotel (534-6835).

Points of Interest

U.S. ARMY CORPS OF ENGINEERS

BIG SANDY LAKE

The site of a trading post in the early 1800s. Gravestones mark an Indian burial mound. From McGregor, 13 miles north on MN 65.

BIG STONE LAKE

Fishing, hunting, hiking, cross-country skiing, and nature watching are only some of the activities taking place in this 10,700-acre wildlife refuge. From Ortonville, 8 miles southeast on MN 7 and 1 mile south on US 75.

CROSS LAKE (PINE RIVER LAKE)

Located in the heart of Crow Wing State Forest, at the headwaters of the Whitefish Chain Lakes. From Brainerd, east on US 210, 8 miles north on MN 25, right on County Road 3, and 18 miles north to Cross Lake.

LAC QUI PARLE

In a rich agricultural area, the nearby Mission Park Historical Site contains replicas of early Indian life. From Montevideo, 9 miles northwest on MN 7 and MN 59.

POKEGAMA LAKE

Features a nature trail, scenic drives, and an abundance of wildlife. Nearby mining/paper mill tours available. From Grand Rapids, 2 miles west on US 2.

FISH AND WILDLIFE SERVICE

MINNESOTA VALLEY NATIONAL WILDLIFE REFUGE

This is one of only a few urban wildlife refuges in the nation, a place where wild coyotes, bald eagles, badgers, and beavers live next door to 2.2 million people. Withing this 34-mile corridor of marsh, grassland, and forest, you'll find over 300 species of animals, and opportunities for a wide range of outdoor and educational activities. Minnesota Valley National Wildlife Refuge is one of many refuges in the Great Lakes—Big Rivers Region (Region 3).

U.S. Fish and Wildlife Service
Minnesota Valley National Wildlife Refuge
3815 E. 80th St.
Bloomington, MN 55425
612-854-5900

For further information on Minnesota's other fish and wildlife refuges, contact:

U.S. Fish and Wildlife Service
1 Federal Drive
BHW Federal Building
Fort Snelling, MN 55111
http://www.fws.gov

MISSOURI

GEORGE WASHINGTON CARVER NATIONAL MONUMENT

70 miles west of Springfield, MO.

5646 Carver Road
Diamond, MO 64840
417-325-4151
http://www.nps.gov/gwca

Born as a slave, George Washington Carver ascended to national prominence as a scientist by the age of 55. Throughout his career, Carver refused to respect the "boundaries" among science, art, and religion; he drew from one realm to strengthen concepts in another. Unlike other agricultural researchers of his time, Carver saw the need to devise farming methods that were practical for use in the South. Perhaps his greatest gift was a talent for drawing others into the spirit of his research. The monument consists of 210 acres of the original 240-acre Moses Carver Farm, and contains Carver's birthplace cabin, the Moses Carver 1881 period dwelling, the three-quarter-mile Carver Trail with wayside exhibits, the Carver Family Cemetery, and the Carver Museum. Carver himself is buried at the Tuskegee Institute.

HARRY S TRUMAN NATIONAL HISTORIC SITE

Independence, MO.

223 North Main Street
Independence, MO 64050-2804
816-254-7199
http://www.nps.gov/hstr

 **Eastern National.** (446 North Lane, Conshohocken, PA 19428; 800-355-5566)

Known as the "Summer White House" during the presidency of Harry S Truman, the house at 219 North Delaware Street in Independence originally belonged to Truman's mother-in-law, Madge Gates Wallace. Truman maintained his permanent residence here from the time he married his wife, Bess, in 1919, until his death in 1972. On the eve of the 1948 election, he addressed the country by radio from his living room, and it was here that he received word of the invasion of South Korea in June 1950. After his death in 1972, his widow kept the house as it was during his lifetime and, upon her death, bequeathed it to the country.

SAM'S TIPS

- Other sites in the Independence area that feature the history of the Trumans include the Harry S Truman Library, the Harry S Truman Railroad Station, and

The Civil War and Carver's Upbringing

Born into slavery on the Moses Carver farm in the early 1860s, George, along with his birth mother, was kidnapped by Confederate bushwhackers when he was a newborn. George was found in Arkansas and returned to the Carvers, but his mother was never seen again. The identity of George's father was unknown—although Carver believed he was a slave on a neighboring farm. Moses and Susan Carver raised George and his brother Jim as their own children. The Carver family showed the children abundant love and guidance and encouraged them to expand their minds and imaginations. The influence of the Carvers allowed George to explore his desire to understand his natural surroundings, which led to his study of the sciences.

the Trinity Episcopal Church, where Bess and Harry Truman were married. The Jackson County Courthouse features a program about Truman and Independence in the Truman Courtroom, where the future president served as a presiding county judge.

- The Harry S Truman Farm Home, located 20 miles south of Independence, was the site of the Truman family farm, which operated from 1906 to 1917. It is open Friday, Saturday, and Sunday in May through August.

JEFFERSON NATIONAL EXPANSION MEMORIAL

Downtown St. Louis.

11 North 4th Street
St. Louis, MO 63102
314-425-4010
http://www.nps.gov/jeff

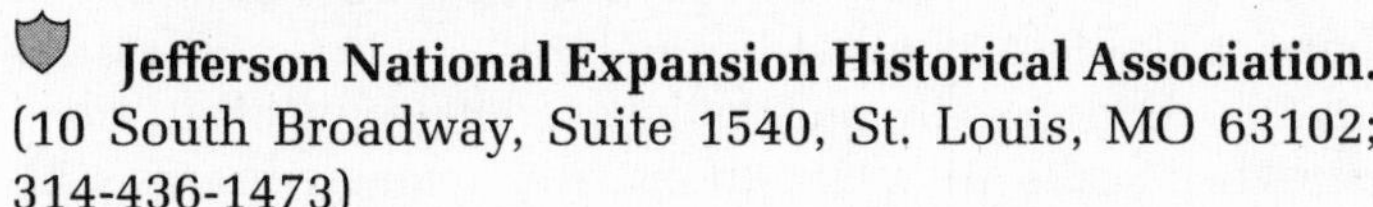

Jefferson National Expansion Historical Association. (10 South Broadway, Suite 1540, St. Louis, MO 63102; 314-436-1473)

The Jefferson National Expansion Memorial commemorates the westward growth of the United States between 1803 and 1890. The park is a memorial not only to Thomas Jefferson and the Louisiana Purchase but also to the pioneers who settled the West. The memorial contains the Gateway Arch of St. Louis, the symbolic "Gateway to the West," which is 630 feet tall (75 feet taller than the Washington Monument and more than twice as tall as the Statue of Liberty). Another famous site in the park is the Old Courthouse, the scene of the famous 1850 Dred Scott

The Gateway Arch

The Arch is America's tallest monument, though several nonmonumental buildings outside the United States are taller. In the world, the only monumental structure taller than the Gateway Arch is the 984-foot Eiffel Tower, in Paris. The trams that take visitors to the top of the Arch are a hybrid of elevator and ferris wheel, moving passengers both horizontally and vertically, while staying level. They were designed in two weeks by Dick Bowser, a University of Maryland dropout.

 **FOREST SERVICE SCENIC BYWAY**

Glade Top Trail

The 23-mile Glade Top Trail crosses narrow ridgetops above the surrounding rolling countryside, and travelers are treated to numerous views that reach to the Springfield Plateau to the northwest and to Arkansas's Boston Mountains to the south. The area is also well known for its beautiful fall colors. *Contact Mark Twain National Forest.*

lawsuit for freedom from slavery, as well as numerous rallies, meetings, and speeches of national significance. The Museum of Westward Expansion, located beneath the Arch, contains exhibits, films, and artifacts to help visitors understand what it was like to go west in the 19th century.

MARK TWAIN NATIONAL FOREST

95 miles southwest of St. Louis.

401 Fairgrounds Road
Rolla, MO 65401
573-364-4621
http://www.fs.fed.us/

Ozark Interpretive Association, Inc. (PO Box 1270, Mountain View, AR 72560; 870-757-2211)

Mark Twain National Forest, Missouri's only national forest, encompasses 1.5 million acres of mountains, rivers, streams, and wilderness areas. Located in southern Missouri, the forest lies mostly within the Ozark Plateau, dotted with remnant hills from America's oldest mountains, the Ozarks. The forest ranges from gently rolling plains to deep sinuous valleys containing clear, cool, spring-fed rivers and streams. Peaks, hills and knobs, and open glades are scattered throughout.

OZARK NATIONAL SCENIC RIVERWAYS

150 miles southwest of St. Louis.

PO Box 490
Van Buren, MO 63965
573-323-4236
http://www.nps.gov/ozar

 **Eastern National.** (446 North Lane, Conshohocken, PA 19428; 800-355-5566)

Devils Well

Within the Ozark Riverways are over 300 caves, numerous large springs, and more than 130 miles of clear-flowing streams. In the northern part of the Riverways are enormous underground air- and water-filled chambers called "Devils Well," which serve as a natural reservoir for heavy rain in the spring. Over millions of years, water from the surface flowed over decaying plants, became slightly acidic, and dissolved the underlying dolomite along tiny cracks or joints. As water flowed from crack to crack, small underground chambers gradually became larger and longer. The entrance to Devils Well, an open sinkhole, was formed when the ceiling of an underground chamber collapsed. Devils Well is open during daylight hours, and visitors are permitted into the entrance.

Facts about Devils Well:

- *Height from the viewing platform to the water: 80 to 100 feet, depending on the lake level.*
- *Size of main chamber: 400 feet by 100 feet.*
- *Deepest part of the lake: 100 feet.*
- *Lake content: 22 million gallons of water.*
- *Daily flow from Cave Springs: 32 million gallons.*
- *Air-filled chambers: 4 known.*
- *Age of rock (eminence dolomite) in which Devils Well was formed: 400 to 500 million years.*

Encompassing more than 134 miles of the Current and Jack Fork Rivers, the Ozark National Scenic Riverways pass through mixed pine and hardwood forests. Limestone bluffs rise abruptly above some stretches of the rivers, and a climb to the top offers a good view over the surrounding countryside. Canoeing and floating on tubes are the most popular activities at Ozark. A series of record floods struck the area in the past few years, leaving changed channels, new gravel bars, and rootwads to test navigational skills.

ULYSSES S. GRANT NATIONAL HISTORIC SITE

St. Louis.

7400 Grant Road
St. Louis, MO 63123
314-842-3298
http://www.nps.gov/ulsg

Jefferson National Expansion Historical Association. (10 S. Broadway, Suite 1540, St. Louis, MO 63102; 314-436-1473)

President Ulysses S. Grant established Yellowstone, the country's first National Park. President George Bush, 117 years and approximately 360 park units later, designated Grant's home, White Haven, a National Historic Site. Currently, the National Park Service is renovating and restoring White Haven as a tribute to Grant and his family. There are five historic structures on the 10-acre property: a two-story residence, an outbuilding, a barn, an ice house, and a chicken house.

HOW TO ENJOY A GOOD FLOAT

The Ozark Riverways offer these tips:

Floating. Learning to read the water is the key to a good float. In a Class II river, the main current is always the best place to be. In straightaways, look for smooth, glassy water. In bends, the reverse is true: the smooth water may be too shallow, while the water with riffles and small waves will carry you through. Avoid the outside of the bend, where you may run into overhanging obstacles or collections of debris. Float with the water, moving with just enough speed to control your boat; keep the keel of the canoe parallel to the current.

The chute. As you approach a series of obstacles, look for a long glassy "V" pointing downstream. This is the chute, the safest route through.

Swamping. If you get hung up on a rock or a submerged log, lean downstream. If you lean upstream, rushing water will tend to roll the hull over and fill the canoe. If you capsize, stay upstream from the canoe to avoid being pinned against the obstruction by the water-filled canoe.

Gravel bar camping. Camping on a gravel bar is one of the delightful aspects of floating. In the heat of summer, this will usually be one of the cooler places and will have fewer mosquitoes. Set up your tent out of sight of any nearby dwelling, and use existing firepits. Always pay attention to changes in the river's level; set up a stick at water's edge as a gauge. As the river starts to rise, time the rate so you will know whether danger is imminent. Plan an escape route to higher ground. Don't underestimate the river. Never go back on the river during high water.

WILSON'S CREEK NATIONAL BATTLEFIELD

10 miles southwest of Springfield.

6424 W. Farm Road
Republic, MO 65738
417-732-2662
http://www.nps.gov/wicr

 **Eastern National.** (446 North Lane, Conshohocken, PA 19428; 800-355-5566)

The bloody Battle of Wilson's Creek, in 1861, was one marker of the beginning of the Civil War in Missouri. At the battle's end, the Confederate Army held the field and claimed victory even though Union forces controlled key areas of Missouri, such as St. Louis and Kansas City.

Today, visitors can tour battlefield sites such as Bloody Hill, where approximately 1,700 Union and Confederate soldiers were killed or wounded, and the Historic Overlook, where the Union army passed through during the advance to and the retreat from Bloody Hill. Also on the site is The Ray House, the only existing dwelling that dates back to the time of the battle. Once used as a Confederate hospital, The Ray House has been restored and is open for tours.

POINTS OF INTEREST

U.S. ARMY CORPS OF ENGINEERS

CLEARWATER LAKE

Located near three state parks and several historical sites, such as Gads Hills, where the notorious Frank and Jesse James gang staged the world's second train robbery in 1874. From Piedmont, go west 5 miles. From St. Louis, south 100 miles on US 67, then west on MO 34.

HARRY S TRUMAN DAM AND RESERVOIR

Adjacent to the Lake of the Ozarks, Truman features excellent fishing, a regional visitor center, and a powerplant exhibit area. Rugged hills, scenic bluffs, hardwood forest, and prairie offer some of the best scenery in Missouri. From Kansas City, 19 miles south on US 71, 75 miles east on MO 7 to Warsaw, then 1 mile north.

FISHING IN THE NATIONAL FORESTS

The U.S. Forest Service has issued an incredible guide to fishing in the national forests. It lists every forest and what kinds of fishing you can expect to find there. There are separate entries for saltwater, ice, warm water, and cold water fishing. Looking to catch a particular fish? Here are the species you can catch within the national forests:

- 15 species of trout and char.
- 7 species of salmon.
- 5 species of catfish.
- 7 species of bass.
- 4 species of perch.
- 2 species of sunfish.
- 3 species of pike.
- 15 species of saltwater fish.
- 10 other species of fish.

You can get a copy of *Fishing Your National Forests* by writing to any regional office of the Forest Service.

THE JUNIOR RANGER CODE

To be a Junior Ranger at Ozark National Scenic Riverways (MO), I promise to:

1. Explore other national parks.
2. Collect litter while I'm exploring.
3. Learn more about different animals, plants, and parks.
4. Leave animals, plants, and historic objects in the Riverways undisturbed.
5. Take pride in America! Help keep the place we live clean, safe, and beautiful for everyone.

LONG BRANCH LAKE

Beautiful shoreline vistas, and abundant hunting and fishing opportunities. Long Branch State Park provides a variety of water-related recreation opportunities. From Columbia, 59 miles north on US 63 to Macon, then 2 miles west on US 36.

POMME DE TERRE

Cool, clear spring waters make this lake the "Gem of the Ozarks." From Springfield, 53 miles north on US 65, 5 miles west on US 54, and 4 miles south on MO 254.

SMITHVILLE LAKE

Within 30 minutes of downtown Kansas City, this 7,190-acre lake offers a regional visitor center and an 18-hole golf course, in addition to water-related recreation activities. From Kansas City, north on I-29, north on US 169 for 15 miles, and 2 miles east on MO Road.

NEBRASKA

AGATE FOSSIL BEDS NATIONAL MONUMENT

400 miles northwest of Lincoln; 23 miles south of US 20 at Harrison, on State Highway 29; and 34 miles north of US 26 at Mitchell, on State Highway 29.

301 River Road
Harrison, NE 69346-2734
308-668-2211
http://www.nps.gov/agfo

Oregon Trail Museum Association. (PO Box 27, Gering, NE 69341-0027; 308-436-2975)

Agate Fossil Beds National Monument features a concentrated collection of 19-million to 21-million-year-old Miocene mammalian fossils and an outstanding collection of 19th- and 20th-century Oglala Lakota artifacts of beads and quillwork. The Visitors' Center and Museum contains a life-size diorama of the Miocene mammals, including Dinohyus, Moropus, Paleocaster, and beardogs, as well as a room displaying the Oglala materials and memorabilia of the fossil and artifact collector, James Cook. There are two trails around the fossil deposits, and picnic areas are available at the Visitors' Center. All this is set within the upper Niobrara River Valley, which has extensive wetlands and some historic structures.

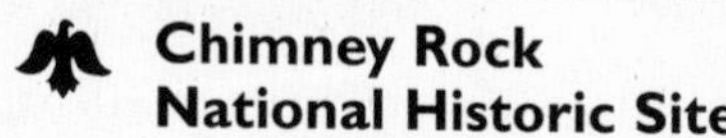

Chimney Rock National Historic Site

"Seeing the Elephant" was the phrase uttered long ago by pioneers upon glimpsing Chimney Rock, perhaps because its spire seems to rise in the air like a huge trunk. Chimney Rock served as a milepost for early travelers and heralded the astounding rock formations ahead. Today, the Visitor Center tells the story of the thousands who trekked west on the Oregon and Mormon trails. For more information write to PO Box F, Bayard, NE 69334-0680; 308-586-2581.

HOMESTEAD NATIONAL MONUMENT OF AMERICA

40 miles south of Lincoln.

RFD 3
Box 47
Beatrice, NE 68310
402-223-3514
http://www.nps.gov/home

Eastern National. (446 North Lane, Conshohocken, PA 19428; 800-355-5566)

The Homestead Act of 1862 brought millions of settlers to the western prairies and plains. The Act declared that any citizen or intended citizen could claim 160 acres—one quarter square mile—of surveyed government land. Claimants had to improve the plot with a dwelling, and grow crops. If, after five years, the original filer was still on the land, it was his property, free and clear. Homestead

National Monument of America commemorates one of America's first documented homesteads. The Monument includes an original homestead, a historic log cabin typical of those in eastern Nebraska, a one-room school, and trails that wind through the restored tallgrass prairie.

NEBRASKA NATIONAL FOREST

360 miles northwest of Omaha.

125 North Main Street
Chadron, NE 69337-2118
308-432-0300
http://www.fs.fed.us

Pine Ridge National Recreation Area

Located in the Nebraska National Forest, southeast of Crawford, the Pine Ridge National Recreation Area offers back-country recreation in a natural ponderosa pine forest that is an extension of the forests of the Black Hills. Activities include hiking, horseback riding, hunting, nature study, and cross-country skiing. Motorized vehicle recreation is not permitted, and there are no developed sites in this smallest (6,600 acres) of the U.S. Forest Service national recreation areas. For details, contact the Recreation Area at HC 75, Box 13A9, Chadron, NE 69337; 308-432-4475.

Badlands Natural History Association. (Box 6, Interion, SD 57750; 605-433-5361)

The Nebraska National Forest includes the largest hand-planted forest in the Western Hemisphere. Nearly 1.1-million acres are scattered within a large arc extending from central Nebraska west to the northern panhandle, into southwestern South Dakota, and east to the state's center. The forest is part of a larger protected area of the northern Great Plains ecosystems that includes three National Grasslands: the Buffalo Gap and Fort Pierre, in South Dakota; the Oglala, in Nebraska; and the Samuel R. McKelvin National Forest, in Nebraska. Grass is the primary vegetation in the forest, from the short grass prairies of extreme western South Dakota and Nebraska to the taller, more diverse grass prairies of central South Dakota and the Nebraska Sandhills. Toadstool Geologic Park, on the Oglala National Grassland, is a moonscape of eroded Badlands features. Museums around the world contain 30-million-year-old mammal fossils from this area. The 10,000-year-old Hudson-Meng Bison Bonebed, located on the Oglala National Grassland, contains the western hemisphere's largest concentration of remains from an extinct bison species.

NIOBRARA/MISSOURI NATIONAL SCENIC RIVERWAYS

North Central Nebraska, off US 20 and US 83; Missouri Recreational River: 150 miles NW of Omaha.

PO Box 591
O'Neill, NE 68763
402-336-3970
http://www.nps.gov/nimi

Here is where East meets West. The Niobrara's river corridor, which is bisected by the 100th meridian, has long been known to Nebraskans as a beautiful river with superb canoeing. In 1991, a 70-mile section of the river, from east of Valentine to the Highway 37 bridge, was designated a National Scenic River. The Missouri National Recreational River, totaling 98 miles, includes 39 miles from Fort Randall Dam east to the headwaters of Lewis and Clark Lake, and a 59-mile section from Gavins Point Dam, near Yankton, SD, to Ponca, NE. The free-flowing stretches of the Missouri still exhibit the river's dynamic character in its islands, bars, chutes, and snags.

Sam's Tips

- The portion from Cornell Dam downstream 25 miles has the most popular canoeing.
- The Niobrara/Missouri Scenic Riverways is not a traditional park area with traditional park services. The US Fish and Wildlife Service and the US Army Corps of Engineers, along with state, local, and private facilities, provide river access, interpretive activities, and camping.

SCOTTS BLUFF NATIONAL MONUMENT

380 miles west of Lincoln.

PO Box 27
Gering, NE 69341-0027
308-436-4340
http://www.nps.gov/scbl

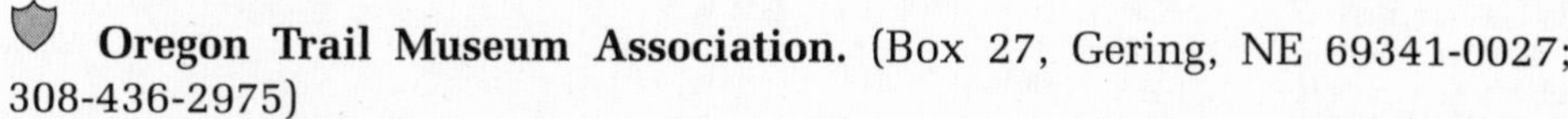

Oregon Trail Museum Association. (Box 27, Gering, NE 69341-0027; 308-436-2975)

Scotts Bluff, an immense sandstone and siltstone formation, was an important landmark for pioneers crossing Nebraska's grassy plains. Travelers could spot the bluff days before they actually reached it; once they passed the formation, the emigrants from the East knew that they had traveled one-third of the Oregon

Snakes of the Prairie

The western rattlesnake is the only venomous snake you are likely to find on the Great Plains. Rattlers belong to the pit viper family of snakes, characterized by temperature-sensitive pits on either side of the face between the eye and the nostril. These pits aid the snake in locating its warm-blooded prey. Prairie rattlesnakes are also distinguished by a broad, triangular head, vertical eye pupils and, of course, rattles. Although the snakes gain a rattle each time they shed their skin, the number of rattles is not a reliable indicator of age because old rattles may break off and be lost. Rattlesnakes are usually well camouflaged. They are not aggressive but may bite if molested. It is possible for a dead rattlesnake to bite, through a reflex action, so all rattlesnakes, alive or dead, should be treated with caution and respect.

WHAT TO DO IF YOU ARE LOST

The Rogue River National Forest offers this wilderness safety advice if you become lost.

Keep calm; don't panic. Check the surrounding country and try to orient yourself. Do not walk aimlessly. Carry and trust the map and compass. If you can reach a road, trail, or telephone line, follow it until you can determine you are moving in the right direction. As a last resort, travel downhill parallel to a stream or drainage.

Select a sheltered spot and prepare camp and firewood well before dark. Remember that shelter, warmth, and liquid intake are much more important than food. If unsuccessful in attempts to find your way, stay in one place, conserve your strength, and build a fire so that smoke may be seen by searchers.

Trail. Today, even as wind and water dismantle the rock grain by grain, visitors can explore the bluff and its surrounding prairie. The Visitor Center displays artwork by William Henry Jackson, a noted pioneer photographer and artist; the human history of the westward migration; and the geology of the area.

POINTS OF INTEREST

U.S. ARMY CORPS OF ENGINEERS

HARLAN COUNTRY LAKE

Located in the south-central part of the state, this is the second-largest lake in Nebraska and is well-known for its excellent spring walleye fishing. From Lincoln, take I-80 14 miles southwest, and then take US 183 for 41 miles south.

PAPIO CREED WATERSHED LAKE PROJECT

Three small lakes near Omaha: Glen Cunningham Lake, near 96th and I-680; Wehrspann Lake, near 156th and Giles Road; and Zorinsky Lake, near 156th and Center.

STANDING BEAR LAKE

This lake, in northwest Omaha, has facilities for fishing, non-motorized boating, hiking, cycling, nature study, and winter sports, near 132nd and Fort.

U.S. BUREAU OF RECLAMATION

BOX BUTTE RESERVOIR

Box 30370, Lincoln, NE 68503; 308-762-5605. Located 10 miles north of Hemingford. Nearest highway: Nebraska 385. Reservoir open 24 hours. Good access roads. Fishing season year-round. Species include northern pike, walleye, largemouth bass, yellow perch, and channel catfish.

CALAMUS RESERVOIR

HC Box 201, Burwell, NE 68823; 308-346-5666. Located 5 miles northwest of Burwell. Nearest highway: Nebraska 91. Reservoir open 24 hours. Good access roads. Fishing season year-round. Species include walleye, northern pike, largemouth bass, rainbow trout, and crappie.

DAVIS CREEK RESERVOIR

Box 129, Ord, NE 68862; 308-745-0230. Located 5 miles south of North Loup. Nearest highway: Nebraska 11. Reservoir open 24 hours. Fair access roads. Species include walleye, crappie, yellow perch, channel catfish, and bullhead. Fishing season year-round.

ENDERS RESERVOIR

RR 1, Box 4B, Enders, NE 69027; 308-394-5118. Located 2 miles east of Enders. Nearest highway: US 6. Reservoir open 24 hours. Good access roads. Fishing season year-round. Species include walleye, crappie, white bass, channel catfish, and wipers.

HUGH BUTLER RESERVOIR

RR 1, Box 145, McCook, NE 69001; 308-345-6507. Located 10 miles north of McCook. Nearest highway: Nebraska 83. Reservoir open 24 hours. Fair access roads. Species include walleye, crappie, white bass, channel catfish, and wipers.

HARRY STRUNK RESERVOIR

RR 2, Box 95, Cambridge, NE 69022; 308-697-4667. Located 9 miles northwest of Cambridge. Nearest highway: US 34. Reservoir open 24 hours. Fair access roads. Species include walleye, crappie, white bass, channel catfish, and wipers. Fishing season year-round.

LAKE MINATARE STATE RECREATION AREA

Box 188, Minatare, NE 69356; 308-783-2911. A state recreation area managed by the Nebraska Game and Parks Commission, Lake Minatare has slightly more than 7 miles of shoreline and is a part of the North Platte National Wildlife Refuge. Walleye, channel catfish, and gizzard shad are stocked in the reservoir annually. The area is open to the public from January 15 to September 30.

LAKE ALICE

North Platte National Wildlife Refuge, Box 1346, Scottsbluff, NE 69363; 308-635-7851. Lake Alice lies almost entirely within the North Platte National Wildlife Refuge. The west side of the reservoir features an undisturbed bird sanctuary. The reservoir is nearly drained during the irrigation season, so there is no viable sport fishing in the lake. No services or facilities.

MERRITT RESERVOIR

420 East First Street, Valentine, NE 69201; 420-684-2921. Located 21 miles southwest of Valentine. Nearest highway: Nebraska 97. Reservoir open 24 hours. Good access roads. Fishing season year-round.

SHERMAN RESERVOIR

RR 2, Box 117, Loup City, NE 68853; 308-745-0230. Located 5 miles northeast of Loup City. Nearest highway: Nebraska 92. Reservoir open 24 hours. Good access roads. Fishing season year-round.

STATELINE RESERVOIR

Managed by the Mountain View Ranger District, Wasatch-Cache National Forest, PO Box 129, Mountain View, WY 82939; 307-782-6555. Situated 20 miles south of Mountain View, at a 9,160-foot elevation in a timber setting. Managed recreation season is June through October.

WINTERS CREEK LAKE

North Platte National Wildlife Refuge, Box 1346, Scottsbluff, NE 69363; 308-635-7851. Most of the Winters Creek Lake lies within the North Platte National Wildlife Refuge. The northeast side features an undisturbed bird sanctuary. Walleye are stocked in the reservoir annually. Nonpowered boats only. Open to the public from January 15 to September 30, during daylight hours.

FISH AND WILDLIFE SERVICE

CRESCENT LAKE NATIONAL WILDLIFE REFUGE

Crescent Lake Refuge, which occupies some 70 square miles, is a haven for wildlife and for people who enjoy the sweep of grassland and the sight and sound of waterfowl, grouse, and deer.

The refuge is best reached from Oshkosh, NE, by going north on a dirt road for 28 miles. Few sandhill roads are surfaced, and although travel with almost any vehicle is possible over the better roads, the side trails require a four-wheel-drive truck.

For further information on this site, contact:

Refuge Manager
Crescent Lake National Wildlife Refuge
HC 68, Box 21
Ellsworth, NE 69340
308-762-4893
http://www.fws.gov

OHIO

CUYAHOGA VALLEY NATIONAL RECREATION AREA

10 miles northwest of Akron.

15610 Vaughn Road
Brecksville, OH 44141
216-526-5256
http://www.nps.gov/cuva

 **Eastern National.** (446 North Lane, Conshohocken, PA 19428; 800-355-5566)

Situated between Akron and Cleveland, the Cuyahoga Valley National Recreation Area contains 33,000 acres of woodlands, rolling meadows, gentle farmlands, ravines, gorges, ledges, river beds, and streams. You can travel the area by car, along scenic drives on back-country roads, or by hiking, biking, riding horseback, and skiing. The dominant feature of the valley is the Cuyahoga River, named centuries ago by the Indians whose word, "ka-ih-ogh-ha," means crooked.

Hale Farm and Village

Located in the recreation area, Hale Farm and Village is a restored, mid-19th-century farm with 21 buildings open to the public. The Museum Shop features hand-crafted items made at the farm; the Gatehouse (visitor center) has artifacts and exhibits from the mid-1800s. The Hale Farm and Village also offers one-week summer camp sessions for boys and girls ages 9 to 14.

SAM'S TIPS

- Book a ticket on the Cuyahoga Valley Scenic Railroad and watch the beautiful scenery of the valley from the comfort of a train seat. The railroad features special fall color train tours during October. Call the Cuyahoga Valley Scenic Railroad at 800-468-4070.
- The Cuyahoga Valley Environmental Education Center, nestled on 500 acres within the recreation area, is an outdoor learning center with programs for schools and other groups. For more information, call 216-657-2796.

DAYTON AVIATION HERITAGE NATIONAL HISTORICAL PARK

Dayton.

22 S. Williams Street
PO Box 9280, Wright Brothers Station
Dayton, OH 45409
937-225-7705
http://www.nps.gov/daav

The Dayton Aviation Heritage National Historical Park preserves the legacy of Wilbur and Orville Wright and the work of poet Paul Laurence Dunbar, a classmate and friend of the Wright brothers. The park consists of four separate units across the metropolitan area: (1) the building in which the brothers operated their printing and bicycle businesses; (2) the Huffman Prairie Flying Field, now part of Wright-Patterson Air Force Base, where the brothers learned how to fly; (3) Wright Hall, where the Wright Flyer III, the world's first practical airplane, is displayed; and (4) the Dunbar House State Memorial.

HOPEWELL CULTURE NATIONAL HISTORICAL PARK

45 miles south of Columbus.

16062 State Route 104
Chillicothe, OH 45601
614-774-1125
http://www.nps.gov/hocu

Eastern National. (446 North Lane, Conshohocken, PA 19428; 800-355-5566)

> **Hopewell Pipes**
>
> Hopewell artisans produced two types of pipes that have been found at Mound City—a plain platform pipe with a cylindrical bowl, and an effigy platform pipe with a bowl carved in the shape of a bird, mammal, or other animal. In addition to providing insight into the ceremonial life of the Hopewell people, the effigy pipes prove the existence of certain animals during the Hopewell Period.

The area known today as Mound City, a 2,000-year-old cemetery in the Hopewell Culture National Historical Park, was an ancient ceremonial and burial site for people living along the Scioto River between 200 B.C. and 500 A.D. Early speculation held that the mounds had been built by a "lost race" of mysterious origin. That notion was laid to rest after further extensive excavations demonstrated that the mounds were built by early American Indians. These "Hopewell people" left many historical clues for scientists, including pipes and other artifacts. The site was declared a National Monument in 1923 but only after many of the mounds were destroyed by construction of a World War I training facility.

JAMES A. GARFIELD NATIONAL HISTORIC SITE

35 miles northeast of Cleveland.

8095 Mentor Avenue
Mentor, OH 44060
216-255-8722
http://www.nps.gov/jaga

 **Western Reserve Historical Society.** (same address as above)

In 1876, James A. Garfield purchased a 117-acre farm with a rundown 1½ story house for his wife, mother, and 5 children. He soon gained an additional 40 acres and, in 1880, oversaw a major addition to the house. His wife added nine more rooms in 1885, four years after Garfield's death. These rooms now house the first presidential memorial library. The house remained in the Garfield family until 1936, when the President's children gave it to the Western Reserve Historical

Society. The home has been restored to the period 1880–1904, the time President Garfield campaigned for office.

PERRY'S VICTORY AND INTERNATIONAL PEACE MEMORIAL

40 miles east of Toledo.

PO Box 549, 93 Delaware Avenue
Put-in-Bay, OH 43456
419-285-2184
http://www.nps.gov/pevi

 **Eastern National.** (446 North Lane, Conshohocken, PA 19428; 800-355-5566).

Monuments to peace are rarely associated with military victories, but Oliver Hazard Perry's victory over a British fleet on Lake Erie in the War of 1812 so contributed to a lasting peace that the Perry's Victory and International Peace Memorial on Lake Erie is a fitting tribute to both. The granite memorial, topped by an 11-ton bronze urn, is 352 feet tall—taller than the Statue of Liberty—and houses the remains of the 3 British and 3 American officers killed in the battle.

Sam's Tips

- The memorial site, located on South Bass Island in Lake Erie, is open daily from late April until late October. In season, automobile ferries operate daily from Catawba Point and Port Clinton. The memorial is open only by appointment through the winter; the Port Clinton and Sandusky airports have year-round air service to and from the island.

WAYNE NATIONAL FOREST

60 miles southeast of Columbus.

219 Columbus Road
Athens, OH 45701
614-592-6644
http://www.fs.fed.us

Eastern National Forests Interpretive Association. (PO Box 70, East Tawas, MI 48730; 517-362-7511)

Located in southeastern Ohio, the Wayne National Forest is a blend of forested hillsides and pastures. The history of the area shows itself in vintage oil wells, a partially restored Civil War iron furnace, century-old covered bridges, and the ancient Adena Indian mounds. The forest came into being in the mid-1930s, after the Great Depression drove farmers out of the area. As the expanse of tax-delinquent land grew, the legislature asked the federal government to purchase land for use as a national forest. The forest now offers abundant recreational opportunities, including those of the Leith Run Recreation Area, many off-road vehicle trails, and the Covered Bridge Scenic Byway.

WILLIAM HOWARD TAFT NATIONAL HISTORIC SITE

Mount Auburn section of Cincinnati.

2038 Auburn Avenue
Cincinnati, OH 45219-3025
513-684-3262
http://www.nps.gov/wiho

 **Eastern National.** (446 North Lane, Conshohocken, PA 19428; 800-355-5566)

The William Howard Taft National Historic Site is the country's only memorial to its 27th president and 10th chief justice. The house has been restored to its appearance when Taft lived there as a child and young adult. By 1938, the house had undergone numerous modifications since being sold by the Tafts 39 years earlier and was ready for the wrecking ball. The movement to save the house from demolition began in 1938 with the establishment of the William Howard Taft Memorial Association. Louise Taft's letters to her family in Massachusetts provided details of decorating plans and furniture purchases that guided the restoration.

POINTS OF INTEREST

U.S. ARMY CORPS OF ENGINEERS

BERLIN LAKE

A historic area with an old stagecoach station in Deerfield. John Brown was born near here. From Deerfield, 2 miles east on OH 224.

CAESAR CREEK LAKE

The regional visitor center for the Corps of Engineers is located at the dam. There is also a reconstructed pioneer village on the southeast side of the project. Located just east of Waynesville on OH 73.

CHARLES MILL LAKE

Malabar Farm, home of Louis Bromfield, a Pulitzer Prize-winning novelist, is maintained near here by the state. In Mansfield, see the Kingwood Center formal gardens in bloom, April–October. From Lucas, east 5 miles on US 30, then south 4 miles on OH 603.

DOVER DAM

No permanent pool, but day-use facilities are along the river. The restored village of Zoar is 5 miles north of the dam. Nearby attractions include Shoebrunn State Park, operated by the Ohio Historical Society, and the Warther Museum, which has 56 hand-carved, operating, miniature locomotives. From Dover, northeast 4 miles on OH 800.

NORTH BRANCH OF KOKOSING LAKE
A small, quiet fishing lake located 1.5 miles from Fredericktown, just off OH 13.

PAINT CREEK LAKE
Impressive prehistoric Indian sites in the central Scioto River basin are in the vicinity of this lake. Located 24 miles southwest of Chillicothe, off US 50.

TOM JENKINS DAM (BURR OAK LAKE)
Within an hour's drive of the caves and cliffs of Hocking Hills State Park. From Athens, north 20 miles on US 33 and OH 13.

WILLIAM H. HARSHA LAKE
A 2,160-acre lake made popular by Cincinnati boaters; also the site of two abandoned gold mines. Located southeast of Batavia, just south of OH 32.

ASK AN (INTERNET) HISTORIAN

Do you have a specific question about the national parks, the National Park Service, or American history? To get your answer, use the Internet to access experts at the National Park Service. Categories of subjects include:

Alaska's history
Appalachian history
Archaeology
Architectural history
Aviation history
Civil War
Early American history
Historic preservation
Labor history
Maritime history
Military history
Mining history
National historic landmarks
Native American history
Technology
Western history
Women's history

You'll find the names of more than two dozen authorities on various subjects, ready to answer your question. Use the online e-mail form and get an answer within days. This terrific site can be found at: http://www.nps.gov/crweb1/history/askhist.htm.

OKLAHOMA

CHICKASAW NATIONAL RECREATION AREA

75 miles southeast of Oklahoma City.

PO Box 201
Sulphur, OK 73086
405-622–3165
http://www.nps.gov/chic

Southwest Parks and Monuments Association. (221 N. Court Avenue, Tucson, AZ 85701; 520–622-1999)

The park is named in honor of the Chickasaw Indian nation, the original occupants of this land. These partially forested, rolling hills of south-central Oklahoma are dotted with springs, streams, and lakes, and offer swimming, boating, and fishing as well as camping and hiking. Archaeologists believe that this area may have been inhabited for as long as 7,000 years. The ancient people called this the "Peaceful Valley of Rippling Waters" and believed in the healing power of the strong-smelling mineral water. Today, people still come to drink water from several mineral springs.

Three Special Forest Sites of Oklahoma

The Ouachita National Forest lies mostly in Arkansas, but three Oklahoma areas within the Ouachita have been designated as National Forest System Special Places:

- The Beech Creek National Scenic and Botanical Area attracts visitors because of its solitude and native vegetation. Beech trees, rare in Oklahoma, and American holly are found here in abundance.
- The Indian Nations National Scenic Area lies on the north slopes of Winding Stair Mountain, and during the spring and fall provides a panorama of beautiful colors. The Talimena Scenic Drive provides vantage points from which the entire area can be seen. Deer and turkey hunting are very popular.
- The Talimena Scenic Drive, which winds past scenic vistas and historical sites, leads to Winding Stair National Recreation Area. The area reportedly contains more plant species than any other place between the Rockies and the Appalachians. Environmental education programs are offered at the Nature Center. Visitors can go trekking in the remote Black Fork Mountain Wilderness or the Upper Kiamichi River Wilderness.

For details, contact: Ouachita National Forest, HC 64, Box 3467, Heavener, OK 74937; 918-653-2991.

TAX INCENTIVES FOR HISTORIC REHABILITATIONS

A community's historic buildings are the tangible links with its past. The Federal government encourages investment in historic buildings and the revitalization of historic districts through tax incentives. Find out more at http://www2.cr.nps.gov/tps/taxact.html.

WASHITA BATTLEFIELD NATIONAL HISTORIC SITE

140 miles west of Oklahoma City.

PO Box 890
Cheyenne, OK 73628
580-497-2742
http://www.nps.gov/waba

Washita Battlefield National Historic Site provides for the preservation and interpretation of the Battle of Washita, November 27, 1868, one of the largest engagements between Plains tribes and the U.S. Army on the Southern Great Plains. The Battle of Washita symbolized the struggle of the Southern Great Plains tribes to maintain their traditional lifeways and not to submit to reservation confinement. The core area includes the site of Black Kettle's village, Custer's command post, and troop and Indian positions recently discovered during a November 1995 survey of the battlefield. The site was designated a Historic Site on November 12, 1996, and at present there are no federal facilities. The Black Kettle Museum run by the Oklahoma Historical Society (PO Box 252, Cheyenne, OK 73628; 580-497-3929) has the most in-depth information available.

Sam's Tips

- An overlook operated by the Oklahoma Historical Society consists of a historical plaque, monument commemorating the site, and a panel indicating approximate route, approach, and attack of Custer and approximate location of the Indian village.
- The National Park Service plans to install an interpretive trail from the Overlook to connect with key features of the battlefield—Black Kettle's Village, Custer Command Knoll, and site of the pony herd slaughter.

Points of Interest

U.S. ARMY CORPS OF ENGINEERS

BROKEN BOW LAKE

The McCurtain County Wilderness Area at the lake's north end retains its primitive, natural beauty. From Broken Bow, north 7 miles on US 259, then east 2 miles on OK 259-A.

CANTON LAKE

Named for a pioneer Army post or "cantonment" at the halfway point between Forts Reno and Supply. Deactivated in 1882, the post also served as a Mennonite school for Indians. From Fairview, south 13 miles on OK 58 and west 2 miles on OK 58A.

EUFAULA LAKE

One of the largest Corps lakes. Outlaw Belle Starr lived near here in the turbulent days between the 1830s and the Civil War. From McAlester, north 23 miles on US 69, east 16 miles on OK 9, and north 6 miles on OK 71.

FORT GIBSON LAKE

The Fort Gibson Stockade, a restored frontier fort, is located near the lake. Fort Gibson is the oldest town in Oklahoma. From Fort Gibson, north 6 miles on OK 80.

GREAT SALT PLAINS LAKE

Visit Great Salt Plains National Wildlife Refuge, one of the chain of refuge areas for ducks and geese on the Continental Central Flyway. From Enid, northwest 31 miles on US 64 to Jet, then 8 miles north on OK 38.

HEYBURN LAKE

Located near Kellyville in the Sandstone Hills of the Osage Section central lowlands. Good hunting and fishing. From Sapulpa, southwest 8 miles on US 66 and west 5 miles on County Road.

HUGO LAKE

The Oklahoma Department of Wildlife Conservation manages over 18,000 acres of land and water that are open to hunting, plus an additional 8,000 acres managed by the Corps. Wildlife around the lake includes waterfowl, bobwhite quail, dove, white-tailed deer, mink, fox, and beaver. Located on the Kiamichi River about 7 miles east of Hugo.

HULAH LAKE

Oil discoveries here made the Osage Indian tribe the wealthiest in America. Woolaroc Museum is nearby. From Bartlesville, north 12 miles on US 75, then west 12 miles on OK 10.

KAW LAKE

On the Arkansas River in Kay and Osage counties in Oklahoma and Crowley County in Kansas, this 17,000-acre lake offers camping and picnicking; 24,000 acres in both states are open to hunting and other activities. Game include: deer, turkey, quail, dove, waterfowl, rabbit, and prairie chicken. From Ponca City, east 9.5 miles on US 60, then north on County Road.

LAKE TEXOMA

The second most popular Corps lake in the country (after Lake Sidney Lanier, GA). Old Fort Washita is maintained as a museum by the Oklahoma Historical Society. From Denison, TX, northwest 5 miles on TX 75A.

OPTIMA LAKE

Located in an area once known as "No Man's Land," in the Oklahoma Panhandle, this lake is set in a scenic area of sand hills, rock outcroppings, and rolling grasslands. From Guymon, east 30 miles on OK 3, then north 3 miles on County Road.

TENKILLER FERRY LAKE

The area around this beautiful, clear lake is rich in the history of the Cherokee Nation. A nearby point of interest is Tsa-La-Gi, an authentic recreation of a Cherokee village of the 1700s. The Trail of Tears drama is presented here. From Muskogee, southeast 21 miles on OK 10, then east 7 miles on OK 10A.

U.S. BUREAU OF RECLAMATION

ALTUS LAKE

Quartz Mountain State Park, Route 1, Box 40, Lone Wolf, OK 73655; 405-563-2238. Nearest highway: 44. Nearest city: Lone Wolf. The lake is approximately 6,500 acres of open water. Accessible from numerous roads. Several boat ramps and camping facilities. Fishing year-round.

ARBUCKLE LAKE

Chickasaw National Recreation Area, PO Box 201, Sulphur, OK 73086; 405-622-3161. Nearest highway: 7. Nearest city: Sulphur. Approximately 2,300 acres of open water. Accessible from numerous roads. Several boat ramps and camping facilities. Fishing year-round.

FORT COBB LAKE

Fort Cobb State Park, Fort Cobb, OK 73005; 405-643-2249. Nearest highway: 146. Nearest city: Anadarko. The lake is approximately 4,000 acres of open water. Accessible from numerous roads. Several boat ramps and camping facilities. Fishing year-round.

FOSS RESERVOIR

Foss Lake State Park, Foss, OK 73647; 405-592-4433. Nearest highway: 44. Nearest city: Elk City. The lake is approximately 6,800 acres of open water. Accessible from numerous roads. Several boat ramps and camping facilities. Fishing year-round.

LAKE THUNDERBIRD

Little River State Park, Route 4, Box 277, Norman, OK 73071; 405-364-7634. Nearest highway: 9. Nearest city: Norman. The lake is approximately 6,000 of acres open water. Accessible from numerous roads. Several boat ramps and camping facilities. Fishing is year-round.

MCGEE CREEK RESERVOIR

McGee Creek State Park, Route 1, Box 6A, Farris OK 74542; 405-364-7634. Nearest highway: 3. Nearest city: Atoka. The lake is approximately 3,800 of acres open water. Accessible from numerous roads. Several boat ramps and camping facilities. Fishing year-round.

TOM STEED LAKE

Great Plains State Park, Mountain Park, OK 73006; 405-569-2032. Nearest highway: 183. Nearest city: Mountain Park. The lake is approximately 6,400 acres of open water. Accessible from numerous roads. Several boat ramps and camping facilities. Fishing permitted throughout the year.

CELEBRATE WILDFLOWERS

National Wildflower Week, which takes place during May of each year, launches a year-long program called "Celebrating Wildflowers," which emphasizes the aesthetic, recreational, biological, medicinal, and economic values of our native flora on 640 million acres of public lands in the United States.

Various events throughout the year are sponsored by Uncle Sam to promote the importance of conservation and management of native plants and plant habitats, and to stress the aesthetic, recreational, biological, medicinal, and economic values of wildflowers.

To find out about "Celebrating Wildflowers" events, call the Wild Hot Line at 800-354-4595 (April–July). To see what events are scheduled for your state, go to the "Celebrating Wildflowers" Website at the National Park Service: http://www.aqd.nps.gov/natnet/npci/events.htm.

WISCONSIN

APOSTLE ISLANDS NATIONAL LAKESHORE

215 miles northwest of Green Bay, 90 miles east of Duluth, MN.

Route 1, Box 4
Bayfield, WI 54814
715-779-3397
http://www.nps.gov/apis

 **Eastern National.** (446 North Lane, Conshohocken, PA 19428; 800-355-5566)

Near the western end of Lake Superior lies a forested archipelago of 22 islands known as the Apostles. Twenty-one of those islands and a 12-mile strip of Wisconsin's north coast comprise the Apostle Islands National Lakeshore. Emerald green in summer, gold and crimson in fall, the wooded islands are studded with bogs and beaver ponds and trimmed with sea caves. Among these forested, sheltered islands on the world's most expansive freshwater lake, early traders built posts for shipping furs bound for Europe. Loggers worked the islands extensively in the late 19th and early 20th centuries, and the sandstone cliffs on the lake's edge were quarried to provide building materials for the Midwest's growing cities. The six historic light stations in the park, placed to aid navigation through the Great Lakes, are the most found in any park in the national park system.

 **Artists-in-Residence**

Each summer, Apostle Islands National Lakeshore hosts several professional artists who spend two or three weeks in a rustic lakeside cabin. They share their experiences with island visitors, make a presentation to the general public, and donate one of the works inspired during their residency to the National Park Service. Artists-in-Residence have included landscape and watercolor artists, writers, photographers, songwriters, and performers.

 **Sam's Tips**

- Some of the park's most spectacular scenery centers around intricate caves carved into the sandstone cliffs along the coast of the lakeshore. The caves are best seen by boat, but visitors can walk along the top of the cliff above the Squaw Bay caves, or even visit by walking across the ice during the winter.
- Daily cruises include a 3-hour non-stop Grand Tour and two others that make scheduled stops on 5 islands and include tours of lighthouses. Camping is allowed on 18 of the 21 isalnds, but a permit is required. Twelve islands have public docks. Some of the islands are very remote; Outer Island, the farthest away from shore, features a lighthouse, old-growth forest, and an abandoned logging camp. Devil's Island has sea caves and a lighthouse. Both are accessible only by private boat or an expensive water taxi.

CHEQUAMEGON NATIONAL FOREST

120 miles southeast of Superior, WI.

1170 4th Avenue South
Park Falls, WI 54552
715-762-2461
http://www.fs.fed.us

Eastern National Forests Interpretive Association. (PO Box 70, East Tawas, MI 48730; 517-362-7511)

The Chequamegon is both a scenic mix of northern hardwoods, pines, and meadowlands, and home to several hundred wildlife species. The forest has bountiful lakes, rivers, and streams and is punctuated with rock outcroppings and scenic overlooks.

SAM'S TIPS

- Each winter, the Birkebeiner Ski Race, North America's largest cross-country ski race, is held in the forest. During the summer, the Birkebeiner trail is

Chequamegon Tourist Highlights

Scenic Views

Marengo River Valley Overlook, Mondeaux Dam Recreation Area, St. Peter's Dome, and Morgan Falls.

The Penokee Range Great Divide and Overlook.

Water Recreation

Lake fishing: 373 remote lakes with muskie, largemouth and smallmouth bass, walleye, crappie, northern pike, yellow perch, panfish, trout.

Cold water streams: 74 trout streams.

Campgrounds: 23 campgrounds on lakes, and 2 on rivers.

Canoe trails: spring high-water canoe trails: east fork of Chippewa River, Namekagon River, south fork of Flambeau River, Yellow River.

Semiprimitive Nonmotorized Areas

11 areas totaling 52,000 acres for camping, hiking, hunting, mountain biking, skiing, horseback riding.

Wilderness Areas

Porcupine Lake Wilderness: 4,450 acres for primitive camping. Access from the North Country Trail and from Porcupine Lake.

Rainbow Lake Wilderness: 6,600 acres for camping, hiking, and fishing. Access from North Country Trail, Anderson Grade, and Beaver Lake.

FOREST SERVICE SCENIC BYWAY

Great Divide Highway

These 29 miles of State Highway 77 showcase the beauty of the Upper Great Lakes' forests, lakes, marshes, and streams. *Contact Chequamegon National Forest.*

used for the Chequamegon Fat Tire Festival, the largest off-road bike race in the United States.

- St. Peter's Dome is a red granite summit from which it is often possible to see Lake Superior, about 20 miles to the north. About halfway up to the dome, hikers see Morgan Falls, a 70-foot cataract falling over a steep cliff.

NICOLET NATIONAL FOREST

105 miles northwest of Green Bay.

68 South Stevens Street
Rhinelander, WI 54501
715-362-1300
http://www.fs.fed.us

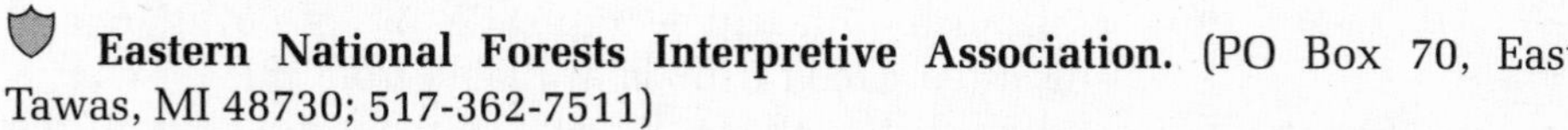

Eastern National Forests Interpretive Association. (PO Box 70, East Tawas, MI 48730; 517-362-7511)

Known as the "Cradle of Rivers," the Nicolet National Forest contains the headwaters of the Wolf, Pine, Popple, Oconto, Peshtigo, Deerskin, and Wisconsin rivers within its 661,889 acres. The forest is comprised of glacial terrain with gently rolling hills, 1,200 lakes, 1,100 miles of trout streams, and more than 400 spring ponds. Most of the lakes are crystal clear, providing good fishing for trout, pike, and bass. Three wilderness areas and several nonmotorized, walk-in areas provide more than 33,000 acres for year-round backpacking and primitive camping opportunities.

Sam's Tips

- The forest rents 8 rustic cabins at Lost Lake; for information, contact the Florence Natural Resource Center at 715-528-4464.

ST. CROIX NATIONAL SCENIC RIVERWAY

55 miles northwest of Eau Claire.

Ice Age National Scientific Reserve

In its nine properties spread across the state, the Ice Age National Scientific Reserve exhibits evidence of great glacial advances that occurred as recently as 12,000 years ago. The Wisconsin glaciation stage covered much of the northern United States from the Atlantic coast to the Rocky Mountains, but nowhere is evidence of the glaciers better preserved than here in Wisconsin. The Reserve was established in 1971 to protect these landforms, but the individual units are managed for various purposes, including wildlife management, recreation, and scientific study. For more information write c/o Bureau of Parks and Recreation, PO Box 7921, Madison, WI 53707; 608-266-2181.

PO Box 708
St. Croix Falls, WI 54024
715-483-3284
http://www.nps.gov/sacr

Eastern National. (446 North Lane, Conshohocken, PA 19428; 800-355-5566)

Free flowing and unpolluted, the Namekagon and St. Croix rivers wind through some of the most scenic and least developed country in the upper Midwest. Today, 252 miles of these rivers are preserved as part of the St. Croix National Scenic Riverway. The wilder upper ends of the rivers offer challenges for canoeists—although none of the Riverway's waters is classified as whitewater—while the lower ends provide calmer entertainment for boaters, fishers, birdwatchers, campers, and picnickers.

SAM'S TIPS

- Rapids along the Riverway are rated as Class I, but high water can raise the difficulty level to Class II or Class III. Local outfitters provide canoes, paddles, life vests, and assistance with trip planning. A list of outfitters and suggested canoe trips is available from the Wisconsin address listed above. Be sure to request a copy of the Riverway's publication, *Two Rivers Guide.*

POINTS OF INTEREST

U.S. ARMY CORPS OF ENGINEERS

BLACKHAWK PARK
Direct access to the main channel and some of the best fishing on the Upper Mississippi River at Pool 9, near La Crosse, WI. Several historical landmarks of the Blackhawk Wars are located near the park, along WI 35. From La Crosse, south 20 miles on WI 35.

EAU GALLE LAKE
Located in a scenic area with steep hills, valleys, bluffs, streams, and lakes. From St. Paul, east 40 miles on I-94, then south 10 miles on County Road 29.

GRANT RIVER

A well-developed camping area with numerous conveniences and a boat ramp. Turn left off WI 133 at the sign near the southern edge of Potosi, WI, then go 2 miles and turn right on the first improved road.

STURGEON BAY AND LAKE MICHIGAN SHIP CANAL

On the west shore of Lake Michigan. From Milwaukee, north on US 141 to Manitowoc, north on WI 42 to Sturgeon Bay, and right on Memorial Drive.

THE NATIONAL PARK FOUNDATION

For 30 years, the National Park Foundation (NPF) has been the official, nonprofit partner of the National Park Service. Chartered by Congress in 1967, the Foundation channels private resources into programs that directly benefit Uncle Sam's national parks.

The NPF raises money for the parks through gifts from individuals, corporations, and private foundations, and through cause-marketing programs. NPF's grants support education and public outreach; natural resource conservation and stewardship; National Park Service volunteers, and the professional development of National Park Service employees. Since 1990, the National Park Foundation has awarded more than $10.4 million to the national parks.

NPF's Board of Directors is comprised of 25 civic and business leaders, including the Secretary of the Interior.

NPF donors have the opportunity to invest directly in park wildlife conservation, environmental education, preservation of historic structures, preservation of archaeological and cultural sites, and development of media products, such as films, wayside exhibits, and other means of teaching the public about the unique values of the site. Gifts can be planned for specific sites, ecosystems, species, or issues. All contributions to the Foundation are tax-deductible.

For more information, contact:

The National Park Foundation
1101 17th Sreet, NW, Suite 1102
Washington, DC 20036
202-785-4500; fax: 202-785-3539
http://www.nationalparks.org

One of NPF's greatest contributions is its book, *The Complete Guide to America's National Parks.* This authoritative and comprehensive resource can be ordered by writing to the address above or by calling 800-533-6478. Bulk sales are available at a 50 percent discount. Proceeds from *Guide* sales—and all other NPF products—directly support the parks.

THE ELEMENTS OF THE NATIONAL PARK SERVICE

National Battlefield

The parks under this general title include national battlefields, national battlefield parks, national battlefield sites, and national military parks.

National Historic Site

This designation, derived from the Historic Sites Act of 1935, applies to the second largest number of units in the national park system. The title has been applied to an array of historic sites, from forts to the homes of notable Americans. In general, a national historic site contains a single historical feature that was directly associated with its subject. Examples include Fort Union Trading Post in North Dakota, Theodore Roosevelt Birthplace in New York, and Weir Farm in Connecticut.

National Historical Park

The National Historical Park designation has generally been applied to parks that extend beyond single properties or buildings, such as Independence National Historical Park in Philadelphia, with its several structures; Boston National Historical Park, with nine separate components; and Colonial National Historical Park in Virginia (originally a national monument), with its separate Jamestown and Yorktown units.

National Lakeshore

Congress authorized Pictured Rocks National Lakeshore (MI) in October 1966, and Indiana Dunes (IN) in November of the same year. The last two national lakeshores, Apostle Islands (WI) and Sleeping Bear Dunes (MI), were authorized in 1970. The lakeshores, all on the Great Lakes, closely parallel the seashores in character and use.

National Memorial

A national memorial is purely commemorative of a particular historic person or episode. The first National Park Service property classified as a national memorial was the Washington Monument, begun in 1848.

National Monument

President Theodore Roosevelt proclaimed and reserved the first national monument, Devils Tower (WY), in 1906. National monuments are smaller than national parks and lack the diversity or range of attractions that national parks have.

National Park

A national park designation has generally been assigned to the greatest natural attractions of the national park system. The term is meant to imply a large, spectacular, natural place having a wide variety of attributes, at times including significant historic assets. Hunting and mining are not authorized.

National Parkway

Four units of the national park system fall into this classification, although none has "national parkway" in its name: George Washington Memorial Parkway, in Virginia, dates from 1930; the Blue Ridge Parkway and the Natchez-Trace Parkway, each more than 400 miles long, were begun in the mid-1930s; John D. Rockefeller, Jr., Memorial Parkway, linking Yellowstone and Grand Teton national parks, was designated in 1972. The title "parkway" refers to the parkland paralleling the road as well as the roadway itself.

National Preserve

In 1974, Big Cypress (FL) and Big Thicket (TX) became the first of the national preserves. Ten national preserves are in Alaska, all established by the Alaska National Interest Lands Conservation Act of 1980. Seven of these preserves border national parks of the same name; all allow sport hunting, which is prohibited in the national parks. Many of the existing national preserves would, without sport hunting, otherwise qualify for designation as national parks.

National Recreation Area

The first unit with this designation was Lake Mead National Recreation Area, renamed Boulder Dam National Recreation Area when the National Park Service assumed responsibility for it in 1936. Twelve national recreation areas in the NPS are centered on large reservoirs. The first urban national recreation areas were Gateway (NY) and Golden Gate (CA), authorized by Congress in 1972. These urban parks combine scarce open spaces with the preservation of significant historic resources and important natural areas, in locations that can provide outdoor recreation for large numbers of visitors.

National Scenic River

The first area with this title was authorized in 1964—Ozark National Scenic Riverways—extending 140 miles along two rivers in Missouri. Other river units bear variations of this title that reflect their differences: national river and recreation area, national scenic river, national recreational river, and wild river.

National Scenic Trail

The Appalachian National Scenic Trail, the first such park in the National Park system, was so designated by the National Trails System Act of 1968. The trail extends some 2,100 miles from Katahdin, Maine, to Springer Mountain, Georgia. The title aptly describes these linear parklands and their use.

National Seashore

Cape Hatteras National Seashore (NC) was the first such area to be authorized, in 1937. Nine more have been established on the Atlantic, Gulf, and Pacific coasts, the last being Canaveral National Seashore (FL), in 1975. Some national seashores have roads, parking, and other facilities to accommodate heavy beach visitation. Others are in a relatively primitive state and include wilderness areas.

Wild and Scenic Rivers

To be eligible for WSR designation, a river must be free-flowing and contain at least one "outstandingly remarkable value"—scenery, recreation, geological formations, fish, wildlife, historic or cultural resources, and other similar values. Although most rivers are designated by an Act of Congress, the Secretary of the Interior can also designate a river upon a State Governor's request.

Wilderness Area

The Wilderness Act, which created the National Wilderness Preservation System, was passed by Congress in 1964. The legislation stated that wilderness is "an area where the earth and its community of life are untrammeled by man, where man himself is a visitor who does not remain." It provided for use and enjoyment of wilderness, but in a manner that leaves such areas unimpaired for future use and enjoyment as wilderness.

The Rocky Mountain Region

NATIONAL PARK SERVICE HANDBOOKS— THE ROCKY MOUNTAIN REGION

National Park Service handbooks highlight popular visitor sites across the country. Use them to learn about the historic significance and natural beauty of your next vacation destination. All are generously illustrated with photos, maps, and diagrams. Sites in the Rocky Mountain Region for which these authoritative handbooks are available include:

Site	*Stock No.*	*Price*
Craters of the Moon (ID)	024-005-01077-7	$2.75
Devils Tower (WY)	024-005-00899-3	4.25
Grand Teton (WY)	024-005-00903-5	4.50
Fort Laramie (WY)	024-005-00900-1	7.50
Wind Cave National Park (SD)	024-005-00766-1	7.00

You can order these documents by phone (202-512-1800) or fax (202-512-2250) or by writing to: Superintendent of Documents, PO Box 371954, Pittsburgh, PA 15250-7954. (Use stock number when ordering. Prices may change.) The 24 local Government Bookstores located around the country carry titles of regional interest. Check the appendix for the one nearest to you.

COLORADO

ARAPAHO AND ROOSEVELT NATIONAL FORESTS

Fort Collins is 50 miles north of Denver. The forests' boundaries extend north to the Wyoming border and south past Interstate 70.

Arapaho and Roosevelt National Forests
1311 South College
Fort Collins, CO 80524
970-498-2770
http://www.fs.fed.us/arnf

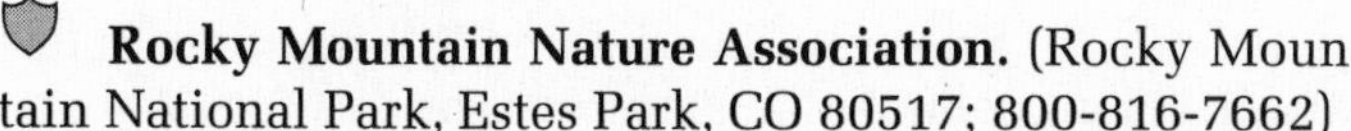

Rocky Mountain Nature Association. (Rocky Mountain National Park, Estes Park, CO 80517; 800-816-7662)

Historical Highlights

Ancestors of the Ute, Cheyenne, Arapaho, and Pawnee probably lived in this area as far back as 11,000 years ago. Around 1810, agents of the Hudson's Bay Company and the American Fur Company explored the region, establishing trapping sites. Gold was discovered in 1859 at Russell Gulch near Idaho Springs, and for the next four decades prospecting was intense.

Because of their nearness to major population centers and to the Rocky Mountain National Park, the Arapaho and Roosevelt rank among the top national forests for year-round recreation use. Camping, hiking, hunting, fishing, skiing, mountain biking, and driving for pleasure are popular activities. The Continental Divide and the front range of the Rocky Mountains form the "backbone" of the forests. Along the flanks of the glacially carved peaks—some reaching over 14,000 feet—lie high plateaus, rolling foothills, and open stretches of high prairie. Mountain peaks, alpine tundra, and towering canyon walls create breathtaking vistas. Over 400 species of wildlife make their home here, including deer, bighorn sheep, Rocky Mountain goats, marmots, and beavers. Much of the forests is managed for more primitive recreational activities, such as hike-in camping.

SAM'S TIPS

- Selecting a tree from designated cutting areas for holiday decorating is popular in early December each year.
- The highest paved road in the United States, the Mount Evans Scenic Byway, takes travelers up to the arctic-like high-alpine zone.
- The downhill ski areas within the park include Winterpark, Eldora, and Loveland Pass. For snowmobilers, Colorado's best snow and facilities are in Grand County.
- Rafting and kayaking are popular pastimes on the Cache la Poudre River. Canoeing is enjoyed on many forest lakes, including Lake Granby and Chambers Lake.

Arapaho National Recreation Area

The "Great Lakes of Colorado" are the major attractions of the Arapaho National Recreation Area, located just southwest of Rocky Mountain National Park, in the Arapaho–Roosevelt National Forests. Excellent campground and marina facilities are available. Visitors who want more than water sports can hike a portion of the Continental Divide National Scenic Trail in the headwaters of the Colorado River, visit the historic Monarch Lake logging camp site, or enjoy the vistas of the neighboring Rocky Mountain National Park. For details, contact Arapaho National Recreation Area, PO Box 10, Granby, CO 80446; 970-887-4100.

Pawnee National Grassland

The Pawnee National Grassland, 90 miles from Denver, CO, is a Great Plains shortgrass prairie backed by a panorama of beige and orange-hued rock ledges. The Pawnee Buttes—referred to as the "Rattlesnake Buttes" by James Michener, in his popular novel *Centennial*—are a well-known landmark in the Grassland. The prairie is home to over 200 bird species, including many birds of prey, as well as pronghorn antelope, coyote, and prairie dogs. The 193,000 acre grassland is divided into two sections. The western half is called the Crow Valley, and the eastern is called the Pawnee. For further information contact the Arapho and Roosevelt National Forest which manages the area.

BENT'S OLD FORT NATIONAL HISTORIC SITE

175 miles south of Denver, 250 miles north of Santa Fe, NM.

35110 Highway 194 East
La Junta, CO 81050-9523
719-384-2596
http://www.nps.gov/beol

Bent's Old Fort Historical Association. (same address as above; 719-384-2800)

Bent's Old Fort appears today as it did in 1845–1846, when the fort was a center of trading activities for the Mexican territory, the Plains Indians, and the commercial East. Ceran St. Vrain and Charles and William Bent maintained a giant commercial empire at the fort for 17 years. Their downfall began when the federal government designated the adobe trading post as an advance base for Stephen Watts Kearney's invasion of New Mexico. As the war progressed, the Army's increasing presence disturbed wildlife, especially bison, and polluted some water sources. With the commencement of Indian warfare in 1847, trading suffered. Finally, after an outbreak of cholera, the fort was abandoned.

BLACK CANYON OF THE GUNNISON NATIONAL MONUMENT

200 miles southwest of Denver; 200 miles north of Santa Fe, NM; 15 miles east of Montrose, CO, via US 50 and CO 347.

102 Elk Creek
Gunnison, CO 81230
970-641-2337
http://www.nps.gov/blca

The Southwest Parks and Monuments Association. (same as park)

Carved by the Gunnison River, the Black Canyon combines sheer walls, extraordinary narrowness, and great depth to magnificent effect. Slanting rays of sunlight keep the canyon's deep rock walls in heavy shadows—hence, the name. The canyon is 53 miles long, but only the most spectacular 12 miles of the gorge lie within the monument boundaries.

Authentic Reproductions

The Bent's Old Fort Historical Association store is a throwback to the heyday of the fort; its list of goods is similar to one that you might have found had you visited in the 1840s. In fact, the association requires that most items sold are documented to the 1830s and 1840s and are approved by the National Park Service. Almost all of the items stocked are reproductions, with the exception of the 4-point Whitney blanket, which has been in production since 1669 and is still produced in Whitney, England, by the original company. Another original item is the Sheffield knife, which has been in continuous production since 1819. For a complete list and price sheet of these and other interesting period items, write to the Bent's Old Fort address or call 719-384-2800.

SAM'S TIPS

- *Currents,* the Visitor Information Guide for the monument, has plenty of tips on what to do with anywhere from 2 days to 2 hours of time. Hikers: There are no marked trails into the canyon. If you plan to make a descent, a backcountry permit is required, and it is essential to check with a park ranger who can tell you which routes to use.
- The South Rim of the canyon is the most accessible. The road to the North Rim is graveled and closed in winter. Both roads take you to the very edge of the canyon.
- At the Narrows View, on the North Rim of the canyon, the distance between the rims (1,150 feet) is less than the depth (1,725 feet) of the canyon.

Parks as Classrooms

The Black Canyon of the Gunnison National Monument and Curecanti National Recreation Area Outreach Education Program provides programs for 10,000 K-12 students on the western slope of Colorado. Field trips using the parks resources are scheduled Monday through Thursday excluding federal holidays. Curriculum offerings include:

Preschool: "Feathers or Fur?" and "Trees"
Kindergarten: "Ice, Snow, Water and Mist" and "Changing with the Seasons"
First Grade: "Who Goes There?" and "The Five Senses"
Second Grade: "Fascinating Fossils!" and "Weather, Weather All Around Us"
Third Grade: "Globes, Maps, and GPS" and "DAMS"
Fourth Grade: "Die, Adapt, or Move" and "Colorado Geology"
Fifth Grade: "Habitats and Satellites"
Sixth Grade: "Energy in Our World"
Seventh Grade: "Paleontology: Putting Together the Pieces"
Eighth Grade: "The Active Earth"
High School Units: "Water Quality/ Macro-Invertebrates"

Program dates should be reserved in advance. For more information, call 970-641-2337 ext. 203 or 204.

- Because of its sheer, steep walls, Black Canyon is a great rock-climbing park, but not for beginners.
- Camping is first-come, first served. Curecanti National Recreation Area, and the Ridgeway Lake and Crawford Lake state recreation areas—Black Canyon's neighboring parks—have plenty of camping and picnicking spots if the canyon is crowded.
- The canyon walls on the North Rim are almost vertical, offering some of the most impressive views found in the monument. It is reachable only by gravel road from Crawford, Colorado.

COLORADO NATIONAL MONUMENT

265 miles west of Denver; 280 miles southeast of Salt Lake City.

Fruita, CO 81521
970-858-3617
http://www.nps.gov/colm

Colorado National Monument Association. (same address as above)

This plateau-and-canyon country, with its towering naturally sculpted rock, is representative of the grand landscapes of the American West. Thirty-two square miles of up-and-down terrain are filled with great views and remote canyons. The high country of Colorado National Monument rises more than 2,000 feet above the Grand Valley of the Colorado River. Situated at the edge of the Uncompahgre Uplift, the park is a part of the greater Colorado Plateau, which also embraces such scenic wonders as the Grand Canyon, Bryce Canyon, and Arches National Park.

John Otto

When John Otto moved into Grand Junction, Colorado, in 1906, he found an area that "felt like the heart of the world to me." He lived alone in the desolate canyons and spent his time building miles of trails so that others could enjoy the beauty of the land. He also campaigned tirelessly for the area to be set aside as a national park. The citizens of Grand Junction rallied behind him and swamped officials in Washington, DC, with letters. In 1911, the Colorado National Monument was established, and Otto was rewarded by being offered the job of caretaker. He accepted and held the position until 1927, for $1 a month.

SAM'S TIPS

- The easiest way to see the monument is via Rim Rock Drive, which climbs from the Grand Valley of the Colorado River to the park's high country, then winds along the plateau rim, offering 23 miles of breathtaking views.
- The Serpent's Trail, the Crookedest Road in the World, has 50 switchbacks and can be hiked in about 2 hours. This historic trail, engineered by John Otto in the early 1900s, was once the main road into the high country.
- The largest free-standing rock formation in the park is Independence Monument, which has been carved by erosion over millions of years. You can view it from the Independence Monument Viewpoint, 2 miles south of the Visitor Center. Or, hike the 12-mile (round trip) Monument Canyon Trail, a steep 600-foot descent from the plateau into the bottom of the canyon.

Comanche National Grassland

The 435,000-acre Comanche National Grassland is made up of two units in southeastern Colorado: the Timpas Unit, near La Junta, and the Carrizo Unit, near Springfield. The Grassland was named for the Comanche Indian tribe, highly respected fighters in the southern Plains. The Grassland's landscape varies from steep canyons with scarce trees to gently rolling slopes covered with yucca and sagebrush. This area is home to the lesser prairie chicken, which is a threatened species in Colorado. Within the Grassland is Picture Canyon, which has served as an oasis for travelers and settlers for thousands of years. Whether through the rock art drawings preserved on sandstone walls, or through other artifacts, such as the Birthing Stone, the Canyon's past inhabitants have left the marks of their cultures. Panel drawings include animal figures, human figures, and a series of vertical incised lines that have been likened to an ancient Celtic writing style called Ogam. Write to PO Box 127, Springfield, CO 81073; 719-523-6591.

CURECANTI NATIONAL RECREATION AREA

200 miles southwest of Denver; 200 miles north of Sante Fe, NM.

102 Elk Creek
Gunnison, CO 81230
970-641-2337
http://www.nps.gov/cure

 **The Southwest Parks and Monuments Association.** (same address as above; 970-641-2337)

The construction of three dams on the Gunnison River has turned a semiarid shrubland into a recreation mecca. Three lakes—Blue Mesa, Morrow Point, and Crystal—offer a variety of water sports. The surrounding mesas are capped with cliffs and rocky spires that are the result of violent volcanic eruptions some 30 million years ago.

 **Sam's Tips**

- Boat tours on Morrow Point Lake are offered on a regular schedule during the summer. An interpreter on board relates the lake's story and gives you a water-level view of the Curecanti Needle (a 700-foot granite spire) and the sheer walls of Black Canyon. For schedules and information, call 970-641-0402 between Memorial Day and Labor Day.
- Blue Mesa Lake, the largest and most accessible of the three lakes, is the focus of most of the water sports and recreation activities. The 20-mile-long lake has three large basins—the Iola, Cebolla, and Sapinero—with suitable expanses for fishing, sailing, sailboarding, and waterskiing. Curecanti's lakes are cold, so beware of hypothermia.

The Little Railroads

Almost toylike in appearance, narrow gauge railroad trains used rolling stock only two-thirds the size of regular train cars. The term "narrow gauge" comes from the short distance (3 feet) between the rails on which the trains rolled. The entire system was designed to facilitate the building of a railroad through the high country of the Rocky Mountains. The lighter rails could be bent sharply to make the necessary curves around mountainsides. Although the trains were able to carry enough cargo to make the lines economically feasible, one problem doomed narrow gauge from the start: where the 3-foot rails met the standard-gauge rails, all loads had to be transferred to a different train. In spite of this and other problems, the narrow gauge railroads served the mountain areas from the late 1800s until almost 1950. The rise of the automobile eventually doomed these "little railroads."

- The National Park Service's Cimarron site has a superb railroad exhibit. Locomotive #278, its coal tender, a boxcar, and a caboose stand atop the last remaining railroad trestle along the Black Canyon of the Gunnison route. These restored pieces are excellent examples of the types of trains used on this branch of the Denver and Rio Grande Narrow Gauge Railway in its heyday. The trestle is on the National Register of Historic Places.
- The Dillon Pinnacles Trail is a four-mile round trip with a panoramic view of the volcanic Dillon Pinnacles and Blue Mesa Lake. The Dillon Pinnacles have four distinct rock layers visible above water level.
- The Black Canyon of the Gunnison National Monument (see entry) is adjacent to the eastern boundary of Curecanti. Scenic Highway 92 provides the best views of the Black Canyon's North Rim.

Finding the Fossils

Paleontologists did not have to dig far to find fossils at Dinosaur National Monument. In fact, the first fossils discovered were sticking out of the top of a tall jagged ridge. Here's why. The sandbar that held the ancient dinosaur fossil beds was buried under thousands of meters of rock until the Rocky Mountains began to rise to the east. As they rose, the area that is now Dinosaur National Monument went along for the ride. Instead of pushing the rock layers up from below, the mountains squeezed them from the side, warping and tilting them, while cracking and shifting the rock along fault lines. Rain, frost, wind, and gravity steadily wore away layer after layer of the uppermost strata, revealing the older rocks underneath, including the fossil bed at Dinosaur. Thus, when Earl Douglass found the first brontosaurus bones in 1909, the rock layer that had once been a sandy river bed was instead a tilted ridge of rock protruding sideways from the earth. Since the Douglass discovery, thousands of bones—including several nearly complete skeletons of the stegosaurus, brontosaurus, camptosaurus, and allosaurus—have been removed from the site.

DINOSAUR NATIONAL MONUMENT

330 miles west of Denver, CO; 165 miles east of Salt Lake City, UT.

4545 Highway 40
Dinosaur, CO 81610-9724
970-374-3000
http://www.nps.gov/dino

Dinosaur Nature Association. (1291 East Highway 40, Vernal, UT 84078; 800-845-DINO)

Located on the border between Colorado and Utah, Dinosaur National Monument is home to one of the most unique fossils beds ever discovered—a "time capsule" from the world of the dinosaurs, which is preserved in the sands of an ancient river. But dinosaur bones are only a part of this unique monument. The lesser-known canyon country to the east of the Dinosaur Quarry is a harsh, beautiful landscape cut by the Green and Yampa Rivers on their way south to the Colorado.

Sam's Tips

- The canyon country east of the Dinosaur Quarry is worth at least half a day. A trip on the Harpers Corner Scenic Drive and then a short hike on the Harpers Corner Trail lead to spectacular views of Echo Park and Whirlpool Canyon.
- The best way to see the canyons is to take a river-rafting trip on the Green or Yampa Rivers. Day trips are generally available, even on short notice. A river permit is required for private trips, and can only be obtained though a lottery system or by contacting a river concessionaire.
- Several examples of Freemont Indian rock art can be found in Dinosaur. The most easily accessible sites are along Cub Creek, a few miles to the east of the Dinosaur Quarry.

Unique Fish

The Colorado River Basin once had a unique fish population. The widely varying stream flows (roaring floods in spring, mere trickles by late summer), turbulent and muddy water, and high summer water temperature created an environment in which only a few species adapted. Of the river system's 14 native species, 6 are found nowhere else in the world. Dams have greatly altered the character of these rivers, and the native fish are unable to adapt to the changes. Nonnative species thrive in the dam-calmed waters and eat the young of native fish. The result is that four native fishes—the Colorado squawfish, humpback chub, bonytail chub, and razorback sucker—are now endangered species. Dinosaur National Monument contains some of the last wild rivers in Colorado, providing an important sanctuary for native fish.

THE ROCKY MOUNTAIN NATURE ASSOCIATION

Cooperating associations are on the front lines as providers of vital information to millions of visitors to America's national parks, forests, and other public lands. These nonprofit associations work closely with the management of the parks and forests toward the production of quality publications, maps, videos, and theme-related merchandise. One of the largest associations is:

Rocky Mountain Nature Association
Rocky Mountain National Park
Estes Park, CO 80517
800-816-7662
http://www.rmna.org/bookstore

This Association produces material for these public lands:

Arapaho–Roosevelt National Forest (CO)
Florissant Fossil Beds National Monument (CO)
Medicine Bow National Forest (WY)
Pike–San Isabel National Forest (CO)
Rio Grande National Forest (CO)
Rocky Mountain National Park (CO)
Shoshone National Forest (WY)
U.S. Forest Service Regional Office (CO)
White River National Forest (CO)

FLORISSANT FOSSIL BEDS NATIONAL MONUMENT

100 miles south of Denver; 38 miles west of Colorado Springs on US 24.

PO Box 185
Florissant, CO 80816
719-748-3253
http://www.nps.gov/flfo

Rocky Mountain Nature Association. (same address as above; 800-816-7662)

The area that is now Florissant Fossil Beds was once a 12-mile lake stretching through a forested valley. Violent volcanic eruptions trapped animal and plant life in layers of sediment that settled at the bottom of the lake. Thirty-four million years after the eruptions, early settlers from Missouri named this land of meadows, forests, and wildflowers "Florissant," French for "flowering." The monument preserves some of the finest fossil-bearing deposits of the Eocene Epoch found anywhere in the world.

Fossil Insects

The volcanic ash mixture that fell on Lake Florissant was finer than talcum powder and ideal for the delicate job of preserving insect fossils. More than 1,100 insect species have been identified from the fossils retrieved from the shale. The insects are usually preserved as exquisitely detailed impressions in the shale, colored black or brown by a thin residue of organic matter—all that remains of the actual living entity. Some insects look perfect, others are crushed, and some are just parts: a wing fragment or a headless body.

The fossils are evidence that insects have not changed much in the past 34 million years. However, many of the types that once habitated Lake Florissant are no longer in Colorado. One example is the tsetse fly, which no longer exists in North America. Other insect species have become extinct.

Sam's Tips

- Rangers conduct both classroom visits and field trips to the Fossil Beds. Seminar and group tours are available. Call or write the monument office to make a reservation.
- The Petrified Forest Loop Trail leads to several petrified stumps, including Big Stump, the remains of a giant sequoia 38 feet in circumference. Surface exposures of the paper-thin fossil-bearing shale rock occur in only a few locations, and the rock erodes easily. Collecting of fossils is not permitted.
- The Hornbek Homestead recreates the life of pioneers in 1878. The site includes the original cabin and a reconstructed barn, carriage shed, and root cellar.
- Among the fossils found at Florissant are: butterflies, tsetse flies, redwood trees, opossums, and ancient ancestors of the horse and pig. The insects are a special rarity; their detailed fossils are found in only a few other places because insects are so fragile and are not usually preserved.

NATIONAL FOREST USER ETHICS

The slogan of the U.S. Forest Service is "Caring for the Land and Serving People." The Forest Service is involved with several programs to help visitors use the forests in a manner that will minimize the impact of their visit. Two of these programs are *Tread Lightly!* and *Leave No Trace. Tread Lightly!* provides information about enjoying off-highway vehicle travel and other back-country travel. Call 801-627-0077, or write *Tread Lightly!* Inc., 298 24th Street, Suite 325, Ogden, UT 84401. *Leave No Trace* provides information and materials on nonmotorized back-country recreation skills and ethics. Call toll free 800-332-4100 or write *Leave No Trace,* 288 Main Street, Lander, WY 82520.

GRAND MESA, UNCOMPAHGRE, AND GUNNISON NATIONAL FORESTS

Throughout southwestern Colorado; Delta is 50 miles southeast of Grand Junction.

2250 Highway 50
Delta, CO 81416-2485
970-874-6600
http://www.fs.fed.us

Western Colorado Interpretive Association. (2250 Highway 50, Delta, CO 81416; 970-874-6600)

The jointly managed Grand Mesa, Uncompahgre, and Gunnison National Forests, which comprise almost 3 million acres extending into 10 Colorado counties, make up the third largest national forest area in the lower 48 United States. The mostly forested, mountainous lands located on the western slope of the Colorado Rockies are notable for their spectacular scenery, natural features, and abundant wildlife, and for the recreational activities that attract over 2 million visitors a year. In addition to 9 separate mountain ranges, the forests contain the Grand Mesa, the world's largest flat-top mountain, which is dotted with over 300 lakes and reservoirs. The Slumgullion Slide Area, 4 miles southeast of Lake City, was created about 700 years ago when a gigantic flow of earth moved down a nearby mountain and dammed the Lake Fork of the Gunnison, creating Lake San Cristobal. Eight separate Wilderness areas offer primitive camping and hiking opportunities in a solitary environment. The 1,850 miles of trails that provide access to the back-country areas include 50 miles groomed for cross-country skiing and 200 miles of trails groomed for snowmobiling. Other areas and trails are open for mountain biking, horseback riding, and off-road vehicle use.

SAM'S TIPS

- Six scenic highways pass through the boundaries:
  1. The Grand Mesa Scenic and Historic Byway crosses the world's largest flat-top mountain and travels through numerous ecological transitions, including desert canyons, aspen foothills, lily ponds, and alpine forests.
  2. The San Juan Skyway loops through the San Juan Mountains, passing ancient Indian ruins.
  3. The Silver Thread National Scenic Byway winds for 75 miles through the San Juan Mountains in the Gunnison and Rio Grande National Forests and crosses the 700-year-old Slumgullion Earthflow, which is still moving at a rate of 28 feet per year.
  4. The West Elk Loop circles the West Elk Wilderness and passes the Black Canyon of the Gunnison, Curecanti National Recreation Area, Blue Mesa Reservoir, Crawford State Recreation Area, and Paonia State Recreation Area.

5. The Alpine loop, a nationally famous four-wheel-drive loop, is actually a series of old mining roads built in the late 1800s during the silver, gold, lead, and zinc booms.
6. The Unaweep and Tabeguache Scenic and Historic Byway includes ancient structures built by Native Americans, petroglyphs, and a wooden water flume, hanging to the edge of stone cliffs and left over from mining operations.

- Mountain climbers can tackle one of the "fourteeners" (peaks above 14,000 feet) in Uncompahgre, Lizard Head, or Mount Sneffels Wilderness Areas.
- Some of the forest's most popular camping areas include Amphitheater Campground near Ouray; Sunshine and Matterhorn Campgrounds south of Telluride; and the Taylor River Canyon northeast of Gunnison.
- At an elevation over 11,500 feet, the 1882 Alpine Tunnel, near Pitkin, was the highest point ever reached by a railroad in its time. The tunnel was the first railroad bore drilled in the United States and the first to carry tracks under the Continental Divide.
- The Dry Mesa Dinosaur Quarry, discovered in 1968, has yielded skeletons of the world's largest plant-eating dinosaur ever found and the largest carnivorous dinosaur from the Jurassic Period.

Where Did the Name Come From?

Mount Sneffels, the prominent 14,150-foot peak, received its name from the Jules Verne novel *Journey to the Center of the Earth.* Sneffels, the Nordic word for "snow field," was the crater in which Verne's expedition party descended into the earth.

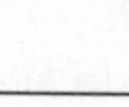

GHOST TOWNS ON THE BACK COUNTRY BYWAYS

Many historic mining sites are located on the federal lands managed by the Bureau of Land Management (BLM). These spots can be wonderful destinations for school or family field trips. A number of sites are located along the BLM's "Back Country Byways"—roads that pass through outstanding scenic, historic, and cultural treasures located on federal lands. In Colorado, the Alpine Loop Back Country Byway, linking Lake City, Silverton, and Ouray, follows roads built by miners over 100 years ago. It passes entrances to old mines, mining camps, mill ruins, tram lines, and ghost towns.

The ghost town of Garnet, Montana, stands along the Garnet Range Back Country Byway east of Missoula. At its peak in 1898, Garnet's population climbed to almost 3,000. Today, Garnet is Montana's best preserved ghost town, with more than 30 wooden structures still standing. For more information about Back Country Byways, contact your local BLM office. Byways are also located in Arizona, California, Colorado, Idaho, Montana, Nevada, New Mexico, Oregon, South Dakota, Utah, and Wyoming.

Of All Places, Why Are There Dunes Here?

Seeing the sand dunes for the first time can be disconcerting. Dunes belong near the shore of an ocean or near lakes, not at the base of the Sangre de Cristo Mountains. And yet, the ingredients for dunes—sand, wind, and time—all exist here. The Rio Grande, which runs through the valley, has been depositing sediment on the river banks for thousands of years. These deposits were left exposed as the river changed its course. Wind picked up the sand and sediments and carried them toward the mountain range. The lighter sediments were carried by the wind over the mountains, and the sand and heavier sediments were deposited at the base. Over time, the large dunes emerged.

GREAT SAND DUNES NATIONAL MONUMENT

240 miles south of Denver; 184 miles north of Santa Fe, NM.

11999 Highway 150
Mosca, CO 81146
719-378-2312
http://www.nps.gov/grsa

 **The Southwest Parks and Monuments Association.** (same address as above)

Tucked between the San Juan Mountains and the Sangre de Cristo Mountains are the tallest sand dunes in North America. Built by the wind from tiny grains of sand, these dunes reach heights of over 750 feet and cover approximately 39 square miles. The winds continue to blow, sometimes at velocities above 40 miles per hour, shaping and reshaping the surface of the dunes.

HOVENWEEP NATIONAL MONUMENT

200 miles southwest of Denver; 25 miles southwest of Pleasant View.

McElmo Route
Cortez, CO 81321
970-529-4461
http://www.nps.gov/hove

 **The Mesa Verde Association.** (same address as above)

Hovenweep was established in 1923 to protect six groups of Pueblo Indian ruins. The inhabitants of Hovenweep occupied the Four Corners region until almost 1300, when a prolonged drought drove them south toward the Rio Grande. Today, the remains of multiroom pueblos, small cliff dwellings, and towers constructed of excellent coursed-stone masonry still stand more than 20 feet high in some places.

MESA VERDE NATIONAL PARK

400 miles southwest of Denver; 247 miles northwest of Albuquerque, NM. Park entrance is midway between Cortez and Mancos, off US 160.

PO Box 8
Mesa Verde, CO 81330-0008
970-529-4461
http://www.nps.gov/meve

Mesa Verde Museum Association (PO Box 38, Mesa Verde National Park, CO 81330; 970-529-4445)

At Mesa Verde National Park, immense stone cities built into cliff faces are the spectacular remnants of the ancestral Puebloan people, dating back thousands of years. Mesa Verde occupies part of a large plateau rising high above the Montezuma and Mancos Valleys. The remains of the Puebloan stone cities are the primary attraction of the park.

Sam's Tips

- Hiking is restricted to six developed trails within the park. Aptly named Petroglyph Trail is the only trail with petroglyphs open to visitors. Register in advance for this hike.
- The largest cliff dwellings open to the public are in the southern part of the park, at Chapin Mesa and Wetherill Mesa. The long and winding road to Wetherill is closed during the winter.
- The only place in the United States where four states abut (Colorado, Utah, Arizona, and New Mexico) is just southwest of Mesa Verde. The most spectacular view in what is known as the Four Corners region is from Park Point, in the northern part of the park.

No Forwarding Address?

About 1,400 years ago, a group of Native Americans chose Mesa Verde for their home. For the next 700 years, their descendants lived and flourished here, eventually building elaborate stone cities in the sheltered recesses of the canyon walls. Their basic construction material was sandstone, which they shaped into rectangular blocks. Mortar between the blocks was a mix of water and mud. Some dwellings were three stories tall and were joined together into units of 50 rooms or more.

Then, in the late 1200s, within the span of one or two generations, they left their homes and moved away. With no written records, archaeologists can only provide guesses about the reasons for their sudden departure.

PIKE AND SAN ISABEL NATIONAL FORESTS

The Pike National Forest's 1.1 million acres begin west of Colorado Springs and extend west across the Rocky Mountains.

San Isabel National Forest consists of several geographically separate parcels beginning 45 miles southwest of Colorado Springs, extending south, and terminating near the border of New Mexico.

1920 Valley Drive
Pueblo, CO 81008
719-545-8737
http://www.fs.fed.us

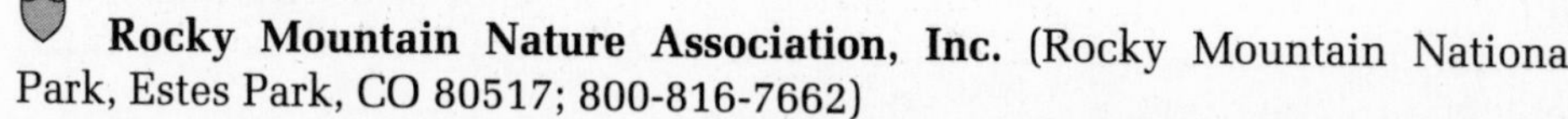

Rocky Mountain Nature Association, Inc. (Rocky Mountain National Park, Estes Park, CO 80517; 800-816-7662)

The Pike National Forest is marked on its northern end by 14,264-foot Mount Evans, which is surrounded by the Mount Evans Wilderness. Except for Geneva and Jefferson Creeks, the recreation resources in this large expanse of Park County remain primarily primitive and undeveloped, accessible mainly by four-wheel drive, horse, or foot. Four miles northwest of Alma is the Windy-Ridge Bristlecone Pine Scenic Area, which contains a unique grove of beautifully deformed bristlecone pine trees. The San Isabel forest contains numerous ghost mining towns. Cross-country skiing and snowmobiling are popular in many undeveloped areas of the forest.

Sam's Tips

- Some of the popular fishing and camping areas in the Pike National Forest, such as Lost Park, Tarryall Creek, and Elevenmile Canyon, remain undeveloped in a remote, natural setting.
- The Pike and San Isabel National Forests are home to big game animals, such as deer, elk, Rocky Mountain bighorn sheep, goats, bear, and antelope, along with smaller game, such as rabbit, raccoon, coyote, mountain lion, bobcat, badger, marten, and mink. Hunting and fishing are permitted in all government and some privately owned lands within the forests' boundaries, subject to state hunting regulation. For more information, write the Colorado Division of Wildlife, 6060 Broadway, Denver, CO 80216.
- Among the area's most majestic mountains are 14,433-foot Mt. Elbert, Colorado's highest, and Pike's Peak, Colorado's most famous.
- Turquoise Lake Recreation Area and Twin Lakes Reservoir, near Leadville, are open for water skiing, boating, fishing, and camping.
- The Pike's Peak Toll Road is a well-known 19-mile drive to the summit of Pike's Peak. The Mount Manitou Park and Incline Cog Railroad provides an alternative means to reach the summit.
- Rafting and whitewater kayaking have become popular activities on the Arkansas River between Buena Vista and Cañon City, an area managed by multiple agencies.

LAND ABOVE THE TREES: ALPINE ZONE

In the land above the treeline, trees are less than eight feet tall. This beautiful but fragile landscape of rugged alpine plants needs your help.

- Don't be a tundra trampler! Stay on the trail or step carefully from rock to rock, avoiding any plants.
- Camp only below the treeline or where snow is two or more feet deep.
- Use a backpacking stove. Wood fires are generally not allowed in forests above the treeline.

ALTITUDE ACCLIMATIZATION

The U.S. Forest Service urges anyone coming into the high mountains from low altitudes to allow a few days to acclimatize before attempting a climb. Going too high too fast may cause "mountain sickness." The symptoms are vomiting, diarrhea, and a general feeling of being very ill. Pulmonary edema, a major medical emergency, also can occur above the 9,000-foot level. Its symptoms include extreme fatigue or collapse, shortness of breath, a racking cough, bubbling noises in the chest, and bloody sputum. The following schedule lists the approximate length of time you should spend at various altitudes in order to become acclimatized:

Day 1 = 0 ft.–7,000 ft.
Day 2 = 7,000 ft.–10,000 ft.
Day 3 = 10,000 ft.–12,000 ft.
Day 4 = 12,000 ft.–14,000 ft.

RIO GRANDE NATIONAL FOREST

South-central Colorado.

1803 West Highway 160
Monte Vista, CO 81144
719-852-5941
http://www.nps.gov/srnf

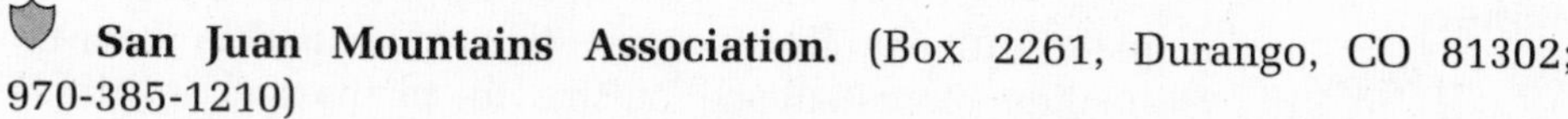

San Juan Mountains Association. (Box 2261, Durango, CO 81302; 970-385-1210)

The Rio Grande National Forest encompasses almost 2 million acres on the eastern slope of the Continental Divide. The forest surrounds the San Luis Valley, one of several high basin valleys ringed by mountains within Colorado, and contains parts of two spectacular mountain ranges: the San Juan to the west and the Sangre de Cristo to the east. The headwaters of the third longest river in the country are within the forest—the Rio Grande de Norte—"the Great River to the North," as it was known to the early Indian and Spanish inhabitants of the Southwest. The forest's 80 high lakes and 150 tumbling streams offer great fishing opportunities. The forest also contains campgrounds, picnic areas, trailheads, scenic overlooks, and eight boat ramps. Most of these facilities are accessible from major US/State highways.

Sam's Tips

- The forest contains many historical points of interest. One popular tour goes to Bachelor Town which is the gravesite of Bob Ford, the "dirty little coward" who killed Jesse James.

- Photography and wildlife-watching opportunities are excellent, especially along the 75-mile Silverthread Scenic Byway (Colorado Highway 149 from Southfork to Lake City).
- Other forest highlights include the Wheeler Geological Area near Creede, the Chama Basin, and three Wilderness Areas: the South San Juan, the La Garita, and the Weminuche.

The Alpine Tundra

Tundra, the Russian word for "land of no trees," is an extremely fragile landscape. Areas at Rocky Mountain that were damaged when opened to the public in 1932 and closed for study in 1952 have shown almost no signs of recovery. High winds (up to 170 mph) and long winters make new growth very slow. In a typical year, there are only 40 frost-free days, and temperatures stay below freezing for over 5 months. Step lightly when walking on tundra. Trampled places may take centuries to heal.

ROCKY MOUNTAIN NATIONAL PARK

65 miles north of Denver; 91 miles southwest of Cheyenne, WY.

Estes Park, CO 80517-8397
970-627-3471 (Kawuneeche Visitor Center, on the west side of the Park)
970-586-1206 (Park Headquarters, on the east side of the Park)
http://www.nps.gov/romo

 **Rocky Mountain Nature Association.** (same address as above; 800-816-7662)

The tenth oldest national park, Rocky Mountain is a high-altitude back-country hiking and mountain-climbing paradise. It boasts 114 named peaks above 10,000 feet. Douglas fir, Engleman spruce, and subalpine fir forests cover the mountainsides. At higher altitudes, the trees become twisted, hugging the ground. They then give way to the harsh landscape of the alpine tundra. Over one-third of the park is above the treeline. More than one-fourth of the plants here can also be found in the Arctic.

Bighorn Sheep

Bighorn sheep in Rocky Mountain National Park are a welcome sight. Hunting, and diseases introduced by domestic sheep, almost caused their extinction, but bighorn sheep are well adapted to the harsh climate and terrain of the park. Excellent eyesight, sense of smell, and hearing allow them to detect danger at great distances. Soft and flexible hooves aid them in rock jumping and allow them to climb on sharp cliff faces as they seek to escape predators. Their four-part stomach lets them eat large quantities of food and then retreat to the cliffs to rechew and digest it.

SAM'S TIPS

- Among the best day hikes are: the Lulu City Trail (7.2 miles), which leads to the remains of a once-booming mine town; the Tundra Nature Trail (½ mile), a short, paved trail that highlights the alpine environs; the Never Summer Ranch Trail (1 mile), which tells the story of homesteading and dude-ranch life during the early 20th century; and the Wild Basin Trail (16 miles), located in a wild corner of the park that offers scenic valleys, streams, and waterfalls.
- Trail Ridge Road (the highest continuous paved highway in the United States) is open from Memorial Day to mid-October, depending on the snowfall. The magnificent alpine highway winds up to 12,183 feet above sea level into a world of tundra surprisingly similar to the Arctic regions.

Back-Country Camping

The *Backcountry Camping Guide*, a park brochure, is an excellent starting point for planning a hiking and camping trip. It offers these tips:

1. *Get further information.* Rocky Mountain has many free publications that will be useful on your trip. Ask for them from the park itself. Then call the Rocky Mountain Nature Association and order one or more of these inexpensive publications: *Trails Illustrated Topographic Map of Rocky Mountain National Park; Backpacking One Step at a Time;* and *Rocky Mountain National Park Hiking Trails.*
2. *Plan ahead.* Use a topographical map to select your campsites. Take into consideration the physical condition of the weakest member of your party, and remember that most trails begin at 7,000 feet above sea level. Rangers recommend spending at least one night at 7,000 to 8,000 feet, to get acclimated before hiking.
3. *Get a permit.* You must have a back-country permit to camp overnight in the Rocky Mountain back-country. Permits are limited, so it is better to write or call ahead of time (write to the park address, Attn: Back-country Permits, or call 970-586-1242). For all reservations, you must include (a) your name, address, and zip code; (b) the dates you plan to enter and leave the back-country; (c) the number of people who will be in your party; and (d) an itinerary with dates corresponding to campsites or cross-country zones where you plan to stay overnight.

- Bear Lake Road is one of the few paved roads in the Rockies that leads to the heart of a high mountain basin. The lake sits at 9,400 feet and is the starting point for many trails. The half-mile nature trail around the lake is an easy walk.
- Additional camping and recreation opportunities nearby include the Arapaho and Roosevelt National Forests (see entry) and the Arapaho National Recreation Area.

ROUTT NATIONAL FOREST

Straddling the Continental Divide in the north central part of the state; 180 miles west of Denver.

Supervisor's Office
2468 Jackson Street
Laramie, WY 82070
307-745-2300
http://www.fs.fed.us/mrnf

Yampatika Outdoor Awareness Association. (PO Box 773342, Steamboat Springs, CO 80477; 970-879-1870)

This forest, which covers nearly 1.5 million acres, was once the favored meeting area for Indian tribes—including the Utes, Arapaho, Gros Ventres, Sioux, and

Cheyenne—attracted by the ample hunting and fishing, and the easy accessibility. This also became a favorite fur trapping ground, from 1825 to 1845. Year-round activities at the forest are horseback riding, hiking, and camping; winter activities include snow shoeing, snow mobiling, cross-country skiing, and ice fishing. Hunters find this area one of the best in Colorado for deer and elk.

Sam's Tips

- The forest's unique features include Fish Creek Falls, near Steamboat Springs, where water tumbles 263 feet over sheer rock walls, creating a mist to cool the visitor in summer. The Devils Causeway, an unusual geological formation with sharp drop-offs on either side, is located in the Flat Tops wilderness.
- A great place for ice fishing is Big Creek Lake, one of the state's largest natural lakes.

LOW-IMPACT CAMPING AND HIKING

In all wilderness areas, visitors are encouraged to practice low-impact camping and hiking. The San Juan National Forest (CO) offers these guidelines on how to use wilderness areas responsibly:

- Limit party size to 25 people and/or livestock.
- Camp at least 200 feet from water and trails.
- Do not cut switchbacks in trails. It causes erosion and actually uses more energy.
- Do not feed wild animals.
- Pack it in; pack it out! If you bring something in with you, make sure it leaves with you.
- Bury human waste and wash-water at least 6 to 8 inches underground and 200 feet from water, camp, and trails.
- Wash dishes, using a bucket, well away from water sources, and remember, even biodegradable soap pollutes water and can harm fish.
- Select a less popular area to visit, or plan a spring, fall, or midweek trip.
- Camp in areas where you won't disturb soil and can minimize any trampling of vegetation. Stay in one place no longer than four days.
- Use a gas stove rather than building a fire. Avoid creating new fire circles.
- Burn small sticks rather than cut down dead or green trees.
- Before breaking camp, make sure any earlier fire is cold to the touch, and bury the fire scar.
- Observe common courtesy; keep pets under control; don't make unnecessary noise that will disturb wildlife or other visitors; leave flowers, rocks, and other natural features where you found them.

SAN JUAN NATIONAL FOREST

Southwestern corner of Colorado, due west of Durango.

701 Camino Del Rio
Durango, CO 81301
970-247-4874
http://www.fs.fed.us/srnf

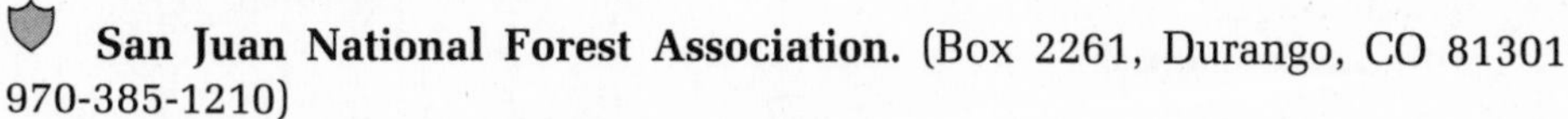

San Juan National Forest Association. (Box 2261, Durango, CO 81301; 970-385-1210)

Ride on the Durango and Silverton Narrow Gauge Railroad as it winds its way through the upper Animas River Canyon on a spectacular and historic route. The train will drop you off in Colorado's largest Wilderness Area, the Weminuche, where you can enjoy primitive back-country camping. The forest has over 40 developed campsites; the most popular ones are located around the major water attractions, such as the McPhee, Vallecito, Williams Creek, and Lemon reservoirs. The 2-million-acre forest boasts some of the most outstanding high mountain scenery anywhere in the world, as well as a variety of canyons, waterfalls, and lakes, and the headwaters of four major streams: the San Juan, Piedra, Animas, and Dolores.

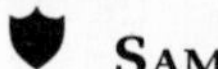

Sam's Tips

- The forest contains ruins from the ancient Anasazi culture of the southwest. Guided tours of the Chimney Rock Anasazi ruins are offered only in the summer.
- Stay overnight in the Jersey Jim Fire Lookout Tower, which rises from an aspen-lined meadow in the San Juan at nearly 10,000 feet above sea level. The tower's living quarters, or cab, come equipped with original furniture and propane heating and lighting.
- Heli-ski or cross-country ski in the back-country or try Purgatory's famous downhill runs. Water skiers, wind surfers, and wildlife watchers will enjoy McPhee and Vallecito reservoirs.
- The forest is fast becoming a prime destination for mountain bikers, who are finding a wide variety of trails for their use.

FOREST SERVICE SCENIC BYWAY

San Juan Skyway

The San Juan Skyway winds for 232 miles through the San Juan and Uncompahgre national forests, offering views of spectacular, rugged, and primitive country as well as cultural and historical sites. *Contact San Juan National Forest.*

WHITE RIVER NATIONAL FOREST

60 miles west of Denver; the forest extends east–west 150 miles, from the Continental Divide to east of Grand Junction.

PO Box 948
9th and Grand
Glenwood Springs, CO 81602
970-945-2521
http://aspen.com/forest

Rocky Mountain Nature Association, Inc. (Rocky Mountain National Park, Estes Park, CO 80517; 800-816-7662)

The area's natural scenic beauty, along with its many services, have made White River one of the top five most popular national forests for total recreation use. The forest offers camping, hunting, hiking, fishing, horseback riding, and backpacking. Activities at the forest's reservoirs include boating, wind surfing, and water skiing. The White River is home to the largest elk herd in the country. Its eleven downhill ski areas, including the Vail/Beaver Creek Resorts, the Aspen/Snowmass complex, and all the Summit County resorts, make it the national leader in ski area capacity. Within the forest's 751,756 acres of wilderness are such nationally renowned areas as the Maroon Bells, Trapper's Lake (home of the wilderness management concept), and Mountain of the Holy Cross.

SAM'S TIPS

- The Fryingpan wilderness is in a spectacular red sandstone canyon, with steep timbered slopes and three Gold-Medal Waters—Roaring Fork, Fryingpan, and Crystal River—as well as world-class trout fishing. A paved road follows the river as it descends from Ruedi Dam down to Roaring Fork, with many pull-offs for easy streamside access.
- If you're interested in back-country hut-to-hut skiing, contact the 10th Mountain Hut Association (1280 Ute Avenue, Suite 21, Aspen, CO 81611; 970-925-5775) for a map of its hut system.

YUCCA HOUSE NATIONAL MONUMENT

Yucca House National Monument
c/o Mesa Verde National Park
Mesa Verde National Park, CO 81321
970-529-4461

Ruins of these large prehistoric Indian pueblos are as yet unexcavated. The monument is not open to the public.

Points of Interest

U.S. ARMY CORPS OF ENGINEERS

BEAR CREEK LAKE

Fishing, boat launching facilities, camping, picnicking, game fields, and winter sports are available. Located just west of Denver, near Morrison, on CO 8.

CHATFIELD LAKE

This lake features a heron and marsh-bird observatory and a sailboat harbor. Snowmobiling, ice fishing, ice skating, ice boating, and cross-country skiing are popular during the winter months. The barrier-free design of the facilities provides convenient access for the handicapped. Located off I-25, directly south of Denver.

CHERRY CREEK LAKE

Camping, picnicking, water skiing, a skeet range, a model airplane airstrip, archery, rifle ranges, dog training areas, and a wildlife management section are a few of the amenities offered here. On the southeast fringe of Denver.

BUREAU OF LAND MANAGEMENT

THE ANASAZI HERITAGE CENTER

This museum, devoted to prehistoric cultures in the Four Corners region, has almost 2 million records and artifacts from the Dolores Archaeological Program. A theater, programs, exhibits, and a special gallery provide interpretation of the Anasazi.

Southwest Colorado
27501 Highway 184
Dolores, Colorado 81323
970-882-4811

GOLD BELT TOUR BACK-COUNTRY BYWAY

This 122-mile loop consists of three routes with diverse landscapes. Phantom Canyon follows the historic Florence and Cripple Creek Railroad grade; the Shelf Road provides access to the Garden Park Fossil Area and Shelf Road climbing area; and the High Park Road provides scenic views of Pike's Peak.

South-central Colorado
Cañon City District Office
3170 East Main Street
Cañon City, CO 81212
719-269–8500

These are just a few of the many Bureau of Land Management points of interest in Colorado. For further information, contact:

Bureau of Land Management
Colorado State Office
2850 Youngfield Street
Lakewood, CO 80215
303-239–3600
http://www.co.blm.gov

U.S. BUREAU OF RECLAMATION

CARTER LAKE

Managed by Larimer County Parks Department, 1800 South County Road 31, Loveland, CO 80537; 303-679-4570. Developments include 5 campgrounds with 151 campsites and 3 boat-launch ramps. A concession-operated public marina is located at the north end of the lake. Primary recreation activities include fishing, camping, power boating, and sailing. Water levels are low in late summer because of seasonal drawdown. A public swim beach and snack bar/restaurant are available.

EAST PORTAL RESERVOIR

Managed by Estes Valley Recreation and Park District, PO Box 1379, Estes Park, CO 80517; 303-586-8191. One concession campground for overnight camping accommodates 90 campsites. A day-use picnic area is located nearby. All boating is prohibited. Although not managed as a ishery, an occasional rainbow trout is caught in this regulatory reservoir. The site has a trailhead that provides access to Rocky Mountain National Park.

GREEN MOUNTAIN RESERVOIR

Managed by the US Forest Service, PO Box 620, Silverthorne, CO 80498; 303-468-5400. Recreational developments include 6 campgrounds, 208 campsites, and 2 boat-launch facilities. Fishing is the primary recreational activity, followed by power boating and camping.

LAKE ESTES

Recreation is managed by the Estes Valley Recreation and Park District, PO Box 1379, Estes Park, CO 80517; 303-586-8191. Facilities include a 9-hole golf course, 5 picnic and associated day-use areas, and a marina.

MARY'S LAKE

Recreation is managed by the Estes Valley Recreation and Park District, PO Box 1379, Estes Park, CO 80517; 303-586-8191. A concession-developed campground accommodating 270 campsites, including both RV sites with utility hookups and tent camping sites, has been constructed adjacent to the site. No boating is allowed.

PUEBLO RESERVOIR

Recreation is managed by the Colorado Division of Parks and Outdoor Recreation, Pueblo State Park, 640 Reservoir Road, Pueblo, CO 81005; 719-561-9320 or 719-561-4909. Facilities include 4 campgrounds with a modern shower and restrooms, 2 boat ramps, and 2 marina complexes. A water recreation area, downstream from Pueblo Dam, includes a swim beach and bathhouse area. A state-of-the-art fish hatchery has been constructed downstream from the dam. Approximately 16,500 acres of wildlife lands are managed by the Colorado Division of Wildlife.

TWIN LAKES RESERVOIR

Recreation is managed by the US Forest Service, 2015 North Poplar, Leadville, CO 80461; 719-486-0749. Facilities consist of 2 campgrounds, accommodating approximately 100 campsites and 2 boat-launch ramps. In winter, ice fishing is a popular activity.

ESSENTIALS FOR OFF-ROAD VEHICLES

The Bureau of Land Management urges drivers of off-road vehicles (ORVs) to be sure to take this equipment on all outings:

- Area or road maps.
- Bailing wire.
- Compass.
- Equipment parts and repair tools.
- Extra fuel and oil.
- Full water can.
- Knife.
- Signaling flares.
- Several sources of fire.
- Tow chain or strap.

In areas subject to overcrowding or where recreational use may impact natural resources, permits and fees may be required for individual and family outings. Each agency has its own list of rules and regulations. For maps or additional information, contact the specific site you plan to visit.

IDAHO

BOISE NATIONAL FOREST

Less than 10 miles northeast of Boise.

1249 South Vinnell Way
Boise, ID 83709
208-373-4100
http://www.fs.fed.us

Boise Basin Interpretive Association. (PO Box 350, Idaho City, ID 83631; 208-392-6681)

Occupying over 2.6 million acres of land from north to east and southeast of Idaho's capital city, the Boise National Forest features steep mountains carved by swift rivers. Most of the main roads follow rivers or scenic creeks. Blue-ribbon trout streams weave their way through the sagebrush country on the south side. Hunting opportunities abound, from upland birds to elk and moose. The Boise contains over half a million acres of forest growth, and includes the Lucky Peak Nursery, the birthplace of millions of new trees for forests elsewhere. The Boise (from the French *bois* for "wood") has trails for mountain biking, motorcycles, hiking, and skiing (both downhill and cross-country) and snowmobiling. The reservoirs and whitewater rivers also give visitors the chance to water ski, fish, boat, and raft.

CARIBOU NATIONAL FOREST

Five separate sections, starting in Pocatello and extending to the southeastern border of Idaho.

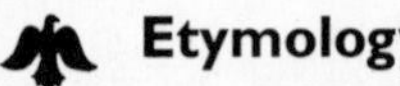

Etymology

The Caribou Forest's name came from Jesse Fairchild, a gold miner who bore the nickname "Cariboo Jack." In 1870, Fairchild, who had achieved local fame for his tall tales of the Canadian Caribou country, discovered gold near what is now Caribou Mountain. The resulting gold rush lasted 20 years, and produced $50 million worth of placer gold. Abandoned relics of this era can still be found near the Caribou Mountain.

Federal Building
250 South Fourth Avenue
Pocatello, ID 83201
208-236-7500
http://www.fs.fed.us/

Southeast Idaho Interpretive Association. (2877 US 89, Fish Haven, ID 83287; 208-847-1531)

Created in 1907 by President Theodore Roosevelt, this 1-million-acre forest is located mostly in southeastern Idaho; small portions are in Utah and Wyoming. The Curlew National Grasslands, near Malad, are also administered by the forest and are known for their upland game birds. Snowmobiling, horseback and trailbike riding, and backpacking are popular activities on the forest's 1,200-mile trail system. The most popular attraction in the area is Minnetonka Cave, located 10 miles west of St. Charles.

CHALLIS NATIONAL FOREST

Central Idaho.

RR 2, Box 600
Highway 93
South Salmon, ID 83467
208-756-5100
http://www.fs.fed.us

Sawtooth Interpretive and Historical Association. (PO Box 75, Stanley, ID 83278; 208-774-3380)

Situated among towering mountains, alpine lakes, and clear streams, the Challis National Forest encompasses over 2 million acres. There are many areas, near roads, for camping, mining, fishing, hiking, and sightseeing. And there's plenty of the latter to do. Idaho's 25 highest mountains all lie within or on the border of the forest. The Visitor Center is at the junction of Highways 75 and 93.

Sam's Tips

- The Middle Fork of the Salmon Wild and Scenic River—part of the Frank Church–River of No Return Wilderness—is one of the outstanding whitewater rafting rivers in the nation.
- Mount Borah, the highest park peak in Idaho (12,635 feet), can generally be climbed without special equipment. The mountain is located four miles east of Dickey.
- The Lemhi Mountain Range, which boasts 100 miles of hiking trails and numerous high-country lakes, is a roadless wilderness area within the forest's boundaries.

CITY OF ROCKS NATIONAL RESERVE

Southern Idaho, near the Utah border: 125 miles northwest of Salt Lake City, UT.

PO Box 169
3010 Elba–Almo Road
Almo, ID 83312-0169
208-824-5519
http://www.nps.gov/ciro

Named by pioneers for its silent skyline of 60 rock pinnacles, City of Rocks was a landmark for travelers to California

Caves, Arches, Bathtubs, and Hollow Boulders

The shaping of the granite towers at City of Rocks is a result of weathering and case hardening. When the top of the rock formation is dissolved by rainwater, various minerals, such as iron oxide, are deposited and form a top more resistant to weathering. When this harder top is gone, the inner granite is molded into caves, arches, bathtubs, and hollow boulders by a process called exfoliation. Exfoliation occurs when water that has seeped into the cracks of the rocks freezes and expands, chipping off pieces of rock. The process is very gradual—the City of Rocks that you see looks much the same as it did to early pioneers.

and Oregon in the 1800s. It was on one of the principal routes used during the California Gold Rush, when it was still partly in Mexican territory. Portions of the trails are still visible, as are the names of many of the early travelers, written in axle grease on the rocks.

Sam's Tips

- City of Rocks rivals Yosemite National Park as a western favorite for technical rock climbers.
- Because the reserve is relatively new—it was opened in 1988—facilities with hook-ups are 30 minutes away.
- One of the lowest pollution rates in the country makes City of Rocks a favorite place for amateur astronomers.

CLEARWATER NATIONAL FOREST

250 miles north of Boise; 175 miles west of Missoula, MT; 150 miles east of Spokane, WA.

12730 Highway 12
Orofino, ID 83544
208-476-4541
http://www.fs.fed.us

The 1.8-million-acre Clearwater National Forest includes high, rugged ridges interspersed with deep, forested canyons and tumbling whitewater. For centuries, the ridges between the canyons have provided travel corridors for wildlife and humans alike. The forest is known for its large herds of elk, moose, and other big game animals. Lewis and Clark followed Indian routes through the area on their way to the Pacific. (Ask for the brochure, *Lewis and Clark Across Lolo Trail,* for more information.) Today's visitors follow these same historic pathways through an area that is little changed.

Compression Fossils

Most fossils found today are *impression* fossils. Leaves, flowers, and insects trapped by silt millions of years ago left their imprint behind as they decomposed. Some fossils, however, still contain original organic material. These *compression* fossils, usually found in deeper silt layers, where weathering has not yet penetrated, contain actual leaves, flowers, and insects. The outer and inner layers of specialized cells remain intact and can be studied under a microscope. Scientists have extracted DNA genetic codes from compression fossils of the ancient forests. Oviatt Creek, near the town of Elk River, is one of the few places in the world that contain well-preserved specimens of these fossils.

Sam's Tips

- Unlike many other national forests, Clearwater permits rockhounding and fossil hunting (for personal use, not economic gain). Smokey quartz and tourmaline crystals are scattered across the forest, and garnets and fossils of plant remains can be found on the western edge of the forest.
- The Lochsa Historical Ranger Station is a relic from the time before 1952, when the area was inaccessible by road. All the materials used to build the station were either harvested onsite or packed in by mule.

CRATERS OF THE MOON NATIONAL MONUMENT

180 miles east of Boise; 270 miles northwest of Salt Lake City, UT.

PO Box 29
Arco, ID 83213-0029
208-527-3257
http://www.nps.gov/crmo

The Craters of the Moon Natural History Association. (same address as above)

According to one early traveler, the Craters of the Moon landscape is "the strangest 75 square miles on the North American continent." The distinctive geology that visitors discover here began to form 15,000 years ago, when the earth cracked along the Great Rift and started to spew lava across the land. Fissure vents, volcanic cones, and lava flows were periodically active until about 2,000 years ago. Today, the landscape is dominated by balsitic lava and cinder deposits pockmarked with numerous lava-tube caves, cones, and craters that are home to numerous wildflowers, birds, and mammals.

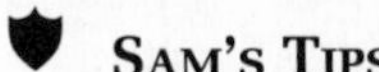

Sam's Tips

- The lava rocks that make up Craters of the Moon are very sharp; sturdy shoes and long pants are a must. In summer it is very hot and dry, so be sure to carry plenty of water. If you plan to go into lava-tub caves, wear a hat and bring a flashlight.

A Typical Eruption at Craters of the Moon

During a typical eruption at Craters of the Moon, the force of rising magma caused a section of the Great Rift to pull apart. As the magma rose through the crack, gases contained within the magma expanded. The frothy magma was very fluid and charged with gas. Eruptions, called "curtains of fire," began as a long line of tall fountains along a crack that may have extended more than a mile.

After hours, or days, the initial expansion of gases decreased and the eruption became less violent. Some sections of the fissure sealed off, and the eruption became more localized. Cinders were thrown high into the air, and may have built up in huge piles around individual vents, forming cinder cones.

As the amount of gas contained in the magma continued to drop, the volcanic activity again changed. Huge outpourings of lava flowed from various fissures and vents. These lava flows typically continued for days to a few months, but may continue for more than a year. They were the source of most of the volcanic rock in the park.

HAGERMAN FOSSIL BEDS NATIONAL MONUMENT

95 miles southeast of Boise; 200 miles northwest of Salt Lake City, UT.

221 North State Street
PO Box 570
Hagerman, ID 83332-0570
208-837-4793
http://www.nps.gov/hafo

 **Craters of the Moon Natural History Association.** (same address as above)

The Origin of the Beaver

No one is sure whether beavers originated in North America or evolved in Europe and entered North America. The earliest beaver fossils found in the United States are 30 million years old. These fossil beavers were not aquatic but lived on land in burrows, with a lifestyle similar to that of today's prairie dogs (burrows can be seen at Nebraska's Agate Fossil Beds National Monument). The first fossils of the ancestor to the modern aquatic beavers in North America and Europe occur in rocks of almost identical age. Paleontologists hope that fossils preserved in the Hagerman Fossil Beds will provide clues to resolve the national origin of the present-day beaver.

Beneath the surface at the Hagerman Fossil Beds National Monument lies the largest variety of fossilized animals from the Pliocene Epoch anywhere in the United States. Thousands of remains have been found, some as old 3.2 million years, representing at least 105 species of animals, many now extinct. Rivers and marshes that once covered the area supported animals like beavers, otters, mastodons, and saber-toothed cats. First explored by a Smithsonian expedition in 1929, the area became famous for its "horse quarry," where more than 150 individual zebralike horse skulls and bones, along with scores of smaller animals, have been found. Hagerman is one of three National Park Service units that offers interpretive markers of the Oregon Trail.

Sam's Tips

- Hagerman is a relatively young National Park Service site (established in 1988). Its limited facilities include two short wheelchair-accessible trails with interpretive exhibits. The Visitors' Center includes visual programs and fossils on display. Public tours are given during the summer. The schedule for them, and for other park interpretive programs, is listed in *The Fossil Record,* published by the park seasonally.
- Those who enjoy Hagerman Fossil Beds might consider planning a trip around other western fossil sites. Fossil Butte National Monument (WY) is 200 miles to the southeast, and Dinosaur National Monument (CO and UT) is about 75 miles beyond Fossil Butte (see entries). A bit farther away are the John Day Fossil Beds National Monument in central Oregon, Florissant Fossil Beds National Monument in central Colorado, and Agate Fossil Beds National Monument in western Nebraska (see entries).

IDAHO PANHANDLE NATIONAL FORESTS

Idaho panhandle (northern, narrow part of the state).

3815 Schreiber Way
Coeur d'Alene, ID 83814
208-765-7223
http://www.fs.fed.us/outernet/ipnf

Northwest Interpretive Association. (909 First Avenue, Suite 630, Seattle, WA 98104-1060; 206-220-4140)

The Idaho Panhandle National Forests lie in northern Idaho, where quaint villages snuggle up against soaring peaks or hug the shores of deep blue lakes. Back-country trails guide the traveler through evergreen forests to remote lakes and spectacular views. Quiet country lanes take the motorist by abandoned mining towns, and trace military wagon roads that date back to the mid-1800s. Over 4,000 miles of rivers and vast lowland lakes are home to world-class sport fisheries. Foam-flecked rapids challenge the whitewater rafter. Glassy-quiet runs beckon the canoeist to travel where steamboats once carried miners with dreams of riches gouged from the earth.

Sam's Tips

- Three of Idaho's largest lakes—Coeur d'Alene, Priest, and Pend Oreille—are nearby and offer a variety of fishing and water-related activities.
- The Idaho Panhandle Forests make good camping or resting points on a trip east from Washington State toward Glacier National Park (MT), about 50 miles to the east.

NEZ PERCE NATIONAL FOREST

North-central Idaho, between Oregon and Montana.

Route 2, Box 475
Grangeville, ID 83530
208-983-1950
http://www.fs.fed.us

Northwest Interpretive Association. (909 First Avenue, Suite 630, Seattle, WA 98104-1060; 206-220-4140)

Nearly half of the Nez Perce's 2.2 million acres has been set aside as protected wilderness. Four wild and scenic rivers and several recreational rivers have carved deep canyons into the surrounding mountainous terrain. The nearly 7,000-foot vertical drop in Hells Canyon, between He-Devil Mountain and the nearby Snake River, is the deepest gorge in the country. Large elk herds and outstanding steelhead runs provide exciting hunting and fishing. The forest is on land rich with the history of both the Nez Perce Tribe and early gold mining.

Sam's Tips

- The Nez Perce National Forest offers some of the best trophy elk hunting in the continental United States. If you are looking for big game, set out on your own or with a licensed outfitter to hunt trophy whitetail, mule deer, elk, bighorn sheep, moose, mountain goat, black bear, or mountain lion.
- Some of the best fishing in the world can be found on the Clearwater and Salmon Rivers. For hunting/fishing issues, contact the Idaho Department of Fish and Game (1540 Warner Avenue, Lewiston, ID 83501; 208-799-5010).
- Thousands of private and outfitted rafters, kayakers, and jetboaters come here each year to experience the 200 miles of internationally renowned Salmon River and Selway River whitewater.
- A great spot to photograph bald eagles is on the South Fork of the Clearwater River.

NEZ PERCE NATIONAL HISTORIC PARK

Throughout Idaho, Oregon, Washington, and Montana; Spalding is 80 miles southeast of Spokane, WA.

Route 1, Box 93
Spalding, ID 83551
208-843-2261
http://www.nps.gov/nepe

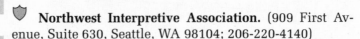

Northwest Interpretive Association. (909 First Avenue, Suite 630, Seattle, WA 98104; 206-220-4140)

For thousands of years, the valleys, prairies, and plateaus of north-central Idaho and adjacent areas in Oregon and Washington have been home to the Nez Perce Indians. Created in 1965, the Nez Perce National Historic Park originally consisted of 24 separate sites in Idaho, each commemorating an important moment in Nez Perce history. In 1992, fourteen additional sites in Oregon, Washington, Idaho, and Montana were designated part of the park. Road markers show their locations; two crossed feathers indicate each site's number. Because a complete tour of the 24 sites in Idaho alone is about a 400-mile trip, visitors often tour the park in segments. One Visitor Center is located in Spalding, the other at Big Hole National

Hells Canyon Corridor

Once called the "Grand Canyon of the Snake River," the Hells Canyon corridor is known for its extremely rugged landscape. There are few points of entry into Hells Canyon, so traveling in this corridor takes time and effort. Once there, however, visitors are rewarded with beautiful scenery and exciting whitewater on the Wild and Scenic Snake River. Pittsburg Landing has a boat launch area as well as facilities for campers, hikers, and stock users. For a high-elevation experience on the Idaho side, a trip to Heavens Gate offers a 360-degree panoramic view of the Salmon River country, the Seven Devils Mountains, and Hells Canyon.

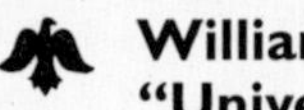

William T. Sherman's "Universal Praise"

General William T. Sherman called the Nez Perce War of 1877 "one of the most extraordinary Indian wars of which there is a record. The Indians displayed a courage and skill that elicited universal praise; they abstained from scalping, let captive women go free, did not commit indiscriminate murder of peaceful families . . . and fought with almost scientific skill. . . ."

Battlefield. Write to the park for brochures that explain the background and locations of all 24 sites.

PAYETTE NATIONAL FOREST

The forest stretches across central Idaho and is bordered on the north by the Salmon Wild and Scenic River and on the west by the Snake River.

PO Box 126
800 West Lakeside Avenue
McCall, ID 83638
208-634-0700
http://www.mccall.net/pnf

Northwest Interpretive Association. (909 First Avenue, Suite 630, Seattle, WA 98104-1060; 206-220-4140)

Containing some of the largest remaining tracts of undeveloped land in the United States, the Payette National Forest has extreme climate diversity. Annual precipitation on the forest varies from 12 inches at lower elevations to over 60 inches in the high country; elevations can range from 1,500 feet in Hells Canyon to over 9,500 feet in parts of the Frank Church–River of No Return Wilderness; and winter temperatures can drop to –40°F, and summer temperatures can exceed 100°F. Pristine high-mountain lakes lie along the ridge between the South Fork Salmon River and the North Fork Payette River drainages. The forest administers lands from two neighboring wildernesses: 2.4 million acres of the Frank Church River of No Return Wilderness, the largest designated wilderness outside Alaska, and some 24,000 acres of the Hells Canyon Wilderness. The Payette is also home to several gold mining operations.

SALMON NATIONAL FOREST

North-central Idaho.

PO Box 600
Salmon, ID 83467
208-756-5100
http://www.fs.fed.us

Sawtooth Interpretive and Historical Association. (PO Box 75, Stanley, ID 83278; 208-774-3380)

Known as the "Whitewater Capital of the World," the Salmon Wild and Scenic River offers day floats and week-long adventures that take you down the River of No Return. Float through steep and narrow canyons, witness sacred Indian pictographs, and view remnants of abandoned gold mines and homesteads. The Salmon National Forest's rugged and remote terrain also offers opportunities for fishing, hunting, sightseeing, biking, and hiking on 1,200 miles of trails.

 RUSTIC CABINS AND LOOKOUTS IN IDAHO

Many of Idaho's National Forests offer lodging in rustic guard stations and fire lookout towers. These cabins, scattered around eight National Forests, are out-of-the-way gems, located in the middle of some of America's most pristine lands.

Most cabins are accessible via narrow, winding, dirt or gravel roads, or, in winter, by snowmobile or cross-country skis. Facilities are spartan: a table, chairs, wood stove and bunks (some with mattresses, some without). You might need to bring your own drinking water and cut your own firewood. Expect to use outdoor privies, and don't expect a telephone. The Forest Service recommends that children under 12 not stay in lookout towers.

These cabins can be a remarkable place to stay amidst Idaho's beautiful National Forests. Prices range between $20 and $35 a night, with some cabins also requiring an $8.75 reservation fee. Cabins house as few as four or as many as ten or more guests. Call for more information and to make reservations, which are required.

Boise National Forest (15 cabins)
Idaho City Ranger District (mostly summer-only)
PO Box 129
Idaho City, ID 83631
208-392-6681

Mountain Home Ranger District (summer-only)
2180 American Legion Boulevard
Mountain Home, ID 83647
208-587-7961

Emmett Ranger District (summer-only)
1805 Highway 16, Room 5
Emmett, ID 83617
800-280-2267

Lowman Ranger District (winter-only)
HC 77 Box 3020
Lowman, ID 83637
208-259-3361

Caribou National Forest (3 cabins, year-round)
Soda Springs Ranger District
421 West 2nd South
Soda Springs, ID 83276
208-547-4356

Salmon and Challis National Forests (5 cabins, year-round)
Salmon-Cobalt Ranger District
Highway 93 South
Salmon, ID 83467
208-756-5122

Targhee National Forest (2 cabins, 1 lookout tower, year-round)
Ashton Ranger District
46 Highway 20
PO Box 858
Ashton, ID 83420
208-652-7442

Clearwater National Forest (2 cabins, 4 lookout towers, mostly autumn-only)
Lochsa Ranger District
Route 1, Box 398
Kooskia, ID 83539
208-926-4275

Pierce Ranger District
Route 2, Box 191
Kamiah, ID 83536
208-935-2513

North Fork Ranger District
1225 Ahsahka Road
Orofino, ID 83544
208-476-3775

Idaho Panhandle National Forest (2 cabins, 1 lookout tower, summer- and autumn-only)
Bonners Ferry Ranger District
Route 4, Box 4860
Bonners Ferry, ID 83805
208-267-5561

Nez Perce National Forest (2 cabins, 1 lookout tower)
Elk City Ranger District (year-round)
Box 416
Elk City, ID 83525
208-842-2245

Selway Ranger District (summer-only)
HCR75, Box 91
Kooskia, ID 83539
208-926-4258

SAWTOOTH NATIONAL FOREST

South-central Idaho, stretching from Raft River Mountain Range, UT, to the Salmon River.

2647 Kimberly Road East
Twin Falls, ID 83301-7976
208-737-3200
http://www.northrim.net/sawtoothnf

Sawtooth Interpretive and Historical Association. (PO Box 75, Stanley, ID 83278; 208-774-3380)

With elevations ranging from 4,500 feet on Rock Creek near Twin Falls to 12,009 at Hyndman Peak near Sun Valley, the Sawtooth National Forest has a remarkable combination of geographic features that contribute to recreational use. There are more than 1,100 lakes here, most of which hold trout and other game fish, as well as 193 developed recreation sites, including ski areas, campgrounds, picnic areas, boat ramps, scenic overlooks, trail heads, interpretive sites, and visitor centers. The famous Sun Valley ski resort is located on the forest. Other downhill ski areas are Soldier Mountain, Pomerelle, and Magic Mountain.

Sawtooth National Recreation Area

"I don't want to ever die unless I can be an angel and come back twice a year to Stanley Basin in June and October to see the clustered spires of the Sawtooth Range reaching up among the stars," wrote "Fitz-Mac," a reporter of the *Challis-Messenger* in 1902. One of the largest National Recreation Areas in the country, the Sawtooth is surrounded by majestic mountain ranges—the Sawtooths, Boulders, White Clouds, and Smokeys—with over 40 peaks 10,000 feet or higher. There are over 1,000 high-mountain lakes here, as well as the headwaters of four major rivers in Idaho: the Salmon, South Fork of the Payette, Boise, and Big Wood. Recreational activities in the summer and fall include camping, horseback riding, mountain climbing, nature trails, wildlife viewing, mountain biking, motor biking, off-road vehicle travel, bird watching, airplane tours, llama trekking, lake canoeing, swimming, kayaking, water skiing, and whitewater boating. During the winter, visitors enjoy rock and ice climbing, ice fishing, skiing, sledding, snowmobiling, ice skating, and winter camping. For more information contact: Star Route, Ketchum, ID 83340; 208-727-5013.

 **FOREST SERVICE SCENIC BYWAY**

Mesa Falls Scenic Loop

Mesa Falls Scenic Loop, on the Targhee National Forest in eastern Idaho, travels from open farmland through forested canyon to the lip of the largest volcanic caldera in the United States. Winding throughout the Greater Yellowstone Area, it offers glimpses of the Grand Teton Mountain Range, Mesa Falls (on the Henrys Fork of the Snake River), and wildlife such as elk, moose, and deer. *Contact Targhee National Forest.*

TARGHEE NATIONAL FOREST

Along the southeastern border of Idaho and Wyoming, with lands bordering on Yellowstone National Park.

420 North Bridge Street
PO Box 208
St. Anthony, ID 83445
208-624-3151
http://www.fs.fed.us/tnf

 **Grand Teton Natural History Association.** (PO Box 170, Moose, WY 83012; 307-739-3403)

The Targhee National Forest, centered on the headwaters of the Snake River, lies partially in Wyoming, but the majority of its 1.8 million acres are in Idaho. The forest lies along the Continental Divide; Yellowstone and Grand Teton National Parks make up most of the eastern border. Hiking, horseback riding, and ATV and motorcycle use are especially popular. Winter activities include cross-country and downhill skiing. Much of the Targhee is in grizzly bear country.

POINTS OF INTEREST

U.S. ARMY CORPS OF ENGINEERS

ALBENI FALLS DAM (PEND OREILLE LAKE)

Forests and mountains, clear water, sandy beaches, and excellent trout fishing are a few of the many attractions of this large lake. From Spokane, 50 miles northeast on US 2.

LUCKY PEAK LAKE

On the state highway route that connects the city of Boise with the Sawtooth National Recreation Area, the project provides developed and primitive recreation sites in the scenic mountains of southeastern Idaho. From Boise, 10 miles southeast on ID 21.

BUREAU OF LAND MANAGEMENT

UPPER SNAKE RIVER DISTRICT

The Oregon Trail

In the mid-1800s, pioneers followed the Oregon Trail for 2,000 miles from Missouri to Oregon in search of a better life. However, the Oregon Trail was never just one route. Some emigrants deviated from the main trail in search of water and livestock forage; others found shortcuts and better routes, to avoid difficult terrain. Two segments of the primary route—the North Trail and Sinker Creek—are located in southwestern Idaho, and visitors today can still see original wagon ruts.

Bonneville Point, 16 miles southeast of Boise; Milner Site, 4 miles west of Burley
BLM Pocatello Resource Area, 208-236-6860

THE UNITED STATES YOUTH CONSERVATION CORPS

Are you a person between the ages of 15 and 18 who is trying to decide what to do this coming summer? Consider joining the Youth Conservation Corps. Administered jointly by the National Park Service, the Fish and Wildlife Service, and the Forest Service, the YCC is a great opportunity to develop an appreciation of your natural environment and heritage *and* get paid for it. Participants might build trails, construct campground facilities, plant trees, clear streams, or improve wildlife habitats.

There are residential and nonresidential positions available. Applications are accepted from the beginning of the year until April 15. For more information, write to the Forest Service at:

The Auditor's Building
201 14th Street, SW
PO Box 96090
Washington, DC 20090-6090
202-205-1760

Great Rift Backcountry Area

The rupture in the earth's surface for which this area is named is believed to be one of the largest in the United States: 65 miles long and 800 feet deep. This proposed Wilderness Area has thousands of acres of lava dotted with buttes and *kipukas* (islands of vegetation).

45 miles east of Idaho Falls
BLM Shoshone Resource Area, 208-886-2206

Salmon Falls Creek Reservoir

The Salmon Falls Dam was built in 1910 to provide water for irrigation to farms. Anglers will find brown trout, chinook and kokanee salmon, yellow perch, black crappie, channel catfish, small mouth bass, and walleye. Ice fishing is possible in January and February. Day-use and overnight facilities and campsites are available at nearby Lud Drexler Park.

22 miles south of Twin Falls
BLM Snake River Resource Area, 208-677-6641

St. Anthony Sand Dunes

This 10,600-acre playground of clear, shifting, white quartz sand is known for its recreation opportunities: dune buggy and motorcycle riding, as well as horseback riding. Winter activities include sledding and tubing.

10 miles north of St. Anthony
BLM Medicine Lodge Resource Area, 208-524-7500

LOWER SNAKE RIVER DISTRICT

Snake River Birds of Prey National Conservation Area

This 483,000-acre area supports the densest nesting concentration of raptors in North America. More than 800 pairs of falcons, eagles, hawks, and owls gather here each spring to mate and raise their young. The best time for viewing raptors is from mid-March through June, in the morning and early evening hours, especially from the viewing site on the Dedication Point Trail.

15 miles south of Boise
BLM Bruneau Resource Area, 208-384-3300

Bruneau and Jarbidge Rivers

The Bruneau Canyon Overlook offers an outstanding vista of spectacular canyons towering 1,200 feet high. The primitive, isolated setting presents challenging hiking and whitewater boating.

12 miles southeast of Bruneau
BLM Bruneau Resource Area, 208-384-3300

UPPER COLUMBIA–CLEARWATER DISTRICTS

Lower Salmon River

Whitewater boaters will find exciting rapids and spectacular beauty on this 112-mile stretch of the longest completely free-flowing river in the lower 48 states. Float trips of one to four days are possible on the Lower Salmon River. Developed and undeveloped recreation areas along the river permit day-use picnicking and overnight camping.

Access from Riggins and White Bird
BLM Cottonwood Resource Area, 208-962-3245

Coeur d'Alene Lake Recreation Area

The Bureau of Land Management manages three recreation sites here. They include Mineral Ridge, the trailhead for the 3.3-mile Mineral Ridge National Recreation Trail, which rises 700 feet above the lake; and Wolf Lodge Bay, a launch area for boats and, in the winter, a premier observation point of endangered northern bald eagles.

Coeur d'Alene
BLM Emerald Empire Resource Area, 208-769-5000

Mackay Reservoir Wildlife Viewing Area/Chilly Slough Wetland

This birdwatcher's paradise comes alive in spring and fall, when thousands of shorebirds and waterfowl flock to the area's mudflats. The Chilly Slough Wetland, 5 miles to the north, features a fantastic view of 12,662-foot Mount Borah.

5 miles northwest of Mackay
BLM Challis Resource Area, 208-756-5400

These are just a sample of Bureau of Land Management points of interest in Idaho. For more information, contact:

Bureau of Land Management
Idaho State Office
3380 Americana Terrace
Boise, Idaho 83706
208-384-3000
http://www.id.blm.gov

U.S. BUREAU OF RECLAMATION

ANDERSON RANCH RESERVOIR

Recreation on this 4,730-acre reservoir southeast of Boise is managed by the Boise National Forest, 1750 Front Street, Boise, ID 83702; 208-364-4100. Anglers will find kokanee, rainbow trout, smallmouth bass, whitefish, yellow perch, and chinook salmon. The season is year-round.

ARROWROCK RESERVOIR

Recreation is managed by the Boise National Forest, 1750 Front Street, Boise, ID 83702; 208-364-4100. Access to this 3,000-acre reservoir is about 15 miles east of Boise via an improved dirt road beginning at Lucky Peak Reservoir.

LAKE LOWELL

This 9,500-acre reservoir lies within Deer Flat National Wildlife Refuge. Managed by the US Fish and Wildlife Service (13751 Upper Embankment Road, Nampa, ID 83686; 208-467-9278), the lake is located 5 miles southwest of Nampa.

MONTOUR WILDLIFE RECREATION AREA

Recreation is managed by the Bureau of Reclamation, 214 Broadway Avenue, Boise, ID 83702; 208-334-9084. This complex of wetlands and ponds, located above Black Canyon Reservoir, has good access via State Route 52.

PALISADES RESERVOIR

This 16,000-acre reservoir managed by the Targhee National Forest, 420 Bridge Street, St. Anthony, ID 83445; 208-624-3151), is located along US Highway 26 near the Idaho–Wyoming border.

RIRIE RESERVOIR

Managed by the Bureau of Reclamation (1359 Hansen Avenue, Burley, ID 83318; 208-678-0461. The reservoir is located 20 miles east of Idaho Falls, off US Highway 26. The fishing season runs from late May to the end of November.

UNCLE SAM'S FIREMEN—THE NATIONAL INTERAGENCY FIRE CENTER

Based in Boise, Idaho, the National Interagency Fire Center (NIFC) is Uncle Sam's primary support center for wildland fire suppression. The NFIC site on the World Wide Web features an "Incident Management Situation Report," which is updated daily. For more information, contact:

NIFC
3833 South Development Avenue
Boise, ID 83705
http://www.nifc.gov

MONTANA

BEAVERHEAD NATIONAL FOREST

Extreme southwest corner of Montana, northwest of Yellowstone Park.

420 Barrett Street
Dillon, MT 59725
406-683-3900
http://www.fs.fed.us/r1/bdnf

Northwest Interpretive Association. (909 First Avenue, Suite 630, Seattle, WA 98104-1060; 206-220-4140)

One of the first areas settled by pioneers in Montana, Beaverhead remains almost as wild and remote as when Lewis and Clark first observed it in the summer of 1805. The forest lies tucked away in a great mountainous bowl in the extreme southwestern portion of Montana. The rugged Bitterroot and Centennial ranges form the western and southern boundaries of the bowl and carry the Continental Divide on their crests. The eastern boundary is formed by the Madison Range. Within the bowl are broad open valleys bisected by high mountain ranges. The valleys contain large cattle and sheep ranches, many of them still owned by descendants of the same family that homesteaded them over 100 years ago. The mountains host the headwaters of the Ruby, Red Rock, Jefferson, Madison, Beaverhead, and Big Hole rivers. Water from the high mountains provides the major source of irrigation for area ranchers, as well as habitat for some of the best trout fishing in the United States. Gently sloped foothills are dominated by sagebrush and grasslands. Visitors can discover abandoned mining towns, travel the route of Lewis and Clark, enjoy 155 high-mountain lakes and 1,500 miles of trails, see the Big Hole Battlefield, where the Nez Perce fought a major battle with the US Army in 1877, and visit the first Territorial Capital of Montana, which is now a State Park.

FOREST SERVICE SCENIC BYWAY

Wise River–Polaris Road

The Wise River–Polaris Road travels 27 miles along the Pioneer Mountain Range of the Beaverhead National Forest and offers spectacular views of stately mountain peaks, magnificent sunrises and sunsets, and abundant wildlife. *Contact Beaverhead National Forest.*

MEET YOUR PARK PERSONNEL

The National Park Service has a varied and experienced staff of national stature—rangers, natural resource managers, archaeologists, historians, interpreters, landscape architects, engineers, and planners—who protect our land and legacy, conduct research, and educate the public. We'd like to introduce you to one of them.

Yvonne Iron, Secretary, Bighorn Canyon National Recreation Area, Yellowtail, Montana, grew up in the Bighorn Canyon country and has worked at Bighorn Canyon National Recreation Area for ten years. Yvonne has this to say about "her" park: "Bighorn Canyon National Recreation Area is part of my life. As I walk the canyon edge on the Om-Ne-A trail, I hear nature's voice greeting me. Standing atop the canyon, the breeze on my face quickens my memory of the story of Chief Big Metal, who was rescued by bighorn sheep, for whom the park was named. The spectacular Madison limestone and Amsden formations of the canyon walls form the Bighorn Lake, patiently waiting for me to launch my boat and exchange feelings of wonder. I value the peace and serenity that Bighorn Canyon offers me and my family. Bighorn Canyon balances the peace as it breaks silence by the laughter of mountain water bouncing from cliff to cliff. What a joy!"

BIG HOLE NATIONAL BATTLEFIELD

150 miles southwest of Helena; 110 miles south of Missoula; 10 miles west of Wisdom, on MT 43.

PO Box 237
Wisdom, MT 59761
406-689-3155
http://www.nps.gov/biho

 **Glacier Natural History Association.** (PO Box 428, West Glacier, MT 59936, 406-888-5756)

Big Hole National Battlefield commemorates the 1877 battle between the Nez Perce Tribe and US Army forces. Big Hole was a stopping point on a 1,300-mile journey by 5 bands of the nontreaty Nez Perce (a wealthy, seminomadic tribe of Native Americans) through Oregon, Idaho, and Montana. Over 100 Nez Perce warriors, US soldiers, and civilians were killed in the day-long fight. The site is located in a high-mountain valley, surrounded by snow-capped peaks and the Beaverhead National Forest.

The Battle of the Big Hole

The Nez Perce arrived in the Big Hole Valley on August 7, 1877, and set up camp. Chief Looking Glass, believing that General Howard and his troops were far behind, did not post guards. Unknown to the Nez Perce, a second military force—Colonel John Gibbon and 162 men of the 7th US Infantry out of Fort Shaw and four other western Montana forts—had joined the chase and were advancing up the Bitterroot Valley toward them.

Gibbon's scouts spotted the Nez Perce teepees on the afternoon of August 8. Before dawn on August 9, US Army troops formed a skirmish line about 200 yards from the Nez Perce campsite. They attacked the camp, surprising the sleeping families and killing tribe members indiscriminately. While the soldiers took possession of the south end of the camp, Nez Perce warriors quickly took up sniper positions. Their deadly shooting forced Gibbon's men to retreat back across the Big Hole River. The troops dug in and were pinned down for the next 24 hours, in need of food, water, and medical supplies.

During the attack, some of Gibbon's men arrived with a Howitzer cannon on the hillside above the siege area. They managed to fire 2 rounds before Nez Perce horsemen galloped forward, captured the gun, and dismantled it, rolling the wheels down the hill.

As the siege continued, some Nez Perce warriors withdrew to help care for the injured and bury the dead. The bulk of the tribe broke camp and headed south. Finally, in the early morning of the second day of fighting, the remaining warriors left to join their people.

The Nez Perce had taken Gibbon's command out of action, and had won the battle, but 60 to 90 of their people had been killed, including 30 warriors. Even so, they continued to fight for another 6 weeks with great determination until convinced that the Army would relentlessly continue its pursuit. Their desperation is echoed in the words Chief Joseph reportedly spoke to Colonel Miles: "Hear me, my chiefs, I am tired; my heart is sick and sad. From where the sun now stands I will fight no more forever."

BIGHORN CANYON NATIONAL RECREATION AREA

Fort Smith is 40 miles southeast of Billings; Lovell is 55 miles northeast of Cody, WY.

PO Box 7458
Fort Smith, MT 59035
406-666-2412
http://www.nps.gov/bica

Southwest Parks and Monuments Association. (221 North Court Avenue, Tucson, AZ 85701; 520-622-1999)

The focus of the area is the 71-mile-long Bighorn Lake, created by Yellowtail Dam near Fort Smith, and including a 55-mile stretch that cuts through the spectacular Bighorn Canyon. Boating, fishing, water skiing, swimming, scuba and skin diving, and sightseeing are the park's principal attractions. Bighorn Canyon borders the Crow Indian Reservation, which is closed to the public.

Sam's Tips

- An orientation film at the Yellowtail Visitor Center highlights the canyon's history and natural features. Exhibits focus on Crow Indian history and the Yellowtail Dam.
- Boating enthusiasts will find a marina, a snack bar, and a boat launch ramp at Horseshoe Bend and Ok-A-Beh. Other boat ramps are at Afterbay Dam and Barry's Landing.
- The Pryor Mountain Wild Horse Range was established in 1968 to provide a sanctuary for wild horses. The herd of 120–140 horses includes descendants of Indian ponies and of horses that escaped from farms and ranches.
- Yellowtail Dam, named in honor of Robert Yellowtail, the former Crow tribal chairman and reservation superintendent, is an arch-type dam about 160 meters high. Tours are conducted by the National Park Service.
- The Bozeman Trail, opened during the Civil War as a shortcut to mines in western Montana, crossed some of the best Indian hunting grounds and was bitterly opposed by the Sioux and Cheyenne. Although the trail crosses through the park near Fort Smith, most of it is on private land in the Crow Indian Reservation. The Bad Pass Trail was used by Native Americans as long as 10,000 years ago.

ADOPTING WILD HORSES AND BURROS

The number of animals roaming public range lands is controlled, in order to maintain healthy herds and protect their habitats from overuse. The Adopt-A-Horse-or-Burro Program has placed over 130,000 wild horses and burros in private care since 1973. For qualified individuals, this is a unique opportunity to care for, then own, a symbol of American history.

A wild horse or burro is an unbranded, unclaimed, free-roaming horse or burro found on Bureau of Land Management or U.S. Forest Service land in the western United States. These animals are descendants of those released by or escaped from Spanish explorers, ranchers, miners, soldiers, or Native Americans.

Each year, between 6,000 and 8,000 horses and 500 to 1,000 burros are offered for adoption. The adoption fees are $125 for wild horses and $75 for wild burros. Adoptions take place at BLM locations and temporary adoption centers across the country.

For more information and an application, call or write the BLM regional office serving the area where you wish to adopt, or phone 800-417-9647, or check the BLM Website at www.blm.gov/whb.

BITTERROOT NATIONAL FOREST

50 miles south of Missoula; 150 miles west of Butte; and 165 miles (est.) west of Helena.

1801 North First Street
Hamilton, MT 59840
406-363-7121
http://www.fs.fed.us

Northwest Interpretive Association. (909 First Avenue, Suite 630, Seattle, WA 98104; 206-220-4140)

Known for spectacular glaciated canyons, plentiful big game, high-mountain lakes, and back-country wilderness recreation, the 1.6-million-acre Bitterroot National Forest is home to the Bitterroot and Sapphire mountain ranges, which are part of the Northern Rocky Mountains. These two ranges, with peaks over 10,000 feet, are bisected by the Bitterroot River Valley, which drops over 6,000 feet between them. The high elevations boast species of subalpine trees that can be found in only a few other locations in the United States.

Sam's Tips

- You can float the Selway Wild and Scenic River. For reservations and information, contact the District Ranger, West Fork Ranger Station, Darby, MT 59829; 406-821-3269.
- There are rustic cabins (no electricity or running water) for rent in remote areas of the forest. Contact the forest for details.

The Flight of the Nez Perce

The Nez Perce War of 1877, one of the most studied and debated Indian Wars in US history, followed a path through Bitterroot. With their land dwindling from the encroachment of settlers, the Nez Perce took up arms and fled east from their reservation in Idaho toward Montana, where they assumed they would find safety. They traveled peacefully down Bitterroot Canyon, through the heart of what is now Bitterroot National Forest, with wary settlers watching at every step. But as they crossed the Continental Divide and left the Bitterroot Valley, they were attacked in their sleep by the U.S. Army 7th Infantry. Big Hole National Battlefield (see entry), 20 miles outside Bitterroot, commemorates this site.

RUSTIC CABINS AND LOOKOUTS IN MONTANA

Many of Montana's National Forests offer lodging in rustic guard stations and fire lookout towers. These cabins, scattered around nine National forests, are out-of-the-way gems, located in the middle of some of America's most pristine lands.

Most cabins are accessible via narrow, winding, dirt or gravel roads, or, in winter, by snowmobile or cross-country skis. Facilities are spartan: a table, chairs, wood stove and bunks (some with mattresses, some without). You might need to bring your own drinking water and cut your own firewood. Expect to use outdoor privies, and don't expect a telephone. The Forest Service recommends that children under 12 not stay in lookout towers.

These cabins, including Hogback Homestead, Priscilla Peak, and Sex Peak, can be remarkable places to stay amidst Montana's beautiful National Forests. Prices range between $15 and $50 a night, and cabins house as few as four or as many as twelve guests. Call for more information and to make reservations, which are required.

Beaverhead-Deerlodge National Forest (20 cabins)
Dillon Ranger District (winter only)
406-683-3900

Wise River Ranger District (year-round)
406-832-3178

Wisdom Ranger District (mostly winter-only)
406-689-3243

Madison Ranger District (autumn-, winter-, and spring-only)
406-682-4253

Deer Lodge Ranger District (year-round)
406-846-1170

Philipsburg Ranger District (year-round)
406-859-3211

Jefferson Ranger District (year-round)
406-287-3223

Bitterroot National Forest (5 cabins, 1 lookout tower)
Sula Ranger District (year-round)
406-821-3201

Darby Ranger District (summer-only)
406-821-3913

West Fork Ranger District (year-round)
406-821-3269

Custer National Forest (1 cabin, year-round)
Ashland Ranger District
406-784-2344

Flathead National Forest (6 cabins, 1 lookout)
Glacier View Ranger District (year-round)
Hungry Horse Ranger District (summer-, autumn-, and winter-only)
406-387-3800

Swan Lake Ranger District (summer-only)
406-837-5081

Gallatin National Forest (25 cabins)
Big Timber Ranger District (year-round)
406-932-5155

Gardiner Ranger District (summer- and winter-only)
406-848-7375

Livingston Ranger District (year-round)
406-222-1892

Bozeman Ranger District (year-round)
406-587-6920

Hebgen Lake Ranger District (year-round)
406-646-7369

Helena National Forest (7 cabins)
Helena Ranger District (year-round)
406-449-5490

Lincoln Ranger District (year-round, except hunting season)
406-362-4265

Townsend Ranger District (year-round)
406-266-3425

Kootenai National Forest (3 cabins, 2 lookout towers)
Rexford Ranger District (year-round)
406-296-2536

Libby Ranger District (summer-only)
406-293-7773

Cabinet Ranger District (summer-only)
406-827-3533

Lewis and Clark National Forest (5 cabins)
Judith Ranger District (winter-only)
406-566-2292

Musselshell Ranger District (winter-only)
406-632-4391

Kings Hill Ranger District (year-round)
406-547-3361

Lolo National Forest (4 cabins)
Missoula Ranger District (year-round)
406-329-3814

Plains Ranger District (year-round)
406-827-3589

CUSTER NATIONAL FOREST

The forest stretches over parts of Montana and the Dakotas.

PO Box 50706
1310 Main Street
Billings, MT 59105-0160
406-657-6361
http://www.fs.fed.us

The sprawling Custer National Forest also includes several National Grasslands; they stretch through 20 counties in Montana, North Dakota, and South Dakota, are scattered from the northeast corner of Yellowstone National Park to the southeastern corner of North Dakota, and total nearly 2.5 million acres. Much of the forest is surrounded by rolling prairie and farmland. Billings, where the forest headquarters is located, is the largest metropolitan area in Montana and is 65 miles from the Beartooth Mountains.

The Cheyenne National Grasslands, the easternmost unit run by the Custer National Forest, is composed of rolling sand dunes vegetated by tall prairie grass. The Cedar and Grand River National Grasslands, located in North and South Dakota, are made up of rolling prairie, some badlands, and river bottoms. The area also offers pheasant, sharptail grouse, waterfowl, antelope, mule, and white-tailed deer hunting.

The Sioux Ranger District, in the southeast corner of Montana and the northwest corner of South Dakota, has eight separate units that have been described as "islands of green in a sea of rolling prairie." These "islands" are hills or mesas of ponderosa pine rising above rolling grasslands. Two official National Landmarks are within the boundaries of the Sioux Ranger District: the Castle—a massive limestone uplift that resembles a medieval castle—and Capitol Rock, another limestone uplift resembling the U.S. Capitol building.

Sam's Tips

- The Beartooth Ranger District includes the Stillwater Complex, which contains the largest known platinum and chrome deposits and the second largest nickel deposits in the United States. Hiking, horseback riding, and mountain climbing are popular activities.
- The magnificent Beartooth Highway, a National Forest Scenic Byway, traverses the mountains from Red Lodge to Cooke City at the northeast entrance to Yellowstone National Park and climbs to the 10,947-foot Beartooth Pass while traveling through the Custer, Gallatin, and Shoshone National Forests.
- Granite Peak, located on the boundary between the Gallatin and Custer National Forests, is the highest point in Montana. The climb to the top is through designated wilderness and is a scramble-type climb, often through areas with virtually no vegetation. Only experienced climbers should attempt to scale Granite Peak.

DEERLODGE NATIONAL FOREST

Surrounding Butte.

420 Barrett Street
Dillon, MT 59725-1630
406-683-3900
http://www.fs.fed.us/r1/bdnf

The Deerlodge National Forest, straddling the Continental Divide and eight separate mountain ranges, includes both low, rolling, semiarid grasslands and rugged rocky peaks towering high above the timberline. There are 1,000 miles of fishing streams; 140 lakes; 22 campgrounds; 629 miles of foot, horse, and motorcycle trails; 200 miles of snowmobile trails; 20 marked ski trails; and 43,629 acres of wilderness. Rental cabins are available at a number of sites in the forest.

FLATHEAD NATIONAL FOREST

The forest is bordered by Glacier National Park to the north and east, the Lolo National Forest to the south, and the Kootenai National Forest to the west.

1935 Third Avenue East
Kalispell, MT 59901
406-758-5200
http://www.fs.fed.us

Glacier National History Association. (PO Box 428, West Glacier, MT 59936; 406-888-5756)

Nearly half of the 2.3-million-acre Flathead National Forest is designated wilderness area. Many of the forest's lakes can be reached by vehicle, horseback, or foot. Some have campgrounds and boat launch facilities. The forest is home to the 15,000-acre Jewel Basin Hiking Area, which includes 27 alpine lakes, mountain streams, meadows, rocky peaks, and a variety of flowers. Thirty-five miles of trails connect most of the lakes.

Sam's Tips

- The Bob Marshall Wilderness Area extends about 60 miles from north to south along the Continental Divide. Main access points are at Pyramid Pass via Holland Lake on the west; Bear Creek, Spotted Bear River, and Meadow Creek on the north; Gibson Reservoir on the east; and the North Fork of the Blackfoot River on the south. Popular activities in the wilderness are: fishing for native black-spotted cutthroat and Dolly Varden trout; hiking; and floating down the South Fork of the Flathead River.
- The National Forest Service in the Northern Region has a Bear Resistant Equipment Loan Program, which, for a recommended minimum donation of $2.00/day, provides materials such as backpacker food tubes, and rope-and-pulley hoisting systems. These are available at the forest's ranger districts: Hungry Horse Ranger District, 406-387-5243; Spotted Bear Ranger District, 406-387-5243 (winter), 406-758-5376 (summer); and Condon Work Center, 406-837-5081 (winter), 406-754-2295 (summer).

GALLATIN NATIONAL FOREST

Extending north and south from Bozeman.

3710 Fallon Street, Suite C
Bozeman, MT 59718
406-587-6920
http://www.fs.fed.us

Yellowstone Association for Natural Science, History, and Education. (Yellowstone National Park, WY 82190; 307-344-7381)

The Gallatin National Forest is made up almost entirely of mountain ranges of the Rocky Mountain chain, including the Bridger Mountains, the Crazy Mountains, the Gallatin Range, the Madison Range, and the Beartooth Mountains. The west side is locally called the Absaroka Range. The three major rivers that pass through the forest—the Gallatin, the Madison, and the Yellowstone—are designated "Blue Ribbon" trout streams and are internationally famous for their superb trout fisheries. The Madison River Earthquake Visitor Center is located at Quake Lake on the Madison River. Built on the site of the great 1959 Madison earthquake and landslide, this facility provides exhibits on the disaster and on the seismic forces that helped shape the region.

GLACIAL LANDFORMS GLOSSARY

Glacier National Park offers this short course in glacial language:

A **HORN** is a steep mountain peak formed when several glaciers carve different sides of the same mountain. Mount Reynolds at Logan Pass is a good example of a horn.

A **CIRQUE** is a large bowl formed at the head of a glacier. Often, the ice melts away and a small lake forms in the depression gouged by the glacier. Avalanche, Iceberg, and Gunsight are all excellent examples of cirque lakes in Glacier National Park.

An **ARÊTE** (French for fish bone) forms when two glaciers work on opposite sides of the same wall, leaving a long narrow ridge. One of Glacier National Parks more prominent features, the Garden Wall, is an arête separating the Lake McDonald Valley from the Many Glacier Valley.

HANGING VALLEYS are formed when large glaciers scour the main valleys, and tributary glaciers work the smaller side canyons. Unable to cut as deep as the valley glaciers, the tributary glaciers have left behind small valleys high up on the mountainsides. Frequently, hanging valleys have waterfalls cascading out of their mouths into the valleys below. Birdwoman Falls plummets from a hanging valley on Mount Oberlin.

MORAINES form at the sides and front of a glacier. Ice flows from the head to the toe of the glacier. This conveyor belt-like flow brings with it the rock and debris trapped in the ice. As it reaches the sides or front, and the ice melts, this trapped material is released and forms large piles called moraines. Moraines from the present glaciers are visible as mounds of rock and gravel along the sides and front of the ice. Plants soon colonize this new soil. Forests and meadows cover many ancient moraines, making them harder to spot.

GLACIER NATIONAL PARK

140 miles north of Missoula; 185 miles northwest of Helena; 125 miles northeast of Spokane, WA.

West Glacier, MT 59936
406-888-7800
http://www.nps.gov/glac

Glacier Natural History Association. (PO Box 428, West Glacier, MT 59936; 406-888-5756)

Established in 1910, Glacier is the tenth most-visited national park, with 2.2 million guests a year. In 1932, Glacier combined with its Canadian neighbor,

Waterton Lakes National Park, to form the Waterton–Glacier International Peace Park—the first international park in the world. The rugged land includes nearly 50 glaciers, numerous glacier-fed lakes and streams, and mountain peaks of over 10,000 feet in height. One highlight of the park is a drive on the famous Going-to-the-Sun Road, which has been called "The Most Beautiful 50 Miles in the World." More than 60 percent of the roadway excavation was through solid rock, using hand-held tools.

SAM'S TIPS

- Because much of Glacier is inaccessible by car, consider these other methods of transportation:
  1. Horse: In the early 1900s, the saddle horse concession at Glacier was the largest of its kind in the world, and it's still a great way to see the park. The Glacier County Tourism Board (800-338-5072) will provide you with more information.
  2. Boat: Scenic cruises on one of Glacier's large alpine lakes are an excellent way to see wilderness views not visible from the road; call the Tourism Board for information.
  3. Foot: There are over 700 miles of trails through Glacier. Order a catalog from the Glacier Natural History Association (address above). *Hiker's Guide to Glacier National Park* ($9.95) and *Short Hikes and Strolls in Glacier National Park* ($5.95) are two of the many fine books that can prepare you for your adventure.

Glaciers

Glaciers can form in any region where it is cold enough for snow to remain year-round. Some have been located on high mountain areas of Mexico as well as near the equator. Ice sheets, or continental glaciers, completely cover the existing landscape, leaving only the tallest mountains above the ice. Glaciers of this type cover the land masses of Greenland and Antarctica. Alpine glaciers—like those in Glacier National Park—are much smaller and form in mountain valleys. Glaciers often pick up huge rocks and carry them miles from their original point. These rocks (known as *erratics*) are responsible for forming Glacier's picturesque "hanging" valleys, which look like gigantic steps in the mountains.

FOOD AND BEARS

Odors attract bears. To prevent a dangerous encounter with a bear, store all edibles (including pet food), food containers (empty or not), and cookware in a hard-sided vehicle or food locker, or hang them from a food pole or cable when not in use, day or night. Glacier National Park offers these additional tips:

- Inspect campsites for bear signs and careless campers nearby.
- Place all trash in bearproof containers; some parks have them for rent.
- Keep pets, especially dogs, under physical restraint.
- Use a flashlight when walking at night.
- If a bear enters your campsite, inform park staff immediately.

- Vehicles over 21 feet long or 8 feet wide are not permitted on some stretches of the Going-to-the-Sun Road. Other options include a bus tour in an open-topped red bus or a car rental in one of the local communities.
- Three other roadways with views of the park are:
  1. US 2, a two-lane highway that winds along the southern boundary of the park for 56 miles between East Glacier and West Glacier Parks and follows the route of the Burlington Northern Railway over Marias Pass.
  2. US 89 (Alberta 2), which connects Waterton Lakes National Park and Glacier National Park via Cardston, Alberta. This main route along Glacier's eastern boundary has a panoramic view of the Continental Divide and Chief Mountain.
  3. The Chief Mountain International Highway, which climbs over glacial debris through aspen groves and lodgepole pine forests while providing great views of Chief Mountain and Mount Cleveland, Water Glacier's highest peak at 10,466 feet. The road is open only from May until September.
- Two interesting geological formations to see in the park: The Garden Wall, near the Logan Pass Visitor Center, a perfect example of a glacial arete—a narrow, jagged, sharp-edged ridge resulting from glacial erosion; and Chief Mountain, a now-isolated mountain that was once part of mountains farther west.

GRANT–KOHRS RANCH NATIONAL HISTORIC SITE

55 miles west of Helena; 85 miles south of Missoula; 40 miles north of Butte; midway between Yellowstone and Glacier National Parks.

Box 790
Deer Lodge, MT 59722
406-846-3388
http://www.nps.gov/grko

Glacier Natural History Association. (same address as above)

The 1860 ranch founded by John Grant became headquarters of legendary Western cattleman Conrad Kohrs. The Grant–Kohrs Ranch, a working cattle ranch, was established to commemorate the frontier cattle era. The 23-room ranch house is the centerpiece of dozens of original historic buildings, furnishings, and flower and vegetable gardens. Rangers in period costume talk about the cowboys, ranching men and women, trail drives, and other topics relating to the frontier.

A Cowhand's Coffee

A Grand–Kohrs Ranch publication, *The Chuckwagon,* offers this recipe: Add two pounds of coffee to two gallons of boiling water. Boil two hours, then throw a horseshoe into the pot and if it sinks, the coffee is not yet done.

 **SAM'S TIPS**

- Each year, on the second full weekend in July, the site commemorates its opening day with a host of special outdoor activities, including branding, chuckwagon cooking, and other demonstrations.

AMERICAN BUFFALO

Bison bison

It is believed that buffalo, or bison, crossed over a land bridge that once connected the Asian and North American continents. Through the centuries, buffalo slowly moved southward, eventually reaching as far south as Mexico and as far east as the Atlantic Coast, extending south to Florida. But the largest herds were found on the plains and prairies from the Rocky Mountains east to the Mississippi River, and from Great Slave Lake in Canada to Texas.

By 1800, the small buffalo herds east of the Mississippi River were gone. Buffalo may have been killed to protect livestock and farmlands in that region. With westward expansion of the American frontier, systematic reduction of the plains herds began around 1830, when buffalo hunting became the chief industry of the plains. Unfortunately, many people at the time also wanted to eradicate buffalo to take away the livelihood and well-being of Native Americans. Native American tribes depended on the buffalo's meat and hides, and many still today believe the animal has special spiritual healing powers, making it an important part of their culture.

Conservation of the buffalo came slowly. In May 1984, Congress enacted a law banning buffalo hunting in Yellowstone National Park. Eight years later, money was appropriated to purchase 21 buffalo from private herds to build up the Yellowstone herd. With adequate protection, this herd has steadily increased until it numbers almost 4,000 animals today. Thousands of buffalo also inhabit the National Bison Range, in the Flathead Valley of Montana; the Wichita Mountains National Wildlife Refuge, in southwest Oklahoma; the Fort Niobrara National Wildlife Refuge, in northern Nebraska; and the Sullys Hill National Wildlife Refuge, in North Dakota.

The present herds, numbering about 200,000 buffalo in all, are not as large as the great herds that once ranged the North American continent, but they are large enough to ensure the continued well-being of the American buffalo for generations to come.

WHAT TO DO IF YOU MEET A BEAR

Although the risk of an encounter with a bear is low, Yellowstone National Park offers these tips—just in case:

- Make bears aware of your presence on trails by making loud noises such as shouting or singing, which lessens the chance of sudden encounters. Hike in groups.
- Do not hike after dark.
- If you encounter a bear, do not run. Bears can run over 30 miles per hour, or 44 feet per second—faster than Olympic sprinters. Running may elicit an attack from otherwise nonaggressive bears. If the bear is unaware of you, detour away from the bear. If the bear is aware of you and nearby, but has not acted aggressively, slowly back away.
- Tree climbing to avoid bears is popular advice but not very practical in many circumstances. All black bears, all grizzly cubs, and some adult grizzlies can climb trees. Running to a tree may provoke an otherwise uncertain bear to chase you.
- Some bears will bluff their way out of a threatening situation by charging, then veering off or stopping abruptly at the last second. Bear experts generally recommend standing still until the bear stops and then slowly backing away. If you are attacked, play dead. Drop to the ground, lift your legs up to your chest, and clasp your hands over the back of your neck. This technique has been especially successful with female bears that have cubs.

HELENA NATIONAL FOREST

West-central Montana, surrounding the capital city, Helena.

2880 Skyway Drive
Helena, MT 59601
406-449-5201
http://www.fs.fed.us

Northwest Interpretive Association. (909 First Avenue, Suite 630, Seattle, WA 98104-1060; 206-220-4140)

The first White men to see this forest were members of the 1805 Lewis and Clark expedition. They traveled up the Missouri River and entered what is now the Helena National Forest at the Gates of the Mountains. In 1864, gold was first discovered in Last Chance Gulch, now the main street of Helena. During that period, a number of settlements and communities, such as Diamond City, Whites City, Hassell, and Old Lincoln, were established. Remnants of these once-booming towns can still be found. The forest, which varies from sagebrush range lands to pristine alpine forests, is roughly divided into two sections. The western portion, with the Continental Divide forming the backbone, extends from the south edge of the Bob Marshall Wilderness to just east of the town of Deer Lodge. The easterly portion, lying in the Big Belt mountain range, extends from the south edge of the Beartooth Game Range to a point just east of Townsend, MT. District ranger offices are located in Townsend, Helena, and Lincoln.

 **SAM'S TIPS**

- The Gates of the Mountains Wilderness contains over 45 miles of scenic trails, many passing through limestone gorges. Water is scarce, but wildlife is usually plentiful. Excursion boats operating on the Missouri River through the Gates of the Mountains offer tours of the area.

KOOTENAI NATIONAL FOREST

Extreme northwestern part of Montana.

506 US Highway 2 West
Libby, MT 59923
406-293-6211
http://www.fs.fed.us

The Kootenai National Forest, bordered on the north by Canada and on the west by Idaho, features high craggy peaks and gently rolling hills in the shadows of the Whitefish Range. The forest is dominated by two major rivers, the Kootenai and Clark Fork. Two dams along the Clark Fork have created the Cabinet Gorge and Noxon Reservoirs within the forest boundary. The Kootenai River is bridled by Libby Dam, creating Lake Koocanusa, which is almost totally encompassed by forest land. The climate of Kootenai is best described as "modified Pacific maritime." It resembles the climate found along the Pacific Coast but is "modified" by occasional arctic air masses more commonly found in the remainder of the state.

 **SAM'S TIPS**

- It is still possible to find gold in the Libby Creek Gold Panning Area. The depth of Libby Creek varies from about 12 inches in autumn to 2–3 feet in the spring. The best place to pan is near the bottom of the gravel piles created by earlier mining operations. The downstream side of large boulders is also a good place to dig. The nearest developed campground is Howard Lake. For more information, contact the Libby Ranger District (406-293-7773).
- Visit the nearby Bull River Ranger Station National Historic Site. This cabin was first inhabited by "Granny" (Granville) Gordon, a cowboy and friend of "Teddy" (President Theodore) Roosevelt. Gordon was appointed the first district ranger at Noxon in 1907. For more information, contact the Cabinet

Wilderness Historical Society (PO Box 618, Noxon, MT 59852) or the Cabinet District Ranger (Cabinet Ranger Station, 2693 Highway 200, Trout Creek, MT 59874).

- The Cabinet Mountains Wilderness area contains some of the most beautiful subalpine scenery in western Montana. The Wilderness offers snow-clad peaks and glacial lakes, cold streams, and cascading waterfalls. A few peaks offer some technical climbing challenges. Wildlife in the area includes: wolverines, deer, elk, moose, grizzly bear, black bear, mountain sheep, and mountain goats. Cutthroat or rainbow trout are found in most of the lakes and streams in the area. Huckleberries and mushrooms are abundant in season.

LEWIS AND CLARK NATIONAL FOREST

90 miles north of Helena; 200 miles northwest of Billings; 170 miles east of Missoula.

1101 15th Street North
PO Box 869
Great Falls, MT 59403
406-791-7700
http://www.fs.fed.us

Situated in north-central Montana, the 1.8 million acres of the Lewis and Clark National Forest are separated into the Rocky Mountain and Jefferson Divisions and scattered into seven separate mountain ranges. The Rocky Mountain Division extends south from the southern border of Glacier National Park. Almost half of the Division comprises the Bob Marshall Wilderness complex. A special attraction for many Wilderness visitors is the huge escarpment known as the "Chinese Wall." Formed as a result of the Ice Age, the wall averages 1,000 feet in height and extends 22 miles along the Continental Divide. The 6 remaining mountain ranges, spread across the Jefferson Division of the forest, seem to spring from the surrounding prairie lands, creating a majestic rise in the flattened agricultural landscape.

Sam's Tips

- A forest visitor's map of each of the Divisions is available at any of the forest offices. The map shows the landownership patterns, the trail and road systems, recreation sites, and motorized vehicle opportunities and restrictions in the forest.

LITTLE BIGHORN BATTLEFIELD NATIONAL MONUMENT

In the Crow Reservation, 65 miles southeast of Billings; 70 miles north of Sheridan, WY.

PO Box 39
Crow Agency, MT 59022
406-638-2622
http://www.nps.gov/libi

Southwest Parks and Monuments Association. (PO Box 190, Crow Agency, MT 59022; 406-638-2622)

Now a National Monument, Little Bighorn Battlefield is the site of the famous 1876 battle between US Army forces, led by Lieutenant Colonel George Custer, and the Lakota (Sioux), Arapaho, and Northern Cheyenne Indians. The Indians won the battle—Custer and the five companies under his immediate command were wiped out—but eventually lost the war. The battle occurred on the ridge and in the valley, over a 4.5-mile area. Today, the hillside and valley have scattered white marble markers, often in pairs, that signify where American soldiers were killed. The Sioux and Cheyenne warriors killed in the battle were removed from the field by friends and relatives.

LOLO NATIONAL FOREST

Western Montana.

Building 24, Fort Missoula
Missoula, MT 59804
406-329-3750
http://www.fs.fed.us/r1/lolo

Northwest Interpretive Association. (909 First Avenue, Suite 630, Seattle, WA; 206-220-4140)

The third largest forest in the Northern Region, the Lolo covers an area 120 miles long and from 40 to 80 miles wide. The topography ranges from remote, high alpine back-country laced with sparkling mountain lakes and whitewater streams to rolling meadows near slow-moving rivers and small towns. Portions of several wildernesses and roadless back-country are within the forest's boundaries. The Lolo is divided into five ranger districts with offices in Missoula, Seeley Lake, Ninemile, Superior, and Plains.

Forest History

The Lolo has played an important role in the history of forest firefighting. Old lookout towers are still perched atop many mountain summits. The Ninemile Remount Station was the site of pioneering developments in firefighting, including innovations in mule-packing to supply fire camps. The first smoke-jumping program was also developed at Ninemile. The firefighting program for the Northern Region is coordinated from the Aerial Fire Depot at Johnson Bell International Airport, outside Missoula. The Depot is busy with smoke-jumping and fire retardant aircraft during the summer months. A Visitor Center has exhibits and tours.

Sam's Tips

- Attractions within the Lolo include the Rattlesnake National Recreation Area and Wilderness; the Lolo Scenic Highway (US 12), which follows a portion of the Lewis and Clark Trail; Seeley Lake; and the Blue Mountain National Recreation Trail.

Points of Interest

U.S. ARMY CORPS OF ENGINEERS

FORT PECK LAKE

The first issue of *LIFE* magazine, in 1936, featured this dam on the cover. Buffalo, elk, deer, antelope, and small game abound in this area, within the Charles M. Russell National Wildlife Refuge. The world's largest known fossil beds are found along the south shore. From Glasgow, southeast on MT 24 for 18 miles.

LIBBY DAM (LAKE KOOCANUSA)

Lake Koocanusa, a 90-mile-long lake, is split between Montana and Canada. In the 48 miles found in the United States, enjoy a variety of water sports, summer and winter sports, and recreational activities, including ranger-led dam tours. The Kootenai River, below the Libby Dam, offers similar opportunities and is a blue-ribbon fishery. From Libby, north on MT 37 for 17 miles.

BUREAU OF LAND MANAGEMENT

BEAR TRAP CANYON WILDERNESS

On Bear Trap Canyon's 6,000 acres, wilderness activities include whitewater floating, hiking, bankside or float fishing, and nature studies.

About 35 miles southwest of Bozeman
406-683-2337

POMPEY'S PILLAR

Just off Interstate 94, visitors will find a famous remnant of the Lewis and Clark Expedition. Captain William Clark climbed this rock and carved his name on July 25, 1806. "Pompey" was Clark's nickname for the young son of Sacajawea, the Corps of Discovery's interpreter.

About 28 miles east of Billings, MT
406-238-1541

GARNET GHOST TOWN AND GARNET BACK COUNTRY BYWAY

Garnet, a historic mining town, is one of the few ghost towns that has been restored but not overcommercialized. More than 30 buildings, some dating back to 1895, have been preserved. Garnet is also the focal point for the Garnet National Winter Recreation Trail, open from January 1 to April 30. More than 100 miles of trails are available for snowmobiling and cross-country skiing. No commercial services are available in the ghost town, but two rustic cabins can be rented for overnight stays.

About 30 miles east of Missoula, off Montana Highway 200
406-329-3884

This is just a sample of Bureau of Land Management sites in Montana. For more information, contact:

Bureau of Land Management
Montana State Office
222 North 32nd Street
PO Box 36800
Billings, MT 59107
406-255-2938
http://www.mt.blm.gov

U.S. BUREAU OF RECLAMATION

CANYON FERRY LAKE

Managed by the Bureau of Reclamation, Montana Area Office, PO Box 30137, Billings, MT 59107; 406-247-6075. Located near Helena; has 76 miles of shoreline, with excellent fishing for rainbow trout, perch, ling, and walleye. Concrete boat ramps, campgrounds, day-use areas, shelters, swimming, and three marinas.

CLARK CANYON RESERVOIR

Administered by the Bureau of Reclamation, 1100 Highway 41, Dillon, MT 59725; 406-683-6472 or 406-683-2307. Located south of Dillon; has 17 miles of shoreline, with good fishing for rainbow and brown trout. Concrete boat ramps, picnic shelters, marina.

FRESNO RESERVOIR

Managed by the Bureau of Reclamation, Montana Area Office, PO Box 30173, Billings, MT 59107; 406-247-6075. Located near Havre; has 65 miles of shoreline. Concrete boat ramp, picnic shelters, and a swimming beach.

NELSON RESERVOIR

Managed by the Bureau of Reclamation, Montana Area Office, PO Box 30137, Billings, MT 59107; 406-247-6075. Located near Saco, on Highway 2; has 30 miles of shoreline.

PISHKUN RESERVOIR
Managed by the Montana Department of Fish, Wildlife and Parks, Capitol Station, Helena, MT 59620; 406-444-2535. Located near the Sun River, west of Great Falls; has 13 miles of shoreline.

DECORATE YOUR LIFE: POSTERS ON THE GREAT OUTDOORS

The government has produced a number of beautiful color posters that are suitable for framing. In addition to spectacular images of landscapes, plants, and wildlife, the posters offer educational material, usually on the reverse side. Some of the available posters are:

Title	*Stock No.*	*Price*
Denali National Park and Preserve, Alaska	024-005-01154-4	$7.00
Everglades National Park, Florida	024-005-00487-4	8.00
Glacier Bay National Park and Preserve, Alaska	024-005-00755-5	8.50
Greater Yellowstone	024-005-01082-3	8.50
The Rocky Mountains	024-005-00967-1	7.00
Yosemite	024-005-01044-1	7.00
Songbirds of the Forest and Field	024-010-00699-4	7.50
Wild Things: America's National Wildlife Refuges	024-010-00713-3	5.00
Desert Wildlife and Plants	024-005-00789-0	7.00
Wetland Wilderness	024-010-00704-4	6.00

You can order these posters by phone (202-512-1800) or fax (202-512-2250), or by writing to: Superintendent of Documents, PO Box 371954, Pittsburgh, PA 15250-7954. (Use the stock number for ordering, and be aware that prices may change.) There are 24 Government Bookstores located around the country. Each carries titles of regional interest. Check the appendix for the one nearest to you.

NORTH DAKOTA

FORT UNION TRADING POST NATIONAL HISTORIC SITE

24 miles southwest of Williston; 21 miles north of Sidney, MT.

R.R. 3, Box 71
Williston, ND 58801
701-572-9083
http://www.nps.gov/fous

 **Fort Union Association.** (same address as above; 800-434-0233)

John Jacob Astor's American Fur Company built Fort Union in 1828, near the junction of the Missouri and Yellowstone rivers. It stood on a grassy plain that stretched one mile to the north, providing ample space for Indians' camps during trading time. The post became the headquarters for trading beaver furs and buffalo hides with the Assiniboin Indians, the Crow Indians on the upper Yellowstone, and the Blackfeet, who lived farther up the Missouri. The stone foundations of the palisades, the main house and its kitchen, the Indian reception building, and the main gate have been excavated. Artifacts such as eating utensils, beer bottles, buttons, metal objects, trapping gear and harnesses, china, pottery, and other glass objects also have been uncovered. Between 1985 and 1989, the National Park Service reconstructed portions of Fort Union Trading Post, including the walls, stone bastions, Indian trade house, and Bourgeois House.

 **SAM'S TIPS**

- A few miles east of Fort Union is Fort Buford State Historic Site which commemorates Sitting Bull's surrender on July 20, 1881. Commanding a northern

 **International Peace Garden**

Dedicated in 1932, the International Peace Garden was the brainchild of Dr. Henry Moore of Islington, Ontario. In 1929, at a convention in Toronto, he presented the idea of a garden commemorating peace between the United States and Canada to the Professional Grounds Management Society. This site was agreed on because it straddles the longest unfortified border in the world, is located on the world's longest north–south road, and is halfway between the Atlantic and Pacific Coasts. The formal gardens are filled with 140,000 flowering annuals, intricate floral designs, reflecting pools, and paths. Lakes, playgrounds, and picnic areas lie around the periphery. The Garden is the home of the International Music Camp, where hundreds of high school students gather each year for intensive training in music and the arts. The Garden is located on Route 1, 14 miles north of Dunseith on the Canadian border. For further information contact: The International Peace Garden, Route 1, Box 116, Dunseith, ND 58329; 701-263-4390.

plains crossroads, Fort Buford offers a museum set in an original military building, a military cemetery, and a picnic area.

KNIFE RIVER INDIAN VILLAGES NATIONAL HISTORIC SITE

60 miles north of Bismarck.

PO Box 9
Stanton, ND 58571
701-745-3300 or 3309
http://www.nps.gov/knri

Theodore Roosevelt Nature and History Association. (PO Box 167, Medora, ND 58645; 701-623-4884)

The park encompasses remnants of historic and prehistoric American Indian villages, last occupied in 1845 by the Hidatsa and Mandan. The park exhibits an array of artifacts of Plains Indian culture, including a 50-foot-diameter earthlodge. The three village sites show evidence of earthlodges, fortification ditches, and cache pits.

THEODORE ROOSEVELT NATIONAL PARK

South Unit is at Medora, 135 miles west of Bismarck on I-94; North Unit is 60 miles southeast of Williston.

PO Box 7
Medora, ND 58645
701-623-4466
http://www.nps.gov/thro

Theodore Roosevelt Nature and History Association. (PO Box 167, Medora, ND 58645; 701-623-4884)

The North Dakota Badlands provide the scenic backdrop to this park named after the 26th president for his enduring contributions to the conservation of our nation's resources. A multitude of prairie animals—including bison, elk, pronghorn antelope, wild horses, and prairie dogs—inhabit the area's grass-and-sagebrush plains. The park is divided into two main sections 72 miles apart from one another. The Elkhorn ranch site is situated roughly midway between them.

Sam's Tips

- The Medora Visitor Center has a museum exhibiting personal items of Theodore Roosevelt, ranching artifacts,

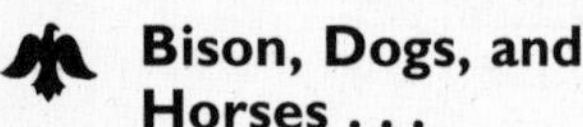

Bison, Dogs, and Horses . . .

The buffalo, the largest mammal on the North American continent, was given its name by early French explorers, who called the animals *boeufs,* meaning "oxen." Over the years, that name went through several changes, from "buffle" to "buffelo" to the present "buffalo." Prairie dogs were originally named *petits chiens,* meaning "little dogs." These highly social animals are not really dogs, but rodents. The modern horse, which became extinct about 10,000 years ago on the North American continent, was reintroduced by the Spanish in the 16th century. Escaped horses became known as "mustangs," from the Spanish *mesteno,* meaning "wild."

and natural history displays. The restored Maltese Cross cabin, used by Roosevelt, is behind the Visitor Center.

- A nearby attraction is the Chateau DeMores State Historic Site. The town of Medora was founded by a wealthy French nobleman, the Marquis DeMores, who named the town after his wife, Medora von Hoffman. Guided tours of the 27-room chateau are usually offered from late May through September.

Points of Interest

U.S. ARMY CORPS OF ENGINEERS

ASHTABULA LAKE

Nearby historic Sibley Trail was used by pioneers moving west. From Valley City, 11 miles northwest on River Road.

BOWMAN–HALEY LAKE

Located on a former Sioux hunting ground where there are treeless slopes and plains. From Bowman, south 13 miles on US 85, then east 9 miles plus 2 miles on a gravel County Road.

GARRISON DAM (LAKE SAKAKAWEA)

This is the Corps of Engineers' largest lake, one of six built to control recurrent flooding on the Missouri River. Sites of early Indian culture and of trading posts and Army posts are located in the area. From Bismarck, north 70 miles via US 83 and ND 200.

U.S. BUREAU OF RECLAMATION

DEVILS LAKE STATE PARK

Managed by the North Dakota Parks and Tourism Department, Route 1, Box 165, Devils Lake, ND 58301; 701-662-8418. Ten miles east and 6 miles south of Devils Lake. Overnight camping, water, and electric hookups.

DICKINSON RESERVOIR

Managed by Dickinson Park and Recreation District, Box 548, Dickinson, ND 58601; 701-225-2074. Public use area open 7 days a week. Overnight camping, water, and electric hookups.

HEART BUTTE RESERVOIR

Managed by the Bureau of Reclamation, Box 1017, Bismarck, ND 58502; 701-250-4592. Fifteen miles south of Glen Ullin.

JAMESTOWN RESERVOIR

Managed by the Stutsman County Park Board, 12 Third Avenue NE, Jamestown, ND 58401; 701-252-4835. Two miles north of Jamestown; modern campground, concession, boat rental, primitive camping. Public use area open 7 days a week.

FISH AND WILDLIFE SERVICE

J. CLARK SALYER NATIONAL WILDLIFE REFUGE

The largest national wildlife refuge in the state follows the Souris River for 50 miles through north-central North Dakota and covers 58,700 acres. The refuge has become a favorite spot for birds to stop on their migrations north and south. Nearly 125 species nest here, and over 300 have been observed since the park was established in 1935. Many species of shorebirds and grebes, white pelican, sandhill crane, lark bunting, longspurs, and sparrows—both Baird's and LeConte's—number among the summer residents.

For more information on the mountain-prairie region's other refuges, contact:

Public Affairs Office
Denver Federal Center
Box 25486
Denver, CO 80225
303-236-7904
http://www.fws.gov

IT'S A PRAIRIE DOG'S LIFE

Early explorers of the High Plains referred to the dominant burrowing animal of the ecosystem as wild dogs of the prairie because of the barking sound they make. These small rodents provide the anchor for ecosystems that are dependent on the complex underground burrows the prairie dogs construct.

For example, prairie dogs churn up dirt, mixing topsoil with underlying soils, making it easier for plants to propagate. Birds often congregate in and around the towns, attracted by the insects that are easily seen in the patches grazed by the prairie dogs. Larger animals such as deer and pronghorn antelope prefer to feed in prairie dog towns because they like the easily digested herbaceous plants that grow in the colonies.

Black-tailed prairie dogs, once numerous on the High Plains, have suffered dramatic declines due to widespread eradication efforts. Some animal populations, such as burrowing owls and swift foxes, are dwindling—in part, because of the decline in prairie dog towns. The black-footed ferret, also dependent on prairie dog towns, has declined to the point of near-extinction.

SOUTH DAKOTA

BADLANDS NATIONAL PARK

85 miles southeast of Rapid City.

PO Box 6
Interior, SD 57750
605-433-5361
http://www.nps.gov/badl

Badlands Natural History Association. (PO Box 47, Badlands National Park, Interior, SD 57750; 605-433-5361)

Badlands National Park is a remnant of an ancient grassland prairie that once stretched unbroken from southern Alberta almost to Mexico, and from the Rockies to Indiana, covering almost a quarter of the United States. For millions of years, rain, wind, and frost have carved steep canyons, sharp ridges, spires, and knobs out of the Dakota prairie, providing a window into the relentless pace of geologic change. Sculpted by erosion, the surreal panoramic landscape that makes up the Badlands National Park contains animal fossils from 26 million to 37 million years ago. The area is mostly arid, but prairie grasslands in the park support bighorn sheep, deer, pronghorn antelope, fox, prairie dogs, and a bison herd of 500. The Stronghold Unit, within the Pine Ridge Reservation, contains the White River Visitor Center. The North Unit, which contains the park headquarters and the campgrounds, is surrounded by the Buffalo Gap National Grassland.

SAM'S TIPS

- The 64,144-acre Sage Creek Wilderness Area is the largest prairie wilderness in the United States. This roadless area is protected from development, but is open for hiking, backpacking, and other nature activities. The only trails within the wilderness are those created by the bison. A topographic map is available for purchase at the park.
- There are two tent/RV campgrounds in the park: Cedar Pass and Sage Creek. Both are open all year, first come, first served. Heavy snows sometimes close campgrounds from December through April.
- The Stronghold Unit is the scene of much Lakota history. The Ghost Dances at Stronghold Table in 1890 were a prelude to the bloodshed at Wounded Knee, 25 miles south of the White River Visitor Center.
- The site of the Wounded Knee Massacre on Pine Ridge Indian Reservation is a short drive south of Badlands National Park. The site is not developed for tourism. It is marked by a sign and a mass grave. If you visit, be considerate. Many of the Lakota (Sioux) people consider it sacred ground.

The Lakotas in "Les Mauvaises Terres . . ."

Though seemingly inhospitable at first glance, the Badlands have supported humans for more than 12,000 years. The area's earliest people were ancient mammoth hunters. Much later, they were followed by tribes whose lives centered on bison hunting. The Arikara were the first Indian tribe known to have inhabited the White River area. By the mid-18th century, they were replaced by the bison-hunting Sioux, or Lakota, who flourished during the next 100 years. French fur trappers, the first of many European arrivals who would supplant the Lakota, called the region *les mauvaises terres ā traverser,* "bad lands to cross." Trappers were soon followed by soldiers, miners, cattlemen, and homesteaders who forever changed the face of the prairie. The following 40 years of struggle culminated in the 1890 Wounded Knee Massacre.

BLACK HILLS NATIONAL FOREST

Western South Dakota and eastern Wyoming; near Rapid City, on I-90.

R.R. 2, Box 200
Custer, SD 57730
605-673-2251
http://www.fs.fed.us/bhnf

 **Black Hills Parks and Forests Association.** (RR 1, Box 190, Hot Springs, SD; 605-745-4600)

Seen from a distance, these pine-covered hills rising several thousand feet above the surrounding prairie appear to be black; hence, their name. The Black Hills cover an area 125 miles long and 65 miles wide in western South Dakota and eastern Wyoming. They encompass rugged rock formations, canyons and gulches, open grassland parks, tumbling streams, deep blue lakes, and unique caves. The forest has 108 developed recreational areas, including camp and picnic grounds, swimming beaches, boat launches, scenic overlooks, and trailheads.

FOREST SERVICE SCENIC BYWAY

Spearfish Canyon Highway

The Spearfish Canyon Highway passes through 20 miles of narrow canyon on the Black Hills National Forest and features views of mountains forested with pine, spruce, aspen, and birch. Bridal Veil Falls and remnants of old mines and mining communities are other attractions along this scenic route. *Contact Black Hills National Forest.*

Hike on a self-guided nature trail near the Visitor Center, or boat, swim, wind surf, and fish in the reservoir. Bismarck, Deerfield, Sheridan, and Stockade Lakes are also open for boating and fishing.

Sam's Tips

- The Black Elk Wilderness area is in the center of the Norbeck Wildlife Preserve. The 9,824-acre Wilderness was named for Black Elk, an Oglala Sioux holy man, and subject of a book, *Black Elk Speaks.*
- Harney Peak, at 7,242 feet above sea level, is the highest point in the United States east of the Rocky Mountains. From a historic lookout tower on Harney Peak, you can enjoy a panoramic view of four states—South Dakota, Nebraska, Wyoming, and Montana—as well as the granite formations and cliffs of the Black Elk Wilderness. Forest Service trails lead to the top of Harney Peak from almost any direction.

JEWEL CAVE NATIONAL MONUMENT

Inside Black Hills National Forest, on Route 16; 13 miles west of Custer.

R.R. 1, Box 60 AA
Custer, SD 57730
605-673-2288
http://www.nps.gov/jeca

Buried beneath the Black Hills is Jewel Cave, named for the crystals that line its chambers and passages and sparkle like brilliant gems when illuminated. This underground spectacle is created by Jewel Cave's most abundant formations—the calcite crystals known as dogtooth spar and nailhead spar. Other formations in Jewel Cave include translucent draperies (up to 30 feet long), scintillites (red rock called chert, coated with sparkling quartz crystals), and hydromagnesite balloons (fragile, silvery bubbles—a cave phenomenon that is as yet unexplained).

Sam's Tips

You can explore Jewel Cave on any of the park's ranger-guided tours:

- The Scenic Tour is a half-mile, 75-minute tour that visits chambers decorated with calcite crystals and colorful stalactites, stalagmites, and draperies. It begins at the Visitor Center with an elevator ride into the cave, and then follows a paved, lighted path up and down more than 700 stairs—a moderately strenuous trip.
- The half-mile Historic Tour takes about an hour and 45 minutes to complete. The tour follows the paths of early Jewel Cave explorers. You see the cave's calcite-coated passages lighted by old-style candle lanterns. The round-trip tour begins at the cave's entrance in Hell's Canyon. This very strenuous tour

Buffalo Gap National Grassland

Located in southwestern South Dakota, this 590,000-acre area was named for the only break in a ring of foothills that surrounds the Black Hills. Bison traveled through this gap in their frequent migrations between hills and prairies. The largest of this region's grasslands, the Buffalo Gap is characterized by gently rolling hills but is better known for its badlands topographic features. Home to many varieties of plants and wildlife especially adapted to the prairie ecosystem, Buffalo Gap is considered a possible reintroduction site for the endangered black-footed ferret and is home to the swift fox, a candidate for federal listing under the Endangered Species Act. Buffalo Gap is also the only grassland in the country with a Visitor Center that interprets the role of National Grasslands. Contact the grassland at 209 North River, Hot Springs SD, 57747-9610; 605-745-4107.

has many steep stairs and requires bending and crawling. Children under 6 years are not admitted.

- Spelunking Tour. This half-mile, 4-hour tour gives you a taste of modern-day cave exploring in a wild, undeveloped portion of Jewel Cave. Old clothes and gloves are recommended; ankle-high laced boots with lug soles are required. The park supplies hard hats and headlamps. To qualify for the tour, you will be required to crawl through an 8.5-foot-by-24-inch concrete block tunnel. Children 15 years and younger are not allowed; children 16 and 17 years must have a parent's or guardian's written permission. Reservations for the Spelunking Tour are required. They can be made up to 1 month in advance by calling or writing to the park.

MOUNT RUSHMORE NATIONAL MEMORIAL

On the northeast border of the Black Elk Wilderness in the Black Hills National Forest; 25 miles southwest of Rapid City.

PO Box 268
Keystone, SD 57751
605-574-2523
http://www.nps.gov/moru

Mount Rushmore History Association. (PO Box 444, Keystone, SD 57751; 605-574-2523, ext. 128)

Frank Lloyd Wright wrote of Mount Rushmore, "The noble countenances emerge from Rushmore as though the spirit of the mountain heard a human plan and itself became a human countenance." The 14-year, $998,000 project was the vision of sculptor Gutzon Borglum, who saw it as "the formal rendering of the philosophy of our government into granite on a mountain peak." Having won fame for his realistic portraiture, Borglum, who in his youth had studied in Paris with Auguste Rodin, chose to give human form to the abstract. His colossal monument to America groups four presidents—Washington, Jefferson, Lincoln, and Theodore Roosevelt—who brought the country from colonial times into the 20th century. Over 2.6 million people come every year to visit the "Shrine of Democracy."

Sam's Tips

- There are no camping or lodging facilities in the park.
- The Sculptor's Studio, constructed in 1939, is a historic building that displays Borglum's tools and original plaster models. The Studio is open only during the summer.
- The park offers on- and off-site school programs for students of all ages. Information packets for classroom and on-site use are available, as well as a film for school loan, entitled *Mount Rushmore, The Shrine.*
- Five miles north of Custer, SD, is the Crazy Horse Memorial. This gigantic statue was begun in 1948 by sculptor Korczak Ziolkowski, who had been one of Borglum's assistants during the carving of Mount Rushmore. Born in Boston, Ziolkowski dedicated his life to the statue, spending several decades alone on Thunderhead Mountain, blasting the image of the legendary Sioux warrior into the mountain. Ziolkowski died in 1982, but the work is continued by his wife and children. On site at the memorial are a scale model of the sculpture, a gift shop, and the Indian Museum of North America, featuring three immense exhibit halls with thousands of artifacts from dozens of tribes throughout the United States. For more information, contact Crazy Horse Mountain Memorial (Avenue of the Chiefs, Crazy Horse, SD 57730-9506; 605-673-4681).

Fort Pierre National Grassland

The Fort Pierre National Grassland was named after a town established in 1826 by the French as one of the first fur trading posts in the Dakota "Territory." It is located where the Bad River empties into the Missouri River. The Fort Pierre National Grassland is recognized as having the best huntable populations of greater prairie chicken and sharptailed grouse in South Dakota. Homesteading failed in this area because of high levels of selenium in the soil. Commonly called "alkali poisoning," selenium accumulates in animals and can cause death. Most of this land was purchased by the US Government because a year-round livestock operation could not be supported. Management practices, such as alternating crops annually and rotating livestock grazing bimonthly, have made farming and ranching on the Fort Pierre possible. Contact the grassland at 124 South Euclid Avenue, Pierre, SD 57501; 605-224-5517.

WIND CAVE NATIONAL PARK

Seven miles north of Hot Springs; 30 miles south of Rapid City.

RR 1, Box 190
Hot Springs, SD 57747
605-745-4600
http://www.nps.gov/wica

The Black Hills Parks and Forests Association. (RR 1, Box 190-WCNP, Hot Springs, SD 57747-9430; 605-745-7020)

"We made our way down the stairway against the very strong wind and then began our descent proper, into the wonderful, indescribably wonderful cave," wrote an 1890 cave explorer. The first recorded discovery of Wind Cave had taken place nine years before, when early settlers of the Black Hills heard a strange whistling sound caused by wind rushing out of a small hole in the ground. This hole can still be seen near the Wind Cave Visitor Center. Wind Cave is one of the longest and most complex caves in the world; its passageways are decorated with beautiful boxwork and delicate calcite crystal formations with names such as "popcorn" "and "frostwork." As of 1996, over 78 miles of the cave had been explored and mapped, but barometric wind studies indicate that only some 5 percent of the total cave has been discovered. Above ground, 28,295 acres of mixed grass prairie, ponderosa pine forest and associated wildlife are the main features of the park.

SAM'S TIPS

- Five types of cave tours are scheduled approximately every twenty minutes, from 8:40 A.M. to 6:30 P.M., daily, June 1 to August. Tour schedules are reduced the remainder of the year. Tours cost from $4.00 to $15.00 per adult depending on the type of tour.

POINTS OF INTEREST

U.S. ARMY CORPS OF ENGINEERS

BIG BEND DAM (LAKE SHARPE)
One of six large lakes on the Missouri River. The area contains numerous sites of early Indian villages. A Visitor Center contains exhibits and displays. From Sioux Falls, west on I-90 to Chamberlain, then north on SD 50.

COLD BROOK LAKE AND COTTONWOOD SPRINGS LAKE
On the south fringe of the Black Hills. Visit nearby Mount Rushmore, Custer State Park, and Wind Cave National Park. About 1 mile north of Hot Springs.

FORT RANDALL DAM (LAKE FRANCIS CASE)

This area, on the Missouri River, contains many historic and archaeological sites. Numerous tributary streams and their embayments afford protected boating and fishing sites. Near Pickstown, on US 18.

GAVINS POINT DAM (LEWIS AND CLARK LAKE)

This Missouri River lake provides a tree-covered shoreline characterized by picturesque chalky bluffs in the lower segment and an interesting view of the Missouri Valley in the upper reach. From Yankton, west on SD 52.

LAKE OAHE

A very large lake on the mainstream of the Missouri River. Rich in historic sites—forts, trading posts, and Lewis and Clark campsites. From Pierre, north 8 miles on SD 1804.

U.S. BUREAU OF RECLAMATION

ANGOSTURA RESERVOIR

Managed by the South Dakota Department of Game, Fish and Parks, PO Box 131-A, Hot Springs, SD 57747; 605-745-6996. Located 9 miles southeast of Hot Springs. Public use area, camping, picnic areas, trailer dump station, concession, boat rental, swimming.

DEERFIELD RESERVOIR

Managed by the US Forest Service, Black Hills National Forest, Star Route, Box 51, Hill City, SD 57745; 605-574-2534. Twenty-five miles west of Rapid City. Public use area, camping, picnic areas, concession, swimming, boating, hiking, and fishing.

PACTOLA RESERVOIR

Managed by the US Forest Service, Black Hills National Forest, 803 Soo San Drive, Rapid City, SD 57702; 605-343-1567. Fifteen miles west of Miles City. Public use area, camping, picnic area, concession, visitor center, swimming, boating, and hiking.

SHADEHILL RESERVOIR

Managed by the South Dakota Department of Game, Fish and Parks, PO Box 63, Shadehill, SD 57635; 605-374-5114. Located 12 miles south of Lemmon. Public use area, camping, picnic areas, trailer dump station, swimming, boating, and hiking.

UTAH

ARCHES NATIONAL PARK

235 miles southeast of Salt Lake City; 100 miles southwest of Grand Junction, CO.

PO Box 907
Moab, UT 84532
435-259-8161
http://www.nps.gov/arch

Canyonlands Natural History Association. (3031 South Highway 191, Moab, UT 84532; 800-840-8978)

Arches National Park contains the largest and densest concentration of natural sandstone arches in the world. More than 2,000 catalogued arches range in size from a 3-foot opening (the minimum considered an arch) to Landscape Arch, which measures 306 feet from base to base. In the heart of southeastern Utah's red rock country, the park lies atop an underground salt bed. Along with above-ground erosion, the salt bed created the arches and spires, balanced rocks, sandstone fins, and eroded monoliths visitors find here.

SAM'S TIPS

- The most popular sites in Arches include: Park Avenue, where the balanced rocks, spires, and eroded fins resemble a city skyline; Courthouse Towers, a

Arches to Arches, Rust to Rust

The red rocks of Arches National Park are the product of erosion from ice and water, as well as of the area's extreme temperatures. This area was covered with ancient seas 300 million years ago. When the seas evaporated, they left behind thousands of feet of salt deposits. Later, layers of sand and sediments covered the salt and were compressed into sedimentary rock. Under the pressure of overlying sediments, underground salt moves and flows like toothpaste in a tube. At Arches, the sandstone layers were pushed up by this salt movement into an anticline, or salt dome. The overlying rock did not bend as easily as the salt did, and so it cracked in parallel fractures. Water ran into these cracks and dissolved much of the salt layer below. The rock remained with nothing to hold it up, and it collapsed. Water carried away sand grains one by one and widened the cracks into narrow canyons. Today, the thin rock walls between these canyons are called "fins." Rain or snow enters tiny cracks in the fins and then freezes and expands, causing little pieces of sandstone to flake off. Soon the tiny cracks break through the fin, and arches are formed.

Cryptobiotic Crust

The maxim "Take only pictures, leave only footprints" does *not* apply here. Footprints are deadly to the fragile cryptobiotic crust that covers the ground at Arches. Sometimes black and bumpy, sometimes almost invisible, this crust is composed of cyanobacteria, lichen, fungi, algae, and moss. It helps to hold desert sands together, retains moisture, and adds critical nutrients to the soil. Decades of growth can be destroyed by one careless footstep.

When walking off trails, stay in dry washes where water runs after rains, or on bare slickrock. Bring a foam pad, and camp on the slickrock. You may need to take long detours to reach your destination without destroying this important and fragile component of the ecosystem.

photographic mecca that boasts huge monoliths; world-famous Balanced Rock; and The Windows section, four large arches seen from the roadway.

- Panorama Point offers a vista of Salt Valley and the Fiery Furnace, which is often brilliantly illuminated when the sun sets.
- Devils Garden is the only developed campground in the park. The tent/RV campground is open all year, on a first-come, first-served basis. It usually fills by midmorning from March to mid-October, so plan to arrive at the park in early morning.
- John Wesley Wolfe, a disabled Civil War veteran, and his son Fred were the first white settlers of this area in 1898. A weathered log cabin, root cellar, and corral remain as evidence of their primitive ranch.

ASHLEY NATIONAL FOREST

Northeastern Utah and southwestern Wyoming; 100 miles east of Salt Lake City via US Highway 40.

355 North Vernal Avenue
Vernal, UT 84078
435-789-1181
http://www.fs.fed.us/r4/ashley

Flaming Gorge Natural History Association. (PO Box 188, Dutch John, UT 84023; 435-885-3305)

A wide range of vegetation and wildlife exists in the Ashley National Forest, where the landscape varies from desert badlands to large open meadows, glaciated basins, high mountain peaks, and steep canyons. The forest is located within three geographical areas: the Uinta Mountains, the largest east–west mountain range in the continental United States; the Wyoming Basin; and the Tavaputs Plateau. Grasses and shrubs in the desert country yield to pinyon and juniper forests on lower mountain slopes. Colorful aspen trees occupy areas above the pinyon and juniper forests. At higher elevations, the vegetation changes to mixed aspen and high-mountain conifers, then to conifer forests of lodgepole pine, fir, and spruce. Wildlife includes bear, mountain lion, moose, elk, mule deer, antelope, and Rocky Mountain bighorn sheep. The high mountains are the source of many rivers and streams that eventually reach the Colorado River. The main recreation attractions are the High Uintas Wilderness, Flaming Gorge National Recreation Area, and Sheep Creek Canyon Geological Area. Two scenic byways and two scenic back-country byways provide the main access to scenic landscapes of the Uinta Mountains.

Flaming Gorge National Recreation Area

A backdrop of bald peaks rises above the timberline on the Uinta Mountains to an altitude of more than 12,000 feet in the Ashley National Forest's Flaming Gorge National Recreational Area. At lower elevations, over 120 miles of trails attract hikers and backpackers to remote mountain lakes and streams. Trophy trout in Flaming Gorge Lake and the Green River (below the dam) have made the area a prime fishing spot. Water sports such as whitewater rafting, sailing, power boating, water skiing, and swimming contrast with the surrounding dusty sagebrush country of the northern desert and the vertical rock of 1,400-foot-deep Red Canyon.

Sam's Tips

- Flaming Gorge Lake, which extends almost 90 miles from the Flaming Gorge Dam to Green River, WY, provides outstanding boating and fishing. Record-breaking German brown trout and large lake and rainbow trout have been caught at Gorge Lake.
- Jarvie Ranch, known as the principal hideout of Butch Cassidy and the Wild Bunch, is located 20 miles east of the Flaming Gorge National Recreation Area (NRA). The ranch has an interpretive center that depicts the era of the Wild Bunch and other outlaws.
- The Flaming Gorge–Uintas Scenic Byway (also known as "The Drive Through the Ages" Scenic Byway) takes you through a panorama of geologic history. As you proceed north from Vernal toward the Flaming Gorge NRA, you will drive 30 miles across edges of exposed rock layers that become progressively older, starting with the Mancos Formation, generally composed of clays that settled to the bottom of a sea that once covered the area.
- Accommodations include primitive and developed camping facilities throughout the forest. Cabins and motel units are located in some of the canyons along the south slope of the Uinta Mountains and at Flaming Gorge NRA.

BRYCE CANYON NATIONAL PARK

80 miles east of Cedar City; 240 miles south of Salt Lake City.

Bryce Canyon, UT 84717
435-834-5322
http://www.nps.gov/brca

Bryce Canyon Natural History Association. (Bryce Canyon, UT 84717; 435-834-4602)

Some of the most colorful and unusual eroded forms in the world stand in horseshoe-shaped amphitheaters along the edge of the Paunsaugunt Plateau in southern Utah. Time and nature have sculpted Claron limestones into thousands of spires, fins, arches, and mazes. Collectively called "hoodoos," these unique and erratically arranged formations are tinted with intense colors. Ponderosa pines, high meadows, and spruce-fir forests border the rim of the plateau, and panoramic views of over 100 miles spread beyond the park's boundaries. This area boasts some of the cleanest air in the country. Visitors to Bryce Canyon can experience the violent beauty of an afternoon thunderstorm, which occurs frequently in late July and in August, or hike to a back-country campsite and enjoy one of the best stargazing areas in the world.

Sunset at Bryce Canyon

As the sun sets, the shadows stretch eastward across this vast landscape until all is darkness. Twenty minutes after sunset, a dark purplish band can be seen lying just above the eastern horizon. This band slowly rises until the darkening sky absorbs it altogether. The purple band is the shadow of the Earth projected onto the atmosphere. This visual splendor occurs because of the ideal atmospheric conditions of southern Utah.

Sam's Tips

- Park rangers offer a variety of conducted programs in the summer, including campfire and children's programs, geology talks, hikes into the canyon, and walks along the rim. Schedules of activities are available at the Visitor Center.
- About half of the park's 1.7 million annual visitors come between Memorial Day and Labor Day. A quieter time to visit is during the winter, when snowshoes are often loaned free of charge at the Visitor Center on a first-come, first-served basis.
- North and Sunset campgrounds total 218 sites (first come, first served); one group campsite is available, by reservation only. Back-country camping is allowed, but a free permit, available at the Visitor Center, is required.
- A drive along the 18 miles of the main park road affords outstanding views of the park and southern Utah's scenery. On crisp winter days, views from Rainbow Point or Yovimpa Point are restricted only by the curvature of the Earth.
- The easiest trail into the canyon is the 1.5-mile round-trip hike into Queen's Garden, which starts from Sunrise Point. The more strenuous Trail to the Hat Shop starts at Bryce Point and takes you through an elevation change of 900 feet. The Peekaboo Loop (4.8 miles, round trip) traverses the canyon bottoms and also serves as a horse trail. The Under-the-Rim Trail covers 22 miles between Bryce Point and Rainbow Point, and has 8 backcountry campsites.

The Namesakes

The mid- to late 1800s brought a group of Mormons (members of the Church of Jesus Christ of Latter Day Saints) to the canyon. Among these religious pioneers were Ebenezer and Mary Bryce, the couple after whom the canyon is named because of their hard work in establishing a road into one of the canyons. The road was used for hauling timber and firewood, making life in the canyon just a little bit easier.

RUSTIC CABINS IN UTAH

Many of Utah's National Forests offer lodging in rustic guard stations. These cabins, scattered around three National Forests, are out-of-the-way gems, located in the middle of some of America's most pristine lands.

Most cabins are accessible via narrow, winding, dirt or gravel roads, or, in winter, by snowmobile or cross-country skis. Facilities are spartan: a table, chairs, wood stove and bunks (some with mattresses, some without). You might need to bring your own drinking water and cut your own firewood. Expect to use outdoor privies, and don't expect a telephone.

These cabins can be a remarkable place to stay amidst Utah's beautiful National Forests. Prices range between $15 and $25 a night, and cabins house as few as four or as many as ten or more guests. For large groups, there's the Gooseberry Facility in Fishlake National Forest, which houses 50 people in three bunk houses, and costs $300 per night. Call for more information and to make reservations, which are required.

Ashley National Forest (3 cabins, year-round)
Vernal Ranger District
353 North Vernal Avenue
Vernal, UT 84078
435-789-1181

Fishlake National Forest (1 cabin, large capacity, summer-only)
Richfield Ranger District
115 East 900 North
Richfield, UT 84701
435-896-9233

Wasatch-Cache National Forest (2 cabins, winter-only)
Ogden Ranger District
2501 Wall Avenue
Ogden, UT 84401
801-625-5306

Evanston Ranger District
1565 Highway 150
Evanston, WY 82930
307-789-3194

UNCLE SAM'S NEWEST NATIONAL MONUMENT: GRAND STAIRCASE ESCALANTE

Established in Utah by President Clinton on September 19, 1996, the newly designated national monument contains paleontological, archaeological, biological, and historical features. The monument extends across fragile and scenic terrain, including red rock canyons, rare rock formations, and high cliffs that provide vistas of up to 60 miles. Thousand-year-old piñon and junipers can be found in the region, as well as prehistoric dwellings, examples of ancient rock art, a world-class fossil trove, millions of years of geologic history, and hundreds of living species of amphibians, birds, mammals, and reptiles.

Our newest National Monument has been at the center of a controversy over drilling rights. The Clinton administration approved exploratory oil drilling within Grand Staircase Escalante against the recommendations of environmental groups who are seeking to overturn the decision.

More information can be found at http://www-a.blm.gov/utah/monument.

CANYONLANDS NATIONAL PARK

220 miles southeast of Salt Lake City.

2282 West Resource Boulevard
Moab, UT 84532
435-259-7164
http://www.nps.gov/cany

Canyonlands Natural History Association. (3031 South Highway 191, Moab, UT 84532; 800-840-8978)

Canyonlands preserves an immense wilderness in the heart of the Colorado Plateau. Water and gravity have been the prime architects of this land, cutting flat layers of sedimentary rock into hundreds of vivid canyons, mesas, buttes, fins, arches, and spires. At center stage are the two great canyons carved by the Green and Colorado rivers. Surrounding the rivers are vast and very different regions of the park. To the north, "Island in the Sky," a broad, level mesa wedged in between the two rivers, serves as the park's natural observation tower. Its many overlooks lead to vistas of almost incomprehensible scope. To the west, "The Maze" is the park at its wildest—it ranks as one of the most remote and inaccessible sections in the United States. The Maze itself is a jumble of canyons that has been described as a "30-square-mile puzzle in sandstone." To the east, the Needles

Upheaval Dome

Upheaval Dome is the oddest geological feature in Island in the Sky. At 1,500 feet deep, the Dome looks more like a crater than a dome. How was it created? One popular theory suggests that slow-moving underground salt deposits pushed layers of sandstone upward. Another more recent theory suggests that the Dome was created from a meteor impact.

Dr. Jekyll and Mr. Hyde

Above their confluence, the Green and Colorado Rivers meander slowly through deep, sheer-walled canyons. Below the confluence, the combined waters begin a 14-mile rush, tumbling through the rapids of Cataract Canyon. It is one of the country's most treacherous whitewater stretches, rivaling any in the Grand Canyon. This Jekyll-and-Hyde personality satisfies those looking for a quiet float as well as those eager for a helter-skelter river run.

is a startling landscape of sculpted rock spires, arches, canyons, grabens, and potholes. The dominant landforms are the Needles themselves—rock pinnacles banded in red and white.

Sam's Tips

- A great way to explore the Needles country is in a high-clearance, 4-wheel-rive vehicle. Angel Arch, located in a side canyon of Salt Creek Canyon, stands 150 feet high. The Grabens lie at the end of another long and challenging journey. To reach these vertical-walled, grass-carpeted valleys requires negotiating the infamous Elephant Hill. With steep, rocky inclines and sharp switchbacks, Elephant Hill tests the skills of the most accomplished rugged-terrain driver. Beyond the Grabens, roads and trails lead to the Confluence Overlook, a point 1,000 feet above the meeting place of the two rivers.
- Traces of the ancient dwellers of these parts, the Ancestral Puebloans, can be found in almost every canyon in the Needles. Many of their stone and mud dwellings and storehouses are remarkably well preserved. Tower Ruin, built high on a cliff ledge in a side canyon of Horse Canyon, is an outstanding example of the Anasazi's architecture.
- The Maze District is the most remote area of the park. The 600-foot descent to the bottom of the Maze is a plunge into the heart of the wild. This area includes 4-wheel-drive roads, hiking routes, and primitive campsites (a back-country permit and fee are required). Many visitors come to the Maze to see the ghostly figures on the walls of Horseshoe Canyon, which were painted by Indians at least 2,000 years ago. The haunting life-size forms are considered among the finest examples of prehistoric rock art in the country.

CAPITOL REEF NATIONAL PARK

The northern tip is 170 miles south of Salt Lake City; the park extends south to a point 40 miles north of the Arizona border.

HC 70
Box 15
Torrey, UT 84775
435-425-3791
http://www.nps.gov/care

Capitol Reef Natural History Association. (same address as above; 435-425-3791, ext. 106)

The Navajo called it the "Land of the Sleeping Rainbow." In this strange and beautiful country, a variety of red, yellow, orange, and white rock cliffs are carved from the Waterpocket Fold. The Fold, a giant, sinuous wrinkle in the

Pickins' at the Park

Apple, cherry, pear, peach, and apricot orchards are located in the historic Fruita area. Visitors may pick fruit when in season. There is no charge for fruit if it is consumed while in the orchard. Bulk picking is also permitted, but a fee is charged. Harvest times vary considerably because of annual climatic changes. A detailed listing is available at the Visitor Center, or call the fruit hotline (435-425-3791). Approximate harvest dates are:

Cherries	June 19–July 6
Apricots	July 1–July 22
Peaches	August 7–September 6
Pears	August 7–September 9
Apples	September 25–October 17

Earth's crust, was created by the same tremendous forces that built the Colorado Plateau 65 million years ago. It stretches for 100 miles across south–central Utah. The park preserves the Fold and its eroded jumble of colorful cliffs, massive domes, spires, monoliths, canyons, and arches. The Capitol Reef National Park, named after the vaulted white rock domes and the nearly impassable ridges that pioneers sometimes called "reefs," is also home to the free-flowing Fremont River. Indians hunted and farmed here more than 1,000 years ago. Later, Mormon pioneers settled to raise their families and grow vegetables and fruit. Today, visitors come to the park to enjoy its spectacular vistas, to pick fruit, hike, mountain bike, climb, camp, or do some 4-wheel-drive touring.

Sam's Tips

- Camping areas range from the historic site of the Mormon pioneer community of Fruita to more remote outposts in the desert. Fruita Campground, the largest tent/RV campground, contains 71 sites and offers picnic tables, fire grills, restrooms, and drinking water. Cathedral Valley and Cedar Mesa Campgrounds, each with five sites, are accessible by dirt roads. Reservations are required for the Fruita Campground. Back-country camping is allowed all year throughout much of the park. A permit is required.
- Technical rock climbing has become an increasingly popular park sport. Natural fracturing has created many climbable crack systems, but many areas of the park are closed to climbing because they contain rock art panels left by the original Indian dwellers of this area.

CEDAR BREAKS NATIONAL MONUMENT

20 miles east of Cedar City; 150 miles northwest of Page, AZ.

2390 West Highway 56, Suite 11
Cedar City, UT 84720
435-586-9451
http://www.nps.gov/cebr

Zion Natural History Association. (Zion National Park, Springdale, UT 84767; 435-772-3265 or 3264)

Cedar Breaks is a natural rock amphitheater carved from the side of the 10,000-foot-high Markagunt Plateau. Subalpine meadows fill with wildflowers in the spring and summer. Early Indian dwellers called it the "Circle of Painted Cliffs." Many years later, early southern Utah settlers renamed the amphitheater for the cedar, or juniper, trees that grow nearby and for its "breaks," another word for badlands. Because the area is located above 10,000 feet in elevation, the road and all facilities in the park are usually closed by deep snow in the winter; but it remains open to cross-country skiers, snowshoers, and snowmobilers.

Sam's Tips

- The Visitor Center is open from early June to mid-October. The rest of the year, information is available at the Kolob Canyons Visitor Center in Zion National Park, located 43 miles southwest of Cedar Breaks.
- The park is home to an uncommon pine tree called the Bristlecone Pine, found only in remote parts of Utah, Colorado, New Mexico, Arizona, California, and Nevada. The oldest specimen, discovered in California in 1957, was determined to be 4,600 years old, making it not only the oldest tree but the oldest living thing on earth. The 1,660-year-old Bristlecones at Cedar Breaks are located on the Spectra Point trail.
- The Rim Drive, a 5-mile scenic road through the high country of Cedar Breaks, is the main route to the park's scenic attractions, overlooks, and trailheads. All visitor services are located along this road or on short side roads.

DIXIE NATIONAL FOREST

Southern Utah.

82 North 100 East
Cedar City, UT 84720
435-865-3700
http://www.fs.fed.us/dxnf

Dixie Interpretive Association. (1696 Tamarisk Drive, St. George, UT 84765; 435-865-3700)

Straddling the divide between the Great Basin and the Colorado River, the Dixie National Forest occupies almost 2 million acres. The forest is divided into four geographic areas. The Markagunt, Paunsaugunt, and Aquarius plateaus are gently rolling hills of high-altitude forests; Boulder Mountain, one of the largest high-elevation plateaus in the United States, is dotted with hundreds of small lakes 10,000 to 11,000 feet above sea level. Elevations in the Dixie National Forest range from 2,800 feet near St. George to 11,322 at Blue Bell Knoll on Boulder Mountain. As a result, vegetation within the forest varies from sparse, desert-type plants at the lower elevations to low-growing pinyon pine and juniper at the mid-elevations and aspen and conifers at

FOREST SERVICE SCENIC BYWAY

Boulder Mountain Highway

Boulder Mountain Highway hosts spectacular views of Boulder Mountain, the Henry Mountains, the slick rock cliffs of the Burr Trail, and the Circle Cliffs. Along the way, visitors can glimpse the only wild, free-roaming herd of bison in the United States, and vistas stretching over 100 miles into Colorado and Arizona. *Contact Dixie National Forest.*

higher elevations. Three national parks (Zion, Capitol Reef, and Bryce Canyon) and two national monuments (Cedar Breaks and Grand Staircase Escalante) are adjacent to the forest. Recreational opportunities at the forest include camping, hunting, hiking, horseback riding, fishing in primitive settings, canoeing, sailing, and swimming, and, in winter, sledding, skiing, and snowmobiling. The forest has 83,000 acres of wilderness in three areas: Pine Valley, Box-Death Hollow, and Ashdown Gorge.

Sam's Tips

- Many of Cedar Breaks National Monument's red limestone formations can be seen from areas within the 6,750-acre Ashdown Gorge Wilderness. For more information about the Wilderness, contact the Cedar City Ranger District (82 North 100 East, PO Box 627, Cedar City, UT 84720; 435-865-3200).
- There are 26 campgrounds and picnic sites on the forest. Those located near lakes and reservoirs—Panguitch Lake, Navajo Lake, and Enterprise Reservoir—offer boating and fishing.

FISHLAKE NATIONAL FOREST

Central Utah; the forest's northern tip is 70 miles south of Salt Lake City; the southern tip is 40 miles northeast of Cedar City.

115 East 900 North
Richfield, UT 84701
435-896-9233
http://www.fs.fed.us

Fishlake Discovery Association. (433 Valley View Drive, Richfield, UT 84701; 435-896-4055)

Small streams within the forest feed gentle valleys and carve canyons framed by colorful walls. Because this is the transition zone between the Colorado Plateau and the Basin and Range Provinces, there is a mix of sedimentary and volcanic rocks. Scenery across the 1.4 million acres varies from almost desert to alpine. Lower elevation lands of rock, sage, pinyon, and juniper appear desert-like, especially in the southeast corner, with its red cliffs. About half of the land is covered with aspen and evergreen trees interspersed with meadows and low sagebrush openings. The forest is crossed by the Fish Lake Shoreline Trail, one of two National Recreation Trails, as well as by the Great Western Trail.

GOLDEN SPIKE NATIONAL HISTORIC SITE

The park is 32 miles west of Brigham City.

PO Box W
Brigham City, UT 84302
435-471-2209
http://www.nps.gov/gosp

Southwest Parks and Monuments Association. (221 North Court Avenue, Tucson, AZ 85701; 520-622-1999)

Completion of the first transcontinental railroad in the United States was celebrated at this site, where the Central Pacific and Union Pacific Railroads met in 1869—an event that drew as much media attention as the first landing on the moon a century later. The event is reenacted every year on May 10. About 1.7 miles of track have been relaid on the original roadbed where the rails were joined, and exact and fully functional replicas of the "Jupiter" and "119" operate during the summer season. This is the only location in the United States where visitors can walk, bike, or jog on the original 1869 railroad grade.

"The Ten-Mile Day"

The "Ten-Mile Day" resulted from a $10,000 bet made by Thomas Durant, vice president of Union Pacific. The previous October, his crew of railroad workers had been able to put down 7 miles and 1,800 feet of track in a single day, and he was willing to bet that the record would never be broken. A track-laying rivalry had begun in 1868 between the Central Pacific and the Union Pacific as they raced to meet each other. When the two teams were only 25 miles apart, the Central Pacific made its move. The mostly Chinese crew was spearheaded by a team of 8 Irish "iron men" whose job was to set each rail in place. The "iron men" earned a place in history books: they laid an average of 2 rails every 2½ minutes. In 11½ hours, they had picked up and put down 3,524 rails, each weighing 560 pounds. The crew put in place 21,142 ties, drove in 84,568 spikes, and bolted the spikes with 3,522 fish plates. Final measurement was 10 miles and 56 feet of track. To this day, this track-laying record has never been broken, notwithstanding modern machinery. Signs that mark the event are located in and near the Visitor Center.

Sam's Tips

- The Annual Railroader's Festival features reenactments of the Golden Spike Ceremony, the World Champion Spike Driving Contest, handcar races and rides, a buffalo-chip throwing contest, and more. Hot food, live music, and handicraft booths are part of the festivities.

MANTI–LA SAL NATIONAL FOREST

3 sections, in central and southeastern Utah.

599 West Price River Drive
Price, UT 84501
435-636-3500
http://www.fs.fed.us

Canyonlands Natural History Association. (3031 South Highway 191, Moab UT 84532; 800-840-8978)

Pictographs, petroglyphs, cliff dwellings, arrowheads, and pottery left by prehistoric cultures tell stories of the area's original inhabitants. Along the eastern Utah border near Moab, the La Sal Mountains rise 12,721 feet above sea level. Narrow roads lead travelers to high mountain passes and into narrow canyons, such as Dark Canyon, where the crystalline rock structure of the peaks is exposed for all to see; or to Mill Creek, where Oowah Lake is set like a small jewel amid spruce trees. The Wasatch Plateau section of the forest is bounded on the east by a sheer escarpment rising as high as 2,000 feet above Castle Valley, and on the west by steep slopes into the Sanpete Valley. The broad rolling ridges of the plateau have forest cover varying from deep green conifers to delicate light-stemmed aspen, and are separated by wild meadows where flowers bloom from snowmelt until fall.

Sam's Tips

- The Fairview to Huntington Byway is a scenic drive through the heart of Utah's energy-producing country and the Manti–La Sal National Forest. The Utah Adventure Highway across the Manti–La Sal National Forest is also known as Skyline Drive. It affords scenic views of the valleys below, passing a variety of high-mountain settings, including reservoirs, glacial cirques, and spruce-fir and aspen forests. Animals are abundant; they include Utah's largest elk herd, deer, bear, moose, and beaver.
- The forest contains two National Recreation Trails: The Left Fork of Huntington Creek Trail and the Fish Creek Trail.

GOLDEN PASSPORTS

The National Park Service has three "passport" programs—Golden Eagle, Golden Age, and Golden Access—that allow individuals (and sometimes their families) access to public lands without additional charge. These programs are an especially good value for people who are frequent visitors to national parks and other sites within the national park system.

To purchase a passport, check with the NPS for the current fees.

All three passports admit the passholder and any accompanying passengers in a private vehicle. Where entry is not by private vehicle, the passport admits the pass holder, spouse, children, and parents.

Golden Eagle Passport

This is an entrance pass to those national parks, monuments, historic sites, recreation areas, and national wildlife refuges that charge an entrance fee. This passport is valid for one year from date of purchase. You may purchase a Golden Eagle Passport at any NPS entrance fee area or by mail. To purchase by writing to National Park Service, 1100 Ohio Drive, SW, Room 138, Washington, DC 20242; Attention: Golden Eagle Passport. As we went to press, the cost was $50.

The Golden Eagle Passport does not cover fees for camping, swimming, parking, boat launching, cave tours, or similar use fees. It is valid for entrance fees only.

Golden Age Passport

This is a lifetime entrance pass for persons 62 years or older. The Golden Age Passport has a one-time processing charge of $10. You must purchase a Golden Age Passport in person, at any NPS entrance fee area. At the time of purchase, you must show proof of age (62 years or older) and of citizenship or permanent residence in the United States. The passport is not available by mail or telephone.

The Golden Age Passport also provides a 50 percent discount on federal use fees charged for camping, swimming, parking, boat launching, cave tours, or similar facilities and services. It does not cover or reduce special recreation permit fees or fees charged by concessionaires.

Golden Access Passport

This is a free lifetime entrance pass for persons who are blind or permanently disabled. It is available to citizens or permanent residents of the United States, regardless of age, who have been determined to be blind or permanently disabled. You may obtain a Golden Access Passport at any entrance fee area by showing proof of medically determined disability and eligibility for receiving benefits under federal law.

The Golden Access Passport also provides a 50 percent discount on federal use fees charged for camping, swimming, parking, boat launching, cave tours, or similar facilities and services. It does not cover or reduce special recreation permit fees or fees charged by concessionaires.

NATURAL BRIDGES NATIONAL MONUMENT

40 miles west of Blanding; 95 miles east of Hanksville.

Box 1
Lake Powell, UT 84533
435-692-1234
http://www.nps.gov/nabr

Canyonlands History Association. (3031 South Highway 191, Moab, UT 84532; 800-840-8978)

Natural Bridges National Monument sits high on Cedar Mesa at an elevation of 6,500 feet. River streams have cut two deep canyons and three massive bridges from the white sandstone that once formed the shore of an ancient sea. At each bridge, trails descend into the canyons from the loop road. A longer trail following the canyon bottom connects the three bridges and returns across the mesa top.

SAM'S TIPS

- The 9-mile Bridge View Drive is a one-way scenic loop starting and ending near the Visitor Center. Overlooks for each of the three bridges, and one cliff dwelling, are reached by short walks from parking areas along the drive. A trailhead for each bridge is located along the drive, as is a small picnic area.
- After Rainbow Bridge, Sipapu is the second largest natural bridge in the world. In Hopi mythology, the sipapu is "the place of emergence," the gateway to the spirit world for souls to enter and exit. The trail down to its base is the steepest in the park. Hiking time is 1 hour.
- Kachina is a massive bridge. The relatively small opening makes it difficult to see from the overlook. In June 1992, about 4,000 tons of rock came crashing down, widening the bridge ever so slightly. Rock art on this bridge

resembles symbols found on kachina dolls—thus the name Kachina, or ghost dancer.

- The hiking trail to Owachomo Bridge, the easiest of the three, takes about 20 minutes to complete. Owachomo means "rock mound" in Hopi.
- The park's 13-site campground is open year-round, but it is not cleared of snow in the winter. There is a 26-foot combined length limit for RVs and vehicles with trailers. If the campground is full, or if your vehicle exceeds 26 feet, you may use the overflow camping area, 6.2 miles from the Visitor Center.
- There are no services in the monument. The closest gasoline is 20 miles west at Fry Canyon; groceries and overnight accommodations are 40 miles away in Blanding or Mexican Hat.

TIMPANOGOS CAVE NATIONAL MONUMENT

In Uinta National Forest, on State Route 92; 30 miles southeast of Salt Lake City; 30 miles north of Provo.

RR 3, Box 200
American Fork, UT 84003
801-756-5239
http://www.nps.gov/tica

Southwest Parks and Monuments Association. (221 North Court Avenue, Tucson, AZ 85701; 520-622-1999)

High on the steep rocky slopes of American Fork Canyon, in the shadow of Mount Timpanogos, are three limestone caves renowned for their dazzling display of stalactites, stalagmites, popcorn, flowstone, and cave pools. What makes these caves special is their exceptional number of helictites and anthodites. These bizarre formations seem to defy gravity as they twist and turn in unpredictable directions. The profusion of white helictites in the Chimes Chamber of Timpanogos Cave is a highlight of any tour. So is the Great Heart of Timpanogos, a giant cave formation of linked stalactites.

Sam's Tips

- Special cave events include periodic costume and flashlight tours. The flashlight tours take place in early morning and are limited to 10 persons. Reservations are required.
- The average temperature in the caves is 45°F. Bring a jacket or a sweater.
- Within 10 miles of the park, American Fork, Pleasant Grove, and Lehi provide gasoline, restaurants, and groceries. There are no campgrounds within the monument's boundaries. For camping, contact the adjacent Uinta National Forest. Lodging and a wider range of services are available at the more distant cities of Orem, Provo, Heber City, and Salt Lake City.

- To get to the caves, visitors must hike the Cave Trail. This is a strenuous hike; the route climbs 1,065 feet over 1.5 miles. The round-trip hike and tour of the cave system takes about 3 hours.
- The 24-mile Alpine Loop Scenic Drive winds through rugged canyons of the Wasatch Range, offering views of Mount Timpanogos and other glacier-carved peaks. The route follows Utah 92 up American Fork Canyon and then continues through Uinta National Forest into Provo Canyon. Along the way is Bridal Veil Falls, a 607-foot waterfall.

UINTA NATIONAL FOREST

The Uinta covers an area along the Wasatch Front extending from the "point of the Mountain" in Salt Lake County south to the city of Nephi in Juab County. The eastern portion of the forest includes the Strawberry and Currant Creek Reservoir areas.

88 West, 100 North
PO Box 1428
Provo, UT 84603
801-377-5780
http://www.fs.fed.us

Uinta Visitor Information Association. (same address as above; 801-377-5780)

The forest ranges from steep canyons along the Wasatch Front to high western desert at Vernon and lofty mountain peaks such as Mount Nebo (11,870 feet). Developed recreation sites include campgrounds, picnic areas, marinas, boat ramps, fishing sites, trailheads, organizational camps, and recreation residences. Some of the game species at the forest are elk, black bear, cougar, moose, Rocky Mountain goat and sheep, and mule deer. The forest contains three Wilderness Areas, as well as the Timpanogos Cave National Monument.

Sam's Tips

- The Alpine Scenic Loop takes you from the mouth of American Fork Canyon until it joins with Highway 189 in Provo Canyon. Along the way, you will pass Timpanogos Cave National Monument and Robert Redford's Sundance Ski and Summer Resort.
- The Strawberry Reservoir Recreation Area is one of Utah's premier fishing sites. It boasts new recreation facilities, including three new campgrounds, numerous day-use and picnic sites, and two paved boat ramps and full-service marinas at Strawberry Bay and Soldier Creek recreation sites. The area is located 23 miles southeast of Heber City.
- The Currant Creek Reservoir Recreation Area is approximately 40 miles southeast of Heber. This recreation site includes a large campground, a paved boat ramp, and many hiking and horseback riding trails.

FOREST SERVICE SCENIC BYWAY

Logan Canyon Highway

The Logan Canyon Highway travels 39 miles along US Highway 89 from Logan to Bear Lake in the Wasatch National Forest. The route features a drive along the Logan River and an outstanding view of the canyon. *Contact Wasatch–Cache National Forests.*

WASATCH–CACHE NATIONAL FORESTS

Northern Utah and southwestern Wyoming. The forest is divided into three major geographic areas; one section is adjacent to Salt Lake City.

8236 Federal Building
125 South State Street
Salt Lake City, UT 84138
801-524-5030
http://www.fs.fed.us/wcnf

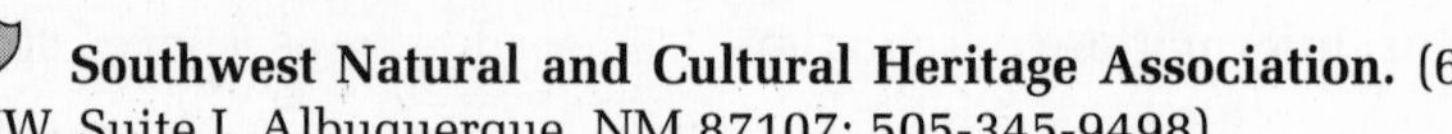

Southwest Natural and Cultural Heritage Association. (6501 4th Street, NW, Suite I, Albuquerque, NM 87107; 505-345-9498)

The Wasatch–Cache National Forest includes lands from the arid Great Basin Desert to lush high-mountain meadows and peaks of the Uinta Mountains. There are two principal mountain ranges within the forest. The Uintas are the largest east–west mountain range in North America. The majestic Wasatch Mountains run north and south along the Salt Lake–Ogden–Logan fronts. Many of the tallest mountains in Utah are found in the Uinta and Wasatch Mountain Ranges. The highest point in the forest is Gilbert Peak at 13,442 feet. There are numerous other peaks in the 12,000-foot range.

Sam's Tips

- Several major ski resorts are found on the forest, including Alta and Snowbird, in Little Cottonwood Canyon; Snow Basin, east of Ogden; and Beaver Mountain, in Logan Canyon. Fluffy, dry powder falls for nearly five months a year.

ZION NATIONAL PARK

320 miles south of Salt Lake City; 300 miles southwest of Grand Junction.

Springdale, UT 84767-1099
435-772-3256
http://www.nps.gov/zion

 **Zion National History Association.** (same address as above; 435-772-3264)

An observer once called Zion "a singular display of nature's art mingled with nonsense." Zion National Park is composed of colorful sandstone canyons, hot rocky deserts, and cool forested plateaus. In Zion Canyon, the Virgin River has carved a spectacular gorge into the red and white sandstone. During a flash flood, the river turns muddy and violent, carrying cottonwoods and boulders like twigs and pebbles; but on most days, the Virgin winds through the canyon peacefully, with Fremont cottonwoods, willows, and velvet ashes along its banks providing shady spots for a picnic or a short walk. The canyon walls loom high above, in most places reaching up 2,000–3,000 feet. East of the Zion–Mount Carmel tunnel, you can see fascinating shapes and patterns at the top of the sandstone layers. In the southern part of the park—a lower, desert area with colorful mesas bordered by rocky canyons and washes—you can view cinder cones from volcanoes and petrified wood from ancient forests. The northern sections of the park are higher plateaus. Cool, green forests overlook broad panoramas of rugged canyon country. Also within the park is a wilderness that contains the 310-foot Kolob Arch, along with other wonders, such as waterfalls and clear back-country pools.

Sam's Tips

- Hiking trails in Zion range from an easy 10-minute walk to a 2-day backpacking trip. The park's Official Map and Guide has a brief guide to Zion's trails. Also available is *Hiking the Zion Narrows,* a booklet that explains the three ways to hike the Narrows, a 20-foot-wide (at its narrowest) canyon cut by the Virgin River.
- Campers can stay along the cottonwood-shaded banks of the Virgin River in Zion Canyon. A more remote camping area is in a high-country forest of ponderosa pine, pinyon, and juniper, atop the Kolob Plateau. The two main

Driving Through Zion

When the Zion–Mount Carmel Highway was completed in 1930, this "almost impossible project" was considered an engineering marvel of its time. Built across rough up-and-down-terrain, it connects lower Zion Canyon with the high plateaus to the east. As you travel the 1.1-mile tunnel, the landscape changes dramatically. On one side is Zion Canyon with its massive cliff walls. The other side is slickrock country, where rocks colored in white and pastels of orange and red have been eroded into hundreds of fantastic shapes. Checkerboard Mesa stands as the most prominent example of this naturally sculpted rock art.

Two roads lead to Kolob, in the northwestern corner of the park, where streams have carved spectacular canyons at the edge of the Kolob Terrace. The Kolob Canyons road penetrates 5 miles into the red-rock Finger Canyons, ending at a high viewpoint. The Terrace Road overlooks the white and salmon-colored cliffs of the Left and Right forks of North Creek. Both routes climb into forests of pinyon and juniper.

BLACK-FOOTED FERRET

Mustela nigripes

The black-footed ferret was once considered the most endangered mammal in the United States. But progress has now been made toward this population's recovery.

Ferrets were once found throughout the Great Plains, from Texas to southern Saskatchewan, Canada. Their range extended from the Rocky Mountains eastward through the Dakotas and south through Nebraska, Kansas, Oklahoma, and Texas. Where prairie dogs were found, so were black-footed ferrets. Ferrets eat prairie dogs and then take over the prairie dog's burrow.

During the fall of 1986 and the spring of 1987, the last of the 19 known wild black-footed ferrets were taken from the wild and placed in a captive breeding facility. This captive population has increased to more than 500 captive black-footed ferrets. The goal of the captive breeding program is to establish 240 breeding adults in captivity, while continuing the return of ferrets to the wild..

If these and future efforts are successful, black-footed ferrets may once again be playing an important role in the dynamics of wild prairie dog towns.

campgrounds (Watchman and South) have services within one mile of the campgrounds, including hot showers, restaurants, and the Zion Nature Center (for children ages 6–12 years).

- Zion Lodge offers guided tram tours of the park and shuttle services for hikers and backpackers from points within Zion National Park to or from trailheads in and immediately adjacent to the park. To make reservations during the Lodge's operating season, call 435-772-3213.

Points of Interest

BUREAU OF LAND MANAGEMENT

THE GREEN RIVER

The Green River enters the Uinta Mountains through the 30-mile-long Red Canyon and meanders through the Desolation–Gray Canyons where, along with the rock art of the Fremont culture, you'll find the best trout fishing in the entire state and a premier wilderness river trip through Utah's deepest canyon.

From northeastern Utah to the Colorado River in southeastern Utah
435-636-3600

THE BONNEVILLE SALT FLATS

Bonneville's 44,000 acres are so flat that you seem to see the curvature of the planet, and so barren that not even the simplest life forms can exist. Since the first land-speed record attempts in 1914, hundreds of records have been set and broken in a variety of automotive and motorcycle classes at the Bonneville Salt Flats. Thousands of visitors, high-speed auto racers, and commercial film-makers make the Bonneville Salt Flats a world-famous destination. Overnight stays are prohibited on the salt flats, but camping is encouraged on surrounding public lands.

North of Interstate Highway 80, near Wendover, Utah
801-977-4300

These are just samples of the many Bureau of Land Management points of interest in Utah. For more information, contact:

Bureau of Land Management
Utah State Office
PO Box 45155
Salt Lake City, Utah 84145-0155
801-539-4001
http://www.blm.gov/utah

ENDANGERED AND THREATENED SPECIES

The Endangered Species Act of 1973 is one of the most far-reaching wildlife conservation laws ever enacted by any nation. It is administered primarily by the U.S. Fish and Wildlife Service in cooperation with other federal, state, and local agencies.

More than 800 native species of plants and animals and over 530 species living in other parts of the world have been placed on the U.S. List of Endangered and Threatened Wildlife and Plants. A species can be listed under one of two categories, endangered or threatened, depending on the degree of threat it faces.

For more information on the Endangered Species Program, visit the FWS's endangered species Website (http://www.fws.gov/~r9endspp/endspp.html) or contact:

U.S. Fish and Wildlife Service
Division of Endangered Species
452 ARLSQ
Washington, DC 20240

For information about protection of whales, seals, and other marine species, write to:

National Marine Fisheries Service
Department of Commerce
1335 East–West Highway
Silver Spring, MD 20910

WYOMING

BIGHORN NATIONAL FOREST

North-central Wyoming.

1969 South Sheridan Avenue
Sheridan, WY 82801
307-672-0751
http://www.fs.fed.us

Rocky Mountain Nature Association. (Rocky Mountain National Park, Estes Park, CO 80517; 800-816-7662)

The Bighorn's 1.1 million acres of forested plateaus and mountains attract visitors throughout the year. Winter sports enthusiasts will find here some of Wyoming's best crosscountry skiing and snowmobiling. Hikers can backpack into remote areas, including the Cloud Peak Wilderness. The forest contains many unique geological formations and historic Native American sites, and it is renowned for its large herds of elk and deer. Other species in the area include bighorn sheep, black bear, coyotes, bald and golden eagles, upland game birds, and songbirds.

BRIDGER–TETON NATIONAL FOREST

Western Wyoming.

Forest Service Building
340 North Cache
PO Box 1888
Jackson, WY 83001
307-739-5500
http://www.fs.fed.us/outernet/btnf

Grand Teton Natural History Association. (PO Box 170, Moose, WY 83012; 307-739-3403)

The 3.4-million-acre Bridger–Teton National Forest includes the mountains south of Yellowstone and Grand Teton national parks; the headwaters of the Green, Snake and Yellowstone rivers; and the canyons of the Hoback and Greys rivers. Areas of special interest are the Gros Ventre Slide Geological Area north of Jackson, where a massive landslide in 1925 created Lower Slide Lake and Periodic Spring in Swift Creek Canyon, the largest of the three existing cold water geysers in the world. The forest has 42 campgrounds, 3 picnic areas, 11 boating areas, 2 alpine ski areas, and many resorts.

FOREST SERVICE SCENIC BYWAY

Bighorn Scenic Byways

The 111 miles of the Bighorn Scenic Byways feature three very different roads. Highway 14 passes through Shell Canyon—a narrow, rocky gorge with panoramic views across the Sheridan Basin. Highway 14A crosses mountainous country with vistas of forests, slopes, rocky alpine tundra, and grasslands. Highway 16 provides close-up views of lodgepole pine forests and spectacular views of the Cloud Peak Wilderness. *Contact Bighorn National Forest.*

DEVILS TOWER NATIONAL MONUMENT

33 miles northeast of Moorcroft; 27 miles northwest of Sundance, WY.

PO Box 10
Devils Tower, WY 82714-0008
307-467-5283
http://www.nps.gov/deto

 **Devils Tower Natural History Association.** (PO Box 37, Devils Tower, WY 82714; 307-467-5283)

In the northeast corner of Wyoming, where the pine forests of the Black Hills merge with the grasslands of the rolling plains, the first national monument in the country, Devils Tower, rises from the plains. Devils Tower is a columnar rock—the remains of the core of an ancient volcano. The Tower rises 867 feet from its base 5,112 feet above sea level. The area of its tear-drop-shaped top is 1.5 acres. Its base diameter is 1,000 feet. For many American Indians Devils Tower, sometimes known as Bears Lodge, is a sacred site of worship.

Climbing Devils Tower

The challenge of scaling the Tower came alive on July 4, 1893, amid fanfare and more than 1,000 spectators, when local rancher William Rogers and Willard Ripley made the first ascent using a wooden ladder they had built that spring for the first 350 feet. (The fact that they already had a flagpole waiting for raising Old Glory suggests that the first ascent might have occurred some days before.) The climbers' wives ran the refreshment stand and sold pieces of the flag as souvenirs. Records of Tower climbs have been kept since 1937, and more than 5,000 climbers come here every year to ascend the Tower's 200+ routes.

FORT LARAMIE NATIONAL HISTORIC SITE

3 miles southwest of Fort Laramie.

HC 72 Box 389
Fort Laramie, WY 82212
307-837-2221
http://www.nps.gov/fola

Fort Laramie Historical Association. (PO Box 218, Highway 160, Fort Laramie, WY 82212; 800-321-5456 or 307-837-2662)

This outpost in the Wyoming wilderness played a crucial role in the transformation of the American West, first as a fur-trading center, then as a military garrison. For over five decades, it was a landmark and way station for trappers, traders, missionaries, emigrants, Pony Express riders, and miners wending their way west. It was also an important staging point for the US Army in its dealings with Plains Indian tribes displaced by migration and settlement. Significant structures of the fort's military period, some dating to 1849, have survived intact. Nearly a dozen of these have been completely restored to their original appearance. Every summer, park rangers dressed in period costume portray the lives of soldiers, laundresses, and civilians who inhabited the fort in the 1870s.

FOSSIL BUTTE NATIONAL MONUMENT

14 miles west of Kemmerer, along US Highway 30.

PO Box 592
Kemmerer, WY 83101
307-877-4455
http://www.nps.gov/fobu

Dinosaur Nature Association. (1291 East Highway 40, Vernal, UT 84078; 800-845-DINO)

Southwest Wymoning is one of the best preserved and most complete paleoecosystems in the world. The Fossil Butte National Monument sits on the limestone lakebed of Fossil Lake, which was the smallest of the three ancient lakes that once existed in this area. The fossils found in the deposits of Fossil Basin are among the best in the world for number, detail, and variety. Many of the fish, for example, retain not only their entire skeleton but their teeth, delicate scales, and fins as well. Preserved here are outstanding examples of animals that lived over 50 million years ago. The delicate bones of a fossil bat, the oldest known in North America, and a remarkably complete fossil snake were found here. Fish, snail shells, insect impressions, crocodiles, freshwater turtles, bird skeletons, and plant remains are part of the buried treasure of fossils preserved here.

GRAND TETON NATIONAL PARK

South of Yellowstone National Park; north of Jackson.

PO Drawer 170
Moose, WY 83012
307-739-3300
http://www.nps.gov/grte

Grand Teton Natural History Association. (PO Drawer 170, Moose, WY 83012; 307-739-3403)

No Rocky Mountain vistas are more impressive than those in the Grand Tetons. As the Teton Range rose through sporadic earthquake-producing jolts, the valley called Jackson Hole subsided. Because of the way in which the mountains formed, there are no foothills to hide jagged peaks and broad canyons. At the base of the range, large lakes mirror the mountains on calm summer days. Grand Teton National Park consists of the most impressive part of the Teton Range, a series of blue-gray peaks rising more than a mile above the sagebrush flats. The park's boundaries lie within the valley called Jackson Hole. Here, you can explore glaciated canyons beneath towering pinnacles, walk through meadows of wildflowers, and experience the Teton back-country through hiking trips that can range from a few hours to a few days. Visitors at the park also can enjoy water-based activities, such as floating, boating, sailing, wind surfing, and fishing in the various lakes and the Snake River.

Sam's Tips

- Floating the Snake River within the park is allowed only in hand-propelled boats and rafts, never in inner tubes. Although the Snake may not seem powerful on the surface, only experienced floaters should attempt this swift, cold river.
- A shuttle boat ride starting at South Jenny Lake to the west side followed by a modest hike to Hidden Falls is a perfect family outing in the park.
- Teton Science School, located in the park, offers a wide variety of in-depth courses year-round. This nonprofit school employs highly qualified instructors to teach a spectrum of topics, for all ages, in natural history and ecology. For information and schedules, write to the Director, PO Box 68, Kelly, WY 83011, or call 307-733-4765.
- The 5-mile Signal Mountain Summit Road starts one mile south of Signal Mountain Lodge and Campground. The road winds to the top of Signal

Free Publications

Many of Grand Teton National Parks' most popular publications are now available for free online, including:

Backcountry Camping—Regulations, permits, tips and more
Boating—Permits and safety suggestions
Floating the Snake River—River mileages, average times of transit, put-in and take-out points, safety suggestions
Journey Through the Past—A short geological history of the park
Day Hikes—A small map with trailhead locations
Snowmobiling—Regulations, route suggestions and route maps
A Walk Through Time—A synopsis of human history in the Jackson Hole area.

To access these and other free publications, go to: http://www.nps.gov/grte/sitepub/freepubs.htm

Arrows of Healing

Where does "Medicine Bow" come from? The generally accepted version is that, in one of the mountain valleys, Native American tribes found mahogany, from which bows of exceptional quality were made. It became the custom of friendly tribes to assemble there annually and construct their weapons. At these assemblies, there were also ceremonial powwows—known as "making medicine" in the hybrid speech that developed between Whites and Indians–for the cure of disease. Eventually, Whites associated the terms "making medicine" and "making bows," and Medicine Bow became the name for the locality. Later, the name gained fame through Owen Wister's novel, *The Virginian.*

Mountain, 800 feet above the valley. Summit overlooks provide panoramic views of the entire Teton Range, Jackson Lake, and most of Jackson Hole. The road is narrow, and parking at overlooks is limited, so trailers or large motorhomes are prohibited.

MEDICINE BOW NATIONAL FOREST

30 miles west of Laramie, on Highway 130.

2468 Jackson Street
Laramie, WY 82070-6535
307-745-2300
http://www.fs.fed.us/mrnf

 **Rocky Mountain Nature Association.** (Rocky Mountain National Park, Estes Park, CO 80517; 800-816-7662)

The Medicine Bow National Forest is located in the southeast quarter of Wyoming and encompasses portions of three mountain ranges: the Laramie, Medicine Bow, and Sierra Madre. The forest has trails for hiking, horseback riding, snowmobiling, and ATVs. In the winter, cross-country skiers can choose between miles of groomed trails or untracked snow. Fishing is popular in the forest during the summer. The forest also contains several unique rock formations, including the rocks at Vedauwoo and Devil's Playground, a jumbled pile of granite boulders.

 **Sam's Tips**

- Laramie Peak is the highest point in the Laramie Mountains. A very steep 5.5-mile trail leads to the 10,272-foot summit and its panoramic views.
- The forest offers interpretive hikes on the nights of the full moon. Each one of the walks (or cross-country skis, in the winter) focuses on a different theme, such as the Spirit Moon at Veedauwoo or the Pika Moon, in the alpine mountains.

FOREST SERVICE SCENIC BYWAY

Snowy Range Highway

The Snowy Range Highway follows 29 miles of State Highway 130 through the Medicine Bow National Forest in southeastern Wyoming and features 12,000-foot Medicine Bow Peak, several campgrounds, and two winter sports areas. *Contact Medicine Bow National Forest.*

FOREST SERVICE SCENIC BYWAY

Beartooth Highway

The Beartooth Highway follows US Highway 212 for 60 miles in northwestern Wyoming and southwestern Montana, on the Custer, Gallatin, and Shoshone National Forests. The route traverses 10,947-foot Beartooth Pass and features outstanding views of snow-capped peaks, glaciers, alpine lakes, and alpine plateaus. Charles Kuralt referred to the Beartooth Highway as "the most beautiful drive in America." *Contact Custer and Shoshone National Forests.*

SHOSHONE NATIONAL FOREST

The eastern part of the Greater Yellowstone Area, in northwestern Wyoming.

808 Meadow Lane
Cody, WY 82414-4516
307-527-6241
http://www.fs.fed.us

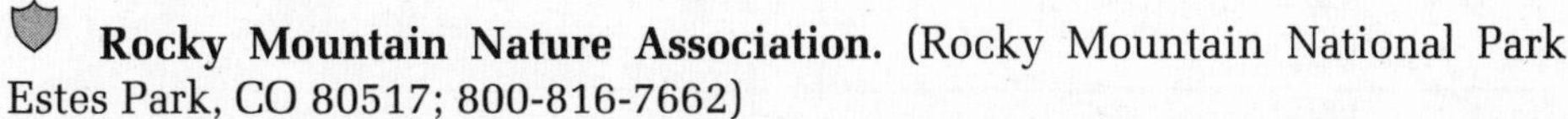

Rocky Mountain Nature Association. (Rocky Mountain National Park, Estes Park, CO 80517; 800-816-7662)

Established in 1891, the Shoshone National Forest was a part of the country's very first forest reserve. The forest now serves as an eastern gateway to Yellowstone National Park. Timberline lakes and mountain streams challenge anglers of all ages. Backpack, bike, ski, and snowmobile in the Wind River Range, or raft the depths of Clark's Fork Canyon. Primitive and developed camp sites offer scenery and solitude. Day activities include hiking, picnicking, and sightseeing by car on one of the Shoshone's three designated National Scenic Byways. The Shoshone manages wildlife habitat for more than 370 species of mammals, birds, reptiles, amphibians, and fish. The Shoshone is the home of the highest concentration of grizzly bears in the Greater Yellowstone area, and the only mountain goats in

FOREST SERVICE SCENIC BYWAY

Wyoming Centennial Scenic Byway

The Wyoming Centennial Scenic Byway passes the badlands west of Dubois, the scenic Snake River, and the National Elk Refuge, where as many as 9,000 elk spend the winter. Located in western Wyoming, the byway winds through the Shoshone and Bridger-Teton National Forests. *Contact Shoshone and Bridger-Teton National Forests.*

THE ORIGINS OF AMERICA'S BEST IDEA: THE NATIONAL PARK SERVICE

The painter, George Catlin, was the first to articulate the idea of a public-owned preserve of special natural and cultural places. Alarmed at the destruction of Indian land and heritage he observed on a trip to the Dakotas in 1832, Catlin wrote of his hope for their conservation " . . . by some great protecting policy of the government preserved . . . in a magnificent park. . . . A nation's park, containing man and beast, in all wildness and freshness of their nature's beauty!"

Our first national park, Yellowstone, was created in 1872 under President Ulysses S. Grant. The first federally protected landscape, Yosemite Valley and the Mariposa Big Tree Grove, was designated in 1864 and given to the State of California. Because Yellowstone was a territory and belonged to no state, it was administered by the government and so became our first, and the world's first, national park. Approximately 1,200 national parks and preserves in over 100 countries around the world have been modeled on Yellowstone.

Harry Yount is considered to have been the nation's first park ranger, although at the time the title was that of "Gamekeeper." He was hired to work at Yellowstone National Park in 1880.

Wyoming. Threatened and endangered species living at Shoshone include the peregrine falcon and the golden eagle.

YELLOWSTONE NATIONAL PARK

Primarily in the northwestern corner of Wyoming, extending into Montana and Idaho; 53 miles west of Cody; 64 miles north of Jackson; 60 miles southeast of Bozeman, MT. There are five entrances to the park:

North Entrance	Highway 89 from I-90 at Livingston, MT
Northeast Entrance	Highway 212 from I-90 at Billings, MT
West Entrance	Highway 191 from Bozeman, MT; Highway 20 from Idaho Falls, ID
East Entrance	Highway 16 from Cody, WY
South Entrance	Highway 89 from Jackson, WY

Address:
PO Box 168
Yellowstone National Park, WY 82190
307-344-7381
http://www.nps.gov/yell

 **The Yellowstone Association.** (same address as above; 307-344-2293)

Yellowstone National Park, the world's first national park, was established in 1872. Old Faithful and some 10,000 other geysers in Yellowstone make this the area with the largest concentration of geysers in the world; in fact, there are more geysers here than in the rest of the world combined. The heart of Yellowstone is volcanism. Two million years ago, again 1.2 million years ago, and then again 600,000 years ago, catastrophic volcanic eruptions occurred here. The latest one spewed out 240 cubic miles of debris. What is now the park's central portion then collapsed, forming a 28-by-47-mile caldera, or basin. The magmatic heat that drove those eruptions still powers the park's famous geysers, hot springs, fumaroles, and mud pots. But as the largest park in the lower 48 states—bigger than Delaware and Rhode Island combined—Yellowstone has many other unique and extraordinary features. The spectacular Grand Canyon of the Yellowstone River provides a glimpse into Earth's interior, with waterfalls that highlight the boundaries of lava flows and thermal areas. At 20 miles long, 14 miles wide, and 320 feet deep at its deepest point, Yellowstone Lake is North America's largest mountain lake. One of the world's premier wildlife habitats, Yellowstone is home to the largest concentration of free-roaming wildlife in the lower 48 states.

SAM'S TIPS

- There are three main areas in the Park:

1. *Old Faithful to Mammoth Springs.* Many of the most famous geysers and hot springs are located on the west side of the park, along the 50-mile stretch of road between Mammoth Hot Springs and Old Faithful. Areas to visit include the Mammoth Hot Springs Terraces, Norris Geyser Basin, Fountain Paint Pots, Firehole Lake Drive, Midway Geyser Basin, Lower Geyser Basin, Biscuit Basin, Black Sand Basin, and the Old Faithful area. Old Faithful is the world's most famous geyser. It's 18 to 22 eruptions each day last for 2 to 5 minutes and rise 100 to 180 feet into the air. Eruption times for other nearby geysers

NOBEL PRIZE-WINNING RESEARCH

Research sponsored by the National Park Service benefits not only the parks but the public as well. For example, Dr. Kary Mullis discovered that the enzymes of *Thermus aquaticus,* a protozoan found in the hot pools of Yellowstone National Park, significantly accelerate (from taking several days to just a few hours) the DNA duplication process that is crucial for medical diagnoses. The technique's increased efficiency benefits not only medicine but also genetic engineering, forensics, and research, where its use is now routine. For his discovery, Mullis was awarded a Nobel prize and, in the words of *The Denver Post,* "*Thermus* was the star of a billion-dollar industry."

Nearby Museums . . .

The story of Yellowstone continues at the Buffalo Bill Historical Center (307-587-4771) in Cody. The Center's Plains Indians Museum tells the story of early humans in the area, and the collections of the Whitney Gallery of Western Art provide artists' interpretations of Yellowstone's landscape and unusual features.

The Museum of the Rockies, in Bozeman, MT, features exhibits on dinosaurs, paleontology, and other topics, and houses the area's only planetarium, for visitors who are interested in taking "the long view" of Yellowstone and its place on the planet.

In Pinedale, WY, the Museum of the Mountain Man (307-367-4101) examines the life of Jim Bridger, one of the first European-Americans to visit Yellowstone, and tells the story of early explorers, mountain men, and fur trappers.

are available at the Old Faithful Visitor Center. The Norris Geyser Basin includes some of the most incredible thermal features in the world. Steamboat Geyser, the world's largest, erupts at irregular intervals of days or years. Echinus Geyser erupts about once per hour. The Porcelain Basin is Yellowstone's hottest exposed area. At Mammoth Hot Springs, travertine (calcium carbonate) forms spectacular mineral terraces, the most famous of which is Minerva Terrace.

2. *Tower Falls and Canyon Village.* Tower Falls, which tumbles 132 feet, was named for adjacent volcanic pinnacles and the Tower Creek, which flows into the Yellowstone River. As you drive south from Tower Falls and look downslope to the east, you'll see prime grizzly bear country along Antelope Creek. From the Washburn Hot Springs Overlook south of Dunraven Pass, there is a good view of the entire Yellowstone Caldera, including the north boundary, Mount Washburn, and the south boundary in the red mountains about 35 miles away. On clear days, the Teton Range is visible beyond the red mountains. The Grand Canyon of the Yellowstone River extends from the Canyon Village area to Tower Junction. However, the most famous and spectacular section can be

The Stories of Jim Bridger

Jim Bridger, one of the greatest mountain men ever and a denizen of Yellowstone country, was a natural at trapping and exploring, but had a tendency to stretch his stories. Once, when he was exploring with another man, he pointed to a tall, flat mountain and said, "Son, when I first came here, that was merely an anthill." He called this mountain his alarm clock and claimed that every night before he went to bed he would yell, "Wake up Jim Bridger, you frost-bit, no-account rascal!" Exactly 7 hours and 56 minutes later, the mountain would echo the message back and wake him up.

Another favorite story was of a lake where the surface of the water was boiling, but the water underneath was cool. He professed that he would catch a fish in the cool water below the surface, and as he brought it up through the hot water, it would cook and be ready to eat when it reached the surface.

RUSTIC CABINS IN WYOMING

Two of Wyoming's National Forests offer lodging in rustic guard stations. These cabins are out-of-the-way gems, located in the middle of some of America's most pristine lands.

Cabins are accessible via narrow, winding, dirt or gravel roads, or, in winter, by snowmobile or cross-country skis. Facilities are spartan: a table, chairs, wood stove and bunks (some with mattresses, some without). You might need to bring your own drinking water and cut your own firewood. Expect to use outdoor privies, and don't expect a telephone.

These cabins can be a remarkable place to stay amidst Wyoming's beautiful National Forests. Cabins are between $20 and $40 a night, and house from five to eight guests. Call for more information and to make reservations, which are required.

Bridger-Teton National Forest (4 cabins, winter-only)
Kemmerer Ranger District
308 Highway 189 North
Kemmerer, WY 83101
307-877-4415

Greys River Ranger District
125 Washington Street
Afton, WY 83110
307-886-3166

Medicine Bow National Forest (1 cabin, year-round)
Laramie Ranger District
2468 Jackson Street
Laramie, WY 82070
307-745-2300

seen from the overlooks along the North and South Rim Roads in the Canyon Village area. Trails run along the rims and into the canyon for closer views of the Upper and Lower Falls and the canyon's famous colors and shapes.

3. *The Yellowstone Lake Area.* With 110 miles of shoreline, Yellowstone Lake is the country's largest mountain lake. The area is prime habitat for a variety of birds and animals, and it draws anglers and boaters as well. Mud Volcano, 6 miles north of Fishing Bridge Junction, and West Thumb Geyser Basin, 22 miles north of the South Entrance, are unique thermal areas. Just north of the lake, the Earth's surface has recently risen as much as 1 inch per year, suggesting future volcanic activity. There is a Visitor Center at Fishing Bridge—which, incidentally, was closed to fishing in 1973—where Yellowstone Lake empties into the Yellowstone River. Here you'll find one of the best places to watch spawning trout for most of the summer. The West Thumb and Grant Village area

includes a geyser basin along the lake's edge. Intense heat in the lake sediment indicates that a shallow thermal system underlies this recent caldera within the larger Yellowstone caldera. If the lake level falls just a few feet, an immense hydrothermal explosion could occur here.

- About 300 designated back-country campsites are scattered throughout the park. All have restrictions on group size, stock use, boating access, and so on. Food-storage poles are provided at most of the sites.
- The Yellowstone Institute is a year-round educational field program that offers a series of short courses in natural history, cultural history, and the humanities. Courses run 1 to 5 days and are generally in session for most of the day. Most courses are offered for graduate and/or undergraduate credit, as well as recertification credit. Contact the Yellowstone Institute (same address as above; 307-344-2294).

FIRE PREVENTION TIPS

The Bureau of Land Management offers this advice:

- Check fire conditions before you go to wildlands, and strictly observe any restrictions that may be in effect. Call or visit the nearest federal or state land management agency to find out whether the fire danger is low, moderate, high, or extreme. Comply with any conditions on campfires, smoking, or equipment use.
- Don't park cars, trucks, or recreational vehicles on dry vegetation. A vehicle's exhaust system can reach over 1,000°F, and it only takes about 500°F to start a wildfire.
- Use an approved spark arrester on all internal combustion-powered vehicles and equipment. This screen, which fits between the exhaust ports of the piston and muffler, helps ensure that sparks generated by vehicles and equipment don't start wildfires. Check and replace spark arresters periodically, to ensure proper functioning.
- Remove all vegetation and debris within 10 feet of a campfire before starting it.
- Keep fire-suppression tools handy. Make sure that you have a bucket of water, a shovel, and other implements nearby, in case your campfire starts to get out of control.
- Make sure the campfire is "dead out" before leaving. Stir water and dirt into the coals with a shovel or stick until the coals are cool enough to touch with your hands.
- Extinguish smoking materials properly. Put out cigarettes, cigars, or pipes only in cleared areas that are free of vegetation or debris.
- Don't use fireworks in wildland areas. Fireworks are illegal on most wildlands.

Points of Interest

BUREAU OF LAND MANAGEMENT

THE POWDER RIVER CANYON

Hidden in the southern portion of the Big Horn Mountains are the hideouts of legendary outlaw Butch Cassidy and the Wild Bunch. Visitors know this area better as a blue-ribbon trout stream and big game range, with elk, mule deer, antelope, eagles, and other wildlife.

From Kaycee, WY, southwest 20 miles
307-684-5586

PRYOR MOUNTAIN NATIONAL WILD HORSE RANGE

The Pryor Range was created in 1968 as the country's first designated wild horse range, now home to about 120 horses. The range's 38,000 acres are characterized by deep, steep-walled canyons, isolated grassy plateaus, and foothill slopes. Cowboys and commercial mustangers captured many of Pryor's horses with the aid of aircraft or motor vehicles until a 1959 federal law prohibited the practice. Wild horses are now federally protected under the 1971 Wild Free-Roaming Horse and Burro Act.

From Lovell, WY, north 13 miles in Carbon County, MT
406-657-6262

This is just a sample of the many Bureau of Land Management points of interest in Wyoming. For more information, contact:

Bureau of Land Management
Wyoming State Office
5353 Yellowstone Road
Cheyenne, Wyoming 82009
307-775-6BLM (6256)
http://www.wy.blm.gov

U.S. BUREAU OF RECLAMATION

BOYSEN RESERVOIR

Boysen State Park, Boysen Route, Shoshoni, WY 82649; 307-876-2796. Located on US 20, 10 miles north of Shoshoni. Fishing year-round (with State fishing license). Good access via shoreline roads and boat ramps. Other activities: big game hunting in season (with State hunting license), rockhounding, and horseback riding. Annual winter carnival held in February. Available services: developed campsites/RV sites with dump stations, drinking water, tables, wind screens, accessible restrooms.

BUFFALO BILL RESERVOIR

Buffalo Bill State Park, 47 Lakeside Road, Cody, WY 82414; 307-587-9227. Located 8 miles west of Cody, on US 14-16-20 (Yellowstone Highway). Fishing year-round (with State fishing license). Good access via shoreline roads and 3 boat ramps. Additional blue-ribbon-quality fishing available on Shoshone River, above and below reservoir. Available services: developed accessible campsites/RV sites with dump stations, drinking water, tables, accessible restrooms, and wind screens; some primitive campsites. Popular wind surfing area.

GLENDO RESERVOIR

Glendo State Park, PO Box 398, Glendo, WY 82213; 307-735-4433. Recreation managed for the Bureau of Reclamation by Wyoming State Parks and Historic Sites. Located on the North Platte River, 6 miles southeast of Glendo, in Platte County. Access from I-25 via County Road 17 (Glendo Park Road). Glendo State Park: 7 campgrounds, 6 boat ramps, and a marina concession. Scenic overlooks and two interpretive nature trails. Glendo Dam Wetlands Trail located along the river, just below the dam; features two fishing/observation piers.

KEYHOLE RESERVOIR

Managed by the Wyoming State Parks and Historic Sites, 353 McKean Road, Moorcroft, WY 82721; 307-756-3596. Eight miles north of I-90 (Exit 165) between Moorcroft and Sundance. Public use area, camping, picnic areas, trailer dump station, concession, swimming, boating, hiking, and fishing.

KORTES RESERVOIR/MIRACLE MILE AREA

Managed by the Bureau of Reclamation, Wyoming Area Office, PO Box 1630, Mills, WY 82644; 307-261-5628. Located on North Platte River, 54 miles southwest of Casper and 34 miles northeast of Rawlins, and in Carbon County. Access from I-80 via Carbon County Rd. 351. Access from U.S. 220 via Natrona County Hwy. 407 and Carbon County roads 291 and 351. Kortes Reservoir is located in a narrow canyon below Seminoe Dam. The Miracle Mile Area extends downstream approximately 5.5 miles from the bottom of Kortes Dam to the boundary of the southern management unit of the Pathfinder National Wildlife Refuge. Eleven primitive camping areas in the Miracle Mile.

PILOT BUTTE RESERVOIR

Wyoming Game and Fish Department, 2055 Missouri Valley Road, Pavillion, WY 82523; 307-856-3007. Located 25 miles west of Riverton, on U.S. 26. Fishing year-round with Wyoming state license. Fish species include trout, ling, and crappie. Limited shoreline access via roads. Available services include picnic/camping shelters, accessible restroom, and boat ramp. No drinking water. Other activities include swimming, hiking, and watchable wildlife.

MOVIES FILMED ON NATIONAL PARK LANDS, 1910 TO 1994

Starting in 1910 with *The Immortal Alamo,* film makers have been coming to national parks year after year to capture majestic scenery for their productions. Courtesy of the NPS Press Office, here is a partial list of films shot on park lands.

Title	*Cast*	*Year*	*NPS Site**	*State*
The Babe	John Goodman	1991	Illinois & Michigan Canal NHS	IL
Bandolero	James Stewart, Dean Martin	1967	Glen Canyon NRA	UT
Betrayed	Debra Winger, Tom Berenger	1987	Illinois & Michigan Canal NHS	IL
Blaze	Paul Newman	1989	Great Smoky Mountains NP	TN
The Blues Brothers	Dan Aykroyd, John Belushi	1978	Illinois & Michigan Canal NHS	IL
Butch Cassidy and the Sundance Kid	Paul Newman, Robert Redford	1969	Zion NP	UT
City Slickers II	Billy Crystal	1993	Arches NP	UT
Close Encounters of the Third Kind	Richard Dreyfuss, Teri Garr	1977	Devils Tower NM	WY
Continental Divide	John Belushi, Blair Brown	1980	Glacier NP	MT
Dances with Wolves	Kevin Costner, Graham Greene	1990	Badlands NP	SD
The Deer Hunter	Robert DeNiro, Meryl Streep	1977	Lake Chelan NRA	WA
Easy Rider	Peter Fonda, Jack Nicholson	1969	Wupatki-Sunset Crater Volcano	AZ
The Firm	Tom Cruise, Hal Holbrook	1993	National Capital Region	DC
Forrest Gump	Tom Hanks	1993	Glacier NP	MT
The Fugitive	Harrison Ford, Tommy Lee Jones	1993	Blue Ridge Parkway	NC
Glory	Matthew Broderick	1989	Boston African-American NHS	MA
The Grapes of Wrath	Henry Fonda, John Carradine	1940	Petrified Forest NP	AZ
Indiana Jones and the Last Crusade	Harrison Ford, Sean Connery	1989	Arches NP	UT
Journey to the Center of the Earth	James Mason, Pat Boone	1959	Carlsbad Caverns NP	NM
Planet of the Apes	Charlton Heston, Roddy McDowall	1968	Glen Canyon NRA	UT
Rocky II	Sylvester Stallone	1978	Independence NHP	PA
Star Wars	Mark Hamill, Carrie Fisher	1977	Death Valley NM	CA
Thelma and Louise	Geena Davis, Susan Sarandon	1990	Arches NP	UT
War Games	Matthew Broderick, Ally Sheedy	1982	Lake Chelan NRA	WA

*NHP = National Historic Park; NHS = National Historic Site; NM = National Monument; NP = National Park; NRA = National Recreation Area.

WESTERN WHITEWATER

Some of the most incredible whitewater in the world is found in the Western United States, on rivers managed by the Bureau of Land Management. Here are some of the best, and how you can find out more about them:

State	*River Name*	*Whitewater Class*	*Address/Phone of BLM Office*
Alaska	Delta	I–V+	PO Box 147, Glennallen, AK 99588; 907-822-3217
	Fortymile	I–V+	1150 University Ave., Fairbanks, AK 99709; 907-474-2368
	Gulkana	I–IV	PO Box 147, Glennallen, AK 99588; 907-822-3217
California	American (North Fork)	III–V+	63 Natoma St., Folsom, CA 95630; 916-985-4474
	Eel	III–IV	555 Leslie St., Ukiah, CA 95482; 707-468-4000
	Kaweah	II–V	4301 Rosedale Hwy., Bakersfield, CA 93308; 805-861-4280
	Kern	III–V+	Same as above
	Merced	III–V+	63 Natoma St., Folsom, CA 95630; 916-985-4474
Colorado	Arkansas	II–V	PO Box 2200, Canon City, CO 81215; 719-275-0631
	Colorado	I–V+	116 Park Ave., PO Box 68, Kremmling, CO 80459; 303-724-3437
	Dolores	II–IV	2465 S. Townsend, Montrose, CO 81401; 303-249-7791
	Gunnison	I–IV	Same as above
	Yampa	I–V+	455 Emerson St., Craig, CO 81625; 303-824-8261
Idaho	Bruneau	III–V+	3948 Development Ave., Boise, ID 83705; 208-384-3300

State	River Name	Whitewater Class	Address/Phone of BLM Office
Idaho (cont.)	Jarbidge	III–V+	Same as above
	Owyhee	III–V+	Same as above
	Salmon	II–IV	PO Box 430, Salmon, ID, 83467; 208-756-5400
	Snake	I–V	PO Box 2B, Shoshone, ID 83352; 208-886-2206
Montana	Madison	III–V+	Dillon Resource Area, Dillon, MT 59725; 406-683-2337
Nevada	Owyhee (South Fork)	III–IV	3900 E. Idaho St., PO Box 831, Elko, NV 89803; 702-753-0200
New Mexico	Rio Grande	I–IV	224 Cruz Alta Rd., Taos, NM 87571; 505-758-8851
Oregon	Deschutes	III–IV	185 E. 4th St., PO Box 550, Prineville, OR 97754; 503-447-8700
	Klamath, Upper	IV	2795 Anderson Ave., Suite 25, Klamath Falls, OR 97603; 503-883-6916
	Owyhee	III–V+	PO Box 700, 100 Oregon St., Vale, OR 97918; 503-473-3144
	Salmon	III–V+	1717 Fabry Road SE, Salem, OR 97306; 503-375-5646
	Sandy	I–IV	Same as above
Utah	Colorado	I–IV	885 S. Sand Flats Rd., Moad, UT 84532; 801-259-8193
	Dolores	III–IV	Same as above
Wyoming	Shoshone	I–IV	1002 Blackburn Ave., Cody, WY 82414; 307-587-2216

For a complete list of all of the rivers that are a part of the BLM river system (including some of the less treacherous rivers, for less adventurous rafters and beginners), write to any BLM office and ask for the brochure *America's Treasures: Rivers and Streams on the Public Lands.*

TEST YOUR PUBLIC LANDS IQ

1. *What are federally owned public lands?*
   a. National Parks and National Forests;
   b. lands managed by the Bureau of Land Management;
   c. U.S. Fish and Wildlife Service refuges;
   d. lands that are owned by all Americans;
   e. all of the above.
2. *Which federal agency manages the greatest number of acres of public lands?*
   a. the Forest Service;
   b. the National Park Service;
   c. the Army Corps of Engineers;
   d. the Bureau of Land Management.
3. *How many acres of federally owned public land are managed by the Bureau of Land Management (BLM)?*
   a. 57 million acres (2.53 percent of U.S. acreage);
   b. 100 million acres (4.44 percent of U.S. acreage);
   c. 225 million acres (10 percent of U.S. acreage);
   d. 270 million acres (12 percent of U.S. acreage).
4. *What are the uses of the public lands managed by the Bureau of Land Management?*
   a. recreational uses, such as fishing, hiking, off-road vehicle use, and camping;
   b. commercial uses, such as mining, grazing, forestry, power transmission rights-of ways, scenery for advertising, and motion picture filming;
   c. conservation of plant, fish, and animal specimens and habitats, wild horse and burro ranges, archaeological and historic properties;
   d. all of the above.
5. *Commercial uses of the public lands managed by the Bureau of Land Management generate how much revenue for federal, state, and local governments annually?*
   a. none;
   b. over $140 million;
   c. over $1 billion;
   d. just under $100 million.
6. *Total revenues paid to the federal government by companies that conduct energy and mineral operations on BLM public lands exceeded which of the following dollar amounts in 1994?*
   a. $1 million;
   b. $400 million;
   c. $750 million;
   d. over $1 billion.

Solutions to the Quiz
1. e; 2. d; 3. d; 4. d; 5. b; 6. d.

The Southwest Region

NATIONAL PARK SERVICE HANDBOOKS—THE SOUTHWEST REGION

National Park Service handbooks highlight popular visitor sites across the country. Use them to learn about the historic significance and natural beauty of your next vacation destination. All are generously illustrated with photos, maps, and diagrams. Sites in the Southwest for which these authoritative handbooks are available include:

Site	*Stock No.*	*Price*
Saguaro National Park (AZ)	024-005-00912-4	$5.00
Fort Union National Monument (NM)	024-005-00893-4	3.75
Big Bend National Park (TX)	024-005-00908-6	6.00
Fort Davis National Historic Site (TX)	024-005-00187-5	2.50

You can order these documents by phone (202-512-1800) or fax (202-512-2250) or by writing to: Superintendent of Documents, PO Box 371954, Pittsburgh, PA 15250-7954. (Use stock number when ordering. Prices may change.) The 24 local government bookstores located around the country carry titles of regional interest. Check the appendix for the one nearest to you.

RIPARIAN RIBBON OF LIFE—THE SAN PEDRO RIVER

Riparian areas—the lush green areas of vegetation bordering lakes, ponds, rivers, streams, and wet meadows—are lifelines in the desert. More than 90 percent of the historic riparian areas in the Southwest have been lost due to the damming of rivers. One of the most important riparian areas in the United States runs through the Chihuahuan Desert and the Sonoran Desert in southeastern Arizona, along the San Pedro River. Despite the dryness of the surrounding land, it sustains one of the richest wildlife populations in the country. Legislation passed by Congress in 1988 designated this segment of more than 22,400 hectares a Riparian National Conservation Area. According to the Bureau of Land Management, this "ribbon of life," which represents the most extensive and healthy riparian ecosystem remaining in the desert Southwest, is home to 82 species of mammals, 12 species of fish, 47 species of reptiles and amphibians, and 100 species of breeding birds. It provides an invaluable habitat for another 250 species of migrant and wintering birds, including yellow-billed cuckoos, green kingfishers, vermilion flycatchers, and elf owls. The gray hawks on the San Pedro River represent about 30 percent of the nesting gray hawks in the United States.

ARIZONA

APACHE–SITGREAVES NATIONAL FOREST

180 miles northeast of Phoenix.

309 South Mountain Avenue
Box 640
Springerville, AZ 85938
520-333-4301
http://www.fs.fed.us

Arizona Natural History Association. (Box 1633, Flagstaff, AZ 86002; 520-527-3450)

The 2 million acres of the Apache–Sitgreaves National Forest have some of the most spectacular scenery in the Southwest. Elevations range from 3,500 feet in the Upper Sonoran desert zone, covered by prickly pear and yucca, to nearly 11,500 feet in the alpine zone, where stands of fir and spruce are interwoven with green meadows. Southwestern city dwellers find the forest an oasis from the summer heat. In the winter, the area is popular for cross-country skiing, snowshoeing, snowmobiling, camping, and ice fishing in the higher-elevation lakes.

SAM'S TIPS

- The Blue Range Primitive Area, one of Arizona's little-known gems, is the last remaining primitive area in the national forest system. There are 200,000

FOREST SERVICE SCENIC BYWAYS

Coronado Trail Scenic Byway

The Coronado Trail Scenic Byway covers 123 miles of US Highway 666 from Clifton to Springerville and follows the path of Coronado's conquistadors in their search for the legendary seven cities of gold. Mountains, lakes, forests, and meadows abound on this route through the Apache–Sitgreaves National Forest. *Contact Apache–Sitgreaves National Forest.*

White Mountains Scenic Highway

The White Mountains Scenic Highway wanders for 123 miles through ponderosa pine forests, crosses several mountain streams, and passes through an area rich in Apache Indian culture. The byway is located on the Apache–Sitgreaves National Forest in eastern Arizona. *Contact Apache–Sitgreaves National Forest.*

acres of wilderness recreation available, and over 450 miles of streams. Apache–Sitgreaves is known as one of the top ten forests for fishing.

- The Coronado Scenic Byway weaves south through the forest, from Springerville to Clifton, and has exceptional views. This drive makes a good day-trip.

CANYON DE CHELLY NATIONAL MONUMENT

200 miles northeast of Flagstaff, AZ, 245 miles northwest of Albuquerque, NM.

Box 588
Chinle, AZ 86503
520-674-5500
http://www.nps.gov/cach

Southwest Parks and Monuments Association. (221 North Court Avenue, Tucson, AZ 86701; 520-622-1999)

The canyons of Canyon de Chelly National Monument sheltered prehistoric Pueblo Indians for 1,000 years and served as an ancestral stronghold of the Navajo Indians. Today, these beautiful, steep-walled canyons are famous for their plentiful ruins of prehistoric Indian dwellings, set below towering cliffs or on high ledges. Present-day Navajo Indian homes are scattered along the canyon floors.

SAM'S TIPS

- The best views of the park are from the South and North Rim Drives, each about 30 miles round trip. Highlights include views of White House Ruin (the best known Anasazi cliff dwelling in the canyon), Spider Rock (an 800-foot sandstone spire rising from the canyon floor), Antelope House (named for colorful Navajo drawings done 150 years ago), and Mummy Cave (considered one of the most spectacular dwellings in the park).
- Pictographs are common throughout the canyons. Some date from the prehistoric Basketmaker and Pueblo periods, but the finest are those done by the Navajo. Look for them in Antelope House.

FOREST SERVICE SCENIC BYWAY

Apache Trail

The Apache Trail consists of 78 miles of awe-inspiring desert scenery along State Highway 88 in the Tonto National Forest. Less than 30 miles from Phoenix, the byway features impressive rock formations, giant saguaro cactus, and narrow canyons. *Contact Tonto National Forest.*

- Visitors are not allowed to travel in the canyon without a park ranger or authorized guide. The only exception is along the 2½-mile (round trip) trail to White House Ruin.

CASA GRANDE RUINS NATIONAL MONUMENT

50 miles southeast of Phoenix, 80 miles northeast of Tucson.

1100 Ruins Drive
Coolidge, AZ 85228
520-723-3172
http://www.nps.gov/cagr

Southwest Parks and Monuments Association. (221 North Court Avenue, Tucson, AZ 86701; 520-622-1999)

The mysterious Great House at Casa Grande Ruins National Monument was completed sometime before 1350 by the Hohokam, hunter-gatherers who lived in Arizona for several thousand years. Established in 1892, this was the first archaeological preserve in the United States. The house's walls face the four cardinal points of the compass. A circular hole in the upper west wall aligns with the setting sun during the summer solstice, and additional openings align with the sun and moon at other specific times. Apparently, the builders of the Great House gathered inside to ponder the heavens, possibly for very practical purposes: Knowledge of the changing appearances of celestial objects meant knowing the proper times for planting, harvest, and celebration.

Immigrants from Mexico

Mexico is 50 miles to the south, yet the Chiricahua Mountains' special mix of life is more like that found in the Mexican Sierra Madres than in typical southwestern highlands. Many southern trees, wildflowers, and animals have crossed the border into Chiricahua National Monument. Most conspicuous of the Mexican influences are the area birds, such as Sulphur-bellied flycatchers, Mexican chickadees, and Elegant trogan. (Bird sightings vary according to the season of the year.) The Mexican influence is also seen among the area's mammals—including the Chiricahua fox, squirrel, coatimundis, and peccaries—and in trees like the Chihuahua pine and Apache pine.

CHIRICAHUA NATIONAL MONUMENT

120 miles east of Tucson, 200 miles southeast of Phoenix.

HCR #2
Box 6500
Willcox, AZ 85643
520-824-3560
http://www.nps.gov/chir

Southwest Parks and Monuments Association. (221 North Court Avenue, Tucson, AZ 86701; 520-622-1999)

This park in the northwest corner of the Chiricahua Mountains harbors towering rock spires, massive stone columns, and balanced rocks, weighing hundreds of tons,

HAPPY CAMPERS—THE WONDERFUL OUTDOOR WORLD (WOW) PROGRAM IN ARIZONA

Bringing nature to the city is the concept of WOW, a national program designed to give urban children the chance to cook on a camp stove, sleep under the stars, and learn about the environment—right in their own neighborhood parks.

The WOW program was conceived when a network of public and private partners recognized a trend; fewer families were spending free time on family camp-outs, the traditional way children are introduced to the environment and lifelong outdoor activities. WOW was developed as a cost-effective means of bringing camping experiences into the cities. Their motto: "If you can't take kids to the outdoors, bring the outdoors to the kids." WOW was successfully piloted by the City of Los Angeles in 1995. Building on California's success, leaders from Arizona's federal, state, and local agencies, private organizations, and businesses expanded the program to Arizona.

WOW is offered at no cost to participants. National sponsors provide trailers, tents, stoves, and other camping gear. Local sponsors provide sleeping bags, T-shirts, food, and other items for campers. For more information on this program, or to start a WOW program in your area, contact the regional offices of the Bureau of Land Management.

that perch on small pedestals. Geologists presently believe that the rock forms were created about 27 million years ago by volcanic eruptions and subsequent erosion of the ash and dark volcanic rock.

COCONINO NATIONAL FOREST

In and around Flagstaff, off I-17; about 115 miles north of Phoenix.

2323 E. Greenlaw Lane
Flagstaff, AZ 86004
520-527-3600
http://www.primenet.com/~iink/coco/coform.html

Arizona Natural History Association. (Box 1633, Flagstaff, AZ 86002; 520-527-3450)

From the snow-covered San Francisco Peaks to desert highlands along the Verde River, this forest's 1.8 million acres cover a variety of altitudes and landscapes. Here, you can climb the highest mountain in Arizona, fish in crystal-clear lakes, swim in desert creeks under red rock cliffs and magnificent sycamore trees, hang glide, ski through meadows and ponderosa pine, and hunt elk, deer, antelope, bear, mountain lion, or wild turkey. You also may want to visit Lava River Cave, which has an entrance that is actually a hole in the ground.

Sam's Tips

- Protected species in the forest include wintering bald eagles, nesting osprey and other raptors, and various songbirds. Mormon Lake and Lake Mary are popular viewing sites for migrating waterfowl.
- If you live near the forest, it is possible to take a bit of Coconino home with you. The forest allows people to collect firewood on a free-use and paid-permit basis, and during the Christmas season, it holds a Christmas Tree Harvest. Contact Coconino for further information.

CORONADO NATIONAL FOREST

Headquartered in Tucson and covering most of the mountain ranges south, east, southeast, and northeast of Tucson.

300 West Congress
Tucson, AZ 85701
520-670-4552
http://www.azstarnet.com/public/nonprofit/coronado/cnfhome.htm

Southwest Natural and Cultural Heritage Association. (6501 Fourth Street, NW, Suite I, Albuquerque, NM 87107; 505-345-9498)

In search of gold, the Spanish explorer Don Francisco Vasques de Coronado and his expedition came north from Mexico in 1540 and passed through what is now southern Arizona. What they found were vast grassy hills, cactus, and scattered, rugged mountain ranges, including the Chiricahua, Santa Catalina, Santa Rita, Piñaleno, Huachuca, and Dragoon. These mountains, now known as sky islands because they rise out of the desert like islands out of a sea, capture rain and snow. In the arid southwest, these highlands provide precious water to the low-lying desert below. The Coronado, the only forest that shares a border with Mexico, was an ancient hunting site, and later hosted prehistoric farming villages and, in the 19th century, homesteaders and miners. The five small lakes in the higher-elevation pine forests provide recreation opportunities that are unique in a desert environment.

Sam's Tips

- Sabino Canyon, a low-elevation streamside oasis on the forest border nearest Tucson, attracts over 1 million visitors a year.
- Indian reservations in the area include Pascua Yaqui, Tohono O'odham Nation, and San Carlos Apache.
- Three National Park Service sites adjoin the forest: Saguaro National Park, Coronado National Memorial, and Chiricahua National Monument.

CORONADO NATIONAL MEMORIAL

75 miles southeast of Tucson.

4101 East Montezuma Canyon Road
Hereford, AZ 85615
520-366-5515
http://www.nps.gov/coro

Southwest Parks and Monuments Association. (221 North Court Avenue, Tucson, AZ 86701; 520-622-1999)

Coronado National Memorial lies on the United States–Mexico border within sight of the San Pedro River valley through which the Coronado expedition first entered the present-day United States in search of the fabled Cities of Cibola. Montezuma Pass is the most outstanding physical feature found in the memorial. At an elevation of 6,575 feet, the pass offers sweeping views of the San Pedro River Valley to the east and the San Rafael Valley to the west.

FORT BOWIE NATIONAL HISTORIC SITE

100 miles east of Tucson.

Box 158
Bowie, AZ 85605
520-847-2500
http://www.nps.gov/fobo

Southwest Parks and Monuments Association. (221 North Court Avenue, Tucson, AZ 86701; 520-622-1999)

Fort Bowie commemorates the bitter conflict between the Chiricahua Apaches and the U.S. military. For more than 30 years, Fort Bowie and nearby Apache Pass were the focal points of military operations. The conflict culminated in the surrender of Geronimo in 1886 and the banishment of the Chiricahuas to Florida and Alabama. Today, the remains of Fort Bowie are carefully preserved. The adobe walls of various post buildings and the ruins of a Butterfield Stage Station can still be seen.

SAM'S TIPS

- No road runs through the ruins. They can be reached by a 1½-mile foot trail that begins midway in Apache Pass Road.
- The trail to the fort passes a number of historic features: the Butterfield Stage Station ruins, the post cemetery, Apache Spring, and the original Fort Bowie.

BUREAU OF INDIAN AFFAIRS ON THE WORLD WIDE WEB

The homepage of the Bureau of Indian Affairs (http://www.doi.gov/bureau-indian-affairs.html) has a list of tribal Internet sites that provide details about opportunities to visit reservations. Throughout the United States, 554 federally recognized tribes are considered sovereign domestic nations. Some tribes offer a wealth of experiences for visitors: parks, historic sites, golf courses, hiking trails, fishing, skiing, hotels, casinos, motels, restaurants, and museums. Although many tribes welcome visitors on their lands, you should be aware that customs and regulations may vary from tribe to tribe.

GLEN CANYON NATIONAL RECREATION AREA

120 miles north of Flagstaff.

Box 1507
Page, AZ 86040
520-608-6404
http://www.nps.gov/glca

 **Glen Canyon Natural History Association.** (32 North 10th Avenue, Suite 9, Box 581, Page, AZ 86040; 520-645-3532)

The waters of the Colorado River and its tributaries back up for almost 200 miles behind the Glen Canyon Dam, forming Lake Powell, the second largest manmade reservoir in the United States (after Lake Mead). Glen Canyon itself is now beneath the waters of Lake Powell, and the park lies in the midst of the nation's most rugged canyon country. The lake and more than 1 million acres of desert-and-canyon country offer great fishing and boating, hiking along canyons and cliffs, and evidence of prehistoric and more recent human inhabitants.

Sam's Tips

- Downriver from Glen Canyon Dam, Lees Ferry lies in the break between Glen and Marble canyons. Lees Ferry has a Ranger Station, and most river trips through the Grand Canyon begin here. Permits are required, and can be secured a year or more in advance. For more information, contact Grand Canyon National Park, Grand Canyon, AZ 86023.
- The Dangling Rope Marina and Rainbow Bridge National Monument (see entry) areas, accessible only by boat, are about 50 miles by water from the city of Page. Rainbow Bridge, the world's largest natural bridge, spanning

 **FOREST SERVICE SCENIC BYWAY**

Kaibab Plateau–North Rim Parkway

Described as "the most beautiful 44 miles in America," the byway begins at Jacobs Lake, travels through dense forests that open on beautiful, high alpine meadows and small lakes, and ends at the North Rim of the Grand Canyon. *Contact Kaibab National Forest.*

275 feet at a height of 290 feet, can be reached by rough trails across the Navajo Reservation. Hiking permits must be obtained from the Navajo Nation, Recreational Resources Department, Box 9000, Window Rock, AZ 86515; 520-871-6647.

- The canyons of the Escalante are reminiscent of Glen Canyon before the dam was built. Natural bridges, arches, narrow canyons, and remains of prehistoric inhabitants are just some of the region's attractions.
- The Hite area was originally named Dandy Crossing because it was the best place to ford the Colorado above Lees Ferry. Prehistoric people used this crossing, and remains of their structures can be seen nearby. Many people find this region to be the most scenic in the Recreation Area.
- Water sports are the dominant recreational activity at Glen Canyon. Concessionaires offer boat tours lasting from 1 hour to all day, and they provide boat rentals at Wahweap, Hite, Bullfrog, and Halls Crossing Marinas. Canoes, power boats, jet skis, and houseboats are all common sights on the lake.

GRAND CANYON NATIONAL PARK

The South Rim of the canyon is 78 miles north of Flagstaff and 291 miles from Las Vegas. The North Rim is 267 miles from Las Vegas and 221 miles from Flagstaff.

Box 129
Grand Canyon, AZ 86023
520-638-7888
http://www.nps.gov/grca

Grand Canyon Association. (Box 399, Grand Canyon, AZ 86023; 520-638-2481)

Located entirely in northern Arizona, the Grand Canyon National Park encompasses 277 miles of the Colorado River and adjacent uplands and is the most popular natural attraction in the United States. One of the most spectacular examples of erosion anywhere in the world, Grand Canyon is unmatched in the vistas awaiting visitors from all points on the rim. The Grand Canyon was known only to Native Americans and a few explorers until 1869, when Major John W. Powell, a one-armed Civil War veteran with a thirst for science and adventure, made a pioneering journey through the canyon on the Colorado River with nine men in four small wooden boats. (Only six men completed the journey.) While most visitors see the canyon only from overlooks along the rim, those who venture into the canyon can experience it in the same manner as the first explorers: on foot, by mule, or by raft.

Sam's Tips

- As with any visits to national parks, be sure to plan well ahead of time. Reservations for overnight lodging or camping and mule trips in Grand Canyon are often booked a year in advance. Send the park a written request for a *Trip Planner* or, if you are interested in overnight hikes into the Canyon, ask for the *Backcountry Trip Planner.*
- Advance reservations for lodging, specialized tours, and mule rides can be made by contacting Amfac Parks and Resorts (Grand Canyon National Park Lodges), Attn: Reservations, 14001 East Iliff, Aurora, CO 80014; 303-297-2757, fax 303-297-3175. For same-day lodging reservations, call 520-638-2631. Reservations can also be made on-line at http://www.amfac.com.
- Warm deserts to the east, west, and south guarantee access to the South Rim during most of the year. On the North Rim, however, deep side canyons to the east and west pose a challenge. The only easy route to the North Rim is across the Kaibab Plateau, which rises to 9,000 feet and may receive up to 25 feet of snow in the winter. But the North Rim has its advantages: 4.5 million of the 5 million visitors who come to the Canyon annually choose the South Rim, which makes the north one a good place to find relative solitude while still enjoying the Grand Canyon experience.

Where Did It Come From?

Grand Canyon was formed from erosion by the Colorado River over the past 5 to 6 million years—only yesterday, considering the age of the rocks through which the canyon is carved. Some of the rocks are from the Precambrian Era and are as old as 2 billion years. The rocks at the Grand Canyon are not unique—similar rocks are found throughout the world. But the wide variety of rocks, the clarity with which they're exposed, and the complex geological history they reveal make the canyon unique.

Grand Canyon owes its distinctive shape to the fact that different rock layers in the walls respond to erosion in different ways. Some form slopes, some form cliffs, some erode more quickly than others. The vivid colors of many of these layers are due mainly to small amounts of various minerals; most contain iron, which imparts subtle shades of red, yellow, or green to the canyon walls. Climate plays an important role. If the climate at Grand Canyon were wetter, the walls might be covered with lush vegetation.

Virtual Visitor Centers

Many of the larger national parks have partnered with non-profit and private sector groups to develop state-of-the-art web sites which are linked directly from their Park Service sites. The Grand Canyon is a superb example. Its expanded web pages include a Trip Planner (camping and lodging information, reservations, and more), a guide to commercial river outfitters (with addresses and phone numbers), and frequently updated park news. Be sure to use this web resource—developed by the National Park Service, the Grand Canyon Association and Canyon Web—in planning your Grand Canyon adventure: http://www.thecanyon.com/nps.

- Many overlooks are accessible by car. The East Rim Drive follows the canyon rim for 26 miles east of Grand Canyon Village and brings you to the east entrance to the park. The West Rim Drive follows the canyon from Grand Canyon Village to Hermits Rest, but this part of the drive is closed to private vehicles during the summer. You can board a free shuttle bus that runs along the West Rim and stops at scenic points along the way.
- The inner canyon is accessible only by mule, on foot, or by raft on the Colorado River. Mule rides can be arranged through Amfac (303-297-2757). Taking a mule all the way to the Colorado River at the bottom of the Canyon requires a two-day round trip. A one-day trip goes part way into the canyon. (Overnight riders stay and eat at Phantom Ranch.) Mule trips may be booked eleven months in advance, and bookings fill up early. A waiting list is maintained for cancellations, but the chances of obtaining reservations on a waiting list are slim. Mule rides are also available from the North Rim, but they do not go all of the way to the river.
- Hiking below the rim is a popular but strenuous activity. Permits are not required for day hikes, but the park recommends that you do not attempt to hike all of the way to the river and back in one day. Overnight hikers may arrange to stay and eat at Phantom Ranch, but reservations are required (303-297-2757). All overnight camping (including overnight hiking, horseback riding, and cross-country skiing) below the rim requires a permit, available from: Backcountry Office, Grand Canyon National Park, PO Box 129, Grand Canyon, AZ 86023; 520-638-7888. Beware of developing the "Kaibab shuffle," a condition arising from sore, inflamed muscles and tendons. Be prepared with a first-aid kit that includes material for blister prevention, a supportive elastic wrap, and an over-the-counter medication to reduce inflammation and pain.
- The Grand Canyon Field Institute (GCFI) hosts a yearly series of walks, hikes, and river trips led by expert instructors. Participants can study wilderness skills, geology, ecosystems, photography, human history, birds, and art. For further information, call 520-638-2485 or write to GCFI, PO Box 399, Grand Canyon, AZ 86023.
- Train rides are available from Williams, through the plains and pine forests of Arizona's Old West to the South Rim of the Grand Canyon. A round trip takes 8 hours. For more information, call 1-800-THE-TRAIN.

PREVENTING HEAT STRESS

The Southwestern National Forests report that heat stress occurs when body temperature rises beyond safe limits. When water lost through sweating is not replaced, the body's heat control system breaks down, subjecting the body to heat stress. Maintaining a high level of physical fitness is one of the best ways to protect yourself. The physically fit person has a well-developed circulatory capacity, as well as increased blood volume for regulating body temperature. Another good way to protect yourself is to acclimatize yourself to heat. The body adjusts to heavy exertion in hot climate in four to eight days by:

- Increasing sweat production.
- Improving blood distribution.
- Decreasing skin and body temperature.
- Decreasing heart rate (beats per minute for the same job may drop from 180 to 150).

According to the Forest publication *On Your Own in Southwestern Mountains and Wilderness and Primitive Areas,* acclimatization may be hastened in several ways, such as by taking 250 milligrams of vitamin C daily and by performing about 1½ hours of work daily in hot conditions. You won't acclimatize overnight; be sure to adjust to hot weather activity gradually. Set a sensible pace, take frequent breaks, replace fluids, and don't expect full production for the first few days.

HOHOKAM PIMA NATIONAL MONUMENT

35 miles south of Phoenix.

c/o Casa Grande Ruins National Monument
1100 Ruins Drive
Coolidge, AZ 85228
520-723-3172
http://www.nps.gov/pima

Preserved here are the archaeological remains of the Hohokam culture. Hohokam is a Pima Indian word meaning "those who have gone." Located near Casa Grande Ruins National Monument, the Monument is not open to the public.

HUBBELL TRADING POST NATIONAL HISTORIC SITE

On the Navajo Nation, 165 miles northeast of Flagstaff, and 55 miles west of Gallup, NM.

Box 150
Ganado, AZ 86505
520-755-3475
http://www.nps.gov/hutr

Southwest Parks and Monuments Association. (221 North Court Avenue, Tucson, AZ 85701; 520-622-1999)

John Lorenzo Hubbell bought out an old trader in Ganado in 1878 and became one of the foremost Navajo traders of his time. He was not only a merchant to the Navajos, but also their guide and teacher in understanding the ways of the White man. He participated in politics as Sheriff of Apache County, as a member of the Territorial Council, and as a state senator who helped guide Arizona to statehood. Hubbell died in 1930 and is buried on nearby Hubbell Hill. Business at the trading post is still done in the traditional way. As it was for their great-grandparents, the post serves as a bridge between cultures for many Navajos. Native American products, including rugs, blankets, and silverwork, are sold at the post today.

KAIBAB NATIONAL FOREST

The forest's office at Williams is 30 miles west of Flagstaff.

800 South Sixth Street
Williams, AZ 86046
520-635-8200
http://www.fs.fed.us/r3/kai

Southwest Natural and Cultural Heritage Association. (6501 Fourth Street NW, Suite I, Albuquerque, NM 87107; 505-345-9498)

This 1.5-million-acre tract has the distinction of being divided by the Grand Canyon. Elevations reach more than 10,000 feet, and the forest includes mountain peaks, plateaus, canyons, and beautiful high-country forests and meadows, as well as deer and buffalo herds and the unique forest squirrel. The area offers camping, hiking along historic trails, prehistoric rock art sites, and legendary US Route 66.

SAM'S TIPS

- The Visitor Center in Williams is in a restored 1901 train station. The Grand Canyon Railway, which first ran in 1901, has service from Williams to the South Rim of the Grand Canyon. For information and schedules, call 1-800-THE TRAIN.

- The Kaibab Plateau–North Rim Parkway has been described as "the most beautiful 44 miles in Arizona." This scenic byway runs through the northern part of the forest and provides access to the North Rim of the Grand Canyon. A Visitors' Center operates seasonally at Jacob Lake.

MONTEZUMA CASTLE NATIONAL MONUMENT

50 miles south of Flagstaff; 90 miles north of Phoenix.

Box 219
Camp Verde, Arizona 86322
520-567-3322
http://www.nps.gov/moca

Southwest Parks and Monuments Association. (221 North Court Avenue, Tucson, AZ 85701; 520-622-1999)

This site is not actually a castle nor did it ever belong to Montezuma. Early settlers to the area assumed the structure was connected to the Aztec emperor, but the castle was abandoned almost a century before Montezuma was born. The 5-story, 20-room cliff dwelling served as a "high-rise apartment building" for Sinagua Indians more than 600 years ago. Tucked into a limestone recess above the Verde Valley, it is one of the best preserved prehistoric ruins in North America. Close by are the Montezuma Well, a limestone sink formed by the collapse of an underground cavern, and Tuzigoot National Monument (see entry), the remnant of a Sinaguan village built between 1100 and 1400.

NAVAJO NATIONAL MONUMENT

140 miles northeast of Flagstaff; 160 miles west of Durango, CO.

HC 71
Box 3
Tonalea, AZ 86044-9704
520-672-2366
http://www.nps.gov/nava

Southwest Parks and Monuments Association. (221 North Court Avenue, Tucson, AZ 85701; 520-622-1999)

Ancient Anasazi farmers built the impressive cliff dwellings that are preserved at Navajo National Monument. The mostly stone structures include homes and harvest storage chambers. The need to store food also hastened this culture's development of pottery, which accounts for the many pottery fragments found

A GUIDE TO NAVAJO RUGS

A lovely 42-page full-color booklet written by Susan Lamb gives an excellent overview of the 16 major styles of Navajo rugs. Brief descriptions give the reader a window into the traditions behind Navajo weaving and the thoughts of various Navajo weavers. Order from the Southwest Parks and Monuments Association, 221 North Court Avenue, Tucson, AZ 85701; 520-622-1999.

at the site. This farming culture abandoned the whole area around 1300 A.D. Centuries later, the Navajo found the ruins left by the Anasazi.

Sam's Tips

- The half-mile-long Sandal trail leads to an overlook and a fine view across the canyon to the ancient village of Betatakin. A visit to the cliff dwellings requires more strenuous hiking.
- Tours to the ruins are given only during the warmer months. One or 2 trips (25 people per trip) a day are scheduled—and they fill up quickly. The round trip takes about 5 hours. The other major village ruin, Keet Seel, is 8½ miles from the Visitor Center, and only 20 hikers a day are allowed to make the trip. Neither site may be entered without a park ranger.
- A third set of ruins, called Inscription House, is exposed to the weather and is deteriorating more quickly than Betatakin and Keet Seel. It has been closed to the public since 1968.
- At the peak of Anasazi culture, there were three important regional centers: (1) the Kayenta, which is represented by this park; (2) Mesa Verde, represented by Mesa Verde National Park, in Colorado; and (3) the Chaco, represented by Chaco Culture National Historic Park, in New Mexico.

ORGAN PIPE CACTUS NATIONAL MONUMENT

120 miles south and west of Tucson.

Route 1
Box 100
Ajo, AZ 85321
520-387-6849
http://www.nps.gov/orpi

Southwest Parks and Monuments Association. (221 North Court Avenue, Tucson, AZ 86701; 520-622-1999)

Organ Pipe Cactus National Monument celebrates the life and landscape of the Sonoran Desert. Here, you can drive a lonely road, hike a back-country trail, camp beneath a clear desert sky, or just soak in the warmth and beauty of the American Southwest. The Monument also is a showcase for creatures that have adapted themselves to extreme temperatures, intense sunlight, and desert aridity. The Monument's namesake, the organ pipe cactus, is common in Mexico but relatively rare in the United States.

PETRIFIED FOREST NATIONAL PARK

The north-end Visitor Center is 25 miles northeast of Holbrook, 100 miles east of Flagstaff.

PO Box 2217
Petrified Forest National Park
AZ 86028
520-524-6228
http://www.nps.gov/pefo

Petrified Forest Museum Association. (Box 2277, 1 Park Road, Petrified Forest NP, AZ 86028; 520-524-6228, ext. 239 or 261)

In the mid-1800s, U.S. Army mappers and surveyors returned East with stories of a remarkable "Painted Desert and its trees turned to stone." By 1900, extensive removal of the wood, changed to multicolored stone, led to an effort to preserve areas containing large deposits. The park exists for this purpose. In addition to viewing the colorful Painted Desert and petrified wood, visitors can see ancient Indian dwellings like Puerco Pueblo, occupied as far back as 1100, and Agate House, a partially restored petrified wood pueblo. Newspaper Rock, a huge sandstone block covered with petroglyphs, is visible from an overlook on the park road. Nearby are the "tepees"—badland formations colored by iron, manganese, and other minerals—and the Blue Mesa, containing what are know as "pedestal logs."

Sam's Tips

- Collecting samples is not permitted at the park. Petrified wood, of the same quality as the wood found in the park, can be bought from commercial dealers outside the park. Small pieces are sold rough, tumbled, or polished. Artists and craftspeople work larger pieces into decorative objects such as jewelry, bookends, and clocks.
- There are no campgrounds in the park, although back-country, wilderness camping is allowed. Free permits are available in the visitor centers located at either end of the park.
- Hiking along one of the park's short trails is the best way to see the major features of the park up close. The Painted Desert Rim Trail (1-mile round trip) offers views from the rim into the Painted Desert, a brightly colored land of scant vegetation among deeply eroded soft clay hills. The Puerco Pueblo

What Is a Petrified Forest?

A forest becomes petrified when its wood is turned to stone by mineral water. Now a high and dry tableland, this forest was at one time a large floodplain, crossed by many streams. To the south, tall pinelike trees grew along the headwaters. The trees fell and were washed by swollen streams into the floodplain. There, they were covered by silt, mud, and volcanic ash. This blanket of deposits cut off oxygen and slowed the logs' decay. Gradually, silica-bearing groundwaters seeped through the logs and, bit by bit, encased the original wood tissues with silica deposits. Slowly, the silica crystallized into quartz, and the logs were preserved as petrified wood. Minerals and impurities, which were deposited while the wood was petrifying, added the bright colors and interesting patterns.

That was about 225 million years ago, in the late Triassic Period. After that time, the area sank, flooded, and was covered with freshwater sediments. Later, the area was lifted far above sea level, and this uplift created stresses that cracked the giant logs.

In recent geological time, wind and water wore away the layers of hardened sediments. Now, the petrified logs, plus fossilized animal and plant remains, are exposed on the land's surface. Wind and water continue to remove sediments, break down the giant logs that lie exposed, and reach for the logs and other remaining fossils still buried below the surface.

Trail (½-mile loop) leads to the remains of a 100-room ancient Indian pueblo. The Crystal Forest Trail (.8-mile loop) includes the petrified remains of trees that once hid large amounts of beautiful smoky quartz, clear quartz, and purple amethyst crystals. In the late 1800s, before the establishment of the park, profit-seekers dynamited many logs in search of these gems. Long Logs (.6-mile loop) leads through the largest concentration of petrified wood in the park. The logs here lie across each other in a log-jam type of formation. The trail is open for only limited hours, so check the day's schedule at the visitor center or entrance station.

PIPE SPRING NATIONAL MONUMENT

130 miles northwest of Flagstaff; 150 miles northeast of Las Vegas, NV.

HC 65
Box 5
Fredonia, AZ 86022
520-643-7105
http://www.nps.gov/pisp

Zion Natural History Association. (Zion National Park, Springdale, UT 84767; 801-772-3264)

In the dry Arizona landscape, Pipe Spring's free-flowing water has attracted travelers and settlers for centuries. Basketmaker and Pueblo Indians lived near the spring more than 1,000 years ago. Later, other Indians lived in the area. By the 1860s, Mormons were ranching here. It is now a monument to western pioneer life. The historic structures, including an impressive fort built in the 1870s, were made of native sandstone, trees, and earth. Pioneer life is also reflected in the furnishings, tools, and possessions now on exhibit.

PRESCOTT NATIONAL FOREST

70 miles northwest of Phoenix; 70 miles southwest of Flagstaff. The town of Prescott is located on the northern border of the forest.

344 South Cortez Street
Prescott, AZ 86303-4398
520-771-4700
http://www.sedona.net/vvcenter

Arizona Natural History Association. (Box 1633, Flagstaff, AZ 86002; 520-527-3450)

Grief Hill, Yellowjacket Gulch, Lonesome Pocket, Blind Indian Creek, Battle Flat, and Horsethief Basin—the names tell the story of the harsh times in this area of the frontier. Although portions of the forest are much the same as they were when Sam Miller searched for gold in Lynx Creek and was wounded by a wildcat, there are plenty of opportunities to camp, fish, hike, and ride. Pleasant daytime winter temperatures allow visitors to enjoy the forest year-round.

Sam's Tips

- Travel in the wilderness is limited to hiking or horseback riding. Granite Mountain Wilderness is the most popular area both because of its proximity to Prescott—only 20 minutes away, on a paved road—and because it offers hiking among huge granite boulders and rock formations, and an outstanding view of the surrounding area from the top of Granite Mountain.

CAMPING ON BLM LANDS

Most of the public lands in the Western states offer the chance to camp near natural, scenic, and historical resources. Contact the BLM office nearest your destination for more information. Reservations are not usually required, but fees are charged at some sites. The National Park Service Golden Age Passport and Golden Access Passport entitle the holder to use BLM campgrounds for half the usual fee.

RAINBOW BRIDGE NATIONAL MONUMENT

150 miles north of Flagstaff.

c/o Glen Canyon National Recreation Area
Box 1507
Page, AZ 86040
520-608-6404
http://www.nps.gov/rabr

Glen Canyon Natural History Association. (PO Box 581, Page, AZ 86040; 520-645-3532)

Rainbow Bridge, the world's largest natural bridge, is considered a sacred place by many Native Americans. Carved by a stream winding toward the Colorado River, it arches to a height of 290 feet and sits nestled among canyons. The arch is 42 feet thick and 33 feet wide at the top. Afternoon sunlight makes the sandstone and reddish-brown colors at the base especially brilliant. Most people travel by water to the site and then follow one of the two trails to the bridge. Both trails begin on the Navajo Nation. For the required hiking permits, contact the park (see above).

Sam's Tips

- Rainbow Bridge is approximately 50 miles by boat from Wahweap, Bullfrog, or Halls Crossing, Utah. From the courtesy dock landing in Bridge Canyon, the bridge is a half-mile walk along a moderate trail.
- The park's concessionaire, Aramark, has boat tours daily from May to September, and intermittently in other months. For further information, call 800-528-6154.
- If you want to use your own boat, launch ramps and marinas with boating and camping supplies are available at Wahweap, Halls Crossing, Bullfrog,

Respect for Tradition

To the five neighboring nations (Navajo, Hopi, San Juan Southern Paiute, White Mesa Ute, and Kaibab Paiute), Rainbow Bridge is a sacred religious site. They travel to Rainbow Bridge to leave prayers and offerings nearby. Special prayers are said before passing beneath the bridge because neglecting them might bring misfortune or hardship.

Both hiking trails traverse the Navajo Nation. The National Park Service asks that visitors respect the land and the privacy of the people living there. In previous years, visitors have walked under Rainbow Bridge. Out of respect for Indian beliefs, they are now asked to stay on the trail, avoid walking beyond the viewing area at the end of the trail, and enjoy Rainbow Bridge silently.

and Hite. Dangling Rope, 10 miles northwest of Rainbow Bridge, is the closest marina.

- You can reach the bridge via two foot trails: from Navajo Mountain Trading Post, 14 miles, and from abandoned Rainbow Lodge, 13 miles. Required permits and detailed information on routes, water sources, and supplies may be obtained from the Navajo Nation, Recreational Resources Department, Box 9000, Window Rock, AZ 86515.

SAGUARO NATIONAL PARK

The park has two locations; each is 12 miles to the west or east of Tucson.

3693 South Old Spanish Trail
Tucson, AZ 85730-5699
520-733-5158 (Saguaro West)
520-733-5153 (Saguaro East)
http://www.nps.gov/sagu

 **Southwest Parks and Monuments Association.** (221 North Court Avenue, Tucson, AZ 85701; 520-622-1999)

Saguaro are the largest cacti in the United States. The big, numerous flowers on these cacti bloom and color the desert in late April, May, and June, but the giant cacti are perhaps best known for the eerie human shapes they assume. The park is divided into two sections: east and west. Saguaro East encompasses an aging saguaro forest and other desert communities at the foot of the majestic Rincon Mountains. Saguaro West embraces a wide variety of Sonora Desert life against a backdrop of the rugged Tucson Mountains.

Sam's Tips

- The Saguaro wilderness has more than 100 miles of trail open to horses and pack animals.

The Life of the Saguaro

A single saguaro cactus produces tens of thousands of seeds in a year, and as many as 40 million in a lifetime of 175 to 200 years, but out of all the seeds that a saguaro produces in its life, probably only one will survive to adulthood.

A Saguaro's growth is extremely slow. At the end of a year, a seedling may measure only ¼ inch. After 15 years, it may be barely a foot tall. At about 30 years, the cactus flowers and produces fruit. By 50 years, it can be as tall as 7 feet. After about 75 years, it may sprout its first branches, or "arms." The branches begin as prickly balls and then extend outward and upward. By 100 years, the saguaro can be as tall as 25 feet. Those that live 150 years or more attain the grandest sizes, towering as high as 50 feet and weighing 8 tons or more.

- Places of interest near Saguaro West include the Arizona–Sonora Desert Museum and its live collection of about 200 desert animals and 300 kinds of plants. To the south, Tucson Mountain County Park has hiking, horse trails, and campgrounds. Kitt Peak National Observatory, 45 miles to the west, has the largest collection of optical telescopes in the world.
- Places of interest near Saguaro East include Coronado National Forest (see entry), which has campgrounds, hiking trails, and picnic areas and Colossal Cave.
- Parents should ask about the Junior Ranger Discovery Pack Program, which allows children to borrow such items as field guides, binoculars, and a magnifying glass, to help them complete a series of fun activities and increase their appreciation of the park.

SUNSET CRATER VOLCANO NATIONAL MONUMENT

15 miles northeast of Flagstaff.

Route 3
Box 149
Flagstaff, AZ 86004
520-526-0502
http://www.nps.gov/sucr

Southwest Parks and Monuments Association. (221 North Court Avenue, Tucson, AZ 85701; 520-622-1999)

The eruption of Sunset Crater Volcano, in the year 1065, blanketed the region with black cinder. Today, the volcano's rim of red and yellow cinders, and the lava flows near the cone have cooled and hardened to a jagged surface. Squeeze-ups and spatter-cones are just two of the fascinating volcanic features you'll encounter while exploring the park.

Sam's Tips

- There is no camping in the Monument. Bonito Campground, operated by the U.S. Forest Service, is located across from the Visitor Center and is generally open from late May through mid-October. Overnight accommodations, food, supplies, and gasoline are available in Flagstaff, about 15 miles away.
- Nearby attractions include Walnut Canyon National Monument and Wupatki National Monument (see entries).

THE TEN ESSENTIALS FOR GOING INTO A WILDERNESS AREA

As provided by the Southwestern National Forests:

1. *Motivation*—a reason for traveling, and reasons for wanting to get out again.
2. *Physical conditioning*—general good health, and preparation matched to what you plan to do.
3. *Knowledge of the area*—acquired through prior study of maps and information on terrain, distances, hazards, and so on.
4. *Basic outdoors skills*—how to hike, orient oneself, make a fire, cook, maintain warmth, and similar activity.
5. *Mature judgment*—the ability to decide what is important and what is not, to weigh alternatives and handle emergencies.
6. *Adaptability*—the ability to "make-do," improvise, and alter plans constructively when necessary.
7. *Outside contact*—someone who knows your plans and can send help if you are overdue because of accident or other problems.
8. *Adequate clothing*—sturdy, comfortable clothing suitable for the conditions, plus extra items for unforeseen necessary changes.
9. *Food*—simple, nutritious, and sufficient for the trip.
10. *Minimal equipment*—that which is necessary for carrying, cooking, sleeping, shelter, and personal health and safety.

TONTO NATIONAL FOREST

The park begins 25 miles either north or east of Phoenix.

2324 East McDowell
Phoenix, AZ 85006
602-225-5200
http://www.fs.fed.us

One of the largest national forests in America, the Tonto covers nearly 3 million acres of rugged, scenic landscapes ranging from cactus-studded desert to pine-covered mountains. (Zane Grey fans will recall the forest setting from the bestselling author's classic, *Under the Tonto Rim*.) Recreational opportunities abound on the forest's rivers, lakes, and trout streams. You can take horseback camping trips or boat camp at a remote spot on the shore of one of the reservoirs.

Sam's Tips

- The Apache Trail National Forest Scenic Byway runs from Apache Junction, east of Phoenix, to Roosevelt Lake in the heart of the forest.

- Shoofly Village, a Hohokam and Salado Indian village built around 1000 A.D., is northeast of Payson in the northern part of the forest. The ruins contain 87 rooms and many courtyards in a 4-acre area surrounded by a compound wall.

TONTO NATIONAL MONUMENT

75 miles east of Phoenix.

HC 02
Box 4602
Roosevelt, AZ 85545
520-467-2241
http://www.nps.gov/tont

Southwest Parks and Monuments Association. (221 North Court Avenue, Tucson, AZ 85701; 520-622-1999)

Shallow caves overlooking the Tonto Basin shelter masonry ruins nearly 700 years old. This was home to the prehistoric Salado people, who made their living here as farmers for two centuries. Bonding rocks with mud, the Salado built apartment-style dwellings in hillside alcoves. The pueblo now called the Lower Ruin consisted of 16 ground-floor rooms, 3 of which had a second story. Next to this was the 12-room annex. The Upper Ruin, located on a nearby ridge, was much larger—32 ground-floor rooms, 8 with a second story. Terraces and rooftops provided level, open space for work and play. The surrounding topography—a river valley surrounded by steep slopes rising some 2,000 feet—created different local environments, each with its own community of wildlife. For unknown reasons, the Salado left the Basin between 1400 and 1450.

SAM'S TIPS

- To see the Salado cliff dwellings up close, climb the half-mile foot trail that runs 350 vertical feet to the Lower Ruin. Allow about an hour for the round-trip walk. Visits to the Upper Ruin are by guided tour only, November through April. Call the park for reservations.
- The Monument is near Roosevelt Lake and the Tonto National Forest.

TUMACACORI NATIONAL HISTORICAL PARK

The main unit is 45 miles south of Tucson and 16 miles north of Nogales, on the United States–Mexico border.

Box 67
Tumacacori, AZ 85640
520-398-2341
http://www.nps.gov/tuma

Southwest Parks and Monuments Association. (221 North Court Avenue, Tucson, AZ 85701; 520-622-1999)

Three early Spanish colonial missions, begun by Jesuits in 1691, have been reunited to form the Tumacacori National Historical Park. The history of these missions is a sad one; all three of them suffered from the circumstances of the time. First were the hardships of frontier life, including Apache raids and the disruption of the Mexican-American war. The missions also fell victim to Old World diseases, such as smallpox and measles. Today, the most extensive remains of the religious colonies are those of the mission church of San José de Tumacacori. The self-guided walking tour includes an associated cemetery and mortuary chapel. The ancient patio garden displays plants of the mission period. Other ruins include some still-standing walls of Calabazas, and the remains of the church of Guevavi though these sites are not open to the public.

Sam's Tips

- The Tubac Presidio State Historic Park 40 miles north of Tumacacori has a museum, exhibits, and an underground archaeological display. San Xavier del Bac, an active Franciscan mission on the outskirts of Tucson, is one of the finest examples of Spanish colonial architecture in the United States. Self-guided tours are available year-round. Call 520-294-2624 for information.
- The Tumacacori Fiesta is held on the first Sunday in December. Visitors can see crafts and ceremonial dances, and sample the foods of the Tohono O'odham, Yaqui, Apache, Mexican, and Southwest cultures. A historic high Mass, sung in Latin and Pimean, is held in April and October; all Mass attendees must be dressed in period costumes. Call the park for reservations.
- The first section of the Juan Bautista de Anza National Historic Trail open to the public begins near the northwest corner of Tumacacori National Historical Park. It commemorates the historic Anza colonizing expedition from Culiacan, Mexico, to San Francisco in 1775–1776.

TUZIGOOT NATIONAL MONUMENT

65 miles south of Flagstaff; 90 miles north of Phoenix.

Box 219
Camp Verde, AZ 86322
520-634-5564
http://www.nps.gov/tuzi

Southwest Parks and Monuments Association. (221 North Court Avenue, Tucson, AZ 85701; 520-622-1999)

Tuzigoot, the remnants of one of the largest pueblos built by the Sinagua Indians, lies on a ridge high above the Verde River. An Apache word meaning "crooked water," Tuzigoot was built between the period 1100 to 1400 and consisted of 2 stories and 110 rooms. The structure and other sites in the area provided shelter for hundreds of occupants. The Visitor Center maintains collections of Sinaguan artifacts in Arizona.

WALNUT CANYON NATIONAL MONUMENT

15 miles northeast of Flagstaff.

Walnut Canyon Road
Flagstaff, Arizona 86004-9705
520-526-3367
http://www.nps.gov/waca

Southwest Parks and Monuments Association. (221 North Court Avenue, Tucson, AZ 85701; 520-622-1999)

For 600 years, the cliff dwellings here apparently stood deserted, undisturbed, and unknown; the earliest report of them appeared in 1883. Until the National Park Service took the dwellings over in 1933, vandals removed much of the cultural material that had been left by the Sinagua, and even damaged and defaced the dwellings themselves. Our present understanding of the sites is largely derived from investigation of other sites. The scattered cliff dwellings and rim-top sites were linked by a system of trails, most of which are now obscured by vegetation.

SAM'S TIPS

- The Island Trail, a paved mile-long foot trail, leads to 25 of the cliff dwelling rooms.
- Much can be seen from the rim of the canyon, along the short and fairly level Rim Trail, which is accessible by wheelchair (with help) and offers a view of the canyon and ruins from two overlooks. An excavated pit house and above-ground pueblo lie along the Rim Trail.
- In the summer, the Park Service offers daily talks on the Rim Trail every day at 2 P.M. Also, during the summer months, ranger-guided walks into rugged

The Sinagua

Sometime before 600 A.D., groups of people from southeastern Arizona set out for the area east of San Francisco Peaks. There they established permanent settlements and made their living by hunting and gathering and farming. These were the people now called the Sinagua—Spanish for "without water"—named for the high desert region they inhabited. As time went on, scattered families united into villages. Walnut Canyon became an important community between about 1125 and 1250. The homes we see today beneath the canyon's limestone overhangs were built during this period, when Sinagua culture flourished.

The Sinagua lived in Walnut Canyon for almost 150 years, before vacating their homes. Drought, depleted soil, warfare, or disease may have caused them to leave the canyon. Anthropologists believe that their descendants live today among the Hopi Indians of northeastern Arizona, whose villages date from 1000 A.D.

terrain off the designated trail are offered. These ranger-guided walks are strenuous and require reservations.

- Other sites of interest in the area include Wupatki National Monument and Sunset Crater Volcano National Monument (see entries).

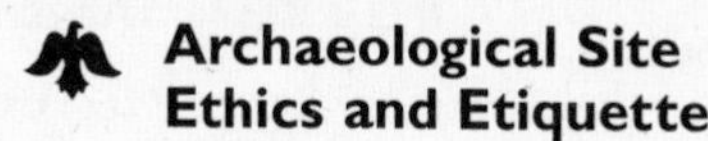

Archaeological Site Ethics and Etiquette

The rules for visiting archaeological sites like Wupatki are dictated mostly by common sense. As when exploring a museum full of rare, fragile, and priceless objects, watch where you step and sit, and what you touch. Stepping in, around, or on rock walls or other masonry accelerates their destruction. Don't disturb artifacts; once moved and taken out of context, they lose much of their ability to help explain the past and may even lead to false conclusions.

WUPATKI NATIONAL MONUMENT

35 miles northeast of Flagstaff, off Highway 89.

HC 33
Box 444A
Flagstaff, AZ 86004
520-679-2365
http://www.nps.gov/wupa

Southwest Parks and Monuments Association. (221 North Court Avenue, Tucson, AZ 85701; 520-622-1999)

Ruins of red sandstone pueblos built by farming Indians about 1120 A.D. are preserved at Wupatki National Monument. The modern Hopi Indians are believed to be partly descended from these people. Wupatki (wu-POT-ki) is a Hopi word that means "tall house." Wupatki Pueblo is the largest in the monument—it had approximately 100 rooms. Ruins here also include Wukoki, which means "big house"; Box Canyon Ruin, named for the narrow canyon rim on which it rests; and Lomaki, the "beautiful house" ruins.

Sam's Tips

- You can visit both Wupatki and Sunset Crater Volcano National Monuments by driving the 35-mile loop road that meets Highway 89 at both ends.
- Overnight camping is not allowed in the monument, but forest service campgrounds are near the Sunset Crater Visitor Center.

Points of Interest

U.S. ARMY CORPS OF ENGINEERS

ALAMO LAKE
One of the best lakes for bass fishing in Arizona. North of Wenden, off I-10.

PAINTED ROCK DAM
Famous for rockhounds. Painted Rock Park is nearby. From Gila Bend, 30 miles west via I-8 and Painted Rock Road.

BUREAU OF LAND MANAGEMENT

HISTORIC ROUTE 66 BACK COUNTRY BYWAY

"Get your kicks on Route 66" has echoed for decades across America, and Arizona showcases 42 miles of the "Mother Road" from Kingman to Topock at the California border and the Colorado River. Visit the old gold mining town of Oatman and the tristate overlook.

5 miles south of Kingman, Arizona
Kingman Resource Area, 520-757-3161

HOT WELL DUNES

An oil-drilling operation in 1928 hit water instead of oil, and the 106°F artesian well has been flowing ever since. Rolling mesquite and creosote-studded sand dunes stretch out in all directions around the hot well, making the area extremely popular with off-highway vehicle users. Small cattail-lined ponds provide habitat for fish and wildlife. Camping, picnicking, and hunting are all nearby. The site is open year-round, but summers can be extremely hot.

32 miles northeast of Safford, Arizona
San Simon Resource Area, 520-428-4040

PAINTED ROCKS RECREATION AREA

The Gila River winds through this rugged volcanic region. The Mormon Battalion Trail and the Butterfield Stage Route run through the campground. Mountain biking, off-highway vehicle trails, hiking, and bird watching are popular activities in the area.

30 miles northwest of Gila Bend
Lower Gila Resource Area, 602-780-8090

For more information on these and other Bureau of Land Management sites in Arizona, contact:

Arizona State Office
3707 North 7th Street
PO Box 16563
Phoenix, AZ 85011
602-650-0500
http://www.az.blm.gov

NEVADA

GREAT BASIN NATIONAL PARK

385 miles southeast of Reno; 286 miles northeast of Las Vegas.

Baker, Nevada 89311
702-234-7270
Fax: 702-234-7331
http://www.nps.gov/grba

 **Great Basin Natural History Association.** (Baker, NV 89311; 702-234-7270)

Located near the Utah–Nevada border, the Great Basin National Park is part of the Great Basin—a vast region of sagebrush-covered valleys and narrow mountain ranges that sweeps across Nevada from the Wasatch Mountains of Utah to California's Sierra Nevada. The South Snake mountain range is often called a desert island because a rich variety of plants and animals that could not survive in the lower desert live in the higher elevations. The park includes streams, lakes, a small glacier, a stone arch, golden eagles, alpine plants, and a variety of forest types, including groves of ancient, twisted bristlecone pines.

CAVES AND CAVERNS EVERYWHERE

Did you know that the National Park Service has eight areas designated specifically to protect limestone or marble caves? Each NPS cave system protects a unique underground ecosystem that provides an incomparable wilderness experience to visitors.

The National Park Service caves are:

1. Carlsbad Caverns National Park (NM)
2. Great Basin National Park (NV)
3. Jewel Cave National Park (KY)
4. Mammoth Cave National Park (KY)
5. Oregon Caves National Monument (OR)
6. Russell Cave National Monument (AL)
7. Timpanogos Cave National Monument (UT)
8. Wind Cave National Park (SD)

Several other National Park Service areas, although not designated specifically for caves, do contain caverns—for example, Crystal Cave in Sequoia National Park (CA). Other areas contain lava tube caves like those found at Lava Beds National Monument (CA). Of all the National Park Service areas, nearly one in seven contains a cave or rock shelter.

It also includes numerous limestone caverns, including Lehman Caves, among the most richly decorated caves in the country, on the eastern flank of Wheeler Peak.

Sam's Tips

- During the spring, summer, and fall, rangers lead programs such as patio talks, activities for children, and evening campfire programs. A limited number of advance tickets are available each day for various programs. Also, *The Bristle Cone,* published yearly, provides information on events, tour times, and educational programs.
- Wheeler Peak, the second highest peak in Nevada, reaches 13,063 feet. The Wheeler Peak Scenic Drive starts at the Visitor Center and goes to the Wheeler Peak Campground, gaining 3,400 feet in elevation along the way.
- About 18 miles south of the Visitor Center is 6-story Lexington Arch. Getting there can be half the fun. Drive west 12 miles on a gravel road just off Utah State Highway 21. Then continue on a strenuous 1-mile hike up an obscure trail to the arch. Check at the Visitor Center for detailed directions and road conditions.

RUSTIC CABINS IN NEVADA

Nevada's Humboldt and Toiyabe National Forests offer nightly lodging in three rustic guard stations. These cabins are out-of-the-way gems, located in the middle of some of America's most pristine lands.

Most are accessible via narrow, winding, dirt or gravel roads, or, in winter, by snowmobile or cross-country skis. Facilities are spartan: a table, chairs, wood stove and bunks (some with mattresses, some without). You might need to bring your own drinking water and cut your own firewood. Expect to use outdoor privies, and don't expect a telephone.

These cabins can be a remarkable place to stay amidst Nevada's beautiful National Forests. Prices range between $15 and $30 a night, and cabins house as few as four or as many as ten or more guests. Call for more information and to make reservations, which are required.

Mountain City Ranger District (year-round)
405 Davidson Street
Mountain City, NV 89831
702-763-6691

Jarbidge Ranger District (year-round)
1008 Burley Avenue
Buhl, ID 83316
208-543-4129

HUMBOLDT NATIONAL FOREST

220 miles northeast of Reno; 310 miles north of Las Vegas.

2035 Last Chance Road
Elko, NV 89801
702-738-5171
http://www.fs.fed.us/htnf

Named for the German naturalist Alexander Von Humboldt, this National Forest has 9 separate divisions covering 2.5 million acres. The lower elevations of sagebrush-dominated rangelands give way to alpine meadows and sparkling streams in the upper reaches. The forest contains 8 wilderness areas and the Lamoille Canyon Scenic Area, which extends to the top of the Ruby Mountains and is marked by glaciated canyons, towering peaks, and beautiful crystal-clear alpine lakes.

LAKE MEAD NATIONAL RECREATION AREA

25 miles southeast of Las Vegas.

601 Nevada Highway
Boulder City, NV 89005-2426
702-293-8990
http://www.nps.gov/lame

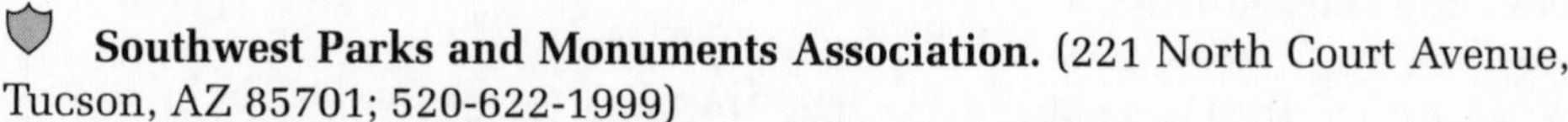

Southwest Parks and Monuments Association. (221 North Court Avenue, Tucson, AZ 85701; 520-622-1999)

Lake Mead National Recreation Area boasts a startling contrast of desert and water, mountains and canyons, primitive back country and modern technology (the Hoover Dam). In one of the hottest, driest regions on Earth, two huge lakes—Lake Mead and Lake Mohave combined are twice the size of Rhode Island—are centerpieces of the country's first national recreation area.

Sam's Tips

- Lake Mead and Lake Mohave feature 9 marinas that rent boats ranging from personal watercraft to houseboats. Water enthusiasts will enjoy swimming, boating, rafting, fishing, canoeing, and kayaking.
- Seven-eighths of the Recreation Area protects a vast area of the eastern Mohave Desert. The best way to explore is on foot, traveling across open expanses of rock formations that contain all the colors of the rainbow. The best season for hiking is November through March, when the temperatures are cooler. Summer temperatures reach 120°F in the shade.
- The Railroad Hiking Trail takes you past the only remaining section of the Hoover Dam Railroad that is not under water. The trail passes through five

tunnels. A portion of the track was used in the motion picture *The Gauntlet,* starring Clint Eastwood.

- Nearby visitor attractions include the Hoover Dam, the Grand Canyon Caverns, and Oatman, a historic mining town. The Grand Canyon is approximately 200 miles away.

From Mead to Mexico: Exploring the Lower Colorado River

Millions of people every year play in the Colorado River's cool waters, hunt and fish from its banks, camp on adjacent lands, hike up nearby mountains, and explore historic sites. The River, its lands, and wildlife are carefully preserved and managed by a number of federal agencies working under the auspices of the Department of Interior. Some of these agencies, and their addresses in this region, are:

- **The Bureau of Land Management** administers land for camping, fishing, hunting, boating, wildlife observation, and many other recreational activities. Contact: Bureau of Land Management, Arizona State Office, Siete Square Building, 3707 North 7th Street, Phoenix, AZ 85014; 602-943-2279.
- **The U.S. Fish and Wildlife Service** administers four refuges and one fish hatchery. Activities include wildlife observation, hunting, fishing, and hiking. The Imperial National Wildlife Refuge offers hunting for ducks, geese, cottontail rabbit, dove, gambell's quail, and deer, as well as nature photography of migrating waterfowl on backwater lakes. For more information, contact: U.S. Fish and Wildlife Service, Refuges and Wildlife, Region 2, PO Box 1306, Albuquerque, NM 87103.
- **The Bureau of Reclamation** maintains numerous facilities for the delivery of water to irrigation districts, municipal users, and other customers. Facilities include dams, canal systems, and pumping and processing plants. Activities include tours of facilities, boating and canoeing, fishing, and nature observation. Contact the Bureau of Reclamation, Lower Colorado Regional Office, Box 61470, Boulder City, NV 89006-1470; 702-293-8419.
- **The National Park Service** administers Lake Mead National Recreation Area, which includes Lake Mohave, and oversees a comprehensive visitor services program. NPS concessionaires on Lakes Mead and Mohave rent boats and houseboats and operate resorts that may include marinas, RV parks, stores, food services, and motels. Recreation within the 1.5-million-acre park includes day use and overnight camping along 700 miles of shore; boating, swimming, sailing, and fishing; back-country driving on unimproved roads; hiking. Hunting and trapping are permitted in most areas. For more information, contact the National Park Service, Lake Mead NRA, 601 Nevada Highway, Boulder City, NV 89005; 702-293-8906.

TOIYABE NATIONAL FOREST

5 miles east of Reno; 330 miles northwest of Las Vegas.

1200 Franklin Way
Sparks, NV 89431
702-331-6444
http://www.fs.fed.us/htnf

Eastern Sierra Interpretive Association. (PO Box 1008, Lone Pine, CA 93545; 619-876-5324)

The largest forest outside of Alaska, the mountainous Toiyabe National Forest contains approximately 4 million acres and is divided into 5 districts. Popular activities in the forest include camping, hiking, fishing, hunting, skiing, canoeing, and horseback riding.

POINT OF INTEREST

BUREAU OF RECLAMATION

HOOVER DAM

Since its completion in 1935, the Hoover Dam has been the tallest concrete dam in the United States. During its construction, enough concrete was used to pave a standard sidewalk all the way around the equator. Guided tours of the dam and the power plant are offered daily from 8:45 A.M. to 5:45 P.M. Tours venture 520 feet into the solid andesite canyon wall to view the inner workings of the 2,000-megawatt hydroelectric power plant. There are more than 5 miles of tunnels, and 2 wings, each 650 feet long and 8 stories high. Hoover Dam's electrical output is primarily used by California; the remainder is divided between Arizona and Nevada. The plant generates less than 5 percent of Las Vegas's electricity.

Bureau of Reclamation
Lower Colorado Field Office
PO Box 61470
Boulder City, NV 89006
http://www.hooverdam.com

NEW MEXICO

AZTEC RUINS NATIONAL MONUMENT

118 miles northwest of Santa Fe.

PO Box 640
Aztec, NM 87410-0640
505-334-6174
http://www.nps.gov/azru

Southwest Parks and Monuments Association. (221 North Court Avenue, Tucson, AZ 85701; 520-622-1999)

Despite the name, the buildings and structures at Aztec Ruins National Monument were not built by the Aztecs of central Mexico. The Aztecs lived centuries after the rise and fall of this ancestral Puebloan town, but, inspired by popular histories of Cortes's conquest of Mexico, early Anglo settlers dubbed the site Aztec, and the town took its name from the ruins. The monument is remarkable for its wealth of archaeological remains concentrated in a small area. Besides the mammoth West Ruin and the enigmatic Hubbard triwall site, there are remnants of many buildings, roads, and kivas on nearby river terraces and bottomlands.

BANDELIER NATIONAL MONUMENT

12 miles southeast of Los Alamos; 47 miles northwest of Santa Fe.

HCR 1
Box 1, Suite 15
Los Alamos, NM 87544
505-672-0343
http://www.nps.gov/band

Southwest Parks and Monuments Association. (221 North Court Avenue, Tucson, AZ 85701; 520-622-1999)

Named for Adolph Francis Bandelier, the first scholar to study and report on the archaeological sites of the ancestral Pueblo people in Frijoles Canyon, this monument is filled with rich history of native civilization. On the canyon-slashed slopes and canyon bottoms of the Pajarito Plateau are the remains of cliff houses and other dwellings of 12th- to 16th-century Pueblo Indians. The Frijoles Canyon Visitor Center has a 10-minute introductory slide program, plus exhibits on prehistoric and historic Pueblo culture. There is a science museum dedicated to the development of the atomic bomb in nearby Los Alamos.

Sam's Tips

- The detached Tsankawi section of the monument is 11 miles north of Frijoles Canyon on NM 4. This large unexcavated site, situated on a high mesa, provides sweeping views of the Rio Grande Valley, the Sangre de Cristo Mountains to the east, and the Jemez Mountains to the west. A 2-mile trail leads from the highway on a circular route through the prehistoric village.
- Bandelier contains 23,267 acres of designated wilderness with 70 miles of back-country trails. Permits, free of charge, are required for all overnight travel into the backcountry. The Dome Fire of April 1996 affected almost 5,000 acres in the park and almost 12,000 acres outside the west boundary. Portions of the monument may be closed due to fire damage.

CAPULIN VOLCANO NATIONAL MONUMENT

200 miles northeast of Santa Fe; 260 miles northeast of Albuquerque.

PO Box 40
Capulin, NM 88414
505-278-2201
http://www.nps.gov/cavo

Southwest Parks and Monuments Association. (221 North Court Avenue, Tucson, AZ 85701; 520-622-1999)

Have you ever wanted to walk into a volcano? Capulin Volcano National Monument is one of the few places in the world where you can do just that. A trail goes to the vent area at the bottom of the crater of a volcano active 50,000 to 60,000 years ago. Evidence of activity can be seen in the scores of nearby hills: every peak you see around Capulin was once an active volcano. The symmetry of Capulin Volcano was preserved because lava did not flow from the main crater but from a fissure located near the western base of the cone. Cinder cones do not erupt again after they are extinct; therefore, Capulin should not erupt again.

Bats

As part of the mammal family, bat "pups" are born, not hatched. And pups don't need a nest—they hang upside down. Contrary to popular perception, bats are not blind; in fact, in low-light situations, they can see much better than humans. Of 1,000 species of bats worldwide, only three kinds use blood for food (none of these types live in the United States) and none have fangs. All bats that live in Bandelier (and in New Mexico) are insect eaters. The bats can catch up to 500 insects an hour, and many prefer such unpopular creatures as moths and mosquitoes. There is a maternity colony located right above the main trail; the bats are usually there from late May to mid-September.

CARLSBAD CAVERNS NATIONAL PARK

150 miles northeast of El Paso, Texas.

3225 National Parks Highway
Carlsbad, NM 88220
505-785-2232
http://www.nps.gov/cave

Carlsbad Caverns–Guadalupe Mountains Association. (PO Box 1417, Carlsbad, NM 88221-1417; 505-785-2322, ext. 483)

Lechugilla Cave

In June 1984, a group of Colorado cavers requested permission from the National Park Service to do some limited excavating to see if an airflow that was first noticed in the 1950s was coming from a hidden cave. Exploration began and, by the end of 1987, the cave was measured at 37,500 feet long and 1,501 feet deep. As of July 1995, the cave was explored to 85.75 miles and 1,567 feet. The cave, which provides the only known transversable cross section through one of the world's largest Permian Age fossil reefs, is one of the most physically demanding wild caves in the United States, beginning with a 90-foot vertical drop at its entrance. Only individuals who are extremely proficient in vertical caving skills and are in top physical condition are allowed to join expeditions.

The park's highlight, Carlsbad Cavern, features one of the world's largest subterranean chambers and many colorful, complex cave formations. The cavern and numerous other nearby caves were originally part of a Permian Age fossil reef, formed as a result of erosion and evaporation. Now, they are filled with million-year-old stalagmites, stalactites, flowstone formations, crystal-clear Mirror Lake, and the Bottomless Pit, a black hole 140 feet deep. Carlsbad Cavern also offers two modern-day surprises—an underground lunchroom and an elevator back to the surface. In addition to ranger-guided cave tours, other popular activities in the park include attending evening bat-flight programs and exhibits on animals, geology, history, and caves.

Sam's Tips

- You can become a "new bat parent" and support the park at the same time. Adoptive parents will receive an official certificate, educational information, a bat photograph, and a bumper sticker. Proceeds from the Adopt-A-Bat program benefit educational programs and research projects within the park.
- An amphitheater at the natural entrance just east of the Visitor Center is used for evening bat-flight programs during the summer and for other special events. Recently, cave swallows have joined the nightly show, setting the stage for the entrance of more than 250,000 Mexican free-tailed bats.
- The cavern temperature is a constant 56°F, so a light jacket or sweater is recommended for the trip. Also recommended is a pair of good walking shoes with rubber soles. Open-toed shoes, plastic soles, or high heels are not safe on the steep and wet cavern trails.
- Slaughter Canyon Cave (formerly New Cave) is one of the more spectacular sites within the park. Visitors can join park rangers on a flashlight tour, but be aware that to reach the cave you have to climb 500 feet in one half-mile, equivalent to ascending a 50-story building.

CARSON NATIONAL FOREST

45 miles northeast of Santa Fe; 100 miles northeast of Albuquerque.

208 Cruz Alta Road
Taos, NM 87571
505-758-6200
http://www.laplaza.org/gov/fed/carson

Spanning 1.5 million acres of north central New Mexico, the Carson National Forest features high desert grasslands, Ponderosa pine and spruce fir forests,

DO YOU THINK BATS ARE YUCKY?

You may be surprised to know that bats are among the gentlest, most benign animals on earth. They are the primary predators of vast numbers of insect pests that cost farmers and foresters billions of dollars annually. Bats also pollinate flowers and disperse the seeds that make the rain forests grow and the deserts bloom. Consider these bat facts:

- A single little brown bat can catch and devour 600 mosquitoes in just 1 hour.
- A colony of 150 big brown bats can eat 18 million cucumber beetles to protect local farmers from the beetles' rootwork larva each summer.
- The 20 million Mexican free-tails from Bracken Cave, TX, eat 250 tons of insects nightly.
- Tequila is produced from agave plants whose seed production drops to 1/3,000th of normal without bat pollinators.
- Bat droppings in caves support entire ecosystems of unique organisms, including bacteria useful in detoxifying wastes, improving detergents, and producing gasohol and antibiotics.

Bats are in serious decline. Of the 43 species living in the United States and Canada, nearly 40 percent are endangered or are candidates for that status. Bats and their ecosystems must be properly managed and protected. The Bureau of Land Management, the U.S. Forest Service, and the Bat Conservation International have joined forces to conserve bats, their habitats, and the ecosystems they support. If you would like to learn more about bats, contact the U.S. Forest Service, the Bureau of Land Management, or the Bat Conservation International National Headquarters, PO Box 162603, Austin, TX 78716; 512-327-9721.

alpine meadows, and sagebrush mesas, as well as rich cultural, historical, and archaeological resources. The Pot Creek Cultural Site and the Taos Pueblo are both testimonies to the fact that this land has been continuously occupied by Native Americans for more than 9,000 years.

CHACO CULTURE NATIONAL HISTORICAL PARK

130 miles northwest of Santa Fe; 120 miles northwest of Albuquerque.

PO Box 220
Nageezi, NM 87037
505-786-7014
http://www.nps.gov/chcu

 **Southwest Parks and Monuments Association.** (221 North Court Avenue, Tucson, AZ 85701; 520-622-1999)

Chaco Pottery

Using ceramic analysis to identify the temper in the pottery, archaeologists can determine where an object was created. They also learn a lot just by studying the pottery's designs. The pottery in the Chaco Canyon suggests a settled lifestyle. It is heavy, fragile, and not easily moved. Moreover, agriculture encourages a settled lifestyle, which influences the building of permanent structures and the creation of ceramics.

Chaco Canyon was the center of life for the Anasazi, who farmed the land and built towns connected by a wide-ranging network of roads. By 1000 A.D., Chaco had become the political, religious, and economic center of the San Juan Basin. As many as 5,000 persons lived in some 400 settlements in and around the area. A new masonry technique—the use of masonry walls with rubble cores and shaped stones—allowed walls to rise more than 4 stories high. Some large buildings show signs of being planned from the start, in contrast to the usual Anasazi custom of adding rooms as needed. The decline of Chaco possibly coincided with a prolonged drought in the San Juan Basin between 1130 and 1180, but as the people began drifting away, they left behind impressive evidence of their former influence. The best known ruin is Pueblo Bonito, which, in its final form, contained some 600 rooms and 40 kivas and rose 4 stories high. Casa Rinconada, on the south side of the canyon, is the largest "great kiva" in the park. There are a dozen significant archaeological sites at the monument.

CIBOLA NATIONAL FOREST

East of Albuquerque.

2113 Osuna Road, NE
Suite A
Albuquerque, NM 87113-1001
505-761-4650
http://www.fs.fed.us

Southwest Natural and Cultural Heritage Association. (6501 Fourth Street, NW, Albuquerque, NM 87103; 505-345-9498)

The Cibola National Forest is made up of 13 separate parcels of land totalling 1.6 million acres, scattered eastward from Albuquerque to northeastern New Mexico, the panhandles of Texas and Oklahoma, and western Oklahoma. The forest landscape is generally mountainous, with numerous canyons, washes, and mesas. Elevation ranges from about 5,660 feet in the lowland desert to 11,301 feet at Mount Taylor. The lower elevations of the forest are rolling hilly terrain cut by sand washes and small canyons. Much of the forest shows evidence of past cultures—with numerous prehistoric and historic sites.

Sam's Tips

- The National Park Service sites adjacent to the Cibola National Forest include El Malpais National Monument, El Morro National Monument, and Salinas Pueblo Missions National Monument (see entries). Nearby pueblos also have visitor centers and offer tours to the public.

- Nearby Acoma/Sky City, dating back to 1150 A.D., is the oldest continuously inhabited pueblo in the United States. Shops there sell the famous Acoma pottery.
- The unpaved Zuni Mountain Historic Auto Tour travels from the Museum of Mining to Bluewater Creek, with several natural and historical sites in between.

The New Mexico Mining Museum

Located just a short distance from El Malpais, the New Mexico Mining Museum is the only uranium mining museum in the world. A tour gives you the opportunity to see, touch, and feel the underground world where thousands of men and women worked to mine this precious ore.

EL MALPAIS NATIONAL MONUMENT

87 miles southeast of Santa Fe; 47 miles west of Albuquerque.

PO Box 939
Grants, NM 87020
505-783-4774
http://www.nps.gov/elma

Southwest Parks and Monuments Association. (221 North Court Avenue, Tucson, AZ 85701; 520-622-1999)

El Malpais means "the badlands," an appropriate name for a spectacular volcanic area composed of cooled lava flow blankets, mountain ranges, mesas, and jagged spatter cones. The monument also contains a 17-mile-long lava tube system, wilderness areas, failed log homesteads, sandstone bluffs, prehistoric petroglyphs of ancient Pueblo Indians, and fragile ice caves. (Despite seasonal heat, some lava tubes contain ice year-round.) One of the surprising sights found in the area is a number of Douglas fir trees thriving in the midst of rugged lava-covered terrain. In fact, the overall diversity of life at El Malpais illustrates many stories of unique adaptation to a challenging environment. The area also features the La Ventana Natural Arch—the largest of New Mexico's readily accessible natural arches. Popular activities include hiking across lava fields, lava "bridges," and ancient Indian trails, and along craters, trenches, sinkholes, and lava caves. Seasonal flower displays are spectacular. The Pueblo people of Acoma, Laguna, and Zuni, and the Ramah Navajo, continue their traditional uses of the area.

SAM'S TIPS

- Two wilderness areas, the Cebolla Wilderness and the West Malpais Wilderness, allow you to explore more deeply the petroglyphs, old homesteads, and lava flows. The Sandstone Bluffs Overlook offers excellent views of the lava flows and the countryside.
- The El Calderon area of the monument offers above-ground explorations of lava trenches, sinkholes, and the El Calderon crater. To explore the lava caves at the Big Tubes Area, be sure to wear a hard hat, protective clothing, boots, and gloves. And bring water and light sources to the cave—it is a tricky area.

- Nearby attractions include the Pueblo of Acoma, the oldest continually inhabited city in the United States, and El Morro, an immense rock carved with evidence of the cultures that lived and passed through here during prehistoric times.
- Chain of Craters Wilderness Study Area is located along the western edge of the El Malpais National Conservation Area. The area was named for a line of volcanic cinder cones that roughly follows the Continental Divide. Mountain bikes are allowed on the existing dirt roads, which wind between the cinder cones.

EL MORRO NATIONAL MONUMENT

56 miles southeast of Gallup, NM, via Highways 602 and 53.

Route 2
Box 43
Ramah, NM 87321-9603
505-783-4226
http://www.nps.gov/elmo

Southwest Parks and Monuments Association. (221 North Court Avenue, Tucson, AZ 85701; 520-622-1999)

El Morro National Monument, which rises above the surrounding plains of the New Mexico desert, is a wonderful example of a geological formation know as a *cuesta,* a long formation with a gentle upward slope that drops off abruptly at one end. A protective layer of hard rock at the top of El Morro has delayed erosion longer than was possible for the surrounding land, which once rose as high. The sandstone face developed cracks that gradually weathered into the long vertical "joints" that are prominent today. The ruins of two Anasazi pueblos sprawl atop the mesa. The smaller north pueblo is an unexcavated mound blanketed with cacti and shrubs. The larger pueblo was unearthed by archaeologists and has been stabilized. The pueblos were abandoned around 1400, when the people moved to larger, consolidated villages in the valley.

SAM'S TIPS

- Inscription Rock, located on the Inscription Rock Trail Loop, is covered with pictographs, petroglyphs of ancient Indians, and carved names and inscriptions from earlier Spanish and American explorers.

FORT UNION NATIONAL MONUMENT

95 miles northeast of Santa Fe; 150 miles northeast of Albuquerque.

PO Box 127
Watrous, NM 87753
505-425-8025
http://www.nps.gov/foun

Southwest Parks and Monuments Association. (221 North Court Avenue, Tucson, AZ 85701; 520-622-1999)

When New Mexico became a United States territory after the Mexican War, the army established garrisons in towns scattered along the Rio Grande, to protect the area's inhabitants and travel routes. Fort Union was established to guard the mountain and the Cimarron Branches of the Santa Fe Trail. During the 1850s, mounted riflemen from the fort campaigned against several Indian tribes of the southwest. A massive earthwork fort, built in 1861, was designed to defend the territory against a threatened Confederate invasion. The third and last fort included not only a military post and arsenal, but a separate quartermaster depot with warehouses, corrals, shops, offices, and quarters.

GILA CLIFF DWELLINGS NATIONAL MONUMENT

44 miles north of Silver City, NM, on Highway 15.

Route 11
Box 100
Silver City, NM 88061
505-536-9461
http://www.nps.gov/gicl

Southwest Parks and Monuments Association. (221 North Court Avenue, Tucson, AZ 85701; 520-622-1999)

Surrounded by the Gila National Forest, the Gila Cliff Dwellings National Monument offers a glimpse into the lives of the people who lived in the area from the late 1280s through the early 1300s. The surroundings probably look today very much like they did when the cliff dwellings were inhabited. The term "cliff dwellers" refers to Pueblo people who built their homes in the natural caves, but Pueblo people also built in the open, and the monument contains examples of both types of settlements. Seven natural caves occur high in the southeast-facing cliff of a side canyon, and five of the caves contain the ruins of dwellings—a total of about 40 rooms.

GILA NATIONAL FOREST

190 miles southwest of Albuquerque; 250 miles southwest of Santa Fe.

3005 E. Camino del Bosque
Silver City, NM 88061
505-388-8211
http://www.fs.fed.us

The Gila National Forest, 3.3 million acres of publicly owned forest and range land rising above the desert country of southwestern New Mexico, is a rugged realm of cactus and grass, juniper and pine, spruce and aspen. The Gila contains more federal land than any other national forest outside Alaska. The Continental Divide meanders for 170 miles through this canyon country, once the stronghold of Apache warrior Geronimo and his followers. The mountain ranges of the Gila include the Mogollon, Tularosa, Diablo, Big Burro, San Francisco, and Mangas Mountains, and the Blank Range. Elevations start at 4,500 feet in the desert and rise to almost 11,000 feet on the often snow-covered crest of Whitewater Baldy.

SAM'S TIPS

- The Catwalk National Scenic Trail is a 250-foot metal causeway clinging to the side of Whitewater Canyon; in some places, the canyon is only 20 feet wide and 250 feet deep.
- The Gila River flows through some of the most rugged and spectacular areas of the wilderness and is excellent for rafting. The forest will provide you with a list of Outfitter Guides who are permitted to operate in the forest. Although the river can be run in canoes, kayaks, and tubes, the recommended form of travel is by specialized whitewater craft.
- Apache Creek Archaeological Interpretive Site is a classic Mimbres village of ancient walls and great kiva lying along the Tularosa River. The site tells the story of a people famed for their pottery and art. A nearby trail leads to the mesa top and interprets petroglyphs scattered along the rimrock.

FOREST SERVICE SCENIC BYWAY

Inner Loop/Gila Cliff Dwellings Scenic Byway

This 110-mile byway includes a side trip to the Gila Cliff Dwellings National Monument, where travelers can visit the remains of a once-thriving Mogollon Indian community. Overlooks along the loop allow visitors to stop and view the beauty of the surrounding countryside, including panoramic views of the Gila Wilderness, the nation's first designated wilderness area. A visit to Pino Altos, a historic mining town, and fishing, camping, and hiking opportunities are available along the byway. *Contact Gila National Forest.*

LINCOLN NATIONAL FOREST

207 miles southeast of Albuquerque; 221 miles south of Santa Fe.

Federal Building
1101 New York Avenue
Alamogordo, NM 88310
505-434-7200
http://www.fs.fed.us

Southwest Natural and Cultural Heritage Association. (6501 Fourth Street NW, Suite I, Albuquerque, NM 87107; 505-345-9498)

Located mostly in south-central New Mexico, the Lincoln National Forest covers over 1.1 million acres stretching north from the Guadalupe Mountains across the Sacramento Mountains and through the Capitan Mountains. Travelers will find spectacular sunsets across the desert, as well as breathtaking views of the Tularosa Basin and White Sands National Monument. Higher elevations offer mountain meadows—mixtures of pine, fir, aspen, oak, and other vibrant greens broken by the brilliance of wildflowers and blossoming plants and trees that change with the season. The forest is also the birthplace of Smokey Bear. In 1950, after the Capitan Gap wildfire, a black bear cub was found clinging to a charred tree in the Lincoln National Forest. Nicknamed Smokey by firefighters and nursed back to health, Smokey was then flown to Washington, DC, to reside in the National Zoo. The little cub became a living symbol of wildfire prevention.

Sam's Tips

- The White Mountain and Capitan Mountain Wildernesses offer adventurers spectacular vistas in their 83,000 acres, all of which are limited to foot and horse traffic.
- The forest is home to two ski areas. Ski Apache, located near Ruidoso, is operated by the Apache Mescalero Indian Tribe. Snow Canyon, the southernmost ski area in the United States, is adjacent to the small village of Cloudcroft in the Sacramento Mountains.
- Points of interest near the forest include the Smokey Bear Historical State Park, the Desert Lake Golf Course, and the Space Hall of Fame.

FOREST SERVICE SCENIC BYWAY

New Mexico State Highway 6563

Commonly called the "Sunspot Highway," this byway travels the front rim of the majestic Sacramento Mountains. Spectacular views range from the Tularose Basin to the ceaselessly shifting sand dunes of the White Sands National Monument. *Contact Lincoln National Forest.*

Kivas

The Pecos Indians, like many other Pueblo groups, enjoyed a rich cultural tradition, highlighted by an elaborate religious life. Their pueblos were filled with kivas, most of which have what's called a *sipapu*—a hole in the floor that symbolizes the place of mankind's emergence and the point of entry for the spirits below.

PECOS NATIONAL HISTORICAL PARK

25 miles southeast of Santa Fe, 40 miles west of Las Vegas.

PO Box 418
Pecos, NM 87552-0418
505-757-6414
http://www.nps.gov/peco

Southwest Parks and Monuments Association. (221 North Court Avenue, Tucson, AZ 85701; 520-622-1999)

In a passage through the Sangre de Cristo Mountains, the ruins of Pecos Pueblo and a Spanish mission share a small ridge that embraces 8,000 years of human history. Around 800, the first Puebloans began building pit houses immediately south of this ridge. During 1100–1300, about two dozen modest villages rose, including one where Pecos Pueblo stands today. By the time the Spanish missionaries arrived and began building their mission 460 years ago, Pecos Pueblo was a firmly established well-planned frontier fortress, 5 stories high, with a population of 2,000. Today, visitors can explore the ruins and reconstructed areas that help explain the life of the Pueblo people and Spanish missionaries, and the later trading and ranching communities of the park.

SAM'S TIPS

- The Forked Lightning Ranch, built near the ruins, was originally owned by "Tex" Austin, a rodeo producer who produced the first rodeos in New York, Wichita, Chicago, and London. His Forked Lightning brand still marks the original fixtures in the living and dining rooms.

PETROGLYPH NATIONAL MONUMENT

Albuquerque.

6001 Unser Boulevard NW
Albuquerque, NM 87120
505-839-4429
http://www.nps.gov/petr

Southwest Parks and Monuments Association. (221 North Court Avenue, Tucson, AZ 85701; 520-622-1999)

More than 15,000 prehistoric and historic Native American and Hispanic petroglyphs—images carved in black volcanic rock—stretch 17 miles along Albuquerque's west mesa escarpment. For many Native Americans, the site is a sacred space for worship and ceremony. Congress declared the site a national monument in order to protect it from the urban sprawl underway in Albuquerque.

Petroglyphs

Petroglyphs are symbols that reflect the complex society and religion of the Pueblo people. The images are made up of a variety of shapes and symbols. Animal figures, masks, sprials, stars, and geometrics are just a few examples of what can be seen at the monument.

Techniques for the exact dating of petroglyphs are still being developed by archaeologists. Often the best way to determine the origin of a particular petroglyph is to compare the image to pottery or murals of a known date. Experts guess that most of the petroglyphs were created between A.D. 1300 and 1650, but some of them might be even older. Easiest to date are petroglyphs created by Conquistadors from the Spanish Colonial Period.

Besides petroglyphs, the site is known for its unique geology, which includes five volcanos.

Sam's Tips

- Adjacent attractions include the Natural History Museum of New Mexico, the Old Town area of Albuquerque, and Coronado State Monument, a pueblo ruin site.

SALINAS PUEBLO MISSIONS NATIONAL MONUMENT

75 miles southeast of Albuquerque.

PO Box 517
Mountainair, NM 87036
505-847-2585
http://www.nps.gov/sapu

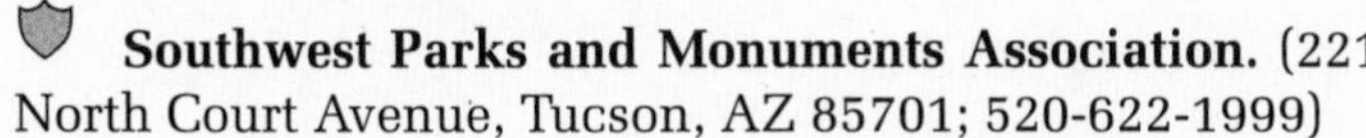

Southwest Parks and Monuments Association. (221 North Court Avenue, Tucson, AZ 85701; 520-622-1999)

Two extinct southwestern cultures, the Mogollon and the Anasazi, resided in the Salinas Valley more than three centuries ago. The Mogollon were agricultural people, living in pit houses or adobe jacales. When the Anasazi moved into the valley, the area became a major economic center. Architecturally, the area changed as well. The simple jacales of the Mogollon village evolved into large and complex stone buildings. Today, visitors can tour three ruins of these pueblo communities and the ruins of the Salinas Valley, named by the Spanish for the lakes where the Indians once mined their salt. The "Salt Missions Trail" traces prehistoric trade routes through historic ruins, parks, forests, and the city of Albuquerque.

Churches

Spaniards first visited the Salinas Valley in 1581. In the century that followed, a great effort was made to convert the residents and change the dominant culture to Christianity. This conversion effort is obvious in that ruins of a Christian church are found at each of the three pueblo sites. The church at Abo, San Gregorio de Abo, featured an organ and a trained choir and was built with a sophisticated buttressing technique that was unusual in 17th-century New Mexico.

SANTA FE NATIONAL FOREST

Santa Fe.

1474 Rodeo Drive
PO Box 1689
Santa Fe, NM 87504
505-438-7840
http://www.fs.fed.us

Southwest Natural and Cultural Heritage Association. (6501 Fourth Street NW, Suite I, Albuquerque, NM 87107; 505-345-9498)

Some of the finest mountain scenery in the Southwest is found in the more than 1.5 million acres of the Santa Fe National Forest. The Jemez Mountains on the west side are composed of narrow V-shaped canyons that separate gently to form moderately steep mesas. Volcanic plugs and cones are common. The Sangre de Cristo Mountains on the east side are more rugged, with numerous deep canyons and steep hillsides. The ridges are generally narrow and rocky. Vegetation ranges from grasslands at the drier, lower elevations, through pinyon-juniper, ponderosa pine, mixed conifer, and Engelmann spruce/subalpine fir forests.

SAM'S TIPS

- Hikers, mountain bikers, horseback riders, and 4-wheel drivers will enjoy exploring 1,002 miles of trails; during the winter, many of the trails become cross-country skiing and snowmobile trails.
- Dead-and-down firewood permits can be obtained from all Santa Fe National Forest offices. Christmas tree permits can be purchased by mail or over-the-counter at selected Districts.

FOREST SERVICE SCENIC BYWAY

Santa Fe Scenic Byway

Beginning at the Palace of Governors, the oldest government building in the United States, the Santa Fe Scenic Byway travels 15 miles through rolling foothills and the picturesque Tesuque Canyon and on up into dense stands of ponderosa pine. *Contact Santa Fe National Forest.*

SOUTHWEST NATURAL AND CULTURAL HERITAGE ASSOCIATION

Southwest Natural And Cultural Heritage Association
6501 North Fourth Street, Suite I
Albuquerque, NM 87107
505-345-9498

Information is provided for the following sites:

Aransas National Wildlife Refuge (TX)
Bosque del Apache National Wildlife Refuge (NM)
California BLM State Office (CA)
California Desert Information Center (CA)
El Malpais National Conservation Area (NM)
Hagerman National Wildlife Refuge (ID)
Imperial National Wildlife Refuge (AZ)
Laguna Atascosa National Wildlife Refuge (TX)
Lincoln National Forest (NM)
New Mexico BLM State Office (NM)
Santa Ana National Wildlife Refuge (TX)
Santa Fe National Forest (NM)
Tonto National Forest (AZ, NM)
Williams/Kaibab National Forest Visitor Center (AZ)

WHITE SANDS NATIONAL MONUMENT

221 miles southeast of Albuquerque; 235 miles southwest of Santa Fe.

PO Box 1086
Holloman AFB, NM 88330-1086
505-479-6124
http://www.nps.gov/whsa

 **Southwest Parks and Monuments Association.** (221 North Court Avenue, Tucson, AZ 85701; 520-622-1999)

At the northern end of the Chihuahuan Desert, in a mountain-ringed valley called the Tularosa Basin, is one of the world's greatest natural wonders—the glistening sands of White Sands National Monument. Here, great wavelike dunes of gypsum sand have engulfed 275 square miles of desert and created the world's largest gypsum dune field. The brilliant white dunes are ever changing—growing, cresting, then slumping, but always advancing. Within the extremely harsh environment of the dune field, even life adapted to desert conditions struggles to

Where Does All the Sand Come From?

The answer lies in the mountains. The nearby ranges, the Sacramento Mountains, and the San Andres Mountains, contain layers of limestone, which contain a soluble rock called gypsum. When rain falls in the area, the gypsum dissolves and runs down the mountains into the Tularosa basin, which has no rivers running through it. As a result, the water collects and forms at the lowest spot of the basin floor, called Lake Lucero. As the water begins to evaporate, gypsum forms a crust on the lake bed. Some of the gypsum forms beautiful crystals called selenite, which eventually break down into grains of sand. The sand at White Sands National Monument is almost pure gypsum crystals.

survive. Only a few species of plants grow rapidly enough to survive burial by moving dunes, but several types of small animals have evolved a white coloration that camouflages them in the gypsum sand.

Sam's Tips

- The Alkali Flat Trail is a 4.6-mile round-trip path that leads through the heart of the dunes to the ice-age lake bed where the sand is formed.
- The park is surrounded by the White Sands Missile Range, an important testing site for experimental weaponry and space technology. For safety reasons, both the park and the nearby roadways may be closed while tests are being conducted. In general, these closures occur about twice a week and last from 1 to 2 hours.
- The Monument offers curriculum-based programs in desert ecology, geology, area history, bio-diversity, environmental ethics, and endangered species that relate park resources to teaching in the classroom.
- Nature walks and evening programs are given every night from Memorial Day weekend to mid-August. On full-moon nights, the park stays open later. Past programs have included talks on endangered species, the spreading deserts, the invasion of exotic plants in the west, landscaping with nature, and astronomy of ancient Americans. Contact the monument for the Full Moon Program Schedule.
- Points of interest in nearby Alamogordo include the International Space Hall of Fame, the Toy Train Depot, and the Alameda Park Zoo.
- Twice a year, on the first Saturdays in April and October, the Alamogordo Chamber of Commerce and the White Sands Missile Range sponsor a visit to the Trinity Site, the site of the world's first above-ground atomic explosion. The device was exploded one week after White Sands was established, creating a (since filled in) crater one-half mile across and eight feet deep. For information, call the Space Center Museum at 800-545-4021.

Points of Interest

U.S. ARMY CORPS OF ENGINEERS

ABIQUIU DAM

This reservoir offers some of the finest fishing in northern New Mexico. Reptile fossils 200 million years old have been found in the area. A fine panoramic view of the Cerro Pedernal can be seen from the dam. From Espanola, west 30 miles on US 84, then 2 miles south on NM 96.

CONCHAS LAKE

Petroglyphs testify to the area's early cultures. From Tucumcari, 34 miles northwest on NM 104.

TWO RIVERS DAM

Visitors can see antelope here during the fall months. The reservoir is dry except for limited storage during spring runoffs. From Roswell, 14 miles west on US 70/380, and 7 miles south on the project's access road.

BUREAU OF LAND MANAGEMENT

THE FRANCES CANYON PUEBLITO

The Frances Canyon Pueblito, one of the largest and best preserved Navajo Pueblitos, was occupied after the Pueblo Revolt in 1680.

For more information on the many Bureau of Land Management sites in New Mexico, contact:

Bureau of Land Management State Office
1474 Rodeo Road
Santa Fe, NM 87505
505-438-7400
http://www.nm.blm.gov

BLACK-FOOTED FERRET

Mustela Nigripes

The black-footed ferret was once considered the most endangered mammal in the United States. But progress has now been made toward this population's recovery.

Ferrets were once found throughout the Great Plains, from Texas to southern Saskatchewan, Canada. Their range extended from the Rocky Mountains eastward through the Dakotas and south through Nebraska, Kansas, Oklahoma, and Texas. Where prairie dogs were found, so were black-footed ferrets. Ferrets eat prairie dogs and then take over the prairie dog's burrow.

During the fall of 1986 and the spring of 1987, the last of the 19 known wild black-footed ferrets were taken from the wild and placed in a captive breeding facility. This captive population has increased to more than 500 captive black-footed ferrets. The goal of the captive breeding program is to establish 240 breeding adults in captivity, while continuing the return of ferrets to the wild..

If these and future efforts are successful, black-footed ferrets may once again be playing an important role in the dynamics of wild prairie dog towns.

TEXAS

ALIBATES FLINT QUARRIES NATIONAL MONUMENT

30 miles northeast of Amarillo; 350 miles northwest of Dallas.

PO Box 1460
Fritch, TX 79036
806-857-3151
http://www.nps.gov/alfi

Southwest Parks and Monuments Association. (221 North Court Avenue, Tucson, AZ 85701; 520-622-1999)

Archaeological traces of prehistoric Indians—homes, workshops, and campsites—dot the entire Canadian River region of the Texas Panhandle, but few sites are as dramatic as Alibates Flint Quarries, where for 12,000 years people quarried flint for tool making. Indians of the Ice Age Clovis Culture used Alibates flint for spear points to hunt the Imperial Mammoth before the Great Lakes were even formed. The flint usually lies just below the surface at ridge level, in a layer up to 6 feet thick.

AMISTAD NATIONAL RECREATION AREA

150 miles west of San Antonio; 340 miles west of Houston.

HCR-3
Box 5J
Del Rio, TX 78840-9350
210-775-7491
http://www.nps.gov/amis

Big Bend Natural History Association. (PO Box 68, Big Bend National Park, TX 79834; 915-477-2236)

The Amistad National Recreation Area, located on the United States–Mexico border, was developed through the combined efforts of both countries. "Amistad" means "friendship," and the site symbolizes an international playground for citizens of both countries—and others. The reservoir, created by the 6-mile-long Amistad Dam on the Rio Grande, has more than 850 miles of shoreline, 540 of which are in Texas. The water's extraordinary blueness results from the underlying limestone character and the lack of loose soils.

Sam's Tips

- The Amistad area is also known as the Lower Pecos Region, which refers to an artistic style of rock art exclusive to the Amistad National Recreation Area and its surrounding lands. Carved into the rock are pictographs as old as 4,000 years and as recent as the 16th and 17th centuries. Visitors can view isolated works and murals over 100 feet long.

- Panther Cave and Parida Cave, Amistad's two major rock art sites, are accessible by boat, but only at normal lake levels.
- One highlight of Del Rio is the Whitehead Memorial Museum, where historic buildings have been preserved and are opened to the public. American visitors can cross over into Mexico to visit Ciudad Acuna, the sister city of Del Rio, Texas.

BIG BEND NATIONAL PARK

325 miles southeast of El Paso; 230 miles southwest of Odessa.

PO Box 129
Big Bend National Park, TX 79834
915-477-2251
http://www.nps.gov/bibe

Big Bend Natural History Association. (PO Box 196, Big Bend National Park, TX 79834; 915-477-2236)

According to a Native American legend, the Great Spirit who made the earth simply dumped all the leftover rocks on the Big Bend, resulting in the spectacular mountains and canyons we see today. In contrast to the mountains, the desert runs along the great bend of the Rio Grande, where grit-laden waters run through deep-cut canyon walls. Here, Big Bend National Park administers 234 miles of the river for recreational use. The park offers outstanding walking and hiking, ranging from short self-guided nature trails to cross-park treks. This is also a birder's paradise; during migratory seasons, as many of 450 species have been spotted by watchers. To see how the river has carved colossal canyons out of solid stone, take a canoe down the Rio Grande.

Dinosaurs

In 1971, Douglas Lawson, a graduate student from the University of Texas at Austin, found a large radius bone of a pterosaur in the Javelina Formation in Big Bend. Seventy-five percent of the wing skeleton was eventually recovered, and the pterosaur proved to be the largest flying creature ever found. Dinosaur remains are found in the nonmarine Aguja and Javelina Formations in the park. Although remains are relatively uncommon at Big Bend, skeletal remains of duck-billed, horned, and the large sauropod and carnivorous dinosaurs have been found.

SAM'S TIPS

- Several seminars are offered through the Big Bend Natural History Association. Past topics have included "Introduction to the Wildflowers of Big Bend National Park" and "Dinosaurs of the Big Bend." For more information, contact the association at the address above.

ROCK ART OF THE LOWER PECOS

The lower Pecos River region's rock art is considered by experts to be world-class, comparable in significance to sites in Europe, Australia, and America's Baja California. With 250-plus known sites within a 100-square-mile area, the region has one of the densest concentrations of archaic rock art in the western hemisphere and is among the largest multicolored areas in North America.

While traveling through Amistad National Recreation Area in Texas, you can see some of this famous rock art by visiting Panther Cave, accessible by boat. Parida Cave, on the Rio Grande, is also accessible by boat if water levels permit. When lake levels are low, Parida Cave is sometimes accessible by foot via a primitive three-mile trail. Check with park rangers before embarking on this potentially dangerous hike.

Visitors who don't have boats can see spectacular rock art on guided tours at nearby Seminole Canyon State Historical Park.

BIG THICKET NATIONAL PRESERVE

Beaumont, 80 miles northeast of Houston.

3785 Milam
Beaumont, TX 77701
409-246-2337
http://www.nps.gov/bith

Southwest Parks and Monuments Association. (221 North Court Avenue, Tucson, AZ 85701; 520-622-1999)

People have called Big Thicket an American ark and a biological crossroads of North America because so many species coexist here. Among the major North American biological influences that bump up against each other are: southeastern swamps, eastern forests, central plains, and southwest deserts. Bogs sit right near arid sandhills. Eastern bluebirds nest near roadrunners. Four of America's five types of insect-eating plants live within the preserve, which is also home to a rarely seen population of alligators. The preserve—12 units comprising 86,000 acres (soon to be expanded by 10,766 acres)—was designated an International Biosphere Reserve by the United Nations.

SAM'S TIPS

- The backwaters of the Neches River provide some of the preserve's most scenic places. Unless you are familiar with the area, trying to find access to these waters is difficult. Ask Big Thicket for a canoe-access brochure that lists local canoe rental outfitters and provides maps to help you find your way to put-in and take-out points.

- There are four types of poisonous snakes in North America, and the Big Thicket has them all: cottonmouths, copperheads, coral snakes, and rattlesnakes. Treat all snakes with respect; a bite from a nonpoisonous snake can still be painful. Should you get bitten by a snake, try to identify the species. Thanks to safety guidelines posted throughout the park, there have been very few on-site snake bites in the past couple of years.
- Nearby attractions include The Nature Conservancy's Roy E. Larsen Sandyland Sanctuary (409-385-2863), and the Alabama–Coushatta Indian Reservation (800-444-3507). Other popular adjacent attractions include several museums in Beaumont that relate the history of the timber and petroleum industries, and Heritage Village in Woodville, which recreates the early settlement of the Big Thicket.

CHAMIZAL NATIONAL MEMORIAL

El Paso.

800 South San Marcial
El Paso, TX 79905
915-532-7273
http://www.nps.gov/cham

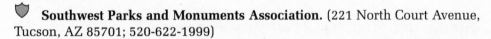

Southwest Parks and Monuments Association. (221 North Court Avenue, Tucson, AZ 85701; 520-622-1999)

The Chamizal National Memorial is devoted to international cooperation and goodwill. More than a century ago, Chamizal was cut off from Mexico when the Rio Grande changed its course between the small settlements that grew into El Paso and Ciudad Juarez. In 1895, Mexico laid formal claim to the tract, a seemingly insignificant piece of land less than 3 square kilometers. The Mexican claim spawned counterclaims by the United States, and over the years the dispute became a major impasse. In an atmosphere heavy with pride and distrust, Chamizal became a symbol of disharmony—a rallying point for Mexican nationalism and a locked gate in U.S. policy. In 1962, Presidents John F. Kennedy and Adolfo Lopez Mateos moved to break the deadlock. The result was a new concrete-lined channel for the Rio Grande that cuts through both Chamizal and Cordova. All land south of the center of this channel is now in Mexico; all to the north is in the United States.

SAM'S TIPS

- The National Park Service has year-round special programs to broaden cultural understanding. Past events have included theater performances and art exhibits. A film called *This Most Singular Country,* which highlights the boundary struggle between the two countries, is shown throughout the day.

- Directly across the Rio Grande, Mexico has established a companion park, featuring landscaped grounds and formal gardens. Visitors from the United States are invited to use the park.

FORT DAVIS NATIONAL HISTORIC SITE

160 miles southwest of Odessa; 300 miles north of Lubbock.

PO Box 1456
Fort Davis, TX 79734
915-426-3224
http://www.nps.gov/foda

Southwest Parks and Monuments Association. (221 North Court Avenue, Tucson, AZ 85701; 520-622-1999)

Fort Davis was a key post in the defense of West Texas. From 1854 to 1891, troops based at the post guarded immigrants, freighters, and stagecoaches on the San Antonio–El Paso road and fought with the Comanche and Apache Indians. Today, the remnants of Fort Davis are more impressive than those of any other southwestern fort. Through a continuing program of restoration, half of the more than 50 original structures have been saved.

GUADALUPE MOUNTAINS NATIONAL PARK

110 miles east of El Paso; 55 miles southwest of Carlsbad.

HC 60
Box 400
Salt Flat, TX 79847-9400
915-828-3251
http://www.nps.gov/gumo

Carlsbad Caverns–Guadalupe Mountains Association. (PO Box 1417, Carlsbad, NM 88221-1417; 505-785-2322)

Located on the border of Texas and New Mexico, the Guadalupe Mountains National Park captures the rugged spirit and diverse terrain of this pioneer countryside. Rising from the desert, this mountain mass contains portions of the world's most extensive and significant ancient marine fossil reef, formed about 250 million years ago when a tropical ocean covered portions of Texas and New Mexico. Also featured: Guadalupe Peak, the highest point in Texas at 8,749 feet; El Capitan, a massive limestone formation; and McKittrick Canyon, popular for its variety of plant and animal life, rugged twisting gorge, high cliffs, peaceful shady creek, and trails. Located in the high country is the "bowl," a 2-mile wide depression atop the mountains where the forest is especially lush and offers 80 miles of scenic trails. Other attractions include the Pinery, ruins of a stagecoach station, and Smith and Manzanita Springs, two small oases with freshwater springs, full of wildlife and near the historic Frijole Ranch.

Sam's Tips

- One of the park's most popular areas is McKittrick Canyon, where desert gives way to forest. Near the mouth of the canyon, desert plants and animals predominate. As you travel further along, the canyon narrows and its walls loom higher. Further up the canyon, you enter a riparian woodland of maple, hickory, oak, ash, and pine.
- Williams Ranch, a ranch on the remote west side of the Guadalupe Mountains, is set in the shadows of high rock cliffs. The 7-mile road to the ranch is open only to 4-wheel-drive vehicles. Parts of the road follow the historic Butterfield Trail. Travelers of this road must obtain a key to the entrance gates at the visitor center.
- The park maintains two museums: the Museum of Natural and Geological Histories, located in the Visitor Center, and the Cultural History Museum in the Frijole Ranch House, 1.5 miles from the Headquarters Visitors Center. Exhibits are also located at the McKittrick Canyon Visitor Center.

LAKE MEREDITH NATIONAL RECREATION AREA

30 miles northeast of Amarillo; 350 miles northwest of Dallas.

PO Box 1460
Fritch, TX 79036
806-857-3151
http://www.nps.gov/lamr

Southwest Parks and Monuments Association. (221 North Court Avenue, Tucson, AZ 85701; 520-622-1999)

Lake Meredith lies on the dry and windswept High Plains of the Texas Panhandle in a region known as Llano Estacoado, or Staked Plain. Through this plain—as flat as any surface in the world—the Canadian River has cut and recut 200-foot canyons called breaks. Lake Meredith was created by Sanford Dam on the Canadian River and now fills many breaks whose walls are crowned with white limestone caprock, scenic buttes, pinnacles, and red-brown, wind-eroded coves. Above the canyons lie the mesquite, prickly pear, yucca, and grasses of arid plains.

LYNDON B. JOHNSON NATIONAL HISTORICAL PARK

50 miles west of Austin; 60 miles north of San Antonio.

PO Box 329
Johnson City, TX 78636
210-868-7128
http://www.nps.gov/lyjo

Southwest Parks and Monuments Association. (221 North Court Avenue, Tucson, AZ 85701; 520-622-1999)

The Lyndon B. Johnson National Historical Park contains two distinct areas: Johnson City and the LBJ Ranch. In Johnson City, the principal points of interest are the Boyhood Home of Lyndon Johnson and the Johnson Settlement, a complex of restored historic structures that trace the ancestry of Lyndon Johnson and the evolution of the Texas Hill Country. The LBJ Ranch includes the one-room school first attended by Johnson, his reconstructed birthplace, the Johnson Family cemetery where the President is buried, the ranch house or "Texas White House," and views of the ranch and its registered Hereford cattle.

Sam's Tips

- Access to the LBJ Ranch is by tour only. Buses leave from the LBJ State Park Visitor Center for the LBJ Ranch on a regular schedule. Call the park for more information.
- The Lyndon B. Johnson Library, on the campus of the University of Texas at Austin, is operated by the National Archives and Records Service of the General Services Administration. It is both a center of scholarly research and a historical museum. Three floors of exhibits highlight President Johnson's long public career.

NATIONAL FORESTS IN TEXAS

Various locations.

701 North 1st Street
Lufkin, TX 75901
409-639-8501
http://www.fs.fed.us

Ozark Interpretive Association. (PO Box 1279, Mountain View, AR 72560; 870-757-2211)

The national forests and grasslands in Texas comprise about 675,000 acres and are divided into four units: the Angelina, Davy Crockett, Sabine, and Sam

Houston and two grasslands: Lyndon B. Johnson and Caddo. The forests provide a variety of recreational opportunities, including hiking, camping, hunting, fishing, wildlife viewing, and water activities. Birdwatchers delight in the fact that these East Texas forests lie right in the migratory path of warblers, vireos, and other species of neotropical migrants. Spring and Fall are excellent times to watch the migrations.

The Davy Crockett and Sam Houston national forests are located where the pine forests of the southeastern United States join the blackland prairies of central Texas. The result is a mix of eastern and western species of birds and other wildlife found nowhere else in the state.

The Sabine and Angelina national forests are located on the shores of Toledo Bend and Sam Rayburn reservoirs, two large East Texas lakes featuring fishing and other water sports. Nestings of bald eagles also can be found close to the water's edge. Lake Conroe and Lake Livingston offer water-related outdoor recreation activities on or near the Sam Houston National Forest.

PADRE ISLAND NATIONAL SEASHORE

Corpus Christi.

9400 South Padre Island Drive
Corpus Christi, TX 78418
512-949-8068
http://www.nps.gov/pais

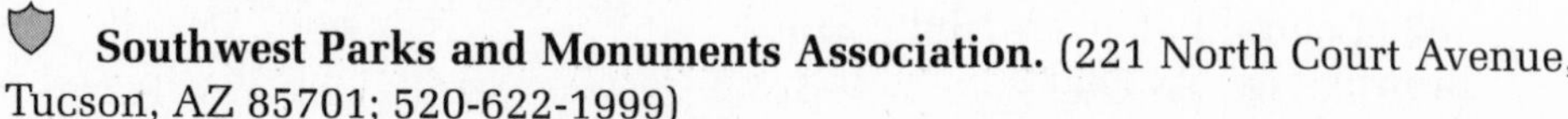

Southwest Parks and Monuments Association. (221 North Court Avenue, Tucson, AZ 85701; 520-622-1999)

Padre Island is one of a chain of islands that stretches along the Atlantic and Gulf coasts of the United States from Maine to Texas. Seaside homes, fishing villages, and lighthouses line many of these low-lying islands, but on Padre Island the handiwork of nature predominates. The many environments of Padre Island—beach, dunes, grasslands, and tidal flats—are shaped and reshaped daily in response to the breezes, the waves, the rhythmic tides, and, occasionally, the violent battering of tropical storms and hurricanes.

SAM'S TIPS

- Winter brings the best time for shelling, especially after storms (called "Northers") disturb the water and push more shells ashore.
- Portuguese-men-of-war, found along the seashore year-round, are attractive blue jellyfish that can cause a painful sting if they come in contact with the skin. Even if the men-of-war are washed up on the beach and appear dead, give them a wide berth.
- During the summer, the park sponsors its Junior Seashore Ranger Program, a series of fun educational programs for children between the ages of 5 and 13.

Sea Turtles

From 1978 to 1988, 2,000 sea turtle eggs were collected yearly along the beaches at Rancho Nuevo, Mexico, transported to a laboratory at Padre Island, and incubated. After hatching, the young turtles were released on the beach and allowed to crawl to the surf, in the hope that the short journey would leave them with a lasting impression of the beach. Following a short swim in the Gulf of Mexico, the baby turtles were recaptured and transported to the National Marine Fisheries Service Lab in Galveston, TX. The turtles were raised for one year, growing large enough to avoid most predators, and were finally released permanently into the Gulf of Mexico. In 1997 a second breeding colony was discovered established from the eggs of two returning tagged turtles.

Park rangers and other staff lead the small groups and present a badge and certificate to each child upon completion of the program. Past programs have included: tidepooling, sea turtles, birds, photography, nature and writing, conservation, and weather forecasting. For more information on the summer schedule, call 512-949-8068.

PALO ALTO BATTLEFIELD NATIONAL HISTORIC SITE

120 miles south of Corpus Christi.

1623 Central Boulevard, Suite 213
Brownsville, TX 78522
956-541-2785
http://www.nps.gov/paal

Southwest Parks and Monuments Association. (221 North Court Avenue, Tucson, AZ 85701; 520-622-1999)

The Palo Alto Battlefield National Historic Site preserves the first battle site of the 1846–1848 Mexican–American War. Nearly all land within the authorized park boundary is in private ownership and not open to the public. However, a small portion of government-owned property at the junction of Highway FM 1847 and Highway FM 511 has been set aside as a commemorative park, developed and maintained by the Brownsville Kiwanis. Tours are offered by appointment only.

RIO GRANDE WILD AND SCENIC RIVER

The river begins in Big Bend National Park, 260 miles southeast of El Paso.

c/o Big Bend National Park
PO Box 129
Big Bend National Park, TX 79834
915-477-2251
http://www.nps.gov/rigr

The Rio Grande Wild and Scenic River, managed by Big Bend National Park, has no separate facilities, address, or handouts. All of the pertinent information on the river is included in Big Bend National Park information.

SAN ANTONIO MISSIONS NATIONAL HISTORICAL PARK

San Antonio.

2202 Roosevelt Avenue
San Antonio, TX 78210
210-534-8833
http://www.nps.gov/saan

Southwest Parks and Monuments Association. (221 North Court Avenue, Tucson, AZ 85701; 520-622-1999)

The chain of missions established along the San Antonio River in the 18th century is a reminder of one of Spain's most successful attempts to extend its New World dominion northward from Mexico. The missions flourished between 1718 and 1793, enjoying strong economies and a relatively peaceful coexistence between mission Indians and Spanish settlers. Later in the century, increased tensions from Apaches and Comanches, coupled with inadequate military support stemming from the decline of Spain's empire in Mexico, weakened the missions. Disease reduced the surrounding Indian population, further accelerating the missions' decline. In 1824, the secularization of the San Antonio Missions begun in 1792, was completed. Today, four of the San Antonio missions have been designated as national historical sites. Mission San Antonio de Valero, commonly called the Alamo, was founded in 1718, the first mission on the San Antonio River. The Alamo, a state Historic Site, has been under the care of the Daughters of the Republic of Texas for the state of Texas since 1905.

Points of Interest

U.S. ARMY CORPS OF ENGINEERS

ADDICKS AND BARKER RESERVOIRS
These normally dry reservoirs contain the largest municipal park in the nation and provide a different recreational experience for the metropolitan area. They contain facilities for golf, hiking, picnicking, field sports, horseback riding, shooting ranges, model airplane flying, a velodrome, and other activities. From Houston, west on I-10 to TX 6.

BENBROOK LAKE
Nearby Fort Worth offers stock shows, an indoor rodeo, and botanical gardens. From Benbrook, south 1 mile on US 377 and east 2.5 miles on County Road.

DENISON DAM (LAKE TEXOMA)
The second most popular Corps lake in the country features Old Fort Washita, now maintained as a museum by the Oklahoma Historical Society. From Denison, northwest 5 miles on TX 75A.

LAKE O' THE PINES
Fishing is popular on this 19,780-acre lake. From Jefferson, west 4 miles on TX 49 and continue on FM 729 and FM 726.

LAVON LAKE
The Heard Natural Science Museum and Wildlife Sanctuary in nearby McKinney features natural history exhibits and nature trails. From Wylie, east 3 miles on TX 78, then north 1 mile on County Road.

LEWISVILLE LAKE
This 540-acre park includes a golf course. From downtown Lewisville, northeast a half-mile to I-35E.

NAVARRO MILLS LAKE
Points of interest include the ghost town of Dresden near Dawson. From Corsicana, southwest 20 miles on TX 31, then north 1 mile on FM 667.

SAM RAYBURN DAM AND RESERVOIR
A 114,000-acre lake in the Big Thicket country of Texas. From Jasper, northwest 15 miles on TX 63, then east on TX 255.

SOMERVILLE LAKE
Nearby points of interest include Bluebonnet Trails, Independence Day Trek, and Salt Grass Trek. From Somerville, 1 mile west on TX 36.

WHITNEY LAKE
See the reconstructed Fort Graham, traces of the Old Chisholm Trail, and the dinosaur tracks at nearby Glen Rose. From Whitney, southwest 5 miles on TX 22.

U.S. BUREAU OF RECLAMATION

LAKE MEREDITH
Lake Meredith National Recreation Area, National Park Service, PO Box 1460, Fritch, TX 79036; 806-857-2002. Nearest highway: State 136. Nearest city: Sanford. The lake provides over 100 miles of shoreline with 200-foot, steep-walled canyons. Accessible from numerous roads with several boat ramps and camping facilities. Open year-round for fishing which includes white, largemouth and smallmouth bass; crappie, walleye, and several species of catfish.

LAKE TEXANA
Lake Texana State Park, PO Box 760, Edna TX 77957; 512-782-5718. Nearest highways: U.S. 59 and State 111. Nearest city: Edna. The lake provides over 11,000 acres of water surface. Several boat ramps and camping facilities. Fishing year-round.

TWIN BUTTES RESERVOIR
San Angelo Water Supply Corporation, PO Box 160, San Angelo, TX 79602; 915-655-9140. Nearest highways: U.S. 67 and 277. Nearest city: San Angelo. Several boat ramps and some camping facilities. Open year-round for fishing.

THE SOUTHWEST PARKS AND MONUMENTS ASSOCIATION

Cooperating Associations are on the front lines as providers of vital information to millions of visitors to America's national parks, forests, and other public lands. These nonprofit associations work closely with the management of the parks and forests toward the production of quality publications, maps, videos, and theme-related merchandise. One of the largest associations is:

Southwest Parks and Monuments Association
221 North Court Avenue
Tucson, AZ 85701
520-622-1999

This Association produces material about these public lands:

Aztec Ruins National Monument (NM)
Bandelier National Monument (NM)
Bighorn Canyon National Recreation Area (MT)
Big Thicket National Preserve (TX)
Black Canyon of the Gunnison National Monument (CO)
Canyon de Chelly National Monument (AZ)
Capulin Volcano National Monument (NM)
Casa Grande Ruins National Monument (AZ)
Chaco Culture National Historic Park (NM)
Chamizal National Memorial (TX)
Channel Islands National Park (CA)
Chickasaw National Recreation Area (OK)
Chiricahua National Monument (AZ)
Coronado National Memorial (AZ)
Curecanti National Recreation Area (CO)
El Malpais National Monument (NM)
El Morro National Monument (NM)
Eugene O'Neill National Historic Site (CA)
Fort Bowie National Historic Site (AZ)
Fort Davis National Historic Site (TX)
Fort Larned National Historic Site (KS)
Fort Scott National Historic Site (KS)
Fort Union National Monument (NM)
Gila Cliff Dwellings National Monument (NM)
Golden Spike National Historic Site (UT)
Great Sand Dunes National Monument (CO)
Hubbell Trading Post National Historic Site (AZ)
John Muir National Historic Site (CA)

Lyndon B. Johnson National Historical Park (TX)
Lake Mead National Recreation Area (NV)
Little Bighorn Battlefield National Monument (MT)
Montezuma Castle National Monument (AZ)
Navajo National Monument (AZ)
Organ Pipe Cactus National Monument (AZ)
Padre Island National Seashore (TX)
Palo Alto Battlefield National Historic Site (TX)
Pecos National Historic Park (NM)
Petroglyph National Monument (NM)
Pinnacles National Monument (CA)
Saguaro National Park (AZ)
Salinas Pueblo Missions National Monument (NM)
San Antonio Missions National Historical Park (TX)
Santa Monica Mountains National Recreation Area (CA)
Sunset Crater Volcano National Monument (AZ)
Timpanogos Cave National Monument (UT)
Tonto National Monument (AZ)
Tumacacori National Historical Park (AZ)
Tuzigoot National Monument (AZ)
Walnut Canyon National Monument (AZ)
Whiskeytown–Shasta–Trinity National Recreation Area (CA)
White Sands National Monument (NM)
Wupatki National Monument (AZ)

THE NORTHWEST INTERPRETIVE ASSOCIATION

Cooperating associations are on the front lines as providers of vital information to millions of visitors to America's national parks, forests, and other public lands. These nonprofit associations work closely with the management of the parks and forests toward the production of quality publications, maps, videos, and theme-related merchandise. One of the largest associations is:

Northwest Interpretive Association
909 First Avenue, Suite 630
Seattle, WA 98104
206-220-4140

The Association produces material on these public lands:

Beaverhead National Forest (MT)
Bitterroot National Forest (MT)
Clearwater National Forest (ID)
Colville National Forest (WA)
Columbia River Gorge National Scenic Area (OR)
Coulee Dam National Recreation Area (WA)
Deerlodge National Forest (MT)
Deschutes National Forest (OR)
Fort Vancouver National Historic Site (WA)
Fremont National Forest (OR)
Gifford–Pinchot National Forest (WA)
Idaho Panhandle National Forests (ID)
John Day Fossil Beds National Monument (OR)
Klamath National Forest (CA)
Klondike Gold Rush National Historical Park (AK)
Lassen National Forest (CA)
Lewis and Clark National Forest (MT)
Lolo National Forest (MT)
Malheur National Forest (OR)
Mount Baker–Snoqualmie National Forest (WA)
Mount Hood National Forest (OR)
Mount Rainier National Park (WA)
Nez Perce National Forest (ID)
Nez Perce National Historical Park (ID)
North Cascades National Park (WA)
Ochoco National Forest (OR)
Okanogan National Forest (WA)
Olympic National Forest (WA)
Olympic National Park (WA)
Rogue River National Forest (OR)
San Juan Island National Historical Park (WA)
Shasta–Trinity National Forest (CA)
Siskiyou National Forest (OR)
Siuslaw National Forest (OR)
Six Rivers National Forest (CA)
Umpqua National Forest (OR)
Umatilla National Forest (OR)
Wallowa-Whitman National Forest (OR)
Wenatchee National Forest (WA)
Whitman Mission National Historic Site (WA)
Willamette National Forest (OR)
Winema National Forest (OR)

The Pacific Region

NATIONAL PARK SERVICE HANDBOOKS—THE PACIFIC REGION

National Park Service handbooks highlight popular visitor sites across the country. Use them to learn about the historic significance and natural beauty of your next vacation destination. All are generously illustrated with photos, maps, and diagrams. Sites in the Pacific for which these authoritative handbooks are available include:

Site	*Stock No.*	*Price*
Exploring the American West	024–005-00834–9	$6.50
Overland Migration Settlers to California, Oregon, and Utah	024–005-00932–9	5.50
Sequoia and Kings Canyon (CA)	024–005-01095–5	7.00
North Cascades (WA)	024–005-00975–2	7.00

You can order these documents by phone (202-512-1800) or fax (202-512-2250) or by writing to: Superintendent of Documents, PO Box 371954, Pittsburgh, PA 15250-7954. (Use stock number when ordering. Prices may change.) The 24 Government Bookstores located around the country carry titles of regional interest. Check the appendix for the one nearest to you.

ALASKA

ALAGNAK WILD RIVER

The river runs 25 miles north of King Salmon.

c/o Katmai National Park and Preserve
PO Box 7
King Salmon, AK 99611
907-246-3305
http://www.nps.gov/alag

Flowing from Kukaklek Lake in Katmai National Preserve, the Alagnak River sports 69 miles of outstanding whitewater rafting. The river is also noted for abundant wildlife and sport fishing for five species of salmon. Portions of the main stem lie outside and west of Katmai.

ANIAKCHAK NATIONAL MONUMENT AND PRESERVE

150 miles south of King Salmon; 450 miles south of Anchorage.

PO Box 7
King Salmon, AK 99613
907-246-3305
http://www.nps.gov/ania

Unknown to all but native inhabitants until the 1920s, the 586,000 acres of Aniakchak are among the least visited in the National Park System. Aniakchak volcano, 6 miles wide and 2,000 feet deep, is part of the active volcanic Ring of Fire along the rim of the Pacific Ocean. About 3,500 years ago, a dramatic explosion collapsed the 7,000-foot mountain that once rose here, leaving a relatively flat-floored, ash-filled bowl. Many lesser eruptions have created the small cinder cones, lava flows, and explosion pits dotting the bowl's floor today. Surprise Lake, source of the Aniakchak river, also cascades through a 1,500 foot gash in the crater wall. Prehistoric and historic people hunted, trapped, and fished the Aniakchak area, but modern exploration began only 70 years ago.

Sam's Tips

- Anchorage has daily commercial service to King Salmon. Air charters, from King Salmon, land at Meshik Lake, Surprise Lake, in the caldera, or at Aniakchak, Amber, or Kujulik bays on the Pacific Ocean.
- Be prepared to be self-sufficient; there are no marked trails, campgrounds, or services. All camping is primitive, and small backpacking stoves are

SUMMITS OVER 15,000 FEET

The ten highest peaks in the United States are all located in Alaska. They are:

Summit	Elevation (feet)
1. Mount McKinley	20,320
2. Mount St. Elias	18,008
3. Mount Foraker	17,400
4. Mount Bona	16,500
5. Mount Blackburn	16,390
6. Mount Sanford	16,237
7. Mount Vancouver	15,979
8. South Buttress	15,885
9. Mount Churchill	15,638
10. Mount Fairwether	15,300

necessary for cooking in what is essentially a treeless tundra. King Salmon offers the most extensive travel facilities, services, and supplies.

- Spawning runs of sockeye salmon fight their way up the Aniakchak River and into Surprise Lake. Fishing is permitted with an Alaska fishing license. Sport hunting is permitted in the preserve but not in the monument area.
- The Aniakchak River provides one of the most interesting river-rafting trips in the world, beginning inside the Aniakchak volcano caldera (at Surprise Lake) and then flowing rapidly downhill through treeless tundra to the sea. Beware, though, weather on Aniakchak is severe; life-threatening conditions can develop rapidly.

BERING LAND BRIDGE NATIONAL PRESERVE

70 miles northeast of Nome; 40 miles southeast of Kotzebue.

PO Box 220
Nome, AK 99762-0220
907-443-2522
http://www.nps.gov/bela

The 55-mile stretch of sea water that separates Alaska and Siberia was dry land about 20,000 years ago. Most archaeologists agree that it was across the 1,000-mile-wide Bering Land Bridge, also called Beringia, that humans first passed from Asia to populate the Americas. This 2.7-million-acre preserve is accessible in the summer by bush planes and small boats, and, in the winter, by small planes on skis, snow machines, or dogsleds. Preserve activities include strenuous tundra hiking; snowmobiling; cross-country skiing; hunting and fishing (under state regulations); and exploration of remains from the Gold Rush era and from early Eskimo life. Some small villages are nearby, but, very often, you are absolutely alone in the preserve.

Sam's Tips

- From the towns of Nome and Kotzebue, served daily by jets from Anchorage, bush planes and small boats provide most summer access into the preserve.
- Summer days are long, almost without darkness; winter days are short, with only a few hours of light.
- Park scenery includes Serpentine Hot Springs, tucked into a haunting valley marked by imposing granite spires called tors; extensive lava flows and ash/steam explosion craters, now turned to lakes called maars; dynamic coast and beach environments of barrier islands and low sand dunes; and a wide range of both wet tundra plant communities on the coast and alpine tundra on mountains in and near the park.
- Facilities are limited, although there are a few trails, and six shelter cabins are scattered throughout the preserve. The cabins are mostly for emergency winter use. One bunkhouse-style cabin at Serpentine Hot Springs sleeps 15 to 20 people. All cabins are unreserved, and bush etiquette may require sharing with strangers.
- Camping is relatively unrestricted; there are no formal campsites in the park. For safety purposes, stop by preserve headquarters to file an itinerary with the park.

HOW A SLIVER OF TECHNOLOGY TAMED THE ARCTIC

Archaeological evidence suggests that it wasn't until 14,000 to 13,000 years ago that humans migrated into North America by crossing from Siberia to Alaska via the Bering land bridge. Most researchers agree that, to survive in arctic and subarctic environments, ancient humans had to be able to make clothing that was generally form-fitting and relatively weather-tight. The invention of the awl, a pointed implement used for stitching together animal skins for garments and other uses, was the technological breakthrough that most likely enabled ancient peoples to begin to colonize cold regions before moving on to settlements to the south. The eyed needle, which evolved from the awl and is found on 30,000-year-old Russian campsites, would have allowed strong, weather-tight, and, in some cases, water-tight clothing seams to be made.

Thus, according to the BLM, it can be said that this simple tool and those skilled in its use were responsible, in part, for the human occupation of the New World.

CAPE KRUSENSTERN NATIONAL MONUMENT

10 miles northwest of Kotzebue; 500 miles northwest of Fairbanks.

PO Box 1029
Kotzebue, AK 99752
907-442-3890
http://www.nps.gov/cakr

Alaska Natural History Association. (401 West First Avenue, Anchorage, AK 99501; 907-274-8440)

The 114 beach ridges of Cape Krusenstern tell the history of the changing shorelines of the Chukchi Sea and an estimated 4,000 years of prehistoric human use. The park is administered along with nearby Kobuk Valley National Park and Noatak National Preserve. Collectively, the three units were once known as the Northwest Alaska Areas. Now, after the recent merger with Bering Land Bridge National Preserve, the four units are known, administratively, as "Western Arctic National Parklands." In summer, the tremendous show of wildflowers coloring the beach ridges and nearby hills competes with the huge numbers of birds that come to the coastal area for nesting. Inupinq Eskimos still hunt marine animals along the outer beaches, and local rural residents are allowed to hunt in the monument for subsistence resources.

SAM'S TIPS

- The park is accessible via scheduled airlines from Fairbanks or Anchorage.
- There are no roads into the park.

CHUGACH NATIONAL FOREST

130 miles southeast of Anchorage.

3301 C Street, Suite 300
Anchorage, AK 99503
907-271-2500
http://www.fs.fed.us

Alaska Natural History Association. (401 West First Avenue, Anchorage, AK 99501; 907-274-8440)

Pronounced "Chew'-gatch," this 5.6-million-acre forest—roughly the size of Massachusetts and Rhode Island combined—is the most northern of the national forests, only 500 miles south of the Arctic Circle. One-third of the forest is made up of rocks and moving ice—glaciers. The remainder is a tapestry of the mountains, lakes, and rivers of the Kenai Peninsula; the islands and glaciers of Prince William Sound; and the wetlands of the Copper River Delta. For more than 100 years, the area has been continually inhabited by Alaskan Eskimos

FOREST SERVICE SCENIC BYWAY

Seward Highway

Connecting the cities of Anchorage and Seward, the 127-mile Seward Highway travels through a mix of saltwater bays, ice-blue glaciers, knife-edged ridges, and alpine valleys. This is the most popular travel route in Alaska. *Contact Chugach National Forest.*

and Indians. Across the centuries, the forest has attracted Spaniards seeking empires; Russians seeking furs; English looking for a northwest passage to the Pacific; and Americans seeking whale oil, petroleum, fish, gold, copper, coal, furs, timber, and strategic defense.

SAM'S TIPS

- The forest is widely known for its salmon, lake and rainbow trout, and other species.
- The only major road through Chugach is the Seward Highway Scenic Byway, winding south from Anchorage on its way to Seward. Most of the forest is accessible by aircraft or boat, or on foot. A number of commercial operators and outfitters provide boat and plane access to some of the wildest areas.
- Nearby points of interest include Kenai Fjords National Park, near Seward; Kenai National Wildlife Refuge, along the western boundary of the forest; Chugach State Park and the city of Anchorage, near the northwest corner of the forest; and Wrangell–St. Elias National Park and Preserve, bordering the northeast edge.
- The forest contains portions of the Historic Iditarod Trail, which can be hiked, biked, skied, and, of course, dogsledded.

DENALI NATIONAL PARK AND PRESERVE

240 miles north of Anchorage; 120 miles south of Fairbanks.

PO Box 9
Denali Park, AK 99755
907-683-2294
http://www.nps.gov/dena

 **Alaska Natural History Association.** (401 West First Avenue, Anchorage, AK 99501; 907-274-8440)

 **Denali Foundation.** (PO Box 212, Denali National Park, AK 99755)

Denali, the "High One," is the name Athabascan native people gave Mount McKinley. At 20,320 feet, it is North America's highest mountain and, according to geologists, it is still rising. The massive snowy peak crowns the volcanic, 600-mile-long Alaska Range that runs through the Denali National Park and Preserve. Earthquake tremors frequently occur. Denali's 6 million acres of unspoiled wilderness encompass a complete subarctic ecosystem with miniaturized plants and large mammals such as grizzly bears, wolves, caribou, and moose.

Sam's Tips

- Private vehicles are restricted beyond the Savage River (14 miles into the park). Bus traffic is limited, although buses travel regularly from the Visitor Access Center to other sites in the park. (Some trips can take as long as 11 hours, round trip.) There are two bus systems operating in the park. Tour buses feature a narrated bus tour and wildlife viewing. Lunch is provided. Seats are in heavy demand, and waits of up to 2 days are normal during peak season. For tour bus reservations, call 800-276-7234. Visitors wishing to day-hike, camp, backpack, or picnic in the park should use shuttle buses. Reservations are made by calling 800-622-7275.
- The Alaska Railroad provides daily summer passenger and freight service to the park from Anchorage and Fairbanks. For more information, write: Alaska Railroad Corporation, Passenger Services, PO Box 107500, Anchorage, AK 99510-7500, or call 800-544-0552 (Continental United States and Hawaii), 907-265-2494 (Anchorage), or 907-456-4155 (Fairbanks).
- All Mount McKinley and Mount Foraker climbers must register 60 days prior to their ascent and pay a climber's fee. For more information, write Talkeetna Ranger Station, PO Box 588, Talkeetna, AK 99676, or call 907-733-2231.

Park History

Charles Sheldon, a naturalist and hunter, first traveled here in 1906 and again in 1907 with a packer and guide named Harry Karstens, who later made the first ascent of Mount McKinley's south peak and served as the park's first superintendent. Sheldon devoted much of his 1907 travels to studying boundaries for the proposed national park, which would include territories suitable for a game refuge. When he returned to the East in 1908, the Game Committee of the Boone and Crockett Club, of which he was chairman, launched the campaign to establish a national park. Largely due to these efforts, Mount McKinley National Park was established in 1917. Mount McKinley, however, was not wholly included in its boundaries—the park was originally established to protect large mammals, not because of majestic Mount McKinley.

In 1980, the boundary was expanded to include both the Denali caribou herd's wintering and calving grounds and the entire Mount McKinley region. Now more than tripled in size, the park became Denali National Park and Preserve.

THE ALASKA NATURAL HISTORY ASSOCIATION

Alaska Natural History Association
605 West 4th Avenue, Suite 85
Anchorage, AK 99501
907-274-8440

Information on these public lands is available from the association:

Alaska Maritime National Wildlife Refuge
Cape Krusenstern National Monument
Chugach National Forest
Denali National Park and Preserve
Glacier Bay National Park and Preserve
Innoko National Wildlife Refuge
Katmai National Park and Preserve
Kenai Fjords National Park
Kenai National Wildlife Refuge
King Salmon Visitor Center
Kobuk Valley National Park
Kodiak National Wildlife Refuge
Koyukuk Nowitna National Wildlife Refuge
Lake Clark National Park and Preserve
Noatak National Preserve
Sitka National Historical Park
Tetlin National Wildlife Refuge
Tongass National Forest
Wrangell–St. Elias National Park and Preserve
Yukon Delta National Wildlife Refuge

GATES OF THE ARCTIC NATIONAL PARK AND PRESERVE

200 miles northwest of Fairbanks; 20 miles northeast of Bettles or Evansville.

PO Box 74680
Fairbanks, AK 99707-4680
Headquarters: 201 First Avenue
907-456-0281
http://www.nps.gov/gaar

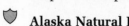

Alaska Natural History Association. (401 West First Avenue, Anchorage, AK 99501; 907-274-8440)

Gates of the Arctic is located in the northernmost Rocky Mountains. Along with adjacent Noatak National Preserve and Kobuk Valley National Park,

Gates of the Arctic comprises one of the world's largest parkland areas. This arctic wilderness was established to protect the environment's natural features, including six national wild rivers; to give access to wilderness recreational activities; and to protect the habitat for the western and central Arctic caribou herds.

Sam's Tips

- Scheduled flights from Fairbanks land at Bettles/Evansville and Anaktuvuk Pass. From these points, or from Fairbanks, you can charter small aircraft into either the park or the preserve areas. It's common to wait days for decent flying weather. Contact the park headquarters for a list of licensed air taxis, guides, and outfitters.
- There are no developed facilities in the park and preserve. Limited lodging is available in the neighboring communities of Bettles, Anaktuvuk Pass, and Coldfoot.
- The main ranger stations are located in Fairbanks and Bettles. The Bettles ranger station is staffed throughout the summer, but the stations at Anaktuvuk Pass and Coldfoot are open only periodically.

GLACIER BAY NATIONAL PARK AND PRESERVE

Headquarters is located at Bartlett Cove, 65 miles west of Juneau.

PO Box 140
Gustavus, AK 99826
907-697-2232
http://www.nps.gov/glba

Alaska Natural History Association. (401 West First Avenue, Anchorage, AK 99501; 907-274-8440)

Visitors to Glacier Bay can cruise along shorelines that were completely covered by ice just 200 years ago. By 1879, the ice had retreated up the bay 48 miles; four decades later, the ice had backed up another 17 miles. Scientists are studying this rapid glacial retreat to learn more about glaciers, climate, and how plants get started in previously ice-covered terrain. The bay is an ancestral home to Tlingit Indians, the original inhabitants, and the park offers exhibits on their culture as well as the area's natural history. Glacier Bay is also a whalewatching mecca where minke, humpback, and orca whales can be spotted. Although large cruise ships often schedule stops in the bay, few people live in this largely isolated and undeveloped area.

Sam's Tips

- Planes from Juneau land at Gustavus, very close to the southeastern corner of the park. Bus and taxi service into the park is available there.

- If you want to hike in the back-country, you'll need to arrange a boat or float plane dropoff. Learn the rules about visiting the back-country; and secure a permit at Bartlett Cove before you go.

KATMAI NATIONAL PARK AND PRESERVE

290 miles southwest of Anchorage.

PO Box 7
King Salmon, AK 99613
907-246-3305
http://www.nps.gov/katm

Alaska Natural History Association. (401 West First Avenue, Anchorage, AK 99501; 907-274-8440)

The Novarupta Volcano, one of five volcanoes in the Katmai Group, erupted in 1912. If the eruption had occurred in New York City, it would have been heard in Chicago, the fumes would have tarnished brass in Denver, acid rain could have burned skin in Toronto, the ash would have been a foot deep in Philadelphia, and Manhattan would have had no survivors. Today, the surface geothermal features have cooled. At Katmai Park and Preserve, you can visit the Valley of Ten Thousand Smokes, which, after the eruption, contained tens of thousands of smoke vents curling up from the fissured floor, a few of which remain active. Other activities include bear viewing from one of two bear-viewing platforms along the Brooks River; world-class sportfishing for salmon and trout; a major archaeological site dating back 4,000 years, including, at Brooks Camp, a reconstructed, partially underground house like those used for shelter by the Brooks River area natives; scenic flights over coastal waterfalls and glacier-covered mountains; boating on enormous lakes and bays; and floating on Katmai's rushing rivers.

Bear Behavior

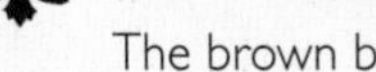

The brown bears, or grizzlies, that live in Katmai are huge, weighing up to 900 pounds. In summer, North America's largest land predators gather along streams to feast on salmon runs. They enter their dens in November and emerge in April. Mating occurs from May to mid-July, and the cubs are born in the dens in midwinter.

Cubs generally weigh 1 pound. They stay with their mother for 2 years, and the interval between litters is usually at least 3 years.

Bears are, of course, unpredictable. Visitors to Katmai are prohibited from intentionally approaching or remaining within 50 yards of a bear, or within 100 yards of a bear with cubs. Viewing platforms are available, where bears may be safely seen at close distances.

SAM'S TIPS

- Daily commercial flights connect Anchorage with King Salmon, about 6 miles from the park's west boundary. Air taxis operate daily between King Salmon and Brooks Camp from June to September; a few offer year-round charter service. Write to the park for a list of authorized air-taxi operators and guides for flightseeing, backpacking, canoeing, and fishing.
- Back-country campers should get a permit from the Brooks Camp Visitor Center or the park's King Salmon headquarters. Be sure to hang your food or use a bear-proof container.

KENAI FJORDS NATIONAL PARK

130 miles south of Anchorage via the Seward Highway; 40 miles southwest of Seward.

PO Box 1727
Seward, AK 99664-1727
907-224-3175
Recorded park information:
907-224-2132
http://www.nps.gov/kefj

Alaska Natural History Association. (401 West First Avenue, Anchorage, AK 99501; 907-274-8440)

Kenai Fjords is home to: valley and tidewater glaciers; one of the last remaining ice fields (35 miles long by 20 miles wide) in the world; one of the four major ice caps in the United States; waterfalls and mountain streams; sweeping mountain ranges; craggy cliffs; Native American archaeological sites; isolated gold extraction locations; and such wildlife as moose, bear, thousands of seabirds, sea lions, sea otters, and seals. The park is named for the glacier-carved fjords along the coast of the Kenai Peninsula. Today, at the seaward end of the park, mountains are slipping into the sea from the collision of two tectonic plates in the Earth's crust. What were once alpine valleys filled with glacier ice are now deepwater mountain-flanked fjords. A 1964 earthquake dropped the shoreline in Seward 6 feet in just 1 day. Visitors explore the park in a number of ways—boat tours, flightseeing tours, driving tours, hiking, skiing, and dogsledding.

Sam's Tips

- The park has five public-use cabins that cost approximately $30 per day. For reservations and information, contact the park.
- The town of Seward, one of Alaska's more popular winter destinations, hosts special events like family-oriented full-moon ski trips, dogsled races, and the Polar Bear Jump-Off Festival.
- The Alaska Sealife Center is a state-of-the-art facility for marine mammal research and wildlife rehabilitation. It is being paid for out of the state and federal *Exxon Valdez* Oil Spill Restoration funds. For more information, contact the Alaska Sealife Center, Box 1329, Seward, AK 99664; 907-224-3080.

KLONDIKE GOLD RUSH NATIONAL HISTORICAL PARK

85 miles northwest of Juneau; the southern tip of the park starts at Skagway.

PO Box 517
Skagway, AK 99840
907-983-2921
http://www.nps.gov/klgo

Alaska Natural History Association. (401 West First Avenue, Anchorage, AK 99501; 907-274-8440)

In 1897, when a steamer from Alaska put in at Seattle with a ton of gold aboard, it set off the last of the great gold rushes. Klondike Gold Rush National Historical Park preserves historic buildings from this period in Skagway, which is now a regular port of call for cruise ships and has a lively nightlife. Attractions include the Trail of '98 Museum, the Gold Rush Cemetery, hikes to the mountains above town, and a trip to the townsite of Dyea, reached from Skagway via a 9-mile dirt road. Backpacking is popular in this spectacular geographic area of islands, mountain passes, glaciers, rivers, lakes, and forest.

SAM'S TIPS

- To follow in the footsteps of the gold rush stampeders, hike the 33-mile Chilkoot Trail, a difficult hike that usually takes 3 to 5 days.
- Skagway has year-round scheduled and chartered air service, via Juneau, Haines, and Whitehorse. By car and bus, use the Alaska and Klondike Highways. You also can take a ferry from Bellingham, Prince Rupert, Ketchikan, Wrangell, Petersburg, Sitka, Juneau, and Haines. Reservations are needed for ferry travel; contact the park office for information.

KOBUK VALLEY NATIONAL PARK

60 miles east of Kotzebue.

PO Box 1029
Kotzebue, AK 99752
907-442-8300
http://www.nps.gov/kova

Alaska Natural History Association. (401 West First Avenue, Anchorage, AK 99501; 907-274-8440)

Located entirely north of the Arctic Circle, Kobuk Valley National Park has a dry, cold climate approximating that of the late Pleistocene era. Here, in the northernmost extent of the boreal forest, you'll find Arctic wildlife such as caribou, grizzly and black bear, wolf, and fox. The 25-square-mile Great Kobuk Sand Dunes lie just south of the Kobuk River, against the base of the Waring

Mountains. Archaeological sites revealing at least 9,000 years of human occupation are the benchmarks by which all other Arctic sites are measured. The park is administered jointly with nearby Cape Krusenstern National Monument and Noatak National Preserve. Collectively, these sites are known as the Northwest Alaska Areas.

LAKE CLARK NATIONAL PARK AND PRESERVE

150 miles southwest of Anchorage.

Headquarters
4230 University Drive, Suite 311
Anchorage, AK 99508
907-271-3751

Field Headquarters
Port Alsworth, AK 99653
907-781-2218
http://www.nps.gov/lacl

Alaska Natural History Association. (401 West First Avenue, Anchorage, AK 99501; 907-274-8440)

The sparsely populated Lake Clark National Park and Preserve is primarily accessible by aircraft. The spectacular scenery stretches from the shores of Cook Inlet, across the Chigmit Mountains, to the tundra-covered hills of the western interior. The Chigmits, where the Alaskan and Aleutian ranges meet, are a jagged array of mountains and glaciers and include two active volcanoes—Mount Redoubt and Mount Iliamna. Fifty-mile-long Lake Clark and many other lakes and rivers within the 4-million-acre park are critical salmon habitat to the Bristol Bay salmon fishery, one of the largest sockeye salmon fishing grounds in the world. The lakes and rivers also offer excellent float trips, fishing, kayaking, and wildlife viewing.

SAM'S TIPS

- Float planes may land on the many lakes throughout the area. Wheeled planes land on open beaches, gravel bars, or private airstrips in or near the park. A 1- to 2-hour flight from Anchorage, Kenai, or Homer will provide access to most points within the park and preserve.
- Park service facilities, besides the field headquarters, are minimal. Backcountry patrol cabins, staffed on a limited basis, are located at Telaquana Lake, Twin Lakes, Crescent Lake, and Chinitna Bay.

NOATAK NATIONAL PRESERVE

25 miles northwest of Kotzebue; 85 miles west of Bettles and Evansville.

PO Box 1029
Kotzebue, AK 99752
907-442-8300
http://www.nps.gov/noat

Alaska Natural History Association. (401 West First Avenue, Anchorage, AK, 99501; 907-274-8440)

Noatak National Preserve, which is north of the Arctic Circle, protects the largest undeveloped river basin in the United States. The Noatak River runs the length of the preserve, from Mount Igikpak in the east to the western end of the park and then south to the Kotzebue Sound. Along its 425-mile course, it has carved out the Grand Canyon of the Noatak, which is ideal for kayaking and canoeing. Among the large mammals in the preserve are grizzly bears, caribou, wolves, and lynx. Summer brings migratory birds from as far away as Asia and the tip of South America.

SAM'S TIPS

- Charter flights arrive at the preserve out of Kotzebue and Bettles/Evansville, which are served by air from Fairbanks or Anchorage.

SITKA NATIONAL HISTORICAL PARK

595 miles southeast of Anchorage.

106 Metlaktla Street
Sitka, AK 99835
907-747-6281
http://www.nps.gov/sitk

Alaska Natural History Association. (401 West First Avenue, Anchorage, AK, 99501; 907-274-8440)

Alaska's oldest federally designated park was established in 1910 to commemorate the Battle of Sitka (from the Tlingit name for the area, *Shee Aitka,* meaning "the people on the outside [i.e., seaward side] of Shee [Baranoff Island]"). Russians arrived here in 1799, but they didn't mix well with the Tlingit natives, who had been living in this chilly, rain-drenched Alaskan panhandle for centuries. Tlingit warriors attacked Redoubt St. Michael, a nearby Russian settlement, in 1802, killing nearly all the Russians. Two years later, the rebuilt Russian community drove the natives from their village and built a fortified town, which they called New Archangel (Novo Archangelsk in Russian). The Russian Bishop's

House is one of four surviving examples of Colonial Russian log architecture in North America. The park contains 1.6 miles of wooded trails lined with replicas of the totem poles brought back to Sitka in 1905 from the Louisiana Purchase Exposition. The originals, made by Tlingit and Haida villagers for the Exposition, are now in storage.

Sam's Tips

- No roads reach Sitka from the mainland. Visitors arrive by cruise ship, Alaska State Ferry, chartered plane, or regularly scheduled flights from Anchorage or Seattle. There are also accommodations for private boats and planes.
- Seven miles up the coast from Sitka, near the Alaska State Ferry landing, is the site of the destroyed Russian settlement, Redoubt St. Michael. Shuttle buses transport sightseers and ferry passengers to town.

TONGASS NATIONAL FOREST

Juneau, Sitka, and Skagway are all within the area of this national forest.

204 Siginaka Way
Sitka, AK 99835
907-747-6671
http://www.alaska.net/~tnfhp1

Alaska Natural History Association. (401 West First Avenue, Anchorage, AK 99501; 907-274-8440)

Named for the Tongass clan of Tlingit Indians, who lived on a small island off its southern edge, this 17-million-acre forest, the largest in the national forest system, extends 500 miles northward from the Alaska–Canada border to just north of Skagway. The forest brings together ice fields, glaciers, and the long, deepwater fjords carved by glaciers. Many of the glaciers, unexplored and unnamed, are waiting for their first visitors.

Sam's Tips

- This southeast part of Alaska is serviced by airlines and cruise ships, but the main transportation is the Alaska Marine Highway Ferry System. For information, call 800-642-0066 (Juneau).
- A large population of bald eagles and grizzly bears lives in the park. All five species of Pacific salmon spawn in the rivers and streams.
- Forest recreation includes backpacking, fishing, hunting, photography, boating, nature study, and camping. The forest rents more than 140 public recreation cabins.

Misty Fjords National Monument and Wilderness

Located in southeastern Alaska, next to the Canadian border, Misty Fjords is a coastal ecosystem comprised of long fjords that were formed by glacial erosion and are now lined with sea cliffs rising for thousands of feet. The rest of the monument (the western border is 25 air miles from Ketchikan) consists of forested areas of Kitka spruce, western hemlock and cedar, and still-active glaciers along the Canadian border. Killer whales, sea lions, harbor seals, and Dall porpoises use the saltwater bays and passages in the area. The National Forest Service maintains 17 cabins and approximately 20 miles of trails. For more information, contact Misty Fjords National Monument and Wilderness, 3031 Tongass Avenue, Ketchikan, AK 99901; 907-225-2148.

For a complete on-line directory of Forest Service cabins to rent in the Tongass and Chugach forests, go to: http://www.midnightsun.com/usfs.htm.

- Other points of interest: Southeast Alaska Indian Cultural Center, 907-747-8061; Totem Heritage Center, 907-225-5900; and Alaska Chilkat Bald Eagle Preserve, 907-766-2292.

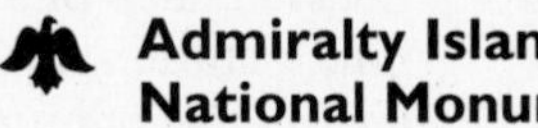

Admiralty Island National Monument

Inside the Tongass National Forest, 15 miles west of Juneau, is Admiralty Island, 937,396 acres of rain forest, alpine tundra, and ice fields accessible only by boat or floatplane. The spruce–hemlock rain forest gradually changes to alpine tundra and permanent ice fields above the 2,000-foot timberline. Among the numerous bays and inlets is Seymour Canal, on the east side of the island, which supports the largest concentration of bald eagles in southeast Alaska. For more details, contact Admirality Island National Monument, 8461 Old Dairy Road, Juneau, AK 99801; 907-586-8790.

WRANGELL–ST. ELIAS NATIONAL PARK AND PRESERVE

190 miles northeast of Anchorage; 180 miles southeast of Fairbanks.

PO Box 439
Copper Center, AK 99573
907-822-5234
http://www.nps.gov/wrst

Alaska Natural History Association. (401 West First Avenue, Anchorage, AK 99501; 907-274-8440)

At Wrangell–St. Elias National Park and Preserve, the number and scale of everything are simply enormous. At more than 13 million acres—the size of 6 Yellowstones—this is the largest U.S. national park. It includes 9 of the 16 highest mountain peaks in the United States. One of the glaciers, Malaspina, is larger than Rhode Island and carries so much glacial silt that plants and trees take hold on its extremities, grow to maturity, and topple over the edge as the glacier melts. The park is the meeting point of four major mountain ranges; the Wrangells, the Chugach, the St. Elias, and the Nutzotin and Mentasta. The high country is covered with snow year-round. The Bagley Ice Field, near the coast, is the largest subpolar ice field in North America. Vegetation in the park varies from dense forest to low-lying shrubs. The park also contains a variety of wildlife. Dall sheep and mountain goats patrol the peaks, herds of caribou feed on the lichen, and moose browse in the bogs.

YUKON–CHARLEY RIVERS NATIONAL PRESERVE

100 miles east of Fairbanks; 10 miles north of Eagle.

PO Box 167
Eagle, AK 99738
907-547-2234
http://www.nps.gov/yuch

Alaska Natural History Association. (401 West First Avenue, Anchorage, AK 99501; 907-274-8440)

Located deep in the interior of Alaska, this preserve is wilder and less populated now than it was 80 years ago. The area is largely untouched by glaciation and mostly free of human imprint—only 30 or so year-round residents live in an area the size of New Jersey. The Yukon River, which flows under 6 feet of ice in the winter, runs from the town of Circle, at the northwestern corner of the preserve, to Eagle, at the southeastern corner. The rest of the preserve is remote mountainous and forested wilderness. Good wilderness survival skills are a necessity for all visitors.

Sam's Tips

- Scheduled air taxis serve Eagle and Circle year-round.
- There are no accommodations, roads, maintained trails, or maintained public airstrips in the national preserve. In summer, Eagle, Circle, and Circle Hot Springs offer basic services.

Points of Interest

U.S. ARMY CORPS OF ENGINEERS

CHENA RIVER LAKES

Gently rolling slopes characterize the landscape of this area, dotted with ponds, peat bogs, oxbow lakes, and meandering streams. The clear waters of the rivers, ponds, and lakes provide excellent fish habitat. From Fairbanks, 17 miles east on Richardson Highway.

BUREAU OF LAND MANAGEMENT

WHITE MOUNTAINS NATIONAL RECREATION AREA

This 1-million-acre area is named for the unusual limestone cliffs found here, and is most popular in winter when cross-country skiers, snow machiners and dog mushers take advantage of the winter solitude. The Bureau maintains a number of public recreation cabins and about 300 miles of winter trails.

80 miles northeast of Fairbanks.

PINNELL MOUNTAIN NATIONAL RECREATION TRAIL

This 27-mile trail in the Steese National Conservation Area traverses high, scenic alpine ridges offering outstanding vistas of the surrounding terrain. It is passable only in summer and is known for its outstanding wildflower displays and vistas of the "midnight sun" in June.

100 miles northeast of Fairbanks.

For information about these and other Bureau of Land Management Alaska sites, contact:

Alaska State Office
222 West Seventh Ave. #13
Anchorage, AK 99513
907-271-5960
http://www.ak.blm.gov

FISH AND WILDLIFE SERVICE

ARCTIC NATIONAL WILDLIFE REFUGE

This is the nation's largest and most northerly national wildlife refuge. South Carolina could almost fit inside its borders, and it has 8 million acres of wilderness, the most of any refuge. It includes three major physiographic areas (arctic

RUSTIC CABINS IN ALASKA

Alaska's Chugach and Tongass National Forests offer nightly lodging in many rustic guard stations. These cabins are out-of-the-way gems, located in the middle of some of America's most pristine lands.

Cabins are accessible via trail, floatplane, or boat. Facilities are spartan: a table, chairs, wood stove and bunks (some with mattresses, some without). You might need to bring your own drinking water and cut your own firewood. Expect to use outdoor privies, and don't expect a telephone. The National Forest Service recommends that children under the age of 12 not stay in their rustic guard stations as many of them are over 60 feet above ground.

These cabins can be a remarkable place to stay amidst Alaska's beautiful National Forests. Cabins cost $25 a night, plus an $8.25 reservation fee. Cabins house as many as eight guests. Call for more information and to make reservations, which are required.

Chugach National Forest
USFS Reservation Center
PO Box 900
Cumberland, MD 21502
800-280-2667
fax: 301-722-9802

For current information on reservations at Tongass, or for specific information on the dozens of cabins available in both these National Forests, contact:

USFS Information Center
101 Egan Drive
Juneau, AL 99801
907-586-8751

tundra, Brooks Range, and boreal forest), glaciers, and 18 major rivers, of which 3 are designated wild. Because of its size and diversity, the refuge accommodates the greatest variety of plant and animal life of any conservation area in the circumpolar north. Birds of 180 species from 4 continents have been observed here, and endangered peregrine falcons are common. Land mammals of 36 species are inhabitants, including Porcupine caribou and all three species of North American bear. Nine marine mammal species live along its coast, and 36 fish species swim in its rivers and lakes. There are no trails, roads, or developments. Visitors must fly, boat, or walk to get there.

For more information on this site, contact:

Arctic National Wildlife Refuge
101 Twelfth Avenue
Box 20
Fairbanks, AK 99701
907-456-0250
http://www.r7.fws.gov/nwr/arctic/arctic.html

For more information on Alaska's 15 other national wildlife refuges, contact:

The Public Affairs Office
1011 East Tudor Road
Anchorage, AK 99503
907-786-3486
http://www.r7.fws.gov

CALIFORNIA

ANGELES NATIONAL FOREST

20 miles northeast of Los Angeles.

701 North Santa Anita Avenue
Arcadia, CA 91006
818-574-1613
http://www.fs.fed.us

San Gabriel Mountains Interpretive Association. (7 North Fifth Avenue, Arcadia, CA 91006)

This 693,667-acre forest, which covers one-fourth of the land in Los Angeles County, is located in the hills north and northeast of Los Angeles. Elevations range from 1,200 to 10,064 feet. The Big Santa Anita Canyon area of the forest includes 55-foot Sturtevant Falls, one of the highest waterfalls in the park, and the Mount Wilson Skyline Park, which offers a spectacular view across the Los Angeles Basin to the Pacific Ocean. The Mount Wilson Observatory, located in the forest, is home to one of the world's largest telescopes.

CABRILLO NATIONAL MONUMENT

San Diego.

1800 Cabrillo Memorial Drive
San Diego, CA 92106-3601
619-557-5450
http://www.nps.gov/cabr

 **Cabrillo Historical Association.** (same address as above)

Juan Rodriguez Cabrillo set out to explore the "Northern Mystery" just 50 years after Christopher Columbus sailed from Europe, but Cabrillo was killed after breaking his leg during a scuffle with the Island Chumash Indians in the Channel Islands. In his honor, Cabrillo's men named the land that he discovered after him. The monument established in his honor overlooks his landing site in San Diego Bay and includes a lighthouse furnished in original and period pieces from the 1800s, demonstrating the life of a typical lighthouse keeper and his family. Remnants of World Wars I and II military structures are also on the site.

SAM'S TIPS

- The annual migration of the gray whale takes place between late December and the end of February, when more than 20,000 whales make the trip from

Alaska to Baja, California. Their return trip in February/March signals the arrival of spring. There is a whale overlook at the monument so that visitors can witness this amazing sight.

- On the rocky western side of Point Loma are tidepools filled with anemone and 100 other species of plants and animals. The best time to explore these pools is during the low tides of fall, winter, and spring.
- Cabrillo is rich with birds of prey, including the bald eagle, the peregrine falcon, and the zone-tailed hawk.

CHANNEL ISLANDS NATIONAL PARK

60 miles from Los Angeles; 30 miles from Santa Barbara.

1901 Spinnaker Drive
Ventura, CA 93001
805-658-5730
http://www.nps.gov/chis

Southwest Parks and Monuments Association. (221 North Court Avenue, Tuscon, AZ 85701; 520-622-1999)

Lying just off California's southern coast, the Channel Islands appear quite close on clear days, but their isolation has kept them relatively undeveloped. Five of the eight islands and one nautical mile of the surrounding ocean, including kelp forests, have been set aside as parkland because of their unique natural and cultural resources. More than 2,000 terrestrial plants and animals exist within the park—145 of which are found nowhere else in the world. Marine life ranges from microscopic plankton to the blue whale. Popular activities

Diving in the Channel Islands

In the waters surrounding the Channel Islands lay the remains of over 100 shipwrecks, spanning the history of the European presence in the New World. These shipwrecks attract a significant amount of marine life and are popular with divers. Here are some of the most interesting animals you might encounter:

Gray whale
Steller sea lion
California sea lion
Northern elephant seal
Northern fur seal
Guadalupe fur seal
Pacific white-sided dolphin
Spiny lobster
Giant squid
Soft coral
Sea lettuce
Leather star
Sponge
Sea palms

include scuba diving, snorkeling, kayaking, whale watching, sailing, and tide-pool exploration.

Sam's Tips

- The main Visitor Center for the Channel Islands is on the waterfront in Ventura. Boat transportation to the islands is provided through the Island Packers Company (805-642-1393).
- These treeless islands are extremely windy; if you're camping, be prepared for winds of up to 30 miles per hour.
- No rentals or supplies are available once you reach the islands, so rent all necessary equipment before you leave the mainland.

CLEVELAND NATIONAL FOREST

San Diego.

10845 Rancho Bernardo Road
Suite 200
San Diego, CA 92127-2107
619-673-6180
http://www.fs.fed.us

Laguna Mountain Volunteer Association, Inc. (3348 Alpine Boulevard, Alpine, CA 91901; 619-445-6235)

Cleveland National Forest, separated into 3 districts, is located approximately 3.5 miles east of San Diego and extends northward approximately 130 miles. The southernmost district is noted for the Laguna Mountains, the timbered campsites of the Laguna Mountain Recreation Area, and the Hauser and Pine Creek Wilderness areas. The central district includes Palomar Mountain, with the famed Palomar Observatory, the rugged Agua Tibia Wilderness, and high desert landscapes. The northern district contains the San Mateo Wilderness, nearly 40,000 acres of rugged southern California chaparral wildland, with steep canyons and arduous hiking trails.

DEATH VALLEY NATIONAL PARK

300 miles northeast of Los Angeles; 120 miles northwest of Las Vegas, NV.

Death Valley, CA 92328
760-786-2331
http://www.nps.gov/deva

Death Valley Natural History Association. (PO Box 188, Death Valley, CA 92328; 760-786-3285)

Death Valley—the name is foreboding and gloomy, yet in this desert valley, much of it below sea level, or in the surrounding high mountains, visitors find

Ghost Towns

The mining boom came and left very quickly in Death Valley. Here are short histories of the towns that were in or around what is now Death Valley National Park.

Ballarat

The Radcliffe Mine at Ballarat, a few miles to the west of Death Valley, produced 15,000 tons of gold ore between 1898 and 1903. At its peak, the town was home to 400 people.

Chloride City

Chloride City sprang up in 1905, when the Bullfrog strike brought people into the area to rework old mining claims, and was completely abandoned the following year.

Greenwater

This town was built around a copper strike in 1905. Water had to be hauled in and was sold for $15 a barrel. The town was once home to 2,000 people and was known for a lively magazine called the *Death Valley Chuckwalla*. By 1909, the region's mining industry had collapsed and people left for other areas.

Harrisburg

Originally, the town was to be named Harrisberry after the two men who found the gold that launched it in 1905. Shorty Harris took credit for the strike and changed the name to Harrisburg after himself, but Peter Aguereberry, one of the original strike finders, still spent 40 years working his claims in the Eureka gold mine. Aguereberry's home and mine are all that remains of the town today.

Leadfield

Copper and lead claims had been filed in the area as early as 1905, but the claims were not heavily mined until 1926. By April of that year, Charles Julian, the flamboyant promoter who was president of the town's leading mining company, brought great numbers of people in, and the town was laid out with 1,749 lots. The town died in 1927, brought down by Julian's financial downfall.

Panamint City

Outlaws found silver in Surprise Canyon in 1873 and gave up their life of crime. By 1874, the town had a population of 2,000 citizens. In 1876, a flash flood destroyed most of the buildings.

Rhyolite

Once the biggest town in the Death Valley area, boasting a population as high as 10,000 citizens, Rhyolite had 2 churches, 50 saloons, 18 stores, 2 undertakers, 19 lodging houses, 8 doctors, 2 dentists, a stock exchange, and an opera house. The ghost town, which still has many remains, is located on Bureau of Land Management property just outside the northeast border of the park, in Nevada.

Skidoo

Founded in 1906, when 2 prospectors who were on their way to the strike at Harrisburg found gold here, the town became famous as the site of the only hanging to take place in Death Valley. As legend has it, a saloon owner named Hootch Simpson, who had fallen on hard times, attempted to rob a bank, failed, and later went back and shot the bank's owner. During the middle of the night, he was hanged by the townspeople. He was then hanged a second time to accommodate the news photographers who had missed the first hanging.

many signs of life. Attractions include spectacular wildflower displays, snow-covered peaks, beautiful sand dunes, abandoned gold and borax mines and industrial structures, the hottest spot in North America and the lowest point in the Western Hemisphere, a mostly cloudless deep-blue sky, spectacular mountain range views, the 2,400-foot-wide Ubehebe Crater, the Devil's Golf Course (where the surface is covered with jagged rock salt spikes), and colorful badlands and canyon country. Death Valley got its name from the severity of the environment. Visitors can find several ghost towns here, most of which were established during the mining periods of the early 1900s. Covering more than 3.3 million acres, Death Valley is the largest national park outside of Alaska.

Sam's Tips

- In 1994, over 1.3 million acres were added to the park. The new sections, located primarily to the northwest of the old boundary, include the highest peak in the Last Chance Mountains, the highest peak in the Funeral Mountains, and the ghost town of Panamint City. Many of these new sections are accessible only by four-wheel-drive vehicle or cross-country hiking.
- First-time visitors to Death Valley may be surprised that it is not an endless sea of sand. In fact, less than 1 percent of the land area of Death Valley is covered with dunes. The highest dunes in the park (and in California) are the Eureka Dunes (700 feet high), located in the northern part. The most accessible are the Death Valley Dunes; the highest rises about 100 feet.
- The Telescope Peak Trail is a hiker's dream. At 11,300 feet above the valley floor, the peak is the highest point in Death Valley National Park. The hike begins at the head of Wildrose Canyon, at an elevation of 8,133 feet, and includes spectacular views of Mount Whitney, the White Mountains, Panamint Valley, and, of course, Death Valley. The 14-mile round-trip trek takes between 6 and 9 hours.
- Death Valley's size and the distances between its major features require precaution. Gasoline is sold at only four places within the park and, because overheating of engines is common, radiator water is available from tanks alongside the park roads.

DEVILS POSTPILE NATIONAL MONUMENT

315 miles east of San Francisco; 340 miles north of Los Angeles.

785 North Main Street
Bishop, CA 93514
760-872-4881
http://www.nps.gov/depo

Sequoia Natural History Association, Inc. (HCR 89, Box 10, Three Rivers, CA 93271-9792; 209-565-3758)

This 800-acre monument on the western slopes of the Sierra Nevada preserves Devils Postpile and Rainbow Falls. Their formation is a story of fire and ice. The story began about 100,000 years ago when a volcano erupted in the valley of the Middle Fork of the San Joaquin River and covered it with lava 400 feet deep. As the lava cooled, it cracked, forming a pattern on the surfaces of the flow. These cracks eventually deepened and formed basalt columns 40 to 60 feet high, resembling a giant pipe organ or fenceposts (postpiles, to early ranchers). Some 10,000 years ago, a glacier flowed through the valley, leaving a sheer wall of columns exposed—Devils Postpile, among the world's finest examples of columnar-jointed basalt. Sometime after the last glacier melted, part of the river was diverted. At Rainbow Falls it rejoins its original course, cascading 101 feet over a cliff of volcanic lavas, andesite, and rhyodecite.

Sam's Tips

- The park is open from late June until late October, weather permitting. Call the park for exact dates and opening times.
- The bottom of Rainbow Falls may be reached by a stairway and short trail and is best visited noon through early afternoon.
- Hiking opportunities include the John Muir Trail, which links Yosemite with Sequoia and Kings Canyon national parks, as well as a portion of the Pacific Crest Trail.

ELDORADO NATIONAL FOREST

30 miles east of Sacramento; 90 miles northeast of San Francisco.

Headquarters
100 Forni Road
Placerville, CA 95667
916-622-5061
http://www.r5.pswfs.gov/eldorado/frames.htm

Eldorado National Forest Interpretive Association. (3070 Camino Heights Drive, Camino, CA 95709; 916-644-6048)

Located between the historic Mother Lode region and the peaks of the Sierra Nevada crest, the Eldorado National Forest overlooks the Lake Tahoe Basin. Its proximity to many metropolitan areas has made the forest one of the most popular year-round vacation areas in northern California. There are 2 wilderness areas, 12 reservoirs for water-related recreation, and plenty of campgrounds.

Sam's Tips

- The Forest Service's Institute of Forest Genetics is open to people who call ahead for tours. Nearby is the Placerville Nursery, where more than 18 million seedlings are grown annually for planting.

FOREST SERVICE SCENIC BYWAY

Carson Pass Highway

The Carson Pass Highway coves 58 miles on State Highway 88, from Dew Drop to Woodfords, through the Eldorado and Toiyabe national forests in northern California. Considered one of the most beautiful of the trans-Sierra highways, it has won national honors for its design and scenic vistas. *Contact Eldorado and Toiyabe National Forests.*

EUGENE O'NEILL NATIONAL HISTORIC SITE

25 miles east of San Francisco; 45 miles south of Sacramento.

PO Box 280
Danville, CA 94526
510-838-0249
http://www.nps.gov/euon

Southwest Parks and Monuments Association. (221 North Court Avenue, Tucson, AZ 85701; 520-622-1999)

After being awarded the Nobel Prize for Literature in 1936, Eugene O'Neill, author of such plays as *The Emperor Jones, Anna Christie, Desire Under the Elms,* and *Strange Interlude,* and his wife, Carlotta, took the accompanying stipend and built Tao House, which O'Neill referred to as his "final harbor." Over the next six years, before ill health forced him to give up writing, O'Neill completed the great dramas of his fifties: *The Iceman Cometh* and *Long Day's Journey into Night.* The house is now open to the public for tours.

FORT POINT NATIONAL HISTORIC SITE

San Francisco.

PO Box 29333
Presidio of San Francisco
San Francisco, CA 94129-0333
415-556-1693
http://www.nps.gov/fopo

Golden Gate National Park Association. (Fort Mason, Building 201, San Francisco, CA 94123; 415-561-3000)

Originally constructed by the US Army Corps of Engineers to prevent a hostile fleet from sailing into San Francisco Bay, the fort was designed to mount 126 massive cannons and was rushed to completion at the beginning of the Civil

War. With the advent of faster, more powerful rifled cannon, brick forts such as Fort Point were rendered obsolete. The last troops began leaving in 1880. The fort was used by the Army for storage and training purposes and then served as the base of operations for the construction of the Golden Gate Bridge. Fort Point is well preserved and includes several exhibits of early 19th-century armaments and military life.

GOLDEN GATE NATIONAL RECREATION AREA

San Francisco.

Fort Mason
San Francisco, CA 94123
415-556-0560
http://www.nps.gov/goga

Golden Gate National Park Association. (Fort Mason, Building 201, San Francisco, CA 94123; 415-561-3000)

Golden Gate National Recreation Area is the largest urban national park in the world—nearly 2½ times the size of neighboring San Francisco. None of the historic, urban, and natural features is more than an hour from downtown San Francisco. One of the most famous views within the park is the harbor entrance at the Golden Gate Bridge. Other sights include:

- Alcatraz Island, close to the city yet off-limits for years as a prison; an easy ferry trip from Fisherman's Wharf.
- Aquatic Park and Fort Mason, which have panoramic views of the city and bay. Fort Mason also serves as Park Headquarters and is home to the Fort Mason Center, which houses art galleries and museums.
- The Presidio, one of the oldest military posts in the nation. Besides the main post and Visitor Center, it has one of the west coast's oldest golf courses, constructed in 1895.
- Crissy Field, Baker Beach, Ocean Beach, and China Beach, which lie in the San Francisco portion of the Recreation Area. The best swimming is at China Beach and Crissy Field; the strong riptides of Ocean Beach and Baker Beach make the water too dangerous for swimming. Crissy Field is also one of the most popular wind surfing spots in the country.
- Fort Funston, with its high cliffs and strong winds, is a prime location for hang gliding.

TREASURE BENEATH THE WAVES: SHIPWRECKS WITHIN THE NATIONAL PARK SYSTEM

For more than half its history, American commerce was conducted almost solely by ships. Inevitably, there were losses of ships to storms and coastlines, to wars and accidents. Each wreck became a time capsule buried by sand and water. Hundreds of these sites lie within areas managed by the U.S. National Park Service. In all, 59 parks have identified important submerged cultural resources within their boundaries. Among the most notorious sites are:

Cape Hatteras National Seashore (NC)

More than 500 shipwrecks lie along the Outer Banks of Virginia and North Carolina. The earliest is the *Tiger,* a British ship sunk in 1585.

Cape Cod National Seashore (MA)

The seashore coastline and associated shoals carry the remains of more than 500 vessels, including the *Sparrowhawk* of 1623, and the 64-gun *H.M.S. Somerset,* wrecked in 1778 during the Revolutionary War.

Dry Tortugas National Park (FL)

More than 200 known vessels lie within the park's boundaries, including the *Nuestra Senora del Rosario,* sunk in 1622.

Golden Gate National Recreation Area (CA)

More than 100 barks, schooners, steamers, and other ships lie in offshore waters, including the medium clipper ship *King Philip,* sunk in 1856.

Isle Royale National Park (MI)

Ten major vessels lie in the offshore waters of this park, including the sidewheel steamship, *Cumberland,* sunk in 1877, and the package freighter *Kamloops,* lost in 1927 with no survivors.

Point Reyes National Seashore (CA)

Of more than a dozen shipwrecks here, the most significant is the Spanish galleon, *San Agustin,* wrecked in 1595 while making a survey of the California coast.

U.S.S. Arizona Memorial (HI)

In addition to the *U.S.S. Arizona,* there are the remains of the *U.S.S. Utah* and of aircraft lost in the Japanese attack on Pearl Harbor in 1941.

Mono Basin National Forest Scenic Area

In the heart of the Inyo National Forest is the Mono Basin National Forest Scenic Area. Mono Lake itself is located in the middle of a broad shallow basin, along the eastern access route to Yosemite National Park. Classic volcanic domes and craters and the towering Sierra Nevada contrast sharply with the picturesque lake. The brine shrimp and alkali flies that thrive in the lake's water by midsummer provide a plentiful food supply for more than 70 species of migratory birds. Notable migrants include the eared grebe, Wilson's phalarope, the red-necked phalarope, and the California gull, which nests on the lake's islands. Contact the Scenic Area directly (PO Box 429, Lee Vining, CA 93541; 760-647-3044).

INYO NATIONAL FOREST

180 miles southeast of San Francisco; 100 miles northwest of Las Vegas, NV.

873 North Main Street
Bishop, CA 93514
760-873-2400
http://www.r5.pswfs.gov/inyo

Eastern Sierra Interpretive Association. (308 West Line Street, Suite D, Bishop, CA 93514; 760-872-3070)

Extending 165 miles along the California/Nevada border between Los Angeles and Reno, the forest is comprised of 1.9 million acres of pristine lakes, fragile meadows, winding streams, rugged Sierra peaks, and the arid Great Basin Mountains. Habitats support vegetation ranging from semiarid deserts to alpine fell-fields. The Pacific Crest Trail, which extends from Canada to Mexico, traverses the forest from one end to the other.

JOHN MUIR NATIONAL HISTORIC SITE

25 miles northeast of San Francisco; 60 miles southwest of Sacramento.

4202 Alhambra Avenue
Martinez, CA 94553
510-228-8860
http://www.nps.gov/jomu

Southwest Parks and Monuments Association. (221 North Court Avenue, Tucson, AZ 85701; 520-622-1999)

As one of the founding members of the Sierra Club in 1892, John Muir, nicknamed "John of the Mountains," helped establish conservation as a critical element in managing the environment and its resources. Before moving into his home near Mount Wanda, Muir had already walked several thousand miles, pondering nature's role in maintaining civilization and human values. The site preserves the mansion where he lived from 1890 until his death in 1914.

GRANDMA PRISBEY'S BOTTLE VILLAGE, SIMI VALLEY, CALIFORNIA

Tressa "Grandma" Prisbrey started the bottle village—an imaginative world created out of milk of magnesia bottles, automobile headlights, flat irons, and cement—in 1956, as a place to display her pencil collection. Grandma became a daily fixture at the local dump, the source for many of her building materials. She embedded her findings into concrete and created an amazing series of structures over the one-third-acre site. Bottle Village includes a "rumpus room" made of green and clear glass bottles, a wishing well composed of blue milk of magnesia bottles, and "Cleopatra's Bedroom" composed entirely of amber-colored bottles. Through the building winds a mosaic walkway; alongside it runs a wall of television tubes. In her later years, Grandma would give tours of her creation, for a small fee, to visitors. A unique local tourist attraction and the subject of a highly acclaimed documentary on folk art, the Bottle Village has recently been placed on the National Register of Historic Places.

JOSHUA TREE NATIONAL PARK

140 miles east of Los Angeles; 100 miles northeast of San Diego.

74485 National Park Drive
Twentynine Palms, CA 92277
760-367-5500
http://www.nps.gov/jotr

Joshua Tree National Park Association. (same address as above; 760-367-1488)

Two desert ecosystems are joined together at Joshua Tree National Park. The low desert, below 3,000 feet, is dominated by creosote bush with spidery ocotillo and jumping cholla cactus. The higher, cooler, and wetter Mojave Desert is the special habitat of the Joshua tree, extensive stands of which occur throughout the western half of the park. The park also boasts rugged mountains of twisted rock and exposed granite monoliths. Pinto Basin Culture, one of the Southwest's earliest peoples, lived here, hunting and gathering along the river that once ran through the now dry Pinto Basin. Later, American Indians, explorers, cattlemen, miners from the 1800s, and homesteaders from the 1930s came to live off the land. Remnants left behind include Barker Dam, the Lost Horse and Desert Queen mines, and the Desert Queen Ranch. Today, visitors come to the National Park to enjoy the desert beauty, the green islands of the oases, and some of the most interesting and rugged geologic displays in California's deserts.

What Is a Joshua Tree?

Joshua trees, like giant saguaro cactus, are symbols of the unique deserts of the American Southwest. These "tree yuccas"—found only in California, Arizona, Utah, and Nevada—acquired their strange name from Mormon pioneers, who thought that the branches resembled the arms of Joshua beckoning them farther west.

Sam's Tips

- The California Desert Protection Act of 1994 added 234,000 acres to Joshua Tree National Monument and promoted it to National Park status. Most of the newly designated land is not easily accessible by automobile but includes parts of the Pinto, Coxcomb, Eagle, and Little San Bernardino Mountains.
- One of the best times to observe the Joshua trees is during April and May, the spring blooming period.
- The Oasis of Mara, first inhabited by Native Americans and later by prospectors and homesteaders, is now home to the Oasis Visitor Center and the park headquarters.

KLAMATH NATIONAL FOREST

240 miles northeast of San Francisco; 180 miles north of Sacramento on Interstate 5.

1312 Fairlane Road
Yreka, CA 96097
916-842-6131
http://www.r5.pswfs.gov/klamath

Northwest Interpretive Association. (909 First Avenue, Suite 630, Seattle, WA 98104; 206-220-4140)

The river canyons and grasslands of Klamath National Forest, along the California–Oregon border, offer unspoiled environments and some of the least crowded conditions in the west. The Klamath is heavily forested with tree species that vary with elevation. Yreka, the county seat, is a restored mining town dating to the late 1800s. The Pacific Crest Trail runs through the 227,000-acre "Marbles," a

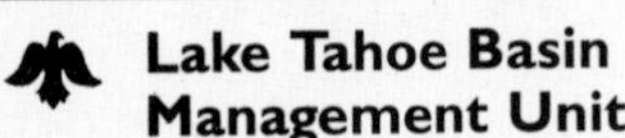

Lake Tahoe Basin Management Unit

Lake Tahoe, measuring 1,645 feet at its deepest point, is the second deepest lake in the United States (after Crater Lake) and the tenth deepest in the world. Its 72 miles of shoreline were formed by faulting and a glacier meltdown. Landscapes range from the rugged, exposed heights of Freel Peak to the numerous glacial lakes of the Desolation Wilderness and the Jeffrey pine–white fir forest at lake level. The Forest Service manages 150,000 acres within Tahoe Basin. During the "Era of Opulence" brought in by the Gold Rush, Lake Tahoe was a popular getaway spot for the wealthy from nearby cities. Resorts like "Lucky" Baldwin's remodeled Point House offered guests a lavish hotel, a casino, a ballroom, and a host of activities. Point House no longer exists, but other luxurious estates remain and are available to visitors. For more information, contact Lake Tahoe Basin Management Unit, 870 Emerald Bay Road, South Tahoe, CA 96150; 916-573-2600.

portion of the forest that contains one of the West's deepest and most complex limestone cave systems. Visit the forest service Website to find extensive recreational information from fishing and boating on 200 miles of rivers and streams to driving directions to 35 campgrounds.

LASSEN NATIONAL FOREST

135 miles northeast of Sacramento; 190 miles northeast of San Francisco.

55 South Sacramento Street
Sousanville, CA 96130
916-257-2151
http://www.r5.pswfs.gov/lassen/lassenwelcome.html

Northwest Interpretive Association. (909 First Avenue, Suite 630, Seattle, WA 98104; 206-220-4140)

Located in northeastern California, the Lassen National Forest's landscape varies from the oak-covered foothills on the northeastern side of the Sacramento Valley to the pine and fir ridges and peaks of the northern Sierra Nevada and southern Cascades. Topography varies from rugged river canyons to sagebrush flats below high mountain peaks. Lakes, rivers, and creeks located throughout the forest accent its natural beauty. The forest has three designated wildernesses. The newest, the Ishi, contains the grasslands and canyons of Mill and Deer creeks.

Sam's Tips

- The most scenic roads within the forest are State Highway 44/89 along Hat Creek, State Highway 44 from Susanville to Old Station, and the 181-mile Lassen Scenic Byway.
- Lassen Volcanic National Park (see entry) is located in the center of the forest.
- There are numerous campgrounds, many of which have a "host"—a resident camper who provides information, monitors use, and contacts forest officers in the event of problems.

LASSEN VOLCANIC NATIONAL PARK

50 miles east of Redding, on Highway 44.

PO Box 100
Mineral, CA 96063-0100
916-595-4444
http://www.nps.gov/lavo

Lassen Loomis Museum Association. (same address as above; 916-595-4444)

In May 1914, Lassen Peak erupted, beginning 7 years of sporadic volcanic outbursts. The climax of this episode came in 1915, when the peak blew an enormous mushroom cloud some 7 miles into the stratosphere. Before the 1980 eruption of Mount Saint Helens in Washington, Lassen Peak was the most recent volcanic outburst in the lower 48 states. Current active volcanism includes hot springs, steaming volcanic vents, and mudpots (springs filled with usually boiling mud). Today, Lassen Volcanic National Park is a place for scientists and tourists alike to study and view how volcanic activity can forever change the landscape of an area.

Sam's Tips

- Lassen's geothermal area on the south and southeast sides of the volcano includes Sulphur Works, Bumpass Hell, Little Hot Springs Valley, Boiling Springs Lake, Devils Kitchen, and Terminal Geyser. Scientists say that some of these bubbling mud pots, steaming fumaroles, and boiling waters are getting hotter and that Lassen Peak and Mount Shasta are the most likely candidates in the Cascades to join Mount Saint Helens as an active volcano.
- The Devastated Area on the northeast side of the volcano was leveled by the 1915–1916 eruptions and mudflows but has since undergone a successful process of revegetation. Strangely, other areas where eruptions occurred in the 18th century, at Cinder Cone and Fantastic Lava Beds, show no significant vegetative recovery.

LAVA BEDS NATIONAL MONUMENT

100 miles northeast of Sacramento; 52 miles south of Klamath Falls, OR.

Box 867
Tulelake, CA 96134
916-667-2282
http://www.nps.gov/labe

Lava Beds Natural History Association. (PO Box 865, Tulelake, CA 96134; 916-667-2282)

For a million years, the Medicine Lake Shield Volcano spewed forth lava, gases, and cinders, creating an incredibly rugged landscape punctuated by cinder cones made of cooled lava, lava flows, spatter cones, lava-tube caves, and pit craters. During the Modoc War of 1872–1873, the Modoc Indians used these lava flows to their advantage. Under the leadership of Captain Jack, the Modocs took refuge in "Captain Jack's Stronghold," a natural lava fortress. From this base, a group of 53 fighting men and their families held off US Army forces up to 20 times their strength for 5 months. Perhaps one of the most striking volcanic features in Lava Beds is the phenomenon of lava-tube caves. When lava flows from a volcano, the outer edges and surface cool rapidly and begin to harden. This outside layer acts as insulation while the rest of the flow beneath it remains hot and fast moving. When the eruption stops and the river of lava drains, a tunnel or tube has been formed.

How to Make Hardtack

Because it lasted forever, hardtack was the standard-issue field ration (12 crackers a day) for frontier soldiers of the 19th century. If it had weevils, a soldier needed only to rap it against a rock or a table to knock them off. If it was moldy, he rubbed the mold off or ate it in the dark. The recipe was simple—a combination of flour, salt, and water, baked for 2 to 4 hours.

Sam's Tips

- There are over 300 known lava-tube caves in the park. Many of the caves have been developed for public use: as a simple trail to the entrance, a stairway or ladder into the cave, or developed trails and stairways within the cave. Mushpot is connected to the Visitor Center and has lights and signs explaining various formations. Twenty other developed caves include such features as lava tubes within other tubes, waterfalls, natural bridges and balconies, and places where ice remains year-round, even when the temperature outside the cave approaches 100°F. Lava is a good natural insulator.

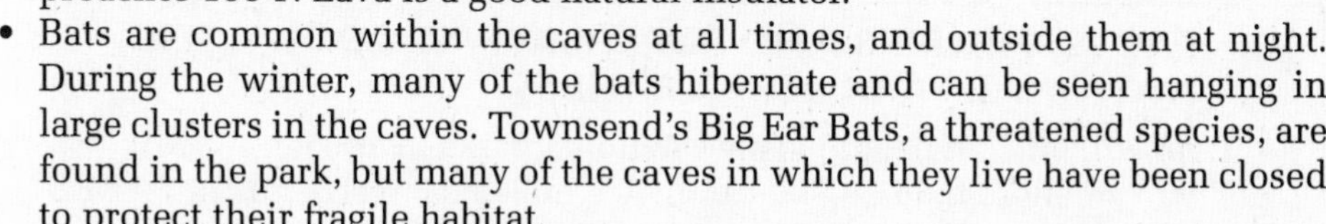

- Bats are common within the caves at all times, and outside them at night. During the winter, many of the bats hibernate and can be seen hanging in large clusters in the caves. Townsend's Big Ear Bats, a threatened species, are found in the park, but many of the caves in which they live have been closed to protect their fragile habitat.
- Native American pictographs and petroglyphs can be found in Lava Beds. The pictographs at Big Painted Cave are painted on boulders within the cave and on either side of the cave entrance.
- A 1.2-mile trail from the Black Crater parking area leads to the Thomas–Wright Battlefield, one of the main battle sites of the Modoc War. At this site, Army troops were besieged in a surprise attack, and over half of the men lost their lives.

LOS PADRES NATIONAL FOREST

125 miles northwest of Los Angeles. The forest extends 220 miles from the west boundary of Los Angeles County to mid-Monterey County in the north.

6144 Calle Real
Goleta, CA 93117
805-683-6711
http://www.r5.pswfs.gov/lospadres

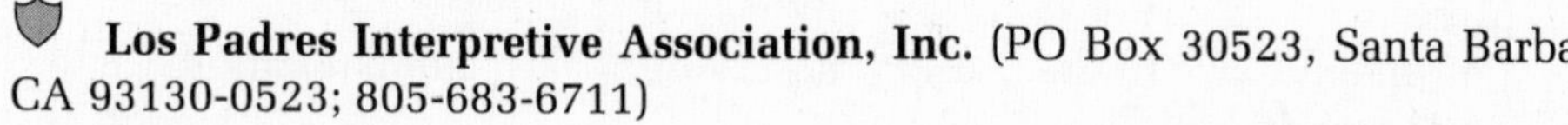

Los Padres Interpretive Association, Inc. (PO Box 30523, Santa Barbara, CA 93130-0523; 805-683-6711)

Encompassing almost 2 million acres in the coastal mountains of central California, the Los Padres National Forest ranges from the semidesert of the Cuyama Badlands to the coniferous forests of Mount Pinos, and is home to diverse wildlife and plant species. Because there are virtually no roads in the forest (nearly half of the forest is designated wilderness), almost nothing gets between visitors and nature.

Sam's Tips

- There are 1,500 miles of trails and 90 developed sites in the forest, including camping and picnic areas and beaches.
- The Chula Vista Winter Sports Area, on Mount Pinos, provides a cold climate for cross-country skiing and other outdoor winter activities.
- The famed San Andreas Fault, California's major earthquake-producing fault, goes through part of the Mount Pinos district of the forest.
- Big Sur, a 75-mile-long stretch along the Pacific Ocean, contains some of the most beautiful coastline in the world.

FACTS, FIGURES AND SUPERLATIVES ABOUT THE NATIONAL PARK SERVICE (NPS)

- Over 270 million people visited national parks in 1995.
- There are more than 25,700 campsites in 548 campgrounds in 77 NPS areas.
- The NPS has 15,000 buildings and 13,000 miles of trails.
- The NPS's largest area is Wrangell–St. Elias National Park and Preserve (AK): 13.2 million acres.
- The NPS's smallest area is the Thaddeus Kosciuszko National Memorial (PA): .02 acre.
- The highest point in North America is in Denali National Park and Preserve (AK), where Mt. McKinley's summit towers 20,320 feet above sea level.
- The lowest point in the western hemisphere is in Death Valley National Monument (CA).
- The longest cave system in the world is in Mammoth Cave National Park (KY), where more than 345 miles of caves have been mapped.
- The deepest cave in the country is in Carlsbad Caverns National Monument (NM): 1,593 feet deep.
- The largest gypsum dunefield in the world is in the White Sands National Monument (NM). It covers 275 square miles and is 60 feet high.
- The deepest lake in the country is in Crater Lake National Park (OR): 1,932 feet deep.
- The world's largest living things are the Sequoia trees in the Sequoia National Forest (CA).
- The world's largest carnivores are the Alaskan brown bears.

MANZANAR NATIONAL HISTORIC SITE

250 miles northeast of Los Angeles; 12 miles north of Lone Pine.

PO Box 426
Independence, CA 93526-0426
760-878-2932
http://www.nps.gov/manz

In 1942, two months after the bombing of Pearl Harbor, President Franklin D. Roosevelt signed an order that required all people of Japanese ancestry living on the west coast—most of whom were American citizens—to be placed in relocation camps. The first of these camps, the Manzanar War Relocation Center, now serves as a reminder of how easily hysteria and distrust can shatter the American dream. Among the remains are the camp auditorium, the stonework shells of the pagoda-like police post, the sentry post and portions of other buildings in the administrative complex, and concrete foundations and portions of the water and sewer systems throughout the camp.

 **SAM'S TIPS**

- This monument was established in 1992; to date, there are no facilities for visitors to the site.
- The Eastern California Museum (760-878-0258), 5 miles north of the camp in Independence, has a good collection of photos, drawings, paintings, and artifacts associated with the Manzanar camp.

MENDOCINO NATIONAL FOREST

140 miles northwest of San Francisco; 135 miles northwest of Sacramento.

825 North Humboldt Avenue
Willows, CA 95988
916-934-3316
http://www.r5.pswfs.gov/mendocino/index.htm

The Mendocino National Forest extends from the Yolla Bolly Mountains in the north to Clear Lake in the south. Elevations range from 1,000 feet to over 8,000 feet, hosting a variety of vegetation and wildlife. Archaeological evidence suggests that Indians lived in the area for thousands of years; historical settlements, however, date to the 1860s.

 **SAM'S TIPS**

- Hang gliding is popular on the Mendocino; all sites are for the intermediate or advanced hang glider.
- Offroading is one of the most popular activities in Mendocino. The south end of the forest offers some of the most enjoyable and challenging OHV trails found in the country.

- During the winter, permits are available for families who want to cut down their own Christmas trees.
- It has been said that visitors can see a greater variety of birds here, within 3 or 4 miles, than in any other place in northern California. The best bird-watching is along the trails at the Lake Red Bluff Recreation Center.

MODOC NATIONAL FOREST

355 miles northeast of San Francisco; 180 miles northwest of Reno, NV.

800 West Twelfth Street
Alturas, CA 96101
916-233-5811
http://www.fs.fed.us

The Modoc National Forest, set in the northernmost corner of California, is the most remote forest in the state. Forest vegetation varies from lichens, on extensive recent lava flows, to stately red fir trees in the higher elevations. In between lies the largest western juniper forest in the world as well as vast expanses of sagebrush. The Modoc also boasts more acres of wetlands than any other national forest in California.

SAM'S TIPS

- The Modoc is one of the least crowded forests in California. Its 20 developed campgrounds are rarely crowded, except on holiday weekends.
- The forest was the site of the 1993 hang gliding world championships. Sugar Hill is said to be one of the state's best spots for the sport.

MOJAVE NATIONAL PRESERVE

80 miles northeast of Los Angeles; 120 miles north of San Diego.

222 East Main Street
Suite 202
Barstow, CA 92311
760-255-8800
http://www.nps.gov/moja

Death Valley Natural History Association. (PO Box 188, Death Valley, CA 92328; 760-786-3285)

The desert in the Mojave National Preserve ranges in elevation from less than 1,000 feet to almost 8,000 feet and is home to nearly 300 different species of animals, including desert bighorn sheep, mule deer, coyotes, and desert tortoises. Golden eagles and several species of hawks can be seen soaring on the thermal updrafts. Evidence of the people who have lived in and made a living from the desert can be found in the petroglyphs and pictographs etched and drawn on the rocks throughout the region. Old mines, ranches, and the ruts cut into the desert floor by wagons tell of later arrivals to the desert.

Sam's Tips

- Come prepared for extreme temperatures and a scarcity of water. The best months for visiting are October through May. In the summer, daytime temperatures average more than 100°F. When hiking, carry at least a gallon of water per person per day.
- A variety of roads offer visitors access to sand dunes, a historic railroad depot, scenic canyons, and cinder cones. Some roads are marked, but many require a map.

MUIR WOODS NATIONAL MONUMENT

12 miles north of the Golden Gate Bridge in San Francisco.

Mill Valley, CA 94941
415-388-2595
http://www.nps.gov/muwo

Golden Gate National Park Association. (Fort Mason, Building 201, San Francisco, CA 94123; 415-776-0693)

In 1905, after noticing that Redwood Creek contained one of the last uncut stands of old-growth redwood in the Bay Area, Congressman William Kent and his wife, Elizabeth Thatcher Kent, purchased 295 acres of woods for $45,000. Kent then donated the land to the federal government in order to protect the redwoods. When President Theodore Roosevelt declared the area a national monument, Kent suggested that the area be named after John Muir, one of the founding members of the Sierra Club. In this "tree-lovers monument," the most popular activity is hiking through the grove of majestic coastal redwoods.

Sam's Tips

- Cathedral and Bohemian Groves contain Muir Woods's largest redwoods. The tallest is 252 feet, the thickest is nearly 14 feet across. The oldest redwood is nearly 1,000 years old. Most of the mature trees are between 500 and 800 years old. The Hillside and Ocean View Trails through Redwood Canyon are the best way to see these groves.
- Educational programs for groups are available, including slide programs about redwoods that teachers can borrow off-site. Call 415-388-2596 for more information.

The Naming of Muir Woods

Here is a transcription of the correspondence between President Roosevelt and William Kent, and John Muir's response to the naming of Muir Woods.

The White House
Washington
January 22, 1908

My Dear Mr. Kent:

I have just received from Secretary Garfield your very generous letter enclosing the gift of Redwood Canyon to the National Government to be kept as a perpetual park for the preservation of the giant redwoods therein and to be named the Muir National Monument. You have doubtless seen my proclamation of January 9th, instant, creating this monument. I thank you most heartily for this singular generous and public spirited action on your part. All Americans who prize the natural beauties of the country and wish to see them preserved undamaged, and especially those who realize the literally unique value of the groves of giant trees, must feel that you have conferred a great and lasting benefit upon the whole country.

I have a great admiration for John Muir; but after all, my dear sir, this is your gift. No other land than that which you give is included in this tract of nearly 300 acres and I should greatly like to name the Monument the Kent Monument if you will permit it.

Sincerely yours,

Theodore Roosevelt

Kentfield, California
January 30, 1908

To the President,
Washington, D.C.

My Dear Mr. Roosevelt:

I thank you from the bottom of my heart for your message of appreciation, and hope and believe it will strengthen me to go on in an attempt to save more of the precious and vanishing glories of nature for a people too slow of perception.

Your kind suggestion of a change of name is not one that I can accept. So many millions of better people have died forgotten that to stencil one's own name on a benefaction seems to carry with it an implication of mundane immortality, as being something purchasable.

I have five good, husky boys that I am trying to bring up to a knowledge of democracy and to a realizing sense of the rights of the "other fellow," doctrines which you, sir, have taught with more vigor and effect than any man in my time. If these boys cannot keep the name of Kent alive, I am willing it should be forgotten.

I have this day sent you by mail a few photographs of Muir Woods, and trust that you will believe before you see the real thing (which I hope will be soon) that our nation has acquired something worthwhile.

Yours truly,

William Kent

The White House
Washington
February 5, 1908

My Dear Mr. Kent:

By George! you are right. It is enough to do the deed and not to desire, as you say, to "stencil one's own name on the benefaction." Good for you, and for the five boys who are to keep the name of Kent alive! I have four who I hope will do the same thing by the name of Roosevelt. Those are awfully good photos.

Sincerely yours,

Theodore Roosevelt

Martinez
Feb. 6, 1908

Dear Mr. Kent:

Seeing my name in the tender & deed of the Tamalpais Sequoias was a surprise of the pleasantest kind. This is the best tree-lover's monument that could possibly be found in all the forests of the world. You have done me great honor, & I am proud of it. Schools here & there have planted "Muir trees" in their playgrounds, & long ago Asa Gray named several plants for me, the most interesting of which is a sturdy frost-enduring daisy that I discovered on the shore of the Arctic Ocean near Icy Cape; a Sierra peak also & one of the Alaskan glaciers bears my name, but these aboriginal woods, barring human action, will outlast them all, even the mountain & glacier. Compared with Sequoia glaciers are young fleeting things, & since the first Sequoia forests lifted their domes and spires to the sky, mountains great and small, thousands of them, have been weathered, ground down, washed away & cast into the sea; while two of the many species of Sequoia have come safely through all the geological changes & storms that have fallen upon them since Cretaceous times, surviving even the crushing destroying ice sheets of the glacial period.

Saving these woods from the axe & saw, from money-changers and water-changers, & giving them to our country & the world is in many ways the most notable service to God & man I've heard of since my forest wanderings began. A much needed lesson & blessing to saint & sinner alike & credit & encouragement to God. That so fine divine a thing should have come out of money made in Chicago! Who wad'a' thocht it! Immortal Sequoia life to you.

Ever yours,

John Muir

PINNACLES NATIONAL MONUMENT

130 miles southeast of San Francisco; 90 miles southwest of Fresno.

Paicines, CA 95043
408-389-4485
http://www.nps.gov/pinn

Southwest Parks and Monuments Association. (221 North Court Avenue, Tucson, AZ 85701; 520-622-1999)

The Pinnacles are part of the last remains of an ancient volcano, the rest of which is 195 miles to the southeast. Sound confusing? The explanation is that the San Andreas Rift Zone, a series of faults, pulled the part now known as Pinnacles away from the original volcano. Visitors know at once why this park is called Pinnacles—the spires and crags bear no resemblance to the surrounding smooth and rounded hills. Abruptly, the pinnacle rock formations dominate the scenery.

Sam's Tips

- No direct road connects the east side and the west side of the park. There are no federally operated campgrounds on the east side; however, there are several public and private campgrounds nearby. Back-country camping is forbidden, and hiking trails are for day use only.
- Campfire programs are presented at Pinnacles Campground on Friday and Saturday evenings from March through May.
- Two cave systems in the park—Bear Gulch and Balconies—are open for exploration, but bring along a flashlight.

PLUMAS NATIONAL FOREST

90 miles north of Sacramento; 160 miles northeast of San Francisco.

159 Lawrence Street
PO Box 11500
Quincy, CA 95971
916-283-2050
http://www.r5.pswfs.gov/plumas/index.htm

Located in the Sierra Nevada mountains along the border of Nevada and California, Plumas National Forest is known for its geological features, its hundreds of high alpine lakes, and its thousands of miles of clear-running streams. Three branches of the Feather River wind through the forest. The North Fork shares the canyon bottom with Highway 70 and the Union Pacific Railroad; the Middle Fork is designated a Wild and Scenic River. The Wild Zones are in a deep and narrow canyon with numerous large boulders, steep canyon walls, and some impressive waterfalls, including the sixth highest in the United States.

Sam's Tips

- A 75-mile section of the 2,400-mile Pacific Crest Trail extends across the Plumas National Forest, through the canyons of the Middle Fork and North Fork of the Feather River. Elevations range from 2,400 to 7,000 feet. Mid-June is the earliest date for hiking in the area; before then, snow is still prevalent and streams are high. Fall snowstorms can be expected any time after mid-October.
- The upper stretches of the Middle Fork, called the English Bar Scenic and Recreation Zones, are good rafting and canoeing areas with easy access. The North Fork has low flows during the summer and numerous large boulders, both of which make canoeing or rafting dicey.
- The Bucks Lake Wilderness, encompassing 24,000 acres of the northernmost portion of the Sierra Nevada Mountain Range, varies from bare rock slopes and sheer cliffs to high mountain meadows. Small glacial lakes and ponds dot the area at the base of the escarpment. Elevations range from 2,000 feet to 7,067 feet at Mount Pleasant.

X-STREAM DIFFICULTY: THE CLASSIFICATION OF RAPIDS

The Bureau of Land Management provides this guide to the different classes of rapids:

Class I: Moving water with a few riffles and small waves. Few or no obstructions.

Class II: Easy rapids with waves up to 3 feet high and wide clear channels that are obvious without scouting. Some maneuvering required.

Class III: Rapids with high irregular waves, often capable of swamping an open canoe. Narrow passages that often require complex maneuvering. May require scouting from shore.

Class IV: Long, difficult rapids with constricted passages that often require precise maneuvering in very turbulent waters. Scouting from shore is often necessary, and conditions make rescue difficult. Boaters in decked canoes and kayaks should be able to Eskimo roll.

Class V: Extremely difficult, long, and very violent rapids with highly congested routes that nearly always must be scouted from shore. Rescue conditions are difficult, and there is significant hazard to life in the event of mishap. Ability to Eskimo roll is essential for canoes and kayaks.

Class VI: Difficulties of Class V carried to the extreme of navigability. Nearly impossible and very dangerous. For teams of experts only after close study and with all precautions taken.

Port Chicago Naval Magazine National Memorial

This memorial, located on the Concord Naval Weapons Station in Concord, CA, recognizes the critical role Port Chicago played in WWII by serving as the primary munitions facility for the Pacific Theater. It also commemorates the explosion that occurred here on July 16, 1944, which resulted in the largest domestic loss of life during WWII. The memorial is jointly administered by the U.S. Navy and the National Park Service. Visits to the site must be arranged in advance by calling 510-246-5591. Contact the Eugene O'Neill National Historic Site for more information.

POINT REYES NATIONAL SEASHORE

10 miles north of San Francisco, extending 25 additional miles northward along the coast.

Point Reyes Station, CA 94956-9799
415-663-1092
http://www.nps.gov/pore

Point Reyes National Seashore Association. (Point Reyes, CA 94956; 415-663-1155)

Point Reyes National Seashore probably used to be attached to the California mainland. Today, due to movement in the San Andreas Fault Zone, Point Reyes is a peninsula with the California mainland on one side and the Pacific Ocean on the other. The fault zone contains many large and small faults running parallel and at odd angles to one another. Because each plate cannot move freely, tremendous pressures build up. From time to time, this pressure becomes too great, the underlying rock breaks loose, and the surface actually moves. In 1906, during the San Francisco Earthquake, the peninsula leaped 20 feet northwestward. The land continues to move, and although we may not see any change in our lifetimes, Point Reyes is slowly distancing itself from mainland California. The peninsula is noted for its long beaches backed by tall cliffs, lagoons, forested ridges, and offshore bird and sea lion colonies.

Sam's Tips

- The Mount Vision Overlook is an ideal place to get a panoramic view of the entire peninsula. The observation platform at Point Reyes Lighthouse, at the western tip of the peninsula, is the best place to see gray whales on their southward and northward migrations, January to April. Not far from the lighthouse is the Sea Lion Overlook, an excellent spot for viewing harbor seals and sea lions.
- At the northern edge of the park, the road ends at the Tule Elk Reserve, created to reintroduce the tule elk to the peninsula after an absence of nearly 100 years. The Tomales Point Trail leads from the end of this road through the elk reserve to beautiful views of the Pacific from Tomales Point.

REDWOOD NATIONAL PARK

40 miles north of Eureka, extending approximately 60 miles to the north.

1111 Second Street
Crescent City, CA 95531
707-464-6101
http://www.nps.gov/redw

Redwood Natural History Association. (1111 Second Street, Crescent City, CA 95531; 707-464-9150)

North Coast Redwoods Interpretive Association. (Prairie Creek Redwoods State Park, Orick, CA 95555; 707-488-2171)

Redwood national and state parks are home to the world's tallest living thing—the Coastal Redwood. The tallest trees grow to nearly 370 feet—and weigh 500 tons. They are taller than the Statue of Liberty (305 feet) or the dome of the US Capitol (287 feet). These trees, cousins of the giant sequoias that grow larger in diameter but not in height, can live to be 2,000 years old. The thick biological armor of umber bark seems impenetrable to the ravages of fire and insects. In 1769, the redwood forests covered 2 million or more acres. By 1965, they were reduced to 300,000 acres and were under intense logging pressure. In the 1960s and 1970s, the State of California and the US Congress passed legislation to protect these groves. The national and the state parks in this area now encompass 105,516 acres of ancient and second-growth redwood and a variety of animal habitats. The tidepools on Enderts Beach, for example, are filled with organisms such as the Black Turban Snail, hermit crabs, and sea anemone.

SAM'S TIPS

- The Redwood National Park area is a cooperative effort among three state parks and the National Park itself; together, they form both a World Heritage Site and an International Biosphere Reserve. There are four distinct areas to the park, which stretches for 50 miles up the California coast.

1. The Hiouchi Area in the far northern section of the park, east of Crescent City, includes Jedediah Smith Redwoods State Park. Beginning on the far western side of the park, the Howland Hill Road is a scenic unpaved drive through the heart of the redwood forest, ending at South Ford Road near Highway 199. Another unpaved scenic road, Walker Road, winds north and provides access to the Smith River, a popular swimming spot.
2. The Crescent Beach Area has an overlook that is a good place to spot whales while Enderts Beach is the starting point of the Coastal Trail, which allows hikers to traverse nearly the entire length of the park, through grasslands, beaches, former farmlands, and redwood and other forests.
3. The Klamath Area includes False Klamath Cove, which is right across the highway from the popular Redwood youth hostel. (For hostel information, call 707-482-8265.) Klamath Overlook, which stands 600 feet above an estuary at the river's mouth, is another good whale-watching spot, with panoramic views of the ocean. The narrow, partially paved Coastal Drive winds through stands of redwood and offers breathtaking views of crashing surf and the Pacific Ocean.
4. The Orick Area includes the main portions of Redwood National Park. The Tall Trees Grove Trail is a steep, descending, 1.3-mile hike to a grove of some of the world's very tallest trees.

The Coastal Redwood

The world's tallest known tree and one of the world's oldest living trees, the Coastal Redwood has been known to live as long as 2,000 years. For such an immense and grand tree, it has small and delicate foliage. Narrow, sharp-pointed needles are only one-half to three-quarters of an inch long. Redwood cones are about an inch long, and each cone contains between 10 and 24 tiny seeds; it would take more than 100,000 of these to make a pound of seeds.

It is generally believed that the last ice age limited the Coastal Redwoods to their present range, a narrow 450-mile strip along the Pacific Ocean from central California to southern Oregon. The mild, moist climate along this strip, a rarity in the world today, was once much more common, and redwoods were found throughout what is now the western United States and Canada, and along the coasts of Europe and Asia. Although some of the redwood fossils found elsewhere are more than 160 million years old, the trees are relatively recent arrivals to California—the earliest fossil records of redwoods in the state are less than 20 million years old.

THE FOREST SERVICE'S SPECIAL PLACES

Are you trying to find an unusual or distinctive forest for your next recreational adventure? Some of Uncle Sam's 155 forests offer especially scenic and recreational opportunities found nowhere else in the world; others are, well, forests. To steer you to the most noteworthy places among the national forests, Uncle Sam in 1965 designated a number of places within the national forests as "Special Places." Here are some examples:

- Mount St. Helens: a volcano that erupted in 1980 after 123 years of inactivity (Gifford–Pinchot National Forest, WA)
- Hells Canyon: the deepest gorge in North America, at 8,000 feet (Wallowa-Whitman National Forest, OR)
- Oregon Dunes: a unique series of sand dunes that rise as much as 500 feet above sea level (Siuslaw National Forest, OR)
- Sawtooth National Recreation Area: rugged peaks and high glacial valleys in the heart of Idaho (Sawtooth National Forest, ID)

For a brochure that describes these places, and more, in detail, write to any regional U.S. Forest Service office, and ask for *Discover Special Places in Your National Forests.*

SAN BERNARDINO NATIONAL FOREST

80 miles east of Los Angeles; 90 miles north of San Diego.

1824 South Commercenter Circle
San Bernardino, CA 92408-3430
909-383-5588
http://www.r5.pswfs.gov/sanbernadino

San Bernardino offers many types of mountain country, from gentle flatlands and rolling hills to sheer escarpments and rock-ribbed peaks; hot slopes covered in thorny chaparral; and cool subalpine forests of pine and fir. The forest is located within 2 hours' drive from Los Angeles.

 **SAM'S TIPS**

- Hikers can choose from over 663 miles of trails, including 193 miles of the Pacific Crest Trail.
- The Children's Forest, located in the heart of the San Bernardino Mountains, is a 3,400 acre reserve where kids care for the the forest and practice their skills in leadership, research, teaching, and decision making. Follow interpretive signs designed by kids or take a guided walk with youth naturalists. For more information, contact Children's Forest, PO Box 350, Sky Forest, CA 92385; 909-337-5156.

SAN FRANCISCO MARITIME NATIONAL HISTORICAL PARK

San Francisco.

Building E
Lower Fort Mason, Room 265
San Francisco, CA 94123
415-556-1659
http://www.nps.gov/safr

National Maritime Museum Association. (Fort Mason, Building 35, San Francisco, CA 94123; 415-929-0202)

Part of the Golden Gate National Recreation Area, the San Francisco Maritime National Historical Park is a tribute to the people and ships that shaped the development of the Pacific Coast of the United States. Located west of Fisherman's Wharf, the park features the Maritime Museum, with exhibits on the exploration of and expansion on the West Coast, and models and displays on steam technology. There are also four historic ships to tour at the Hyde Street Pier. Researchers will enjoy the park's J. Porter Shaw Library, with its extensive collection of books, ship plans, historic photographs, and artifacts.

SANTA MONICA MOUNTAINS NATIONAL RECREATION AREA

Santa Monica, which is adjacent to Los Angeles, and extending 35 miles westward.

401 Hillcrest Drive
Thousand Oaks, CA 91360
818-597-9192 ext. 201
http://www.nps.gov/samo

Southwest Parks and Monuments Association. (221 North Court Avenue, Tucson, AZ 85701; 520-622-1999)

The Santa Monica Mountains rise above Los Angeles, widen to meet the curve of the Santa Monica Bay, and reach their highest peaks facing the open ocean. Coastline alternates between rocky shore and narrow sandy beaches. Spread over 40 miles, the recreation area has beaches, campgrounds, tennis courts, historic sites, and even a television filming site.

Sam's Tips

- Will Rogers State Historic Park features walking tours of Will Rogers's home and grounds.
- The Paramount Ranch has been used by Hollywood studios since 1927 to produce films and television westerns. It is currently the filming site of the TV series *Dr. Quinn, Medicine Woman.* Visitors are often permitted to watch; contact the ranger on duty for specific guidelines and information.
- Summer events in the area include guided hikes, concerts at the Peter Strauss Ranch, the Malibu Art Festival, and treasure hunts. Contact the Thousand Oaks address above for more information.

SEQUOIA AND KINGS CANYON NATIONAL PARKS

55 miles east of Fresno; 400 miles west of Las Vegas, NV.

Three Rivers, CA 93271
209-565-3341
http://www.nps.gov/seki

Sequoia Natural History Association, Inc. (HCR 89, Box 10, Three Rivers, CA 93271-9792; 209-565-3341)

Sequoia National Park, created in 1890, features the 275-foot General Sherman Tree, the world's largest living organism. Its trunk weighs an estimated 1,385 tons; the circumference at the ground is 103 feet; its largest branch is 7 feet in diameter; and, each year, it grows enough to make a 60-foot-tall tree of usual proportions. These giant sequoias grow naturally only on the west slope of the Sierra Nevada.

Kings Canyon National Park, established in 1940, contains Grant Grove, a great place to view giant sequoia groves and to hike miles of scenic trails. The focal point is the General Grant Tree, referred to as the Nation's Christmas Tree. It's also a designated national shrine—a living memorial to Americans who gave their lives for freedom. The parks have been managed jointly since the mid-1940s. They include the snowcapped peaks of the Great Western Divide; 14,495-foot Mount Whitney, the highest mountain in the 48 contiguous states; and Tulainyo Lake, the highest-altitude lake in the United States.

SAM'S TIPS

- There are two entrances to the parks: Highway 198 East enters Sequoia National Park, and Highway 180 East enters Kings Canyon National Park. The Generals Highway, through the parks, connects the two entrances.
- The Grant Grove area of Kings Canyon National Park contains giant sequoias, including the General Grant Tree, where the annual Christmas Tree ceremony is held every second Sunday of December.
- The Giant Forest of Sequoia National Park is one of the best places to see the giant trees. Over 40 miles of trails wind through this grove, which includes the General Sherman Tree. Crescent Meadow Road will take you to Moro Rock for spectacular views and will pass through the Tunnel Log, a fallen giant sequoia with a tunnel that allows an automobile to pass through.
- Lodgepole, Atwell Mill, and Grant Grove campgrounds are all situated near sequoia groves.

SEQUOIA NATIONAL FOREST

55 miles east of Fresno; 400 miles west of Las Vegas, NV.

900 W. Grand Avenue
Porterville, CA 93257
209-784-1500
http://www.r5.pswfs.gov/sequoia

Three Forests Interpretive Association. (33685 Frazier Road, Auberry, CA 93602; 209-855-3450)

After hunter A.T. Dowd discovered the High Sierra giant sequoias in 1852, spectators flocked to the Sierra Nevada area to see for themselves. Some enterprising promoters even cut down the larger trees for public display. Today, the Sequoia National Forest is home to 38 of the 75 known groves of these tall trees. In all, the groves cover approximately 20,000 acres inside the forest, which also has chaparral, hardwood, conifer woodlands, and conifer forests. The giant sequoia groves are located within the conifer forests, on the western slopes of the Sierra Nevada.

Sam's Tips

- Highway 180, a designated Scenic Byway, climbs 4,000 feet through the western foothills of the Sierra Nevada on its way to Sequoia and Kings Canyon National Parks (see entry).
- The Chicago Stump, all that remains of a giant sequoia cut down and transported to Chicago for the 1893 Columbia Exhibition, lies in the Converse Basin portion of the forest. Also in the Converse Basin is the Boole Tree, the largest tree inside any national forest (Sequoia National Park has the largest in the United States) and one of the largest trees in the world at 269 feet tall and 35 feet in diameter.
- Lake Isabella is one of the largest reservoirs in southern California. Its fishing, boating, and camping make it one of the best year-round freshwater recreation areas near Los Angeles and Bakersfield.

SHASTA–TRINITY NATIONAL FORESTS

200 miles north of San Francisco; 160 miles northwest of Sacramento.

2400 Washington Avenue
Redding, CA 96001
916-246-5222
http://www.r5.pswfs.gov/shastatrinity/index.htm

Northwest Interpretive Association. (909 First Avenue, Suite 630, Seattle, WA 98104; 206-220-4140)

Once a center of Gold Rush activity, the 2.1-million-acres of Shasta–Trinity National Forests are dominated by Mount Shasta, whose height (elevation, 14,162 feet) and configuration dominate the view from all directions. In the Trinity Alps Wilderness, granite peaks and alpine lakes dot the rugged terrain and create high-elevation adventure for visitors.

Sam's Tips

- Hiking Mount Shasta takes about 8 to 12 hours for people in good physical condition, but it is best split into 2 days because of the steep rise in elevation (7,000 feet). The Mount Shasta Ranger District Office (916-926-4511) provides information on wilderness permits and regulations, climbing, and licensed outfitter and guide services that are available.
- Whitewater rafting is very popular; there are rapids for every skill level. One of the favorite routes is down the main fork of the Trinity River. For rafting information, contact the Big Bar Ranger District Office, 916-623-6123.
- The Lewiston Lake/Trinity River Hatchery is an official state wildlife viewing site and a prime spot to watch herons, beavers, black-tailed deer, northern orioles, and bald eagles. Shasta Lake is home to the largest breeding population of eagles in California.

TREES NEED THEIR SKIN TOO!

Every season, countless visitors to public lands damage trees by removing their bark. Tree wounds are unsightly and frequently do not heal. Exposed wood is attacked by decay, fungi, and insects. Larger wounds then develop and the tree may become unsafe. The loss of trees diminishes the beauty of the natural environment. The U.S. Forest Service offers these do's and don'ts:

- Removal and piercing of bark by nails, axes, and other objects driven into it expose the tree to fungi and harmful parasites; do not embed knives or axes in tree trunks.
- Hanging lanterns on trees is harmful because the heat kills the adjacent bark.
- Hanging your clothes and leaving the clothesline may eventually kill the tree. As the tree grows, the cord will strangle the trunk.
- Be careful not to bump trees with your vehicle; neither the tree nor the vehicle was built for it.
- Do not drive over roots, and avoid soil unsuitable for heavy traffic. Overuse of such areas will severely compact and erode the soil. As a result, roots will suffer from exposure and a lack of air and water below ground.
- Hitting trees with sticks or other objects can bruise and kill the bark.
- Dog chains attached around tree bases can saw through bark as the animal moves.

SIERRA NATIONAL FOREST

130 miles southeast of San Francisco; 200 miles northwest of Los Angeles.

1600 Tollhouse Road
Clovis, CA 93611-0532
209-297-0706
http://www.r5.pswfs.gov/sierra

Three Forests Interpretive Association. (33685 Frazier Road, Auberry, CA 93602; 209-855-3450)

The California Gold Rush is still alive in the Sierra National Forest, which continues to house four active gold mines, one tungsten mine, and a number of small, occasionally worked mines. Recreational gold panning and dredging are still popular in the area and are permitted where they do not infringe on existing claims. The forest terrain ranges from gently rolling, oak-covered foothills along the edge of the great San Joaquin Valley, to the majestic snowcapped

 **FOREST SERVICE SCENIC BYWAY**

Sierra Vista National Scenic Byway

The Sierra Vista National Scenic Byway meanders 100 miles through the Sierra Nevada Mountains and offers a variety of views, including sheer canyon walls, domes, and surrounding majestic peaks. A gentle half-mile walk from the byway leads to the top of Fresno Dome. The route travels from grasslands to oak and pine forests and passes by the Nelder Grove Giant Sequoia area, home to the Bull Buck, one of the largest and oldest trees in the world. *Contact Sierra Vista National Forest.*

peaks of the Sierra Nevada crest. The Ansel Adams Wilderness contains spectacular alpine scenery. There also are a number of fairly large lakes and streams, and several small glaciers. Barren windswept granite outcroppings and steep-walled gorges afford challenges for experienced mountain climbers.

SIX RIVERS NATIONAL FOREST

300 miles northwest of San Francisco; 300 miles northwest of Sacramento.

1330 Bayshore Way
Eureka, CA 95501-3834
707-442-1721
http://www.r5.pswfs.gov/sixrivers

 **Northwest Interpretive Association.** (909 First Avenue, Suite 630, Seattle, WA 98104; 206-220-4140)

 **Smith River National Recreation Area**

Inside the Six Rivers National Forest. The Smith River's clear and free-flowing waters are well known for salmon and steelhead runs. More than 300 miles of the Smith River system have been designated as a wild and scenic river, the most extensive one managed by the Forest Service. On their way to the Pacific, various forks and tributaries of the river wind their way through steep, forested mountains of the Six Rivers National Forest. Kayaking, inner-tubing, and rafting are increasingly popular sports. The region includes seven established botanical areas that protect unusual plant communities. More than 300 species of wildlife are found here, including bald eagles, peregrine falcons, and spotted owls. For details, contact Smith River National Recreation Area, PO Box 228, Gasquet, CA 95543; 707-457-3131, or the Interpretive Association, at the address given above.

FOREST SERVICE SCENIC BYWAYS

Smith River Scenic Byway

This scenic byway travels 33 miles along the Smith River and provides many spectacular views of deep green pools, whitewater rapids, and waterfalls. Large coastal redwood forests laced with rhododendron, azaleas, and beds of ferns compete with the riverfront wildlife for travelers' attention. From November through April, visitors can watch or fish for Chinook salmon and steelhead along the river. *Contact Six Rivers National Forest.*

The Six Rivers National Forest gets its name from the six major rivers and dozens of tributaries that tumble down the mountain slopes toward the Pacific Ocean. Stretching in a narrow band along the western slopes of the Klamath ranges, the six rivers together make up 35 percent of the state's wild and scenic rivers located on federal lands. Only 6 hours from San Francisco and Sacramento, the forest is a relatively undiscovered gem.

STANISLAUS NATIONAL FOREST

70 miles southeast of Sacramento; 110 miles northeast of San Francisco.

19777 Greenley Road
Sonora, CA 95370
209-532-3671
http://www.r5.pswfs.gov/stanislaus/index.htm

Three Forests Interpretive Association. (33685 Frazier Road, Auberry, CA 93602; 209-855-3450)

The Stanislaus National Forest, on the western slope of the central Sierra, is quite similar to neighboring Yosemite National Park in both beauty and recreational activities. There are over 800 miles of rivers and streams, and many lakes are tucked into the back-country. Created in 1897, it is among the oldest of the national forests.

SAM'S TIPS

- River experts consider the Tuolumne River one of the most challenging rafting runs in California. The Groveland Ranger District Office (209-962-7825) can provide more information on running the rivers.

THE FOREST SERVICE VIDEO LIBRARY

A terrific resource at the U.S. Forest Service is a video library where you can borrow a variety of videos for a school or group function. The choices include:

- *A Precious Legacy,* a five-minute video introduction to the history and mission of the national forest system.
- *Commencement 2000: Tomorrow's Caretakers,* an 11-minute video designed to introduce inner-city and minority students to the field of natural resources. Emphasis is on career development.
- *Gifford Pinchot: America's First Forester,* a 57-minute public television adaptation of Gary Hines's one-man play about the first Chief of the Forest Service. The video incorporates historic photos and footage as Hines traces Pinchot's colorful life, including his friendships with John Muir and Theodore Roosevelt.
- *Landscape of History: The Nez Perce National Historic Trail,* a 20-minute program that takes you on the 1,170-mile journey of the Nez Perce tribe in 1877. Pursued by the United States Army, 750 Nez Perce men, women, and children made a heroic yet futile flight seeking freedom and peace far from their homeland. The program highlights the need to preserve and interpret this landscape of history.
- *Silent Witness,* a 31-minute video, narrated by Robert Redford, explores the alarming destruction and desecration of American Indian archaeological sites on public lands. Pueblo Indians, archaeologists, and national park rangers examine the crisis and the loss it represents.

To find out more about these and other videos, go to the complete catalog on the U.S. Forest Service Website: http://www.r5.pswfs.gov/video.

For further information, contact:

Forest Service Video Library
c/o Audience Planners
5341 Derry Avenue, Suite Q
Agoura Hills, CA 91301
800-683-8366; fax: 818-865-1327

Except for return postage, there is no other cost or charge.

TAHOE NATIONAL FOREST

45 miles northeast of Sacramento; 115 miles northeast of San Francisco.

631 Coyote Street
Nevada City, CA 95959
530-265-4531
http://www.r5.pswfs.gov/tahoe

Tahoe Outdoor Partners Organization. (17506 Blue Tent School Road, Nevada City, CA 95959; 916-478-1224)

During the California Gold Rush, pioneers crossed the Tahoe National Forest seeking their fortunes. Today, the forest retains evidence of those days, in museums and historical sites in the surrounding communities, and in Gold Rush mining camps. The forest is located between Lake Tahoe on the east and the Sacramento Valley on the west. The land rises from 1,500 feet in the west, where there are steep-walled river canyons, to 9,400 feet in the rugged rolling ridges at the Sierra Crest on the east.

Sam's Tips

- The infamous Donner Party became lost in the area that is now this National Forest and was reduced to cannibalism to try to survive. Learn about the tragedy of the Donner Party at the Donner Picnic Area, on the eastern side of the park.

WHISKEYTOWN–SHASTA–TRINITY NATIONAL RECREATION AREA

140 miles north of San Francisco; 115 miles northwest of Sacramento.

PO Box 188
Whiskeytown, CA 96095-0188
916-246-1225
http://www.nps.gov/whis

Southwest Parks and Monuments Association. (221 North Court Avenue, Tucson, AZ 85701; 520-622-1999)

About the time of the California Gold Rush, as a pack mule with a barrel of whiskey on its back was being led across Clear Creek, the barrel came loose and spilled whiskey into the creek. This event earned Clear Creek the nickname "Whiskey Creek," and the settlement on the eastern side of the creek became known as Whiskeytown. Today, the site of Whiskeytown is covered by Whiskeytown Lake, a focal point of the Whiskeytown–Shasta–Trinity National Recreation Area. Whiskeytown is the smallest of the recreation area's three impounded lakes, but its constant level in the summer makes it ideal for recreational use.

Shasta Lake, the largest reservoir in California, has as a beautiful backdrop the dormant Mount Shasta Volcano.

SAM'S TIPS

- The Shasta and Trinity Units of the National Recreation Area are managed by the National Forest Service. For detailed information on the Shasta–Trinity Area, contact the Forest Service at 2400 Washington Avenue, Redding, CA 96001; 916-246-5222.
- A variety of ranger-led activities are available in the recreation area, from a tour of the 1852 Camden House to panning for gold. Children's activities include a junior ranger program.
- Mountain bikers will find the Whiskeytown area challenging. Elevations rise from 1,210 feet to 6,209 feet.

YOSEMITE NATIONAL PARK

125 miles east of San Francisco.

PO Box 577
Yosemite, CA 95389-0577
209-372-0200
http://www.nps.gov/yose

Yosemite Association. (PO Box 230, El Portal, CA 95318; 209-379-2646)

One of America's most revered—and overcrowded—national parks, Yosemite embraces a vast tract of scenic wildlands set aside in 1890 to preserve a portion of the Sierra Nevada in California's eastern flank. Glacier Point, a sheer rock cliff about 3,200 feet straight down, affords a bird's-eye view of the entire Yosemite Valley. Across the valley is the 2,425-foot drop of Yosemite Falls, and beyond the falls, the panoramic expanse of the High Sierra stands out. Tuolumne Meadows, at 8,600 feet, is the largest subalpine meadow in the Sierra. The meadows, abounding in wildflowers and wildlife, are spectacular in midsummer. The Mariposa Grove is the largest of three giant Sequoia groves in Yosemite; the grove's Grizzly Giant, 2,700 years old, is presently thought to be the oldest living giant Sequoia. Other attractions in the Yosemite Valley include Mirror Lake, which is silting up and will eventually be a meadow; the Ansel Adams Gallery; and the sheer rock walls of

Getting In

The four entrances to Yosemite are:

1. South Entrance, on Highway 41 North (from Fresno).
2. Arch Rock Entrance, on Highway 140 West (from Merced).
3. Big Oak Flat Entrance, on Highway 120 West (from Modesto).
4. Tioga Pass Entrance, on Highway 120 East (from Lee Vincing) and Highway 395.

Recent floods, however, have caused serious damage to Highway 140 West. Repairs are scheduled to continue through most of 1998. Visit the Yosemite Website to learn the latest road conditions.

Yosemite Camping

There are more than 1,700 campsites in 15 campgrounds located throughout the park. On busy days, every site is occupied. The Yosemite Website is especially valuable in planning your trip. It includes maps of most campsites and a listing of available facilities (showers, laundry, etc.), as well as nearby campgrounds that are outside the park. For further information, call 209-372-0200 and choose a campground option from the recorded menu. The same number will direct you to lodging information.

El Capitan. In all, elevations vary from 2,000 feet to over 13,000 feet.

Because of its popularity and recent flooding damage, traveling to Yosemite requires advance inquiries and preparation.

Sam's Tips

- Perhaps the most famous part of the park is the Yosemite Valley, known for its waterfalls, cliffs, and unusual rock formations. It is probably the world's best example of a glacially carved canyon. The impressive monoliths left behind by the receding glacier include the vertical cliffs of El Capitan and Cathedral Rocks. The most prominent waterfalls in the canyon are the Yosemite, Bridalveil, Vernal, Nevada, and Illiouette; the falls are at their highest flow in May and June.
- Other notable stops within the valley are the Indian Cultural Exhibit, a display of the history of the Miwok and Paiute people in the region, and the reconstructed Indian Village of Ahwahnee; the Wilderness Center, where back-country hikers can obtain permits up to 24 weeks in advance (209-372-0740); the Ansel Adams Gallery, offering works of Ansel Adams and contemporary photographers; and Mirror Lake. During the summer, the Yosemite Theater, held in the Visitor Center auditoriums, offers programs in the performing and film arts that bring Yosemite and its history to life.
- The Mariposa Grove and Wawona Area, near the park's south entrance includes the Pioneer Yosemite History Center, a collection of historic buildings associated with the people who shaped the national park idea in Yosemite.
- At Glacier Point, an overlook high above Yosemite Valley, the 2,425-foot Yosemite Falls can be seen on the far side of the Valley. Sunset and full-moon nights are the ideal times to visit the point.
- The Crane Flat area, a pleasant forest and meadow, is located 16 miles from Yosemite Valley. The Tuolumne Grove of giant sequoias is accessible from this point.
- The Tioga Road is a scenic drive that winds through forests and past the meadows, lakes, and granite domes that lie between Crane Flat and Tuolumne Meadows. From the many turnouts along this road, visitors can enjoy broad and beautiful vistas, including one at Tioga Pass, which crosses the Sierra's crest at 9,945 feet and is

Wilderness Permits

Wilderness permits are required year-round for all overnight trips into the back-country, but they are not required for day hikes. Maximum group size is 15 people for trail travel and 8 people for off-trail travel. Permits are available at the Yosemite Valley Visitor Center from 9:00 A.M. to 4:00 P.M. daily for Valley trailheads and via 24-hour self-registration at Big Oat Flat Information Station, Hetch Hetchy Entrance Station, Wawona Information Station, and Badger Pass Ranger Station for non-Valley trailheads. Permit reservations may be made by calling 209-372-0740.

Yosemite Fun Facts

The Yosemite Concession Services Corporation annually supplies Yosemite National Park's visitors with:

- Over 100,000 gallons of milk
- 275,000 hamburgers
- 2,400,000 eggs
- 100,000 hot dogs
- 68,000 steaks
- 125,000 pounds of chicken
- 1,500,000 soft drinks
- 2,500,000 cups of coffee
- 30,000 gallons of ice cream
- 70,000 flashlight batteries
- 5,000,000 pounds of ice
- 160,000 rolls of film
- 2,250,000 meals

Wilderness Areas within Yosemite

Hetch Hetchy

Hetch Hetchy Reservoir, located in the northwest part of the park, is the gateway to many of the less populated areas in Yosemite. Laurel Lake, Lake Vernon, Rancheria Falls, and Tiltill Valley are all within 15 miles of the reservoir. Hikers may elect to begin longer trips here as well, toward either Tuolumne Meadows or the northernmost reaches of the park.

The Tioga Road

This scenic 45-mile drive covers almost 4,000 feet of elevation change, beginning at Crane Flat and ending at Tioga Pass. The road is generally open to vehicles from late May until the first major snowstorm after November 1. There are several first-come, first-served campgrounds along the road, including Tamarack Flat, Yosemite Creek, White Wolf, and Porcupine Flat.

Tuolumne Meadows

At over 8,600 feet in elevation, Tuolumne temperatures average 15 to 20 degrees cooler than Yosemite Valley. Snow is not uncommon as late as June or as early as September. Some peaks retain snow throughout the summer and provide breathtaking views. Eight different trailheads lead backpackers and day hikers into a broad variety of wilderness adventures. Check guidebooks and Visitor Centers for more information. The Tuolumne Meadows campground is available by advance and same-day reservation.

Yosemite Valley

Trailheads here lead hikers up the sheer granite walls that form the valley. To reach the top of such spectacles as Yosemite Falls, Glacier Point, Half Dome, and El Capitan, the hiker will encounter steep terrain, switchbacks, and rapidly changing weather conditions. Pack plenty of water, food, and warm clothes. Many of the areas reached around the rim of the Valley area are day-use-only zones.

Glacier Point

At an elevation of 7,200 feet, Glacier Point is the trailhead for many popular day hikes, including the Panorama and Pohono trails, as well as short hikes to Taft Point and Sentinel Dome. Glacier Point Road offers access to trails in the Clark Range and the southern portion of the park. The 16-mile road begins at the Chinquapin junction of Highway 41. Driving time from Yosemite Valley is about 1 hour. Permits for trails leaving the Glacier Point Road may be obtained from the Wawona or Yosemite Valley Permit Stations. The Bridalveil Creek campground, located on the Glacier Point Road, is available on a first-come, first-served basis June through September.

Wawona

Historic Wawona, just inside the park's southern boundary, serves as an access point to a variety of beautiful, less-frequented areas. The Mariposa Grove of giant sequoias and Chilnualna Falls are popular day hikes. Beautiful meadows, lakes (Chilnualna, Grouse, Crescent, Royal Arch, and Buena Vista), and the little used Alder Creek trail can be accessed from the south end of the park. Wawona Campground is available on a first-come, first-served basis.

the highest automobile pass in California. Tuolumne Meadows, near the east end of the Tioga Road, is graced by the winding Tuolumne River and surrounded by majestic peaks and domes. The Tioga Road, the only east–west highway through the park, closes during the winter months (approximately November through May).

Points of Interest

U.S. ARMY CORPS OF ENGINEERS

BAY MODEL REGIONAL VISITOR CENTER

The model simulates San Francisco Bay conditions such as tidal action, sediment disposition, and freshwater/saltwater interaction. Corps rangers explain how engineers and scientists conduct laboratory tests in their search for solutions to the problems of maintaining the bay's water environment. From Golden Gate Bridge, north 3 miles on US 101 to Sausalito exit, then to 2100 Bridgeway Boulevard.

BLACK BUTTE LAKE

Situated at the northern end of the Central Valley, an hour's drive south of Red Bluff, this quiet park, surrounded by beautiful, dark volcanic buttes, is well known for outstanding fishing and sailing. From Orland, 10 miles west via Newville Road.

EASTMAN LAKE

Just an hour's drive north of Fresno, in the Sierra Nevada foothills. Rolling oak-covered hills provide a scenic and restful setting for fishing, boating, and hiking. Located 25 miles east of Chowchilla, at the north end of County Road 29.

ENGLEBRIGHT LAKE

Only an hour's drive north of Sacramento, on the historic Yuba River. A grand and rugged canyon hides many boat-access campsites. From Maryville, 20 miles east on CA 20.

FULLERTON DAM

Facilities accommodate fishing, picnics, hardcourt ball games, and field sports. On State College Road in Fullerton, off CA 57 south of Imperial Highway.

HANSEN DAM

Extensive day-use facilities, including a golf course and riding stables, are available at this site in the San Fernando Valley. Exit I-210 at Osborne Street.

HENSLEY LAKE

Less than an hour's drive north of Fresno, in the foothills of the Sierra Nevada. A gateway to Yosemite National Park, with excellent water skiing and a fishing lake. Located 17 miles northeast of Madera, on County Road 400.

MARTIS CREEK LAKE
Less than an hour's drive west of Reno, near world-famous Lake Tahoe, the Martis Creek area features exciting trout fishing in the lake and surrounding streams. From Truckee, southeast 5 miles on CA 267.

LAKE MENDOCINO
Two hours' drive north of San Francisco, near the redwood country, this beautiful park is popular with local residents exploring the northern California coast. Fishing, hiking, and boating are all available. From Ukiah, 3 miles north on US 101, then east on Lake Mendocino Drive.

MOJAVE RIVER DAM
In the high desert wilderness at the foot of the San Bernardino Mountains. Camping and equestrian facilities are available. Near Hesperia, 15 miles east of I-15, via CA 138 and CA 173.

NEW HOGAN LAKE
About an hour's drive east of Stockton, near historic gold rush towns of the California Mother Lode. This scenic setting in the Sierra Nevada foothills features exciting fishing, water skiing, and hiking. From Stockton, 35 miles east via CA 26.

PINE FLAT LAKE
Less than an hour east of Fresno, in the Sierra and Sequoia national forests. The rugged Kings River Canyon is the location of this beautiful park where fishing, boating, and water skiing are all available. From Fresno, 32 miles east via CA 180.

SANTA FE DAM
Swimming, fishing, nonpowered boating, hiking, and picnicking are available. Of special interest are five distinct biological communities representing the last vestige of a complex plant life system that was important to the Indians and early settlers. Exit I-210 onto I-605 in the City of Irwindale.

LAKE SONOMA
In the wine-growing region of Sonoma County, this picturesque lake has secluded vehicle and boat-in camping available for fishing and boating. From Healdsburg, 10 miles northwest on Dry Creek Road.

STANISLAUS RIVER PARKS
Just a few minutes northeast of Modesto in the central valley. A series of small parks, located along the Stanislaus River, provides exciting fishing, rafting, and canoeing opportunities. From Modesto, 10 miles north via CA 99.

SUCCESS LAKE
At the southern end of the central valley, this scenic setting with the Sierra Nevada in the background provides great fishing and boating. From Porterville, 5 miles east on CA 190.

BUREAU OF LAND MANAGEMENT

AFTON CANYON

The sheer walls of this miniature Grand Canyon tower 300 feet above the Mojave River. Four major trails of varying lengths take visitors past these varicolored cliffs and through the haunts of Native American peoples, Spanish missionaries and explorers, and mountain men.

35 miles east of Barstow
Barstow Resource Area, 760-255-8700

THE BLYTHE INTAGLIOS

Centuries ago, native peoples of the lower Colorado River Valley engraved on the ground surface gigantic human, animal, and geometric figures, known to archaeologists as "intaglios." There are a total of six figures in three locations, including a human figure at each location and an animal figure at two of the locations. The largest human figure measures 171 feet from head to toe. According to the Mojave and Quechan tribes of the Lower Colorado River area, the human figures represent Mastambo, creator of Earth and all life. The animal figures represent Hatakulya, one of two mountain lion-persons who helped in the Creation.

From Blythe, go 15 miles north
El Centro Resource Area, 760-337-4400

SACATONE OVERLOOK

The Sacatone Overlook provides an impressive view of the Carrizo Gorge and the desert beyond. The vantage point commemorates the centenary of the elite 10th Cavalry ("the Buffalo Soldiers"), who patrolled the area from their station in nearby Campo. There is also a trestle of the Impossible Railroad, built in 1919 at a cost of $19,000,000. The railroad, an early link between San Diego and the East, remained in use until the 1970s when maintenance problems and Hurricane Kathleen caused irreparable damage.

McCain Valley, San Diego County
El Centro Resource Area, 760-337-4400

For information on these and other Bureau of Land Management recreational sites in California, contact:

California State Office
2800 Cottage Way
Sacramento, CA 95825
916-978-4400
http://www.ca.blm.gov

FISH AND WILDLIFE SERVICE

SAN FRANCISCO BAY NATIONAL WILDLIFE REFUGE

Covering a hillside above miles of salt marshes, tidal sloughs, mudflats, and salt ponds, this refuge makes it easy to see and explore the natural wonders of the South Bay. The Visitors' Center, located near the Dumbarton Bridge toll plaza in Fremont, features an observation deck and an auditorium available by reservation for meetings of educational and environmental organizations. The Environmental Education Center, at the southern end of San Francisco Bay, can accommodate school groups and is designed for education. Teachers and group leaders who wish to schedule special activities should call the center at least one month in advance. The refuge's naturalists and volunteers offer a wide variety of guided programs, walks, and other activities.

The refuge is crisscrossed by miles of hiking trails (with a boardwalk) to introduce visitors to the San Francisco Bay environment and local wildlife. Boating (but not motorboating) is permitted and there are public launch ramps at Redwood City, the Palo Alto and Alviso marinas, and near the Refuge Visitor Center. Be aware of the tide schedule; many sloughs are empty of water at low tide.

For more information, contact:

San Francisco Bay National Wildlife Refuge
PO Box 524
Newark, CA 94560
510-792-0222
http://www.r1.fws.gov/sfbnwr/sfbnwr.html

For more information on wildlife refuges throughout the Pacific region, contact:

Fish and Wildlife Service, Region 1
911 Northeast 11th Avenue
Portland, OR 97232
503-231-6828
http://www.r1.fws.gov/test/welcome.html

HAWAII

HALEAKALÄ NATIONAL PARK

35 miles southeast of Kahului.

PO Box 369
Makawao, Maui, HI 96768
808-572-9306
http://www.nps.gov/hale

Hawaii Natural History Association, Haleakalä Branch. (PO Box 464, Makawao, HI 96768; 808-572-9306)

Haleakalä National Park, on the island of Maui, preserves the outstanding features of Haleakalä Crater, a valley carved by streams and glaciers during the volcano's erosional stage. Streaks of red, yellow, gray, and black trace the courses of recent and ancient lava, ash, and cinder flows. By contrast, the Kipahulu section of the park offers cascading streams, quiet pools, rolling grasslands, forested valleys, upper rain forest, fragile ecosystems, and rare species of plants and birds (more than 90 percent of the native species are found only on these islands).

MEET YOUR PARK RESOURCE MANAGERS

The National Park Service has a varied and experienced staff of national stature—rangers, natural resource managers, archaeologists, historians, interpreters, landscape architects, engineers, and planners—who protect our land and legacy, conduct research, and educate the public. We'd like to introduce you to one of them.

Ron Nagata, Chief of Resource Management, Haleakala National Park, Hawaii, started as a park volunteer in 1976. During that time, Ron spearheaded a creative, experimental fence-building project in which he and his volunteer crew fenced in native life forms, and fenced out the nonnative feral creatures that threaten them. The park, Ron explains, is a critical habitat for seven endangered bird species and twelve threatened and endangered plants. At Haleakala, Ron relates that although "tens of thousands of feral animals were removed, the void was quickly filled by animals from lands adjoining the park." Innovative park managers planned, designed, and constructed approximately 48 miles of both barrier and boundary fences. The feral animals were removed by resource management crews, allowing the native species to prosper. Ron anticipates that the fences will be maintained in perpetuity in order to favor native species.

Several hundred years have passed since the last volcanic activity near Mäkena (on the southern part of the island), but scientists believe Haleakalä could erupt again.

Sam's Tips

- The Haleakalä Visitor Center, 11 miles from the park entrance, is near the summit of Mount Haleakalä and has a magnificent view of the volcanic valley.
- There are various campgrounds and cabins within the park, but roads lead only to the ones at Hasmer Grove and Kipaholu. Back-country campgrounds are accessible only on foot. Reservations are required (3 months in advance for cabins) and can be obtained through park headquarters.

HAWAII VOLCANOES NATIONAL PARK

The park's Kilauea Visitor Center is 35 miles southwest of Hilo.

PO Box 52
Hawaii National Park, HI 96718
808-985-6000
http://www.nps.gov/havo

Hawaii Natural History Association. (PO Box 74, Hawaii National Park, HI 96718; 808-985-6000)

Situated on two active volcanoes, Hawaii Volcanoes National Park is a habitat for endangered plant, bird, insect, spider, and snail species from sea level to 14,000 feet; a spiritual place for native Hawaiians; and a last vestige of Hawaii as it was hundreds of years ago. Once celebrated as islands of evolution, the islands in the Hawaiian Archipelago are now islands of extinction. The arrival of people changed forever the conditions that fostered the original diversity of life. The park is a shelter for what remains of the once rich tapestry of Hawaiian life.

Sam's Tips

- At the Halema'uma'u Overlook, only a 10-minute hike from the crater's edge, native Hawaiians practice their ancient traditions. The Devastation Trail is a 30-minute walk through the cinder outfall of the 1959 Kilauea Iki eruption. For an update on current volcanic activity, call 808-985-6000.
- The 11-mile Crater Rim Drive circles the summit caldera and craters of Kilauea, passing through rain forest and desert.
- The 20-mile Chain of Craters Road, which intersects with the main Crater Rim Drive, descends 3,700 feet to the coast and then dead ends where a 1995 lava flow crossed the road. This road takes you through some of the most active volcanic areas of the park.
- Backpackers hike the 18-mile trail to the summit of Mauna Loa, at nearly 14,000 feet. All back-country hikers must register at the Kilauea Visitor Center prior to their trip.

KALAUPAPA NATIONAL HISTORICAL PARK

20 miles northeast of Maunaloa, on the island of Molokai.

Kalaupapa, Molokai, HI 96742
808-567-6102
http://www.nps.gov/kala

Located on the northwestern corner of the Molokai Forest Reserve and northeast of the Phallic Stone Palaau State Park, this park contains the site of the Hansen's disease (leprosy) settlement that existed from 1886 to 1969. The park features the Kauhako Crater, Molokai Lighthouse, and Kalaupapa Trail. It also is a habitat for rare and endangered species.

KALOKO–HONOKÖHAU NATIONAL HISTORICAL PARK

2 miles northwest of Kailua; 40 miles southwest of Waimea.

73-4786 Kanalani Street, # 14
Kailua—Kona, HI 96740
808-329-6881
http://www.nps.gov/kaho

Hawaii Natural History Association. (PO Box 74, Hawaii National Park, HI 96718; 808-985-6000)

The site of important Hawaiian settlements before the arrival of European explorers, the park includes coastal areas, large fishponds, house sites, and other archaeological remnants. The park is intended to preserve the native culture of Hawaii. There are no federal facilities in the park.

PU'UHONUA O HONAUNAU NATIONAL HISTORICAL PARK

20 miles southeast of Kailau.

PO Box 129
Honaunau, Kona, HI 96726
http://www.nps.gov/puho

Hawaii Natural History Association. (PO Box 74, Hawaii National Park, HI 96718; 808-985-6000)

This 180-acre park is the best preserved of a system of pu'uhonua or safe havens that dotted the islands. For anyone who broke a sacred law, called a *kapu,* the punishment was death; otherwise, the gods might send lava flows, tidal waves, famine, or earthquakes. But, if you could make it to a *pu'uhonua,* you could go through a ceremony of absolution and return home safely. It also provided sanctuary for defeated warriors and noncombatants during times of battle.

PU'UKOHOLA HEIAU NATIONAL HISTORIC SITE

12 miles southwest of Waimea-Kohala.

PO Box 44340
Kawaihae, HI 96743
808-882-7218
http://www.nps.gov/puhe

Hawaii Natural History Association. (PO Box 74, Hawaii National Park, HI 96718; 808-985-6000)

This last major religious structure of ancient Hawaiian culture is set high on a hill above the Pacific Ocean. The stone *heiau,* or temple, was built by Kamehameha I in 1790–1791 on Pu'ukohola, the "hill of the whale," and was dedicated to his family war god, Kukailimoku. It has been abandoned for 150 years, and the National Park Service is now working to repair damages to the structure.

USS ARIZONA MEMORIAL

25 miles west of Waikiki, Oahu.

1 Arizona Memorial Place
Honolulu, Oahu, HI 96818-3145
808-422-2771
http://www.nps.gov/usar

Arizona Memorial Museum. (same address as above; 808-422-5905 or 808-422-5664)

The *USS Arizona* Memorial honors those who died in the December 7, 1941, attack on Pearl Harbor. The 184-foot-long memorial structure spans the midportion of the sunken battleship, the final resting place for 1,177 of its crewmen. It has an entry room, an assembly room, and a shrine room, where the names of those killed on the *Arizona* are engraved on the marble wall.

SAM'S TIPS

- The Visitor Center and the *USS Arizona* are located on the Pearl Harbor Navy Base. First, get a free ticket at the Visitor Center, hear a brief talk by a park service ranger, watch a 20-minute documentary on the Pearl Harbor attack, and then board a Navy shuttle boat to the memorial.

OREGON

COLUMBIA RIVER GORGE NATIONAL SCENIC AREA

18 miles northeast of Portland on I-84; 80 miles northeast of Salem.

902 Wasco Avenue
Suite 200
Hood River, OR 97031
541-386-2333
http://www.fs.fed.us/r6/columbia

Northwest Interpretive Association. (909 First Avenue, Suite 630, Seattle, WA 98104; 206-220-4140)

Carved into the volcanic rock of the Cascade Mountain Range, the Columbia River Gorge is a spectacular canyon, 80 miles long and up to 4,000 feet deep. As the only sea-level route through the Cascades, it is both an important transportation corridor and an essential source of water and power for industries, cities, farms, and schools throughout the Pacific Northwest.

Sam's Tips

- The Historic Columbia River Highway is a twisting two lane road that passes cascading waterfalls and breathtaking vistas.
- The stone-masoned Vista House, perched on the pinnacle of Crown Point, offers a 30-mile view of the Columbia Gorge. Built between 1916 and 1918, it also has views of two extinct volcanoes, Mount Pleasant and Mount Zion, looming directly across the river.
- Beacon Rock, named by Lewis and Clark in 1805, is an 848-foot-high volcanic core that signified to native inhabitants the end of obstructions between themselves and the ocean.
- The Mount Hood Columbia Gorge Loop is a prime sightseeing excursion that weaves through the Columbia River Gorge and the Hood River Valley and then circles Mount Hood.
- Rooster Rock State Park, named for its landmark rock spire, is popular with wind surfers when the strong east winds are blowing. The entire gorge is known as a prime wind surfing site. The unique climate at some of the geological formations creates a wind-tunnel effect with spectacular waves of air currents.

Facts about Crater Lake

Greatest depth: 1,932 feet.

Lake surface elevation: 6,176 feet above sea level.

Widest point: 6 miles.

Narrowest point: 4.5 miles.

Average lake temperature: 38° F.

Lake surface area: 21 square miles.

Highest peak along the rim: Hillman Peak.

Last time the lake froze: 1949.

Height of Wizard Island: 764 feet.

CRATER LAKE NATIONAL PARK

80 miles northeast of Medford.

PO Box 7
Crater Lake, OR 97604
541-594-2211
http://www.nps.gov/crla

Crater Lake Natural History Association. (PO Box 157, Crater Lake, OR 97604; 541-594-2211)

Deep-blue Crater Lake lies inside the top of an ancient volcano. After Mount Mazama erupted some 7,700 years ago, its peak collapsed, creating a deep basin. Over the course of about 350 to 500 years, rain and snowmelt filled the basin, creating Crater Lake. At 1,932 feet, it's the nation's deepest lake. Shamans in early historic time forbade most Indians to view the lake, and the Indians said nothing about it to trappers and pioneers, who for 50 years did not find it. It was discovered in 1853 by prospectors who were searching for the Lost Cabin Gold Mine. Crater Lake National Park was established in 1902.

Sam's Tips

- The Cleetwood Cove Trail, located on the north side of Crater Lake, is the only safe and legal access to the lake. Over the course of a mile, the Cleetwood Trail climbs 700 feet in elevation, making it shorter but slightly steeper than trails into the Grand Canyon. It translates into climbing 65 flight of stairs.
- The Sinnott Memorial Overlook, located below the caldera rim at Rim Village, is open to visitors daily from July through September and features an unobstructed view of the lake.
- Hikers should be sure to get a copy of the comprehensive brochure, *Day Hikes at Crater Lake National Park* from the park. Hikes are categorized by length (short, medium, and longer) and defined in terms of time, length, elevation, and degree of difficulty.

Skiing around Crater Lake

For the advanced skier, a trip around Crater Lake can be a memorable way to experience the solitude of the park's back-country. A complete trip around the lake takes 2 to 3 days—longer during snowstorms. Snow camping is required; there are no shelters along the 30-mile route. This trip should be attempted only by experienced and properly equipped skiers. A free back-country permit is required.

DESCHUTES NATIONAL FOREST

75 miles east of Eugene; 80 miles southeast of Salem.

1645 Highway 20 E
Bend, OR 97701
541-388-2715
http://www.empnet.com/dnf

Northwest Interpretive Association. (909 First Avenue, Suite 630, Seattle, WA 98104; 206-220-4140)

 **FOREST SERVICE SCENIC BYWAY**

Cascade Lakes

This highway traverses 93 miles of forests and meadows on the Deschutes National Forest and provides year-round access to the Cascade Mountains in central Oregon. The route provides outstanding views of volcanic peaks and offers access to eight resorts, dozens of lakes, and the largest ski resort in the Northwest. *Contact Deschutes National Forest.*

The Deschutes National Forest, part of the rugged lands between the Rocky Mountains and the Cascades Mountain Range, was once well traveled by native Indians, fur trappers, explorers, and miners. Set against a scenic background of the volcanic mountains that form the crest of the Cascade Divide, the forest boasts six wild and scenic rivers, volcanic attractions, dense evergreen growths, mountain lakes, caves, desert areas, and alpine meadows. The Lava Lands Visitor Center includes: Lava Butte, which overlooks lava fields and a fire lookout; Lava River Cave, where you can rent a lantern and explore a lava tube; and the Lava Cast Forest Geologic Site.

 **SAM'S TIPS**

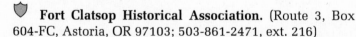

- Ride the Summit Express Chairlift to the top of 9,065-foot Mount Bachelor, and view three states, the Cascades mountain chain, and Three Sisters Wilderness.
- The excellent rafting on the upper Deschutes River, below Benham Falls, is attributed to a lava flow that dammed and narrowed the river channel, creating thunderous, cascading rapids. Be sure to have a map of the river: There are numerous put-ins and take-outs to avoid waterfalls.

FORT CLATSOP NATIONAL MEMORIAL

5 miles southwest of Astoria; 100 miles northwest of Portland.

Route 3, Box 604-FC
Astoria, OR 97103
503-861-2471
http://www.nps.gov/focl

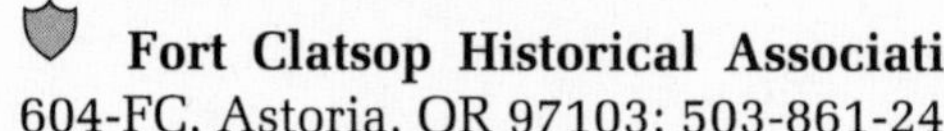

Fort Clatsop Historical Association. (Route 3, Box 604-FC, Astoria, OR 97103; 503-861-2471, ext. 216)

Named after a local Indian nation, Fort Clatsop was built by the Lewis and Clark expedition party during the winter of 1805–1806. While there, the explorers prepared scientific

 **Newberry National Volcanic Monument**

Located about 10 miles south of Bend, Newberry Volcano's huge caldera contains two sparkling lakes, trails, two rustic resorts, and one of the largest obsidian flows in North America. From the summit of 8,000-foot Paulina Peak, visitors enjoy a spectacular overview of an internationally significant volcanic region, including lava flows where NASA astronauts have trained. Three major waterfalls can be seen along the Deschutes River near the monument. For more information, contact the monument at 1230 NE 3rd Street, Bend, OR 97701; 541-388-5664.

accounts of the data they had gathered on their trip west from the mouth of the Missouri River. After Lewis and Clark's party left, the empty fort decayed and eventually disappeared. Today, a replica of the fort, built in 1955, is open for touring; it includes captains' quarters, enlisted men's quarters, and a storeroom. In summer, costumed demonstrations at the fort bring to life the skills of the explorers, such as flintlock muzzle loading, candle making and hide tanning and sewing.

Sam's Tips

- The Lewis and Clark National Historic Trail, which extends from near St. Louis, Missouri, to Les Shirley Park in Oregon, passes through the fort area.
- The Saltworks, located 15 miles southwest of the park, in Seaside, commemorates the location where the expedition set up a salt-making operation. Using five brass kettles, the saltmakers boiled approximately 1,400 gallons of seawater over a period of several weeks. Three and one-half bushels of salt were produced for the return trip.

FREMONT NATIONAL FOREST

175 miles southeast of Eugene, 275 miles southeast of Portland.

524 North G Street
Lakeview, OR 97630
541-947-2151
http://www.fs.fed.us/r6/fremont

Encompassing some 1.2 million acres in south-central Oregon, the Fremont National Forest is characterized by expansive views, dramatic cliffs, and distinctive rock outcroppings. Slide Mountain Geologic Area, which features a giant, prehistoric landslide, is particularly popular. Open meadows and mixed stands of aspen and pine make for beautifully contrasting colors year-round. The forest includes the rugged and remote Gearhart Mountains and the scenic Gearhart Mountain Wilderness.

Crooked River National Grassland

The Crooked River National Grassland was significant during the homestead era in central Oregon, but the lack of rain, and other brutal conditions, forced most of the farming families to move on. Gray Butte Cemetery is where loved ones were left behind. At Lake Billy Chinook, geological conditions have created a miniature Grand Canyon. Popular activities on the lake include boating and jet skiing. For more information, contact Crooked River National Grassland, 813 Southwest Highway 97, Madras, OR 97741; 541-416-6640.

JOHN DAY FOSSIL BEDS NATIONAL MONUMENT

120 miles east of Bend.

HCR 82
Box 126
Kimberly, OR 97848
541-987-2333
http://www.nps.gov/joda

Northwest Interpretive Association. (909 First Avenue, Suite 630, Seattle, WA 98104; 206-220-4140)

The badlands of the John Day Valley are sedimentary rocks that preserve a 40-million-year fossil record of plant and animal life. Every year, scientists uncover more clues to the Age of Mammals—the period between the extinction of the dinosaurs and the beginning of the Ice Age. Scientists are also finding hidden landscapes—the fossil remains of the jungles, savannas, and woodlands that once flourished here. The 14,000-acre monument is divided into three sections: the Clarno Unit, the Painted Hills Unit, and the Sheep Rock Unit. Painted Hills is 1 hour from Sheep Rock (the location of the Visitor Center); Clarno Unit is 1 hour 45 minutes from Sheep Rock.

Sam's Tips

- The Visitor Center features a fossil museum, indoor and outdoor exhibits, a bookstore, and a theater with orientation films. Ranger-conducted programs include fossil museum talks, trail hikes, and briefings on the area's geology and paleontology. Annual events include fossil identification day, the National Trails Day Hike, and the "Journey Through Time" festival in September.
- The Hancock Field Station at the Clarno Unit, operated by the Oregon Museum of Science and Industry, offers several programs on the geology, paleontology, and ecology of central Oregon. For more information, write to Hancock Field Station, Highway 218, Fossil, OR 97830.

MALHEUR NATIONAL FOREST

260 miles southeast of Salem.

139 Northeast Dayton Street
John Day, OR 97845
541-575-3000
http://www.fs.fed.us/r6/malheur

Northwest Interpretive Association. (909 First Avenue, Suite 630, Seattle, WA 98104; 206-220-4140)

In the Blue Mountains of eastern Oregon lies the 1.46-million-acre Malheur National Forest. Over 200 miles of trails take visitors through forests of pine and fir, timbered slopes with scenic alpine lakes and meadows, or valley grasslands. The Strawberry Mountain Wilderness, with its 9,038-foot peak, extends east to west through the heart of the forest, and the Monument Rock Wilderness overlooks the eastern boundary.

Sam's Tips

- The John Day River features primarily Class III and Class IV rapids for rafting. Magone Lake has a boat ramp, fishing areas, a campground, and a picnic area, and is a favorite site for swimming, hiking, geology study, and wildflower viewing.

McLoughlin House National Historic Site

The McLoughlin House is a tribute to the man who is considered to be the "Father of Oregon." Dr. John McLoughlin was the Chief Factor (president) for the Hudson's Bay Company, Britain's powerful fur-trading company, at Fort Vancouver in the Oregon Country from 1824 until 1845. After resigning from the Hudson's Bay Company, he built his family home on his land claim at Oregon City and spent the last 11 years of his life there. The house is restored as nearly as possible to its appearance during the McLoughlin occupancy. The furnishings are period pieces that belonged to the McLoughlin family, the Hudson's Bay Company, and local residents. The house is located at 713 Center Street, Oregon City, OR 97045; 503-656-5146.

PACKING WITH LLAMAS

With their natural agility, intelligence, and calm, llamas are perfectly suited for packing and traveling in wilderness. In situations where the environment is easily damaged or where easy handling and surefootedness are important, llamas may be a pack animal of choice. In fact, llamas have been used to transport goods across the rugged Andean Mountains in South America for over 4,000 years.

Today, all across the United States and Canada, llamas can be found carrying loads for back-country travelers. Many parks and national forests have concessionaires renting llamas for the length of visitors' expeditions. Contact your destination park or forest for more information. For general information about llamas, contact the International Llama Association, PO Box 37505, Denver, CO 80237; 303-756-9004.

MOUNT HOOD NATIONAL FOREST

28 miles east of Portland; 50 miles northeast of Salem.

16400 Champion Way
Sandy, OR 97055
503-668-1431
http://www.fs.fed.us/r6/mthood

Northwest Interpretive Association. (909 First Avenue, Suite 630, Seattle, WA 98104; 206-220-4140)

The Mount Hood National Forest is located in the Cascade Mountain Range of northwestern Oregon. Visitors delight in the brightly colored wildflowers, cool alpine meadows, and waterfalls along the winding Columbia River. Towering, snow-covered Mount Hood is the central feature of the Mount Hood Wilderness and of the forest.

SAM'S TIPS

- Mount Hood Village, located at the foot of Mount Hood, is an all-season camping resort featuring an indoor heated pool, a fitness center, and tent sites with full hookup. In August, the Mount Hood Festival of Jazz brings top musicians to Mount Hood Community College in Gresham.
- Timberline Lodge, listed on the National Register of Historic Places, has been restored to its original grandeur. Located on the timberline—the highest elevation where trees can grow—the Lodge has historical

Thundereggs

According to legends of the Warm Springs Indians, Mount Hood and Mount Jefferson, two adjacent snowcapped peaks that tower over Central Oregon, at times would become angry with each other. They would rob the nests of the thunderbirds and then, accompanied by thunder and lightning, would hurl spherical masses of rock at each other. The tribes of the central Oregon highlands gave these agate-filled stones the name "thundereggs." The diameter of Oregon thundereggs can range from less than 1 inch to up to 5 feet. The area around Prineville, known as the "Agate Capital of the United States," contains the largest concentration of thundereggs.

exhibits and boasts unsurpassed views of the surrounding countryside.

- At 11,245 feet above sea level, Mount Hood, the highest mountain in Oregon, is high enough to be seen from many places in Oregon and Washington.

Safety Tips for Rockhounding

Rockhounding is a safe and enjoyable hobby, but the forest offers 10 basic rules to follow, for personal safety and for the protection of the resources:

1. Wear heavy shoes.
2. Wear suitable clothes.
3. Wear safety glasses.
4. Disturb as little vegetation as possible.
5. Don't undermine or chop tree roots or trunks.
6. Fill in holes; reinstate all plants and topsoil after digging.
7. Leave gates as you find them.
8. Pack out all your litter.
9. Go with a partner.
10. Don't trespass.

OCHOCO NATIONAL FOREST

120 miles southeast of Salem.

3160 Northeast Third Street
PO Box 490
Prineville, OR 97754
541-416-6500
http://www.fs.fed.us/r6/ochoco

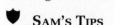

Northwest Interpretive Association. (909 First Avenue, Suite 630, Seattle, WA 98104; 206-220-4140)

The Ochoco National Forest was created in 1911 by combining parts of the Deschutes and Malheur forests. Most of the forest consists of gentle to moderate slopes covered with coniferous evergreens, primarily ponderosa pine, western larch, lodgepole pine, Douglas fir, and western juniper. The foothill areas on the south and west boundaries, including the 106,000-acre Crooked River National Grassland (see entry) are gently rolling with large sagebrush and juniper plant communities. The elevation of the forest ranges from 2,200 feet to over 7,000 feet.

Sam's Tips

- The Prineville and Crook County areas are well known for mineral deposits. Rockhounders may remove small amounts of rock, minerals, or invertebrate fossils for personal use. The Ochoco National Forest and the Bureau of Land Management require no fee or permit for small-scale collection.

OREGON CAVES NATIONAL MONUMENT

125 miles southwest of Eugene; 210 miles southwest of Portland.

19000 Caves Highway
Cave Junction, OR 97523
541-592-2100
http://www.nps.gov/orca

Crater Lake Natural History Association. (PO Box 157, Crater Lake, OR 97604; 541-594-2211)

What is now called Oregon Caves National Monument was originally discovered in 1874 by Elijah Davidson, a hunter who pursued his dog into a deep, dark cave. Over the next few decades, other explorers ventured into the cave, returning home to tell of its beauty and mystery. In 1909, President William Howard Taft proclaimed the 480-acre tract a National Monument. But, during the 1930s, workers blasted tunnels and widened passages in the cave. Waste rocks were put in side passages, and many marble or calcite formations were covered. Changes in air flow patterns then altered the growth of formations and caused greater swings in temperature. The installation of lights in the cave promoted the growth of algae, which turned portions of the cave green and dissolved some formations. Since 1985, the National Park Service has improved conditions here by removing more than a thousand tons of rubble, installing air locks, repairing broken rock formations, and replacing the asphalt trail with cement.

Sam's Tips

- The temptation to reach out and touch can be overwhelming, but formations break easily and oils in your skin will discolor them. Look, but do not touch.
- The cave is cool, wet, and slippery; temperatures inside remain close to 40° F. all year. Wear rubber-soled shoes and warm clothing.
- Special regulations pertain to children. They must be able to climb a set of test stairs unassisted and must be at least 42 inches tall. Children may not be carried through the cave.
- The cave tour route is about a half-mile long and has low and narrow passages. The tour lasts approximately 75 minutes. Persons with walking, breathing, or heart problems should avoid the tour.
- There are no campgrounds in the park; however, the Forest Service operates two campgrounds in the adjoining Siskiyou National Forest (see entry) from late May to mid-September.
- The Chateau, a six-story hotel with a dining room, a soda fountain, and a coffee shop, was completed in 1934 and is listed on the National Register of Historic Places.

ROGUE RIVER NATIONAL FOREST

166 miles southeast of Eugene.

333 West 8th Street
PO Box 520
Medford, OR 97501
541-858-2200
http://www.fs.fed.us/r6/rogue

Northwest Interpretive Association. (909 First Avenue, Suite 630, Seattle, WA 98104; 206-220-4140)

The Rogue River winds through the Rogue River National Forest, carving a dramatic river gorge. The surrounding forest has a rich geological history. To the west, the forest includes the headwaters of the Applegate River, within the geologically complex Siskiyou Mountain Range. The area became "gold country" during the late 1880's, and remnants of mining activities can still be seen today. To the east, the forest contains the upper reaches of the Rogue River, located along the slopes of the volcanic Cascade range. Although the southern Cascades tend to have a gentle relief, several deep canyons, such as the Middle Fork of the Rogue and the South Fork of Little Butte Creek, are located in this part of the forest.

SISKIYOU NATIONAL FOREST

125 miles southwest of Eugene; 180 miles southwest of Salem.

200 Northeast Greenfield Road
PO Box 440
Grants Pass, OR 97526
541-471-6500
http://www.magick.net/~siskiyou

Northwest Interpretive Association. (909 First Avenue, Suite 630, Seattle, WA 98104; 206-220-4140)

Located in the Klamath Mountains, in the southwest corner of Oregon, the 1.1-million-acre Siskiyou National Forest rises from not far above sea level to over 7,022 feet. The forest's unusually large number of rare plants and Limpy Botanical Trail make it a haven for botanists. It also offers hiking, mountain biking, rafting, fishing, and camping. Over 600 miles of trails for hikers and horse riders weave through the park.

SIUSLAW NATIONAL FOREST

40 miles southwest of Salem; 70 miles southwest of Portland.

4077 Research Way
PO Box 1148
Corvallis, OR 97333
541-750-7000
http://www.oregoncoast.com:80/hebord

Northwest Interpretive Association. (909 First Avenue, Suite 630, Seattle, WA 98104; 206-220-4140)

The Suislaw National Forest, located in the coastal mountain range of Oregon, is one of the two forests in the continental United States bordering the Pacific Ocean. Thick Sitka spruce and Douglas fir forests contrast sharply with miles of open sand dunes, beaches, and freshwater lakes.

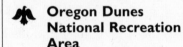

Oregon Dunes National Recreation Area

Located 70 miles southwest of Eugene and 100 miles southwest of Salem, this National Recreation Area has sand dunes that rise as much as 500 feet above sea level. The dunes were created nearly 6,000 years ago, when rocks from nearby rivers tumbled into the area and eroded into sand. The region features a 38-mile-long beach and numerous lakes, marshes, and estuaries. For more information, contact the Recreation Area at 855 Highway Avenue, Reedsport, OR 97467; 541-271-6030.

European Beach Grass Dolls

European Beach Grass, originally imported from Europe to stabilize sand along the coast, is responsible for the prominent coast at the Oregon Dunes National Recreation Area, where European Beach Grass is abundant and may be cut. Dolls made from this beach grass are a popular craft in the area. Write the park and request an instructional booklet so that you can make your own creations when you visit.

The Cape Perpetua Scenic Area and the Oregon Dunes National Recreation Area are the main scenic attractions on the coast. The inland areas of the forest offer three wilderness areas and various recreational opportunities.

Sam's Tips

- Cape Perpetua features an ancient rain forest, volcanic rock, and nearby tidepools. The Interpretive Center offers a movie and exhibits on the natural and cultural history of the Oregon Coast.
- The highest point in the forest is Mary's Peak, with an elevation of 4,097 feet. There are a number of trails to the top, and on a clear day the view is spectacular, stretching from the ocean to the Cascade Range.
- Several salt- and freshwater fishing areas in the forest offer sea perch, flounder, trout, yellow perch, and other species of fish. In the early spring through summer, try clamming.
- Heceta Head, a late 19th-century lighthouse near Devil's Elbow State Park, has been listed on the National Register of Historic Places since 1978. It also operates as a bed and breakfast. For more information and to make reservations, call 541-547-3696.
- The Kentucky Falls are at the end of a steep, narrow 2-mile trail that descends 760 feet to a view of the 80- to 90-foot twin waterfalls spilling over a cliff just before their confluence.

UMATILLA NATIONAL FOREST

170 miles northeast of Portland.

2517 Southwest Hailey Avenue
Pendleton, OR 97801
541-278-3716
http://www.fs.fed.us/r6/uma

Northwest Interpretive Association. (909 First Avenue, Suite 630, Seattle, WA 98104; 206-220-4140)

Located in the Blue Mountains of northeastern Oregon and the southeastern corner of Washington, the Umatilla National Forest consists mostly of V-shaped valleys, narrow ridges or plateaus, and mountainous terrain. *Umatilla* is taken from the Indian word meaning "water rippling over sand." The forest contains three "upside-down" wilderness areas, (so called because they radiate down steep gorges and canyons from high plateaus instead of upward to high peaks and alpine lakes) called Wenaha–Tucannon, North Fork John Day, and North Fork Umatilla. Hikers and horseback riders enjoy the descent into canyon-like wilderness.

FOREST SERVICE SCENIC BYWAY

Blue Mountain Scenic Byway

This 130-mile byway offers panoramic views of Potamus Canyon and the Wild and Scenic North Fork John Day River. History buffs especially will appreciate the former coal and gold mining areas, the Fremont Power House, and four historic Forest Service stations. *Contact Umatilla National Forest.*

Sam's Tips

- The Blue Mountain Scenic Byway traverses 130 miles of paved two-lane roads and passes historical sites, communities, ghost towns, and waterways.
- Over 2,000 personal-use Christmas tree permits are issued each December, and many families make an annual tradition of cutting their own tree.

UMPQUA NATIONAL FOREST

60 miles southwest of Eugene.

PO Box 1008
2900 N.W. Stewart Parkway
Roseburg, OR 97470
541-672-6601
http://www.teleport.com/~umpquanf

Northwest Interpretive Association. (909 First Avenue, Suite 630, Seattle, WA 98104; 206-220-4140)

The Umpqua National Forest extends from the summit of the Cascade Mountain range to western lowlands in southwestern Oregon. The forest is named for the Umpqua Indians, who once fished its rivers and roamed its green timbered slopes.

The 172-mile Rouge–Umpqua Scenic Byway offers a range of natural and recreational opportunities, including wilderness, waterfalls, mountain peaks, old volcanoes, flower-filled meadows, and quiet lakes. It's easy to make a full day of the drive—or longer, if you want to hike any of the side trails.

Sam's Tips

- For a unique experience, spend a night in the Whisky Camp Guard Station, where forest service personnel used to live while protecting the area from blazes. For more information, contact the Roseburg address above.

Cabin Rentals in Oregon and Washington

The Nature of the Northwest Interpretive Center has a Website that lists more than 40 cabins on Forest Service land that can be rented. Plan for a memorable adventure by going to: http://www.naturenw.org/cabin.

- The 30-mile Devils Knob CCC Road traces the history of one of the first Civilian Conservation Corps camps established during the Great Depression. Highlights include camps, a guard station, and lookout areas.
- Acker Rock Lookout offers an expansive view of the upper south Umpqua watershed and the mountains on the watersheds of the Willamette, Rogue, and Deschutes rivers. Sheer cliffs drop off for several hundred feet on the western and southern sides of the lookout. Lodging here is available from June through October by obtaining a Special Use Permit. The fee is approximately $40 a night for up to 3 nights; occupancy is limited to 4 people. Other rentals include Pickett Butte Lookout, a traditional metal lookout tower that sleeps 4 people, and Musick Guard Station, listed in the National Register of Historic Places.

Hells Canyon National Recreation Area

Hells Canyon, North America's deepest river gorge, encompasses a vast and remote region with dramatic changes in elevation, terrain, climate, and vegetation. Carved by the Snake River, the canyon plunges more than 8,000 feet below snowcapped He Devil Peak, in Idaho's Seven Devils Mountains. There are no roads across Hells Canyon's 10-mile-wide expanse, and only three roads lead to the Snake River between Hells Canyon Dam and the Oregon–Washington boundary. The canyon is 150 miles east of Spokane and 125 miles northwest of Boise, ID. For more information, contact the recreation area at 88401 Hwy. 82, Enterprise, OR 97828; 541-426-5546.

WALLOWA–WHITMAN NATIONAL FOREST

300 miles southeast of Portland.

1550 Dewey Avenue
PO Box 907
Baker City, OR 97814
541-523-6391
http://www.fs.fed.us/r6/w-w

 **Northwest Interpretive Association.** (909 First Avenue, Suite 630, Seattle, WA 98104; 206-220-4140)

The Wallowa–Whitman National Forest covers Oregon's Blue and Wallowa mountains, Idaho's Seven Devils Mountains, and Hells Canyon, the deepest river gorge in North America. Visitors enjoy glacial lakes and streams, heavily timbered forests, brilliant colors in the fall, and the diverse scenery of four Wildernesses: Eagle Cap, Hells Canyon, John Day, and Monument Rock. The Snake River segment within the forest is classified as part of the National Wild and Scenic River system; there are seven other wild and scenic rivers in the forest. Remnants of historic gold mining, as well as the early days of logging activities, can still be seen here.

Native American Art

A Nez Perce Indian legend holds that Hells Canyon was dug with a big stick by "Coyote" in order to protect their ancestors from the "seven devils" across the gorge. The canyon's long ties to Native American culture also can be glimpsed in nearly 200 rock-art sites, including abstract petroglyphs, pictographs of red pigment, and geometric scratch designs.

 **SAM'S TIPS**

- The Kirkwood Historic Ranch was built by cattlemen, but the terrain proved too steep and rugged for their herd, so the ranchers turned to more sure-footed sheep.

 **FOREST SERVICE SCENIC BYWAY**

Elkhorn Drive

Elkhorn Drive begins in Baker Valley at an elevation of 3,400 feet and rises to over 7,000 feet in the Elkhorn Range of the Blue Mountains. Along the 106-mile loop, travelers visit Sumpter Valley, where they can see reminders of the earlier gold rush and logging days, enjoy recreation opportunities from swimming to skiing, and take a ride on a restored narrow-gauge railroad. *Contact Wallowa–Whitman National Forest.*

The 16 visitor sites at the ranch range from a cabin museum to a prehistoric pit house village.

- Recreational gold panning continues to be popular in the forest. You're welcome to come and try your luck.
- The Elkhorn Drive Scenic Byway passes through historic Post Office Square in Baker City, the Mason Dam Picnic Area, and the Mowich Loop Wildlife Viewing Area. The road also passes trailheads, overlooks, and the Anthony Lake Ski Area and Campground.
- For 50 years, the Sumpter Valley Railway linked the people and enterprises of northeastern Oregon's Blue Mountain region. In the 1970s, a group was formed to restore parts of the railway, and narrow-gauge excursion trains now run between McEwan and Sumpter.

WILLAMETTE NATIONAL FOREST

70 miles south of Salem.

211 East 7th Avenue
Eugene, OR 97401
541-465-6521
http://www.fs.fed.us/r6/willamette

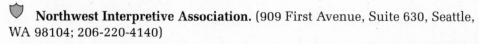

 **Northwest Interpretive Association.** (909 First Avenue, Suite 630, Seattle, WA 98104; 206-220-4140)

Located in the western Cascades of Oregon, the Willamette National Forest is blanketed with Douglas fir trees. Eight wildernesses lie wholly or partially within the forest boundary. Towering, snowcapped Mount Jefferson, among the most beautiful mountains in the world, looks down on deep-blue lakes. Vast plains of lava near Belknap Crater provide desolate landscape in parts of the Mount Washington Wilderness. Wild and mountainous country surrounds the imposing Three Sisters Mountains. Active glaciers lie on the upper slopes while, below, dozens of serene lakes are surrounded by dense, green forest. The Pacific Crest National Scenic Trail crosses through the crest of the Cascades, where numerous waterfalls and mountain lakes delight hikers.

FOREST SERVICE SCENIC BYWAY

Robert Aufderheide Memorial Drive

This drive on the Willamette National Forest parallels for 70 miles the South Fork of the McKenzie River and the North Fork of the Willamette River, offering views of cascading streams and large, old-growth Douglas fir. *Contact Willamette National Forest.*

WINEMA NATIONAL FOREST

140 miles southeast of Eugene; 175 miles southeast of Salem.

2819 Dahlia Street
Klamath Falls, OR 97601
541-883-6714
http://www.fs.fed.us/r6/winema

The Winema National Forest, in south-central Oregon, is named for the heroine of the Modoc War of 1872. Winema, meaning "Woman of a Brave Heart," acted as an interpreter between US troops and the Native Americans, and is credited with saving lives of both the Modoc and the pioneer settlers. Portions of the pristine Sky Lakes Wilderness, encompassing 200 lakes, lie within the forest. The existence here of a pair of unusual volcanic cones, Goose Neck and Goose Egg, is related to the activities of neighboring Mount Mazama, the ancient volcano known today as Crater Lake. The Klamath Basin is the largest waterfowl congregating area on the west coast and has the largest population of wintering and nesting bald eagles in the lower 48 states.

U.S. ARMY CORPS OF ENGINEERS

FOSTER LAKE

A scenic mountain lake with good steelhead and trout fishing. From Sweet Home, northeast 4 miles on OR 20.

HILLS CREEK LAKE

A scenic lake in a narrow canyon of the Willamette National Forest. From Eugene, southeast 45 miles on OR 58.

LOST CREEK LAKE

In the scenic Rogue River Valley, on the route to Crater Lake National Park. From Medford, northeast 30 miles on OR 62

BUREAU OF LAND MANAGEMENT

EUGENE DISTRICT

The four developed recreation areas are: Shotgun Park, Whittaker Creek, Clay Creek, and Sharps Creek. Shotgun Park, in the foothills of the Cascade Range, 4 miles northwest of Marcola, features swimming, horseshoes, volleyball, softball, 5 miles of hiking trails, playground equipment, and individual picnic sites for day use. Whittaker Creek recreation area, located 16 miles southeast of Mapleton, offers 20 camping sites, 9 picnic sites, swimming, fishing, and wildlife viewing.

LAKEVIEW DISTRICT

Landscapes across the 4 million-plus acres of public land include forested mountains and high-elevation desert. The Klamath River offers quality white-water rafting on a stretch of a national scenic river. Scattered reservoirs within the 3.5 million acres in the Lakeview Resource Area offer excellent trout fishing.

MEDFORD DISTRICT

At Tucker Flat Campground, 8 sites are open, May through October, on a no-fee, first-come, first-served basis. It is a remote location with no hookups or potable water, and has only vault toilets. No gas stations or other services are available. Recreation activities are: fishing, camping, picnicking, swimming, hiking.

For more information on these and other Bureau of Land Management sites in Oregon, contact:

Oregon State Office
PO Box 2965
Portland, OR 97208
503-952-6003
http://www.or.blm.gov

WASHINGTON

COLVILLE NATIONAL FOREST

50 miles northwest of Spokane; 150 miles northeast of Seattle.

765 South Main Street
Colville, WA 99114
509-684-7000
http://www.fs.fed.us/cvnf

Northwest Interpretive Association. (909 First Avenue, Suite 630, Seattle, WA 98104; 206-220-4140)

The Colville National Forest—located in the northeast corner of Washington, bordering on Canada—has scenic 7,000-foot mountains, beautiful valleys, picturesque lakes, and rolling wooded slopes, ranging from large lodgepole pine stands in the west to extensive cedar groves on the eastern slopes. The forest's great salmon runs first attracted Native Americans to the area. The discovery of gold brought miners, trappers, and homesteaders. Today, old cabins, mining shafts, and trails are reminders of past times.

SAM'S TIPS

- Recreational activities include wildlife viewing at Sullivan Lake; winter sports at Chewelah Mountain; a geological car tour at Bangs Mountain; and Sherman Pass, the highest pass in Washington.

EBEY'S LANDING NATIONAL HISTORICAL RESERVE

60 miles northwest of Seattle.

PO Box 774
Coupeville, WA 98239
360-678-6084
http://www.nps.gov/ebla

Northwest Interpretive Association. (909 First Avenue, Suite 630, Seattle, WA 98104; 206-220-4140)

At the north end of Puget Sound, on Whidbey Island, lies Ebey's Landing National Historical Reserve, which was created by Congress in 1978 "to preserve and protect a rural community which provides an unbroken historic record from . . . 19th century exploration and settlement in Puget Sound to the present time." In this unique cultural landscape, farms are still farmed, forests are logged, and historic buildings are still actively used today as homes or places of business.

Sam's Tips

- The Washington State Ferry System operates year-round service to the island from Port Townsend and Mukilteo. For the ferry schedule, call 206-464-6400. Ferry lines for both passengers and cars can be extremely long during the summer. The Port Townsend ferry to the Olympic Peninsula is often canceled because of tides and stormy weather conditions.
- Camping is limited on Whidbey Island; for more information, call the two state parks within the reserve: Fort Casey State Park (360-678-4519) or Fort Ebey State Park (360-678-4636).
- The 19th-century seaport town of Coupeville, located in the reserve, features antique shops, restaurants, gift shops, and bed and breakfasts on historic Front Street and Main Street. The reserve contains the greatest number of structures (over 50) on the National Historic Register in Washington State.

FORT VANCOUVER NATIONAL HISTORIC SITE

10 miles north of Portland, OR.

612 East Reserve Street
Vancouver, WA 98601-3897
360-696-7655
http://www.nps.gov/fova

Northwest Interpretive Association. (909 First Avenue, Suite 630, Seattle, WA 98104; 206-220-4140)

Fort Vancouver, an early British stronghold, was the headquarters for the Hudson's Bay Company's fur-trading operations between 1825 and 1849. The fort's warehouses stocked supplies for the fur brigades, the Indian and settler trade, and the 20 other company posts in the department. Since 1966, Fort Vancouver's palisade and nine buildings have been reconstructed on their original locations to create a sense of what life was like when this was the most important settlement in the Pacific Northwest.

Sam's Tips

- The fort has been reconstructed with painstaking detail, from the fire-brick ovens in the bakehouse to the bastion built to protect the fort from American attack. There are 12 sites to tour within the fort.
- Fort Vancouver is at the northwest end of the Oregon Trail, a 2,170-mile path beginning in Independence, Missouri. For more information on the Oregon Trail, write to the Oregon–California Trail Association, 524 South Osage Street, PO Box 1019, Independence, MO 64501-0519.

Mount Saint Helens National Volcanic Monument

On May 18, 1980, Mount St. Helens, located in the heart of the Gifford Pinchot National Forest, erupted after 123 years of volcanic inactivity. About 1,300 feet of the summit exploded from the mountain, transforming the green forest around it into a blown-down gray landscape. Roads wind through forests where a layer of pumice is now the only sign of recent volcanic activity. One lookout, Windy Ridge, is about 4 miles from the crater and provides a startling panorama of the volcano, the building lava dome at its base, and the stark eruption landscape. For details, contact the monument at: 42218 Northeast Yale Bridge Road, Amboy, WA 98601; 360-247-5473; http://volcano.und.nodak.edu/vwdocs/msh.

GIFFORD PINCHOT NATIONAL FOREST

50 miles southeast of Seattle; 25 miles north of Portland, OR.

10600 Northeast 51st Circle
Vancouver, WA 98682
360-891-5000
http://www.fs.fed.us/gpnf

Northwest Interpretive Association. (909 First Avenue, Suite 630, Seattle, WA 98104; 206-220-4140)

Mount Saint Helens, which erupted on May 18, 1980, is the focal point of this national forest, which is named for the founder and first chief of the United States Forest Service. It features an extensive trail system, more than 40 campgrounds, and the 40-million-year-old history of the Columbia Gorge.

Sam's Tips

- The recently opened Johnston Ridge Observatory brings visitors within 5 miles of the north side of the volcano and offers spectacular views of the still-steaming lava dome, crater, pumice plain, and landslide deposit.
- The Coldwater Lake Recreation Area has a variety of recreational opportunities with a view of Mount Saint Helens and surrounding peaks.
- The forest includes some of the best huckleberry picking in the Northwest. The forest office (at the Vancouver address above) will be happy to send you a map that includes all of the best trails where you can pick berries.

KLONDIKE GOLD RUSH NATIONAL HISTORICAL PARK

Seattle.

117 South Main Street
Seattle, WA 98104
206-553-7220
http://www.nps.gov/klgo

Northwest Interpretive Association. (909 First Avenue, Suite 630, Seattle, WA 98104; 206-220-4140)

"At 3 o'clock this morning the steamship *Portland,* from St. Michaels for Seattle, passed up {Puget} Sound with more than a ton of solid gold on board and 68 passengers." When this sentence appeared in the July 17, 1897, issue of *The Seattle Post Intelligencer,* it triggered one of the last—and greatest—gold rushes in the history of North America. The City of Seattle played a significant role in establishing "gold rush fever." Prospectors crowded the docks, hotels, stores, and restaurants of the city during the gold rush years. Klondike Gold Rush National Historical Park, located on the edge of the piers of Elliott Bay, preserves this legacy and evokes a sense of the atmosphere surrounding the gold rush days of 1898.

Sam's Tips

- At 3:00 P.M. on the first Sunday of every month, the park hosts a screening of Charlie Chaplin's *The Gold Rush.*

LAKE ROOSEVELT NATIONAL RECREATION AREA

50 miles northwest of Spokane.

1008 Crest Drive
Coulee Dam, WA 99116-0037
509-633-9441
http://www.nps.gov/laro

Northwest Interpretive Association. (909 First Avenue, Suite 630, Seattle, WA 98104; 206-220-4140)

The creation of this sprawling recreation area began with 24 million tons of concrete and steel. The Grand Coulee Dam was built to turn the power of the Columbia River into electricity and to turn vast deserts into productive farmlands. The dam is open for free self-guided tours year-round; nightly laser light shows on the face of the dam are a popular summer attraction. The recreation area stretches 130 miles along the length of Lake Roosevelt and embraces the lower reaches of many rivers and streams, including the Spokane and Kettle rivers. Most of the water comes from glacial ice, lakes, and snow high in the Canadian Rockies.

Sam's Tips

- Lake Roosevelt has 23 public-access boat ramps; from April through June, though, only a few of these ramps can be accessed, due to the annual drawdown of the lake. Get navigational charts at the Visitor Centers.
- A popular site is St. Paul's Mission, the oldest church on the upper Columbia River.

MOUNT BAKER–SNOQUALMIE NATIONAL FOREST

50 miles west of the Puget Sound metropolitan area.

21905 64th Avenue West
Mountlake Terrace, WA 98043
425-775-9702; 800-627-0062
http://www.wiredweb.com/~mbs

Northwest Interpretive Association. (909 First Avenue, Suite 630, Seattle, WA 98104; 206-220-4140)

On the western slopes of the Cascade Mountains, bordering Canada to the north and Mount Rainier National Park to the south, is the Mount Baker–Snoqualmie National Forest. This lush forest features glacier-honed valley bottoms and the rugged, steep, ice-capped mountains characteristic of the northern Cascades. Special places of interest include Mount Baker, a 10,778-foot dormant volcano that occasionally emits steam and sulfurous fumes; spectacular scenic views from Heather Meadows, Austin Pass, and Artist Point; and the Big Four Ice Caves on the south end of the Mountain Loop Highway.

Sam's Tips

- There are four scenic byways within Mount Baker–Snoqualmie:
  1. The Mount Baker Scenic Byway starts out in a rain forest and ends up with a wonderful view of Mount Baker from Artists Point.
  2. The Mountain Loop Scenic Byway is an easy, pleasant drive with views of the surrounding high peaks and wilderness area and access (via a trail) to the Big Four Ice Caves, which form in late July and stay into September.
  3. The Stevens Pass Scenic Byway follows the path of the old Great Northern Railroad through the Cascades and is a part of the longer Cascade Loop, which includes the North Cascades Scenic Highway.

Mount Baker National Recreation Area

The Mount Baker National Recreation Area is located inside the Mount Baker–Snoqualmie National Forest, on the south flank of Mount Baker, which is part of the volcanic "Ring of Fire" around the Pacific. The area ranges in elevation from nearly 11,000 feet at the glacier-covered summit to 2,000 feet on the lower reaches of the Sulphur Creek Lava Flow, where unique botanical communities are found. In between are four major subalpine meadow systems with some of the most spectacular hiking and horseback riding trails in the North Cascades. Winter recreation includes snowmobiling and back-country skiing. The restored Park Butte Lookout offers panoramic views of the entire area. For more information, contact: Mount Baker Ranger District, 2105 Highway 20, Sedro Woolley, WA 98284; 360-856-5700.

FOREST SERVICE SCENIC BYWAY

Mount Baker Scenic Highway

Near the border of British Columbia, Canada, this scenic highway covers over 24 miles of State Road 542 and offers scenery ranging from dense rain forests to the rugged timberline of the North Cascades. *Contact Mount Baker–Snoqualmie National Forest.*

4. The Mather Memorial Parkway is a classic Cascades drive between the sunny, dry east slopes and the vegetation of the west side. The parkway crosses through the eastern edge of Mount Rainier National Park before it enters the forest.

MOUNT RAINIER NATIONAL PARK

45 miles southeast of Seattle; 75 miles northeast of Portland.

Tahoma Woods, Star Route
Ashford, WA 98304
360-569-2211
http://www.nps.gov/mora

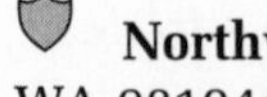

Northwest Interpretive Association. (909 First Avenue, Suite 630, Seattle, WA 98104; 206-220-4140)

The focal point of this fifth-oldest national park in the United States is 14,410-foot Mount Rainier, a relatively young volcano—only 1 million years old. The park is a combination of rugged glaciers, tremendous snowfields, dense forests, and wildflower meadows. Almost 97 percent of the park's 235,612 acres are designated wilderness.

Sam's Tips

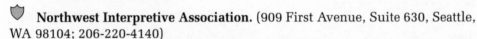

- Five major visitor areas of the park are reachable by road:
  1. The Longmire Area. Site of the Mineral Spring Resort that James Longmire opened in 1884. The road from the Nisqually Entrance to Longmire is one of the world's most beautiful forest roads.
  2. The Paradise Area. Named when one early visitor exclaimed, "This must be what Paradise is like!" The area has outstanding views of Mount Rainier and numerous trails into the subalpine meadows. Snowshoeing, cross-country skiing, and tubing are the most popular winter activities.
  3. The Ohanapecosh Area. Close to the southeast entrance to the park. The Silver Falls Trail travels past hot springs that once supported a health

resort, and then to the spot where the Ohanapecosh River plunges through a slot in ancient volcanic rocks.

4. The Sunrise Area. Situated at 6,400 feet, in the northeastern part of the park. This highest point in the park can be reached by a road. This is the best viewing point of Emmons Glacier, the largest on Mount Rainier.
5. The Carbon River Area. In the far northwest corner of the park. Named for the coal deposits found there, the area has the heaviest rainfall and most luxuriant forests of any of the five park areas. Trails from here lead into the back-country and connect to the Wonderland Trail.

- The National Park Service has outlined certain trails within the park as "Family Day Trip" paths. These are designed for families with young children who are looking for paths that are short, simple, and enjoyable. Free maps for all these trails are available at the visitor centers, wilderness information centers, and ranger stations.

NORTH CASCADES NATIONAL PARK

60 miles northeast of Seattle.

2105 Highway 20
Sedro Woolley, WA 98284
360-856-5700
http://www.nps.gov/noca

Northwest Interpretive Association. (909 First Avenue, Suite 630, Seattle, WA 98104; 206-220-4140)

The North Cascades contain some of America's most beautiful scenery—low valleys, glacier-covered peaks, jagged ridges, slopes, snowfields, and numerous cascading waterfalls. The North Cascades National Park Service Complex's 684,500 acres encompass some 318 glaciers, more than half of all glaciers in the lower 48 states. The Ross Lake National Recreational Area and its North Cascades Highway divide the national park into two sections, neither of which has any paved roads leading into it. At the south end of the national park is the Lake Chelan National Recreational Area. This natural lake is one of the nation's deepest (nearly 1,500 feet). Visitors can enjoy the beauty of Rainbow Falls or a boat tour into the secluded northern region of the 55-mile-long lake.

SAM'S TIPS

- The North Cascades Highway passes Gorge, Diablo, and Ross Lakes in the Ross Lake National Recreation Area. Only Gorge and Diablo can be reached by vehicle from the highway, but roadside turnouts and trails offer views of Ross Lake as well. Just outside the eastern side of the park, Washington Pass (elevation, 5,477 feet) is a good place for breathtaking close-up views of the Cascade Mountains.

Rivers of Ice in the North Cascades

The high country of the North Cascades is one of the snowiest places in the world: 400 to 700 inches of snow fall during a winter season in the high country. When many years' accumulation of snow has been compacted and recrystallized, it begins to flow and slide downhill under its own weight. Once movement begins, the snowfield becomes a glacier. A glacier can be distinguished from a snowfield by the presence of crevasses—cracks in the glacier surface caused by movement over an uneven surface.

The extent of a glacier is controlled by its snowfall budget. "Income" for a glacier comes in the form of winter snowfall. "Spending" is represented by the amount of melting that occurs during the summer. When winter snowfall is high and summer temperatures are low, the budget "surplus" results in an advance; the glacier expands downslope. If winter snowfall decreases and summer temperatures increase—a budget deficit—the downhill flow of ice is exceeded by melting, and the glacier recedes.

- Lower-elevation trails and lakes are usually free of snow from early April through mid-October. Some higher-elevation trails are not open until mid-July.
- The cold waters of Ross, Diablo, and Gorge lakes and Lake Chelan are filled from glacial runoff and melting snowfields. Swimming and other water activities are not recommended because of the danger of hypothermia.

OKANOGAN NATIONAL FOREST

60 miles northeast of Seattle; 45 miles west of Grand Coulee Dam.

1240 South Second Avenue
Okanogan, WA 98840-9723
509-826-3275
http://www.fs.fed.us/r6/oka

 **Northwest Interpretive Association.** (909 First Avenue, Suite 630, Seattle, WA 98104; 206-220-4140)

Just to the east of North Cascades National Park, along the Canadian border, Okanogan National Forest includes the beautiful Pasayten Wilderness and portions of the Lake Chelan/Sawtooth Wilderness. Two features of the forest are: The North Cascades Smokejumper Base, known as the "birthplace of smokejumping," and Washington Pass, the highest point along the scenic highway, which is over a mile above sea level.

North Cascades National Scenic Highway

About 140 miles north of Seattle, this scenic highway runs through the Okanogan and Mount Baker–Snoqualmie National Forests and the Ross Lake National Recreation Area. The scenic highway is managed by the Forest Service as a National Scenic Area. The highway, which is usually closed by avalanches from December through April, affords spectacular views of the highest and most rugged mountains in the state. Recreational activities along the highway include hiking, helicopter skiing, snowmobiling, cross-country skiing, bicycling, rock climbing, and pleasure driving. For more information, contact: Methow Valley Ranger District, District Visitors Center, Bldg. 49, Highway 20, PO Box 579, Winthrop, WA 98862; 509-996-4000.

OLYMPIC NATIONAL FOREST

35 miles northwest of Tacoma.

1835 Black Lake Boulevard, SW
Olympia, WA 98512-5623
360-956-2300
http://www.olympus.net/onf

Northwest Interpretive Association. (909 First Avenue, Suite 630, Seattle, WA 98104; 206-220-4140)

Surrounded on three sides by salt water, the Olympic National Forest (over 95 percent wilderness) is noted for its unique blend of rain forest, lowland forest, montane forest, subalpine forest, and alpine meadows. The diversity of the terrain within the park results in four rain forests characterized by giant trees—Sitka spruce and Western hemlock—and emerald foliage. The forest encompasses over 40 miles of the Olympic range; the highest peak, Mount Olympus, includes five distinct biological zones.

OLYMPIC NATIONAL PARK

113 miles northwest of Tacoma; 68 miles northwest of Seattle, via ferry.

600 East Park Avenue
Port Angeles, WA 98362
360-452-4501
http://www.nps.gov/olym

Northwest Interpretive Association. (3002 Mt. Angeles Rd., Port Angeles, WA 98362; 360-452-4501, ext. 239)

FISHERMEN'S DELIGHT

There are over 155,000 miles of fishable streams and more than four million acres of lakes and reservoirs on Bureau of Land Management (BLM) territory throughout the Western United States. Featured on the BLM website is a clickable map of the country which provides fishing enthusiasts with prime fishing spots, driving directions and an explanation of facilities (boat launch, camping, drinking water, etc.) and fish species.

In the Casper District of Wyoming, for example, there are 54 lakes, creeks, rivers, and reservoirs that are listed. To access this superb resource, go to http://www.blm.gov/nhp/prodserv/rec/fishing.

Olympic National Park, situated in the central part of the Olympic Peninsula, is known for beautiful beaches and alpine country dotted with sparkling lakes, lush meadows, glaciers, and North America's finest temperate rain forest. Annual precipitation averages 145 inches—more than 12 feet—each year. These conditions create a jungle-like atmosphere; fern, Sitka spruce, and bigleaf maple trees grow everywhere in the forest. The Olympic Mountains are not very high—Mount Olympus, the highest, is just under 8,000 feet—but they rise almost from the water's edge.

Sam's Tips

- Temperate rain forests are found only in New Zealand, southern Chile, sections of Canada and Alaska, and here on the northwest coast of the United States, in the valleys of the Quinault, Queets, and Hoh rivers.
- Regularly scheduled ferry service is in operation across Puget Sound, with connections to the Hood Canal floating bridge and Bremerton. Schedules are available from Washington State Ferries, 206-464-6400.
- The most visited glaciers in the park are the Blue and Anderson glaciers. From the Hoh Rain Forest, the upriver hiking trail leads 18 miles up to the snout of the Blue Glacier. Anderson Glacier can be reached by hiking the Dosewallips River Trail for 11 miles or, from the west side, by the East Fork of the Quinault River for 16 miles. To visit other glaciers requires more mountaineering knowledge and time.
- The park contains 60 miles of wilderness coast. Low tide exposes tidepools of red and purple sea urchins, sea anenomes, sea stars, and limpets. Sea otters are often spotted off the coast, and whales migrate into these waters.
- The Olympic Park Institute (111 Barnes Point Road, Port Angeles, WA 98363; 360-928-3720) offers hands-on seminars on topics such as Native Indian art, woodcarving, drum making, canoeing, and geology. The Institute also offers a series of backpacking trips for children ages 11 to 17 years and their families.

SAN JUAN ISLAND NATIONAL HISTORICAL PARK

75 miles northwest of Seattle.

PO Box 429
Friday Harbor, WA 98250
360-378-2240
http://www.nps.gov/sajh

Northwest Interpretive Association. (909 First Avenue, Suite 630, Seattle, WA 98104; 206-220-4140)

In the summer of 1859, San Juan Island was the scene of an international showdown between Great Britain and the United States, each insisting it had jurisdiction. The crisis was brought to a head when an American settler killed a pig belonging to the Hudson's Bay Company. Troops from both countries occupied the island. Today, you can tour the English camp (in the north) and the American camp (in the south). Both contain restored historic buildings with exhibitions on island life and the conflict between the two countries.

WENATCHEE NATIONAL FOREST

75 miles northeast of Seattle.

215 Melody Lane
Wenatchee, WA 98801
509-662-4335
http://www.naturenw.org/forest/wen/index.html

Northwest Interpretive Association. (909 First Avenue, Suite 630, Seattle, WA 98104; 206-220-4140)

The Wenatchee National Forest offers the pristine beauty of alpine meadows, sparkling mountain lakes, and jagged peaks that seem to touch the sky. Visitors can enjoy the manmade splendor of Lake Chelan (depth, 1,500 feet) and the five major reservoirs within the forest boundary.

WHITMAN MISSION NATIONAL HISTORIC SITE

100 miles southwest of Spokane.

Route 2
Box 247
Walla Walla, WA 99362
509-522-6360
http://www.nps.gov/whmi

Northwest Interpretive Association. (909 First Avenue, Suite 630, Seattle, WA 98104; 206-220-4140)

The Whitman Mission—a way station in the early days of the Oregon Trail—was established in 1836 by Marcus and Narcissa Whitman as a Protestant mission for American Indians. What began as a place to teach the Native Americans English and religion ultimately became a shelter for the sick and destitute. After cultural unrest resulted in the killings of Marcus Whitman, his family, and other members of the mission, the mission effort ended in 1847. Today, the site offers a Visitors Center with exhibits on life at a 19th-century mission.

Points of Interest

U.S. ARMY CORPS OF ENGINEERS

CHIEF JOSEPH DAM (LAKE RUFUS WOODS)

Chief Joseph Dam is the Corps' largest power-producing dam. When all 27 generators are operating, the dam can produce over 2.6 million kilowatts—enough power to light 26 million 100-watt lightbulbs. Recreational opportunities including fishing, swimming, wind surfing, and boating at Rufus Woods Lake. From Chelan, north 30 miles on US 7, then east 8 miles on WA 17.

ICE HARBOR LOCK AND DAM (LAKE SACAJAWEA)

Along the Snake River, the waterway of the gold rush days. Visitors can watch Pacific salmon and steelhead trout en route to their spawning grounds. From Burbank, east 8 miles on WA 124.

LAKE WASHINGTON SHIP CANAL

Approximately 85,000 vessels pass through the navigation locks each year. Underground windows offer a rare view of migrating salmon and trout passing through the fish ladder on their way to spawning grounds. Take I-90 west, I-5 north to NE 50th Street, then to 3015 NW 54th Street.

LOWER MONUMENTAL LOCK AND DAM (LAKE HERBERT G. WEST)

Interpretive displays and excellent facilities for viewing Pacific salmon and steelhead trout en route to their spawning grounds on the Snake River. From Kahlotus, south 6 miles.

WYNOOCHEE LAKE

Located in a narrow canyon of the Wynoochee River in the Olympic National Forest below the Olympic Mountains. From Montesano, north 38 miles on county and Forest Service roads.

BUREAU OF LAND MANAGEMENT

SPOKANE DISTRICT

The majority of the Bureau's public lands in Washington are east of the Cascade crest in the central Columbia Basin and in the highlands of northeastern

Washington along the Canadian border. In addition, public lands are found in northern Puget Sound, north of Seattle in San Juan County. These lands are managed for their ACEC (Area of Critical Environmental Concern) values. A full range of habitats is found on the public lands in Washington: the maritime Puget Sound lowlands, the central Columbia Basin sagebrush regime, many riparian zones, and the coniferous forest and subalpine areas of northeast Washington. The lands include one wilderness area, one wilderness study area, 15 ACECs, and numerous areas managed principally for their recreational, riparian, and wildlife values. For details, contact:

Bureau of Land Management
Spokane District Office
1103 North Fancher
Spokane, WA 99212
509-536-1200
http://www.or.blm.gov

Territorial Possessions

THE ESSENTIAL GUIDE BOOKS TO UNCLE SAM'S GREAT OUTDOORS

These two books and three maps are our suggested starting point for anyone planning a vacation in America's Great Outdoors.

National Parks Index

Many guide books profile the different parks within the National Park Service. This is the authoritative NPS guide. Included are descriptive listings (address, phone, etc.) of each park listed by state, a map of the entire system and regional addresses and phone numbers. The book also lists affiliated areas, wild and scenic rivers and national trails. 124 p. $5.00

Lesser-Known Areas

This little-known book is a jewel. With overcrowding such a problem in the larger parks, the NPS highlights more than 200 lesser-known areas such as: Weir Farm in CT; the Channel Islands off the California coast; Big Cypress National Preserve in FL; Cumberland Island National Seashore in GA; Fort Larned and Fort Scott in Kansas; the Big Hole and Little Bighorn Battlefields in MT; and Big Thicket National Preserve in TX. These lesser-known sites aren't often described in the popular outdoors guides found in most bookstores. An especially valuable book for your recreational library. Information is also included on locations, accommodations and attractions. 48 p. $1.75

Outdoors America: Recreational Opportunities on Public Lands

We love this foldout guide because it's the only publication we've seen that gives the "big picture" of all public lands in the U.S. You'll be introduced to all the managing agencies and their missions, from the Interior Department to the Forest Service to the Bureau of Reclamation, with addresses for headquarters and regional offices. The reverse side features a splendid U.S. Geological Survey color map showing all federal recreation lands of the United States. $1.25

National Park System Map and Guide

This map of the United States complements the National Parks Index cited above, showing the locations of parks, historic sites, and other properties operated by the National Park Service. On the reverse side an alphabetical list of each NPS property describes its activities, services and facilities. $1.25

Guide to Your National Forests

This foldout guide provides a listing of national forests in each region by state and includes addresses and telephone numbers of national and regional Forest Service Offices. On the back it features another lovely U.S. map showing locations of the national forests. $1.25

National Wildlife Refuges: A Visitor's Guide

This colorful foldout guide gives state-by-state information on more than 500 national wildlife refuges and includes addresses, a map, seasons, recreational and educational programs, visitor facilities, tips, and more. $1.25

AMERICAN SAMOA

THE NATIONAL PARK OF AMERICAN SAMOA

2,300 miles SSW of Honolulu, just east of the International Dateline.

Pago Pago
American Samoa 96799
684-633-7082
http://www.nps.gov

All the lands of the National Park of American Samoa are leased from private landowners and the American Samoa Government. The park is a wild, scenic rain forest and coral reef area spread out across three rugged volcanic islands of the Samoan archipelago. The three units of the park—on the islands of Tutuila, Ta'u, and Ofu—total nearly 10,500 acres, 2,500 of which are offshore waters extending to the edge of the coral reefs. The Ofu unit features one of the best beaches in the South Pacific.

SAM'S TIPS

- Hawaiian Air provides regular service to American Samoa from Honolulu, HI. Samoa Air and Polynesian Airlines provide interisland service in Samoa.
- English is the second language of a majority of the population. Most of the younger generation speak English, although Samoan is spoken in the home. Outside formal settings, the local Samoan language still prevails.
- Communications are modern; there is telephone service, both government and cable television, and local radio broadcasts. Fax services are also available.

UNCLE SAM, WEATHERMAN

At the *El Nino* page (http://www.elnino.noaa.gov), find out about the now-famous weather disrupter that influences the climate throughout the country.

The National Weather Service (http://www.nws.noaa.gov) has snow cover maps, radar and satellite images, and the explanation of weather map symbols. At the *Interactive Weather Information Network* (http://iwin.nws.noaa.gov/iwin/main.html), choose from graphics or text to find out about flood, hurricane, or thunderstorm warnings.

The National Climatic Data Center (http://www.ncdc.noaa.gov) offers interactive graphs covering rainfall and temperature for any part of the world, from 1900 to 1993. Try not to plan your vacation spot in the middle of the rainy season.

GUAM

WAR IN THE PACIFIC NATIONAL HISTORICAL PARK

Guam.

PO Box FA
Agana, GU 96910-9070
617-477-9362
http://www.nps.gov/wapa

The War in the Pacific National Historical Park commemorates the military personnel of the Pacific Theater campaigns of World War II, and conserves the natural and historic resources on the island of Guam. The park contains seven units located near the villages of Asan, Piti, and Agat on the west side of the island, facing the Philippine Sea. Features include landing beaches, war-related structures and sites, equipment remains, museum exhibits, a battleground, Japanese coastal defense guns, and audio-visual programs in English and Japanese.

COMMONWEALTH OF THE NORTHERN MARIANA ISLANDS

AMERICAN MEMORIAL PARK

120 miles north of Guam; 1,270 miles southeast of Tokyo.

PO Box 5198, CHRB
Saipan, MP 96950
670-234-7207
http://www.nps.gov/amer

Historical Society of the American Memorial Park. (same address as above)

American Memorial Park honors the American and Marianas people who gave their lives during the Marianas Campaign of World War II. The park is designed to be a "Living Memorial," which means that it still offers activities enjoyed over half a century ago by American GIs: water sports, tennis, softball, jogging, and bicycling. Bordering the Park is Micro Beach, one of Saipan's finest white-sand beaches.

Sam's Tips

- Typhoon season falls in late summer, from July through October.

PUERTO RICO

CARIBBEAN NATIONAL FOREST

25 miles east-southeast of San Juan.

PO Box 490
Palmer, PR 00721
787-888-1810
http://www.fs.fed.us

 **Eastern National.** (446 North Lane, Conshohoken, PA 19428; 800-355-5566)

Set aside in 1876 by the Spanish Crown, the Caribbean National Forest (known locally as El Yunque) represents one of the oldest reserves in the Western Hemisphere and the only tropical forest in the national forest system. Up to 240 inches of rain soak the forest annually. The heavy rainfall and warm tropical climate create a dense evergreen forest with 240 native tree species and masses of vines, epiphytes, giant ferns, and mosses, 26 of which are found nowhere else.

SAN JUAN NATIONAL HISTORIC SITE

San Juan.

Fort San Cristobal
501 Norzagaray Street
Old San Juan, PR 00901-2094
Headquarters: 787-729-6777
Visitor services: 787-729-6960
http://www.nps.gov/saju

 **Eastern National.** (446 North Lane, Conshohocken, PA 19428; 800-355-5566)

The 400-year-old castles and battlements that encircle Old San Juan are protected today as part of San Juan National Historic Site. Begun by Spanish troops in the 16th century, these massive masonry defenses are the oldest European-style fortifications within the territory of the United States.

SAM'S TIPS

- The historic streets are narrow and often congested by heavy traffic; parking is extremely limited. Visitors are encouraged to use public transport (buses, taxis, and trolleys) and explore sites on foot.
- The face of colonial Spain still can be seen in Old San Juan: the narrow cobblestone streets, inner patios and courtyards, overhanging balconies, and religious shrines. Of special interest are La Fortaleza (San Juan's oldest fortress, now the home of the governor), Casa Blanca (ancestral home of the Ponce de Leon family, now a museum), and the San Jose Church (the second oldest church in continuous use in the New World).

VIRGIN ISLANDS

BUCK ISLAND REEF NATIONAL MONUMENT

6.5 miles northeast of Christiansted, St. Croix.

PO Box 160
Christiansted, St. Croix, US VI 00820
http://www.nps.gov/buis

Buck Island was used in prehistoric times to gather the area's abundant marine life. The island's original forest was harvested in the mid-1700s to make room for cultivatable space. Goats were grazed there extensively by the mid-1800s. In the early 1960s, the area was established as a preserve for one of the finest marine gardens in the Caribbean. The monument covers 880 acres, 704 of them water. Visitors today can snorkel along a 1,200-foot-long underwater trail, surrounded by coral reefs.

Sam's Tips

- Reach Buck Island Reef from St. Croix through National Park Service-licensed concessionaires. Half-day and full-day trips are available on a variety of vessels, from glass-bottomed boats to catamarans and trimarans. Contact the monument office for a list of concessionaires.
- From the overland hiking trail on Buck Island, visitors can reach an overlook with a beautiful view of the coral reef. On a clear day, St. Thomas and St. John can be seen, 45 miles to the north. The observation tower that used to be located at this overlook was destroyed by Hurricane Hugo, as was over 80 percent of the beach forest.

CHRISTIANSTED NATIONAL HISTORIC SITE

St. Croix.

2100 Church Street, #100
Danish Custom's House, King's Wharf
Christiansted, St. Croix, US VI 00821-0160
809-773-1460
http://www.nps.gov/chri

 **Eastern National.** (446 North Lane, Conshohocken, PA 19428; 800-355-5566)

In 1733, the Danish West India and Guinea Company purchased St. Croix from France to cultivate sugar. When colonization began the next year, the island was divided into 150-acre plantations, which were offered at bargain prices to new settlers. A town was built on the island and named Christiansted in honor of the reigning Danish monarch, King Christian VI. At its peak, population approached

10,000, of which nearly 9,000 were slaves brought from West Africa to work in the fields. The boom years ended in the mid-1800s with the abolition of slavery, bad weather, and problems with sugar prices. In 1917, the United States bought the Danish West Indies to use the islands' strategic harbors. The park was established to preserve the wharf area and related buildings as examples of the town's economy and way of life in Danish colonial times.

SALT RIVER BAY NATIONAL HISTORIC PARK AND ECOLOGICAL PRESERVE

St. Croix.

> 2100 Church Street, #100
> Danish Custom's House, King's Wharf
> Christiansted, St. Croix, US VI 00821-0160
> 809-773-1460
> http://www.nps.gov/sari

The area of Salt River, St. Croix, has been the focus of every major archaeological investigation on the island since 1880. It is the only known site where members of the Columbus expedition set foot on what is now US territory. There is good reason to believe that Salt River was a major religious and cultural center as well as a longtime permanent settlement. Significant artifacts from the Salt River site can be found among the public and private museum collections in the Virgin Islands, the United States, Denmark, and other countries.

VIRGIN ISLANDS NATIONAL PARK

St. John Island.

> 6310 Estate Nazareth
> Charlotte Amalie, St. Thomas, US VI 00802-1102
> 809-775-6238
> http://www.nps.gov/viis

 **Eastern National.** (446 North Lane, Conshohocken, PA 19428; 800-355-5566).

More than half of St. John is national park land; the rest is made up of small towns, shops, homes, and undeveloped territorial or private lands. The park includes a large portion of the offshore waters. The least developed of the US Virgin Islands, St. John offers hiking, sunbathing, fishing, snorkeling, boating, and camping along the clear turquoise waters.

- The Cruz Bay Visitor Center is only a five-minute walk from the public ferry dock. Park rangers can help you plan your visit, which may include guided island hikes, historical tours, snorkeling trips, cultural craft demonstrations, and evening campground demonstrations. Advance registration and transportation fees are required for some activities. Schedules are available, and program reservations for the Reef Bay Hike may be made at Cinnamon Bay Campground (809-776-6339).

- Visitors can hike to the higher elevations, such as Bordeaux Mountain (elevation, 1,277 feet), where the scent of bay rum trees recalls an earlier time when the leaves were harvested to produce St. John's famous Bay Rum Oil. (There is a bay rum still at Cinnamon Bay.)

St. John's History

Archaeological discoveries show that, as early as 710 B.C., South American Indians, migrating northward in canoes, lived on St. John. They hunted and gathered food primarily from the sea. There is evidence that by about 300 A.D., a small Taino Indian population had built villages in sheltered bays, made pottery, and practiced agriculture as they did elsewhere in the Caribbean.

Although Columbus came to the islands, no lasting European settlements existed until the 1720s. The Danes, attracted by the prospects for cultivating sugar cane, took formal possession of the islands in 1694 and established the first permanent European settlement on St. John at Estate Carolina in Coral Bay in 1718. St. John soon supported 109 sugar cane and cotton plantations.

As the plantation economy grew, so did the demand for slaves. Many slaves captured in West Africa were tribal nobles and former slave-owners themselves. In 1733, they revolted, and an islandwide massacre of families occurred. Six months passed before the rebellion was put down.

The 1848 emancipation of slaves was one of several factors leading to the decline of St. John's plantations. By the early 20th century, the main industries were bay rum production and subsistence and cattle farming.

In 1917, the United States purchased the islands. By the 1930s, a tourism industry had begun. In 1956, Rockefeller family interests purchased land here and transferred it to the federal government to establish a national park.

Trails and Parkways

COLLECTING ROCKS, FOSSILS, AND ARTIFACTS

The Bureau of Land Management (BLM) places restrictions on what can be removed from our public lands. In areas specially designated for protection of their scientific and natural values, collecting mineral and fossil resources is prohibited. Arrow heads, pottery, mats, rock art, vertebrate fossils, and old bottles also should be left where found. On public lands, a permit to collect artifacts, ancient or historical, is required and usually is granted only to professionals.

For information on obtaining a permit, contact the Bureau of Land Management's State Offices. For information on where and how to collect rocks, contact the U.S. Geological Survey, Branch of Distribution, PO Box 25286, Denver, CO 80225.

SCENIC TRAILS

APPALACHIAN NATIONAL SCENIC TRAIL

ME, NH, VT, MA, CT, NY, NJ, PA, MD, WV, VA, TN, NC, GA.

Appalachian Trail Project Office
c/o Harper's Ferry Center
Harpers Ferry, WV 25425-0807
304-535-6278
http://www.nps.gov/aptr

 **The Appalachian Trail Conference.** (same address as above; 304-535-6331)

A "super trail" was much talked about in turn-of-the-century hiking circles of New England. The Appalachian Trail evolved from the proposals, in 1921, of Massachusetts regional planner Benton MacKaye to preserve the Appalachian crests as an accessible, multipurpose wilderness belt. One of the two initial components of the national trails system, the trail is also a unit of the National Park Service. This footpath follows 2,144 miles of Appalachian Mountain ridgelines from Katahdin, ME, to Springer Mountain, GA. While most of the 2 million to 3 million yearly visitors use the trail for short hikes, it is also used by hikers who plan to become "2,000 milers." Two-thirds of the people in the United States live within 550 miles of the trail.

Sam's Tips

- The Appalachian Trail is marked with 2-inch by 6-inch vertical white-paint blazes. A double blaze indicates a turn, a junction, or any area that requires hikers to be alert. Blue blazes mark side trails, which usually lead to shelters, water supplies, or special viewpoints.
- For more information contact the Maine Appalachian Trail Club (PO Box 283, Augusta, ME 04332-0283); the Appalachian Mountain Club (Pinkham Notch, Gorham, NH 03581); the Dartmouth Outing Club (PO Box 9, Hanover, NH 03755); the Potomac Appalachian Trail Club (118 Park Street, SE, Vienna, VA 22180; 703-242-0315), or Shenandoah National Park.

CONTINENTAL DIVIDE NATIONAL SCENIC TRAIL

MT, ID, WY, CO, NM.

Forest Service, Region 2
PO Box 25127
Denver, CO 80225

Continental Divide Trail Alliance. (PO Box 628, Pine, CO 80470; 303-838-3760)

Running from the Canadian border in Montana to the Mexican border in New Mexico, the trail follows the Continental Divide along the backbone of the Rocky Mountains. The trail goes through Glacier National Park, Yellowstone National Park, and ten national forests with wildernesses such as the Bob Marshall and Anaconda Pintler; several Bureau of Land Management resource areas; state lands; and short segments of private lands. Over 90 percent of the trail is within 5 miles of the Continental Divide.

FLORIDA NATIONAL SCENIC TRAIL

Florida.

US Forest Service
325 John Knox Road, Suite F-100
Tallahassee, FL 32303
850-942-9300

Florida Trail Association. (PO Box 13708, Gainesville, FL 32604; 800-343-1882)

The Florida trail is primarily a footpath that offers hikers a chance to discover the natural beauty of Florida's wild and rural areas. Added to the national trails system in 1983, the Florida Trail will, when complete, extend 1,300 miles, from Gulf Islands National Seashore, in Florida's western panhandle, to Big Cypress National Preserve, in south Florida. Sections of the trail stretch across some of the state's most picturesque areas; Apalachicola, Ocala, and Osceola national forests; St. Marks National Wildlife Refuge; and Big Cypress National Preserve.

ICE AGE NATIONAL SCENIC TRAIL

Wisconsin.

National Park Service
700 Rayovac Drive, Suite 100
Madison, WI 53711
608-264-5610
http://www.nps.gov/iatr

Ice Age Park and Trail Foundation. (PO Box 423, Pewaukee, WI 53072-0423; 800-227-0046)

At the end of the Ice Age, about 10,000 years ago, glaciers retreated from North America and left behind a chain of moraine hills defining their southern edge. In Wisconsin, the band of hills zigzags across the state for 1,000 miles, from Lake Michigan to the Saint Croix River. A trail along these hills was conceived by Ray

Zillmer in the 1950s and publicized by Rep. Henry Reuss in his book, *On the Trail of the Ice Age*. The trail diverges from the hills to link six of the nine units of the Ice Age National Scientific Reserve and to include significant features of Wisconsin's glacial landscape, with glimpses of the Driftless Area. Today, with help from the State of Wisconsin and the Ice Age Park and Trail Foundation, almost half of the trail (approximately 475 miles) is open to the public.

NATCHEZ TRACE NATIONAL SCENIC TRAIL

MS, TN.

c/o Natchez Trace Parkway
2680 Natchez Trace Parkway
Tupelo, MS 38801
601-680-4025
http://www.nps.gov/natt

 **Natchez Trace Trail Conference.** (PO Box 6579, Jackson, MS 39282)

The Natchez Trace National Scenic Trail extends for 650 miles from Natchez, Mississippi, to Nashville, Tennessee. Portions lie within the Natchez Trace Parkway, which commemorates the historic Natchez Trace, an ancient path that began as a series of animal tracks and Native American trails. It was later used by early explorers and military men, including General Andrew Jackson after his victory at the Battle of New Orleans. Four segments, near Nashville, Tupelo, and Jackson, totaling 110 miles, have been developed as hiking and horseback trails.

NORTH COUNTRY NATIONAL SCENIC TRAIL

ND, MN, WI, MI, OH, PA, NY.

National Park Service
700 Rayovac Drive, Suite 100
Madison, WI 53711
608-264-5610
http://www.nps.gov/noco

North Country Trail Association. (49 Monroe Center NW, Suite 200B, Grand Rapids, MI 49503; 616-454-5506)

Unlike the Appalachian, Pacific Crest, and Continental Divide national scenic trails, which follow mountain ranges, the North Country trail winds through a variety of environments in the northeastern and north-central United States. From the Adirondack Mountains in New York, it meanders westward through the hardwood forests of Pennsylvania, through the countryside of Ohio and southern Michigan, along the shores of the Great Lakes, and through the glacier-carved forests, lakes, and streams of northern Wisconsin and Minnesota. Its western terminus lies in the vast plains of North Dakota. Almost half of the trail is open for public use. Some of the longer segments cross 9 national forests and 2 national park areas along the route.

Sam's Tips

- The National Park Service Official Map of the trail lists the 27 agencies that offer detailed information about particular sections of the trail.

PACIFIC CREST NATIONAL SCENIC TRAIL

CA, OR, WA.

Forest Service, Region 6
PO Box 3623
Portland, OR 97208

Pacific Crest Trails Association. (5325 Elkhorn Boulevard, Suite 256, Sacramento, CA 95842; 800-817-2243)

Lying along the spectacular shoulders of the Cascade and Sierra Nevada mountain ranges from Canada to Mexico, the Pacific Crest is the West Coast counterpart of the Appalachian Trail. It passes through 25 national forests and 7 national parks. One of the two initial components of the national trails system, the Pacific Crest was completed in Oregon and Washington in 1987.

WALKING YOUR DOGS

If you like to bring your dog on a hike, have it under verbal or physical restraint at all times. Be considerate of other hikers. Carry a leash and use it as necessary, especially when around other people. Don't forget to clean up after your dog.

Hiking is hard work. Dogs are a lot like people. If your dog has spent the winter lying on the couch, you can't expect a "super dog" out on the trail. Hiking above the treeline or on rocky, exposed trails can be especially hard on a dog's paws. Watch your dog for signs of stress and fatigue. Make sure to allow plenty of rest and water as needed.

POTOMAC HERITAGE NATIONAL SCENIC TRAIL

DC, MD, PA, VA.

Potomac Field Office
Rivers, Trails Conservation Assistance Program
c/o Chesapeake and Ohio Canal NHP
PO Box 4
Sharpsburg, MD 21782
http://www.nps.gov/pohe

The Potomac Heritage Trail recognizes the unique mix of history and recreation along the Potomac River. Points of interest include: the 184-mile towpath of the Chesapeake and Ohio Canal in the District of Columbia and Maryland; the 18-mile Mount Vernon Trail in Virginia; and the 75-mile Laurel Highlands Trail in Pennsylvania.

HISTORIC TRAILS

CALIFORNIA NATIONAL HISTORIC TRAIL

From points along the Missouri River to points in California; passing through KS, NE, CO, WY, ID, UT, NV, and OR.

National Park Service
Long Distance Trails Office
324 South State Street, #250
Salt Lake City, UT 84145-0155
801-539-4095
http://www.nps.gov/cali

Oregon–California Trails Association. (524 South Osage Street, Independence, MO 64050-0519; 816-252-2276)

Established in 1992, the California Trail is a system of overland routes totaling approximately 5,665 miles. The trail starts at five points along the Missouri River and ends at many locations in California and Oregon. Over these trails passed one of America's great mass migrations; over 200,000 gold-seekers and farmers who believed in the promise of gold and a new life in California in the late 1840s and 1850s. Traces of their struggles and triumphs are still evident at many trail sites.

Sam's Tips

- Information on trail routes (as well as cutoffs, alternate routes, and western routes), the auto tour route, cross-country segments, historic sites, and history is available from the National Park Service Long Distance Trails Office. Information on access and travel conditions along the cross-country segments is best obtained from local offices of the Bureau of Land Management or the National Forest Service. About 2,171 miles of this system and its sites cross public lands and are open to visitors; others are located on private lands.

IDITAROD NATIONAL HISTORIC TRAIL

A 2,300-mile system stretching from Seward to Nome, AK.

Bureau of Land Management
6881 Abbott Loop Road
Anchorage, AK 99507
907-267-1246
http://www.ak.blm.gov/ado/iditnht.html

Iditarod Trail Committee. (PO Box 870800, Wasilla, AK 99687; 907-376-5155)

The Iditarod Trail takes its name from the Iditarod River. Most of the trail is usable only during the 6-month winter, when rivers and tundra are frozen. The Iditarod hosts three annual races: the 210-mile Iditasport race for skiers, mountain bikers, and snowshoers; the Alaska Gold Rush Classic Snowmachine Race; and the renowned Iditarod Trail Sled Dog Race, a 1,150-mile race run on the trail from Anchorage to Nome. The race was first run in 1973 and is held annually in March.

JUAN BAUTISTA DE ANZA NATIONAL HISTORIC TRAIL

A corridor from Tumacacori National Historical Park, AZ, to John Muir National Historic Site, CA.

National Park Service, Western Region
600 Harrison Street, Suite 600
San Francisco, CA 94107-1372
415-556-0560
http://www.nps.gov/pub_aff/naltrail.htm

Heritage Trails Fund, Amigos de Anza. (1350 Castle Rock Road, Walnut Creek, CA 94598; 510-937-7661)

In 1775, a party of Spanish colonists led by Colonel Juan Bautista de Anza left Mexico to establish an overland route to California and to secure the area from the Russians and British by building a presidio and mission. This party of 30 families, a dozen soldiers, and 1,000 cattle, horses, and mules spent 3 months traversing the deserts of the Southwest before reaching the missions of the California coast. Another 3 months were spent traveling up the Pacific coast to where the city of San Francisco now stands.

LEWIS AND CLARK NATIONAL HISTORIC TRAIL

IL, MO, KS, NE, IA, SD, ND, MT, ID, WA, OR.

National Park Service
700 Rayovac Drive, Suite 100
Madison, WI 53711
608-264-5610
http://www.nps.gov/lecl

Lewis and Clark Trail Heritage Foundation, Inc. (PO Box 3434, Great Falls, MT 59403, http://www.lewisandclark.org)

On May 14, 1804, 45 men in a 55-foot keelboat and two pirogues (similar to canoes) set sail up the Missouri River from its confluence with the Mississippi. The Lewis and Clark Expedition (The "Corps of Discovery") was destined to fulfill a long-held dream of Thomas Jefferson: to explore the western half of the continent and to discover the fabled northwest passage to the Pacific Ocean. Their 3,700-mile route extends from the Mississippi River in Illinois to the Pacific Ocean at the mouth of the Columbia River in Oregon. Water routes, hiking trails, and marked highways follow the explorers' outbound and return routes, closely following the explorers' actual route and method of travel. By boat or canoe, by car, or on foot, you can retrace portions of their historic route.

A Notable Partnership

Lewis and Clark's partnership ranks high in the realm of notable friendships. In background and temperament, Lewis and Clark were opposites. The introverted and moody Lewis, refined and well educated, had a philosophical, romantic, and speculative mind; the extroverted and even-tempered Clark was a pragmatic man of action. Each supplied qualities to balance the partnership. This was a rare example of each man sharing the leadership of a dangerous mission without losing the other's respect. Despite the journey's length and the stress, hardships, and other conditions that could easily have bred jealousy, mistrust, or contempt, there is no trace in their letters and diaries of any serious argument between them.

Sam's Tips

- Request the trail's *Official Map and Guide* which describes historical as well as notable interpretive and recreational sites along the way. The Forest Service Northern Region Office also has a map and guide available. It traces the daily challenges confronting the expedition and will help you follow their route on highways and byways.
- The expedition's route over the Missouri and Columbia rivers and their tributaries is impeded now by a series of dams and lakes. Commercial boat trips are available on some segments, such as the Upper Missouri National Wild and Scenic River. The NPS website lists many outfitters to contact.

FADE INTO THE WOODWORK FOR ULTIMATE WILDLIFE WATCHING

The ultimate wildlife watching experience is viewing animals without interrupting their normal activities. The Bureau of Land Management offers these tips:

Wear natural colors and use unscented lotions. Remove glasses that glint.

Walk softly.

Hide your figure behind boulders or vegetation, and try not to throw a shadow.

Resist the temptation to "save" baby animals—their mom is usually watching from a safe distance.

Let animals eat their natural foods.

Let patience reward you: Resist the urge to throw rocks to see a flock fly.

Use binoculars or zoom lenses to get a close-up view of animals.

Give nests a wide berth.

Move slowly, smoothly, and steadily, and approach animals in a roundabout way, never directly.

Avert your gaze; animals may interpret a direct stare as a threat.

MORMON PIONEER NATIONAL HISTORIC TRAIL

This 1,300-mile-long trail passes from Nauvoo, IL, through IA, NE, and WY, to Salt Lake City, UT.

National Park Service
Long Distance Trails Office
324 South State Street, Suite #250
PO Box 45155
Salt Lake City, UT 84145-0155
801-539-4093
http://www.nps.gov/mopi

From 1846 to 1869, more than 70,000 Mormons trekked from Illinois to Utah, establishing thriving communities in what was considered by many to be a worthless desert. The goal of the migration to the Valley of the Great Salt Lake was to find an isolated area where they could permanently settle and practice their religion in peace. The Mormon pioneers traveled in semimilitary fashion, grouped into companies of 100, 50, and 10. Knowing that others would follow, they improved the trail and built support facilities. Businesses were established to help finance the movement. In the end, strong group unity and organization made the Mormon movement more orderly and efficient than other emigrant movements traveling to Oregon and California.

Established in 1978, the Mormon Pioneer National Historic Trail follows the route over which Brigham Young led the Mormons, from Nauvoo, IL, to the site of modern Salt Lake City, UT, in 1846–1847. The 1,297-mile trail can be divided into two parts: the nearly 265-mile-long section across Iowa, and the 1,032-mile segment across the Great Plains and mountains of Nebraska and Wyoming into Utah. The Iowa portion of the trail was mainly used by the Mormons fleeing Illinois in 1846, and by some other Mormons jumping off from Keokuk, IA, in 1853. The second portion of the trail approximated what is sometimes called the Great Platte River Road, or the north branch of the Oregon Trail, which had always been regarded as the most advantageous approach to South Pass, the easiest crossing of the Rocky Mountains.

Sam's Tips

- The *Official Map and Guide* (also available in larger type) describes the most notable interpretive and recreational stops along the trail. An auto tour route, approximating the trail, has been marked. The trailhead, in Nauvoo's historic district, offers 1,100 acres of restored shops and homes—among them, the Brigham Young House.

NEZ PERCE NATIONAL HISTORIC TRAIL

A 1,170-mile corridor from Wallowa Lake, OR, across portions of ID, WY, and MT. It ends at Bear Paw Battlefield, south of Chinook, MT.

US Forest Service, Northern Region
PO Box 7669
Missoula, MT 59807
406-329-3511

Nez Perce National Historic Trail Foundation. (PO Box 20197, Missoula, MT 59801)

This trail route honors the heroic efforts by the Nez Perce Indians to escape capture by the US Army. In June 1877, the Nez Perce were forced to leave their ancestral homelands to move to a reservation east of Lewiston, ID. During this journey, hostilities broke out between White settlers and some groups of the Nez Perce, and the US Army was called in. The resisting bands headed east and crossed the Rocky Mountains, hoping to find refuge in Canada. Led by Chief Joseph and others, they eluded capture for months. Just 40 miles short of the Canadian border, in the Bear Paw Mountains of Montana, most of the party were overtaken after a 6-day siege.

OREGON NATIONAL HISTORIC TRAIL

MO, KS, NE, WY, ID, OR, WA.

National Park Service, Pacific Northwest Region
600 Harrison Street, Suite 600
San Francisco, CA 94101
415-427-1300
http://www.nps.gov/oreg

Oregon–California Trail Association. (524 South Osage Street, PO Box 1019, Independence, MO 64501-0519)

In 1840, the nation's western boundary lay roughly along the Continental Divide, and only three states existed west of the Mississippi River. Beginning in the 19th century as a crude network of rutted traces across the land between the Missouri and Willamette rivers, the 2,170-mile Oregon Trail brought hundreds of thousands of pioneers from the east to the open spaces. The name still evokes the image of an eager group of frontiersmen in their covered wagons hastening to settle the far west.

Sam's Tips

- The Trail's *Official Map and Guide* includes historical background and describes the 125 historic, interpretive, and recreational sites on the trail. Make note of the stops where you can see emigrants' messages carved in rock, notably Register Cliff, inscribed with thousands of emigrants' names, hundreds of which are still legible, and Independence Rock, named by fur trappers on July 4, 1824. An auto route can be followed from Independence, MO, to Oregon City, OR.

OVERMOUNTAIN VICTORY NATIONAL HISTORIC TRAIL

VA, TN, NC, SC.

National Park Service, Southeast Region
75 Spring Street, SW
Atlanta, GA 30303
404-562-3123
http://www.nps.gov

Overmountain History Trail Association. (c/o Sycamore Shoals State Historic Area, Elizabethton, TN 37643)

The 300-mile Overmountain Victory National Historic Trail follows the path of a band of Revolutionary War patriots who gathered in western Virginia and came across the mountains of Tennessee and North Carolina to Kings Mountain, South Carolina, where they decisively defeated an American Loyalist army at the Battle of Kings Mountain, SC, during the fall of 1780. The trail begins on Colonial Road in Abingdon, Virginia.

 **Sam's Tips**

- The *Official Map and Guide,* available from the National Park Service, lists important interpretive and recreational opportunities along the trail.
- The actual battle site is commemorated and interpreted at King's Mountain National Military Park (PO Box 40, King's Mountain, SC 28086; 803-936-7921). The battle is reenacted annually on September 23rd.

PONY EXPRESS NATIONAL HISTORIC TRAIL

An 1,800-mile route from St. Joseph, MO, to Sacramento, CA; passing through KS, NE, CO, WY, UT, and NV.

National Park Service
Long Distance Trails Office
324 South State Street, Suite 250
PO Box 45155
Salt Lake City, UT 84145-0155
801-539-4094
http://www.nps.gov/pub_aff/naltrail.htm

 **National Pony Express Association.** (PO Box 236, Pollock Pines, CA 95726)

For 18 months, during 1860–1861, young men on fast horses carried the nation's mail over an 1,800-mile route between St. Joseph, MO, and Sacramento, CA, on what is now the Pony Express National Historic Trail. They accomplished each trip in the astonishing and then-unprecedented time of just under 10 days. The horse-and-rider relay system became the nation's most direct and practical means of east–west communications before the telegraph. Though in operation only from April 1860 to October 1861, the Pony Express proved the feasibility of a regular overland transportation route to the Pacific coast.

 **Sam's Tips**

- The best-preserved segments of the route can be seen in California and Utah. Of the original 150 Pony Express relay stations, only 50 stations (or station ruins) exist. Many of the sites and segments are on public land and are open to visitors; others are located on private lands, and visitors should obtain the landowners' permission before entry. For information on access, the auto tour route, historic sites, cross-country segments, and travel conditions along the trail, contact local offices of the Bureau of Land Management, the National Forest Service, or the National Park Service Long Distance Trails Office (address above).

SANTA FE NATIONAL HISTORIC TRAIL

The route extends from Old Franklin, MO, through KS, OK, and CO, ending at Santa Fe, NM.

National Park Service
Long Distance Trails Office
PO Box 728
Santa Fe, NM 87504-0728
505-988-6888
http://www.nps.gov/safe

Santa Fe Trail Association. (Santa Fe Trail Center, RR3, Larned, KS 67550; 316-285-2054)

During its colorful history, this route provided a two-way avenue for international commerce between Mexico and the United States, played a crucial role in American expansion westward, and brought both cultural exchange and conflict to three major cultures. Today, the freight wagons no longer roll across the prairies, but evidence of the great days of the trail still exists in the form of buildings and other historic sites. In addition to the landmarks that guided the trail's first travelers, visitors can see the remains of the original ruts worn into the earth by countless wagon wheels.

TRAIL OF TEARS NATIONAL HISTORIC TRAIL

A land and water route traversing the states of TN, KY, IL, MO, OK, AL, and AR.

National Park Service
Long Distance Trails Office
PO Box 728
Santa Fe, NM 87504-0728
505-988-6888
http://www.nps.gov/trte

Trail of Tears Association. (1100 North University, Suite 133, Little Rock, AR 72207; 501-666-9032)

In the late 1830s, 16,000 Cherokee Indians from the southeastern states were forced by the US Army to move to lands in the Oklahoma Territory. Thousands died along the way. Today, the designated trail follows two of the principal routes: a water trail (1,226 miles) along the Tennessee, Ohio, Mississippi, and Arkansas rivers, and an overland route (993 miles) from Chattanooga, TN, to Tahlequah, OK. The journey lasted from June 1838 to March 1839.

Sam's Tips

- Two National Park Service units are affiliated with the trail: Pea Ridge National Military Park (PO Box 700, Pea Ridge, AR 72751-0700; 501-451-8122) and Fort Smith National Historic Site (PO Box 1406, Fort Smith, AR 72902; 501-783-3961).

PARKWAYS

BLUE RIDGE PARKWAY

The parkway passes through western Virginia and North Carolina, with access from several major highways, including I-64, I-81, I-77, I-40, and I-26. Asheville, NC, and Roanoke, VA, are the largest metropolitan areas along the parkway.

Blue Ridge Parkway
400 BB&T Building
One Pack Square
Asheville, NC 28801
704-298-0398
http://www.nps.gov/blri

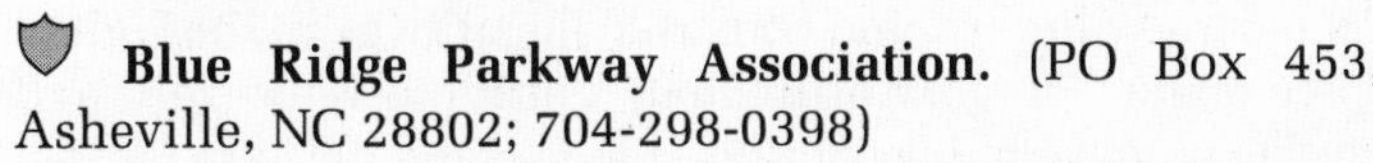

Blue Ridge Parkway Association. (PO Box 453, Asheville, NC 28802; 704-298-0398)

Public Lands along the Blue Ridge Parkway

Shenandoah National Park
Booker T. Washington National Monument
Carl Sandburg Home National Historic Site
Great Smoky Mountains National Park
Appalachian National Scenic Trail
George Washington and Jefferson National Forests
Nantahala National Forest
Pisgah National Forest

Approximately 17 million people per year travel the Blue Ridge Parkway, making it the most visited site in the national park system. The parkway, 52 years in the making, extends 469 miles through the southern Appalachians of Virginia and North Carolina, linking Shenandoah and Great Smoky Mountains national parks along the crest of the Blue Ridge Mountains.

Sam's Tips

- There are 11 Visitor Centers along the parkway, 5 in Virginia and 6 in North Carolina. Visit the "virtual" Visitor Center at the National Park Service Website (www.nps.gov/blri), where you will find maps with mileposts along the entire route. For example, at milepost 86, an area called the Peaks of Otter, you will find a list of places to stay and things to do, with campground, fishing, and other recreational information.
- Locations on the Blue Ridge are described in terms of their milepost location. The motor road is marked every mile by concrete mileposts beginning at Milepost 0, near Shenandoah National Park, and ending at Milepost 469, at Great Smoky Mountains National Park.

- Plan to travel slowly. The parkway speed limit is 45 mph (35 mph in developed areas). Overlooks and trails (ranging from "leg stretchers" to extended hikes) offer breaks during the drive. These are marked with the hiker symbol. To travel the parkway safely from Shenandoah to the Great Smokies will take 2 full days of driving.
- The parkway's nine campgrounds (4 in Virginia and 5 in North Carolina) are open from May through October, except for Otter Creek, VA, and Linville Falls, NC, which are open year-round.
- The Appalachian Trail roughly parallels the parkway from Milepost 0 at Rockfish Gap to Milepost 103.

GEORGE WASHINGTON MEMORIAL PARKWAY

Fairfax and Arlington counties and the city of Alexandria, VA; Montgomery County, MD; Washington, DC.

Turkey Run Park
McLean, VA 22101
703-285-2600
http://www.nps.gov/gwmp

The George Washington Memorial Parkway preserves the natural scenery and resources along the Potomac River. It connects the historic sites, from Mount Vernon, VA, where George Washington lived, past the nation's capital to Great Falls, VA. Within the boundaries of the parkway are the Mount Vernon Memorial Highway, which was the first federally funded and constructed parkway in the United States; memorials to presidents George Washington, Theodore Roosevelt, and Lyndon Baines Johnson; the historic homes of Robert E. Lee and of Clara Barton; numerous monuments to historic events, such as the US Marine Corps War Memorial; two military forts; an old amusement park, and the first inland lighthouse in the United States.

JOHN D. ROCKEFELLER, JR. MEMORIAL PARKWAY

Northwestern Wyoming.

c/o Grand Teton National Park
PO Drawer 170
Moose, WY 83012
307-739-3300
http://www.nps.gov/jodr

Linking West Thumb in Yellowstone with the South Entrance of Grand Teton National Park, this scenic 82-mile corridor commemorates Rockefeller's central role in the establishment of many parks, including Acadia and Grand Teton.

NATCHEZ TRACE PARKWAY

From Natchez, MI, to Nashville, TN; passing through Alabama.

2680 Natchez Trace Parkway
Tupelo, MS 38801
601-680-4025
http://www.nps.gov/natr

 **Eastern National.** (446 North Lane, Conshohocken, PA 19428; 800-355-5566)

This 415-mile historic route generally follows the old Indian trace, or trail, between Natchez, MS, and Nashville, TN. As early as 1733, the French were familiar enough with the land to include it on a map. By 1820, it was an important wilderness road with more than 20 stands to provide simple food and shelter for its bustling travelers. The trail was finally supplanted by steamboats and returned to its former calm. In the late 1930s, the modern parkway's construction was begun and is now over 90 percent complete.

 **SAM'S TIPS**

- The parkway's *Official Map and Guide* lists geographically and thematically the 50-plus sites along its length and correlates them to milepost markers to the nearest tenth of a mile. Mileposts are located along the parkway's east side, beginning at Natchez.

Appendixes

THE NATIONAL PARK SERVICE

Here is a breakdown of 376 different elements managed by the National Park Service:

1	International Historic Site
11	National Battlefields
3	National Battlefield Parks
1	National Battlefield Site
74	National Historic Sites
38	National Historic Parks
4	National Lakeshores
28	National Memorials
9	National Military Parks
73	National Monuments
54	National Parks
4	National Parkways
16	National Preserves
19	National Recreation Areas
2	National Reserves
6	National Rivers
3	National Scenic Trails
10	National Seashores
9	National Wild and Scenic Rivers
11	Parks (other)
376	Total

Units in the National Park Service

International Historic Site (1)
Saint Croix Island, ME

National Battlefields (11)
Antietam, MD
Big Hole, MT
Cowpens, SC
Fort Donelson, TN–KY
Fort Necessity, PA
Monacacy, MD
Moores Creek, NC
Petersburg, VA
Stones River, TN
Tupelo, MS
Wilson's Creek, MO

National Battlefield Parks (3)
Kennesaw Mountain, GA
Manassas, VA
Richmond, VA

National Battlefield Site (1)
Brices Cross Roads, MS

National Military Parks (9)
Chickamauga and Chattanooga, GA–TN
Fredericksburg and Spotsylvania County Battlefield Memorials, VA
Gettysburg, PA
Guilford Courthouse, NC
Horseshoe Bend, AL
Kings Mountain, SC
Pea Ridge, AR
Shiloh, TN
Vicksburg, MS

National Historic Sites (74)
Abraham Lincoln Birthplace, KY
Adams, MA
Allegheny Portage Railroad, PA
Andersonville, GA
Andrew Johnson, TN
Bent's Old Fort, CO
Boston African American, MA
Brown vs. Board of Education, KS
Carl Sandburg Home, NC
Charles Pinckney, SC
Christianstad, VI
Clara Barton, MD
Edgar Allan Poe, PA
Edison, NJ
Eisenhower, PA
Eleanor Roosevelt, NY
Eugene O'Neill, CA
Ford's Theatre, DC
Fort Bowie, AZ
Fort Davis, TX
Fort Laramie, WY
Fort Larned, KS
Fort Point, CA
Fort Raleigh, NC
Fort Scott, KS
Fort Smith, AR–OK
Fort Union Trading Post, MT–ND
Fort Vancouver, WA
Frederick Douglass, DC
Frederick Law Olmsted, MA
Friendship Hill, PA
Golden Spike, UT
Grant–Kohrs Ranch, MT
Hampton, MD
Harry S Truman, MO
Herbert Hoover, IO
Home of Franklin D. Roosevelt, NY
Hopewell Furnace, PA
Hubbell Trading Post, AZ
James A. Garfield, OH
Jimmy Carter, GA
John Fitzgerald Kennedy, MA
John Muir, CA
Knife River Indian Villages, ND
Lincoln Home, IL
Longfellow, MA
Maggie L. Walker, VA
Manzanar, CA
Martin Luther King, Jr., GA
Martin Van Buren, NY

Mary McLeod Bethune Council House, DC
Nicodemus, KS
Ninety Six, SC
Palo Alto Battlefield, TX
Pennsylvania Avenue, DC
Puukohola Heiau, HI
Sagamore Hill, NY
Saint-Gaudens, NH
Saint Paul's Church, NY
Salem Maritime, MA
San Juan, PR
Saugus Iron Works, MA
Springfield Armory, MA
Steamtown, PA
Theodore Roosevelt Birthplace, NY
Theodore Roosevelt Inaugural, NY
Thomas Stone, MD
Tuskegee Institute, AL
Ulysses S. Grant, MO
Vanderbilt Mansion, NY
Washita Battlefield, OK
Weir Farm, CT
Whitman Mission, WA
William Howard Taft, OH

National Historical Parks (38)

Appomattox Court House, VA
Boston, MA
Cane River, LA
Chaco Culture, NM
Chesapeake and Ohio Canal, MD–WV–DC
Colonial, VA
Cumberland Gap, TN–KY–VA
Dayton Aviation, OH
George Rogers Clark, IN
Harpers Ferry, WV–MD
Hopewell Culture, OH
Independence, PA
Jean Lafitte, LA
Kalaupapa, HI
Kaloko–Honokohau, HI
Keweenaw, MI
Klondike Gold Rush, AK–WA
Lowell, MA
Lyndon B. Johnson, TX
Marsh–Billings, VT
Minute Man, MA
Morristown, NJ
Natchez, MS
New Bedford Whaling, MA
Nez Perce, ID
Pecos, NM
Pu'uhonua o Honaunau, HI (formerly City of Refuge)
Salt River Bay, St, Croix, VI
San Antonio Missions, TX
San Francisco Maritime, CA
San Juan Island, WA
Saratoga, NY
Sitka, AK
Tumacacori, AZ
Valley Forge, PA
War in the Pacific, Guam
Women's Rights, NY
Zuni–Cibola, NM

National Memorials (28)

Arkansas Post, AR
Arlington House/Lee Memorial, VA
Chamizal, TX
Coronado, AZ
DeSoto, FL
Federal Hall, NY
Fort Caroline, FL
Fort Clatsop, OR
Franklin Delano Roosevelt, DC
Ulysses S. Grant, NY
Hamilton Grange, NY
Jefferson National Expansion Memorial, IL–MO
Korean War Veterans, DC
Johnstown Flood, PA
Lincoln Boyhood, IN
Lincoln Memorial, DC
Lyndon B. Johnson, Memorial Grove, DC
Mount Rushmore, SD
Oklahoma City, OK
Perry's Victory/Peace Memorial, OH
Roger Williams, RI
Thaddeus Kosciuszko, PA

Theodore Roosevelt Island, DC
Thomas Jefferson Memorial, DC
USS Arizona Memorial, HI
Vietnam Veterans Memorial, DC
Washington Monument, DC
Wright Brothers, NC

National Monuments (73)

Agate Fossil Beds, NE
Alibates Flint Quarries, TX
Aniakchak, AK
Aztec Ruins, NM
Bandelier, NM
Black Canyon of the Gunnison, CO
Booker T. Washington, VA
Buck Island Reef, VI
Cabrillo, NM–CA
Canyon de Chelly, NM–AZ
Cape Krusenstern, AK
Capulin Volcano, NM
Casa Grande, AZ
Castillo de San Marco, FL
Castle Clinton, NY
Cedar Breaks, UT
Chiricahua, AZ
Colorado, CO
Congaree Swamp, SC
Craters of the Moon, ID
Devils Postpile, CA
Devils Tower, WY
Dinosaur, CO–UT
Effigy Mounds, IO
El Malpais, NM
El Morro, NM
Florissant Fossil Beds, CO
Fort Frederica, GA
Fort Matanzas, FL
Fort McHenry, MD
Fort Pulaski, GA
Fort Stanwix, NY
Fort Sumter, SC
Fort Union, NM
Fossil Butte, WY
George Washington Birthplace, VA
George Washington Carver, MO
Gila Cliff Dwellings, NM
Grand Portage, MN
Great Sand Dunes, CO
Hagerman Fossil Beds, ID
Hohokam Pima, AZ
Homestead, NE
Hovenweep, CO–UT
Jewel Cave, SD
John Day Fossil Beds, OR
Lava Beds, CA
Little Bighorn Battlefield, MT
Montezuma Castle, AZ
Muir Woods, CA
Natural Bridges, UT
Navajo, AZ
Ocmulgee, GA
Oregon Caves, OR
Organ Pipe Cactus, AZ
Petroglyph, NM
Pinnacles, CA
Pipe Spring, AZ
Pipestone, MN
Poverty Point, LA
Rainbow Bridge, UT
Russell Cave, AL
Salinas Pueblo Missions, NM
Scotts Bluff, NE
Statue of Liberty, NY–NJ
Sunset Crater Volcano, AZ
Timpanogos Cave, UT
Tonto, AZ
Tuzigoot, AZ
Walnut Canyon, AZ
White Sands, NM
Wupatki, AZ
Yucca House, CO

National Parks (54)

Acadia, ME
Arches, UT
Badlands, SD
Big Bend, TX
Biscayne, FL
Bryce Canyon, UT
Canyonlands, UT

Capitol Reef, UT
Carlsbad Caverns, NM
Channel Islands, CA
Crater Lake, OR
Death Valley, CA
Denali, AK
Dry Tortugas, FL
Everglades, FL
Gates of the Arctic, AK
Glacier Bay, AK
Glacier, MT
Grand Canyon, AZ
Grand Teton, WY
Great Basin, NV
Great Smoky Mountains, TN–NC
Guadalupe Mountains, TX
Haleakala, HI
Hawaii Volcanoes, HI
Hot Springs, AR
Isle Royale, MI
Joshua Tree, CA
Katmai, AK
Kenai Fjords, AK
Kings Canyon, CA
Kobuk Valley, AK
Lake Clark, AK
Lassen Volcanic, CA
Mammoth Cave, KY
Mesa Verde, CO
Mount Rainier, WA
North Cascades, WA
Olympic, WA
Petrified Forest, AZ
Redwood, CA
Rocky Mountain, CO
Saguaro, CA
Samoa, American Samoa
Sequoia, CA
Shenandoah, VA
Theodore Roosevelt, ND
Virgin Islands, VI
Voyageurs, MN
Wind Cave, SD
Wrangell–St. Elias, AK
Yellowstone, WY–MT–ID
Yosemite, CA
Zion, UT

National Preserves (16)

Aniakchak, AK
Bering Land Bridge, AK
Big Cypress, FL
Big Thicket, TX
Denali, AK
Gates of the Arctic, AK
Glacier Bay, AK
Katmai, AK
Lake Clark, AK
Little River Canyon, AL
Mojave, CA
Noatak, AK
Tall Grass Prairie, KS
Timucuan Ecological and Historic, FL
Wrangell–St. Elias, AK
Yukon-Charley Rivers, AK

National Recreation Areas (19)

Amistad, TX
Bighorn Canyon, MT–WY
Boston Harbor Islands, MA
Chattahoochee River, GA
Chickasaw, OK
Coulee Dam, WA
Curecanti, CO
Cuyahoga Valley, OH
Delaware Water Gap, PA–NJ
Gateway, NY–NJ
Gauley River, WV
Glen Canyon, AZ–UT
Golden Gate, CA
Lake Chelan, WA
Lake Mead, NV–AZ
Lake Meredith, TX
Ross Lake, WA
Santa Monica Mountains, CA
Whiskeytown Unit, Whiskey–Shasta–Trinity, CA

National Reserve (2)
City of Rocks, ID
Ebey's Landing, WA

National Seashores (10)
Assateague Island, MD–VA
Canaveral, FL
Cape Cod, MA
Cape Hatteras, NC
Cape Lookout, NC
Cumberland Island, GA
Fire Island, NY
Gulf Islands, FL–MS
Padre Island, TX
Point Reyes, CA

National Parkways (4)
Blue Ridge Parkway, NC–VA
George Washington Memorial Parkway, VA–MD
John D. Rockefeller, Jr. Memorial Parkway, WY
Natchez Trace Parkway, MS–AL–TN

Parks (11)
Catoctin Mountain Park, MD
Constitution Gardens, DC
Fort Washington Park, MD
Greenbelt, MD
National Capital Parks, DC
National Mall, DC
Piscataway Park, MD
Prince William Forest Park, VA
Rock Creek Park, DC
White House, DC
Wolf Trap Farm Park for the Performing Arts, VA

National Scenic Trails (3)
Appalachian National Scenic Trail, ME–GA
Natchez Trace National Scenic Trail, MS–TN
Potomac Heritage National Scenic Trail, VA–PA

National Rivers (6)
Big South Fork River and Recreation Area, TN–KY
Buffalo National River, AR
New River Gorge National River, WV
Niobrara National Scenic River, NE–SD
Mississippi National River and Recreation Area, MN
Ozark National Scenic Trail, MO

National Wild and Scenic Rivers (9)
Alagnak Wild River, AK
Bluestone National Scenic River, WV
Delaware National Scenic River, PA–NJ–NY
Great Egg Harbor National Scenic and Recreational River, NJ
Missouri National Recreation River, NE–SD
Obed Wild and Scenic River, TN
Rio Grande Wild and Scenic River, TX
Saint Croix National Scenic Riverway, MN–WI
Upper Delaware Scenic and Recreation River, NY–PA

National Lakeshores (4)
Apostle Islands, WI
Indiana Dunes, IN
Pictured Rocks, MI
Sleeping Bear Dunes, MI

Affiliated Areas (24)
Aleutian World War II, AK
American Memorial Park, Saipan
Benjamin Franklin National Memorial, PA
Blackstone River Valley National Heritage Corridor, MA–RI
Chicago Portage National Historic Site, IL
Chimney Rock National Historic Site, NE
David Berger National Memorial, OH
Delaware and Lehigh Navigation Canal National Heritage Corridor, PA
Gloria Dei (Old Swedes') Church National Historic Site, PA
Green Springs Historic District, VA

Historic Camden, SC
Ice Age National Scenic Trail, WI
Ice Age National Scientific Reserve, WI
Illinois and Michigan Canal National Heritage Corridor, IL
International Peace Garden, ND–Manitoba
Jamestown National Historic Site, VA
McLoughlin House National Historic Site, OR
Lewis and Clark National Historic Trail, MO–OR
Pinelands National Reserve, NJ
Port Chicago Naval Magazine National Memorial, CA
Quinebaug and Shetucket River Valley National Heritage Corridor, CT
Roosevelt Campobello International Park, New Brunswick, Canada
Sewall–Belmont House National Historic Site, DC
Touro Synagogue National Historic Site, RI

COOPERATING ASSOCIATIONS STATE BY STATE LISTING

Alaska
Alaska Natural History Association
Northwest Interpretive Association

Alabama
Eastern National
Cradle of Forestry in America Interpretive Association

Arkansas
Eastern National

Arizona
Glen Canyon Natural History Association
Grand Canyon Association
Petrified Forest Museum Association
Southwest Parks and Monuments Association

California
Anza-Borrego Desert Natural History Association
Cabrillo Historical Association
Death Valley Natural History Association
Eastern Sierra Interpretive Association
Golden Gate National Park Association
Joshua Tree Natural History Association
Lava Beds Natural History Association
Loomis Museum Association
Point Reyes National Seashore Association
Redwood Natural History Association
Sequoia Natural History Association, Inc.
Southwest Parks and Monuments Association
Yosemite Association

Colorado
Bent's Old Fort Historical Association
Black Hills Parks and Forests Association
Colorado National Monument Association
Mesa Verde Museum Association, Inc.
Rocky Mountain Nature Association
Southwest Parks and Monuments Association

Connecticut
Weir Farm Heritage Trust

Delaware
Eastern National

District of Columbia
Parks and History Association

Florida
Eastern National
Florida National Parks and Monuments Association

Georgia
Eastern National
Fort Frederica Association
Kennesaw Mountain Historical Association, Inc.
Ocmulgee National Monument Association
Cradle of Forestry in America Interpretive Association

Hawaii
Arizona Memorial Museum Association
Hawaii Natural History Association

Idaho
Craters of the Moon Natural History Association
Northwest Interpretive Association

Illinois
Eastern National

Indiana
Eastern National

Iowa
Eastern National

Kansas
Southwest Parks and Monuments Association

Kentucky
Cradle of Forestry in America Interpretive Association
Eastern National
Land-Between-the-Lakes Association

Louisiana
Eastern National

Maine
Eastern National

Maryland
Eastern National
Historic Hampton, Inc.
Parks and History Association
Prince Georges County Parks & Recreation Foundation

Massachusetts
Eastern National

Michigan
Eastern National
Isle Royale Natural History Association

Minnesota
Eastern National
Lake States Interpretive Association
Pipestone Indian Shrine Association

Mississippi
Eastern National

Missouri
Eastern National
George Washington Carver Birthplace Association
Jefferson National Expansion Historical Association
Ozark National Riverways Historical Association

Montana
Glacier Natural History Association

Nebraska
Eastern National
Oregon Trail Museum Association

Nevada
Great Basin Natural History Association
Southwest Parks and Monuments Association
Red Rock Canyon Interpretive Association

New Jersey
Eastern National

New Mexico
Carlsbad Caverns-Guadalupe Mountains Association
Southwest Natural & Cultural Heritage Association
Southwest Parks and Monuments Association

New York
Eastern National
Roosevelt-Vanderbilt Historical Association

North Carolina
Cradle of Forestry in America Interpretive Association
Eastern National

North Dakota
Fort Union Association
Theodore Roosevelt Nature & History Association

Ohio
Eastern National

Oklahoma
Southwest Parks and Monuments Association

Oregon
Crater Lake Natural History Association
Fort Clatsop Historical Association
Northwest Interpretive Association

Pennsylvania
Eastern National
Steamtown Volunteer Association
Valley Forge Park Interpretive Association

Puerto Rico
Eastern National

Rhode Island
Eastern National

South Carolina
Cradle of Forestry in America Interpretive Association
Eastern National

South Dakota
Badlands Natural History Association
Mount Rushmore History Association

Tennessee
Eastern National
Great Smoky Mountains Natural History Association
Cradle of Forestry in America Interpretive Association
Land-Between-the-Lakes Association

Texas
Big Bend Natural History Association
Southwest Parks and Monuments Association

Utah
Bryce Canyon Natural History Association
Canyonlands Natural History Association
Capitol Reef Natural History Association
Dinosaur Nature Association
Southwest Parks and Monuments Association
Zion Natural History Association

Virgin Islands
Eastern National

Virginia
Eastern National
George Washington Birthplace National Monument Association
Parks and History Association
Shenandoah Natural History Association
Cradle of Forestry in America Interpretive Association

Washington
Northwest Interpretive Association

West Virginia
Eastern National
Harpers Ferry Historical Association

Wisconsin
Eastern National

Wyoming
Devils Tower Natural History Association
Fort Laramie Historical Association
Grand Teton Natural History Association
Yellowstone Association

US GOVERNMENT BOOKSTORES

State Offices

Atlanta, GA
First Union Plaza
999 Peachtree Street, Northeast
Suite 120
Atlanta, GA 30309-3964
404-347-1900

Birmingham, AL
O'Neill Building
2021 Third Avenue, North
Birmingham, AL 35203
205-731-1056

Boston, MA
Thomas P O'Neill Building
Room 169
10 Causeway Street
Boston, MA 02222
617-720-4180

Chicago, IL
One Congress Center
401 South State Street, Suite 124
Chicago, IL 60605
312-353-5133

Cleveland, OH
Room 1653, Federal Building
1240 East 9th Street
Cleveland, OH 44199
216-522-4922

Columbus, OH
Room 207, Federal Building
200 North High Street
Columbus, OH 43215
614-469-6956

Dallas, TX
Room IC50, Federal Building
1100 Commerce Street
Dallas, TX 75242
214-767-0076

Denver, CO
Room 117, Federal Building
1961 Stout Street
Denver, CO 80294
303-844-3964

Detroit, MI
Suite 160, Federal Building
477 Michigan Avenue
Detroit, MI 48226
313-226-7816

Houston, TX
Texas Crude Building
801 Travis Street, Suite 120
Houston, TX 77002
713-228-1187

Jacksonville, FL
100 West Bay Street
Suite 100
Jacksonville, FL 32202
904-353-0569

Kansas City, MO
120 Bannister Mall
5600 East Bannister Road
Kansas City, MO 64137
816-765-2256

Laurel, MD
US Government Printing Office
Warehouse Sales Outlet
8660 Cherry Lane
Laurel, MD 20707
301-953-7974
301-792-0262

Los Angeles, CA
ARCO Plaza, C-Level
505 South Flower Street
Los Angeles, CA 90071
213-239-9844

Milwaukee, WI
Suite 150, Reuss Federal Plaza
310 West Wisconsin Avenue
Milwaukee, WI 53203
414-297-1304

New York, NY
Room 2-120, Federal Building
26 Federal Plaza
New York, NY 10278
212-264-3825

Philadelphia, PA
Robert Morris Building
100 North 17th Street
Philadelphia, PA 19103
215-636-1900

Pittsburgh, PA
Room 118, Federal Building
1000 Liberty Avenue
Pittsburgh, PA 15222
412-395-5021

Portland, OR
1305 SW First Avenue
Portland, OR 97201-5801
503-221-6217

Pueblo, CO
Norwest Banks Building
201 West 8th Street
Pueblo, CO 81003
719-544-3142

San Francisco, CA
Marathon Plaza, Room 141-S
303 2nd Street
San Francisco, CA 94107
415-512-2770

Seattle, WA
Room 194, Federal Building
915 Second Avenue
Seattle, WA 98174
206-553-4270

Washington, DC
US Government Printing Office
710 North Capitol Street, NW
Washington, DC 20401
202-512-0132
and

1510 H Street, NW
Washington, DC 20005
202-653-5075

BUREAU OF RECLAMATION

Regional Offices

Pacific Northwest Region

1150 North Curtis Road
Boise, ID 83706
208-378-5012
http://www.pn.usbr.gov

Mid-Pacific Region

2800 Cottage Way
Sacramento, CA 95825
916-978-5000
http://www.mp.usbr.gov

Lower Colorado Region

PO Box 61470
Boulder City, NV 89006
702-293-8411
http://www.lc.usbr.gov

Upper Colorado Region

125 South State Street
Room 6107
Salt Lake City, UT 84138
801-524-3600
http://www.uc.usbr.gov

Great Plains Region

PO Box 36900
Billings, MT 59107
406-247-7614
http://www.gp.usbr.gov

UNITED STATES GEOLOGICAL SURVEY EARTH SCIENCE INFORMATION CENTERS

Regional Offices

Anchorage, AK
Anchorage-ESIC
U.S. Geological Survey
4230 University Drive, Room 101
Anchorage, AK 99508-4664
907-786-7011

Denver, CO
Denver-ESIC
U.S. Geological Survey
Box 25286, Building 810
Denver Federal Center
Denver, CO 80225
303-202-4200

Menlo Park, CA
Menlo Park-ESIC
U.S. Geological Survey
Building 3, MS 532, Room 3128
345 Middlefield Road
Menlo Park, CA 94025-3591
650-329-4309

Reston, VA
Reston-ESIC
U.S. Geological Survey
507 National Center
Reston, VA 20192
703-648-6045

Rolla, MO
Rolla-ESIC
U.S. Geological Survey
1400 Independence Road, MS 231
Rolla, MO 65401-2602
573-308-3500

Salt Lake City, UT
Salt Lake-ESIC
U.S. Geological Survey
2222 W 2300 S, 2nd Floor
Salt Lake City, UT 84119
801-975-3742

Sioux Falls, SD
Sioux Falls-ESIC
U.S. Geological Survey
EROS Data Center
Sioux Falls, SD 57198-0001
605-594-6151

Spokane, WA
Spokane-ESIC
U.S. Geological Survey
U.S. Post Office Building, Room 135
904 West Riverside Avenue
Spokane, WA 99201
509-353-2524

Washington, DC
Washington DC-ESIC
U.S. Geological Survey
U.S. Department of the Interior
1849 C Street, Northwest, Room 2650
Washington, DC 20240
202-208-4047

For further information, go to the ESIC website at: http://mapping.usgs.gov/esic/esic_index.html, or call 800-USA-MAPS.

US ARMY CORPS OF ENGINEERS

District Offices

Alabama
US Army Engineer District, Mobile
PO Box 2288
Mobile, AL 36628-0001
334-690-2511

Alaska
US Army Engineer District, Alaska
PO Box 898
Anchorage, AK 99506-0898
907-753-2504

Arkansas
US Army Engineer District, Little Rock
PO Box 867
Little Rock, AR 72203-0867
501-324-5531

California
US Army Engineer District, Los Angeles
PO Box 2711
Los Angeles, CA 90053-2325
213-452-3967

US Army Engineer District, Sacramento
1325 J Street
Sacramento, CA 95814-2922
916-557-7490

US Army Engineer District, San Francisco
333 Market Street
Room 923
San Francisco, CA 94105-2195
415-977-8600

Florida
US Army Engineer District, Jacksonville
PO Box 4970
Jacksonville, FL 32232-0019
904-232-2241

Georgia
US Army Engineer District, Savannah
PO Box 889
Savannah, GA 31402-0889
912-652-5226

Hawaii
US Army Engineer District, Honolulu
Building 230
Ft. Shafter, HI 96858-5440
808-438-1069

Illinois
US Army Engineer District, Chicago
111 North Canal Street
Suite 600
Chicago, IL 60606-7206
312-353-6400

US Army Engineer District, Rock Island
Clock Tower Building
PO Box 2004
Rock Island, IL 61204-2004
309-794-5224

Kentucky
US Army Engineer District, Louisville
PO Box 59
Louisville, KY 40201-0059
502-582-5601

Louisiana
US Army Engineer District, New Orleans
PO Box 60267
New Orleans, LA 70160-0267
504-862-2204

Maryland
US Army Engineer District, Baltimore
PO Box 1715
Baltimore, MD 21203-1715
410-962-4545

Michigan
US Army Engineer District, Detroit
PO Box 1027
Detroit, MI 48231-1027
313-226-6762

Minnesota
US Army Engineer District, St. Paul
Army Corps of Engineers Centre
190 5th Street East
St. Paul, MN 55101-1638
612-290-5300

Mississippi
US Army Engineer District, Vicksburg
4155 Clay Street
Vicksburg, MS 39180-3435
601-631-5010

Missouri
US Army Engineer District, St. Louis
1222 Spruce Street
St. Louis, MO 63103-2833
314-331-8010

US Army Engineer District, Kansas City
700 Federal Building
Kansas City, MO 64106-2896
816-983-3201

Nebraska
US Army Engineer District, Omaha
215 North 17th Street
Omaha, NE 68102-4978
402-221-3900

New England
US Army Engineer District, New England
Frederick C. Murphy Federal Building 424
Trapelo Road Waltham, MA 02254-9149
718-647-8220

New Mexico
US Army Engineer District, Albuquerque
4101 Jefferson Plaza NE
Albuquerque, NM 87109-3435
505-342-3432

New York
US Army Engineer District, Buffalo
1776 Niagara Street
Buffalo, NY 14207-3199
716-879-4200

US Army Engineer District New York
Jacob K. Javits Federal Office Building
26 Federal Plaza, Room 2109
New York, NY 10278-0090
212-264-0100

North Carolina
US Army Engineer District, Wilmington
PO Box 1890
Wilmington, NC 28402-1890
910-251-4501

Oklahoma
US Army Engineer District, Tulsa
PO Box 61
Tulsa, OK 74121-0061
918-669-7201

Oregon
US Army Engineer District, Portland
PO Box 2946
Portland, OR 97208-2946
503-808-4500

Pennsylvania
US Army Engineer District, Pittsburgh
William S. Moorhead Federal Building 1
000 Liberty Avenue
Pittsburgh, PA 15222-4186
412-395-7103

US Army Engineer District, Philadelphia
Wanamaker Building
100 Penn Square East
Philadelphia, PA 19107-3390
215-656-6501

South Carolina

US Army Engineer District, Charleston
PO Box 919
Charleston, SC 29402-0919
803-727-4344

Tennessee

US Army Engineer District, Nashville
PO Box 1070
Nashville, TN 37202-1070
615-736-5626

US Army Engineer District, Memphis
167 North Main Street, Room B202
Memphis, TN 38103-1894
901-544-3221

Texas

US Army Engineer District, Fort Worth
PO Box 17300
Ft. Worth, TX 76102-0300
817-978-2300

US Army Engineer District, Galveston
PO Box 1229
Galveston, TX 77553-1229
409-766-3001

Virginia

US Army Engineer District, Norfolk
Waterfield Building
803 Front Street
Norfolk, VA 23510-1096
757-441-7601

Washington

US Army Engineer District, Seattle
PO Box 3755
Seattle, WA 98124-3755
206-764-3690

US Army Engineer District, Walla Walla
201 North Third Avenue
Walla Walla, WA 99362-1876
509-527-7700

West Virginia

US Army Engineer District, Huntington
502 8th Street
Huntington, WV 25701-2070
304-529-5395

COOPERATING ASSOCIATIONS ADDRESSES

ALASKA NATURAL HISTORY ASSOCIATION
401 West 1st Avenue, Suite 85
Anchorage, AK 99501
907-274-8440

ANZA-BORREGO DESERT NATURAL HISTORY ASSOCIATION
PO Box 310
Borrego Springs, CA 92004
619-767-3052

ARIZONA MEMORIAL MUSEUM ASSOCIATION
1 Arizona Memorial Place
Honolulu, HI 96818
808-422-5905 or 5664
http://members.aol.com/azmemph/index.htm

BADLANDS NATURAL HISTORY ASSOCIATION
PO Box 47
Badlands National Park
Interior, SD 57750
605-433-5361

BENT'S OLD FORT HISTORICAL ASSOCIATION
35110 Highway 194 East
La Junta, CO 81050
719-384-2800

BIG BEND NATURAL HISTORY ASSOCIATION
PO Box 196
Big Bend National Park, TX 79834
915-477-2236

BLACK HILLS PARKS AND FORESTS ASSOCIATION
Route 1, Box 190—WCNP
Hot Springs, SD 57747-9430
605-745-4600

BRYCE CANYON NATURAL HISTORY ASSOCIATION
Bryce Canyon National Park
Bryce Canyon, UT 84717
801-834-4602

CABRILLO HISTORICAL ASSOCIATION
PO Box 6670
San Diego, CA 92166-0670
619-557-5450

CANYONLANDS NATURAL HISTORY ASSOCIATION
3031 South Highway 191
Moab, UT 84532
800-840-8978
http://www.nps.gov/cany/cnha.htm

CAPITOL REEF NATURAL HISTORY ASSOCIATION
HC 70, Box 15
Torrey, UT 84775-9602
435-425-3791, ext. 106

CARLSBAD CAVERNS–GUADALUPE MOUNTAINS ASSOCIATION
PO Box 1417
Carlsbad, NM 88221-1417
505-785-2322, ext. 483
http://www.caverns.com/~ccgma

COLORADO NATIONAL MONUMENT ASSOCIATION
Colorado National Monument
Fruita, CO 81521
970-858-3617

CRADLE OF FORESTRY IN AMERICA INTERPRETIVE ASSOCIATION
100 South Broad Street
Brevard, NC 28712
704-884-5713

CRATER LAKE NATURAL HISTORY ASSOCIATION
PO Box 157
Crater Lake, OR 97604
541-594-2211, ext. 499

CRATERS OF THE MOON NATURAL HISTORY ASSOCIATION
PO Box 29
Arco, ID 83213
208-527-3257

DEATH VALLEY NATURAL HISTORY ASSOCIATION
PO Box 188
Death Valley, CA 92328
760-786-3285/786-2331

DEVILS TOWER NATURAL HISTORY ASSOCIATION
PO Box 37
Devils Tower, WY 82714
307-467-5283, ext. 109

DINOSAUR NATURE ASSOCIATION
1291 East Highway 40
Vernal, UT 84078
801-789-8807

EASTERN NATIONAL
446 North Lane
Conshohocken, PA 19428
800-355-5566
http://www.EasternNational.org

EASTERN SIERRA INTERPRETIVE ASSOCIATION
PO Drawer 1008
Lone Pine, CA 93545
619-876-5324

FLORIDA NATIONAL PARKS AND MONUMENTS ASSOCIATION
10 Parachute Key #51
Homestead, FL 33034-6735
305-247-1216
http://www.nps.gov/ever/fnpma.htm

FORT CLATSOP HISTORICAL ASSOCIATION
Route 3, Box 604-FC
Astoria, OR 97103
503-861-2471

FORT FREDERICA ASSOCIATION
Fort Frédérica National Monument
Route 9, Box 286-C
St. Simons Island, GA 31522
912-638-3639

FORT LARAMIE HISTORICAL ASSOCIATION
Fort Laramie National Historic Site
PO Box 218, Highway 160
Fort Laramie, WY 82212
800-321-5456/307-837-2662

FORT UNION ASSOCIATION
Route 3, Box 71
Williston, ND 58801
701-572-9083

GEORGE WASHINGTON BIRTHPLACE NATIONAL MONUMENT ASSOCIATION
Route 1, Box 718
Washington's Birthplace, VA 22443
804-224-7895

GEORGE WASHINGTON CARVER BIRTHPLACE DISTRICT ASSOCIATION, INC.
PO Box 38
Diamond, MO 64840
417-325-4151

GLACIER NATURAL HISTORY ASSOCIATION
PO Box 428
West Glacier, MT 59936
406-888-5756
http://www.nps.gov/glac/gnha1.htm

GLEN CANYON NATURAL HISTORY ASSOCIATION
32 North 10th Avenue, Suite 9
PO Box 581
Page, AZ 86040
520-645-3532
http://www.pagelakepowell.com

GOLDEN GATE NATIONAL PARK ASSOCIATION
Fort Mason, Building 201
San Francisco, CA 94123
415-561-3600

GRAND CANYON ASSOCIATION
PO Box 399
Grand Canyon, AZ 86023
520-638-2481
http://www.thecanyon.com/gca

GRAND TETON NATURAL HISTORY ASSOCIATION
Grand Teton National Park
PO Box 170
Moose, WY 83012
307-739-3403

GREAT BASIN NATURAL HISTORY ASSOCIATION
Great Basin National Park
Baker, NV 89311
702-234-7270

GREAT SMOKY MOUNTAINS NATURAL HISTORY ASSOCIATION
115 Park Headquarters Road
Gatlinburg, TN 37738
423-436-0120
http://www.nps.gov/grsm/nhahome.htm

HARPERS FERRY HISTORICAL ASSOCIATION
PO Box 197
Harpers Ferry, WV 25425
800-821-5206
http://www.nps.gov/hafe/hf_shop.htm

HAWAII NATURAL HISTORY ASSOCIATION
PO Box 74
Hawaii National Park, HI 96718
808-985-6000

HISTORIC HAMPTON, INC.
Hampton National Historical Site
535 Hampton Lane
Towson, MD 21286-1397
410-828-9480

ISLE ROYALE NATURAL HISTORY ASSOCIATION
800 East Lakeshore Drive
Houghton, MI 49931
906-482-7860

JEFFERSON NATIONAL EXPANSION HISTORICAL ASSOCIATION
10 South Broadway, #1540
St. Louis, MO 63102
314-436-1473

JOSHUA TREE NATIONAL PARK ASSOCIATION
74485 National Park Drive
Twentynine Palms, CA 92277
760-367-1488

KENNESAW MOUNTAIN HISTORICAL ASSOCIATION, INC.
900 Kennesaw Mountain Drive
Kennesaw, GA 30144
770-422-3696

LAKE STATES INTERPRETIVE ASSOCIATION
3131 Highway 53
International Falls, MN 56649-8904
218-283-2103

LAND-BETWEEN-THE-LAKES ASSOCIATION
100 Van Morgan Drive
Golden Pond, KY 42211
502-924-5897

LAVA BEDS NATURAL HISTORY ASSOCIATION
PO Box 865
Tulelake, CA 96134
916-667-2282

LOOMIS MUSEUM ASSOCIATION
Lassen Volcanic National Park
PO Box 100
Mineral, CA 96063-0100
916-257-2151

MESA VERDE MUSEUM ASSOCIATION, INC.
PO Box 38
Mesa Verde NP, CO 81330
970-529-4445
http://www.nmesaverde.org

MOUNT RUSHMORE HISTORY ASSOCIATION
PO Box 444
Keystone, SD 57751
605-574-2523, ext. 128

NORTHWEST INTERPRETIVE ASSOCIATION
909 First Avenue, Suite 630
Seattle, WA 98104
206-220-4140

OCMULGEE NATIONAL MONUMENT ASSOCIATION
1207 Emery Highway
Macon, GA 31201
912-752-8257

OREGON TRAIL MUSEUM ASSOCIATION
Scotts Bluff National Monument
Box 27
Gering, Nebraska 69341-0027
308-436-4340

OZARK NATIONAL RIVERWAYS HISTORICAL ASSOCIATION
PO Box 490
Van Buren, MO 63965
573-323-4236

PARKS AND HISTORY ASSOCIATION
126 Raleigh Street, SE
Washington, DC 20032
800-990-7275
http://www.parksandhistory.org

PETRIFIED FOREST MUSEUM ASSOCIATION
PO Box 2277, Park Road 1
Petrified Forest NP, AZ 86028
520-524-6228, ext. 239/261

PIPESTONE INDIAN SHRINE ASSOCIATION
Pipestone National Monument
PO Box 727
Pipestone, MN 56164
507-825-5463

POINT REYES NATIONAL SEASHORE ASSOCIATION
Point Reyes National Seashore
Point Reyes, CA 94956
415-663-1155

PRINCE GEORGES COUNTY PARKS AND RECREATION FOUNDATION, INC.
13022 8th Street
Bowie, MD 20720
301-464-6706

RED ROCK CANYON INTERPRETIVE ASSOCIATION
PO Box 26993
Las Vegas, NV 89126-0993
702-363-1921

REDWOOD NATURAL HISTORY ASSOCIATION
1111 Second Street
Crescent City, CA 95531
707-464-9150

ROCKY MOUNTAIN NATURE ASSOCIATION
Rocky Mountain National Park
Estes Park, CO 80517
800-816-7662
http://www.rmna.org/bookstore

ROOSEVELT-VANDERBILT HISTORICAL ASSOCIATION
PO Box 235
Hyde Park, NY 12538
914-229-9300

SEQUOIA NATURAL HISTORY ASSOCIATION, INC.
HCR 89—Box 10
Three Rivers, CA 93271-9792
209-565-3341
http://www.nps.gov/seki/snha.htm

SHENANDOAH NATURAL HISTORY ASSOCIATION
3655 US Highway 211E
Luray, VA 22835
540-999-3581

SOUTHWEST NATURAL AND CULTURAL HERITAGE ASSOCIATION
6501 North Fourth Street, Suite I
Albuquerque, NM 87107
505-345-9498
http://www.nps.gov/shen/snhahome.htm

SOUTHWEST PARKS AND MONUMENTS ASSOCIATION
221 North Court Avenue
Tucson, AZ 85701
520-622-1999

STEAMTOWN VOLUNTEER ASSOCIATION, INC.
150 South Washington Avenue
Scranton, PA 18503
717-346-7275

THEODORE ROOSEVELT NATURE AND HISTORY ASSOCIATION
PO Box 167
Medora, ND 58645
701-623-4884

VALLEY FORGE PARK INTERPRETIVE ASSOCIATION
PO Box 953
Valley Forge, PA 19481-0953
610-783-1076

WEIR FARM HERITAGE TRUST
735 Nod Hill Road
Wilton, CT 06897
203-761-9945

YELLOWSTONE ASSOCIATION
PO Box 168
Yellowstone NP, WY 82190
307-344-2293
http://www.nps.gov/yell/ya/yellassn.htm

YOSEMITE ASSOCIATION
PO Box 230
El Portal, CA 95318
209-379-2646
http://www.yosemite.org

ZION NATURAL HISTORY ASSOCIATION
Zion National Park
Springdale, UT 84767
435-772-3265 or 3264

US FISH AND WILDLIFE SERVICE ADDRESSES

National Headquarters

US Fish and Wildlife Service
Department of the Interior
1849 C Street, Northwest
Washington, DC 20240
202-208-5634
http://www.fws.gov

Regional Offices

US Fish and Wildlife Service Pacific Northwest Region
(CA, HI, ID, NV, OR, WA, Pacific Islands)
911 Northeast 11th Avenue
Portland, OR 97232-4181
503-231-6121
http://www.r1.fws.gov

US Fish and Wildlife Service Southwest Region
(AZ, NM, OK, TX)
500 Gold Avenue, Southwest
PO Box 1306
Albuquerque, NM 87103
505-248-6911
http://sturgeon.irm1.r2.fws.gov

US Fish and Wildlife Service Great Lakes–Big Rivers Region
(IA, IL, IN, MI, MN, MO, OH, WI)
Federal Building, Federal Drive
Fort Snelling, MN 55111-4056
612-725-3519
http://www.fsw.gov/~r3pao

US Fish and Wildlife Service Southeast Region
(AL, AR, FL, GA, KY, LA, MS, NC, PR, SC, TN, VI)
1875 Century Center Boulevard, Northeast
Atlanta, GA 30345
404-679-7289
http://www.fws.gov/~r4eao

US Fish and Wildlife Service Northeast Region
(CT, DC, DE, MA, MD, ME, NH, NJ, NY, PA, RI, VA,VT, WV)
300 Westgate Center Drive
Hadley, MA 01035-9589
413-253-8320
http://www.fws.gov/~r5fws

US Fish and Wildlife Service Mountain–Prairie Region
(CO, KS, MT, ND, NE, SD, UT, WY)
PO Box 25486
Denver Federal Center
Denver, CO 80225
303-236-7904
http://www.r6.fws.gov

US Fish and Wildlife Service Alaska Region
1011 East Tudor Road
Anchorage, AK 99503
907-786-3487
http://www.r7.fws.gov

NATIONAL PARK SERVICE FIELD OFFICES

Field Offices

Alaska Area Field Office
National Park Service
2525 Gambell Street, Room 107
Anchorage, AK 99503
907-257-2696
http://www.nps.gov/pub_aff/akfa.htm

Northeast Area Field Office
National Park Service
US Custom House
200 Chestnut Street, Room 322
Philadephia, PA 19106
215-597-3679
http://www.nps.gov/pub_aff/nefa.htm

Midwest Field Office
National Park Service
1709 Jackson Street
Omaha, NE 68102
402-221-3471
http://www.nps.gov/pub_aff/mwfa.htm

National Capital Field Office
National Park Service
1100 Ohio Drive, Southwest
Washington, DC 20242
202-619-7222
http://www.nps.gov/pub_aff/ncfa.htm

Intermountain Field Office
National Park Service
12795 Alameda Parkway
Denver, CO 80225
303-969-2000
http://www.nps.gov/pub_aff/imfa.htm

Southeast Field Office
National Park Service
100 Alabama Street, Southwest
1924 Building
Atlanta, GA 30303
404-562-3123
http://www.nps.gov/pub_aff/sefa.htm

Pacific West Field Office
National Park Service
600 Harrison Street, Suite 600
San Francisco, CA 94101
415-427-1300
http://www.nps.gov/pub_aff/pwfa.htm

FOREST SERVICE ADDRESSES

National Headquarters

Forest Service
US Department of Agriculture
Auditors Building
201 14th Street, SW
Washington, DC 20250
http://www.fs.fed.us/intro/directory/wo.htm

USDA Forest Service Field Offices

Forest Service, USDA
Northern Region (R.1)
Federal Building
PO Box 7669
Missoula, MT 59807-7669
406-329-3511
http://www.fs.fed.us/r1

Forest Service, USDA
Rocky Mountain Region (R.2)
740 Simms Street
PO Box 25127
Lakewood, CO 80225
303-275-5350
http://www.fs.fed.us/r2

Forest Service, USDA
Southwestern Region (R.3)
Federal Building
517 Gold Avenue, Southwest
Albuquerque, NM 87102
505-842-3292
http://www.fs.fed.us/r3

Forest Service, USDA
Intermountain Region (R.4)
Federal Building
324 25th Street
Ogden, UT 84401-2310
801-625-5354
http://www.fs.fed.us/r4

Forest Service, USDA
Pacific Southwest Region (R.5)
630 Sansome Street
San Francisco, CA 94111
415-705-2874
http://www.fs.fed.us/r5

Forest Service, USDA
Pacific Northwest Region (R.6)
333 Southwest First Avenue
PO Box 3623
Portland, OR 97208
503-872-2750
http://www.fs.fed.us/r6

Forest Service, USDA
Southern Region (R.8)
1720 Peachtree Road, Northwest
Atlanta, GA 30367
404-347-7239
http://www.fs.fed.us/r8

Forest Service, USDA
Eastern Region (R.9)
310 West Wisconsin Avenue, Room 500
Milwaukee, WI 53203
414-297-3693
http://www.fs.fed.us/r9

Forest Service, USDA
Alaska Region (R.10)
PO Box 21628
Juneau, AK 99802-1628
907-586-8863
http://www.fs.fed.us/r10

BUREAU OF LAND MANAGEMENT

Information Access Centers

Washington, DC

Washington Office Information Access Center
1849 C Street, Northwest
Room 750-LS, WO-540
Washington, DC 20240
202-452-5193
http://www.blm.gov

Alaska

Alaska State Office
Information Access Center
Bureau of Land Management
222 West 7th Avenue, #13
Anchorage, AK 99513
907-271-5960
http://www.ak.blm.gov

Arizona

Arizona State Office
Information Access Center
Bureau of Land Management
222 North Central Avenue
Phoenix, AZ 85004-2208
602-417-9528
http://azwww.az.blm.gov

California

California State Office
Information Access Center
Bureau of Land Management
2135 Butano Drive
Sacramento, CA 95825-0451
916-978-4400
http://www.ca.blm.gov

Colorado

Colorado State Office
Information Access Center
Bureau of Land Management
2850 Youngfield Street
Lakewood, CO 80215
303-239-3600
http://www.co.blm.gov

States Bordering and East of the Mississippi River

Eastern States Office
Information Access Center
Bureau of Land Management
7450 Boston Boulevard
Springfield, VA 22153
703-440-1600
http://www.blm.gov/eso

Idaho

Idaho State Office
Information Access Center
Bureau of Land Management
1387 South Vinnell Way
Boise, ID 83709-1657
208-373-3896
http://www.id.blm.gov

Montana, North Dakota, and South Dakota

Montana State Office
Information Access Center
Bureau of Land Management
PO Box 36800
Granite Tower, 222 North 32nd Street
Billings, MT 59107-6800
406-255-2888
http://www.mt.blm.gov

Nevada
Nevada State Office
Information Access Center
Bureau of Land Management
850 Harvard Way
PO Box 12000
Reno, NV 89520-0006
702-785-6500
http://www.nv.blm.gov

Kansas, New Mexico, Oklahoma, and Texas
New Mexico State Office
Information Access Center
Bureau of Land Management
PO Box 27115
Santa Fe, NM 87502-0115
505-438-7400
http://www.nm.blm.gov

Oregon and Washington
Oregon State Office
Information Access Center
Bureau of Land Management
1515 Southwest 5th Avenue
PO Box 2965
Portland, OR 97208-2965
503-952-6001
http://www.or.blm.gov

Utah
Utah State Office
Information Access Center
Bureau of Land Management
324 South State Street, Suite 301
PO Box 45155
Salt Lake City, UT 84145-0155
801-539-4001
http://www.blm.gov/utah

Nebraska and Wyoming
Wyoming State Office
Information Access Center
Bureau of Land Management
5353 Yellowstone Road
PO Box 1828
Cheyenne, WY 82003
307-775-6256
http://www.wy.blm.gov

STATE PARKS

Alabama
Department of Conservation and Natural Resources
64 North Union Street, Room 538
Montgomery, AL 36130
334-242-3333 or 800-ALAPARK

Alaska
Division of Parks and Outdoor Recreation
3601 C Street, Suite 200
Anchorage, AK 99503-5921
907-762-2261

Arizona
State Parks Board
Public Information
1300 West Washington
Phoenix, AZ 85007
602-542-1996

Arkansas
Department of Parks and Tourism
One Capitol Mall, Fourth Floor
Little Rock, AR 72201
501-682-2873

California
Department of Parks and Recreation
PO Box 942896
Sacramento, CA 94296-0001
916-653-7090

Colorado
Division of Parks and Outdoor Recreation
1313 Sherman Street, #618
Denver, CO 80203
303-866-3203, ext. 311

Connecticut
Bureau of Environmental Protection
165 Capitol Avenue, Room 265
Hartford, CT 06106
203-566-6087

Delaware
Division of Parks and Recreation
PO Box 1401
Dover, DE 19903-1401
302-739-4702

Florida
Division of Recreation and Parks
Department of Natural Resources
3900 Commonwealth Boulevard
Tallahassee, FL 32399-3000
904-488-2850

Georgia
Department of Natural Resources
East Tower, Suite 1352
Atlanta, GA 30334
404-656-0779

Hawaii
Department of Land and Natural Resources
PO Box 621
Honolulu, HI 96809
808-587-0330

Idaho
Department of Parks and Recreation
700 West State Street, Department C
Boise, ID 83720
800-635-7820

Illinois
Department of Conservation
600 North Grand Avenue West
Springfield, IL 26706
217-782-6752

Indiana
Department of Natural Resources
402 West Washington Street, Room W298
Indianapolis, IN 46204
317-232-4124

Iowa
Division of Tourism
200 East Grand
Des Moines, IA 50309
800-345-IOWA

Kansas
Parks and Public Lands Division
Department of Wildlife and Parks
512 Southeast 25th Avenue
Pratt, KS 67124
316-672-5911

Kentucky
Department of Parks
500 Mero Street, Capitol Plaza Tower
Frankfort, KY 40601
800-225-8747

Louisiana
Department of Culture, Recreation and Tourism
PO Box 44426
Baton Rouge, LA 70804-4426
504-342-8111

Maine
Department of Conservation
State House Station 22
Augusta, ME 04333-0022
207-287-3821

Maryland
State Forest and Park Service
Department of Natural Resources
580 Taylor Avenue, E-3
Annapolis, MD 21401
401-974-3771

Massachusetts
Division of Forest and Parks
Department of Environmental Management
100 Cambridge Street, 19th Floor
Boston, MA 02202
617-727-3180

Michigan
Parks Division
Department of Natural Resources
PO Box 30257
Lansing, MI 48909
517-373-9900

Minnesota
Division of Parks and Recreation
Department of Natural Resources
500 Lafayette Road
St. Paul, MN 55155-4039
612-296-9223

Mississippi
Office of Parks and Recreation
PO Box 23093
Jackson, MS 39225-3093
800-467-2757

Missouri
Division of State Parks
PO Box 176
Jefferson City, MO 65102
800-334-6946

Montana
Parks Division
Department of Fish, Wildlife and Parks
1420 East Sixth Avenue
Helena, MT 59602
800-847-4868

Nebraska
Game and Parks Commission
PO Box 30370
Lincoln, NE 68503-0370
402-471-5586

Nevada
Department of Conservation and Natural Resources
123 West Nye Lane, Room 207
Carson City, NV 89710
702-687-4370

New Hampshire
Department of Resources and Economic Development
PO Box 1856
Concord, NH 03302
603-271-3255

New Jersey
Division of Parks and Forestry
CN 404, 501 East State Street
Trenton, NJ 08625
609-292-2797

New Mexico
State Park and Recreation Division
PO Box 1147
Santa Fe, NM 87504-1147
505-827-7465

New York
Office of Parks, Recreation and Historic Preservation
Empire State Plaza, Agency Building No. 1
Albany, NY 12238
518-474-0456

North Carolina
Division of Parks and Recreation
PO Box 27687
Raleigh, NC 27611
919-733-4181

North Dakota
Division of Parks and Outdoor Recreation Sites
Parks and Tourism Department
604 East Boulevard
Bismarck, ND 58505
800-435-5663

Ohio
Division of Parks and Recreation
Department of Natural Resources
1952 Belcher Drive, C-3
Columbus, OH 43324
614-265-6561

Oklahoma
Tourism and Recreation Department
2401 North Lincoln, Room 500
Oklahoma City, OK 73105
405-521-3111

Oregon
Parks and Recreation Department
1115 Commercial Street, Northeast
Salem, OR 97310
800-452-5687

Pennsylvania
Department of Environmental Resources
PO Box 8551
Harrisburg, PA 17105-8551
717-783-4356

Rhode Island
Division of Parks and Recreation
2321 Hartford Avenue
Johnston, RI 02919
401-277-2632

South Carolina
Department of Parks, Recreation and Tourism
1205 Pendleton Street
Columbia, SC 29201
803-734-0122

South Dakota
Division of Parks and Recreation
Foss Building, 523 East Capitol
Pierre, SD 57501-3182
800-732-5682

Tennessee
Division of Parks and Recreation
L&C Tower, 7th Floor
Nashville, TN 37243-0446
615-532-0001

Texas
Parks and Wildlife Department
4200 Smith School Road
Austin, TX 78744
512-389-8951

Utah
Division of Parks and Recreation
Department of Natural Resources
1636 West North Temple
Salt Lake City, UT 84116
801-538-7220

Vermont
State Parks Division
Department of Forests and Parks
103 South Main Street
Waterbury, VT 05671-0603

Virginia
State Parks Division
Department of Conservation and Recreation
203 Governor Street, Suite 306
Richmond, VA 23219-2010
800-VISIT-VA

Washington
State Parks and Recreation Commission
PO Box 42650
Olympia, WA 98504-2650
800-544-1800

West Virginia
Parks and Recreation
Division of Tourism and Parks
Capitol Complex, Building 6, Room 451
Charleston, WV 25305
800-225-5982

Wisconsin
Division of Tourism
PO Box 7606
Madison, WI 53707
800-432-TRIP

Wyoming
Division of Tourism
Interstate 25 at College Drive
Cheyenne, WY 82002
800-225-5996

NATIONAL WILDLIFE REFUGES

Note: This list shows only those refuges that provide recreational and educational opportunities.

Check with the Fish and Wildlife Service website (http://www.fws.gov) for the most up-to-date addresses and information.

Always check with the refuge manager (regarding accessibility, activities, fees, weather conditions, etc.) before making a trip to a refuge.

NWR = National Wildlife Refuge
WMD = Wetland Management District

	Best Wildlife Viewing Season(s)																			
	Spring	Summer	Fall	Winter	Visitor Center/Contact Station	Visitor Center/Open Weekends	Walk-In Only Areas	Day Use Only	Food/Lodging Nearby	Refuge Literature	Educational Programs	Auto-Tour Route	Hiking Trails	Wildlife Viewing Sites	Archaeological Sites	Wilderness Areas	Non-Motorized Watercraft	Motorized Watercraft	Hunting	Fishing
ALABAMA																				
Bon Secour NWR, PO Box 1650, Gulf Shores, AL 36542	■		■		■			■	■	■			■	■			■			■
Choctaw NWR, 2704 Westside College Ave., PO Box 808, Jackson, AL 36545				■	■			■		■	■			■			■	■	■	■
Eufaula NWR, Rt. 2, Box 97B, Eufaula, AL 36027 (GA)				■	■			■	■	■	■	■	■	■			■	■	■	■
Wheeler NWR, Rt. 4, Box 250, Decatur, AL 35603			■	■	■	■		■	■	■	■		■	■	■		■	■	■	■
ALASKA																				
Alaska Maritime NWR, 2355 Kachemak Bay Dr. Suite 101, Homer, AK 99603	■	■			■	■	■		■	■	■			■		■		■		
Alaska Peninsula NWR, PO Box 277, King Salmon, AK 99613	■	■	■		■	■			■	■	■		■	■	■	■	■	■	■	■
Arctic NWR, 101-12th Ave., Box 20, Fairbanks, AK 99701		■					■			■						■	■	■	■	■
Becharof NWR, PO Box 277, King Salmon, AK 99613	■	■	■		■	■			■	■	■		■	■	■	■	■	■	■	■
Innoko NWR, Box 69, McGrath, AK 99627		■	■		■					■	■				■	■	■	■	■	■
Izembek NWR, Box 127, Cold Bay, AK 99571	■	■	■	■	■		■		■	■	■		■	■	■	■	■	■	■	■
Kanuti NWR, Box 11, 101-12th Ave., Fairbanks, AK 99701		■	■		■		■		■	■	■				■		■	■	■	■
Kenai NWR, PO Box 2139, Ski Hill Rd., Soldotna, AK 99669	■	■	■		■	■			■	■	■	■	■	■	■	■	■	■	■	■
Kodiak NWR, 1390 Buskin River Road, Kodiak, AK 99615	■	■	■		■	■				■	■			■		■	■	■	■	■
Koyukuk/Nowitna NWR, PO Box 287, Galena, AK 99741		■	■							■	■					■	■	■	■	■
Selawik NWR, PO Box 270, Kotzebue, AK 99752		■	■		■	■				■	■		■		■	■	■	■		
Tetlin NWR, PO Box 779, Tok, AK 99780	■	■	■		■	■	■		■	■	■	■		■			■	■	■	■
Togiak NWR, PO Box 270, Dillingham, AK 99576		■			■				■	■	■			■		■	■	■	■	■

NWR = National Wildlife Refuge
WMD = Wetland Management District

	Best Wildlife Viewing Season(s)																			
	Spring	Summer	Fall	Winter	Visitor Center/Contact Station	Visitor Center/Open Weekends	Walk-In Only Areas	Day Use Only	Food/Lodging Nearby	Refuge Literature	Educational Programs	Auto-Tour Route	Hiking Trails	Wildlife Viewing Sites	Archaeological Sites	Wilderness Areas	Non-Motorized Watercraft	Motorized Watercraft	Hunting	Fishing
Yukon Delta NWR, PO Box 346, Bethel, AK 99559		■	■		■		■		■	■	■					■	■	■	■	■
Yukon Flats NWR, 101-12th Ave., Box 14, Rm. 110, Fairbanks, AK 99701		■					■			■						■	■	■	■	■
ARIZONA																				
Bill Williams River NWR, 60911 Hwy. 95, Parker, AZ 85344	■				■		■	■	■	■	■						■	■	■	■
Buenos Aires NWR, PO Box 109, Sasabe, AZ 85633	■	■	■	■	■	■		■	■	■	■	■	■	■					■	
Cabeza Prieta NWR, 1611 N. Second Ave., Ajo, AZ 85321	■		■		■				■	■					■	■			■	
Cibola NWR, PO Box AP, Blythe, CA 92226 (CA)	■		■	■	■	■		■	■	■				■			■	■	■	■
Havasu NWR, PO Box 3009, Needles, CA 92363 (CA)	■		■	■	■			■	■	■				■	■	■	■	■	■	■
Imperial NWR, PO Box 72217, Martinez Lake, AZ 85365	■		■	■	■	■		■	■	■	■		■	■		■	■	■	■	■
Kofa NWR, 356 W. 1st St., PO Box 6290, Yuma, AZ 85366	■		■	■	■				■	■			■	■		■			■	
San Bernardino NWR, 1408 10th Street, Douglas, AZ 85607	■		■				■	■		■	■		■	■					■	
ARKANSAS																				
Big Lake NWR, PO Box 279, Turrell, AR 72384-0279				■				■	■	■		■		■		■	■	■	■	■
Cache River NWR, PO Box 279, Turrell, AR 72384-0279				■				■	■								■	■	■	■
Felsenthal NWR, PO Box 1157, Crossett, AR 71635	■		■	■	■	■	■		■	■		■	■	■	■		■	■	■	■
Holla Bend NWR, Rt. 1, PO Box 59, Dardanelle, AR 72834-9704				■	■			■	■	■		■	■	■				■	■	■
Overflow NWR, PO Box 1157, Crossett, AR 71635	■		■	■			■			■				■					■	
Wapanocca NWR, PO Box 279, Turrell, AR 72384-0279				■	■			■	■	■	■	■		■			■	■	■	■
White River NWR, Box 308, 321 W. 7th Street, De Witt, AR 72042	■		■	■					■	■							■	■	■	■

NWR = National Wildlife Refuge
WMD = Wetland Management District

Best Wildlife Viewing Season(s): Spring, Summer, Fall, Winter

	Spring	Summer	Fall	Winter	Visitor Center/Contact Station	Visitor Center/Open Weekends	Walk-In Only Areas	Day Use Only	Food/Lodging Nearby	Refuge Literature	Educational Programs	Auto-Tour Route	Hiking Trails	Wildlife Viewing Sites	Archaeological Sites	Wilderness Areas	Non-Motorized Watercraft	Motorized Watercraft	Hunting	Fishing
CALIFORNIA																				
Bear Valley NWR, Rt. 1, Box 74, Tulelake, CA 96134 (OR)				■			■	■	■	■				■					■	
Bitter Creek NWR, PO Box 670, Delano, CA 93216-0670			■	■				■	■											
Cibola NWR, PO Box AP, Blythe, CA 92226	■		■	■	■	■		■	■	■		■		■			■	■	■	■
Clear Lake NWR, Rt. 1, Box 74, Tulelake, CA 96134	■	■	■							■									■	
Colusa NWR, 752 County Rd. 99W, Willows, CA 95988			■	■	■	■	■	■	■	■		■	■	■					■	
Delevan NWR, 752 County Rd. 99W, Willows, CA 95988			■	■															■	
Havasu NWR, PO Box 3009, Needles, CA 92363 (AZ)	■		■	■				■	■	■				■	■	■	■	■	■	■
Hopper Mountain NWR, PO Box 5839, Ventura, CA 93005	■	■	■	■				■												
Humboldt Bay NWR, 1020 Ranch Rd. Loleta, CA 95551-9633	■		■	■			■	■	■	■			■	■			■	■	■	■
Kern NWR, PO Box 670, Delano, CA 93216-0670			■	■	■	■		■	■	■	■	■	■	■					■	
Kesterson NWR, 340 I St., PO Box 2176, Los Banos, CA 93635-2176	■		■	■			■	■	■	■				■					■	
Lower Klamath NWR, Rt. 1, Box 74, Tulelake, CA 96134 (OR)	■		■		■	■		■	■	■	■	■		■					■	
Merced NWR, 340 I St., PO Box 2176, Los Banos, CA 93635-2176	■		■	■	■	■		■	■	■		■		■					■	
Modoc NWR, PO Box 1610, Alturas, CA 96101-1610	■	■	■		■	■		■	■	■		■		■			■	■	■	■
Sacramento NWR, 752 County Rd. 99W, Willows, CA 95988			■	■	■	■	■	■	■	■	■	■	■	■					■	
Sacramento River NWR, 752 County Rd. 99W, Willows, CA 95988			■	■	■	■	■	■		■			■	■						
Salinas River NWR, PO Box 524, Newark, CA 94560-0524	■			■			■	■	■	■				■					■	■
Salton Sea NWR, PO Box 120, Calipatria, CA 92233-0120	■		■	■	■	■	■	■	■	■	■		■	■					■	■
San Francisco Bay NWR, PO Box 524, Newark, CA 94560-0524	■			■	■	■	■	■	■	■	■		■	■	■		■	■	■	■

NWR = National Wildlife Refuge
WMD = Wetland Management District

	Best Wildlife Viewing Season(s)																			
	Spring	Summer	Fall	Winter	Visitor Center/Contact Station	Visitor Center/Open Weekends	Walk-In Only Areas	Day Use Only	Food/Lodging Nearby	Refuge Literature	Educational Programs	Auto-Tour Route	Hiking Trails	Wildlife Viewing Sites	Archaeological Sites	Wilderness Areas	Non-Motorized Watercraft	Motorized Watercraft	Hunting	Fishing
San Luis NWR, 340 I St., PO Box 2176, Los Banos, CA 93635-2176	■	■	■	■	■	■		■	■	■		■		■					■	■
San Pablo Bay NWR, PO Box 524, Newark, CA 94560-0524	■			■			■	■		■			■	■					■	■
Sutter NWR, 752 County Rd. 99W, Willows, CA 95988			■	■															■	
Sweetwater Marsh NWR, 2736 Loker Ave. W., Suite A, Carlsbad, CA 92008	■	■	■	■	■	■	■	■	■	■	■			■						
Tijuana Slough NWR, 2736 Loker Ave. W., Suite A, Carlsbad, CA 92008	■	■	■	■	■	■	■	■	■	■	■		■	■						
Tule Lake NWR, Rt. 1, Box 74, Tulelake, CA 96134	■		■		■	■		■	■	■	■	■	■	■			■		■	
COLORADO																				
Alamosa NWR, 9383 El Rancho Lane, Alamosa, CO 81101-9003	■		■		■		■	■	■	■			■	■	■				■	
Arapaho NWR, PO Box 457, Walden, CO 80480-0457	■	■	■		■			■	■	■		■	■	■					■	■
Browns Park NWR, 1318 Highway 318, Maybell, CO 81640	■		■		■		■			■		■		■	■		■	■	■	■
Monte Vista NWR, 9383 El Rancho Lane, lamosa, CO 81101-9003	■		■		■		■	■	■	■		■		■					■	
Rocky Mtn. Arsenal National Wildlife Area, Bldg. 111, Commerce City, CO 80022-2180	■	■	■	■	■			■	■	■	■			■		■				■
Two Ponds NWR, Box 25486, Denver Fed. Ctr., Denver, CO 80225	■	■	■						■											
CONNECTICUT																				
Stewart B. McKinney NWR, 733 Old Clinton Rd., PO Box 1030, Westbrook, CT 06498-1030	■		■		■	■	■	■	■	■			■	■	■					
DELAWARE																				
Bombay Hook NWR, Rt. 1, Box 147, Smyrna, DE 19977-9764	■		■		■	■		■	■	■	■	■	■	■	■				■	
Prime Hook NWR, Rt. 3, Box 195, Milton, DE 19968-9751	■		■				■	■	■	■			■	■			■	■	■	■

NWR = National Wildlife Refuge
WMD = Wetland Management District

	Best Wildlife Viewing Season(s): Spring	Summer	Fall	Winter	Visitor Center/Contact Station	Visitor Center/Open Weekends	Walk-In Only Areas	Day Use Only	Food/Lodging Nearby	Refuge Literature	Educational Programs	Auto-Tour Route	Hiking Trails	Wildlife Viewing Sites	Archaeological Sites	Wilderness Areas	Non-Motorized Watercraft	Motorized Watercraft	Hunting	Fishing
FLORIDA																				
Arthur R. Marshall Loxahatchee NWR, 10216 Lee Rd., Boynton Beach, FL 33437-4796	■		■	■	■	■	■	■	■	■	■		■	■			■	■	■	■
Cedar Keys NWR, Rt. 1, Box 1193C, Chiefland, FL 32626	■						■	■	■	■							■	■		
Chassahowitzka NWR, 1502 SE Kings Bay Dr., Crystal River, FL 34429	■	■	■	■					■	■						■	■	■	■	■
Crystal River NWR, 1502 SE Kings Bay Dr., Crystal River, FL 34429				■					■	■							■	■		
Egmont Key NWR, 1502 SE Kings Bay Dr., Crystal River, FL 34429	■	■	■	■				■							■			■		
Great White Heron NWR, PO Box 430510 Big Pine Key, FL 33043-0510	■		■	■			■	■								■	■	■		
Hobe Sound NWR, PO Box 645, Hobe Sound, FL 33475-0645	■		■	■	■	■	■	■	■	■	■		■	■	■					■
J. N. "Ding" Darling NWR, One Wildlife Drive, Sanibel, FL 33957	■		■	■	■	■	■	■	■	■	■	■	■	■	■		■	■		■
Key West NWR, PO Box 430510, Big Pine Key, FL 33043-0510	■	■	■	■			■	■								■	■	■		
Lake Woodruff NWR, 4490 Grand Ave., PO Box 488, DeLeon Springs, FL 32130-0488	■		■	■	■		■	■	■	■	■		■	■	■	■	■	■	■	■
Lower Suwannee NWR, Rt. 1, Box 1193C, Chiefland, FL 32626	■			■	■				■	■			■		■	■		■	■	■
Merritt Island NWR, PO Box 6504, Titusville, FL 32780-6504	■		■	■	■	■		■	■	■	■	■	■	■			■	■	■	■
National Key Deer Refuge, PO Box 430510, Big Pine Key, FL 33043-0510	■		■	■	■		■	■	■	■	■		■	■		■	■	■		
Pinellas NWR, 1502 SE Kings Bay Dr., Crystal River, FL 34429	■	■	■	■					■								■	■		■
St. Marks NWR, PO Box 68, St. Marks, FL 32355	■		■	■	■	■	■	■	■	■	■	■	■	■	■	■	■	■	■	■
St. Vincent NWR, 479 Market St., PO Box 447, Apalachicola, FL 32329	■		■	■	■		■	■	■	■			■		■		■		■	■
GEORGIA																				
Banks Lake NWR, Rt. 2, Box 338, Folkston, GA 31537	■	■	■	■				■	■								■	■		■
Blackbeard Island NWR, 1000 Business Center Drive, Savannah, GA 31405	■	■	■	■			■	■		■	■		■			■	■	■	■	■

NWR = National Wildlife Refuge
WMD = Wetland Management District

Best Wildlife Viewing Season(s): Spring, Summer, Fall, Winter

Refuge	Spring	Summer	Fall	Winter	Visitor Center/Contact Station	Visitor Center/Open Weekends	Walk-In Only Areas	Day Use Only	Food/Lodging Nearby	Refuge Literature	Educational Programs	Auto-Tour Route	Hiking Trails	Wildlife Viewing Sites	Archaeological Sites	Wilderness Areas	Non-Motorized Watercraft	Motorized Watercraft	Hunting	Fishing
Eufaula NWR, Rt. 2, Box 97B, Eufaula, AL 36027				■	■			■	■	■	■	■	■	■			■	■	■	■
Harris Neck NWR, 1000 Business Center Drive, Savannah, GA 31405	■	■	■	■			■	■	■	■	■	■	■				■		■	■
Okefenokee NWR, Rt. 2, Box 338, Folkston, GA 31537	■	■	■	■	■	■		■	■	■	■	■	■	■	■	■	■	■	■	■
Piedmont NWR, Rt. 1, Box 670, Round Oak, GA 31038	■	■	■	■	■	■		■	■	■	■	■	■	■					■	■
Pinckney Island NWR, 1000 Business Center Drive, Savannah, GA 31405 (SC)	■		■	■			■	■	■	■	■		■		■		■	■	■	■
Savannah NWR, 1000 Business Center Drive, Savannah, GA 31405	■		■	■			■	■	■	■	■	■	■				■	■	■	■
Wassaw NWR, 1000 Business Center Drive, Savannah, GA 31405	■	■	■	■			■	■		■	■		■				■	■	■	■
HAWAII																				
Hakalau Forest NWR, 154 Waianuenue Ave., Room 219, Hilo, HI 96720	■	■	■	■			■	■		■									■	
Hanalei NWR, PO Box 87, Kilauea, HI 96754			■	■				■	■	■	■		■	■	■					■
Kilauea Point NWR, PO Box 87, Kilauea, HI 96754	■			■	■	■	■	■	■	■	■		■	■	■					
IDAHO																				
Bear Lake NWR, 370 Webster, PO Box 9, Montpelier, ID 83254	■	■					■	■	■	■		■	■	■			■	■	■	
Camas NWR, 2150 E. 2350 N., Hamer, ID 83425	■		■					■	■	■		■							■	
Deer Flat NWR, 13751 Upper Embankment Road, Nampa, ID 83686-0448 (OR)			■	■	■			■	■	■	■		■	■			■	■	■	■
Grays Lake NWR, 74 Grays Lake Road, Wayan, ID 83285	■	■	■		■	■	■	■		■				■	■		■		■	
Kootenai NWR, HRC 60, Box 283, Bonners Ferry, ID 83805	■	■	■		■			■	■	■		■	■	■					■	
Minidoka NWR, Rt. 4, Box 290, Rupert, ID 83350-9414	■	■	■		■	■				■				■			■	■	■	■
ILLINOIS																				
Chautauqua NWR, Rural Route 2, Box 61-B, Havana, IL 62644	■	■	■	■	■			■	■	■	■		■	■	■		■	■	■	■

NWR = National Wildlife Refuge
WMD = Wetland Management District

	Best Wildlife Viewing Season(s)																			
	Spring	Summer	Fall	Winter	Visitor Center/Contact Station	Visitor Center/Open Weekends	Walk-In Only Areas	Day Use Only	Food/Lodging Nearby	Refuge Literature	Educational Programs	Auto-Tour Route	Hiking Trails	Wildlife Viewing Sites	Archaeological Sites	Wilderness Areas	Non-Motorized Watercraft	Motorized Watercraft	Hunting	Fishing
Clarence Cannon NWR, PO Box 88, Annada, MO 63330-0088 (MO)	■		■		■			■	■	■	■			■						
Crab Orchard NWR, PO Box J, Carterville IL 62918-0509	■		■	■	■	■	■	■	■	■	■	■	■	■	■	■		■	■	■
Cypress Creek NWR, Rt. 1, Box 53D, Ullin, IL 62992			■					■	■	■	■		■				■	■	■	■
Emiquon NWR, Rural Route 2, Box 61-5B, Havana, IL 62644		■	■	■			■	■	■	■	■		■	■						
Mark Twain NWR Complex, 1704 N. 24th St., Quincy, IL 62301	■		■		■	■	■	■	■	■	■	■	■	■	■		■	■	■	■
Meredosia NWR, Rural Route 2, Box 61-B, Havana, IL 62644			■	■				■	■	■	■		■	■	■					■
INDIANA																				
Muscatatuck NWR, 12985 East U.S. Hwy. 50, Seymour, IN 47274	■	■	■	■	■	■		■	■	■	■	■	■	■	■		■		■	■
IOWA																				
DeSoto NWR, Rural Rt. 1, Box 114, Missouri Valley, IA 51555			■		■	■	■	■	■	■	■	■	■	■	■		■	■	■	■
Union Slough NWR, 1710 360th Street, Titonka, IA 50480	■		■					■	■	■	■	■	■						■	■
Walnut Creek NWR, PO Box 399, Prairie City, IA 50228-0399	■	■	■		■			■	■	■	■								■	
KANSAS																				
Flint Hills NWR, PO Box 128, Hartford, KS 66854-0128	■		■	■	■		■		■	■			■	■			■	■	■	■
Kirwin NWR, Rt. 1, Box 103, Kirwin, KS 67644	■		■				■	■	■	■		■		■			■	■	■	■
Quivira NWR, Rt. 3, Box 48A, Stafford, KS 67578	■		■		■		■	■	■	■	■	■	■	■					■	■
LOUISIANA																				
Atchafalaya NWR, 1010 Gause Blvd., Bldg. 936, Slidell, LA 70458	■		■	■			■	■	■	■			■				■	■	■	■
Bayou Sauvage NWR, 1010 Gause Blvd., Bldg. 936, Slidell, LA 70458	■		■	■			■	■	■	■	■		■				■	■		■
Bogue Chitto NWR, 1010 Gause Blvd., Bldg. 936, Slidell, LA 70458			■	■			■		■	■	■						■	■	■	■

NWR = National Wildlife Refuge
WMD = Wetland Management District

	Best Wildlife Viewing Season(s)																			
	Spring	Summer	Fall	Winter	Visitor Center/Contact Station	Visitor Center/Open Weekends	Walk-In Only Areas	Day Use Only	Food/Lodging Nearby	Refuge Literature	Educational Programs	Auto-Tour Route	Hiking Trails	Wildlife Viewing Sites	Archaeological Sites	Wilderness Areas	Non-Motorized Watercraft	Motorized Watercraft	Hunting	Fishing
Breton NWR, 1010 Gause Blvd., Bldg. 936, Slidell, LA 70458	■	■			■		■			■					■	■		■		■
Cameron Prairie NWR, Rt. 1, Box 643, Bell City, LA 70630	■		■	■	■			■	■	■			■	■				■	■	■
Catahoula NWR, PO Drawer Z, Rhinehart, LA 71363-0201		■	■	■	■			■	■	■		■	■	■			■	■	■	■
D'Arbonne NWR, Rt. 2, Box 401-B, Farmerville, LA 71241	■		■	■					■	■	■		■				■	■	■	■
Delta NWR, 1010 Gause Blvd., Bldg. 936, Slidell, LA 70458			■	■	■		■	■	■	■					■	■	■	■	■	■
Lacassine NWR, HCR 63, Box 186, Lake Arthur, LA 70549	■		■	■	■		■	■	■	■	■			■	■	■	■	■	■	■
Lake Ophelia NWR, PO Box 256, Marksville, LA 71351-0256	■	■		■			■	■	■	■							■	■	■	■
Louisiana WMD, Rt. 2, Box 401A, Farmerville, LA 71241	■	■	■	■	■		■	■	■					■						
Sabine NWR, Hwy. 27 S., 3000 Main St., Hackberry, LA 70645	■		■	■	■	■	■	■		■		■	■	■			■	■	■	■
Shell Keys NWR, 1010 Gause Blvd., Bldg. 936, Slidell, LA 70458	■	■						■									■	■		■
Tensas River NWR, Rt. 2, Box 295, Tallulah, LA 71282	■		■	■	■	■			■	■	■		■	■		■	■	■	■	■
Upper Ouachita NWR, PO Box 3065, Monroe, LA 71201	■		■	■						■			■				■	■	■	■
MAINE																				
Moosehorn NWR, PO Box 1077, Calais, ME 04619-1077	■	■	■		■	■	■	■	■	■			■			■	■	■	■	■
Petit Manan NWR, Rt. 1, PO Box 279, Milbridge, ME 04658-0279	■	■	■		■	■		■	■	■			■		■					
Rachel Carson NWR, RR 2, Box 751, Wells, ME 04090-9542	■	■	■	■	■		■	■	■	■	■		■	■			■		■	
Sunkhaze Meadows NWR, 1033 S. Main St., Old Town, ME 04468-2023	■	■	■				■	■	■	■			■				■	■	■	■
MARYLAND																				
Blackwater NWR, 2145 Key Wallace Dr., Cambridge, MD 21613-9536	■		■	■	■	■		■	■	■	■	■	■	■			■	■	■	■

NWR = National Wildlife Refuge
WMD = Wetland Management District

	Best Wildlife Viewing Season(s): Spring	Summer	Fall	Winter	Visitor Center/Contact Station	Visitor Center/Open Weekends	Walk-In Only Areas	Day Use Only	Food/Lodging Nearby	Refuge Literature	Educational Programs	Auto-Tour Route	Hiking Trails	Wildlife Viewing Sites	Archaeological Sites	Wilderness Areas	Non-Motorized Watercraft	Motorized Watercraft	Hunting	Fishing
Eastern Neck NWR, 1730 Eastern Neck Rd., Rock Hall, MD 21661-1815	■	■	■		■			■	■	■			■	■	■		■	■	■	
Patuxent NWR, 11400 American Holly Dr., Laurel, MD 20708-4014	■	■	■	■	■	■		■	■	■	■		■	■					■	■
MASSACHUSETTS																				
Great Meadows NWR, Weir Hill Road, Sudbury, MA 01776-1427	■	■	■		■	■		■	■	■	■		■	■			■	■		■
Monomoy NWR, Wiki Way, Morris Island, Chatham, MA 02633-2556	■	■	■	■	■	■	■	■	■	■			■			■	■	■		■
Nantucket NWR, Weir Hill Road, Sudbury, MA 01776-1427	■	■	■	■				■	■								■	■		■
Oxbow NWR, Weir Hill Road, Sudbury, MA 01776-1427	■	■	■				■	■	■	■			■				■	■	■	■
Parker River NWR, Northern Blvd., Plum Island, Newburyport, MA 01950-4315	■		■		■	■		■	■	■			■	■					■	■
Wapack NWR, Weir Hill Road, Sudbury, MA 01776 (NH)	■	■	■				■	■	■				■							
MICHIGAN																				
Harbor Island NWR, HCR #2, Box 1, Seney, MI 49883	■	■	■				■	■						■	■	■			■	
Huron NWR, HCR #2, Box 1, Seney, MI 49883	■	■					■	■		■			■		■	■				
Seney NWR, HCR #2, Box 1, Seney, MI 49883	■	■	■		■	■		■	■	■	■	■	■	■		■	■		■	■
Shiawassee NWR, 6975 Mower Road, Saginaw, MI 48601	■		■		■		■	■	■	■	■		■	■			■	■	■	■
MINNESOTA																				
Agassiz NWR, RR 1, Box 74, Middle River, MN 56737	■	■	■		■			■	■	■		■	■	■		■			■	
Big Stone NWR, 25 NW 2nd St., Ortonville, MN 56278	■		■				■	■	■	■		■	■	■	■		■		■	■
Detroit Lakes WMD, Rt. 3, Box 47D, Detroit Lakes, MN 56501	■		■				■	■	■	■	■						■		■	
Fergus Falls WMD, Rt. 1, Box 76, Fergus Falls, MN 56537	■	■					■	■	■	■	■		■	■			■		■	

NWR = National Wildlife Refuge
WMD = Wetland Management District

	Best Wildlife Viewing Season(s): Spring	Summer	Fall	Winter	Visitor Center/Contact Station	Visitor Center/Open Weekends	Walk-In Only Areas	Day Use Only	Food/Lodging Nearby	Refuge Literature	Educational Programs	Auto-Tour Route	Hiking Trails	Wildlife Viewing Sites	Archaeological Sites	Wilderness Areas	Non-Motorized Watercraft	Motorized Watercraft	Hunting	Fishing
Hamden Slough NWR, Rt. 1, Box 32, Audubon, MN 56511-9713	■	■	■		■			■	■				■	■						
Litchfield WMD, 971 E. Frontage Rd., Litchfield, MN 55355	■	■	■				■	■	■	■							■		■	
Minnesota Valley NWR, 3815 E. 80th Street, Bloomington, MN 55425-1600	■	■	■		■	■	■	■	■	■	■		■	■	■				■	■
Morris WMD, Route 1, Box 877, Morris, MN 56267	■	■	■		■		■	■	■	■	■		■	■					■	■
Rice Lake NWR, Hwy. 65, Route 2, Box 67, McGregor, MN 55760	■		■		■		■	■	■	■		■	■	■	■		■		■	■
Sherburne NWR, 17076 293rd Ave., Zimmerman, MN 55398	■	■	■		■		■	■	■	■		■	■	■			■		■	■
Tamarac NWR, HC 10, Box 145, Rochert, MN 56578-9735	■		■		■	■		■	■	■	■	■	■	■	■	■	■	■	■	■
Upper Miss. River National Wildlife & Fish Refuge, 51 East 4th St., Room 101, Winona, MN 55987	■	■	■	■					■	■	■									
Windom WMD, Hwy. 71 South, Rt. 1, Box 273A, Windom, MN 56101	■	■	■				■	■	■	■							■		■	
MISSISSIPPI																				
Dahomey NWR, PO Box 1070, Grenada MS 38901-1070	■		■	■	■		■	■	■	■		■	■	■			■		■	■
Hillside NWR, Rt. 1, Box 286, Hollandale, MS 38748	■			■				■	■	■			■					■	■	■
Mathews Brake NWR, Rt. 1, Box 286, Hollandale, MS 38748	■			■				■	■	■								■	■	■
Mississippi Sandhill Crane NWR, 7200 Crane Lane, Gautier, MS 39553-7200	■		■	■	■		■	■	■	■			■	■						
Mississippi WMD, Hwy. 8 West, PO Box 1070, Grenada, MS 38901	■		■		■		■	■	■	■			■	■	■	■	■	■	■	■
Morgan Brake NWR, Rt. 1, Box 286, Hollandale, MS 38748	■			■				■	■	■									■	■
Noxubee NWR, Rt. 1, Box 142, Brooksville, MS 39739	■		■	■	■		■	■	■	■			■	■			■		■	■
Panther Swamp NWR, Route 5, Box 25, Yazoo City, MS 39194	■	■	■	■	■	■	■		■	■		■		■			■	■	■	■
St. Catherine Creek NWR, PO Box 18639, Natchez, MS 39122	■		■	■	■		■	■	■	■							■	■	■	■

NWR = National Wildlife Refuge
WMD = Wetland Management District

	Spring	Summer	Fall	Winter	Visitor Center/Contact Station	Visitor Center/Open Weekends	Walk-In Only Areas	Day Use Only	Food/Lodging Nearby	Refuge Literature	Educational Programs	Auto-Tour Route	Hiking Trails	Wildlife Viewing Sites	Archaeological Sites	Wilderness Areas	Non-Motorized Watercraft	Motorized Watercraft	Hunting	Fishing
	Best Wildlife Viewing Season(s)																			
Tallahatchie NWR, PO Box 1070, Grenada, MS 38901-1070	■		■	■	■				■	■										
Yazoo NWR, Rt. 1, Box 286, Hollandale, MS 38748	■			■	■			■	■	■		■	■	■	■				■	
MISSOURI																				
Clarence Cannon NWR, PO Box 88, Annada, MO 63330-0088	■		■		■			■	■	■	■			■						
Mingo NWR, RR 1, Box 103, Puxico, MO 63960-9714	■		■	■	■	■	■	■	■	■	■	■	■	■		■	■		■	■
Squaw Creek NWR, PO Box 101, Mound City, MO 64470	■		■		■	■		■	■	■		■	■	■						■
Swan Lake NWR, Rt. 1, Box 29A, Sumner, MO 64681-0068	■	■			■		■	■		■		■	■	■			■	■	■	■
MONTANA																				
Benton Lake NWR, PO Box 450, Black Eagle, MT 59414	■	■	■		■		■	■	■	■		■		■			■		■	
Bowdoin NWR, HC 65, Box 5700, Malta MT 59538	■	■	■		■	■	■	■	■	■	■	■		■	■				■	
Charles M. Russell NWR, PO Box 110, Lewistown, MT 59457-0110	■	■	■							■		■	■	■		■	■	■	■	■
Hailstone NWR, PO Box 110, Lewistown, MT 59457-0110	■	■	■							■				■			■		■	
Lake Mason NWR, PO Box 110, Lewistown, MT 59457-0110	■	■	■							■				■			■		■	
Lee Metcalf NWR, Third & Main St., PO Box 257, Stevensville, MT 59870-0257	■		■		■		■	■	■	■	■	■	■	■					■	■
Medicine Lake NWR, 223 North Shore Rd., Medicine Lake, MT 59247-9600	■	■	■				■	■	■	■	■	■	■	■	■	■	■		■	■
National Bison Range NWR, 132 Bison Range Road, Moiese, MT 59824	■		■		■	■	■	■	■	■	■	■	■	■						■
Ninepipe NWR, 132 Bison Range Road, Moiese, MT 59824	■	■	■				■	■	■	■	■	■	■	■						■
Northwest Montana WMD, 780 Creston Hatchery Road, Kalispell, MT 59901	■	■	■				■	■	■	■							■	■	■	■
Pablo NWR, 132 Bison Range Road, Moiese, MT 59824	■	■	■				■	■	■	■	■	■		■						■

NWR = National Wildlife Refuge
WMD = Wetland Management District

	Best Wildlife Viewing Season(s): Spring	Summer	Fall	Winter	Visitor Center/Contact Station	Visitor Center/Open Weekends	Walk-In Only Areas	Day Use Only	Food/Lodging Nearby	Refuge Literature	Educational Programs	Auto-Tour Route	Hiking Trails	Wildlife Viewing Sites	Archaeological Sites	Wilderness Areas	Non-Motorized Watercraft	Motorized Watercraft	Hunting	Fishing
Red Rock Lakes NWR, Monida Star Rt., Box 15, Lima, MT 59739		■			■		■	■	■	■			■	■	■	■	■		■	■
Swan River NWR, 780 Creston Hatchery Rd., Kalispell, MT 59901	■		■				■	■	■	■							■		■	■
UL Bend NWR, PO Box 110, Lewistown, MT 59457-0110	■	■	■												■	■	■	■	■	■
War Horse NWR, PO Box 110, Lewistown, MT 59457-0110	■	■	■														■	■	■	
NEBRASKA																				
Crescent Lake NWR, HC 68, Box 21, Ellsworth, NE 69340	■	■			■		■	■		■	■	■					■		■	■
DeSoto NWR, Rural Rt. 1, Box 114, Missouri Valley, IA 51555			■		■	■	■	■	■	■	■	■	■	■	■	■	■	■	■	■
Fort Niobrara NWR, Hidden Timber Rt., HC 14, Box 67, Valentine, NE 69201	■	■	■	■	■	■	■	■	■	■	■	■	■	■	■	■	■			
North Platte NWR, PO Box 125 D, Minatare, NE 69356	■		■			■	■	■	■	■	■				■		■	■		■
Rainwater Basin WMD, PO Box 1686, Kearney, NE 68847-1686	■		■	■			■	■	■	■	■		■	■			■		■	
Valentine NWR, Hidden Timber Route, HC 14, Box 67, Valentine, NE 69201	■		■		■		■	■	■	■							■		■	■
NEVADA																				
Ash Meadows NWR, PO Box 2660, Pahrump, NV 89041-2660	■		■				■	■	■	■		■		■	■		■		■	■
Desert National Wildlife Range, Box 14, HCR 38, Las Vegas, NV 89124	■	■	■		■	■			■	■		■	■	■	■	■			■	
Pahranagat NWR, Box 510, Alamo, NV 89001-0510	■		■	■			■		■	■		■		■			■		■	■
Ruby Lake NWR, HC 60, Box 860, Ruby Valley, NV 89833-9802	■	■			■		■	■		■	■			■	■		■	■	■	■
Stillwater NWR, PO Box 1236, Fallon, NV 98406-1236	■		■		■				■	■		■		■	■		■	■	■	■
NEW HAMPSHIRE																				
John Hay NWR, Weir Hill Road, Sudbury, MA 01776-1427	■	■	■		■	■	■	■	■	■	■		■							

NWR = National Wildlife Refuge
WMD = Wetland Management District

	Best Wildlife Viewing Season(s)																			
	Spring	Summer	Fall	Winter	Visitor Center/Contact Station	Visitor Center/Open Weekends	Walk-In Only Areas	Day Use Only	Food/Lodging Nearby	Refuge Literature	Educational Programs	Auto-Tour Route	Hiking Trails	Wildlife Viewing Sites	Archaeological Sites	Wilderness Areas	Non-Motorized Watercraft	Motorized Watercraft	Hunting	Fishing
Lake Umbagog NWR, PO Box 280, Errol, NH 03579-0280	■	■	■		■		■		■	■			■					■	■	
Wapack NWR, Weir Hill Road, Sudbury, MA 01776-1427	■	■	■				■	■	■				■							
NEW JERSEY																				
Cape May NWR, 15 South Main St., Suite 3, Cape May Court House, NJ 08210-4207	■		■		■		■	■	■	■										
Edwin B. Forsythe (Barnegat) NWR, 70 Collinstown Rd., PO Box 544, Barnegat, NJ 08005-0544	■		■		■			■	■	■	■			■		■	■	■	■	■
Edwin B. Forsythe (Brigantine) NWR, Great Creek Road, PO Box 72, Oceanville, NJ 08231-0072	■	■	■	■	■			■	■	■	■	■	■	■		■	■	■	■	■
Great Swamp NWR, Pleasant Plains Rd., RD 1, Box 152, Basking Ridge, NJ 07920-9615	■		■		■	■		■	■	■	■	■	■	■		■			■	
Supawna Meadows NWR, RD #3, Box 540, Salem, NJ 08079	■			■	■		■	■	■	■					■				■	
Wallkill River NWR, PO Box 383, Sussex, NJ 07461-0383	■		■		■		■	■	■	■			■	■			■			
NEW MEXICO																				
Bitter Lake NWR, PO Box 7, Roswell, NM 88202-0007			■		■	■		■	■	■	■	■	■	■		■			■	
Bosque del Apache NWR, PO Box 1246, Socorro, NM 87801-1246	■		■	■	■	■	■	■	■	■	■	■	■	■	■	■			■	■
Grulla NWR, PO Box 549, Muleshoe, TX 79347-0549			■	■				■		■				■						
Las Vegas NWR, Route 1, Box 399, Las Vegas, NM 87701	■		■	■	■			■	■	■		■	■	■					■	
Maxwell NWR, PO Box 276, Maxwell, NM 87728-0276			■	■	■					■				■				■		■
NEW YORK																				
Elizabeth A. Morton NWR, Smith Rd., PO Box 21, Shirley, NY 11967-0021	■	■	■	■	■	■	■	■	■	■	■		■	■						■
Iroquois NWR, 1101 Casey Road, PO Box 517, Alabama, NY 14003-0517	■	■	■		■	■		■	■	■	■		■	■	■		■		■	■

NWR = National Wildlife Refuge
WMD = Wetland Management District

	Best Wildlife Viewing Season(s)																			
	Spring	Summer	Fall	Winter	Visitor Center/Contact Station	Visitor Center/Open Weekends	Walk-In Only Areas	Day Use Only	Food/Lodging Nearby	Refuge Literature	Educational Programs	Auto-Tour Route	Hiking Trails	Wildlife Viewing Sites	Archaeological Sites	Wilderness Areas	Non-Motorized Watercraft	Motorized Watercraft	Hunting	Fishing
Montezuma NWR, 3395 Route 5/20 East, Seneca Falls, NY 13148-9778	■	■	■		■	■	■	■	■	■	■	■	■	■					■	■
Oyster Bay NWR, Smith Rd., PO Box 21, Shirley, NY 11967-0021	■		■	■					■											■
Target Rock NWR, Smith Rd., PO Box 21, Shirley, NY 11967-0021	■	■	■	■	■	■	■	■	■	■	■		■	■						■
Wertheim NWR, Smith Rd., PO Box 21, Shirley, NY 11967-0021	■	■	■		■		■	■	■	■	■		■	■			■	■		■
NORTH CAROLINA																				
Alligator River NWR, 708 N. Hwy. 64, PO Box 1969, Manteo, NC 27954-1969	■	■	■	■	■		■	■	■	■	■		■	■			■	■	■	■
Cedar Island NWR, Route 1, Box N-2, Swanquarter, NC 27885	■		■	■				■	■	■				■			■	■	■	■
Currituck NWR, State Rt. 615, PO Box 39, Knotts Island, NC 27950-0039	■		■					■	■											
Great Dismal Swamp NWR, 3100 Desert Road, PO Box 349, Suffolk, VA 23434-0349	■		■	■			■	■	■	■	■		■	■	■		■	■	■	■
Mackay Island NWR, State Rt. 615, PO Box 39, Knotts Island, NC 27950-0039	■		■	■	■			■	■	■			■	■			■		■	■
Mattamuskeet NWR, Route 1, Box N-2, Swanquarter, NC 27885			■	■	■			■	■	■		■	■	■	■		■	■	■	■
Pea Island NWR, PO Box 1969, Manteo, NC 27954-1969	■	■	■	■	■	■	■	■	■	■		■	■	■	■		■	■		■
Pee Dee NWR, Rt. 1, Box 92, Wadesboro, NC 28170	■			■	■		■	■	■	■		■	■	■			■		■	■
Pocosin Lakes NWR, Rt. 1, Box 195-B, Creswell, NC 27928				■				■	■	■		■		■			■	■	■	■
Roanoke River NWR, 102 Dundee St., Box 430, Windsor, NC 27983-0430	■		■	■			■	■	■	■				■			■	■	■	
Swanquarter NWR, Route 1, Box N-2, Swanquarter, NC 27885			■	■				■	■	■				■			■	■	■	■
NORTH DAKOTA																				
Arrowwood NWR, 7745-11th St. SE, Pingree, ND 58476-8308	■	■	■		■		■	■	■	■	■	■	■	■			■	■	■	■
Arrowwood WMD, 7745-11th St. SE, Pingree, ND 58476-8308	■	■	■				■		■		■			■			■		■	■

NWR = National Wildlife Refuge
WMD = Wetland Management District

	Best Wildlife Viewing Season(s): Spring	Summer	Fall	Winter	Visitor Center/Contact Station	Visitor Center/Open Weekends	Walk-In Only Areas	Day Use Only	Food/Lodging Nearby	Refuge Literature	Educational Programs	Auto-Tour Route	Hiking Trails	Wildlife Viewing Sites	Archaeological Sites	Wilderness Areas	Non-Motorized Watercraft	Motorized Watercraft	Hunting	Fishing
Audubon NWR, RR 1, Box 16, Coleharbor, ND 58531	■	■	■		■			■	■	■		■							■	■
Crosby WMD, PO Box 148, Crosby, ND 58730-0148	■		■				■	■	■	■									■	
Des Lacs Complex, PO Box 578, Kenmare, ND 58746-0578	■	■	■		■		■	■	■	■		■	■	■	■	■	■		■	
Des Lacs NWR, PO Box 578, Kenmare, ND 58746-0578	■	■	■		■		■	■	■	■		■	■	■	■		■		■	
Devils Lake WMD, PO Box 908, Devils Lake, ND 58301-0908	■	■	■		■		■		■	■									■	
J. Clark Salyer NWR, Box 66, Upham, ND 58789	■	■	■		■		■	■		■	■	■	■	■			■		■	■
Kellys Slough NWR, PO Box 908, Devils Lake, ND 58301-0908	■	■	■				■		■					■					■	
Kulm WMD, PO Box E, Kulm, ND 58456	■		■		■		■	■	■	■							■	■	■	
Lake Alice NWR, PO Box 908, Devils Lake, ND 58301-0908	■	■	■						■	■				■	■				■	
Lake Ilo NWR, Dunn Center, ND 58626-0127	■		■		■			■	■	■	■			■	■		■	■		■
Lake Zahl NWR, PO Box 148, Crosby, ND 58730-0148	■		■				■	■	■	■									■	
Long Lake Complex, RR 1, Box 23, Moffitt, ND 58560																				
Lostwood NWR, RR 2, Box 98, Kenmare, ND 58746	■	■	■		■		■	■	■	■		■	■	■		■			■	
Lostwood WMD, RR 2, Box 98, Kenmare, ND 58746	■	■	■		■		■	■	■								■		■	
Sullys Hill Nat'l. Game Preserve, PO Box 908, Devils Lake, ND 58301-0908	■	■	■		■		■	■	■	■	■	■	■	■						
Tewaukon NWR, RR 1, Box 75, Cayuga, ND 58013-9763	■		■		■			■	■	■	■			■	■		■	■	■	■
Upper Souris NWR, RR 1, Box 163, Foxholm, ND 58718-9523	■	■	■		■			■	■	■	■	■	■	■			■	■	■	■
Valley City WMD, 11515 River Rd., Valley City, ND 58072-9619	■	■	■		■		■	■	■		■						■	■	■	
OHIO																				
Ottawa NWR, 14000 W. State Route 2, Oak Harbor, OH 43449-9485	■		■	■	■	■	■	■	■	■	■		■	■					■	

NWR = National Wildlife Refuge
WMD = Wetland Management District

	Best Wildlife Viewing Season(s): Spring	Summer	Fall	Winter	Visitor Center/Contact Station	Visitor Center/Open Weekends	Walk-In Only Areas	Day Use Only	Food/Lodging Nearby	Refuge Literature	Educational Programs	Auto-Tour Route	Hiking Trails	Wildlife Viewing Sites	Archaeological Sites	Wilderness Areas	Non-Motorized Watercraft	Motorized Watercraft	Hunting	Fishing
OKLAHOMA																				
Little River NWR, PO Box 340, Broken Bow, OK 74728	■		■	■	■				■	■		■							■	■
Optima NWR, Rt. 1, Box 68, Butler, OK 73625-9744	■		■				■	■	■	■									■	
Salt Plains NWR, Rt. 1, Box 76, Jet, OK 73749	■		■	■	■				■	■	■	■	■	■			■	■	■	■
Sequoyah NWR, Rt. 1, Box 18A, Vian, OK 74962	■		■	■	■			■	■	■	■	■	■		■		■	■	■	■
Tishomingo NWR, Route 1, Box 151, Tishomingo, OK 73460			■	■			■		■	■			■	■				■	■	■
Washita NWR, Rt. 1, Box 68, Butler, OK 73625-9744			■	■	■		■		■	■	■			■	■		■	■	■	■
Wichita Mountains Wildlife Refuge, Route 1, Box 448, Indiahoma, OK 73552	■	■	■	■	■	■	■	■	■	■	■	■	■	■	■	■	■	■	■	■
OREGON																				
Ankeny NWR, 2301 Wintel Road, Jefferson, OR 97352	■		■	■	■	■	■	■		■		■	■	■					■	
Bandon Marsh NWR, 26208 Finley Refuge Road, Corvallis, OR 97333	■		■				■	■	■					■					■	■
Baskett Slough NWR, 10995 Highway 22, Dallas, OR 97338	■		■	■			■	■	■	■	■		■	■						
Cape Meares NWR, 26208 Finely Refuge Road, Corvallis, OR 97333	■	■		■	■		■	■	■	■			■	■						
Cold Springs NWR, PO Box 239, Umatilla, OR 97882-0239 (WA)	■		■					■	■	■				■			■		■	■
Deer Flat NWR, 13751 Upper Embankment Road, Nampa, ID 83686-0448 (ID)			■	■	■			■	■	■	■		■	■			■	■	■	■
Hart Mountain NWR, PO Box 21, Plush, OR 97637	■	■	■							■		■	■	■	■	■			■	■
Klamath Forest NWR, HC 63, Box 303, Chiloquin, CA 97624	■		■		■			■	■	■		■	■	■				■	■	■
Lewis and Clark NWR, HC 01, Box 910, Ilwaco, WA 98624-9707	■		■				■	■	■	■				■			■	■	■	■
Malheur NWR, HC 72, Box 245, Princeton, OR 97721	■		■	■	■	■		■		■				■	■	■	■		■	■
McKay Creek NWR, PO Box 239, Umatilla, OR 97882-0239	■		■					■	■	■				■			■	■	■	■

NWR = National Wildlife Refuge
WMD = Wetland Management District

	Best Wildlife Viewing Season(s)																			
	Spring	Summer	Fall	Winter	Visitor Center/Contact Station	Visitor Center/Open Weekends	Walk-In Only Areas	Day Use Only	Food/Lodging Nearby	Refuge Literature	Educational Programs	Auto-Tour Route	Hiking Trails	Wildlife Viewing Sites	Archaeological Sites	Wilderness Areas	Non-Motorized Watercraft	Motorized Watercraft	Hunting	Fishing
McNary NWR, PO Box 308, Burbank, WA 99323-0308 (WA)	■		■	■				■	■	■			■	■					■	
Sheldon NWR, PO Box 21, Plush, OR 97637	■	■	■							■				■	■	■	■		■	■
Upper Klamath NWR, Rt. 1, Box 74, Tulelake, CA 96134	■	■					■	■	■	■				■			■	■	■	■
Umatilla NWR, PO Box 700, Umatilla, OR 97882-0700 (WA)	■		■	■				■	■	■			■	■			■		■	
William L. Finley NWR, 26208 Finley Refuge Road, Corvallis, OR 97333	■		■	■	■	■	■	■	■	■			■	■					■	■
PENNSYLVANIA																				
Erie NWR, RD 1, Wood Duck Lane, Guys Mills, PA 16327-9499	■		■		■	■	■	■	■	■	■		■	■					■	■
John Heinz NWR at Tinicum, Suite 104, Scott Plaza 2, Philadelphia, PA 19113	■		■		■	■	■	■	■	■	■		■	■			■			■
RHODE ISLAND																				
Block Island NWR, Rt. 1A, Shoreline Plaza, PO Box 307, Charlestown, RI 92813-0307	■	■	■	■			■	■	■	■					■					■
Ninigret Complex Headquarters, Rt. 1A, Shoreline Plaza, PO Box 307, Charlestown, RI 92813-0307					■				■	■	■									
Ninigret NWR, Rt. 1A, Shoreline Plaza, PO Box 307, Charlestown, RI 92813-0307	■		■	■			■	■	■	■	■		■	■						■
Pettaquamsutt Cove NWR, Rt. 1A, Shoreline Plaza, PO Box 307, Charlestown, RI 92813-0307	■	■	■	■			■	■	■											■
Sachuest Point NWR, Rt. 1A, Shoreline Plaza, PO Box 307, Charlestown, RI 92813-0307	■		■	■	■	■	■	■	■	■	■		■	■						■
Trustom Pond NWR, Rt. 1A, Shoreline Plaza, PO Box 307, Charlestown, RI 92813-0307	■	■	■	■			■	■	■	■	■		■						■	■
SOUTH CAROLINA																				
Ace Basin NWR, PO Box 848, Hollywood, SC 29449-0848	■		■	■			■	■	■				■	■	■				■	
Cape Romain NWR, 5801 Hwy 17 North, Awendaw, SC 29429	■	■	■				■	■	■	■	■		■	■	■	■	■	■	■	■

NWR = National Wildlife Refuge
WMD = Wetland Management District

Refuge	Best Wildlife Viewing Season(s): Spring	Summer	Fall	Winter	Visitor Center/Contact Station	Visitor Center/Open Weekends	Walk-In Only Areas	Day Use Only	Food/Lodging Nearby	Refuge Literature	Educational Programs	Auto-Tour Route	Hiking Trails	Wildlife Viewing Sites	Archaeological Sites	Wilderness Areas	Non-Motorized Watercraft	Motorized Watercraft	Hunting	Fishing
Carolina Sandhills NWR, Rt. 2, Box 330, McBee, SC 29101-2975	■		■	■	■			■	■	■	■	■	■	■				■	■	■
Pinckney Island NWR, 1000 Business Center Drive, Savannah, GA 31405 (SC)	■		■	■			■	■	■	■	■		■		■		■	■	■	■
Santee NWR, Rt. 2, Box 370, Summerton, SC 29148	■		■	■	■		■	■	■	■			■	■	■		■	■	■	■
SOUTH DAKOTA																				
Huron WMD, 200-4th St., SW, Rm. 113, Federal Bldg., Huron, SD 57350	■		■		■		■	■	■	■							■	■	■	
Lacreek NWR, HWC 3, Box 14, Martin, SD 57551	■	■	■	■	■	■	■	■	■	■	■	■	■	■			■	■	■	■
Lake Andes NWR, RR 1, Box 77, Lake Andes, SD 57356-9653	■		■		■		■	■	■	■			■	■			■	■	■	■
Madison WMD, PO Box 48, Madison, SD 57042	■	■	■		■		■	■	■	■				■			■	■	■	■
Pocasse NWR, RR 1, Box 25, Columbia, SD 57433	■		■				■	■	■								■	■	■	■
Sand Lake NWR, RR 1, Box 25, Columbia, SD 57433	■		■		■		■	■	■	■	■	■	■	■					■	■
Waubay NWR, RR 1, Box 79, Waubay, SD 57273	■	■	■		■			■	■	■	■	■	■						■	
TENNESSEE																				
Chickasaw NWR, 4343 Hwy. 157, Union City, TN 38261	■	■	■	■	■				■	■		■	■	■	■		■	■	■	■
Cross Creeks NWR, 643 Wildlife Rd., Dover, TN 37058	■		■	■	■			■	■	■	■	■	■	■			■	■	■	■
Hatchie NWR, 4172 Hwy. 76 South, Brownsville, TN 38012-0187		■	■					■	■	■							■		■	■
Lake Isom NWR, 4343 Hwy. 157, Union City, TN 38261	■		■	■				■	■	■	■			■			■	■	■	■
Lower Hatchie NWR, 4343 Hwy. 157, Union City, TN 38261	■	■	■	■	■					■		■	■	■	■		■	■	■	■
Reelfoot NWR, 4343 Hwy. 157, Union City, TN 38261	■		■	■	■	■	■	■	■	■	■	■	■	■			■	■	■	■
Tennessee NWR, 810 E. Wood St., PO Box 849, Paris, TN 38242-0849	■		■	■			■	■	■	■	■	■	■	■	■		■	■	■	■

NWR = National Wildlife Refuge
WMD = Wetland Management District

	Best Wildlife Viewing Season(s): Spring	Summer	Fall	Winter	Visitor Center/Contact Station	Visitor Center/Open Weekends	Walk-In Only Areas	Day Use Only	Food/Lodging Nearby	Refuge Literature	Educational Programs	Auto-Tour Route	Hiking Trails	Wildlife Viewing Sites	Archaeological Sites	Wilderness Areas	Non-Motorized Watercraft	Motorized Watercraft	Hunting	Fishing
TEXAS																				
Anahuac NWR, PO Box 278, Anahuac, TX 77514-0278	■		■	■	■				■	■	■	■	■	■			■	■	■	■
Aransas NWR, PO Box 100, Austwell, TX 77950-0100	■		■	■	■	■	■	■		■	■	■	■	■					■	■
Attwater Prairie Chicken NWR, PO Box 519, Eagle Lake, TX 77434-0519	■		■	■	■		■	■	■	■	■	■	■	■						
Big Boggy NWR, PO Box 1088, Angleton, TX 77516			■	■						■							■	■	■	
Brazoria NWR, PO Box 1088, Angleton, TX 77516-1088	■	■	■	■	■			■	■	■	■	■	■	■			■	■	■	■
Buffalo Lake NWR, PO Box 179, Umbarger, TX 79091-0179	■		■		■		■	■	■	■	■	■	■	■					■	
Grulla NWR, PO Box 549, Muleshoe, TX 79347-0549 (NM)			■	■	■			■		■				■						
Hagerman NWR, Rt. 3, Box 123, Sherman, TX 75090-9564	■		■	■	■	■	■	■	■	■	■	■	■	■			■	■	■	■
Laguna Atascosa NWR, PO Box 450, Rio Hondo, TX 78583-0450	■		■	■	■	■		■	■	■	■	■	■	■	■				■	■
McFaddin/Texas Point NWR, PO Box 609, Sabine Pass, TX 77655-0609	■		■	■	■		■	■	■	■							■	■	■	■
Muleshoe NWR, PO Box 549, Muleshoe, TX 79347-0549	■		■	■	■			■		■	■	■	■	■						
San Bernard NWR, Rt. 1, Box 1335, Brazoria, TX 77422	■	■	■	■	■			■	■	■	■	■	■	■			■	■	■	■
Santa Ana NWR, Route 2, Box 202A, Alamo, TX 78516	■		■	■	■	■	■	■	■	■	■	■	■	■	■					
UTAH																				
Bear River Migratory Bird Refuge, 866 So. Main, Brigham City, UT 84302	■	■	■		■			■	■	■		■		■					■	■
Fish Springs NWR, PO Box 568, Dugway, UT 84022-0568	■	■	■	■	■	■	■	■		■		■			■		■		■	
Ouray NWR, 266W 100 North, #2, Vernal, UT 84078	■		■		■	■	■	■	■	■	■	■		■					■	■

NWR = National Wildlife Refuge
WMD = Wetland Management District

	Best Wildlife Viewing Season(s)																			
	Spring	Summer	Fall	Winter	Visitor Center/Contact Station	Visitor Center/Open Weekends	Walk-In Only Areas	Day Use Only	Food/Lodging Nearby	Refuge Literature	Educational Programs	Auto-Tour Route	Hiking Trails	Wildlife Viewing Sites	Archaeological Sites	Wilderness Areas	Non-Motorized Watercraft	Motorized Watercraft	Hunting	Fishing
VERMONT																				
Missisquoi NWR, Rt. 78, PO Box 163, Swanton, VT 05488-0163	■		■				■	■	■	■			■					■	■	■
VIRGINIA																				
Back Bay NWR, 4005 Sandpiper Road, PO Box 6286, Virginia Beach, VA 23456-0286	■		■	■	■	■	■	■	■	■	■		■	■			■		■	■
Chincoteague NWR, PO Box 62, Chincoteague, VA 23336-0062	■	■	■	■	■	■		■	■	■	■	■	■	■					■	■
Eastern Shore of Virginia NWR, 5003 Hallett Circle, Cape Charles, VA 23310	■	■	■		■	■	■	■	■	■	■		■	■						
Great Dismal Swamp NWR, 3100 Desert Road, PO Box 349, Suffolk, VA 23434-0349 (NC)	■		■	■			■	■	■	■	■		■	■	■		■	■	■	■
Mason Neck NWR, 14416 Jefferson Davis Hwy., Suite 20A, Woodbridge, VA 22191-2890	■		■	■				■	■	■	■		■	■	■				■	
Presquile NWR, 6610 Commons Dr., PO Box 189, Prince George, VA 23875-0189	■		■		■		■	■	■	■									■	
WASHINGTON																				
Cold Springs NWR, PO Box 239, Umatilla, OR 97882-0239	■		■					■	■	■				■			■		■	■
Columbia NWR, 735 E. Main St., PO Drawer F, Othello, WA 99344-0227	■		■		■	■	■	■	■	■	■	■	■	■			■	■	■	■
Conboy Lake NWR, 100 Wildlife Refuge Rd., Box 5, Glenwood, WA 98619-0005	■			■	■			■	■	■			■		■				■	■
Dungeness NWR, 1638 South Barr Rd., Port Angeles, WA 98362	■		■	■			■	■	■	■	■		■	■			■	■		■
Julia Butler Hansen Refuge for the Columbian White-Tail Deer, PO Box 566, Cathlamet, WA 98612			■	■	■			■	■	■			■						■	
Lewis and Clark NWR, HC 01, Box 910, Ilwaco, WA 98624-9707 (OR)	■		■				■	■	■	■				■			■	■	■	■
Little Pend Oreille NWR, 1310 Bear Creek Rd., Colville, WA 99114	■			■					■	■			■	■			■		■	■
McNary NWR, PO Box 308, Burbank, WA 99323-0308 (OR)	■		■	■				■	■	■			■	■					■	

NWR = National Wildlife Refuge
WMD = Wetland Management District

	Best Wildlife Viewing Season(s): Spring	Summer	Fall	Winter	Visitor Center/Contact Station	Visitor Center/Open Weekends	Walk-In Only Areas	Day Use Only	Food/Lodging Nearby	Refuge Literature	Educational Programs	Auto-Tour Route	Hiking Trails	Wildlife Viewing Sites	Archaeological Sites	Wilderness Areas	Non-Motorized Watercraft	Motorized Watercraft	Hunting	Fishing
Nisqually NWR, 100 Brown Farm Road, Olympia, WA 98516	■	■	■	■	■	■	■	■	■	■	■		■	■			■	■		■
Ridgefield NWR, 301 N. Third St., PO Box 457, Ridgefield, WA 98642	■		■	■	■	■		■	■	■	■		■	■			■		■	■
San Juan Islands NWR, 100 Brown Farm Road, Olympia, WA 98516	■	■	■	■					■	■			■			■	■	■		
Toppenish NWR, 21 Pumphouse Rd., Toppenish, WA 98948	■		■				■	■	■	■				■					■	
Turnbull NWR, S. 26010 Smith Road, Cheney, WA 99004	■	■			■			■	■	■	■	■	■	■						
Umatilla NWR, PO Box 239, Umatilla, OR 97882-0239	■		■	■				■	■	■			■	■			■		■	
Willapa NWR, HC 01, Box 910, Ilwaco, WA 98624-9707	■		■				■		■	■			■	■	■		■	■	■	■
WEST VIRGINIA																				
Ohio River Islands NWR, PO Box 1811, Parkersburg, WV 26102-1811 (PA)	■	■	■					■	■	■							■	■		■
WISCONSIN																				
Horicon NWR, W. 4279 Headquarters Rd., Mayville, WI 53050			■			■		■	■		■	■	■	■					■	■
Leopold WMD, W. 4279 Headquarters Rd., Mayville, WI 53050	■		■				■	■											■	■
Necedah NWR, W. 7996-20th St. W., Necedah, WI 54646-7531	■	■	■		■			■	■	■	■	■	■	■	■		■		■	■
St. Croix WMD, 146 W. 2nd St., New Richmond, WI 54017	■		■		■		■		■					■			■		■	■
Trempealeau NWR, Rt. 1, Box 1602, Trempealeau, WI 54661-9781	■	■	■	■	■	■		■	■	■	■	■	■	■	■		■		■	■
WYOMING																				
Bamforth NWR, PO Box 457, Walden, CO 80480-0457	■	■	■					■	■											
Hutton Lake NWR, PO Box 457, Walden, CO 80480-0457	■	■	■					■	■	■										
National Elk Refuge, 675 E. Broadway, PO Box C, Jackson, WY 83001	■		■	■	■	■		■	■	■	■	■		■	■				■	■

NWR = National Wildlife Refuge
WMD = Wetland Management District

	Best Wildlife Viewing Season(s)																			
	Spring	Summer	Fall	Winter	Visitor Center/Contact Station	Visitor Center/Open Weekends	Walk-In Only Areas	Day Use Only	Food/Lodging Nearby	Refuge Literature	Educational Programs	Auto-Tour Route	Hiking Trails	Wildlife Viewing Sites	Archaeological Sites	Wilderness Areas	Non-Motorized Watercraft	Motorized Watercraft	Hunting	Fishing
Pathfinder NWR, PO Box 457, Walden, CO 80480-0457	■	■	■					■		■							■	■	■	■
Seedskadee NWR, PO Box 700, Green River, WY 82935-0700	■	■	■	■	■		■	■		■	■	■		■	■		■		■	■
PUERTO RICO AND VIRGIN ISLANDS																				
Buck Island NWR (Virgin Islands), PO Box 510, Boqueron, PR 00622-0510	■	■	■	■			■	■		■								■		
Cabo Rojo NWR, PO Box 510, Boqueron, PR 00622-0510	■	■	■	■	■		■	■	■	■			■	■						
Culebra NWR, PO Box 510, Boqueron, PR 00622-0510	■	■	■	■	■		■	■	■	■							■	■		■
Desecheo NWR, PO Box 510, Boqueron, PR 00622-0510	■	■	■	■						■										
Green Cay NWR (Virgin Islands), PO Box 510, Boqueron, PR 00622-0510	■	■	■	■			■	■		■										
Laguna Cartagena NWR, PO Box 510, Boqueron, PR 00622-0510	■	■	■	■			■	■												

INDEX